MISSIOLOGY
An Ecumenical Introduction

D1366845

MISSIOLOGY
An Ecumenical Introduction

TEXTS AND CONTEXTS OF GLOBAL CHRISTIANITY

Edited by

A. Camps, L. A. Hoedemaker,
M. R. Spindler,

and

F. J. Verstraelen *(general editor)*,
with the special assistance
of J. D. Gort and F. J. Verstraelen
for this English edition

WILLIAM B. EERDMANS PUBLISHING COMPANY
GRAND RAPIDS, MICHIGAN

00 99 98 97 96 95   7 6 5 4 3 2 1

Printed in the United States of America

Library of Congress Cataloging-in-Publication Data

Missiology: an ecumenical introduction: texts and contexts of global Christianity /
edited by F. J. Verstraelen . . . [et al.].
p.   cm.
Includes English translation of Oecumenische inleiding in de missiologie
newly revised by original authors and editors.
Includes bibliographical references.
ISBN 0-8028-0487-X (paper: alk. paper)
1. Missions. 2. Church history. I. Verstraelen, F. J.
II. Oecumenische inleiding in de missiologie.
BV2030.M55   1995
266 — dc20   95-17638
                                                CIP

Chapters 1-23 and 27-29 were translated by John Vriend from *Oecumenische Inleiding in de Missiologie: Teksten en Konteksten van het Wereld-Christendom* (Kampen: J. H. Kok, 1988) and revised by the original authors and editors. Chapter 24 is revised from *International Bulletin of Missionary Research* 16 (1992) 54-60. Chapter 25 is reprinted with emendations by permission of the publishers from *A Century of Church History: The Legacy of Philip Schaff*, edited by Henry Warner Bowden (Carbondale, IL: Southern Illinois University Press, 1988), pages 168-215, copyright © 1988 by the Board of Trustees, Southern Illinois University, Carbondale. Chapter 26 was translated by Elaine Monsma from a paper presented at the twelfth session of CREDIC, held in Verona, Italy, in August 1991. The bibliography is substantially revised from the bibliography that appeared in *Oecumenische Inleiding in de Missiologie*.

Except where otherwise noted, the Scripture quotations in this publication are from the New Revised Standard Version of the Bible, copyright © 1989 by the Division of Christian Education of the National Council of Churches of Christ in the U.S.A., and used by permission.

Contents

CHAPTER 1

Introduction:
What Do We Mean by "Missiology"?

THE EDITORS

Christianity and the World

The Christian faith has sought its way and continues to seek its way in a diverse world of cultures, religions, socioeconomic systems, and political institutions. As it does, it exerts influence on those cultures, religions, systems, and institutions. But the Christian faith itself is also influenced by that varied world: Changes occur in its forms of fellowship, in its self-expressions, and in its theological reflection.

Though we can study these mutual influences of faith and world, there is no longer a preexisting schema by which we can organize our understanding of them. In the past, within the missionary movement that proceeded from European and North American Christianity to the rest of the world, the course of the gospel through the world was seen as coinciding with the course of Western Christianity's expansion. From its beginning, missiology, which arose as a form of critical reflection within the missionary movement, introduced qualifications into this paradigm. The tendency to view and judge world Christianity exclusively from a Western perspective remains a stubborn reality, though it has been increasingly challenged in the twentieth century. New kinds of Christianity originating in parts of the world where Western Christianity is no longer viewed as the norm, together with the development of the ecumenical movement, have made us more aware of a legitimate pluralism and have gradually replaced the paradigm of "expansion" with one of "communication."

The consensus today is that there is no single form of Christianity, or of the Christian faith, standing outside the world's cultural diversity. We cannot stand above culture and regulate the "inculturation" or "contextualization" of our faith from such a vantage point. Christianity itself

1

is fully involved in the dynamics of clashing cultures, religious systems, and institutions. We are caught up today in a *multiplicity of processes* in which forms of Christianity arise, are modified, and sometimes disappear.

This means that missiologists must ask themselves what their field of study is really about. Now that many of the presuppositions of Western missions are no longer valid, missiology is searching for a new working self-definition. Obviously, a book presented as an "ecumenical introduction" to missiology is intended to be part of that search.

The first thing to be noted in this search is that missiology examines the "multiplicity of processes" in which Christianity is involved *from its own angle of interest.* Just what that interest is will be discussed in the next section of this introduction (pp. 3-5 below). What is significant at this point is that missiology does not set itself apart from, for instance, church history, cultural anthropology, the scientific study of religion, sociology, or social psychology. It makes full use of the results of such fields of study. Missiological research can in this light deal with

- changes that specific forms of Christianity have undergone as they are influenced by processes of acculturation,
- the successes and failures of organized mission initiatives, that is, of deliberate efforts to gain admission for the Christian faith in new settings,
- the influence of other religions and ideologies on Christianity, or
- social changes that have consequences for the way in which faith is experienced and interpreted.

In other words, missiology studies the movement of Christianity in the world, the ways in which Christian faith becomes attached to different contexts. The field of inquiry may be very broad in terms of space and time, for example, the influences of racist thought on the rise of Christian churches in southern Africa in the nineteenth and twentieth centuries, or it can have a narrower focus, dealing with, for example, problems in communication encountered in evangelization of youth in a particular city.

Our expression "multiplicity of processes" must be refined in a second way. Missiology is concerned with *both planned and unplanned processes*. By this we mean that it cannot be limited to the study of deliberate missionary expansion and outreach. Such a limitation would force us into a failure to do justice to insights from the study of religion and from the ecumenical experience, specifically that many of the changes and developments in Christianity and Christian faith are complex and cannot be considered the results just of missionary initiatives. History is full of examples of spontaneous unplanned expansion, of sudden mass conversions only superficially linked with the activity of missionaries, of isolated forms of Christianity that persist in some underground fashion, and of events and movements in world history that prompt changes in Christianity. The rise of African-American Christianity, for example, is more the result of a complex of factors — African spirituality, the experience of slavery, the Euro-American version of the Christian faith — than of any "planned" process. Such unplanned processes are not, of course, mechanical events occurring apart from human actions and decisions. But in such cases we are dealing with actions and decisions unprompted by explicit missionary objectives. The need to see at every point a relationship between the Western missionary movement and the expansion of Christianity has somewhat blocked our awareness of these "unplanned processes" in Christianity. But an ecumenical missiology can no longer ignore them.

But there are, of course, planned processes that continue to fall within the purview of missiology. Missiologists still study deliberate missionary initiatives and problems that arise in them:

- The history of organized missions, both Catholic and Protestant,
- problems in communication of the gospel across the boundaries of cultures, religions, socioeconomic systems, and political institutions,
- beneficial and harmful effects of Western missions in non-Western nations,
- dilemmas that emerge in the search for adequate expressions of Christian faith,
- ways in which social issues are dealt with in the work of missions

All these concerns belong to the essence of the field of missiology, though they can just as well be objects of study in church history, cultural anthropology, religious studies, sociology, or social psychology.

The Particular Interest of Missiology

Missiology is a branch of theology in the sense that it is bound up with a faith perspective. The movement of Christianity in the world is studied on the basis of a specific interest arising from this faith perspective. The perspective in question is an original and authentic constituent of the Christian tradition: That tradition views "all the generations of the earth" as the object of God's redemptive will and plan of salvation. Or, in New Testament language, it regards the message of God's "kingdom," made known in Jesus Christ, as intended for "all nations." We meet in such terminology the context in which missiology as a theological discipline seeks to view everything that it studies. In this undertaking we are dealing with the ultimate frame of reference for the "movement of Christianity." In the nature of the case, the definition of this faith perspective is part of the agenda of missiology, and continuous critical examination of this definition is both possible and necessary. Therefore, missiology is closely allied with biblical and systematic theology and keeps a sensitive finger on the pulse of experiences in the different communities of faith. But that missiology is bound to a faith perspective is itself not open to debate. It is, rather, our starting point.

Indeed, the word "mission" has a place only in this faith perspective. It is no longer adequate in an ecumenical missiology to take "mission" in the restricted sense of a mandate that Christians assume with regard to other people. "Mission" is, rather, the dynamic relationship between God and the world: God *sends* himself, his Son, and his church. Those who become actively involved in the vision of his redemptive will understand themselves as *sent* individuals or groups. To let the theological character of the discipline come out in our definition of missiology, we have to speak of — in addition to "the study of the movement of Christianity" — the exposition of the mission of God, of the "sentness" of the church in the observed processes of change, development, contextualization, influence, and assimilation.

We can take the particular theological interest of missiology in two further directions.

First, in the theological interest of missiology we are dealing with faith, that is, with a believing way of looking at the world. This does not mean that because of its faith perspective missiology becomes irrational and unverifiable. Nor does it mean that missiologists are primarily believing people and not also ordinary people involved in their particular work. In the context of the attempt to define missiology the word "believing" means especially that the observed movement of Christianity is interpreted with the aid of and in connection with the dominant concepts of God's redemptive will and kingdom. The link to these concepts *is* open to verification and criticism. In other words, the tendency toward dogmatic bias in the field of missiology is always challenged by ongoing and vital theological discussion. Missiology can never give a priori canonization to specific understandings of God's kingdom and its relation to the world. In missiology every concept and every interpretation is open to discussion. But that discussion is not conducted on the basis of a neutral rationalism but on the basis of an assumed missionary interest.

Second, in this theological interest we are concerned with the whole world, with "the ends of the earth." In missiology "world" is not simply a collective term embracing all geographic and cultural contexts; it represents, rather, the counterpart of God's kingdom. Accordingly, "world" becomes a term for the unity of humankind, for the demolition of walls of separation, for crossing of boundaries, and for reconciliation. The term "kingdom of God" also has its polemical side: It stands for a war against the powers that aim to punish and ruin the world. This understanding of the world is above all a qualitative biblical and theological perspective and only then a quantitative reference to concrete peoples, nations, and cultures. Implied in this is that our understanding of the world must not be only *extensive*, as though it primarily concerned what is at ever-increasing distances from us. Of course, we cannot ignore that aspect of it when we speak of the relationship between God and the world. But "world" is just as much an *intensive* concept: The ends of the earth are near, in our own contexts and lives, present in the processes of change, adaptation, and deepening that we have been discussing.

The Working Method of an Ecumenical Missiology

It might be said that the faith perspective of missiology must involve an aprioristic and dogmatic coloring of the facts with the result that missiology cannot be taken seriously as a legitimate field of study. We can answer this charge only by referring to the ecumenical character of missiology.

Our use of "ecumenical" here means simply that as soon as we attempt to define missiology's "faith perspective," we are faced with a plurality of theological models. It is true also that these models are constantly adjusted and refined in interaction with the study of the movement of Christianity. But they also have roots in different Christian traditions, in which over the centuries different ways of talking and thinking about God and the world have been developed. In missiology these traditions can, in principle, come into dialogue with one another in the context of joint inquiry into the points of contact between Christianity and the world.

Furthermore, any aspect of the movement of Christianity, any process of change, adaptation, or the like, can be studied within more than one frame of reference. For example, one can study the development of Christian churches in Latin America from the perspective of the reevangelization of the continent or from the perspective of the development of a new Christian political self-consciousness among the poor. In the same way, an analysis of church growth in an African country can be undertaken in the context of inquiry into adequate missionary methods or as part of a study of the rise of independent churches in the encounter between African culture and Western Christianity. Several theological starting points may come into play in these different complementary approaches, but they can be brought into fruitful contact with each other because they seek a common goal. That goal is the analysis and interpretation of processes that present themselves in the reality of church and world. The meaning of "ecumenical missiology" thus stands out in sharper relief, and a more traditional understanding of the term "ecumenical" as referring to encounter between different confessional traditions is supplemented and corrected by the reality of global Christianity.

It is essential in all this for missiology to evaluate critically the different views, faith pronouncements, theological conceptions, and intuitive religious responses with respect to "God" and the "world" that play a role in the movement of Christianity. It does not do this according to a standard of canonized and supposedly indubitable faith pronouncements but by the light of insights reached in ecumenical theological discussion and questions posed in that discussion. The objective is inquiry into the degree to which the views, pronouncements, and conceptions stand up in the arena of discussion. In this testing these different understandings can also be examined or compared with a view to discerning hidden ideological motives.

A consequence of all this is that an ecumenical missiology will occupy itself with questions of systematic theology. The concepts that aid us in reflecting on the particular interest of missiology, discussed above, must themselves be weighed and ordered. Our examination of them yields a variety of sketches for a theology of missions and perhaps in time also designs for a "missionary theology," that is, designs in which theology as a whole is related to the starting point and goal of the gospel's journey through the world and the problems encountered on that journey.

The Plan of This Book

In our explanation to this point we have provided all the building blocks of an "ecumenical introduction" to missiology. Many of the subdivisions found in earlier handbooks on missiology will be seen in this book as well: discussions of the history of missionary movements, sections of biblical and theological reflection, sketches of actual missionary praxis, and overviews of different missiological schools and currents. Along with those concerns, we will attempt to do justice to challenges that missiologists of today cannot disregard, the challenges that this introduction has sought to outline.

Part I, "The Diversity of Global Christianity," offers a portrayal of today's polycentric and diverse Christianity. It does this by presenting five carefully selected surveys of the experience of Christianity in particular geographic regions. These surveys include much historical material, but not in order to construct a "history of missions" so much as to document the unique forms, problems, and yearnings that have arisen in each situation that is described.

In Part II, "Word, Mission, and Church," systematic missiology itself speaks. The authors seek to give basic understandings of the ways in which people think and write today about the one mission against the background of the plurality of Christian faith that has been sketched in this introduction.

Only then, in Part III, "The Missionary Movement in History," is the history of Western-based missionary activity reviewed. This review is placed so late in the book to indicate that this particular missionary activity is considered neither the source nor the norm of the movement of Christianity. But it is important and necessary to look at that history because much of what is done and thought in Christianity today began there.

In Part IV, "Missionary Vitality in Contemporary Christianity," we return to the diversity discussed in Part I. But Part IV is a treatment of all the actions, initiatives, and creative thought forms that give depth to the great mission context in which the movement of Christianity can be seen.

Part V, "Mission, Ecumenicity, and Missiology," provides an overview of the present situation of the practice of missiology and of the missionary movement. That in our day only an "ecumenical" introduction to missiology can be written becomes particularly clear in this final section.

Summary

From within a faith interest in the relationship between the world and God's kingdom, missiologists study the movement of Christianity in the midst of cultures, religions, socioeconomic systems, and political institutions. They are concerned both with facing the problems of communicating the gospel to the people of "all nations" and with examining critically the theological concepts by means of which this faith interest is kept alive. Since their context is global Christianity, missiologists are obligated to pursue their discipline from an ecumenical standpoint.

PART I

The Diversity of Global Christianity

The next five chapters examine the manner in which the Christian faith as church and as movement seeks its way in our diverse world. They do so, not by looking at abstract forms of Christianity related to abstract concepts such as "culture," "politics," "religion," or "socioeconomic problems," but by describing concrete experiences. The intent is to sensitize the reader to the plurality of expressions of the Christian faith. Therefore, the topics of these chapters were chosen for their political, socioeconomic, religious, and cultural diversity. They are presented in the chronological order of when Christianity appeared in the different regions treated: the Middle East (chapter 2), western Europe (chapter 3), China (chapter 4), western Africa (chapter 5), Indonesia (chapter 6), and Brazil (chapter 7).

CHAPTER 2

The Middle East: Cradle and Crucible

A. WESSELS

What we most commonly call the "Middle East" (or "Mideast") today was formerly called the "Near East." Both names reflect a Eurocentric perspective on that part of the world, which is in India, for example, called "Western Asia." But even that appellation does not correspond with the self-understanding of the peoples and nations living in the "Middle East." The Arabs themselves call it the "Arabic East" *(Mashrik)*. (The "Arabic West," the *Maghreb*, consists of Morocco, Tunisia, and Algiers.)

But the Middle East includes three non-Arabic states: Israel, Turkey, and Iran. The nations of the Middle East can be divided into Turkey; the nations of the Fertile Crescent, which are Jordan, Israel, Lebanon, Syria, and Iraq, those of the Arabian Peninsula, which are Saudi Arabia, Kuwait, Bahrain, Qatar, the United Arab Emirates, Oman, and Yemen; and Egypt, Sudan, and Libya in northern Africa.

"Middle East" is not so much a geographic term as a historical-cultural and political term. A large majority of the inhabitants of the region are united by a common religion — Islam — and a common language — Arabic. These ties were forged in a common history of thirteen centuries following the rise and swift expansion of Islam beginning in the seventh century A.D.

The Middle East lies at the intersection of three continents: Asia, Africa, and Europe. It is extremely important strategically, because of its oil riches and for other reasons. Recent years have seen the ongoing conflict between Israel and the Palestinians and the Arab nations, the extremely bloody war between Iraq and Iran from 1980 to 1988, and Iraq's takeover of Kuwait, which was ended by a regional and international coalition in 1991.

There are also Middle Eastern minorities who fight for independent states, such as the Kurds, who live in areas belonging to Turkey, Iran, and Iraq, and the Armenians. Already in the 1890s an Armenian revolutionary

11

movement existed in Ottoman Turkey, and Armenian attacks on Turkish diplomatic missions in Europe and the United States continue to be launched in the name of the secret Armenian army (the *Asala*). Maronite Christians in Lebanon are fighting to maintain their political power, which has severely eroded since the outbreak of the civil war in their country.

Because of the Middle East's strategic importance, every one of these conflicts invites international involvement. Therefore, one can say of the whole region what has been said of Syria: "Foreigners are the makers of its history."[1]

Three important world religions originated in the Middle East: Judaism, Christianity, and Islam. But the overwhelming majority of the region's population has over the centuries come to be Islamic. Beginning in the seventh century, Islam, which had its origin in the Arabian Peninsula, quickly became the dominant religion in the Middle East and northern Africa, and then spread far beyond. As Christians converted to Islam or emigrated, their numbers dropped considerably. Today only about ten percent or less of the population of the Middle East is still Christian.

Muslims are divided between Sunnis and Shiites. Most Arabs and Turks are Sunnis, while the majority of Persians are Shiites. Of the several Muslim (and Christian) minorities in Lebanon, the Shiites are the largest Islamic minority. In Syria, by contrast, the Shiites are in the minority (seven percent of the population), but the Shiite sect of the Alawites, under President Hafiz al-Assad, has held uninterrupted power since the end of the 1960s. Though the Shiites are not in power in Iraq, they do form the largest minority. They are found especially in the southern part of the country.

In this chapter we will give short descriptions of the different churches of the Middle East and of the roles that the Roman Catholic Church and Protestant missions play in the region. We will be particularly concerned with how each of these churches relates to its Muslim environment and to Jews.

The Different Forms of Christianity in the Middle East

Christianity originated in the Middle East. In other parts of the world churches were planted by missionaries, but the church was born in the Middle East (not that this has prevented Roman Catholic and Protestant missions from including the Middle East within the radius of their mis-

---

1. W. B. Stevenson, *The Crusaders in the East* (Beirut, 1968) 1.

sionary zeal). The book of Acts tells us that it was in Antioch that followers of Jesus were first called "Christians" (Acts 11:26). Today Antioch is a small town in Turkey called Antakya, but in the first century it was the third largest city of the Roman Empire. At an early stage Antioch became an important church center.

Already in its first centuries the Christian church became divided and schisms began, which have continued to the present. Today the churches of the Middle East are commonly grouped into five families. Together these churches represent fifteen million Christians, of whom nine million still reside in the Middle East. These five families are:

1. Oriental Orthodox or non-Chalcedonian churches, that is, churches that did not accept the decisions of the Council of Chalcedon (held in 451):
   • the Syrian Orthodox Church, also called the Jacobite Church,
   • the Coptic Church of Egypt, and
   • the Armenian Apostolic (or "Gregorian") Church, represented in independent (formerly Soviet) Armenia, in Turkey, and elsewhere in the Middle East;
2. the Eastern Orthodox or Greek Orthodox Church, which is united in doctrine, liturgy, and canon law with the ecumenical patriarch of Istanbul;
3. churches linked with Rome:
   • the Maronite Church,
   • the Roman or Latin Catholic Church, and
   • various churches united with Rome that follow the Eastern rite, such as the Syrian, Armenian, Coptic, Greek, and Assyrian (Chaldean) Catholic Churches;
4. the Assyrian Church of the East; and
5. Protestant churches.

In 1974 The Middle East Council of Churches (MECC) was organized. A precursor of this council began in 1927 as a Protestant missionary council, the Council for Western Asia and North Africa (for Missionary Cooperation). By 1967 the Syrian Orthodox Church belonged to this organization, which in that year became the Near East Council of Churches (NECC). The present Council embraces all the Middle Eastern church families except for the Assyrian and Roman Catholic churches.

Theological Differences

The divisions among these churches exist for a variety of reasons. Both theological and political factors play a role, but only the theological differences are likely to be known in the West. Some of these Eastern churches bear the names of "heresies" with regard to the understanding of Jesus' significance for the salvation of the world that were condemned by the Ecumenical Councils.

The Ecumenical Council of Nicea (A.D. 325) championed the full divinity of Jesus (*vere Deus*). At the Council of Constantinople (381) the church sought to shield itself against the opposite danger and insisted on the fully human nature of Christ (*vere homo*). Once Christ's deity and humanity had thus been defended, the question arose how these two natures relate to each other. Some inferred from the duality of natures in Christ the existence of two persons. This understanding came to be associated with the name of Nestorius and was called Nestorianism. Others concluded that there was only one divine-human nature in Christ. This conception became known as Monophysitism. At the Council of Chalcedon (451) the church rejected both of these views, seeing one as a separation of the two natures and the other as a mingling of them. At the Council of Constantinople (680) the church condemned Monotheletism, that is, belief in the existence of a single divine-human *will* in Christ, an idea closely akin to Monophysitism.

Because of these ecclesiastical pronouncements the churches of the Middle East are distinguished as Chalcedonian and non-Chalcedonian. While Greek Orthodox, Roman Catholic, and Protestant churches follow Chalcedon, the other churches of the region do not.

Political Conflicts

Much more than these theological differences, however, political and national conflicts have played the decisive role in the divisions between the churches. The Councils that we have just described were all convened at or very close to the center of the late Roman Empire. The capital, Constantinople, and nearby Nicea were residences of the emperor. Chalcedon, too, lay close to the capital. The first Ecumenical Council was held in 325 after Christianity had been made the state religion of the Empire in 323 (following the Edict of Toleration in 313). Emperor Constantine saw in the preservation of the church's unity an important factor in reinforcing the Empire's unity. As we will see, loyalty to the imperial state church or lack thereof came to be decisive in the divisions among churches.

Liturgy

Those who would get to know the churches of the East must attend their worship services, whether the public worship service of the Coptic Church with its use of cymbals, the more courtly liturgy of the Byzantines, or the liturgy of Armenian church, in which one catches, as it were, the pathos of its people's suffering over many centuries.

The differences in faith experience can be expressed in this way: While the Roman Catholic believer experiences Christ's presence in the consecration of the elements, for the Protestant this happens in the preaching of the Word, or in some Protestant groups above all in song. These are not, of course, absolute distinctions. The Orthodox faith experience occurs as all the senses are addressed in the liturgy, not only the ear (in the preaching of the Word) but also the eye (viewing the icons) and the senses of touch, taste, and smell: "O taste and see that the LORD is good!" (Psalm 34:8). One who attends any Orthodox liturgy responds as it were to Philip's invitation to Nathanael: "Come and see" (John 1:46). There is express mention of the sense of sight: "Truly I tell you, many prophets and righteous people longed to see what you see, but did not see it, and to hear what you hear, but did not hear it" (Matthew 13:17). Each of the senses — so runs the Orthodox view — is consecrated by the saving action of God. "Sight, as the primary sense, was hallowed through the visible appearing of God in Christ, just as hearing was hallowed through the word of God."[2]

The Churches

The Syrian Orthodox Church

There are three Syrian churches: the Western Syrian, Jacobite, or Syrian Orthodox Church; the Eastern Syrian, Nestorian, or Assyrian Church; and the Maronite Church. Behind these churches' theological differences are political and regional divisions. For centuries before the advent of Islam, the Middle East was controlled by the two warring empires of Persia and Byzantium. The Monophysite Syrian Orthodox Church was especially concentrated in the Byzantine Empire and is known, therefore, as the West Syrian Church.

Certain Christian groups were opposed to other Christians, who

---

2. J. Pelikan, *The Christian Tradition* II: *The Spirit of Eastern Christendom (600-1700)* (Chicago, 1974) 122.

supported the Byzantine imperial power and were therefore called *Melchites* (from Syrian *melkos*, ruler). In Antioch a church of the people grew up beside the Melchite church. In the fifth century a certain Jacob Baradaeus organized such a movement of Syrian nationalist opposition to Byzantium, which came therefore to be called Jacobite. Today this church, called Syrian Orthodox, is found especially in the extreme northeast of Syria. Several of the oldest Syrian Orthodox monasteries, including Dayr al Zafaran and Dayr Gabriel, are located at Tur Abdin, "the mountain of God-worshippers" in Qamishli, an area bordering on southeastern Turkey. Syrian Orthodox believers are also found in the Syrian cities of Aleppo and Homs and in Beirut, Lebanon. The Syrian Orthodox patriarch has his seat in Atshana, Lebanon. In recent decades many Syrian Orthodox people have left southeastern Turkey for Istanbul and Europe. A large number of the so-called "Christian Turks" of Europe are Syrian Orthodox.

The Assyrian (Nestorian) Church

Whether Nestorius, who before his deposition was patriarch of Constantinople, was himself a Nestorian is questionable. The church named after him is sometimes called "the missionary church par excellence." It expanded in the Persian-controlled Middle East and further east because the roads to the West were closed. It is for this reason known as the "East Syrian" Church. The Nestorians then spread to large areas of Asia. In Afghanistan, which today is completely Islamic, there were at one time five Nestorian bishops. A monument discovered at Singanfu in 1625 testifies to the penetration of Nestorianism into China already in the eighth century.

The Mongol invasions of the twelfth and thirteenth centuries, among other factors, led to a sharp numerical decrease in the once widespread Christian church in Asia. It almost completely disappeared, so that one can speak of "the eclipse of Christianity in Asia" (E. G. Browne). The members of this church came to be found primarily in Iraq. But in the 1930s the Assyrians fell victim to British decolonization policies in that part of the Middle East. Many Nestorians lost their lives or fled to the United States, where the patriarch has his residence.

The Maronite Church

A third branch of the Syrian church is associated with the fifth-century Saint Maron. Tensions, mostly of a political nature, with both the Byzantines and the Jacobites led to the independent development of this church. Maronites are usually said to have been Monotheletists at the beginning, though as a rule they deny this, since the Council of Constantinople (A.D. 680), which rejected belief in one divine-human will in Christ, never mentioned the Maronites by name.

With about 700,000 to 750,000 members, the Maronites constitute numerically the largest Christian communion in Lebanon. The president of Lebanon must still, despite all that happened in the 1975-1990 civil war, be, by law, a Maronite. An agreement reached in Ta'if, Saudi Arabia, in 1989 changed the five-to-six proportion of Christians and Muslims in the Lebanese parliament to representation in equal numbers. This agreement was first implemented in the 1992 election. But it did not affect the presidency, so Lebanon has, therefore, the only Christian president in the Middle East, while the prime minister must be a Sunnite. The Phalangist Christian militia (the *Kata'ib*), which has become well known since the outbreak of the Lebanese civil war, consists mainly of Maronites. But the views of the Phalangists cannot be equated with that of the Maronite Church or of Lebanese Christians in general.

The Armenian Apostolic Church

Armenia was formerly an independent kingdom embracing the central highlands of Anatolia and Persia, the Korovalia in Transcaucasia and the Mesopotamian plain. In Iran and Turkey Armenian territory has no separate status, unlike the independent (formerly Soviet) republic of Armenia.

Pious legend has it that the earliest evangelization of the kingdom of Armenia goes back to apostolic times, specifically to the apostle Thaddeus, who is also called the first patriarch of Armenia. The real founder of the Armenian Church was St. Gregory the Illuminator (A.D. 240-322), so that this church is also called the "Gregorian" Church. Gregory won King Tiridates III of Armenia to the Christian faith. Toward the end of the third century, before Constantine accorded Roman state recognition to Christianity, Armenia was already officially Christianized.[3] The Armenian church now has two centers, one in Echmiadzin in independent Armenia and one in Antelias just north of Beirut, Lebanon. A catholicos, as the Armenians call their patriarchs, resides in each of these two centers.

The lot of the Armenians has often been tragic. From 1894 to 1896 there was wholesale slaughter of Armenians. Probably the worst massacre

3. A. Harnack, *The Expansion of Christianity in the First Three Centuries* II (New York, 1905) 344-47.

occurred in Turkey in 1915 and 1916.[4] Different views of what happened and why — and of how many Armenians were killed — have been the source of violent conflicts between Turks and Armenians up to the present.

Without for a moment discounting the tragic character of this bloodbath, which has been called this century's first attempted genocide, we must view it against the background of the collapse of the Turkish Ottoman Empire. The Turks had lost the Balkan Peninsula, which had been the center of their empire, and the Arab nations also won their independence. Only Anatolia was left to the Turks. Mustafa Kemal, later called Kemal Ataturk, fought against, among others, the Greeks, who for a time penetrated deeply into Anatolia. He sought to instill the idea of an Anatolian Turkish homeland, so the Turks came to view their struggle in Anatolia as essential for the preservation of their existence as a people. The struggle between the Turks and the Armenians was, therefore, a struggle for two homelands in one territory.[5]

From 1915 to 1920 many Armenians fled Turkey and went to Syria and Lebanon. Today they are located especially in Aleppo, Syria, in Beirut, Lebanon, and in Anjor, a city they themselves founded in the Beqa 'a Valley of Lebanon. In Iran the Armenian church is the largest Christian communion and is under the jurisdiction of the Catholicos of Cilicia in Antelias.

After the collapse of the Soviet Union, Armenia became independent. War broke out and continues to this day between Armenia and Azerbaijan. An issue in this fighting is the large number of Armenians living in Azerbaijan.

The Coptic Church

"Coptic" means "Egyptian" in the language used by the Coptic Church, which is the largest church in the Middle East. In 1976 the Egyptian government said that there were 2,300,000 Coptic Christians, but the probable number of Copts is now 5,500,000 to 6,500,000. The Church itself claimed 6,600,000 members.

This church, tradition says, was founded in A.D. 42 by the apostle Mark, who is also viewed as its first patriarch. At the Council of Chalcedon the Coptic patriarch Dioskuros of Alexandria was deposed, an act that the Christians of Egypt experienced as a national insult. The resistance of

---

4. See F. Werfel, *The Forty Days of Musadagh* (New York, 1934); J. Lepsius, *Bericht über die Laze des Armenischen Volkes in der Turkei* (Potsdam, 1916); A. Mardgamian, *Auction of Souls* (1920).

5. B. Lewis, *The Emergence of Modern Turkey* (London, 1968) 358.

Coptic Christians to the pronouncements of Chalcedon was theological, since their church is known as Monophysite. But their rejection of Chalcedon was even more a nationalist response to an affront to their leader.

The Coptic Church has always been strongly influenced by monks living in the desert monasteries. As a rule each bishop of the Coptic Church has spent years in one of those monasteries, like the one in Wadi Natrum, or those of Saints Anthony and Paul near the Red Sea. After World War II these monasteries experienced a significant revival, with many young men entering them. This revival has had an important effect on the church through, for example, the church educational work done every Friday (Egypt's day of rest). Every week the Coptic patriarch Anba Shenuda offers such instruction in the cathedral in Cairo, which is attended by thousands of believers. Another influential monk who has come to public attention is Matta al-Miskin (Matthew the Poor).[6]

The Greek Orthodox Church

Beside these national churches — the Syrian Orthodox, Assyrian, Maronite, Armenian, and Coptic churches — the church that was oriented to Byzantium, the Greek-Orthodox church, which until 1054 was united with the church of the West, continues to exist. In the Arab world the Greek Orthodox Church is called *Rum*-Orthodox, in keeping with the Arabic name for Byzantium. The church is said to be Greek in the sense of Byzantine, but its liturgy is Arabic. Since 1898 the patriarch has been not a Greek but an Arab, like the rest of the clergy except in Israel. The present Greek Orthodox patriarch has his seat in Damascus.

Especially after World War II a significant impetus for renewal arose from the Orthodox youth movement, which began in 1942. From it have come many laypersons and clergy who have put an important stamp on later developments, for example, Bishop George Khodr, metropolitan of "Mount Lebanon" *(Jabal Jubnan)*, and Gabriel Habib, secretary general of the Middle East Council of Churches (MECC).

In 1970 an Orthodox theological seminary was founded in Balamand, close to Tripoli, Lebanon. The Greek Orthodox Church is undoubtedly the most Arab of the churches in the Middle East in that it is more aware of being involved in the region's social and political developments. Greek Orthodox Christians play a special role, for example, in the Palestinian question, and also have more of a role than other Christians in Muslim-Christian dialogue.

6. D. B. Barrett, ed., *World Christian Encyclopedia* (Nairobi, 1982) 275.

Rome and the Churches of the Middle East

A long history of disputes led to the open break between the Byzantine Church of the East and the Roman Catholic Church of the West. It was not so much the mutual anathemas of 1054 as the Crusades (1095-1291) that sealed the division. The Fourth Crusade even led to the occupation and plundering of Byzantium (1204). Various attempts to reunify the church failed to effect any lasting results. But in our own time moves have been made toward reconciliation. Athenagoras, the ecumenical patriarch of Constantinople, and Pope Paul VI met in Jerusalem in 1964. This was followed by official visits to Istanbul and Rome in 1967. In 1976 a joint commission for dialogue was established. The commission's report (1978) set reestablishment of full communion of Roman Catholic and Orthodox Christians as the goal of dialogue, and formal dialogue began in 1980 and has continued, though full communion could not be considered close.

Rome has attempted "reunion" also in relation to the non-Chalcedonian churches. With the Maronites this was particularly successful, since their church united with Rome as a body. Already during the Crusades the Maronite Church achieved a closer relationship with Rome, and in 1439 the Council of Florence affirmed that the Maronites were orthodox. In 1736, at the Synod of Luwayzeh, complete reunion was effected. What had always been a shibboleth between Rome and Byzantium, the Roman doctrine that the Holy Spirit proceeded from the Father *and* the Son *(filioque)* and not only from the Father, the Maronites accepted at that time.

With the other national churches rapprochement with Rome took a different course: All attempts at unification led to schisms within these churches, leaving groups of Christians from within them to unite with Rome and form the "Uniate churches."

The Chaldean Church

Already from the time of the Crusades Rome sought closer relations with the Nestorians. In 1551 the Nestorian communion refused to accept its patriarch-elect. A certain monk sent to Rome and subsequently consecrated as patriarch thus became the head of the first Uniate church in the Middle East, since, in distinction from the Maronites, only part of the Nestorian Church united with Rome. But this patriarch was murdered by anti-Catholic Nestorians.

In the seventeenth century a new attempt was made to win the Nestorians. A distinct Chaldean rite was introduced in 1672, and "Chaldean" then became the name for Nestorians united with Rome. In 1845 the Sultan officially acknowledged the Chaldean patriarch as the leader of a distinct *millet*. The current number of Chaldean Christians, whose church is by far the largest in Iraq, is estimated to be between 350,000 and 400,000.

The Coptic Catholic Church

From the days of St. Francis of Assisi the church of Rome has tried to build bridges to the Coptic Church. An attempt at the Council of Ferrara/ Florence (1442) to effect reconciliation with the Copts failed. Although from the sixteenth century on certain orders like the Franciscans and the Jesuits have worked in Egypt, not until the nineteenth century was a Uniate church formed. The first Uniate patriarch, Cyrillus Macarius, took office in 1895. In 1908 he returned to the Coptic Church and defended it in pamphlets against Rome. But just before his death in 1922, he was again "united." Until 1947 the seat of the Coptic Catholic patriarch remained unoccupied.

The Armenian Catholic Church

The Armenian Catholic patriarchate goes back to 1740. The jurisdiction of this patriarch extended from Cilicia, Syria, and Lebanon to Egypt and Mesopotamia. After 1789 it included certain areas in Asia Minor. Groups of Armenian Catholics are also in various parts of Turkey, including Istanbul.

The Protestants

In 1831 the Congregational American Board of Commissioners for Foreign Missions began considerable mission activity in Turkey, first in Istanbul and later in Anatolia. The goal of this mission was to renew the Armenian Apostolic (Gregorian) Church, to save it from formalism, and to accustom it to the preaching of the gospel. Initially, Anglicans chose not to work among the Armenians in order not to compete with the Congregational work. Presbyterians and Anglicans were in agreement on social work and education, but differed on mission policy. Whereas the Presbyterian missionaries sought conversions, the Anglicans wanted to help the churches of the East reform themselves.

In July 1846 the first Protestant church among the Armenians was launched. Its members were excommunicated by the mother church. On

November 19, 1847, the Sultan granted permission for the creation of an independent ecclesiastical organization of Protestant Armenians, which implied acknowledgment of them as a separate *millet*.

In the view of Rufus Anderson, the well-known secretary of the American Board of Commissioners for Foreign Missions, the experience of thirty years showed that the old "dead" Nestorian Church could not be reformed and resurrected to spiritual life. Those who were enlightened were to unite on an apostolic foundation in a separate Protestant church.

At the beginning of the nineteenth century the Anglican missionaries of the Church Missionary Society were the first Protestants to work in Egypt. This organization hoped to stimulate the Eastern churches to spread the Christian faith among Muslims and pagans. It was expressly not the purpose of the Anglican missionaries to start separate churches.

In 1854 the missionaries of the United Presbyterian Church of North America began their work in Asyut, the so-called capital of the Copts, to the annoyance of the Coptic patriarch. He viewed this labor as a serious threat to the unity of his church. Since the patriarch regarded the Protestant church as heretical and "apostate," Copts who joined it were excommunicated.

When the British occupied Egypt in 1882, the Anglicans belonging to the Church Missionary Society, which had left Egypt in 1842, returned. But this time, like the Americans, they formed their own churches there. In 1925 an Anglican church was established in Egypt, and in 1957 it became independent.

Usually Protestant missionaries charged Christians in the Arab world with being insufficiently mission-minded toward their Muslim neighbors. At an early stage the missionaries began to view what they considered the ossification, ritualism, and formalism of these churches as a barrier to any possible missionary breakthrough. Accordingly, they did not wait long before establishing their own Protestant churches, though the Anglicans in Egypt were initially more reluctant to work in that direction. The result was, however, that in each case a Protestant church came into being that, after being accorded recognition by the Sultan, formed a separate *millet* distinct from its environment. Initially, Protestant churches thought that "converted" orthodox Christians would function as leaven, but in place of reform and "revival" what often came was schism and breakups. Conversions from Islam have always been very rare, and one of the ironies of history is that Protestant groups that arrived later, such as the Baptists, Operation Mobilization, and others, have in recent decades accused the older Protestant mission churches of lacking missionary zeal.

The Eastern churches, for their part, have viewed Protestant missions as a form of spiritual imperialism aimed at alienating Eastern Christians from their culture and churches. But no one denies the great contribution that Protestant missions have made in the fields of education, social action, and medical care.[7]

The Revival of Islam

In our time there is much talk about the complex subject of Islamic revival. In part this "revival" has to be interpreted as a largely legitimate form of resistance to foreign — especially Western — economic domination. To many Islam serves as a symbol of such resistance. But most often the term "Islamic revival" is used of an Islamic manifestation of a rightist fundamentalist phenomenon that is not restricted to Islam. Fundamentalism can also be found in the Middle East among Jews and Christians. In Israel the "block of the faithful" (*Gush Emunim*) is sometimes called "Jewish Khomeinism." As an example of Christian fundamentalism one may think of the Phalangists in Lebanon, who primarily operated under the name of "Christian Armed Forces" (not to be confused with the regular Lebanese army). In the case of Islam, the word "revival" immediately brings to mind the Iranian revolution and the coming to power, on February 1, 1979, of the late Imam Khomeini. Since then the Islamic revolution has exerted great influence far beyond the borders of Iran. "Fundamentalism," a term now also used in Arabic, is often called *intégrisme* in the French-speaking world.

But what is referred to with these terms existed in various Arab countries well before the Iranian revolution. One may call to mind the role and influence of the Muslim Brothers, an organization started in the 1920s by Hassan al-Banna. It was this group that in the 1950s and 1960s threatened the presidency of Gamal Abdel Nasser in Egypt. Several attempts were made on his life. In 1966 the well-known leader of the Muslim Brothers, Sayyid Qotb, a thinker whose works were read everywhere in the Islamic world, was hanged on account of his supposed involvement in such an assault. Muhammad Anwar al-Sadat, Nasser's successor, was sympathetic to the Muslim Brothers if not a member. When he came to power, he released some of the "brothers" whom Nasser had imprisoned. But later he himself became the victim of a similar group, which bears the name *takfir wa hijra*.

This name expresses well the views of these and related fundamentalists. It implies that they denounce as "unbelieving" (*takfir*) society as it

7. A. Wessels, *Arabier en christen. Christelijke kerken in het Midden-Oosten* (Baarn, 1983) 129-47.

operates under presidents Nasser, Sadat, and Mubarak. And just as at one time the prophet Muhammad withdrew from pagan Mecca, broke his ties to the city, and emigrated to Medina to found a new society, so now this group wants to break away from an unbelieving society and "migrate" *(hijra)* to a new form of society where the *sharia*, Islamic law, can really be followed. Several extreme fundamentalist movements exist with names like *jihad*. In Lebanon a fundamentalist Shiite movement called Hizbollah, "Party of God," is making itself felt.

These examples show, however, that one cannot simply say that the entire Islamic world is fundamentalistic. Fundamentalism and Islam cannot be equated. It is primarily Muslims themselves who are the victims of these manifestations of fundamentalism. Also, one has to bear in mind that the fundamentalists themselves, such as certain groups in Egypt, have often been the victims of repression, which has radicalized them all the more.

The Church and Islam

Has the church in the Middle East been too divided and imprisoned by group interests, or has it attempted to be relevant in and for the society of the Middle East? This question comes down in important ways to how Christians of the region relate to their Islamic environment, which has not been determined by confessional distinctives. The political context, Palestinian or Lebanese, for instance, plays a large role, and the diversity of attitudes and reactions has everything to do with the history of each group.

For centuries, the Maronites in the mountains of Lebanon have been able to maintain their political independence and autonomy in relation to their Muslim neighbors (and something similar can *mutatis mutandis* be said of the Armenians). And during the Crusades, the colonial period, and even now, the Maronites have had more contact with Western Christians than other Eastern Christian groups have had. Given this relative autonomy vis-à-vis their Muslim neighbors, it is no surprise that the Maronites have come into greater conflict with Muslims than other churches.

Most other Christian groups were quickly constrained to live in the Islamic world as *dhimmi*, protected by the Islamic state but confined to second-class citizenship. They shared the culture of their neighbors but were not genuinely open to their faith. In their Muslim surroundings Armenians have kept their own culture, language, and beliefs. Greek Orthodox Christians have become most consciously Arabic Christians culturally and politically. They fully participated in what G. Antonius called the "Arab awakening" and have played leading roles in Arab nationalism and socialism. In the Arab struggle against Turkey early in the twentieth century, Muslims and Christians in Lebanon and Egypt fought side by side. The founder of the socialist *Ba'ath* party, which is currently in power in Syria and Iraq, was Michel Aflak, a Greek Orthodox man.

A well-known Lebanese Greek Orthodox intellectual, Tarek Mitri, has defined the different political options facing Christians in the Arab East.[8] The first option proceeds from the fact that Christians are a minority. Since some Christians see the Muslim world as wanting nothing to do with the ideal of an egalitarian secular state, and since a secular state appears to be the only guarantee of equality between Muslims and non-Muslims, these Christians are tempted to withdraw from society and to strive for the creation of a separate Christian state.

Another option favored by Christians is that of an Arab nationalism that champions a strong cultural identity and is conscious of the unbreakable bond between Islam and Arab culture. Such Christians thus reject what appears to be an obsession with their minority status. When the Ottoman Empire was deteriorating and after World War I, many Christians played important roles in the development of the "Arab awakening" and in Arab nationalism and socialism.

To many Christians, especially since the Six-Day War of 1967, this last option is no longer viable. In fact, not only Christians, but also some Muslims regard Egypt's defeat in that war as a fiasco for Arab nationalism and socialism. Many Muslims are critical of Arab nationalism because they consider it a movement imported from the West. Its aim, they say, is to divide the Muslim community (the *umma*).

Other Christians — Mitri presumably among them — attempt to take the current renaissance of Islam seriously. Through dialogue with their Muslim co-citizens they search for a model of society that guarantees civic, political, and religious equality between Muslims and non-Muslims. But equality, says Mitri, is inseparably bound up with social justice, democracy, and national liberation. This recalls the markedly Greek Orthodox reflection on mission perspectives in the Middle East of Frieda Haddad, who teaches pastoral theology at the Greek Orthodox seminary in Balamand:

> The future of Christian mission in the Middle East is not to be reduced to mere words in the never-never-land of books. Neither is it to be

---

8. T. Mitri, "Arab Christians in Relation to Their Muslim Co-Citizens and Neighbours," *MECC Perspectives* (Geneva, 1986) 39-42.

advocated through western-type institutions (schools, hospitals, universities) that feed the body and the mind leaving the heart untouched. Our task is to bring Islam, i.e., believers in God, not atheists or agnostics suffering from the currents of thought triggered off by Fichte, Heidegger, Kant, Marx and the like, to distinguish in its own heart the difference between the word that is heard and the word that is seen. The ground has been prepared for us to move from the "Hearken O Israel" of *Exodus* and *Numbers* to "Lift up thine eyes and behold" of *Isaiah* and of the *Psalms*. The liturgical person alone, the one who has acquired an ear for an eye and a heart for a head, who has learned to listen and understand with the heart, will find the right words that will speak to the hearts of one's neighbours.[9]

But Mitri points out that, however strange it may seem, the churches in the Middle East do not generally display any conscious or systematic interest — theological or pastoral — in Islam. He rightly finds this paradoxical because their entire lives are lived among Muslims, in view of which they should, in their theology, pastoral work, and political activities, be able to come to an understanding of their Muslim neighbors.

Another option for Middle Eastern Christians, one little understood by Christians in the West, is to emphasize the survival and identity of their own groups. This option is represented by the Lebanese Phalangists. Such Christians regard the church primarily as an organ for ideological mobilization and as a means of articulating more sharply the cultural identity or particularism of the group. Their paramount goal is to fight for the rights of Christian minorities. For that reason they do not encourage the growth of political pluralism within the Christian community. When survival is at stake, they believe, Christians must close ranks politically. This attitude has been reinforced, Mitri says, by the awakening of Islamic fundamentalism. The result is increased polarization between Christians and Muslims.

The faith and the religious convictions of Arab Christians have, indeed, been steeped in the search for self-preservation. Many Arab Christians point to the benefits of "survival" despite the difficult or at least unfavorable circumstances. They think it unfair that they are expected in their faith and religious practices to be oriented to expansion and mission. Mitri further points out that the drive for self-preservation is less theological than it is psychological, or at least a psychological concern with theological implications. Many Arab Christians who bring up the issue of survival, he says, believe that the Islamic awakening, that is, present-day

9. F. Haddad, "Reflections on Perspectives of Mission in the Arab Middle East," *International Review of Missions* 76 (1987) 75.

Islamic politics, constitutes a danger to them, if not a immediate threat. But they do not always make this assessment in a spirit of objectivity, and the threat is often exaggerated.

The clearest example of this focus on survival is seen not in the Phalangists but in emigrants. During and since the presidency of Sadat, conflicts between Muslims and Christians have increased. As in past times of tension, many Christians have been leaving the Middle East, this time for Europe and especially the United States. For centuries Lebanon was a place of refuge for Christians from other countries in the Middle East, but it, too, has become a threatened nation and so has seen departures. And internal migration has isolated Christians in Christian enclaves inside Lebanon.

Theological Understandings of Islam

Recent decades have seen much reflection on the theological problem of Islam in Protestant and Catholic circles. But it is important for us to listen to Middle Eastern voices. Bishop Khodr made a strong impression in his address at the meeting of the Central Committee of the World Council of Churches in Addis Ababa, Ethiopia, in 1971, in which he dealt with the work of the Holy Spirit and mission.[10] Some of his ideas have been picked up and developed by Tarek Mitri.

Mitri distinguishes four Christian theological understandings of Islam: Some Christians struggle to defend Christian monotheism against Muslim accusations that Christians are polytheists. And they attempt to prove the authenticity of the four Gospels against the Muslim appeal to the apocryphal Gospel of Barnabas as the one original gospel of Jesus Christ.[11]

Other Christians believe that ultimately all religions converge despite the multiplicity of revelations. To them the most important thing is that a person believe in God and live morally. These are usually Christians who have lived together with Muslims for centuries. In their religious understanding and practice Islam is sometimes mixed in with their Christianity. Mitri characterizes this approach as being one more of practical religion than of theology.

A third group of Christians acknowledges the plethora of divine

10. G. Khoder, "The Economy of the Holy Spirit," in *Mission Trends No. 5: Faith Meets Faith,* ed. G. H. Anderson and T. F. Stransky (New York and Grand Rapids, 1981) 36-49.

11. Cf. J. Slomp, "The Gospel in Dispute," in *Islamochristiana* (1978) 67-112.

gifts in the world and of "visitations of the Logos," as the Church Fathers called them. In today's language this means that they believe the Holy Spirit is also actively at work outside the boundaries of visible Christianity, hence also among Muslims. They are particularly interested in those signs and experiences within the Muslim community that manifest such divine activity. They are especially attracted to Muslim mystics.

A fourth school of thought seeks to legitimize Islam. This theology is based on the intuition that mystical grace manifests itself outside Christianity and that there is prophetism outside the Jewish and Christian tradition. Islam is viewed as a natural religion, as Abrahamism, or as Ishmaelism, a reappropriation of Abrahamism.

In this fourth group Mitri is probably thinking of contributions in the "theology of Islam" by Youakim Moubarac and Michael Hayek, both pupils of Louis Massignon. Both of these men have in their own way processed the insights of their teacher and developed them into a Christian view of Islam as the zealous defender of the mystery of God. They refer to certain Nestorian texts in which the prophetic character of Muhammad is defined on the basis of a specific analysis of his message. In their thinking this recognition does not weaken acknowledgment of the centrality and uniqueness of Jesus Christ.[12]

The Church and Judaism

In dealing with the relationship between the church and the world, the church in the Middle East cannot avoid the issue of its relationship to the Jews. For churches in Europe and the United States this issue involves "theology after Auschwitz," the consequences in Christian theology of the Holocaust, which was the nadir of centuries of persecution of European Jews. In the West there is often little awareness that for centuries more Jews lived in the Arab world than in Europe. Often it is said either that Jews there have been exposed to the same anti-Semitism as in Europe or that their situation has been better than that of Jews in Europe.

Both points of view have also been defended by Jewish authors. The Tunisian Jew Albert Memmi concluded that as in Europe so also in the Arab world Jews have been subject to persecutions, pogroms, and discrimination.[13] He described in a novel his struggle to find his own identity:[14]

12. Mitri, *art. cit.*
13. *Portrait of a Jew* (New York, 1962).
14. *The Pillar of Salt* (London, 1956) 95f.

Could I be descended from a Berber tribe when the Berbers themselves failed to recognize me as one of their own? I was Jewish, not Moslem; a townsman, not a highlander. And even if I had borne the painter's name, I would not have been acknowledged by the Italians. No, I'm African, not European. In the long run, I would always be forced to return to Alexandre Mordekhai Benillouche, a native in a colonial country, a Jew in an anti-Semitic universe, an African in a world dominated by Europe.

But André Chouraqui, an Algerian Jew who emigrated to Israel, writes that the occasional outbursts of violence against Jews in North Africa were caused not only by local attitudes toward non-Muslims but also by the horrible wretchedness in which feudalism had immersed the entire population. According to Chouraqui there was never in North Africa a philosophy and tradition of anti-Semitism such as existed in Europe.[15]

However this may be, the fact is that for centuries Jews and Arabs were able to coexist. The Jewish people flourished at times not only in Moorish Spain but also in Iraq. Jews made contributions to the development of Arabic culture, poetry, and philosophy. Jewish poets and thinkers expressed themselves in the Arabic language. A great many Jewish philosophical and theological developments have to be understood against the background of Arabic culture. Jews held the most important positions in economic and political life. Jews in the medieval Arab world were better off and enjoyed more tolerance than those in Christian Europe. The well-known Jewish thinker Maimonides, when he had to flee Spain, sought refuge in the Arab world, where he later died (in Cairo, 1205). Whenever and wherever the Jewish community was threatened, one must ask whether this might have been true of other minority groups as well, particularly in times of economic and political crisis. Often Jews suffered persecution at the same time as Christians. We know of instances where Christians saved their lives in Egypt by wearing Jewish turbans.

Since the establishment of the state of Israel, Jewish communities in several Arab countries have radically decreased in numbers, and some have disappeared. Jews have gone to Israel or emigrated to Europe or the United States. It is with a feeling of sadness that one sees in Stillman's book on the history of Jews in Arab countries[16] pictures of Jewish men, women, and families in various Arab countries living a way of life that no longer exists.

15. A. Chouraqui, *Between East and West: A History of the Jews of North Africa* (Philadelphia, 1968).
16. N. A. Stillman, *The Jews of Arab Lands: A History and Source Book* (Philadelphia, 1979).

Understandably, in our day questions associated with the relationship between the church and the Jews cannot be thought of in the Middle East apart from the issue of the church's relationship to the state of Israel.

This is not the place for a general discussion of the relation between Western Christians and Christianity on the one hand and Jews and Judaism on the other. The attitude of Christians in the Middle East toward Jews is soured by the political tensions surrounding Israel. Tarek Mitri asserts that from the creation of the state of Israel two issues have arisen with regard to the relationship between the churches of the region and Judaism as a religion: First, the establishment of the state of Israel implied that the Palestinian people were robbed of their right to exist as a nation. From the Zionist perspective the Palestinians are simply refugees. Though the Palestinians residing in Israel (inside the pre-1967 borders) are viewed as Israeli Arabs, they are nevertheless regarded as second-class citizens. So far Israel has consistently denied to Palestinians a state of their own. In light of this injustice, says Mitri, the churches in the region speaking in the name of human rights and national self-determination can ask that justice be done. Such a position is not, in his opinion, anti-Semitic. On the contrary, it *repudiates* racial and religious discrimination.

The second issue is that of state religion. In Israel, says Mitri, Judaism is the religion of the state. Islam is the state religion in other countries of the region, though in some cases, as in Syria, the constitution stipulates only that Islam must be the religion of the president. Lebanon has no state religion, though the constitution does require that the president be a Maronite Christian and the prime minister a Sunnite Muslim.

Jewish-Christian dialogue in the region, according to Mitri, will remain blocked as long as the religious dimension of that dialogue is overshadowed by the political dimension and the injustices inherent in it. A remark by the patriarch of the Greek Orthodox Church of Antioch, Ignatius Hazim, points in the same direction. In an address before the Catholic Institute of Paris on June 2, 1983, he said:

> But it is tragic, I repeat with emphasis, it is tragic that the Church of Antioch — the most Semitic, the closest to Judaism in mysticism, compassion and thought — cannot for the moment extend to this religion its effort of peace-making and of dialogue. We cannot forget the annexed Arab City of Jerusalem, the West Bank colonized little by little, Lebanon heavily occupied. Dialogue in this case requires the prerequisite of justice.[17]

17. Mitri, *op. cit.*, 42.

CHAPTER 3

Western Europe — The Netherlands: Emancipation and Pluralization

J. van Raalte

Human history is full of change. Now and then this change bears the character of a mutation of humanity itself."[1] We are living at such a time. As part of Western Europe, the Netherlands is involved in these fundamental changes in human existence.

In this chapter we look at only two broad areas of change that are of particular significance for Western Europe, for the Netherlands, and for Christianity in general:

- changes in power relations among nations and in relationships between the "first" world and the "third" world and
- the rise of a society marked by a plurality of different convictions, views, ideas, experiences, and behaviors.

The first of these sets of changes can be characterized by the term *emancipation*, the second as *pluralization*. Here we will be concerned with describing these changes in the context of the church's mission. How the church fulfills — and should filfill — its mission in the midst of these changes falls outside the scope of our discussion.

Emancipation

With the word "emancipation" I refer to the multiplicity of movements seeking the liberation of groups in society from conditions of juridical, political,

1. F. Boerwinkel, *Inclusief Denken — Een andere tijd vraagt een ander denken* (Hilversum, 1970) 20.

31

or social marginality.[2] This is a relatively vague term, therefore, relating to the acquisition of freedom and of a share in responsibility for society's direction and to the ending of paternalisms. In this chapter it will be used especially of the democratic ordering of society and to decolonization.

Historical Transformations

Government and the People. The French Revolution and the Industrial Revolution marked a profound change in the history of Western European society. In 1789 the national Assembly of the French Republic adopted The Declaration of the Rights of Man and of the Citizen, according to which ultimate power in the state rests with the people: "The law is the expression of the will of the people. All citizens have the right, either personally or through their representatives, to contribute to its establishment."[3]

Before the French Revolution the state consisted of government and subjects. The government could be gentle or tyrannical, but either way it was the bearer of undivided authority. The people had to obey. After the French Revolution the people gained the right and the means, in most cases through representative assemblies, to exert influence on the government. In some countries (Switzerland, for example) the people could now exert direct influence by way of referenda. In the Netherlands parliamentary democracy made its appearance in 1848. Initially only men who paid a stated amount of taxes had the right to vote. In 1917 the right to vote was extended to all men and in 1922 also to women. Since 1986 resident aliens may vote for the members of municipal councils.

The French Revolution was followed in the nineteenth century by the Industrial Revolution. Industrial production required large numbers of laborers, who as a rule led miserable lives on the margins of society. After a period of acquiescence these workers began to organize themselves in order to improve their lot and sought by negotiation to gain better working conditions. Socialist organizations of the proletariat were formed, aimed at overthrowing the existing order to replace it with a society in which laborers would rule. Following the advent in the Netherlands of compulsory education (1900), universal suffrage (1917), and the forty-eight hour workweek (1919), the goal of revolution faded into the background.[4]

2. E. Steinbach, "Emanzipation," *Religion in Geschichte und Gegenwart* II (Tübingen, 1958) 450; J. Hendriks, "Verschillen tussen christenen," *Gereformeerd Theologisch Tijdschrift* 57 (1977) 13-15.

3. H. Bonger, *Leraar der mensenrechten, Thomas Jefferson* (Arnhem, 1951) 66ff.

4. W. Fabian, "Sozialismus I. Geschichtlich und systematisch," *RGG* VI (Tübin-

The French Revolution and the Industrial Revolution thus marked the beginning of the emancipation of the bourgeoisie and the laborers. Power and responsibility no longer rested solely in the hands of the government and employers. Freedom, sharing of responsibility, and the right to influence government have come to be no longer merely dreams. The structure of society has changed. Even so, we cannot say what social relations will look like in the future, whether these changes will continue, or how society will be structured.

Colonialism. The nineteenth-century emancipation of the bourgeoisie and the laborers in Europe was accompanied by the strengthening and expansion of European colonialism elsewhere. In colonization, political domination and economic exploitation usually went hand in hand.[5] The condition of colonialism can be briefly defined as political, cultural, and economic dependence on, and domination by, foreign powers. In the beginning it often involved slavery, but that ended in the nineteenth century, for the Dutch colonies in 1863.[6] In the same century colonial expansion extended to virtually the entire African continent, with Belgium, Germany, and Italy joining the older European colonial powers of Spain, Portugal, Great Britain, the Netherlands, France, and Denmark.

Opposition to colonialism arose in the twentieth century and was especially encouraged by the Soviet Union. From 1920 on advocates there pleaded for an alliance with the victims of colonialism, and anticolonial movements found inspiration and support there.[7] But already certain events had fostered doubts concerning the supremacy of the West, including Turkish participation in the Crimean War against Russia (1854-56) and Russia's defeat in a sea war against Japan (1904-05). Finally, respect for the West was radically undermined by World War I and World War II. The presumption of Western Christian civilization was unmasked.

After World War II, administrative colonialism came to an end, with or without a struggle, nearly everywhere. Among Dutch colonies, Indonesia achieved independence in 1949 and Suriname in 1975. The Dutch An-

gen, 1962) 176-81; J. Hendriks, *Emancipatie, relaties tussen minoriteit en dominant* (Brussels, 1981) 139ff.

5. H. Kraemer, *Godsdiensten en culturen, de komende dialoog* (The Hague, 1963) 57ff.; K. H. Pfeffer, "Kolonialismus," *Religion in Geschichte und Gegenwart* III (Tübingen, 1959) 1723ff.

6. J. van Raalte, *Secularisatie en zending in Suriname; over het secularisatieproces in verband met het zendingswerk van de Evangelische Broedergemeente in Suriname* (dissertation, Wageningen, 1973) 68.

7. J. Verkuyl, *De geest van communisme en kapitalisme en het evangelie van Christus* (Delft, 1950); Pfeffer, *RGG* III, 1723ff.

tilles and Aruba have internal autonomy within the Kingdom of the Netherlands.

That is not to say, however, that these former colonies no longer serve as "institutions and means to *foreign* ends" and that "*foreign* decisions" no longer have decisive influence on the lot of their people.[8] Especially as a result of their weak economic positions, these states have remained dependent on foreign economic and political powers. Attempts to escape from this dependency by means of development programs have not led to the desired results.

I. Wallerstein pointed out that even though "historic capitalism" has brought change, it has not necessarily brought progress. Accordingly, he warned against the prevailing tendency to view history from the perspective of progress.[9] His warning applies equally well to the process of emancipation that began with the French Revolution and the Industrial Revolution and with colonialism in the "third" world. The degree to which we can speak of "progress" in these historical changes must be subjected to closer scrutiny.

Democracy and Emancipation

Democracy. To start on the road toward a democratic ordering of society means to make a beginning with human freedom, responsibility, and independence. Democracy gives people a chance to participate in the progress of society. In this way a society can arise that enjoys the support of the people as a whole. Democracy, emancipation, and progress are thus inseparably bound together.

But we must set three qualifications against this statement. First, the state has begun to play a role in areas where it previously did not. Almost everywhere people have been led to load upon their governments responsibilities for human happiness which no government in previous ages was expected to carry. National governments are widely assumed to be responsible for and capable of providing those things which former generations thought only God could provide — freedom from fear, hunger, disease and want — in a word: "happiness."[10] In this situation emancipation does not mean that the people share responsibility with the government but that they transfer responsibility to the government.

8. Kraemer, 58.
9. I. Wallerstein, *Historisch Kapitalisme* (Weesp, 1984) 81-83.
10. L. Newbigin, *The Other Side of 1984* (Geneva, 1983) 58.

Second, while emancipation means liberation from oppression and paternalism and therefore freedom of religion, conscience, and speech, this freedom can also be interpreted as "freedom to hold property, to trade, and to travel."[11] It is easy — permanently or provisionally, in whole or in part — to make liberation abstract, to separate it from solutions for poverty, sickness, and ignorance. One freedom can be played off against another, in which case emancipation is only partial.

Third, democracy is a system in which minorities must be prepared in advance to submit to decisions of the majority, since every violation of the system would inflict worse damage or entail a greater disadvantage. The only thing a democracy can prevent, therefore, is the dictatorship of a minority over a majority. It has no room for a particular form of the right of might: minority domination. But the right of might continues to exist in democracies, though in a veiled form. Emancipation as coming of age means for the minority little more than the right to protest, provided one gives in to majority rule.

With the establishment of parliamentary democracy a form of emancipation has come into being. The people as a whole are no longer only the object but also the subject and coagent in the exercise of political, social, and economic policy. But liberation from the sins of domination and oppression does not mean that justice and peace will automatically come forth: In a democracy the sins of greed and of the will to dominate are regulated, not banished.

Decolonization. This limited character of political and social emancipation is especially seen in relations between the "third" world and the "first" world. Though administrative colonialism is a thing of the past, foreign powers and institutions continue to have great power in former colonies. Multinational businesses and international banking institutions exercise great influence in poor and dependent countries. Moreover, by means of so-called development aid the wealthier nations are able to exert pressure on recipient nations. As a result of these influences former colonies are incorporated into economic and technological structures in which Western nations and institutions play the dominant role. Administrative decolonization has made it possible for Western nations to interfere in the internal affairs of other nations when it is to their advantage to do so.

Democracy is territorially limited. Poor and dependent people of distant nations can easily, without having any say about it, become the victims of decisions made elsewhere. Democracy is not a system in which all concerned parties exert influence. It is, rather, a system in which admission to a role is dependent on whether common interests are served

11. *Ibid.,* 29.

by it. In the wealthy democratic countries of the West employers and employees negotiate contracts on working conditions. In that context the advantages and disadvantages to both parties are considered. Costs are calculated into the prices of products purchased also by poor people in poor countries, but such people are kept out of the decision-making process because of the disadvantages their influence would have for employers and employees. So for them Western-style democracy means a continuation of colonial oppression.

While decolonization restrains the right of might somewhat, the right of might is simultaneously legitimated and strengthened by being based on democracy. Emancipation seems to be little more than the acquisition of a share in the right of might. The new nations — former colonies — can with more or less success participate in the struggle for profit and power. Therefore, emancipation is by definition not the way to a society characterized by justice and peace.

Christianity and Emancipation

The Influence of Christianity on Emancipation. In describing the influence of Christianity[12] on changes in Western European power structures, one can mention three important factors. First, the advent of Christianity ended the deification of the emperor and of the power of the state. In the *Corpus Christianum* we have "that indissoluble unity of Church, Community, and State"[13] in which the Christian religion and church take the place of pagan state religion and of the culture that accompanied it.[14] But the church was never completely absorbed by the state or society. It always maintained a distance, even though the temptation was present to perpetuate the old religious order in a Christian form.[15] The Christian church was a fellowship around the Word that denied divine status to every institution in this world, including human government. By pronouncing the state a human institution, Christianity helped to open the road to changes in power structures. And it thus unconsciously put a time bomb under its own claims to a position of superiority over the state.[16]

---

12. By "Christianity" I mean here the historical religious phenomenon characterized by faith in Christ, by (fractured) forms of community, by associated organizational and official structures, and by the Christian community's shaping of its faith and message.

13. H. Kraemer, *The Christian Message in a Non-Christian World* (London, 1938) 26.

14. K. Heussi, *Kompendium der Kirchengeschichte* (Tübingen, 1960) 92ff.

15. Van Leeuwen, *Christianity in World History*, 331-33.

16. Cf. Pope Boniface VIII's Bull *Unam Sanctam of 1302*; Heussi, *op. cit.*, 238.

Second, the church was the bearer of a message of far-reaching and all-embracing changes. Jesus overcame the powers and conquered death. He proclaimed the gospel of reconciliation, forgiveness, a new beginning, a new life, and the coming of a kingdom in which God's justice would prevail. This opened the door to initiatives for *actual* change, though it did not guarantee that from then on history would move in the direction of God's kingdom. People can set to work with this message — but they can also undermine the kingdom. The church proclaims a message of essential change, but it can also unleash a syncretistic countermovement to crush the very movement that it has evoked and to legitimize existing structures. But it cannot eliminate the message of hope from the gospel. Despite its own inertia the church has in many cases been a source of resistance.

Finally, the church is the bearer of a message that addresses those who hear it as responsible people. In many Protestant churches this responsibility was given very practical shape in that, by means of elections, its members came to be equal in voice and vote with the preachers in the government of the church. In this way the church was far ahead of the state.

Christianity has thus not only served to confirm "the system"[17] but, often in spite of itself, has been of real significance in the rise of freedom, responsibility, and the escape from paternalism. The church does not bring a gospel of democracy and decolonization. But it has sown seeds of change and has thus contributed to changes that it only rarely envisaged when it sowed those seeds.

Democracy is not a Christian invention. Traces of democratic practice were already present in ancient Greece. In the fifth century B.C. in Athens, the power of the large landowners and the bondage of the poor peasants was ended. "A gathering of able-bodied men" was able to influence the appointment of magistrates. Fifty members were chosen by lot from each of ten tribal communities to occupy for a year a seat in a council charged with governing, "one of the very rare examples of the notion of representation among ancient people."[18] This system lasted for centuries. Even so, the Athenian example is no reason to deny the influence of Christianity on the rise of contemporary political structures in Europe.

The Influence of Emancipation on Christianity. The time of the *Corpus Christianum* is past. In some European countries (Great Britain, Sweden),

17. H. Kuitert, *Everything Is Politics but Politics Is not Everything: A Theological Perspective on Faith and Politics* (Grand Rapids, 1986) 56-61.

18. H. Bolkestein, "De geschiedenis der Grieken," in C. D. J. Brandt and H. van Werveke, ed., *Wereldgeschiedenis — De geschiedenis van de mensheid van de oudste tijden tot heden* II (Antwerp, 1963) 176-253.

the role of the state church is not yet finished. But in the Netherlands it is. There the state guarantees freedom of religion for everyone (Art. 6 of the constitution, February 6, 1983). Church denominations can exist as legal corporations and are governed "by their own by-laws to the extent that they are not in conflict with the law" (*Civil Code* 2.2, 1976). The policy of the government is to extend the separation of church and state and to terminate existing relationships and arrangements, which have been in place for a long time.[19]

Furthermore, the time is past when the church could speak with authority. For the government the voice of the church has as much or as little weight as that of other social groups.[20] The church is heard not because it is a religious institution; its actions and resolutions addressed to the government are judged on the basis of their political significance and objective insight.

But this is not to say that the church no longer has any responsibility for the manner in which the state and other institutions exercise their power. The end of the *Corpus Christianum* does not spell the end of the church's responsibility for the history of the world. Efforts to end poverty, dependence, and voicelessness are still threatened, and for many they are crushed by the right of might. Now that this takes place within the framework of democracy and of the recognition of the independence of almost all nations, the church will have to give fresh form to its responsibility.

Pluralization

Plurality, pluralism, and pluralization are terms that can refer to a variety of situations:

- to differences within a given congregation,[21]
- to differences within Christianity among churches and church traditions,[22]
- to the diversity of religions and cultures, including ideas and movements that judge all religion to be obsolete,[23] and

19. E. K. den Breejen, "Scheiding van kerk en staat — Recente juridische ontwikkelingen in Nederland," *Civis Mundi* 24 (1985) 126-29.

20. G. Dekker, *De mens en zijn godsdienst* (Bilthoven, 1975) 34-39; Kuitert, *op. cit.*, passim.

21. Hendriks, *op. cit.*, 14; J. Plomp, "Eenheid en pluraliteit — vier verkenningen," *Gereformeerd Theologisch Tijdschrift* 77 (1977) 21-48.

22. G. C. Berkouwer, *The Church* (Grand Rapids, 1976) 51-76.

23. Kraemer, *Godsdiensten en culturen*, passim; P. Rossano, "Christ's Lordship

• to cultural, ethical, socioeconomic, and political differences.[24]

In this chapter our main interest is the pluralism of religious and nonreligious insights, concepts, traditions, and behaviors. In this connection cultural, political, and socio-economic aspects also play a role when they are coupled with religious differences.

Between Secularism and Religions

For some time now Western European society has been characterized by religious pluralism — and from the nineteenth century on there has been a growing number of people who view themselves as *non*religious. In the Netherlands the category "no church" occurred in the census for the first time in 1849 and included one-tenth of one percent of the population.[25] Since then this part of the population has risen to fifty-seven percent. This includes those — thirty-six percent of the population — with views and ideas varying from conscious atheism (God does not exist) or agnosticism (God is inconceivable)[26] to a life in which religion can be "neither discovered nor apprehended."[27] Claude Geffré speaks of "post-atheistic" indifference.[28]

We would be going too far if we concluded from this that such people have permanently left behind all religious consciousness and every shadow of religion. Religion appears to be ineradicable. Religious groups that move outside traditional church patterns find resonance, and nonreligious ideologies are often clothed in pseudo-religious forms.[29] Human beings are evidently not content to limit themselves to the world that they can observe and whose structure they can investigate. "[The human person's] nature is apparently such that he cannot resign himself to what is

---

and Religious Pluralism," in G. H. Anderson and T. F. Stransky, ed., *Mission Trends No. 5: Faith Meets Faith* (New York and Grand Rapids, 1981) 20-35.

24. J. Tennekes and A. W. Musschenga, "Minderheden: Dilemma's van een pluralistische samenleving," in *Filosofie en praktijk* 5/3 (1984) 113-28.

25. G. B. Wurth and W. A. Wiersinga, *Het evangelie in een ontkerstende wereld* (Kampen, 1953) 106.

26. J. W. Becker and R. Vink, *Secularistie in Nederland: 1966-1991* (Rijswijk, 1994) 134, 168.

27. J. Hoekendijk, *De kerk binnenste buiten* (Amsterdam, 1964) 69.

28. C. Geffré, "The Outlook for the Christian Faith in a World of Religious Indifference," in *Indifference to Religion*, ed. J.-P. Jossua and C. Geffré (Concilium; New York, 1983) 59.

29. Van Leeuwen, *op. cit.*, 348. The forms which that creed can assume are at most only pseudo-religious.

phenomenal in its relations and relativities."[30] The most fundamental questions of life are religious. We cannot confine ourselves to nonreligious answers. But the claim that every religious answer is untenable and meaningless is, nonetheless, worthy of our attention. That people can choose between religion and some form of secularism[31] is an objective fact. Signs of a break with belief in "something that goes beyond or enfolds human beings and their world"[32] can be seen already in ancient Greek philosophers like Protagoras and Theodoros. Their work was exceptional, however, and produced no areligious movement.[33] Secularism is a "post-Christian" phenomenon.

Even before European Christians had recognized that the exodus from the churches — the break with all religion and the marginalization of church and faith — was occurring, they were confronted with the arrival of comparatively large numbers of adherents of other religions. In the Netherlands today there are about 566,000 Muslims and 71,000 Hindus.[34] The number of adherents of other religions (Buddhism, for example) is unknown. In addition there is among immigrants what we can, for lack of a better term, call folk religion. Adherents of the Winti religion of Suriname are especially striving for recognition.[35]

All the dimensions of pluralism are occurring together in Europe. This pluralism plays important roles both globally and locally. On the global level, the concept of "society" can no longer be restricted to the boundaries of a specific country or continent. None of us belongs any longer to one single nation. We all now belong to the one human race. Plurality has become visible locally because people with different ideas, attitudes, behaviors, and experiences live and work as neighbors and

30. H. Berkhof, *The Christian Faith* (revised ed., Grand Rapids, 1986) 7.

31. By secularism I mean a manner of life and thought in which one takes account only of the phenomena that one can observe and whose inner structure one can investigate and explain. By secularization, on the other hand, I mean the dissolution of the identification of humankind and the world with God. Accordingly, secularism is not the same as secularization, even though the latter term is often used to refer to the progressive loss of all religious notions. Cf. Van Raalte, *op. cit.,* 16-60.

32. H. Küng, "Introduction: The Debate on the Word 'Religion,'" in *Christianity among World Religions,* ed. H. Küng and J. Moltmann (Concilium; Edinburgh, 1986) xv; cf. J. von Ess, H. von Stietencron, and H. Bechert, *Christentum und Weltreligionen — Hinführung zum dialog mit Islam, Hinduismus und Buddhismus* (Munich and Zurich, 1984) 19.

33. G. Mensching, "Atheismus I. Religionsgeschichtlich," *Religion in Geschichte und Gegenwart* I (Tübingen, 1957) 672.

34. C. J. M. Prins, "Islamieten en Hindoes in Nederland," *Maandstatistiek van de bevolking 1994/2* (Centraal Bureau voor de Statistiek, 1994) 22-27.

35. E. D. Caffe, "Worstelen tussen culturen. De rol van Winti in het leven van de Afro-Surinamer," in *Religieuze bewegingen in Nederland, 12. Surinaamse religies in Nederland — winti, hindoeisme, hindostaanse islam* (Amsterdam, 1986) 7-22.

colleagues in the same streets, businesses, and schools. Religions and cultures were originally shaped in bounded societies in which encounters with people unlike oneself were rare and marginal.[36] Our religions and cultures were not designed for plural societies. About the shape of such a society one can at this point speak only with diffidence, but an important start is the Universal Declaration of Human Rights adopted by the United Nations.

Crisis and Kairos

Authors such as Hendrik Kraemer,[37] Peter Berger,[38] and Gerard Dekker[39] have pointed out that pluralization puts every religion and every religious conviction into a competitive position. It entails, that is, the possibility of choice. The adherents of all views are compelled to give account for the meaning and tenability of their convictions and behavior to each other and to themselves. The universal validity and self-evident nature of any single perspective or attitude have been fundamentally called into question. Because plurality implies that people have to make choices, the religions and cultures received from the past are in a situation of crisis.

This is not to say that pluralization is being *experienced* as a crisis. In the first place, people of different views can, as much as possible, limit interpersonal communication. "Hindu, Muslim, and Christian communities living in the same region [are] largely isolated from each other without a common language of discourse at spiritual depth,"[40] writes M. M. Thomas, referring to India. Secondly, people can avoid communication on a spiritual level and limit their interest in each other to superficial everyday matters. Finally, communication can fail because when people do raise ultimate questions, they do so in such different ways. And without mutual participation real communication is impossible. Thomas makes a plea, therefore, for joint participation in nation building and in world communion as the frame of reference for far-reaching dialogue about our final human destiny.

Avoidance of encounter on a spiritual level among members of a

---

36. Kraemer, *op. cit.*, 23-51.

37. Kraemer, *Vormen van godsdienstcrisis* (Amsterdam, 1959), passim; *The Christian Message*, passim.

38. P. Berger, *The Sacred Canopy: Elements of a Sociological Theory of Religion* (Garden City, 1967).

39. Dekker, *op. cit.*, 50-62, 100-106.

40. M. M. Thomas, "Christology and Pluralistic Consciousness," *International Bulletin of Missionary Research* 10 (1986) 106.

plural society is dangerous. Where such avoidance is practiced, there is a strong chance of conflicts that have nothing to do with any real differences in people's approach to and understanding of the final destiny of humanity and human history, though they are interpreted as such. The real sources of tension escape notice. A good example of this occurred in Suriname in 1980, when a small party of the military was able to seize power because the political leaders of the diverse ethnic groups were involved in a power struggle completely unrelated to the real differences among them.

To achieve a set of global transcultural values, it will be necessary for people of different cultures and religions to give themselves fully to communication of what moves them at the deepest levels. Communication on these levels entails a crisis of certainties. A new future can come into being and develop only through the pain of this crisis. The birth and growth of worldwide transcultural values rules out destruction, repression, or oppression of any one culture by another, offenses of which Western Christian culture has been guilty for centuries. Such a transcultural set of values will not come into being as people add something new to the plurality of cultures. Nor will it replace existing cultures or elements in them. It can only arise out of communication on a spiritual level among existing cultures and religions.

Communication *on the local level* among people in their common existence and relationships can be the training school par excellence toward these goals. In the short run avoidance of fundamental encounter may prevent crises and conflicts. But in the long run such an attitude can only produce a crisis with very negative effects. An encounter on a spiritual level produces a crisis that can save humankind from ruin. Viewed in this light pluralization presents a *kairos:* not only a problematic situation but also an opportunity.[41] A Christian has the capacity "to recognise [the demand of the *kairos*] and concretely fulfil its demand."[42]

Pluralization from Below

Finally, following the Ecumenical Association of Third World Theologians (EATWOT), we should notice that pluralization has begun to bear the marks, both globally and locally, of involvement by poor and oppressed peoples. They are entering history from below. We cannot use the concept

41. P. E. Knitter, *No Other Name? A Critical Survey of Christian Attitudes toward the World Religions* (Maryknoll, 1985) 18.
42. G. Delling, *Theological Dictionary of the New Testament* III, 460.

of a pluralistic society to hide this reality. Until now pluralization of society has been marked by political, juridical, social, and economic inequalities. Contemporary pluralization began with colonialism. But it has gone on beyond that stage because poor and oppressed nations and peoples have begun to take steps to participate in human history. EATWOT calls this the "irruption of the Third world."[43]

The "irruption" of poor and oppressed peoples implied the emergence of peoples of other religions and cultures — who generally belong to poor and dependent nations. A number of these people live in Europe, often at the bottom layers of society. Western culture is seen as steeped in a stubborn sense of superiority and an ineradicable drive toward supremacy. Communication among people of different religions and cultures cannot take place outside this context of the social and economic stratification of religions and cultures. But within this context communication is possible and provides perspective in a common effort, both globally and locally, to end forever the existing contrast in power and prosperity in this world.

Christianity and Pluralization

The Significance of Christianity for Pluralization. At first sight it does not seem plausible that Christianity has contributed to the emergence of plural society in its present form. No church can be expected to take steps to end its own religious faith. Furthermore, the initiative for migration into Europe did not proceed from Christianity. The people of different faiths who settled in the West were not attracted by any light shining from Christian churches. Migration to Europe has to do with socioeconomic, political, and other human factors and is not based on religious considerations.

But this is not to say that Christianity has not promoted pluralization despite itself. It is noteworthy that secularism arose in Europe, which has long been Christian. Examined more closely, this is not hard to understand, because the gospel preached by the church is a message that invites people to break with every form of uncritical compliance, whether that compliance be with inherited views and patterns of conduct or with new ideas and norms. The Christian message calls people to account for their choices. Consequently, it calls for the end of religiosity as a matter of course, including the Christian faith itself. Those to whom the gospel has been brought may, after hearing it, reject not only the Christian faith but

43. V. Fabella and S. Torres (ed.), *Irruption of the Third World* (Maryknoll, 1983) 195.

all religion. Secularism is an alternative implied in confrontation with the Christian gospel.

But at the same time the church has also had great influence in the "third" world by its preaching of the gospel there. By its missionary activity the church altered existing religious patterns. The ties to one's own land, people, tribe, and family were relativized. The church also exerted great influence through its mission schools. As a result many people, even if they did not become Christians, came into contact with Western ways of thinking and living. They discovered that the world was larger than their own environments and that it offered possibilities that could be important to them. In this way Christianity removed certain hindrances to migration, which has included both urbanization (migration to cities) and emigration.

So Christianity has contributed to pluralization, though not only because of the church's deliberate message and activity.

The Significance of Pluralization for Christianity. 1. The church has always borne the marks of plurality in its confession. Harnack called dogmatic Christianity, in its conception and in its construction, "the work of the Hellenic spirit upon the Gospel soil."[44] Aulén preferred to speak of "a work of the Christian spirit using Hellenistic terms as building material."[45] The difference is not unimportant, but both authors are saying that Hellenism has influenced the church's confession. In European churches these confessions are still central. But there is still no evidence that in its confession the church has begun to cope with *today's* plural religious context.

2. The old *Corpus Christianum* was also a product of the plural situation in which Christianity found itself. With its state church (from A.D. 380 on), it replaced the pagan *corpus religiosum.* Consequently, the church inherited a position in pluralization and a relationship to the state from a non-Christian religion — even if it came to maintain a certain distance from state and society. It is important to note that resistance to government interference in church affairs arose particularly in connection with doctrinal questions. Such was the case, for example, when the emperor tried to impose Arianism on the church for political reasons. Christianity has since then given up a large part of this syncretistic inheritance. It has lost its monopoly, and its voice can only be heard amid a chorus of religious and nonreligious voices. For Christianity, therefore, present-day plurality means a loss of power and authority. But this has made it possible for Christianity, instead of having to secure and reinforce its own importance, to serve the cause of justice and peace regardless of the consequences for itself.

44. A. Harnack, *Outlines of the History of Dogma* (Boston, 1957) 5.
45. G. Aulén, *Het Christelijk Godsbeeld* (Amsterdam, 1927) 83.

3. Pluralization means that Christianity exists in an embattled position, together with all other religions and ideologies. Like the church of the New Testament (1 Peter 3:15), the church of today is compelled to give an account of the hope that is in it.

4. Finally, Christianity is compelled to engage in self-examination because its mission work was often done in the wake of colonialism and with insufficient distance from colonialism. Often it even legitimized the supremacy of the West. Accordingly, for Western Christianity a plural society implies a painful confrontation with the church's own history and with the question of its responsibility for the dependency and oppression that continue to this day.

Emancipation and Pluralization as the Context for Mission

The church must fulfill its mission in the midst of people who are involved in the far-reaching changes of emancipation and pluralization. We have discussed these changes, but now we will look at them from the perspective of the church's mission.

Emancipation

Emancipation is, as we have seen, an ambiguous process. On the one hand, it involves liberation from paternalism, voicelessness, domination, and exploitation. It makes it possible for humans, those who bear God's image, to show who he is, to live as his allies and therefore as the allies of oppressed, poor, marginalized, and voiceless people. No longer do the powers of destruction and death have the last word. It is now possible and meaningful to devote one's energies to a society characterized by righteousness and peace.

On the other hand, emancipation cannot be divorced from the culture in which it arises. In Western culture it is considered legitimate to accord priority to one's own security, one's own position of power, one's own profit, and one's own material well-being. Alliances and organizations have been and are being created in order to strengthen the ability of peoples to pursue those ends. Emancipation comes to be marked primarily not by self-denial but by self-seeking, not by the struggle to overcome the poverty of others but by the acquisition and increase of one's own wealth, not by solidarity with those who have no rights but by the struggle for one's own rights, not by community in mutual dependence but by the fight for independence, not by the fight to liberate others but by the fight to maintain, protect, and increase one's own freedom over against others, and not by the struggle against sin and death but by participation in the sin of curtailing and destroying defenseless life.

This may not be the goal of emancipation, but it is a consequence of the belief that liberation will automatically lead to the "good" life for everyone. It flows from the myth that in time the best will also prove to be the strongest. The idea is that if people learn to stand up for themselves and are equipped to that end, a society will ultimately come into being in which each person receives his or her due. Newbigin speaks correctly, therefore, of the ideology of capitalism with its "myth of the 'invisible hand' that ensures that the untrammeled exercise of coveteousness by each individual will produce the happiness of all." He calls this myth "one of the most malignant falsehoods that has ever deceived the human race."[46]

Pluralization

Like emancipation, the pluralization of society is ambiguous. It is both a crisis and a *kairos*.

It entails a crisis because in a plural society the tenability of every religious and nonreligious conviction, the firmness of transmitted values and norms, and the continued validity of existing patterns of social relations are all under challenge and attack. Reality can be interpreted and ordered in various ways, none so persuasive as to win a consensus. A plural society is marked by uncertainty and doubt.

Apart from this crisis of certainties, plurality is also a threat to and attack on Western European prosperity and power. The "irruption of the third world" into human history and into Western European society involves the penetration not only of peoples of other religions and cultures but also of poor and dependent nations and people. Consequently, internationally and regionally as well as nationally, the validity, justice, and continuation of existing social, economic, and political structures are being challenged.

Pluralization is a *kairos* in that confronting inequalities in possessions and power can create the awareness, in both the disadvantaged and the advantaged, that present relationships are unjust and in need of change. This awareness and the will to bring about change are to be expected more among the disadvantaged than among those who profit

---

46. L. Newbigin, *Foolishness to the Greeks: The Gospel and Western Culture* (Grand Rapids, 1986) 121.

from these inequalities, for whom the impetus to change is limited by the disadvantages that come to such people from change, as is clear from government policies concerning development cooperation and from policies with respect to foreigners and refugees.

The will to change has a chance insofar as it does not deprive Western Europeans of the opportunity to give priority to their own lives, security, and well-being over that of others. That is to say, structures can change as long as they do not rob people of the opportunity to sin. But it would be wrong to say that any movement of the will toward change among those who would experience the disadvantages of change is impossible. Besides, confrontation with the victims, the disadvantaged, can raise the awareness that injustice exists and that pluralization makes a transformation of these relationships necessary.

Furthermore, encounter, dialogue, and communication among people of different religions, convictions, and cultures not only lead to crisis but also open up new possibilities and perspectives. In this connection it is important not merely that societies enrich one another with their values, norms, views, and goals. It is especially important that from this communication and the tension of the encounter between people of different traditions a transcultural set of views, values, norms, and goals grow up by which all nations and people know themselves bound and to which all can appeal in situations of conflict.

The Relationship of Emancipation and Pluralization

In Western Europe and the Netherlands, emancipation is sometimes regarded as a precondition or means for communication and for the participation of all in a pluralistic society.[47] But this seems to be a misconception. The oppressed and marginal position of some nations and ethnic groups is not an insuperable hindrance to cultural, religious, or ideological change in dominant groups. This is apparent from the history of Greece in the Roman Empire. Hellenism exerted profound cultural and religious influence throughout the empire.[48] And the gospel of Christ was brought to Europe by Jews and propagated by an oppressed and persecuted minority.

This is not to say that a one-sided relationship of dependence can

---

47. Hendriks, *op. cit.*, passim; *Minderhedennota van de Nederlandse regering* (The Hague, 1983).

48. F. C. Grant, "Hellenismus," in *RGG* III (Tübingen, 1959) 209-12; K. Sprey, "De geschiedenis van het Romeinse Rijk," in Brandt and van Werveke, *Wereldgeschiedenis* III (Zeist, 1964) 67-76.

be viewed as conducive to dialogue and communication. Social, economic, and political relationships can promote dialogue and communication, but they are not the only influencing factors. Oppression can also lead to the disappearance of Christianity, as in Asia Minor and North Africa.

Again we must mention that emancipation has a double face. It can go against pluralization and can easily degenerate into acquisition of the skills, tools, and organizational forms needed for participation in Western European society and its sins. Among these sins is investment on behalf of one's own life, prosperity, security, and power at the expense of poor and dependent groups and nations. One thus gains emancipation but loses the values, norms, and goals that could hinder the effort toward emancipation, *even when they are not as such in conflict with it.* In the process the significance of one's own culture and religion comes to be restricted to one's own personal life and relationships. Emancipation thus works to cancel out plurality.

So it can be asked whether such accommodation to Western notions of progress will lead to the desired goal. James Baldwin asserted that poor African Americans of Harlem had given up all hope of improvement by way of accommodation. And he hoped that they would thus be led "to reexamine white standards with the idea of liberating themselves from them."[49]

The mission of the church includes having a critical view and a critical attitude toward the search for emancipation in a plural society. This criticism concerns first of all the dominant group, which thinks it can define the content of emancipation without consulting those whose emancipation is at stake. This criticism further concerns the oppressed nations and groups insofar as they believe that they will profit from a corrupt emancipation. From the perspective of God's coming kingdom, Jesus offers space to all peoples and nations, cultures and religions, and subjects them to his criticism. But in so doing he begins with his own nation and with those who want to preserve their lives, privileges, gains, and power as members of that nation when this takes place at the expense of defenseless fellow human beings, whatever their culture and religion.

---

49. J. Baldwin, "Blanken moeten leven zonder de geruststellende woede van de zwarten," *De Groene Amsterdammer* 111 (1987) 6.

CHAPTER 4

The People's Republic of China: From Foreignness to Contextualization

A. CAMPS

In 1988 the population of the People's Republic of China was 1.0722 billion, almost a fifth of the world's population.[1] A study of the situation of Christianity in this immense country is essential in a book that speaks of our diverse world.

Christianity in China dates from the year 635 and with a few interruptions has been present there ever since. When the Christian faith first entered the country, it encountered a situation of great diversity, including the ancient Chinese religions, Confucianism, Taoism, Buddhism, and folk religions. Following a brief survey of the history of Christianity in China we will give special attention to the situation of Christianity after 1949, when the People's Republic was founded. As has been well said, China is a laboratory for the world church.[2]

The History of Christianity in China

Nestorian Christianity: 635-845

The Nestorian faith moved straight across Central Asia via the silk route and established itself in China in 635. In that year a bishop named Alopen came from the area east of the Euphrates and Tigris rivers into Xian. Nestorian Christianity spread to ten provinces and churches were built in

1. *Pro Mundi Vita Dossiers* 2-3 (Brussels, 1984); E. Tang, *Facts and Figures of the Catholic Church in Asia,* 11, 13.
2. *A New Beginning: An International Dialogue with the Chinese Church, Montreal, October 2-9, 1981* (Toronto, 1983) 118, 144, 146. The statement was made by Bishop K. H. Ting.

more than a hundred cities. In the same year the reigning emperor, Tang
Tai Zung, issued an edict of toleration. Monasteries were built and thirty
Christian books were translated. From a monument built in Xian in 781,
from eighth-century manuscripts discovered in a grotto in Dunhuang at
the beginning of the twentieth century, and from Syriac documents that
came to light later we have come to know a great deal about this Christianity. Stone crosses bearing inscriptions have also been found at many
places.

The Nestorians used Taoist, Confucian, and most often Buddhist
terms and concepts in communicating the gospel. Persecution began in
845 under Emperor Wu Zung. Different reasons are given for this persecution, including overly close ties between the Nestorians and the ruling
authorities, the lack of respect for parents implied by monastic celibacy,
the Christians' lack of permanent ties with their country of origin, too
close a coalescence of their faith with Buddhism, and lack of adequate
Chinese leadership in the churches. On all these points, however, counter-
arguments can be advanced. It is certain, however, that after 845 Nestorianism, the initial contextualization of Christianity in China, nearly disappeared, though there continued to be some Christians in China during the
following four hundred years.[3]

The Franciscans: 1294-1347

In the period of the Mongol-dominated Yuan dynasty (1276-1368) Christianity again asserted itself in China as a result of attempts by the church
in the West and of Western kings in the preceding period to build contacts
with Mongol rulers in central Asia. When the Mongols conquered China
there was reason, therefore, for the Western Christians to seek contact with
China. On the part of the church this was done by the Franciscans.

The first Franciscan arrived in Khanbaliq (Beijing) in 1294. This was
John of Montecorvino, who presented his credentials there to the great
Khan and found Nestorians there. He also found the Alans, descendants of
people deported by the Mongols from the Caucasus a half century earlier
to do military service. The 15,000 or so Alans were Christians of the Greek
rite who had no clergy of their own and who were regarded with hostility

3. A. C. Moule, *Christians in China before the Year 1550* (London, 1930); *idem,
Christianity in China: Some Corrections and Additions* (London, 1940); P. Y. Saeki, *The
Nestorian Documents and Relics in China* (Tokyo, 1951); A. Bürke, "Das Nestorianer-
Denkmal von Si-an-fu. Versuch einer Neuübersetzung," in *Vermittlung zwischen-
kirchlicher Gemeinschaft*, ed. J. Baumgartner (Schöneck-Beckenried, 1971) 125-41;
D. Hickly, *The First Christians of China* (London, 1980).

by the Nestorians. They welcomed John as their spiritual leader. John also encountered Armenians, whom he addressed in their own language. John also spoke Persian and one of the two languages of the ruling class, that is, either Mongol or Turkish. He translated the Gospels and the Psalms into whichever language that was, which he called "Tatar."

John built two churches in Khanbaliq, one close to the imperial palace. He ransomed forty slave boys (probably Chinese), baptized them, and trained them to sing the liturgy in Latin. The emperor loved to listen to them. In the first twelve years John baptized about 6,000 people. He experienced much antagonism from the Nestorians, however, on one occasion barely escaping imprisonment. His converts came from non-Catholic groups who originated in Europe and western and central Asia and were members of the class favored by the Mongol rulers. John lived somewhat apart from the Chinese and, like Marco Polo, saw no benefit in learning their language. His method was first to convert the elite under the assumption that the people would then follow *(cuius regio, illius et religio)*. Apart from a visit in 1304 from another Franciscan, he was cut off from his order.

Not until 1306-07 did two letters from John arrive in Europe. Thereupon he was appointed archbishop of Khanbaliq and patriarch of the entire East (from southern Russia and Asia Minor to China). The pope appointed six other Franciscans as auxiliary bishops, three of whom reached Khanbaliq in 1313 and consecrated John as archbishop. Gerard of Albuini was appointed bishop of the harbor city Quanzhou (Zaiton) and was succeeded by Peregrine of Castello in 1318, who was succeeded by Andreas of Perugia in 1322-23. John also established churches in Hangzhou and Yangzhou. It is noteworthy that the emperor generously supported these missions, that there was freedom of religion, and that "Latin" merchants found support in the mission.

Odoric of Pordenone, a Franciscan, arrived in Guanzhou (Canton) in 1313 and traveled to Quanzhou, where there was already a monastery and cathedral to draw his admiration. He also visited the Catholic communities in Hangzhou and Yangzhou and arrived in Khanbaliq in 1325, where he stayed for three years. In his journal he wrote much about the Mongols and reported that John of Montecorvino always blessed the emperor as the emperor was departing on any journey. From 1328 to 1330 Odoric traveled toward Europe straight across Asia and died in Udine in 1331. John died in 1328-29 at the age of 81. Bishop Andreas of Perugia died in Quanzhou in 1332 and, like John in Khanbaliq, had no successor.

In 1338 emissaries of the Alans in China came to the pope in Avignon to request the appointment of a successor to John. The pope sent a group of clergymen, among them a French theologian from Paris who was intended to be the archbishop of Khanbaliq but who turned back

when he reached Constantinople. One of his companions, John of Marignolli, a Franciscan but not a bishop, arrived in China in 1342 and was
received by the emperor, and left China via Quanzhou in 1347.

The reason for John of Marignolli's early return was probably his
sense that the time of Mongolian domination was running out. Rebel
movements were growing stronger and were to bring about the fall of the
Yuan dynasty in 1368. The Ming dynasty (1368-1644) sought to exclude
all foreign influences and identified Christianity with Mongol domination.
The Christianity introduced by the Franciscans totally disappeared from
China, and the same fate struck the Italian merchant ventures in China.
This second attempt at missionizing in China lacked a feeling for contex-
tuality in terms of actual Chinese culture.[4]

The Jesuits and Other Missionary Orders: 1582-1800

In 1554 the Portuguese gained a foothold in China by building the city of
Macao on a peninsula. From that vantage point missionaries attempted to
enter China, the same thing that had been ventured by Spaniards from a
base in Manila, where a diocese had also been started. The first to be
allowed to establish themselves in China (in 1583) were two Jesuits,
Michael Ruggieri and Matteo Ricci in Zhaoging, near Guanzhou (Canton).
They dressed like Buddhists, diligently learned Chinese, and studied Confucian books and other ancient books (and they printed a map of the
world). But they were expelled because of opposition from the mandarins.
Ruggieri went back to Macao, and Ricci made his home somewhat to the
north in Shaozhou in 1589. He realized that Buddhists were not held in
great esteem and so adopted the garb of a Confucian scholar. He exploited
the secular sciences for the propagation of the faith and began to translate
the four classic works of Confucianism. He attempted by slow degrees to
gain a base in the imperial city of Beijing and succeeded in 1601 when the
emperor gave him a house. When in 1610 Ricci died at the age of 58 he
left "my brothers standing before a gate which can be opened to everyone's
profit, though not without difficulty and danger."

Ricci moved in the circles of the learned, and by 1608 some 2500 of
them had joined him as Christians. He translated Chinese classics and wrote
philosophical works ("On Friendship" and "On the Art of Remembering")
in Chinese. He prepared an edition of the Chinese catechism that Ruggieri

4. A. van den Wyngaert, *Sinica Franciscana* I (Florence, 1929); L. de Hartog,
Europese reizigers naar de Grote Khan (Baarn, 1985); I. de Rachewiltz, *Papal Envoys to the
Great Khans* (London, 1971).

had written, "On the True Doctrine of God." And he wrote many mathematical, geographic, and astronomic works and made European scientific instruments for the Chinese. But above all he effected a generous accommodation to Chinese customs and religious concepts: After baptism Chinese Christians were allowed to continue the practice of venerating their ancestors and Confucius and were permitted to keep Chinese names for God.

Other Jesuits started a congregation in Nanjing. The work continued: In 1636 there were 38,200 believers. Ricci's real successor was Johann Adam Schall von Bell (1630-66) from Cologne, who managed to steer the mission through all sorts of internal and external political disturbances.

The biggest problems arose after 1631 when Spanish missionaries — Dominicans and Franciscans — entered China from the Philippines. They did not understand the work of their Jesuit predecessors, dressed in the habits of their orders, preached the gospel in the streets holding up a cross, and opposed the adaptations begun by Ricci. The conflict led to years of confusion and dispute. Among the Jesuits themselves differences of opinion arose about what was later called "the rites controversy." Initially all this did not adversely affect the mission itself; all the orders gained about the same number of converts.

In 1664, however, persecution broke out. In Beijing Schall von Bell was condemned to death but received a reprieve and was imprisoned. Twenty-five missionaries from all the orders were banished to Guanzhou (Canton). Only the Belgian Jesuit Ferdinand Verbiest and two brothers remained behind. They managed to regain respect by their knowledge of astronomy and other sciences. Schall von Bell was released from prison, as were the other missionaries in 1671. Verbiest became an interpreter for foreign envoys — a task that Catholic missionaries continued to fulfill into the nineteenth century.

Verbiest died in 1688, and ten days later the first five French Jesuits arrived: Joachim Bouvet, Joseph Henri de Prémare, Jean Francois Foucquet, Jean-Alexis de Gollet, and Jean-Francois Lafitau. They built large churches and a library, which later came to be quite famous, and they sent laudatory reports about Chinese culture to Europe. Their reports were later, during the Enlightenment, used in arguments against Christianity. These French Jesuits became known as "Figurists" because they sought to show that Christian doctrines could be found already in the ancient classic Chinese texts, once they were properly interpreted. Conflicts developed over issues of jurisdiction (among the rights of patronage of Portugal and of the *Propaganda Fide* in Rome, Spain, Portugal, and France, each with its own claims where the different orders worked), over the correctness of Figurism, and above all over the rites controversy, which spread as far as Europe, where many theologians addressed it.

Finally, after several papal delegations had gone to China, Pope Benedict XIV (in the Bull *Ex quo singulari* of 1742) condemned the Chinese rites and required missionaries to swear that they would not follow them. Because of this settlement of the rites controversy, which continued in force until 1939, when Pius XII allowed the rites to be used under certain provisions in view of the changed meanings and circumstances, the reputation of the church in China suffered and continues to suffer. Still today, accusations of Western imperialism are made.

Meanwhile, local persecutions of Christians broke out, sometimes with the emperor taking part (particularly in 1717). The persecution of 1784-85 was especially intense. Behind these persecutions lay fear of foreign influences, the sharp attacks of the Jesuits on Buddhism, Taoism, and indirectly on Confucianism, internal disputes among the missionaries, and, of course, the rites controversy.

Nevertheless, a new orientation arose in the mission. The missionaries diligently studied Chinese and adapted their work in many respects — except in the rites. Prayer life was adapted (no private prayer). Chinese women who took vows continued to live in their extended families and in this manner preserved the faith. In churches without priests catechists and other laypeople were given responsibilities (though without the right to polemicize against Chinese ideas), and the need for Chinese priests was admitted. (Though Rome allowed use of the Chinese language in liturgy in 1615, a controversy arose in China over study of Latin.)

Rome saw the necessity of having Chinese bishops in China, but the missionaries had little sympathy for the idea. The greatest difficulty arose in 1762 when the Portuguese minister Pombal gave orders to imprison the Jesuits. In 1773 the pope abolished the order altogether. Finally, Portuguese and French Lazarists took over the Jesuits' tasks and functioned as mandarins or as mathematicians at the emperor's Mathematical Institute in Beijing. The Paris Society for Foreign Missions was most useful in training Chinese priests abroad (in Macao, Indochina, and Malacca). But by 1800 persecution had made the situation of the Catholic Church in China desperate, though in 1815 there were still 89 Chinese priests and 80 European missionaries caring for 210,000 Catholic Christians.

Despite the important gains in this period, great opportunities were missed — because of the rites controversy and other internal disputes. And the faith had not really been contextualized to Chinese culture. In China the dominant conviction was that Christianity was something of and for foreigners.[5]

5. J. Gernet, *China and the Christian Impact* (Cambridge, 1985); H. Bernard, *Matteo Ricci's Scientific Contribution to China* (Peiping, 1935; reprint Westport, 1973); J. D. Spence,

The Churches of the Unequal Treaties: 1800-1949

In the previous period the courage of the Chinese priests was considerable. But it was not possible to find a Chinese successor for the first Chinese bishop, Luo Wenzao. Had one been found history would probably have taken a different turn. It was not until 1926 that Chinese bishops were again appointed — because of pressure exerted by Pius XI.

In this same period Protestant missionaries came onto the field for the first time. The context for mission activity changed fundamentally: External political factors began to play a specific role, the political situation inside China changed, and the strategy of the churches received new accents.

The "period of the unequal treaties" began with Britain's defeat of China in the Opium War (1841-42). From 1833 on the United Kingdom had sought free trade with China. Opium, being much in demand in China, was very profitable, though trade in it was illegal in China, whose leaders sought to put a stop to it before the war. After the war, the treaty of Nanjing stipulated that four ports in addition to Guanzhou (Canton) be opened, that relations be established between Britain and China, that a British consul be posted in every port and concession area, that tariffs for imports and exports be fixed, and that Hong Kong be ceded to Britain in perpetuity. This was only the beginning. By 1912 fifty Chinese treaty ports were in the hands of Britain, Germany, France, Portugal (with Macao), Japan, the United States, and Russia, not only on the coast but also on the larger rivers. China had become a semicolonial country.

The Europeans and Americans lived in separate quarters in the treaty ports, had their own courts of law, and maintained armies. When conflicts arose — such as the Boxer rebellion in 1900 — these foreign troops were deployed to occupy lines of communication and other strategic locations. Sections of Beijing were set aside for foreign legations.

The Memory Palace of Matteo Ricci (London, 1985); G. Minamiki, *The Chinese Rites Controversy from Its Beginnings to Modern Times* (Chicago, 1985); A. Väth, *Johann Adam Schall von Bell S.J.* (Cologne, 1933); M. Ricci and N. Trigault, *Histoire de l'expédition chrétienne au royaume de la Chine 1582-1610* (Paris, 1978); R. A. Blondeau, *Mandarijn en astronoom. Ferdinand Verbiest S.J. (1623-1688) aan het hof van de Chinese keizer* (Bruges, 1970); *idem, Ferdinand Verbiest: missionaris of spion?* (Bruges, 1984); C. von Collani, *P. Joachim Bouvet S.J., sein Leben und sein Werk* (Nettetal, 1985); *idem, Die Figuristen in der China Mission* (Frankfurt, 1981); D. E. Mungello, *Curious Land: Jesuit Accommodation and the Origins of Sinology* (Stuttgart, 1985); *idem, Leibnitz and Confucianism* (Honolulu, 1977); J. Metzler, *Die Synoden in China, Japan und Korea, 1570-1931* (Paderborn, 1980); M. Ricci, *The True Meaning of the Lord of Heaven,* tr. with introduction and notes by D. Lancashire and P. Hu Kuo-chaen, Chinese-English edition by E. J. Malatesta (St. Louis, 1985).

China became powerless and suffered from internal uprisings. Imperial authority was weak.

The movement to turn China into a republic finally succeeded in 1912, ending 2000 years of imperial tradition. Sun Yat-sen (1866-1925) was the great revolutionary leader. He pursued a policy of unity, national dignity, and Westernization, formed the national party, the Guomindang (Kuomintang), and founded a military academy, which gave birth to the nationalist army. Soon after his death general Jiang Jie-shi (Chiang Kai-shek) gained the upper hand. The Communist Party and the Red Army came into being in the 1920s, and in 1935 Mao Zedong (Mao Tse-tung) became their leader. Periods of cooperation between the two parties alternated with periods of intense fighting. There was also a running war with the warlords. The Japanese invasion began in the north in 1931, and after 1945 civil war broke out between the Nationalists and the Communists. On October 1, 1949, the People's Republic was proclaimed at Beijing and the Nationalist government fled to Taiwan.

One must view the revival of Chinese Christianity in this period in the context of these external and internal political developments. The beginning of the nineteenth century found Chinese Catholics in an underground church — and Protestant missionaries were just beginning their work. Both had to find their way in a situation complicated by the influence of foreign powers and by Chinese anti-imperialism, national revival, and interparty fighting. Warlords controlled some regions of the country. Chinese intellectuals were divided between those educated in the West and those who wanted to return to the wisdom of ancient China. In the following paragraphs we can only briefly sketch the positions that Christians assumed in this complex situation.

The Catholic Church. At the beginning of the nineteenth century the Franciscans, Dominicans, and the Paris mission were able to resume their work. In 1841 the Jesuits returned and other missionary groups followed. They entered through the treaty ports and were protected by the foreign powers. Persecution regularly broke out, but the Western powers would then intervene. The Boxer rebellion came to a head in 1900 and cost the lives of thousands of Christians, including numerous priests and the Dutch bishop, Monsignor Hamer of Nijmegen. The foreign powers intervened as far as Beijing, and China was defeated. Heavy economic penalties were imposed, China's sovereignty was humiliatingly restricted, the fate of the ruling dynasty was sealed, and the impetus toward revolution was strengthened.

This cooperation of church and foreign powers was described by the apostolic vicar of Beijing, Monsignor A. Favier: "Once again we have seen the necessity of French protection of the Catholic missions as it has always been exercised and which the church has never wanted to end. Accordingly, one will always see a consulate next to a church. The building where the French tricolor flies will always protect the Catholic cross."[6] The Vatican did want to send a nuncio who would function independently of the Western powers, but France put a stop to that idea. China has never forgotten that church and imperialism thus worked together.

Most of the missionaries and bishops thought they had to keep control in their own hands and not share it with the Chinese clergy. The national Council of Shanghai in 1924 assembled sixty ecclesiastical authorities with the right to vote. Of these, two were Chinese, neither of whom was a bishop. Of the twenty-seven mission heads none was Chinese. There were only nine Chinese priests.[7] Chinese courtesy kept these priests from making known their displeasure. But to this day one can note feelings of frustration among the members of the Catholic Patriotic Society, which consecrates bishops without permission from Rome.

Tensions also existed between the Western bishops in China and the ecclesiastical administration in Rome. In 1922 Monsignor C. Constantini became the apostolic delegate in China. The task of this wise man was to implement the guidelines for the promotion of an indigenous clergy laid down in various encyclicals. After the Council of Shanghai he chose six Chinese priests to be bishops, whom Pope Pius XI himself consecrated at Rome in 1926. When Constantini returned to Rome in 1934, twenty-one mission regions were entrusted to the Chinese clergy. He had founded many regional and central seminaries and started a Chinese religious congregation of priests, a project for which he had received the support of a former Lazarist from Belgium, Vincent Lebbe, who understood the sensitivities of the Chinese.

In 1946 a church hierarchy was established and the first Chinese cardinal was appointed. In 1949 Chinese Catholics numbered 3.25 million, most of them living in the North. Shanghai was also a center of Catholic life. There were by then 139 ecclesiastical provinces, most of them headed by Western bishops. Much good work was being done in schools, hospitals, agricultural cooperatives, and other settings. But the stigma of foreignness remained. Anti-foreign sentiment coincided with anti-church sentiment. The church was viewed as antiintellectual and anti-progressive and as inadequately pro-Chinese.

The Protestant Missions. Protestant missions in China began in 1807 with Robert Morrison, but he had no success and died in 1834. James Legge worked from a base in Hong Kong from 1843 to 1873, translating

6. *Peking, histoire et description* (Lille, 1900) 269.
7. Metzler, *op. cit.*, 200-203.

the Chinese classics into English and leading an English-speaking community. In this early period many missionaries and physicians worked in Guanzhou (Canton) and other treaty ports. Great missionaries like Walter Medhurst and Karl Gützlaff worked alone. Only after the treaties of 1858-60, which forced toleration of Christianity on the Chinese, did possibilities for other kinds of work arise. Hudson Taylor started the China Inland Mission in 1865 and its fifty-four members adopted a Chinese lifestyle. But it was not a great success, and the Boxer rebellion put a stop to the experiment in 1900.

The Taiping uprising (1850-64) showed the marks of Protestant influence. Hong Xiuquan, the leader of the rebellion, had read Morrison's tracts and had been baptized. He controlled Central China and in Nanjing was proclaimed the "heavenly king." In 1864 Chinese, British, and American armies defeated him. He had launched a social program — a form of communism that is being studied today by Chinese scholars. After the uprising had been put down, mission congregations had to endure much suffering.

Contemporary Chinese historians regard the Fourth of May movement, which began in Beijing in 1919, as the birth of Chinese Communism and of the Nationalist Party. Intellectuals believed that China's weakness was caused by the antiforeign and antiprogressive attitude of the Confucianists. They wanted science and democracy and looked with admiration toward Russia, where revolt had succeeded. Among them were both advocates and opponents of Christian faith.

Protestant Christians had more contact with intellectual and socially conscious Chinese than did Catholics. They also tended to view Jesus as a merely human social reformer and emphasized ethical models and values. In 1949 there were 1.4 million Chinese Protestants with thirteen universities and many schools. Their attempts to adapt Christian theology to Chinese culture have been noteworthy.

Despite the differences between them, for both Catholic and Protestant churches the past has remained a burden. To this day cooperation with foreign powers is viewed as foreign imperialism. This burden accounts for much of the thinking and practice of Chinese Christians today.[8]

8. *The Cambridge Encyclopedia of China* (Cambridge, 1982); J. Beckmann, *Die katholische Missionsmethode in China in neuester Zeit 1842-1912* (Immensee, 1931); R. R. Covell, *Confucius, the Buddha and Christ: A History of the Gospel in Chinese* (Maryknoll, 1986); D. W. Treadgold, *The West in Russia and China* II: *China 1582-1949* (Cambridge, 1973); J. Leclercq, *Vie du Père Lebbe* (Tournai, 1961); C. Soetens, *Recueils des archives Vincent Lebbe* (5 vols.; Louvain, 1982-86); J. M. van Minnen, *Accommodatie in de chinese zendingsgeschiedenis* (Kampen, 1951); K. S. Latourette, *A History of Christian Missions in China* (reprint, Taipei, 1975); L. Gutheinz, *China im Wandel. Das chinesische Denken im*

The Churches and Contextualization

The Catholic Church

From 1950 to 1957 the Catholic Church found itself at an impasse with regard to the relationship between the Communist state and "foreign religion." The state opted for atheism and for independence from foreign involvement over modernization. But eighty percent of the bishops were non-Chinese, foreign mission organizations were dominant in the Church, and Catholics owed obedience to a foreign power, the pope in Rome. And the Church spoke an aggressive anti-Communist language. The result of these differences was that all foreigners were expelled and all Church property confiscated. The Church instructed its followers not to cooperate with the state and was regarded as unpatriotic. No way of being both patriotically Chinese and faithfully Catholic was being worked out.

The state sponsored a Chinese Catholic Patriotic Association (as it did with other religious groups) as part of its presentation of a political united front free of foreign influences. The principles of the association, which was founded in 1957, were self-government, financial self-support, and self-propagation. There was fierce resistance to the Patriotic Association in the Catholic community, especially on the part of the Legion of Mary, a lay movement with a strong organization and great influence, especially in Shanghai. Many Chinese bishops, priests, religious, and lay-persons were imprisoned for life or placed in reform camps. In Shanghai, where the bishop was condemned to life imprisonment, resistance was intense. In Guanzhou (Canton) the bishop was imprisoned after being tried twice. But both bishops were freed, in 1985 and 1980 respectively. But some church leaders cooperated with the Patriotic Society in order to save the Church.

Thus the Catholic community became divided from 1957 to 1966. Those who remained faithful to the pope were considered unpatriotic and those who joined the Patriotic Association or cooperated with it were regarded as unfaithful to the pope. An impossible dilemma arose, though in itself to be Chinese and Catholic is not a contradiction. The majority in

---

Umbruch seit dem 19. Jahrhundert (Munich, 1985); R. Laurentin, *Chine et christianisme, après les occasions manquées* (Paris, 1977); B. Wolferstan, *The Catholic Church in China 1860-1907* (London, 1909); *Missionary Ideologies in the Imperialist Era: 1880-1920*, ed. T. Christensen and W. R. Hutchison (Aarhus, 1982); *The Expansion of International Society*, ed. H. Bull and A. Watson (Oxford, 1985); A. Chih, *L'occidente "cristiano" visto dai cinesi verso la fine del XIX secolo, 1870-1910* (Milan, 1979).

the Church chose to practice their faith in an underground manner. The Bureau for Religious Affairs in Beijing started to form provincial and local patriotic societies and promoted the democratic election and consecration of bishops. This was, of course, an appeal to feelings of frustration on the part of Chinese priests with nationalistic sympathies who had suffered under foreign bishops. The candidates proposed by the Bureau were rejected by Rome, which declared that every consecration that it did not approve would automatically lead to excommunication. Some priests and laypersons accused Rome of failing to understand their difficult circumstances, and in these years thirty-five bishops were consecrated without Rome's permission. Pope John XXIII said that these consecrations were paving the way for a regrettable schism, which these bishops deny to this day. There is no real schism — but communication with Rome is broken — and tensions grew between members and nonmembers of the Catholic Patriotic Association.

During the Cultural Revolution (1966-76), all religious groups suffered from the frequently violent action against the whole of China's cultural heritage. All Catholics — patriotic or not — were persecuted and many were jailed. The entire Church went underground, and much church property was destroyed. Education came to a halt. The Church's suffering alongside other Chinese people presented an opportunity to be saved from the stigma of foreignness. And out of that suffering arose local churches, an expression of the faith that is credible in the eyes of all Chinese people. Even without churches and without the right to practice the faith or to pass it on to their children, a large number of believers remained faithful. That after 1976 the popes openly praised Christians for this has done much good in China.

After the Cultural Revolution, freedom of religion was restored and China sought out contact with the outside world. Liberalization and a shift in emphasis from atheism to modernization took place. The help of Catholics was needed, and Catholics received a place in the Chinese People's Political Consultative Conference. The Bureau for Religious Affairs in Beijing and the Catholic Patriotic Association were reorganized. Church buildings were quickly returned to the Church. A bishops' conference for doctrinal matters and a committee for Church matters were organized in 1980. The new state constitution of 1982 recognized the right of religious freedom, provided people did not disadvantage the state and were not dependent on foreign connections. The official teaching of the state was still that religion must go, but it had come to be recognized that this would be a long process.

The period since 1982 has been marked by the reorganization of the Catholic Church. In 1985 an important Chinese personality, Professor Zhao Fusan, vice president of the Chinese Academy for the Social Sciences, stated that religion is neither an "opiate" nor backward, but an important part of the culture and the most direct way to address world problems and to find the meaning of life. So, compared with 1950, matters have changed fundamentally. By 1986 some three million Catholics remained in China, 30,000 baptisms were occurring every year, and more than six hundred churches and more than a thousand places of prayer were open. About fifty bishops (four still appointed by Pope Pius XII) and two to three thousand priests, most of them elderly, were serving and were training laypeople and nuns for new ministries. After 1985 nine seminaries were soon opened with a total of 600 students, and after 1984 there were six novitiates for sisters with 140 novices.

China's social and political situation is in a continual state of flux. As a result, the situation of the Chinese Catholic Church is also continually changing. In 1989 a new policy toward the Catholic Church was introduced by the Communist Party and by the State Council: purely religious relationships with the Holy See were permitted; the Chinese Catholic Bishops Conference was given the highest authority over the Patriotic Association; church property will be returned so that the church can be self-supporting and not dependent on the state; as far as the underground church is concerned, most are to be won over and united and the rest to be isolated and suppressed. Since the June 4, 1989, crackdown the government has adopted stricter measures in its dealings with the underground church. The situation became critical when in the same year a Bishops Conference of the underground church was inaugurated. Many bishops, clergy, and laity were arrested, especially in the provinces of Hebei and Fujian.

In 1992 the Fifth National Catholic Conference was held. It was decided to place the Patriotic Association on the same footing as the Chinese Catholic Bishops Conference. The use of the vernacular in liturgy was approved. In 1994 the party and the government fixed rules for foreigners to observe in their activities. This has often not been understood well by the West. Actually, it was intended to make lawful the seminary teaching that was already being done.

Those among the clergy and laity who had suffered greatly in the past on account of their loyalty to the pope were not willing to cooperate with the official church. Rome addressed Chinese Catholics as one body and avoided distinguishing between the Patriotic Association and the underground Catholics. In reality, however, there is a lack of the spirit of forgiveness on both sides of the division. At the end of 1992 there were some ten million faithful in the recognized Church; 3900 churches and chapels had opened since 1979; 113 dioceses and 69 bishops were recognized by the government; and there were 1200 priests, with 435 ordained since 1979; 21 seminaries with 1000 students; 1200 sisters, and 1000 sisters in formation.

A dynamic Church that is at home in China has come into being. Its members want to be Chinese, Catholic, and autonomous. The problem of past centuries — the problem of foreignness — no longer exists. Rome has moved from condemnation to openness and dialogue. Chinese bishops and laypeople now travel to other countries, and numerous Western bishops, cardinals, and laypersons have traveled to China. A new model of interaction based on equality and mutual respect is emerging. This has created the possibility of solving the problems in relationship to Rome and to the Catholics not affiliated with the Patriotic Association.

The Protestant Churches

In 1949 Protestant churches, both independent Chinese churches and foreign-based churches, were dependent on foreign support, especially from North America. But already in the nineteenth century Protestant missiology was familiar with the three-self principles, self-government, self-support, and self-propagation. Foreign missionaries began to leave with the establishment of the People's Republic, and by 1952 none were left. In 1954 the Chinese Protestant Patriotic Society was born with more than 400,000 members. Almost all Protestant denominations were united into the Church of Christ in China with the aim of serving the country and the cause of world peace.

As it was for the Catholics, the Cultural Revolution was a time of destruction and persecution. But the resurgence after 1979 proceeded more rapidly for the Protestants than for the Catholics. The Protestants have had important and competent leaders like Y. T. Wu (1893-1979), Dr. Wu-yi-fang (born in 1893), and Bishop K. H. Ting. Their number of trained theologians is higher, as one can tell by the level of study in the many theological schools that have reopened. The Bible and other Christian literature is again printed. A large number of church buildings have been restored to their congregations. A dynamic church with numerous foreign contacts — but not dependence — presents itself to the world. A Christian Council of China, with Bishop Ting as president, was organized in 1980.

There are also Protestant house churches — groups of Christians meeting in homes for worship. These groups came into existence especially during the Cultural Revolution and then continued to exist either because there were still too few churches open or because in the villages churches had never been established. Many people attend services both in homes and in churches. But there are also groups — some speak of large movements — that have fundamental objections to the three-self principles of the Patriotic Association. The old contrast between modernists and fundamentalists plays a role. Especially in southern China the number of house churches is rapidly increasing, though a lack of trained leaders is a factor in the rise of Buddhist influences, strange practices, and divisions in some of these groups.

At the end of 1991 the number of Protestants was estimated to be between five and six million. However, in reality they may surpass ten million. There were seven thousand open churches and twenty thousand meeting points. The period from 1989 to 1992 was one of increasingly strict regulation of religious activity. Whereas Catholics were often arrested, Protestants were just more closely supervised.

The national Christian Conference met in 1992 after the promulgation of a new Church Order at the end of 1991. The status of the China Christian Council was not fully clarified. Are the True Jesus Church or Seventh-Day Adventists members of the Chinese Church? What is the relationship between the council and other Christian communities? Is the CCC a national church or one Church among others? Does obedience to Chinese law, regulations, and government policies exclude the faithful from the voice of conscience? Enough is sure that under the circumstances the maintenance of the status quo is to be considered a reasonable achievement. For the time being the discussions on the Three Self Patriotic Movement have calmed down. The Chinese church presents itself as a mainstream conciliar Protestant church with orthodox doctrines and ecclesiology. In 1991 it was accepted into the World Council of Churches.

There are, however, conservative evangelical organizations that give preference to house churches above the official church. House churches and autonomous communities flourish and increase their membership rapidly. Some suspect that very rapid growth will lead to superficial affiliation.

The open churches do not involve themselves in politics. There is an aversion to liberation theology, but also an emphasis on revolution as participation in the people's struggle for a better future. Stress is also placed on the incarnation as Jesus' identification with human suffering, on community as an antidote to Western individualism, on unity as the

end of Western denominationalism, and on the cosmic Christ as the
fulfiller of the whole creation process. A contextual theology is coming
into being, despite all the tensions. Further steps toward unity are
needed.[9]

9. R. C. Bush, *Religion in Communist China* (Nashville, 1970); *idem, Religious Policy
and Practice in Communist China: A Documentary History* (New York, 1972); G. T. Brown,
Christianity in the People's Republic of China (Atlanta, 1983, 1986[2]); A. S. Lazzarotto, *The
Catholic Church in Post-Mao China* (Hong Kong, 1982); E. O. Hanson, *Catholic Politics in
China and Korea* (Maryknoll, 1980); P. E. Kaufman, *China, the Emerging Challenge: A
Christian Perspective* (Grand Rapids, 1982); J. K. Fairbank, ed., *The Missionary Enterprise
in China and America* (Cambridge, MA, 1974); J. Schütte, *Die katholische Chinamission im
Spiegel der rotchinesische Presse* (Münster, 1957); W. Schilling, *Das Heil in Rot-China?* (Bad
Liebenzell, 1975); *Households of God on China's Soil,* compiled and tr. R. Fung (Geneva,
1982); F. Kürschner, *Kleine Kirche im grossen Land. Christen in der Volksrepublik China*
(Breklum, 1985); J. Heyndrickx, "The Chinese Catholic Church and the Churches: The
Search for a New Model of Relationship, Equality and Mutual Respect," in *China and
Europe: Ferdinand Verbiest Foundation Yearbook 1986* (Leuven, 1986) 46-86; E. Wurth, *Papal
Documents Related to the New China* (Maryknoll, 1985); Covell, *op. cit.*; R. Simonato, *Celso
Costantini tra rinnovamento cattolico in Italia e le nuove missioni in Cina* (Pordenone, 1985).
    D. B. Barrett, "Annual Statistical Table on Global Mission: 1987," *International
Bulletin of Missionary Research* 11 (1987) 24, offered the opinion that the Christian com-
munity in China numbered 52,152,000 in that year, but no evidence for this implausibly
high figure. E. Tang and J.-P. Wiest, ed., *The Catholic Church in Modern China: Perspectives*
(Maryknoll, 1993); J. Charbonnier, *Guide to the Catholic Church in China 1993* (Singapore,
1993); J. Chao, ed., *The China Mission Handbook, a Portrait of China and Its Church* (Hong
Kong, 1989); A Hunter and Kim-Kwong Chan, *Protestantism in Contemporary China*
(Cambridge, 1993); B. Whyte, *Unfinished Encounter: China and Christianity* (London,
1988).

CHAPTER 5

Ghana, West Africa: Between Traditional and Modern

F. J. VERSTRAELEN

In the first volume of the eight-volume UNESCO *General History of Africa*, J. Ki-Zerbo writes:

> [Africa played a major role] at the dawn of human history. Placed today on the periphery of the technically developed world, Africa and Asia were in the forefront of progress for the first 15,000-odd centuries of world history. . . . Africa was the principal scene both of man's emergence as the royal species of the planet, and of the emergence of a political society.[1]

This perspective on Africa does not agree with the picture many people have of the continent. We tend to look at Africa through Euro-colonial and imperialistic lenses that keep us from seeing the real face of Africa and its people. In order to break through these persistent prejudices and stereotypes we need to gain insight into the actual course of relations between Europe and Africa. Only from within this historical framework will we be able to describe and evaluate accurately the advent and place of Christianity in Africa.

In view of the great diversity of population groups, cultures, and historical influences in Africa, one cannot speak of Africa as a homogeneous whole. This chapter is limited to western Africa, specifically to Ghana, which was formerly called the Gold Coast. In the precolonial period (1595-1872) there was a strong Dutch trading presence in Ghana. Later and still today, the primary goal for the European presence in Ghana

---

1. J. Ki-Zerbo, "Conclusion: From Nature in the Raw to Liberated Humanity," in *idem*, ed., *General History of Africa* I: *Methodology and African Prehistory* (Paris and Berkeley, 1981) 730.

has been missions. Ghana is of particular interest because the black population of Brazil, the Caribbean, and North America has its roots especially
in this part of Africa.

We will deal first with the history of relations between Europe and
western Africa, focusing especially on the significance of the slave trade
and the opposition to colonial domination on the Gold Coast. We will then
concentrate on the place and significance of Christianity in the religio-
cultural and sociopolitical context of modern Ghana.

The Changing Relationship between Western Africa and Europe

From Trading Partners to Losers

The first Europeans to reach the Gold Coast were the Portuguese in 1471.
But a great deal of history had already passed in this part of Africa. For
centuries empires and states had formed there. In the ninth century there
was a Kingdom of Ghana, a strong state that traded in gold. This kingdom
was succeeded in the eleventh century by an even greater empire called
Mali, which extended to Nigeria. From the thirteenth century on in this
region, the Yoruba developed a new political system. Their art in terra-
cotta and bronze belongs to the best in the world and shows continuity
with a much older culture, the Nok culture, which was present in the
region centuries before the Christian era.[2]

After the Portuguese a host of traders followed from France, England, Holland, Brandenburg, and Denmark. The coastal inhabitants with
whom they came into contact were loosely organized in clans and small
political units. But to the north, in the rain forest and savanna regions,
larger states existed. Contact was made with the offshoots of these states:
the Akwamu, Akim, Denkyira, and Adansi. It took some time before the
focus of trade of these peoples shifted from a northward orientation
toward the coast. The Europeans acquired primarily gold and slaves from
this trade. The Africans acquired firearms and other European goods. With
the permission of local chiefs European traders of different nations built
trading forts — forty of them on a coastline of 400 km. With the growing
profits, rivalries among Europeans and among African groups increased.

The European nations most influential on the Gold Coast were first
the Portuguese, then the Dutch, and then the British. In 1637 the Portuguese were forced to yield their large fort at Elmina (called São Jorge da

2. B. Davidson, *Guide to African History* (second ed., London, 1966) 26-36.

Mina) to the Dutch, who were the strongest maritime power at the time. In 1872 the British won the fort in a treaty with the Dutch. The European monopoly position of Britain on the Gold Coast was thus sealed.[3]

For a long time relations between Europeans and Africans were marked by equality. It was easier for the Europeans to fight each other than to gain a firm grip on the Africans, who easily exploited European rivalries to their own advantage. Trade partnerships between Africans and Europeans proved stronger than any disputes between them.[4]

In this context of commercial and political partnerships, the slave trade was not a one-sided European enterprise. Basil Davidson has shown that in the Middle Ages slavery and serfdom were generally accepted institutions in both Europe and Africa. But the Europeans did come to dominate the relationship, they greatly expanded the slave trade, and they ensured their own advantage at the Africans' expense.[5]

Clear European domination of the rest of the world did not come about until the nineteenth-century Industrial Revolution. But European trade with western Africa, with all its ramifications, produced the prosperity that made possible industrial capitalism. The movement of slaves to North and South America was increased enormously by the European traders. It caused dislocations for Africa but was one part of the "great circuit" of trade, which was very profitable for Europe. This circuit also took consumer goods to western Africa and sugar and cotton to Europe. It has been calculated that from 1492 to 1870 the Atlantic slave trade brought from 9.5 to 12 million Africans to the Americas alive. About 1.5 million died during the crossing, and millions also died before shipment. It was truly an African holocaust.[6]

Those who wanted to abolish slavery succeeded not only on the basis of moral and humanitarian considerations but also, and especially, because of an underlying change in economic interests and balances.[7] On Africa's western coast society had more or less accommodated itself to the two-centuries-old slave trade with Europe. Discontinuation of that trade

---

3. W. E. F. Ward, *A History of Ghana* (fourth ed., London, 1967) 64-136. See also D. Coombs, *The Gold Coast, Britain and the Netherlands, 1850-1874* (London, 1963).

4. K. Y. Daaku, *Trade and Politics on the Gold Coast 1600-1720* (Oxford, 1970).

5. B. Davidson, *The African Slave Trade* (Boston, 1980) 206. This book is an expanded version of *Black Mother: A Study of the Precolonial Connection between Africa and Europe* (London, 1961).

6. Davidson, *African Slave Trade*, 95-101. The heartrending autobiography of the emancipated West African slave Olaudah Equiano (1745-97) went through nine printings in his own lifetime: O. Equiano, *The Life of Olaudah Equiano or Gustavus Vassa, the African, Written by Himself* (two vols. in one, Boston, 1837).

7. H. Porter, *The Abolition of the Slave Trade in England, 1784-1807* (1970).

— in 1807 in England and in 1814 in the Netherlands — brought about a social crisis. This crisis and the accompanying uncertainty and confusion were wrongly regarded in Europe as signs that Africans were by nature unsuited for self-government. The negative consequences of the breakup of the old partnership in the slave trade were now interpreted as results of "leaving the Africans to themselves."[8] But the problem was that the Africans had not, in fact, been left to themselves. Europeans hypocritically waved the banner of "guardianship and civilization." The progress that Europe had made at the expense of Africa now led to a European sense of superiority.

The slave trade had in the end the opposite effect for Africans. Increasingly confronted with the Europeans' material wealth, technical skills, and sense of superiority, Africans often fell into a sense of inferiority, sometimes even of guilt and shame. To end this sense of inferiority, which still affects people today, relations between Europe and Africa have to be placed within a correct historical perspective, specifically with regard to the slave trade. African scholars are struggling to see the history of their continent from an African perspective.[9] What has emerged from this historical study is a truer picture of the perseverance of Africans in the fight for existence, of their skill in relating to partners and adversaries, of the ease with which they assimilate new things, of their courage in resisting intruders and oppressors both native and foreign, of their wisdom in social organization, and of their powers of expression in language, dance, and the visual arts.

The Persistent Resistance to European Imperialism

The course of colonization in Ghana shows that the advent of the European powers was not simply "I came, I saw, I conquered." At first, the goal was not imperialism, and once that goal emerged it was merely one component in a complex network of political and sociocultural interrelationships.[10]

The European corporations that established themselves in trading posts and forts on the coast were interested in trade (first gold and later mainly slaves), not in politics. Since they brought profit, the traders were

8. Davidson, *African Slave Trade*, 254; see further 253-57, 269-86.

9. See the eight-volume *General History of Africa* (note 1 above), which is being edited by internationally recognized African historians such as J. Ki-Zerbo, B. A. Ogot, J. F. A. Ajayi, A. A. Boahen, and A. A. Mazrui. A reinterpretation of West African church history is taking place at the universities of Ibadan, Lagos, Accra, and elsewhere.

10. The information in this section comes mainly from Ward, *op. cit.*, and J. D. Fage, *Ghana: A Historical Interpretation* (Madison, 1966).

tolerated, but they were neither loved nor feared. They were dependent on their African neighbors for essentials like wood and water and they had to pay rent for the land they occupied. In 1699, the rent agreement that the Dutch had concluded for the fort of Elmina passed from the Denkyira to the Ashanti, because the former had been defeated by the latter. This was the start of the Ashanti's direct involvement in the trade politics of the coast.

Power in this region was gradually concentrated in the hands of two nations, one European, one African. Among the Europeans the British gained a European monopoly on the Gold Coast after the Danes sold their forts in 1850 and the Dutch gave up ownership of Elmina in 1872. Among the African nations the Ashanti emerged as the strongest power. The nations on the coast, especially the Fante, felt threatened and sought a link with the other Europeans, but without surrendering their sovereignty. In 1844 relations between the Fante and the British were formalized in a declaration made by a number of chiefs. In this "Alliance" judicial and police matters (e.g., human sacrifices), but not administrative matters, were transferred to British authority.

As a result of British misrule, new attacks by the Ashanti, and a sharp drop in trade, the British government decided in 1865 to withdraw from the Gold Coast altogether as soon as possible in view of the obligations that it had assumed. There was also some thought of transferring the administration to the local people with a view to ultimate withdrawal. A number of educated Fante men — most of them Christian — responded to this development by forming, in 1871, the Fante Confederation, which at a meeting at Mankesim formulated a constitution. Their idea was to organize a national government in which the leaders would take over the entire administration after the departure of the British. This constitution also contained a development plan with a special accent on schooling — to include girls, which was unusual — and the opening up of economic resources.

Meanwhile the tide had turned as a result of an imperialistic wind that was beginning to blow from Europe. The authors of the Mankesim constitution were viewed as traitors to the queen of England, to whom they had never sworn allegiance. After a military expedition against the Ashanti, the Gold Coast, a coastal area of about 330 by 50 miles, was declared a colony in 1874. In 1896 the Ashanti were coerced into recognizing the British protectorate; this was followed in 1902 by the incorporation of their land as a colony while the northern "hinterland" became a protectorate. Part of Togoland was added to this protectorate in 1922. This sequence of events set the boundaries of what is Ghana today.

As the British began to take their colonial administration more seriously, the influence of the local leaders in the colony was increasingly rolled back. But the drive toward self-rule and independence that had manifested itself in the Alliance and even more in the Fante Confederation sought out new means and new goals. About 1900 the Aborigines' Rights Protection Society, in which African jurists and businesspeople championed the rights of the coastal chiefs and their territories, was established. In 1918 Caseley Hayford formed the National Congress of (British) West Africa, which insisted on complete representative government for all West African colonies.

The colonial government sought cooperation more among the traditional leaders than among the educated elite, who increasingly regarded the chiefs as stooges of the colonial administration, which the elite wanted to destroy. The ranks of this intellectual elite were strengthened by a large new class of individuals who had been emancipated in their attitudes — partly through the experiences of World War II — office people, shopkeepers, technicians, cocoa farmers, teachers, and young men, all seeking to detach themselves from the traditional communal social order in favor of a modern society.

In 1947 the United Gold Coast Convention, the first real political party, was founded under the leadership of Dr. J. B. Danquah. It was surpassed in radicalism by the Convention People's Party (CPP), organized by Kwame Nkrumah in 1949. With the slogan "Self-Government Now!" Nkrumah managed to unite the people around the CPP. In the first general election in 1951, Nkrumah — then in prison — received 22,780 votes out of 23,122 in Accra.

After being a formal British colony for only fifty-five years — a status that the people of the Gold Coast had steadfastly resisted — the territory defined by the British became the independent state of Ghana. The country's name was chosen by Dr. Danquah. By means of it he sought to revive the traditions of a connection between the Gold Coast and the most ancient known West African empire and thereby to break with the European precolonial and colonial past.

The Expansion and Diversity of Christianity in Ghana

Christianity has been in Africa nearly from the beginning. Africans are mentioned in the Bible and played a significant role in the life and expansion of the early church. The Coptic Church in Egypt, which is still very much alive today, and the Ethiopian Orthodox Church had their beginnings in the first centuries of Christian history. Many African Christians draw their encouragement and inspiration from this fact: African Christianity is not a purely colonial phenomenon but a reality that has been rooted on the African continent already for centuries.[11]

But Europeans also brought their Christianity with them. When in 1471 the Portuguese first landed in Ghana at Shama, they planted a cross. A mass was celebrated for the first time in 1482. The priests who came to minister to the Portuguese also worked outside the forts. The village of Elmina had four hundred Christians in 1632. Before the large fort there was surrendered to the Dutch in 1637, church objects and images were hastily moved to the homes of local Christians.

With the Dutch came preachers who intended only to work among their own people, not to spread the gospel. The Dutch Calvinist merchants adopted a very pragmatic attitude toward "pagan" religion: They paid an annual stipend to the priest who conducted the worship of Benya, the tutelary spirit of Elmina, but "papists" were forbidden to conduct public services. About the changing of the guard Ward writes, "From the point of view of Christian influence in the country as a whole, the replacement of the Catholic priest by the Dutch predikant was a great loss."[12] In 1743 the majority of the people at Elmina proved to be still "papist." But in fact their Catholic Christianity had been absorbed into traditional religion. Traces of a Catholic past were encountered by the Society of African Missions fathers who came in 1880 to do systematic mission work: They encountered the Santonafo, a group of people who venerated the remains of an image of St. Anthony from the Portuguese period.[13]

Organized missions, both Catholic and Protestant, began in the nineteenth century. The Evangelical Mission Society of Basel began its work in 1828 from a base in the fort of Christiansborg. The Wesleyan Methodist Mission Society started in 1834 from the fort at Cape Coast, followed in 1847 by the North German Mission Society (the Bremer Mission). In 1897 the apostolic prefecture of the Gold Coast was begun and entrusted to the Society of African Missions, whose first two priests settled in Elmina in 1880. Out of these missionary efforts have come the Presbyterian Church of Ghana (1950),[14] the Methodist Church (1961),[15] and the Catholic Church (established as an ecclesiastical province in 1950).[16]

11. Cf. L. Sanneh, *West African Christianity: The Religious Impact* (Maryknoll, 1983) 1-13.

12. Ward, *op. cit.*, 80.

13. R. M. Wiltgen, *Gold Coast Mission History 1471-1880* (Techny, 1956) 142-52.

14. N. Smith, *The Presbyterian Church of Ghana, 1835-1960: A Younger Church in a Changing Society* (Accra, 1966).

15. F. L. Bartels, *The Roots of Ghana Methodism* (London, 1965).

16. Wiltgen, *op. cit.*; H. M. Pfann, *A Short History of the Catholic Church in Ghana* (Cape Coast, 1965).

Missionaries came to Ghana not only from Europe but also from North America. Interest in Africa in the United States was aroused, for example, by the Education Society (1773) and the American Colonization Society (1816), both seeking to repatriate former slaves to Africa. Evangelization and missionizing were among the various motives for this movement.

While Liberia was the main goal of repatriation efforts, mission work was also done in other British colonies in West Africa. In 1898 the American Methodist Episcopal Zion Church began its mission work at Cape Coast and Keta in Ghana. Because this church was totally African American, it strongly attracted those Africans in whom color-consciousness had been awakened. Its emotionally charged celebrations made it a forerunner of the independent African churches.[17]

Besides the mission churches there also arose in Ghana — as in so many other African countries — the "independent" churches. These churches originated either by separation from "established," that is, mission-based, churches or by independent initiatives.

The Akonomsu ("water drinkers") are viewed as the first group to secede from a mission church. The group was formed in 1862 in protest against the Methodist Church's weak reaction to use of alcohol. A clear movement of ecclesiastical independence was seen only from the 1920s on and was exemplified by the African Faith Tabernacle Church (founded in 1919), the Christ Apostolic Church (1921), and the Army of the Cross of Christ (1922). This movement came into the foreground only after Ghana won political independence in 1957. Just before that time there were seven such churches in Accra, the capital, but in 1970 there were at least a hundred.

Because of recent developments in Christianity in Ghana we have to make some distinctions in order to present the full variety of churches in this country. Besides the independent churches that originated in Ghana and are usually referred to as "spiritual churches" *(sunsum sore)*, there are two types of pentecostal movements: The first type is the classical pentecostal movement, which began in the West and reached Ghana in the 1920s (Assemblies of God, Pentecost Churches, etc.); the second type consists of neopentecostal or charismatic interdenominational fellowships (e.g., the Full Gospel Businessmen's Fellowship International and Women Aglow Fellowship International). In the mainline churches we find charismatic renewal groups like Catholic Charismatic Renewal, and Bible study and prayer groups in Protestant denominations. Out of the neopentecostal

17. J. K. Agbeti, *West African Church History: Christian Missions and Church Foundations 1482-1919* (Leiden, 1986) 113-19; H. W. Debrunner, *A History of Christianity in Ghana* (Accra, 1967) 234-37.

fellowships have developed new charismatic churches that are distinct from classical pentecostal and African independent churches because of a predominantly youthful and urban membership, use of English language, and adoption of American Christian styles of music, preaching, and other aspects of worship. A central issue in popular Christianity pervading almost all Christian groups is "deliverance," which aims at helping people break free from the influence of Satan and his allied evil spirits, which causes bad habits, suffering, sickness, and failure in life.[18]

The number of people who follow traditional religion exclusively is drastically declining, because traditionalists tend to be members of Christian churches or, less often, Muslims. In 1975, 27.3% of Ghana's population was still purely traditionalist, but Barrett believes that in 2000 this will be only 5.6%.[19] The largest concentration of pure traditionalists is found in northern Ghana, where 60% to 90% of certain population groups adheres to traditional religion. But, as we will see, much of the picture of the world and of human society inherent in traditional religion has been carried into African Christianity.

Islam also has its largest number of adherents in the north. In the fifteenth century Islam came into northern Ghana with merchants. It plays an important role in the more centralized northern states (Gonja, Dagomba, Mamprusi); in the decentralized (acephalous) groups its influence is weak and reaches at most 30% of the population. After the Ashanti victory over the Gonja and Dagomba (1744-45), educated Muslims were welcomed at the court of the Asantehene (king of the Ashanti) because of their powerful religion of Allah and Koran and were employed as bodyguards and to negotiate with the British.

Now non-Muslim migrants from the north tend to become Muslim rather than Christian. People in the south are better educated and more likely to be Christians. They tend to look down on the people of the north

18. On independent churches in Ghana, see C. G. Baeta, *Prophetism in Ghana: A Study of Some "Spiritual" Churches* (London, 1962); C. Hulsen and F. Mertens, "Independent Religious Movements," in *Survey of the Church in Ghana* (Cape Coast, 1972) 23-42; D. M. Beckmann, *Eden Revival: Spiritual Churches in Ghana* (St. Louis, 1975); J. R. Leferink, *Independent Churches in Ghana* (Africa Dossier 32; Brussels, 1985); Asempa Publishers, *The Rise of Independent Churches in Ghana* (Accra, 1990). For charismatic movements see A. O. Atiemo, *The Rise of the Charismatic Movement in the Mainline Churches in Ghana* (Accra, 1993); *idem*, "Deliverance in the Charismatic Churches in Ghana," in *Numen* (1994); C. N. Omenyo, *Charismatic Renewal in Mainline Churches: The Case of the Bible Study and Prayer Group of the Presbyterian Church of Ghana* (M. Phil. thesis, University of Ghana, Legon, 1994).

19. This estimate is from D. B. Barrett, ed., *World Christian Encyclopedia: A Comparative Survey of Churches and Religions in the Modern World A.D. 1900-2000* (Nairobi, 1982); on Ghana see pp. 323-26.

and still regard them more or less as slaves. Christian churches tended to be absent from the poorer sections where these migrants live. Nowadays churches, especially evangelical missionary groups, show, however, more concern for making the Christian gospel known to people living in the North and to migrants from the North settling in the South, many of whom are non-Muslim.[20]

In the mid-1980s Ghana was 15.7% Muslim, and half of the Muslims represented Ahmadiyya, a more modern form of Islam originally from Pakistan and brought to Ghana by a group of Fante Muslims. It is estimated that by 2000 Muslims will constitute 18% of Ghana's population and 11% of the total population will be Ahmadiyyas.

According to Barrett 62.6% of the population in 1980 was Christian and 43.9% were registered church members. He estimates that in the year 2000, 75% will be Christian and 52% registered church members. In 1980, of the total population 25% called themselves Protestant, 18.7% Catholic, and 16% were affiliated with independent churches. Barrett estimates that in 2000 these figures will have changed to 18.8%, 25%, and 28%. In mid-1993 the 10,202,700 Christians were 62.29% of the total population of 16,379,300, "traditional/no religion" accounted for 21.71% (3,555,500), and Muslims constituted 16% of the population, with 2,621,000.[21]

Christianity, Tradition, and Development

African culture has a great diversity of languages, sets of customs, and forms of socio-political and economic organization. But there is a shared substratum with two interrelated focuses: the extended family as a center of life and experience and religion oriented to everyday life. For the African the powers of life and vitality are pivotal. The function of religion is to make life possible and to maintain it (food supply, human and animal fertility, mutual relationships) and to protect it against illness, misfortune,

---

20. R. Kuitse, "Islam in Africa Project: Ghana Survey," *Bulletin of Christian Institutes of Islamic Studies* 3 (1970) 34-50. For further study see J. S. Trimingham, *Islam in West Africa* (London, 1967 [1959]); I. M. Lewis, ed., *Islam in Tropical Africa* (London, 1966); P. B. Clarke, *West Africa and Islam: A Study of Religious Development from the 8th to the 20th Century* (London, 1982); H. Hoeben, *Islamic Inroads into West Africa* (Africa Dossier 25; Brussels, 1983). Islam, in recent times, is becoming more visible in Ghana, and presents itself with self-confidence, also in the South, supported in its activities by oil money from Arab countries. For greater Christian concern regarding the northern people see "3.2 Million Unreached Northern and Alien People in Northern Ghana," *National Church Survey: 1993 Update* (Accra, 1993) 101-2, and "2.3 Million Unreached and Alien People in Southern Ghana," *ibid.*, 99-100.

21. *National Church Survey: 1993 Update*, 103.

enemies, and death. The whole world is viewed as an arena of forces affecting life for good or ill. African traditional religion seeks contact with the powers that control life and bestow life and vitality: ancestors (the "living dead"), spirits, magic, witchcraft, and the Supreme Being (God). At the center of these powers the human person tries to placate the powers for his or her own well-being and happiness. Traditional African life and culture are permeated by religion.[22]

It is striking to see that despite the vast changes occurring in various areas of African life the traditional African picture of the world and of human society is still powerfully present and operative. It is equally striking that Africans never allow themselves to be boxed in by outsiders in terms of religion or ideology. We will demonstrate this with a few examples from the Akan group, which constitutes 46.1% of the total population of Ghana, and of which the Ashanti are the largest sub-group (with 13.3% of Ghana's total population). (Other ethno-linguistic groups in Ghana include the Mole-Dagbani in the north with 17%, the Ewe in the east with 13%, and the Ga-Adangme in the area around Accra with 8.3%.)

The Traditional Worldview and Christianity

Traditional culture and religion are not static. Originally they were bound to the society of the small village, in which ancestors were venerated in order to insure order and prosperity. As a result of changes brought on first by commercial contacts with Europeans and then by colonial administration — and by the money economy — physical and psychological tensions increased and, in consequence, so also did witchcraft.[23]

In the 1930s the Ghanaians, observing that their own tutelary spirits — such as the Ashanti river gods Tano and Pra — had lost power, imported new cultures from the north, like the medicine cult of the Tigare and Blekete, which were considered more powerful because they had been less exposed to the influences of colonialism. While the shrines of these medicine cults come and go, they do as such still exert much influence on the lives of many Ghanaians. Traditional psychiatric techniques are some-

22. F. J. Verstraelen, "Afrika en zijn godsdiensten," in *Wat geen oog heeft gezien* (Amersfoort, 1981) 24-42 (bibliography); J. G. Platvoet, "The Akan Believer and His Religions," in P. H. Vrijhof and J. Waardenbur, ed., *Official and Popular Religion: Analysis of a Theme for Religious Studies* (The Hague, 1979) 543-606; J. B. Danquah, *The Akan Doctrine of God: A Fragment of Gold Coast Ethics and Religion* (London, 1944; second ed., 1968); G. Parrinder, *West African Religion* (London, 1949; second ed., 1961).

23. H. Debrunner, *Witchcraft in Ghana: A Study on the Belief in Destructive Witches and Its Effect on the Akan Tribes* (Kumasi, 1959).

times combined with ethical principles, organizational forms, and rituals taken over from Christian churches and organizations.[24] The imported medicine cults were a religious response to changing situations within the tradition, whereas the independent churches, responding to changes in the traditional world-view, attempted to provide a Christian answer.

In religious matters Africans, including Ghanaians, are very pragmatic. If one religious power does not help, another is tried. In the words of a traditional Ashanti priest: "We in Ashanti dare not worship the Sky God alone, or the Earth Goddess alone, or any one spirit. We have to protect ourselves against, and use when we can, the spirits of all things in the Sky and upon Earth."[25]

Ghanaians' understanding of Christianity fits into this framework of thought. They were not disturbed that Christianity was an import. The important thing was the power for prosperity and well-being that it would offer them in the new situation. They tended to see it as the religious dimension of the "modern life" that had entered their society through European contacts and colonization. Missionaries, both Catholic and Protestant, regarded Christianity as the faith that was to replace traditional religion. But Ghanaians saw it as a new religious power to be added to the totality of existing supernatural powers that they could use.[26]

European Christianity and Ghanaian Christians

Christian missions brought to Ghana a number of blessings such as formal education, scientific health care and agricultural methods, and a variety of technical conveniences. The missionaries saw and presented themselves primarily as messengers of God — and were easily accepted as such.

In the process of change and expansion, the traditional concept of God came increasingly and naturally to the fore. Ancestors linked to family and clan and spirits linked to places and to the ongoing existence of nature offered neither explanation nor direction for the "new world" that was forcing its way in everywhere, especially during the colonial period. Only the divine creator and life-giver continued to hold up. *Nyame,* the Supreme Being of traditional culture, proved to be a clear point of contact for the two world religions that presented themselves in Ghana: Islam and Christianity.[27]

24. Beckmann, *op. cit.,* 29-34.
25. R. S. Rattray, *Ashanti* (London, 1923) 150.
26. Smith, *op. cit.,* 241f.
27. Verstraelen, *op. cit.,* 32. See also R. Horton, "African Conversion," *Africa* 41 (1971) 85-108.

So at one level, that of "modern" life, Ghanaians found links with Christianity, but at another level Christianity itself had a very difficult time finding links with the totality of Ghanaian life. In his study of the Presbyterian Church in Ghana (1835-1960) Noel Smith remarks: "The church has failed rather to integrate itself into African society and has not succeeded in coming to terms with the social and religious conditions of its environment but has emerged in a marked degree as a bourgeois association largely out of touch with the mass of the people."[28] Although this statement applies in the first place to the Presbyterian church, it is also true — with minor modifications — for other mission-based churches, certainly as it concerns the relationship to the prevailing Ghanaian culture.

The missionaries believed that in both religion and culture they had something better to offer: Traditional religion would have to be replaced by Christianity, and traditional cultural institutions and customs would have to give way to proven and scientifically responsible institutions and forms. Within this mindset the Christianity of the missions had no need for dialogue with representatives of traditional religion and culture. Their attitude was: "Take it or leave it."

Existential Dialogue. Africans who became Christian found themselves in an ambivalent position. The Christianity of the missionaries gave them access to the "great tradition" of Western civilization, by which they could relate to the modern technical-industrial world with its new and hitherto unknown possibilities. At the same time they remained firmly and completely rooted in the "little tradition" of family and clan and of the concepts of religion and ritual bound up with family and clan.[29] To give up the "little tradition" would be self-annihilation, since life existed and received its spiritual and cultural nourishment in family and clan. What the missions as institutions did not know how to bring about was, in fact, realized by their converts: The dialogue that did not occur officially took place in the lives of African Christians who, to save themselves, combined elements of tradition with Christian elements.

This process of existential dialogue has been analyzed in a fascinating way in John Middleton's study of the Presbyterian Church in Akropong.[30] Although the missionaries in Akropong sought to build a com-

28. Smith, *op. cit.*, 246.
29. The expressions "great tradition" and "little tradition" are from R. Redfield, *Peasant Society and Culture* (Chicago, 1956) and are not intended to imply a value judgment.
30. J. Middleton, "One Hundred and Fifty Years of Christianity in a Ghanaian Town," *Africa* 53 (1983) 2-19. Comments on Middleton's work by historian P. Jenkins ("150 Jahre christliche Präsenz in Akropong aus der Sicht eines Ethnologen") and theologian J. S. Pobee ("Akropong der Stolz der Basler Mission aus der Perspective eines Afrikanischen Theologen") are in *Zeitschrift für Mission* 12 (1986) 213-18, 219-25.

munity in accordance with their own model, that of a Schwabian country village, and put much emphasis on quality Western schooling, in many ways the Akan tradition is still decisive today. That tradition is especially symbolized by the king of Akwapim and his court in Akropong and is also still clearly present in family life and in the plurality of religious centers.

This does not mean that the Christians of Akropong think in terms of a polarity between the Christian church and the traditional community. They live on the basis of "a single religious complex," as Middleton puts it. It means only that many serious Christians are not always able to meet all the demands of the church. They are heterogenous, so to speak, in their ecclesiastical status but homogeneous in their desire to make the gospel normative for their lives.[31] This church community proves to have fascinating ties with the traditional culture and with the main representatives of that tradition.

In this regard the role of elders — women as well as men — is important. In both church and society they fulfill a much-appreciated role as arbiters, especially in inheritance cases. In this way they mediate between the traditional matriarchal judicial system and the modern nuclear family.[32]

The Ghanaian View of the European Missionary Establishment. The missionaries regarded themselves as the bearers of the one true religion and of a higher civilization. They considered what they had superior to what Africa had in religion and culture. Most Africans agreed that the new material goods marked an improvement, but did not share the Europeans view in regard to religion and culture.

To most African Christians, Christianity is part of a much larger religious whole. While the missionaries regarded such a view as superstitious, the Africans thought that the missionaries evidenced "abysmal ignorance of supernatural things."[33] Their incomprehension was especially manifest in relation to the most evident phenomena, such as entrancement. To a Ghanaian Catholic anthropologist, Bishop Peter Sarpong, it is clear that, as long as questions remain about everything that can happen to people, faith in witchcraft and magic will continue in Ghana for centuries to come.[34]

31. A. Dankwa, "Tradition and Christianity at Cross-roads," a paper presented at the triennial consultation meeting of the Presbyterian Church, Aburi, September, 1982.

32. Middleton, *op. cit.*, 14f.; Jenkins, *op. cit.*, 217f.

33. M. J. Field, *Search for Security: An Ethno-Psychiatric Study of Rural Ghana* (London, 1960) 54.

34. P. Sarpong, *Ghana in Retrospect: Some Aspects of Ghanaian Culture* (Accra, 1974) 50.

Already at an early stage in Ghana, when colonialism was easily seducing missionaries into a posture of superiority toward all that was African, there was criticism from the side of Christian intellectuals. Beginning in 1897 an "emancipation" literature arose that was forthrightly critical of missionaries and their work. This criticism came from Ghanaian Protestants who were dedicated Christians as well as dedicated nationalists. They spoke against not only the social distance maintained by missionaries and the ecclesiastical forms that they imposed ("just as in England"), but also against the manner in which Christianity was interpreted vis-à-vis traditional religion. Thus Casely Hayford (1903) called the missionary "a simple soul" who was unable to see the good in traditional religion, such as veneration of ancestors. J. B. Danquah (1928) pleaded for some combination of "stool-worship" and "African Christianity"; otherwise the Akan-Fanti nations were bound to remain non-Christian for a long time. The objections of these and other critics concerned mistakes not in the theology of the missionaries but in their anthropology.[35]

Beginning in the 1920s similar criticism came to expression among educated Catholic laypersons. In the monthly *Catholic Voice*, starting in 1926, they asked that the church pay attention to local customs and religious usages. A Catholic program of action in 1938 concerned itself with the "Christianization of indigenous customs at births, marriages, and funerals."[36]

The period when Ghana achieved political independence was marked by systematic interest in local culture. In 1955 the Christian Council of Ghana organized a day of workshops on "Christianity and African Culture." In the Catholic Church the archbishop, at the urging of the Lay Conference, appointed a commission to study African customs relating to funerals, widowhood, and *abam* (twins). Its first product was a report on libations, which prohibited Catholics from taking part in this "superstitious" religious tradition. But ten years later a conference on the lay apostolate urged a review of the report.[37]

Apart from the new openness that developed under the influence of political independence and church renewal, which was inspired in part by Vatican II and the World Council of Churches, a "stuckness" also existed among Ghanaian Christians and their leaders: Some Christians had internalized the negative attitudes of the missions toward their own African culture and religion and were afraid to introduce changes. Con-

35. H. W. Mobley, *The Ghanaian Image of the Missionary* (Leiden, 1970) passim.
36. F. J. Verstraelen, "Missionaris-boodschap-cultuur in Ghana. Historisch-missiologische notities," *Wereld en Zending* 15 (1986) 216f.
37. F. J. Verstraelen, ed., *Christians in Ghanaian Life: Report of the National Seminar on Lay Apostolate, Kumasi, August 31-September 5, 1967* (Accra, 1968) 16-25, 27.

sequently the new insights did not automatically lead to new attitudes and forms.

African Christianity

In the mission-based churches increased attention and openness to the values of traditional culture and religion thus emerged only with difficulty. But in the so-called "independent churches," unhindered by European rules and controls, an African Christianity grew that responded to the reality of the African cultural and religious complex.

One cannot overestimate the importance for this of the appearance of the Bible in African languages. Charismatically gifted men and women acquired in the Bible an independent frame of reference by which to judge the Christianity brought by Western missionaries. But even more important was the discovery that many things in the Bible seemed to correspond with the worldview and aspirations of these indigenous leaders, for example, recognition of the influence of spirits and the central place of Jesus' healing power.

In the assemblies of the independent churches everyone participates by clapping, shouting exclamations, and dancing, and everyone with problems of health, marriage, work, and so on receives personal attention.[38] In Ghana there are some five hundred independent churches, often called "healing churches" because of their emphasis on healing. They are also sometimes called "spiritual churches," but this expression is easily misunderstood. "Spiritual church" represents *sunsum asore.* In Twi, the Akan language, *sunsum* is that part of the human personality which can wander away from the body in dreams and visions. A strong *sunsum* is said to be the best defense against malicious spiritual powers. The Holy Spirit is known as *sunsum kronkron,* and glossolalia, ecstasy, visions, spiritual protection, and miraculous healing are thought to be the Holy Spirit's main province.[39] The term "spiritual churches" refers therefore not to something purely "spiritual" but to the "power" that people experience in these churches in their struggle for life and in their yearning for the expansion of their lives.

The Role of Women. Independent churches, both large and small, tend to attract people of all levels of society, but especially women. Barrett has shown that in many African cultures women occupy important posi-

38. D. B. Barrett, *Schism and Renewal in Africa: An Analysis of Six Thousand Contemporary Religious Movements* (Nairobi, 1968) 127-29.
39. Beckmann, *op. cit.,* 12f.

tions, especially in matrilineal societies like that of the Akan in Ghana.[40] Because they were responsible for agriculture, women exercised economic control. Polygyny, though not an expression of equality, gave them status, security, and a considerable measure of economic and religious power. Women played an important role in the cult of Mother Earth and exerted influence on politics. In the Ashanti war against British imperialism in 1900, the center of inspiration was Yaa Asantenwa, the queen mother of Ejisu.

In the missionary system certain categories of women lost much of their earlier position. At the baptism of a polygamous man he would choose a favorite wife; the others were sent away and sometimes became prostitutes. As a rule there was no place for women in office or in any position of executive responsibility. The missionaries themselves were daunted by the influence that women sometimes had in cultures with strong emotional and sexual rites. And in many other respects the inflexibility of the institutional churches — for example, the refusal to baptize illegitimate children — was experienced primarily by women.

An extensive survey of the Catholic Church in Ghana conducted in 1972 addressed, among other issues, the status of women. It made clear that women did not have the same level of rights as men, that they were considered inferior to men, and that much was prohibited to them. They were represented hardly at all in parish councils and were not allowed to have leading roles in churches or in other groups that included men. It became evident, in fact, that women had lost status by joining the Catholic Church. That many of them were joining independent churches had something to do with this issue of status: In independent churches women sometimes play very prominent roles.[41]

The dissatisfaction of women does not always lead them into other churches. They often find an escape valve in women's societies such as the Manyano groups in southern Africa or in "pious associations" in western Africa. But women do often become fervent followers of independent prophets, and many independent movements are initiated by women themselves. Barrett mentions several hundred such movements begun over the last few decades. The women leading them are often remarkably young, sometimes only seventeen to thirty years old.

As an example of such women, Mama Mary, a formerly Catholic

40. Barrett, *Schism and Renewal*, 146-53. See also the study of the status and influence of women among the LoBir in Ghana by B. L. Hageman, *Beer and Matriliny: The Power of Women in a West African Society* (Ann Arbor, 1977).

41. C. Hulsen and F. Mertens, "Status of Women in the Church," in *Survey of the Church in Ghana*, 35-37. Cf. L. Lagerwerf, *"They Pray for You. . .": Independent Churches and Women in Botswana* (IIMO Research Pamphlet 6; Leiden, 1984).

woman, founded the "Church of the Holy Spirit" *(Sunsum Kronkron Donhye)* in Kumasi, Ghana. A fundamental reason that she did so was that as a woman with leadership skills she always aroused suspicion among church administrators. In any case, in the Catholic Church she had met no one prepared to accept that her gifts might have religious value or that she could be a chosen instrument of the Lord. The bishop of Kumasi, Peter Sarpong, did send an official representative to the solemn inauguration of Mama Mary's church, thereby both recognizing the genuineness of her aspirations and also admitting with regret the impossibility of doing justice to them within the Catholic Church.[42]

In general, women can go to independent churches with their problems of infertility, childlessness, and domestic issues, problems that the mission churches as a rule do not want to deal with. And in the independent churches they acquire status by occupying responsible posts as evangelists, ordained ministers of sacraments, healers, and prophetesses. Not until they joined the independent church movement did the relatively underprivileged status that many women had in the mission churches make any significant change for the better.

Relationships between Established Churches and Independent Churches. For a long time the significance of the independent church movement in Ghana was played down in mission circles. The Catholic Church in particular believed that the independent churches held no attraction for its members. But it has become evident that the bulk of the membership in independent churches comes from the "established" churches, including the Catholic Church.

At a congress on the lay apostolate in Kumasi in 1967, the following reasons were given that Catholics had gone over to independent churches:

- They were thus attempting to find help for various forms of physical and spiritual distress,
- they experienced in the independent churches strong feelings of solidarity, and
- in contrast to what they experienced in the Catholic Church they felt completely accepted despite marital problems.[43]

The 1972 survey confirmed this picture and added other reasons. Moreover, it pointed out that some people have membership in both the Catholic Church and in the independent churches. For example, more than

---

42. W. Eggen, "Charisme prophétique d'une femme et institution," *Spiritus* 24 (1983) 278-86.

43. Verstraelen, ed., *Christians in Ghanaian Life*, 27f.

20% of the members of the Nazarene Healing Church in Accra also belonged to an "established" church, and nearly half of those were Catholics.[44] Prof. Noah K. Dzobo of the Cape Coast University explains this by saying that the originally Western churches confer social respectability while the independent churches are seen as reflecting a faith that works, an "affirmative Christianity." That is, they offer a faith that enters a person's life in order to expand and enrich it, not to confine it.[45]

One would expect that the independent churches would have become the predominant form of African Christianity in independent Africa. Around the time Ghana achieved political independence (1957) there was a sharp increase in the number of these churches. But many African government leaders found them too small, too poor, and too circumscribed to mean much for the development of their countries. Despite frequent verbal criticism of the "colonialism" of the missions, in the end African leaders still expected more from the better organized "established" churches.

"Independent" churches and "established" churches, both Catholic and Protestant, have clearly grown closer together, both in fact and in the minds of their leaders. In the established churches there has been increasing recognition of the values of the independent churches with their smaller scale and their direct attention to individuals. It is increasingly understood that the church must not start at the top but from within the life situation of people. Ghanaian theologian John S. Pobee puts it this way: The real success of missionary activity does not lie in the number of adherents gained or the number of schools and hospitals built but in "whether mission and local anthropological factors have entered into a meaningful mutual relationship."[46]

The independent churches understand that they need more training and theological schools, which then requires the formation of larger ecclesiastical units. Some independent churches have also joined organizations created by the "established" churches. The Eden Revival Church, for example, is a member of the Christian Council of Ghana. For training purposes the Good News Training Institute was founded at Accra in 1971.[47]

The interrelationship that offers complementation and enrichment for both kinds of churches can be described briefly: The "independent" church has fellowship and is searching for organization; the "established"

44. Hulsen and Mertens, *op. cit.,* 28.
45. Leferink, *op. cit.,* 27 (from an address given by Dzobo on January 25, 1981).
46. Probee, "Akropong," 224.
47. E. Weaver and I. Weaver, *From Kuku Hill: Among Indigenous Churches in West Africa* (Elkhart, 1975).

church has organization and is searching for fellowship. Only fellowship and institution together are able to meet the religious challenges of the Ghanaian people and their society today.[48]

Organizationally, the churches in Ghana today demonstrate a great diversity. The churches resulting from the pioneer missions have formed three major councils and conferences: the Christian Council of Ghana (with fourteen member churches), the Bishops' Conference of the Catholic Church of Ghana (with nine dioceses), and the four Conferences of the Seventh Day Adventist Church in Ghana. The older African independent churches (the "spiritual churches") have some major groupings like the African Faith Tabernacle, Apostles Revelation Society, and Savior Church of Ghana, but many are of the "one-man" type. The classical pentecostal churches have formed the Ghana Pentecostal Council (formerly called the Ghana Evangelical Fellowship) with currently sixty-six member denominations. Then there is an incoherent group of mission-related churches and denominations, each originating from or otherwise related to an overseas church or missionary society; in Ghana there are twenty-four such mission enterprises, but there is no organizational relationship among the churches in this category. Finally, the new Charismatic Churches, which emerged in the late 1970s and are experiencing phenomenal growth in recent years, have not yet produced a council comparable to the Christian Council or the Ghana Pentecostal Council.[49] Diversity in itself is, of course, an expression of living unity. But if each group does not relativize its specificity this easily leads to divisions that in the end cannot but do damage to the credibility of the missionary message of Christ, their common Lord and Savior.

Church and State in Ghana

The missions and later the churches that came out of them have always been in contact with political leaders, since churches and politicians have had to deal with the same people and the same society. That encounter has been one of cooperation, of tension, and of open conflict. In Ghana's colonial period, cooperation was the rule in education and medical care. But there were also tensions and conflicts. For example, the colonial rule of "peace and order" was used to block missionary work in northern

---

48. See A. Hastings, *A History of African Christianity 1950-1975* (London, 1979), 268: "One has community and is searching for institution; one has institution and is searching for community."

49. See *National Church Survey: 1993 Update*, 12, 107-9.

Ghana, which was considered a bulwark of Islam — despite the attempts of missionaries to convince the colonial administration that Christians would be more loyal than Muslims. In northern Ghana the first mission posts could not be opened until 1906 (the Catholic White Fathers) and 1913 (the Methodist mission).[50]

At the inauguration of the Nkrumah government in 1951, during the period of transition from internal self-government to complete self-government, it became clear at once that this government wanted more control over education. This was understood by the churches as an attempt to keep religion out of the schools. What Nkrumah was in fact striving for was a socialist society in which all the means of production would be centralized in the hands of the government. This orientation and the goals of Nkrumah's "Plan for Education" were foreign to most church leaders, who insisted on democracy for the new Ghana. Compromises were made with regard to education, but the fundamental differences were never genuinely discussed.[51]

Many other areas of friction arose between the churches and the Nkrumah government. Particular concerns were the use of religious language for political matters, the "divinization" of Nkrumah, the transformation of his place of birth into a shrine (with direct reference to Bethlehem) in order to make it the Mecca of African politics, and the inception of the Ghana Young Pioneer Movement, in which, some believed, Nkrumah took the place of Christ.

There was of course much reason for criticism, certainly when religion in an absolute sense appeared to be linked to nationalistic politics and to the person of Nkrumah. But frequently the protest of the churches evidenced an unenlightened attitude toward African traditions. For example, when the honorific title Osagyefo ("Savior") was applied to Nkrumah, the churches regarded this as the arrogation of a title that could only be used of Christ. But in the Fante tradition this title was conferred on chiefs who went to war as "saviors in battle," as deliverers. By concentrating on the real or imagined blasphemous use of religion, the churches failed to reflect on more central issues.

The rapid social and political transformation of the Gold Coast made it necessary for adjustments to be made. In this readjustment the Church was perhaps slow; she sometimes failed to realize that she lived in a pluralistic society and could no longer be accorded a privileged

---

50. Kuitse, *op. cit.*, 44. See also B. Der, "Church-State Relations in Northern Ghana, 1906-1940," *Transactions of the Historical Society of Ghana* XV, 41-61.

51. J. S. Pobee, "Church and State in Ghana 1949-1966," in *idem*, ed., *Religion in a Pluralistic Society* (Leiden, 1976) 121-44.

position; she failed to understand Nkrumah's philosophy and sometimes even made no effort to understand it.[52]

Christian churches in Ghana were still firmly tied in theology and ethos to
the churches in Europe and America that had started them — and their
theological education still occurred in the framework of a colonial theology.[53]

In the Nkrumah period church and state clashed, though it was a
relatively mild clash. Many Christians and church leaders did no better than
the politicians and showed a lack of moral conviction. The churches failed
to give Ghanaians a more critical and rational view of their situation. "The
problem of winning moral authority for creating a new Ghana was difficult
and that partly because the church failed to give the proper moral leadership."[54]

Nkrumah was a charismatic personality with a grand vision, but he
was toppled because he concentrated more on the unification of Africa than
on the increasing problems in his own country. Since his time things have
not gotten better, despite the three military coups and the two republics that
followed the first republic under him. Israeli political scientist Naomi
Chazan views Ghana as a microcosm of political processes in Africa, a paradigm of the revolutions and general stagnation shared by so many African
countries. Although economic progress is officially central, a shift has in fact
taken place from industrialization to rural development, from growth to
prevention of a total collapse, from a food production surplus to maintenance of a minimum. In Ghana decolonization consisted in the takeover
of the colonial center, not in improvement or modification of that center.
Ghana was Africanized in form, but not in substance. The dissonance between center and periphery characteristic of the colonial period continued.
Truly, as Chazan remarks, when God wants to test his angels, the only thing
he has to do is send them to govern a newly independent country.[55]

52. *Ibid.*, 142. See also John S. Pobee, *Kwame Nkrumah and the Church in Ghana
1949-1966* (Accra, 1988); *idem, Religion and Politics in Ghana* (Accra, 1991).
53. K. A. Dickson, "Religion and Nkrumah: A Study in Church and State Relations in the First Republic," a paper presented at a symposium on Nkrumah organized
by the Institute of African Studies of the University of Ghana, Legon, May 27-June 1,
1985, 21. This paper has been published in Kwame Arhin (ed.), *The Life and Work of
Kwame Nkrumah* (Accra, 1991) 135-51 under the title "Religion and Society: A Study in
Church and State Relations in the First Republic."
54. Pobee, "Church and State," 144. See also F. J. Verstraelen, "Ghana after the
'Coup' and Vatican II (Is the Church to Blame?)," *Catholic Voice* 43 (Cape Coast, 1968) 69f.
55. N. Chazan, *An Anatomy of Ghanaian Politics: Managing Political Recession,
1969-1982* (Boulder, 1983) passim. Cf. D. Austin, "Progress in Ghana," *Ghana Observed*
(1976) 154, cited in Chazan, 4.

Economic stagnation increased the inequalities in society. The decline of the state's power and authority prompted the politicizing of practically all the larger segments of the Ghanaian population: ethnic communities, local and regional agglomerates, students, trade unions, intellectuals, women, and religious groups. Indeed, women who in 1974 joined ranks in the National Council on Women constitute a force to be reckoned with in Ghanaian politics. The principal overarching religious organizations with public influence are the National Catholic Secretariat and the Christian Council of Ghana, which represent over 40% of the population, and the Ghana Muslim Organization, which can speak nationally for 25% of the population.

Do the churches understand what their mission is in independent Ghana? Do they know how to give relevant shape to that mission? They have been more courageous in pointing with conviction to the failings and mistakes of those in power than they were in the Nkrumah period. Besides continuing dialogue behind closed doors the churches now also speak openly against violations of human rights by successive government leaders, such as Acheampong and Rawlings.[56] But pronouncements remain relatively easy and do not furnish solutions.

The credibility of the churches will grow when they not only make pronouncements but also work out programs that promote social justice and economic equality. But can they do this without a revolution in their own ranks — a revolution that attempts to discover and put into practice the core of the gospel and to give up matters of secondary importance, a revolution that carries out a shift from concern for institutional prestige to the service of people, who are, after all, those to whom the Good News is directed?[57]

56. See J. S. Pobee, "Church and Politics," *Bulletin de Théologie Africaine* 7 (1985) 330f.; cf. L. A. Abadamloora, *Ghana in the Wake of the Revolution: An Urgent Need for Christian Social Principles* (Accra, 1982); J. N. Kudadjie and R. K. Aboagye Mensah, *The Christian and National Politics* (Accra, 1991); idem, *The Christian and Social Conduct* (Accra, 1992).

57. Cf. K. Adu-Opako, *Economic Patterns in West Africa: A Challenge to the Church* (Africa Dossier 24; Brussels, 1983) 28.

CHAPTER 6

Indonesia: A Christian Minority in a Strong Position

K. A. Steenbrink

The History of Indonesian Christianity

Though the churches in Indonesia may not always want to remember it, the roots of Indonesian Christianity lie in the country's colonial period. The first Catholic missionaries arrived with Portuguese merchants and soldiers. The Spanish and Portuguese method of conversion aimed for quick success and therefore made no permanent imprint for Catholicism. Portuguese domination of part of the Moluccas began in 1522, with varying political and religious success. On both the political front and the religious front the great adversary was the Islamic sultanate. Francis Xavier conducted a campaign in 1546, but despite his concern for follow-up, little was done to achieve it. After 1600, when the Portuguese were replaced by the Dutch, those first "converts" quietly entered the Protestant churches.

The great period of colonialism began in the nineteenth century when a large number of independent kingdoms in the archipelago — first the coastal regions, then the inland areas — came under the Dutch central administration of Batavia, which is now known as Jakarta. The inland areas of the main island of Java were permanently subjugated in the Java War of 1825-30. The "rebel" Diponegoro, a central figure in that war, was also viewed as a Muslim reformist. West Sumatra experienced the same fate in 1838 after the Padri Wars, waged by extremist Muslims; the victorious Dutch were allied with the nonreligious party. Palembang fell in 1822, the remaining areas of South Sumatra (Lampong) between 1840 and 1850. Jambi was subjugated in 1899, and war went on in Aceh from 1873 to 1912, with the same outcome. But in the Batak areas of North Sumatra the mission preceded the arrival of the colonial administration: In 1876

88

the German missionary Nommensen reached Lake Toba, though the area itself was not "pacified" until years later.

The completion of this colonial empire, which began as a mere chain of trading posts, constituted the "reunification" of the Indonesian archipelago. Politicians and historians still debate whether the empires of Sriwijaya, ruled from Sumatra in the sixth through the ninth centuries, and Majapahit, ruled from Java in the thirteenth through the fifteenth centuries, were such unifying states. Politicians stress that they were in order to give the present unified nation of Indonesia deeper roots. At any rate, from a great variety of empires, kingdoms, and cultures a unified empire came into being in the first few years of the twentieth century, beginnng in the western part of the present nation. Then this empire was extended: The war with Banjarmasin (1857-60) resulted in the conquest of an important part of Kalimantan (i.e., Borneo, the largest island of Indonesia). Lombok came under the colonial administration in 1894, as did the area belonging to the Torajas on Celebes in 1905 and the island of Bali in 1908, in each case after fierce wars. The definitive subjection of the island of Flores occurred in 1908, and in the same period, slowly but surely, the Dutch also acquired hegemony over the other eastern islands.

The memory of struggle against colonial powers continues to play a significant role in the political life of the nation. At the beginning of the 1980s "the history of the national struggle" became a required school subject from the elementary grades to the end of secondary school. This teaching serves the ideological strengthening of Indonesia as a unified state. Official formulations from the Ministry of Education and Culture consistently try to find a balance: *Internal* struggles in the formation of the nation are glossed over as much as possible, and all the country's regions and religions are portrayed as having been involved in the national struggle. Considerable attention is paid to the religious motivation of Muslims in the fight for nationhood. But other groups are not ignored. Prominence is given to Christina Martha Tiahahu, a Moluccan, doubly important because she is a Christian. In the gallery of national heroes women are reasonably well represented.

Well into the nineteenth century Indonesian Christianity was closely tied to colonialism. Outside the Moluccas there had been virtually no converts, and churches were in the main content to serve their European members. Missionary élan really began to assert itself only toward the end of the nineteenth century. Even then, this occurred in a way that, though it certainly did not entail identification with the colonial administration, exhibited much more cooperation with the administration than opposition to it. In areas where the government had no secure foothold the missions were entitled to a "cultural subsidy," and during

World War I the government paid German missionaries whose salaries were cut off by the war.[1]

In many ways the missions and the government cooperated with each other and Christians were favored at the expense of adherents of other religions. But there were also many conflicts, which made identification between Christianity and the colonial government impossible, even in the eyes of outsiders. For a period neither Catholic nor Protestant missions were allowed to operate in certain areas, such as Islamic Atjeh and Hindu Bali. But in general, love overruled hatred in the marriage of convenience between government and church.[2]

The Ideological and Political Context

National Unity and Pancasila as Pseudo-Religion

After the proclamation of independence in 1945 and Dutch recognition of independence at the end of 1949, the Indonesian republic still had to go to great lengths to keep the colonial legacy of a unified state. Up to the early 1960s separatist movements arose, some from Islamic protests against the compromise of 1945, in which it was agreed that Indonesia would be neither an Islamic state nor a secular state, but a state based on the "five-pillar doctrine," which is called *Pancasila.* The first of the five pillars is "belief in the one almighty deity"; the other four are nationalism, humanism, democracy, and social justice. For some Muslims this was not acceptable, and in some areas, especially West Java, South Kalimantan, and Atjeh, there was an extended struggle for the establishment of an Islamic state.

Christians were generally more able to accept this ideology of the state, but they too had problems with it. They certainly did when, beginning in August, 1982, the word from government circles was that *Pancasila* would have to be accepted as "the sole basis" of government, not only by political parties and groups but by all groups in society, including churches. An appeal to colonial and Dutch legislation, which accords special status to church denominations, did not help in the debate. Some groups, both Muslim and Christian, that had always been ready to defend *Pancasila* as a historic compromise, now began to be frightened. Studies

1. On this subject there is interesting material in M. C. Jongeling, *Het Zendings-consulaat in Nederlands-Indië, 1906-1942* (Arnhem, 1966).

2. On Bali, see H. Kraemer, *De strijd over Bali en de zending* (Amsterdam, 1933). On the manner in which Christian missions have been favored over Islam in the Batah area, see L. Castles, *The Political Life of a Sumatran Residency: Tapanuli 1915-1940* (New Haven, 1972), especially 91-170.

and declarations of *Pancasila* were issued that spoke of it as a pseudo-religion or a state religion. Accordingly, a meeting of church councils in October, 1984, at Ambon adopted as article 3 of the constitution of the new Communion of Indonesian Churches this statement: "The Communion of Indonesian Churches has its foundation in Jesus Christ, Lord and Savior, in agreement with God's Word in the Bible." Article 5 then continues: "In the light of the foundation described in Article 3 above, the Communion of Indonesian Churches fully accepts its responsibility to recognize, realize, and promote *Pancasila* as the only basis of social, national, and political life in Indonesia." Though there may be no clear distinction between "foundation" and "basis," those meeting in Ambon wanted first of all to secure the theological basis.

Many Muslims who initially regarded *Pancasila* as too great a concession to the Christian minority in Indonesia began to view it as a good defense against Communism. An increasingly Islamic understanding of the *Pancasila* formula, which was in fact already monotheistic, grew. Conversely, various Christian groups have felt increasing reserve toward *Pancasila*, regarding it as a pseudo-religion. This is so partly because the term "only basis" *(azas tunggal)*, which is now officially accepted by the churches, does sound weighty to people who are used to applying it only to the Bible or to Jesus. For some it is impossible to attribute it to an ideology of the state. It was, therefore, Christian pupils who in Middle Java in mid-1985 were no longer willing to take part in the numerous and often pseudo-religious nationalistic ceremonies at school, such as bowing before the flag and saluting it. But among both Christians and Muslims, opponents of *Pancasila* are in the minority, which recalls the fact that from the beginning *Pancasila* was open to a variety of interpretations.[3]

At all schools, from kindergarten through the end of secondary school, *Pendidikan Moral Pancasila*, that is, ethics according to *Pancasila*, is part of the required curriculum. It often overlaps with what is taught in religion classes, which are also required, and this sometimes causes problems. One can perhaps compare the status of *Pancasila* ethics with that of the teaching of Confucius in early China: Confucius provided standards of conduct for social and political life, just as *Pancasila* does in Indonesia. For answers to questions concerning the hereafter or problems of sickness

3. Cf. B. Boland, *The Struggle of Islam in Modern Indonesia* (The Hague, 1971; second ed. 1982). The Conference of Catholic Bishops delayed for a considerable time its acceptance of *Pancasila*. At a large conference in November, 1986, it accepted a formulation which bears strong resemblance to that of the Council of Churches. The decision was kept confidential until January 7, 1987, when a report of the conference was submitted to the president.

and death the Chinese sought counsel from the Buddha, just as in Indonesia Islam provides solutions to these problems for most people.

The third current within ancient China, Taoism, is comparable to what takes place in Indonesia outside the reach of bureaucrats and religious leaders, school curriculum and religious writings. This is what comes down through old practices, remnants of animism, and *guna-guna*, a variety of magical practices and beliefs, including an almost completely secularized folklore. Anthropologist C. Geertz introduced the term *abangan* for this complex, his term coming from the word for red, the color of the earth, in contrast particularly to "whites," that is, rigorous Muslims.[4]

Geertz did his research in East Java in 1954-55 during a time of elections. Muslims and Christians both made a show of their ideological independence and were linked to particular political parties. The same period even witnessed the institutional organization of groups of "reds" or *abangan* into new religions. The polarizations culminated in the upheavals of 1965, as a result of which Sukarno was replaced as head of state by Suharto. Then religion was again depoliticized and the conflicts became less intense. There was eventually relative harmony among the three main traditions. This development has made it clear that any characterization of such a culture is provisional and subject to alteration.

Van Baal, a scholar and government administrator in western New Guinea, which is now a province of Indonesia as Irian Jaya, concluded in his study of the religion in Marind-Anim that it presented an example of "the peaceful coexistence of two separate and nevertheless mutually complementary cultic communities."[5] This model is also applicable to other areas of Indonesia, certainly on Java, though we would have to speak of *three* such coexisting communities.

From Party Politics to Lobbying

After a period of "free democracy" marked by a luxuriant growth in the number of political parties — until there were more than a hundred — President Sukarno, the proclaimer of independence and the first president, returned in 1959 to a presidentially guided democracy in which little power was left to the parties. The Suharto administration began after the failed Communist coup of September 30, 1965, or formally after 1967.

---

4. C. Geertz, *The Religion of Java* (Glencoe and New York, 1960).
5. J. van Baal, *Ontglipt Verleden* I (Franeker, 1986) 273. This book offers a number of noteworthy and critical comments on mission methodology and mission ideals that do not simply come out of the old feuds between anthropologists and missionaries.

Under Suharto the function of the political parties was reduced even further. Besides the government party only two groups remained. One was a coalition of four Islamic parties. The other was a federation of the remaining parties, among them the Catholic and Protestant parties.

All these political parties have accepted *Pancasila* as their basis. Because the contribution of the Christian parties to this federation is relatively small there is no clear input from any Christian political power block via a parliamentary group. Currents of political influence flow to the government directly from the Communion of (Protestant) Churches or from the (Catholic) Bishops' Conference through a system of lobbying or personal contacts.

High government functions such as ministries and regional military commands are distributed in accordance with a scheme designed to insure that all regions and all religions will, if possible, be properly represented. Therefore, there have always been one or more Catholic and Protestant ministers in the cabinet. But no clear tie exists between church and politics. The position of supreme military commander has frequently been Catholic or Protestant, in view of the proportion of Catholics and Protestants in the population. But that could be, as rumor has it, so that the commander would be a member of a minority group and would therefore never be able to entertain presidential aspirations.

The Ministry of Religion

For administration of matters relating to religions Indonesia has opted for a separate Ministry of Religion.[6] Many matters dealt with by religious groups fall under the jurisdiction of this ministry, including theological training, solemnization of marriages, building of mosques, organization of religious education, and translation of sacred books. The last is done among Muslims and Hindus and to some extent among Christians by and at the initiative of the civil servants of this ministry.

Christians have always had some difficulty with the position of this ministry. Because Indonesia is not an Islamic state the ministry has departments for Catholics, Protestants, Hindus, and Buddhists as well as Muslims.[7] Funds and training centers for administrators are designated

6. This is a literal translation of *Departemen Agama*. The translation "Ministry of Religious Affairs" is also frequently used.

7. After long discussions the *aliran kepercayaan,* the "new religions," which tend to be *abangan* ("red"), have for the time being come under the Ministry of Education and Culture for administrative purposes. In the distribution of television time and in the rotation system governing prayers at official state occasions, they are treated equally

for all these groups. Catholics and Protestants have consistently viewed the ministry as unnecessary ballast and have never placed their most qualified people there. So their departments in the ministry are weakly staffed. Christian theological training schools have almost always sought state recognition for their diplomas in the Ministry of Education and Culture rather than in the Ministry of Religion — except American faith missions, which beginning in the 1970s started a number of training schools, usually Bible schools, and almost always sought permission and recognition from the Ministry of Religion. But, unlike the Muslims, most churches are reluctant to ask for assistance from the Ministry of Religion in publishing books, building churches, and other activities.

The Socio-Economic Context: The Minority Status of Christians

Exports of raw materials and of lightly processed products have kept the Dutch East Indian and later the Indonesian economy afloat for centuries. There has always been much to export from this richly endowed country. In the nineteenth century, after the period of the spices, indigo, tobacco, tea, and especially sugar were exported. The twentieth century added primarily rubber, coal, and oil. After independence, oil replaced sugar as the key commercial product. It is currently followed, at a great distance, by tropical hardwoods.

Anyone who ever witnessed a gathering of Protestants or Catholics from all of Indonesia is bound to be impressed by the variety of peoples represented. Christians live especially in the periphery of the country, from what used to be called the Outlying Areas: They are Bataks, Menadonese, Moluccans, Dajaks, Torajas, Florinese, and Timorese. Now lucrative raw materials, especially oil, which are sold abroad and bring in foreign currencies, come mainly from such areas. These "minority" areas have therefore proven to be important on several fronts, not only for the nation's unity but also for its prosperity.

In the years of high oil prices, about 1975-84, two-thirds of the

---

with the "real" religions. But in general they are not accorded recognition as real religions, though there are local differences.

Dances and ceremonies of tribal religions are permitted in the "secularized" form of cultural presentations. Such religions are generally viewed as "folklore" and their adherents as those who have yet to choose a religion. The government pressures them to join one of the "five big ones," among which Catholics and Protestants are counted separately. Weddings must usually take place in accordance with the ritual and regulations of one of these five recognized religions.

government's budget came from oil revenues. The yield from local taxes, income taxes, and the like is still very low. This allows the central government to play a forceful role in the entire economy: It is from the government that money and initiatives come. Proposals for economic expansion generally came from above and are brought into effect "with the cooperation" of the people.[8] Programs for birth control, municipal credit, cooperatives, reforestation, and adult education are all centrally planned and regulated in Jakarta. There the goals for each region are set. All this is, then, implemented locally through provincial and regional offices.

Of the approximately 180 million Indonesians, 105 million live in Java (as of 1993). Java is very densely populated, and emigration projects take people from there to other parts of the country, especially South and Central Sumatra, Kalimantan, and West Irian. This movement of people has considerable potential for creating problems — and fresh opportunities. In some heavily Islamic areas it often means a first encounter with groups of Christian Javanese.

The older missiology often distinguished direct and indirect methods. Where preaching and Bible reading are not yet possible, there indirect methods, especially education and care of the sick, have to be used in order in the end to gain access to the people. Because of this approach, Christian schools and hospitals have often been among the best in heavily Islamic parts of Indonesia. Christians today no longer view such projects just as aids toward a more noble goal, that of proclamation of the gospel. They tend to see them rather as the realization of a Christian task as such, that of development. But Hindus and Muslims sometimes continue — often correctly — to regard such Christian projects as indirect and frequently ill-disguised means of propaganda. This is all the more true when such projects are started amid populations with hardly any Christians, as in Bukittinggi, where in the 1970s a group of Baptists wanted to open a hospital. This led to a fairly unpleasant dispute, because Bukittinggi is situated in a very self-consciously Islamic area, namely in the cultural heart of West Sumatra (Minangkabau).

In 1980, 3% of the Indonesian population was Catholic and 5.8% was Protestant. Church responses to measures designed to regulate relations among religions sometimes appear to be exaggerated by this minority status. For example, in 1978 the minister of religion took a number of measures to curtail overly direct religious propaganda. Direct distribution of pamphlets, home visitations, and other aggressive methods that are

---

8. For a critical comparison of ethical politics under the colonial administration and the Suharto regime, see M. Ricklefs, *A History of Modern Indonesia* (London, 1981), especially 272f.

frequently used by faith missions were prohibited. Use of foreign personnel and money was subjected to a stricter policy of permits. From the reactions to these measures it was apparent that as a minority Christians felt threatened.

Conversely one can also fairly describe Muslims as "a majority with a minority mentality."[9] Rigorous Muslims, the "whites," had to give up not only the ideal of an Islamic state but even "the seven words" of the Jakarta Charter, which stipulated that in the Indonesian state Muslims would live under Islamic law. These concessions were part of the historic compromise of 1945 in which the unified state was given its shape.[10]

The country is dominated economically by a small Chinese minority. Part of this minority has clear Catholic or Protestant sympathies, and virtually none want to convert to Islam. Culturally and in the sphere of public welfare Muslims are forced to recognize that in the largest cities the best schools (elementary and secondary, not necessarily universities) and the best hospitals are Catholic and Protestant. The Muslims have no national daily paper of any standing, while the recognized paper of distinction is Catholic (*Kompas*, sometimes interpreted as "Kommando Pastor"). In all these spheres Muslims feel like a minority and react as such: They close ranks and attempt to strengthen their own position. It is Muslims who attempt to have proselytism condemned and who seek clear lines of demarcation among religions.[11]

But a similar defensive attitude is present among Christians. When it appears that Christians' rights will be affected, they often react with vehemence. Early in 1985 the Ministry of Religion decided that a religious census had to be made of pupils in the state schools and that religious instruction would be given in a class only if there were ten pupils of a given religion in the class. Parents were required to fill out forms specifying religion.[12] The Catholic bishops and the Council of Churches immediately issued a protest. Even though the measure was intended only for government schools, people were afraid that in time it would be applied

---

9. W. F. Wertheim, *Indonesië van vorstenrijk tot neo-kolonie* (Meppel, 1978) 209-30.

10. K. Steenbrink, "Indonesian Politics and a Muslim Theology of Religions: 1965-1990," *Islam and Christian-Muslim Relations* 4 (1993) 223-46.

11. See, among others, the account of an "ethical code" for religious interaction formulated at Yogyakarta in 1984 in K. Steenbrink, "Indonesian Churches 1978-1984: Main Trends, Issues, and Problems," *Exchange* 39 (1984) 1-31.

12. The general view is that Islamic religious education is more difficult for students than Christian religious training. In Islamic training students are graded on their ability to memorize a fair number of Arabic formulas. Many Christian lessons proceed from "the child's own world of experience" and are consequently much easier. To get higher grades less committed Muslim children therefore opt for Christianity at school.

also in religious schools, with the result that in those schools instruction in the Christian faith could no longer be compulsory for all students, including non-Christians. A Jesuit father said to me in connection with this matter, "Jesus said that if someone should strike us on the one cheek we should turn the other, but now we hit back *before* we have been struck."

Christians in Indonesia: A Separate Class

Indonesian Christians tend to be better off than other Indonesians in education, health care, and financial resources. This does not mean that there are no poor Christians. A number of Christians come from notoriously depressed areas, but aid organizations, cooperatives, and the flow of help from abroad tend to be of more help in those areas there than elsewhere. Churches have what they need: sound organizational structures, buildings, theological training of international standing, good radio and television broadcast facilities — and also internal conflicts and here and there an occasional schism.

We can divide the churches in Indonesia into three large groups: Catholics, evangelicals, who are generally the product of American faith missions begun after 1960, and Protestants of the Communion of Indonesian Churches *(Persekutuan Gereja-gereja di Indonesia)*, largely stemming from Dutch and German missions. No overarching Council of Churches exists but each of these three groups has its organization. Catholics have their bishop's conferences. The evangelicals and their theological schools work within a loose federation. Among the older Protestant churches, the struggle to arrive at a united church failed (the tendency is rather to increase in numbers), but in order nevertheless to register some form of success their Council of Churches became a "Communion" in 1984.

It is clear that the evangelicals are advancing more rapidly than the other Protestants, while in a number of areas Catholics are also experiencing rapid growth. Especially after the revolution in 1965 many people wanted an umbrella group. The Christian churches are strongly anti-Communist. Communism and the possibility of an Islamic state are both perceived as threats to what has been accomplished by Christian missions. But many ex-Communists have become Christians: From 1965 to 1985 the number of Christians in the ancient feudal city of Surakarta increased from less than 5% to 25%. Though such growth is not seen everywhere, the churches are becoming larger. The evangelicals often offer a bit more enthusiasm and personal warmth than the somewhat more businesslike and "dry" older Protestant groups and than the efficient Catholics.

Catholics are especially hard at work to make their churches less massive and clerical by creating (one should rather say "allowing") small base communities under lay leadership to serve as focal points of the faith experience. In a church and a society whose mentalities are strongly hierarchical, this is no small feat. Among Protestants the reaction against massiveness and growth has come in the charismatic movement. The emphasis so far has been on "house churches" based on the Pentecostal movement or on the faith missions. In a number of places the charismatic movement has assumed forms that resemble the other "new Javanese religions," especially by their focus on a charismatic guru who gathers a small group of adherents around him.

Unlike Latin America, whose liberation theology is viewed with some suspicion in Indonesia because of its links with Marxist thought, unlike Africa, with its independent churches and its theologians who dip into native traditions, and unlike the theologians of India, who are engaging both old and new traditions of Hinduism in dialogue, Indonesian churches have not yet developed a clear identity of their own. Perhaps they are too new for that. Perhaps there are just too many cultures with which to enter into dialogue. Perhaps Indonesian society is caught up in too much change. And perhaps the number of first-generation Christians is too overwhelming. Hardly any dialogue with Muslims is happening. In general the strategy of Christians is to minimize the significance of the Islamic contribution to the total culture and to cooperate in the government's program of dialogue, the primary aim of which is to prevent marriage problems, to enable the building of new churches, to regulate religious holidays, and the like. This stance is understandable, but from a theological perspective more can be done.

The Indonesian churches are convinced of the dynamism that Christian traditions have given them and are clearly at work to make their position permanent. Up to now this has produced much good for their own communion and for the whole country. In generations to come even greater influence may proceed from this base, reaching even beyond the borders of the country.

CHAPTER 7

Brazil: Old Christianity and New

R. G. van Rossum

Brazil is the world's fifth largest country. More and more of its 152 million people, representing all the races of humankind, live in a growing number of enormous cities. Life for those still in the rural areas is ever more problematic. Brazil's economy is the world's eighth largest, though the benefits of that economy are very unequally distributed and in large part must be transferred to North Atlantic countries. This places a heavy burden on Brazil's political order. Brazil is also the world's largest Catholic country, but it displays great religious creativity and has many faiths. Its Catholic Church has been driven by the Spirit toward the poor of the land. This chapter will, therefore, discuss first the land, people, and cities of Brazil, then its economic and political situation, its religious diversity, and finally developments in its Catholic Church.

For decades Brazil has been called the land of the future. But for millions of people, that future remains elusive.

Land, People, and City

The World's Fifth Largest Country

The history of the nation of Brazil began with Portuguese discovery and conquest. The "legitimacy" of that conquest goes back to the treaty of Tordesillas in 1494, in which Spain and Portugal, under papal supervision, divided the New World between them. That the New World had been inhabited for some ten millennia before Christ did not confer the legitimacy adhering to the name "Christian."

Pedro Alvares Cabral, who arrived on the coast of Brazil in 1500, took possession in the name of the king of Portugal. It was not until 1532 that the first Portuguese settlement was established in São Vicente. Soon

99

afterward, in 1534, importation of black slaves began. Civil and ecclesiastical authorities — a governor, a bishop, and especially members of the
Jesuit order — arrived in 1549. Little by little the Portuguese cobbled together the 8,511,965 square kilometers that today make Brazil the fifth
largest country in the world.

That Brazil has that ranking carries a lot of feeling for its people,
and the term "cobble together" is intentional. It is natural for people in
small countries to direct their attention outward, but for a Brazilian it is
normal to think that this nation has everything it needs — that the whole
world is wrapped up in it. This gigantic country seems always to be
seeking solutions to its problems, such as the need for land reform, by
moving those problems further inland. The "receding horizon" of its vast
land causes everything to lose its focus. It makes exploration more reward-
ing in the short term than investment, and improvisation easier than
planning. This has been the case not only recently but also in, for instance,
the inland expeditions of the "bandeirantes" from 1600 on, the opening
of the Amazon basin in 1639, and the risky opening of the frontier to the
Rio de la Plata (Uruguay) in 1680.

In consequence of these moves the treaty of Madrid (1750) recognized that the boundaries drawn for the Portuguese in Tordesillas had
been greatly exceeded. Wars with Paraguay (1865) and negotiations with
Bolivia regarding the Acre region did not lead to any substantial change
in those boundaries, though to this day many poor Brazilians looking for
land cross those very boundaries. The military regime that governed Brazil
in 1964-85 made geopolitics the centerpiece of its ideology of security.
Projects such as the "Transamazonica" and the hydroelectric project at
Itaipú, which were in themselves economically unsound, were justified in
terms of world politics.

Apart from the mountain range on the northern border, all Brazil
has in real mountains is concentrated in the southeast. Forty percent of its
land surface rises to an elevation of two hundred meters. Only the northeast has insufficient precipitation. There are five large drainage systems.
The Amazon drains half the country. The Rio São Francisco and the Rio
Parana are next in size of the area drained. Colonists used those two rivers
to open the country to settlement. Finally, there are the drainage areas of
the Rio Paraguay and Rio Uruguay, which did not really come into the
Brazilian purview until the eighteenth century, after the Portuguese and
Spaniards had put an end to the "sacred experiment" of the Jesuits and
Indians in the mid-eighteenth century.

Descriptions of Brazil use a variety of geographical divisions, including:

- center and periphery,
- southeast, interior, and northeast, and
- south, southeast, north, midwest, and northeast.

The center is Brazil's economically strongest region, with a well-developed and modern agrarian sector, industrial activity on the largest scale, and a growing service industry. In the periphery the north and northeast are notable, the north because it has not yet been truly integrated into the rest of Brazil — it could be a separate country, the northeast because it is Brazil's biggest problem area.

One Hundred Fifty Million People from All the Countries of the World

In 1992 Brazil had 151,381,000 inhabitants; it is expected that by 2000 this number will have grown to 173 million. In 1990 35.2% of the population was under 15 years old, 28% was between 15 and 29 years old, and only 1.5% was older than 75. Average life expectancy is 66.3. These figures show clearly the dominance of youth. In global terms this burden of youth is comparable to the pressure exerted by senior citizens in wealthy countries.

Around 1500 the population of Brazil was between 1 and 5 million. After that the number of inhabitants gradually increased, but the indigenous population decreased. Since the beginning of the twentieth century the population has grown rapidly, doubling from the mid-1960s to the mid-1980s. The increase in population has contributed greatly to the increase of poverty and threatens to make living conditions steadily worse.

Brazilian society embraces a variety of races and cultures coexisting more or less in balance. This balance between one's own identity and that of others is based on values of tolerance. Already in the time of Cabral's exploration in 1500, people from many nations began to settle in this Indian land — or were taken there as slaves or contract laborers. All these peoples intermingled to some degree and frequently changed their places of residence within Brazil. Movement and migration continue constantly. Some 40 million people are regularly in search of employment and places to live.

There are three main elements in the population:

1. Brazilian *Indians* are lowlanders clearly distinguishable from the highland Indians of Peru and Mexico with their monumental cultures of the past. They continue to have a way of life very much their own based on hunting, fishing, gathering of wild plant foods, and agriculture done

according to a system of shifting cultivation. This way of life requires large amounts of land. Now that the Amazon basin is being caught up in the development of Brazil, the situation of Brazil's Indians is becoming more precarious every day. The expansion of agribusiness in southern and western Brazil is so extensive that small farmers are moving in huge numbers to the Amazon region. There they are preparing the way for the destruction of the rain forest, despite strong national and international efforts to prevent that outcome.

2. The *Portuguese* element in Brazil's population dates back, of course, to the beginning of exploration in 1500. Portuguese culture, which was permeated by Catholic Christianity, became dominant in the country. Today Brazil is considered the largest Catholic country in the world.[1]

3. The *African* element in Brazil's population began with the importation of the first slaves in 1542 to work on sugar plantations. From 1500 to 1850 some 3 million to 18 million Africans were brought to Brazil. Indians had proven to be ill-suited for agricultural work because agriculture was foreign to them, because they had no immunity to the Europeans' diseases, and because they often rebelled, committed suicide, or fled further inland, where they could elude European pursuers. Only in work in which Africans were less efficient did Indians continue to be enslaved — into the eighteenth century. Africans came to be indispensable to the development of Brazil. They had more experience in agriculture than the Portuguese and advanced the development of a variety of technical skills. Though they were put to work first in agriculture — sugar, cotton, tobacco, and coffee — they then became indispensable for mining in the eighteenth century. Slavery broke up their social and cultural structures, which may explain why they rapidly absorbed elements of other cultures. But the history of colonial Brazil also shows that Africans did not simply and submissively accept their fate. The *quilombos*,[2] places in the interior where runaway slaves created their own sanctuaries, are permanent signs of resistance.

Neither the Indians nor the Africans formed homogeneous groups. The two broad ethnic terms conceal the fact that we are dealing with innumerable varieties and tribes of people. Nor have we referred here to the tracks left behind by temporary occupants and refugees from France, the Netherlands, Spain, and Britain. And from the middle of the nineteenth century on Brazil experienced massive immigration from Europe and in the twentieth century from Japan. Each group has influenced and con-

1. Cf. T. C. Bruneau, *The Church in Brazil: The Politics of Religion* (Austin, 1982) 18.

2. Cf. E. B. Burns, *A History of Brazil* (New York, 1980) 54.

tinues to influence Brazilian culture. Several terms have come into use for those whose parents represent more than one of these many ethnic groups, such as *mulatto* (African + European), *mameluco* (European father + Indian mother), *branco* (fully European), *criollo* (fully African), *cafuso* (African + Indian), and *caboclo* (fully Indian).

City and Interior

Brazil's cities have exploded in population. This growth was especially dramatic in the 1950s. In 1940 about 31% of the population lived in cities, in 1982 about 67%. This urbanization has taken place especially along the coast, particularly in the southeast, though the northeastern cities of Recife, Fortaleza, and Belem have also seen enormous expansion. The main reasons for this strikingly rapid urbanization have been the sharp drop in Brazil's death rate, the accompanying high birth rates, and constant migration from the countryside.

Three classes of people can be distinguished in the cities:

1. The upper class has wealth and power. To a large extent that power is still bound up with a system of rewards that permeates all of urban society. This system consists of a network of personal loyalties based on a simple principle: Scratch my back and I'll scratch yours. For example, a politician will offer money or promise benefits in exchange for votes.

2. The middle class did not really begin to grow until after World War II. It is the class of which one can say in general that it lives beyond its means. Its members want to take part in the modern world of television, automobiles, and vacations but do not really have the means. Therefore, friendships and group solidarity are very important. On the one side, the rewards system binds members of the middle class to members of the upper class. On the other side, the living standard of the middle class can only be maintained by their making the most use economically of the poor.

3. The poor, for their part, have a very hard time keeping their heads above water. Many of them are new arrivals from the country and have experienced the intense culture shock that the transition to the city entails. In the city they are severed from everything that seemed meaningful in the country and that gave them a modest place in the sun. The uprooting of their lives can lead to disintegration of their families, of which children are especially the victims.

Urban housing problems are horrendous. Around the frequently supermodern city centers grow huge slums, the *favelas*. But even in the *favelas* there is great diversity. In the squatter areas people build their own simple dwellings, which may be subleased many times over. In other areas people buy pieces of land and build their homes themselves gradually over years. In government housing areas people buy their land and the government builds. The character of these areas changes over just a few years because people unable to pay their debts are pushed further to the outer margins of the cities and often have to give up their property to members of the lower middle class. There are gradations of poverty. The *favelas* are mainly populated by younger people, while the populations of the urban centers are aging.

Besides the constant effort to get a board, a piece of corrugated metal, or a real roof, the poor are continually involved in the problem of how to survive (*luta da vida:* the struggle to live). Since they no longer own land to grow crops, they have to buy everything and so need an income. Husband and wife both seek jobs, no matter how high the unemployment rate. Unless a job is landed in a modern industry — which is unlikely — a job must be sought with one of the small supply companies that "modern businesses" use — and get rich on.

The poor person thus takes his or her first step into the reward system. In exchange for the favor of a job, he or she must live with low and changeable wages and no benefits. And thousands are waiting in line for every vacated job. If a person cannot get into the job market in this way, he or she can look for work in the informal sector, as a shoeshiner, peddler, dockworker, concession stand worker, or prostitute. The whole family is focused on making money and spending as little as possible. Survival calls for enormous resourcefulness: Almost nothing is thrown away, and what others regard as trash can be utilized in a thousand ways.

As we have stated, an ever decreasing percentage of the Brazilian population lives in the countryside. In 1940, 16.3% of the population lived in the central agricultural and dairy state of Minas Gerais; today that figure is 11.2%. In 1990 more than one-third of the Brazilian population lived in the nine largest cities. Until the 1950s Brazil was an agrarian country.

The big problem in the countryside now is land distribution. In traditional agrarian societies, land (usually along with water) is the most important source of wealth. The problem now is that a few Brazilians have too much and many have too little. But concentration of land ownership in the hands of the few characterizes all of Latin America. In 1965 7% of Brazil's farms had 94% of the land at their disposal. A consequence of this unequal distribution of land is a serious underutilization of the soil: The bigger the farm, the less efficient its use of the soil. The United Nations FAO (Food and Agricultural Organization) has determined that this concentration of land ownership is the chief barrier to more efficient agriculture and thus to a more just society.

In 1980 the Brazilian bishops issued a sketch of the problems in land ownership that still gives a picture of the situation as it exists today: 52% of the population consisted of people who each owned less than ten hectares of land, and this group as a whole owned 2.8% of all the land. 47% of the population consisted of people owning ten to 1000 hectares of land, and this group owned 54.4% of all the land. The remaining 1% of the population (actually 0.8%) consisted of people owning more than 1000 hectares of land, and this group as a whole owned 42.8% of all the land. But even these impressive figures fail to show the full seriousness of the situation, since many wealthy landowners own several farms, many small farms are not owned but leased by those who live and work on them, and countless farm workers neither own nor lease land and have only seasonal employment.

Another development that has been making country life more difficult is the takeover of farms and dairy operations by large agribusiness corporations. Foreign multinational companies are often involved. This development has caused enormous land speculation and "little wars for the land." On account of the modern methods used in such operations, they offer few job opportunities. In the north and midwest agribusiness is mainly involved in cattle operations; in other parts of the country it is seen mainly in production of soybeans, grown for the Common Market countries, and sugar for, among other purposes, alcohol as a replacement for gasoline.

The concentration of land ownership, which began with Portuguese colonization, has led to a situation in which, apart from the "European" southern part of Brazil, the country has hardly any villages or village culture. This has serious consequences for the people's church life and for the development of education and health care. As soon as a farmer can manage, he gets himself a house in the city: There he displays his wealth and looks out for his well-being.

Economics and Politics

A Future World Power?

It is easy, in view of Brazil's economic problems, to forget that Brazil is the world's tenth or eleventh largest economy. Expectations that the Brazilian economy would surpass that of France or Italy by the year 2000 have been stymied by the economic stagnation of the 1980s. The day is long past, however, when Brazil produced only sugar, coffee, and iron ore. High quality Brazilian technology is calling forth import restrictions in North America. In the powder keg of the Middle East negotiators are eager to exchange oil for advanced Brazilian weapons systems. Brazilian cars are conquering the market in Africa. In the rest of Latin America cries of distress over the dominance of Brazil's economy cover walls, and Dutch television tube manufacturing is disappearing in favor of Philips of Brazil. These are all examples indicating how, since World War II, Brazil has been doing much to "get ahead" and what success it has had. But success for whom? And for how long?

Brazil's economy is marked by up-and-down cycles. It began with the sugar cycle and its lasting consequences: concentration of land owner-ship in the hands of the few, slavery, the beginning of the destruction of the northeast, and increasing dependence on foreign capital, which was pulled out when there was more money to be made in sugar elsewhere. Then toward the end of the eighteenth century came the mining cycle with its lasting consequences: mass migration within the country and continu-ing decline of the northeast. Portugal was under British financial control at the time, and slave labor in Ouro Preto and other small towns of Minas Gerais helped to finance Britain's industrial revolution.

Then at the beginning of the nineteenth century the focus in Brazil shifted to the coffee plantations. In 1830 Brazil delivered 40% of the world production of coffee. Coffee exhausts the soil. And because five years must pass before it can be harvested, it requires financial means available only to large landowners. Coffee plantations began virtually at the city limits of Rio de Janeiro and left their destructive trail all the way to the border of Paraguay.

Brazil was an exporting nation and therefore a free trade nation, which made it impossible — up to the 1930s — for it to build up any industry that could be competitive in world trade. By the end of the nineteenth century the capital of Amazonia, Manaus, had become a kind of wonder of the world — but not for the hundreds of thousands of *Nor-destinos* who, as "rubber soldiers," wasted away in the jungle. By then the abolition of slavery had led to the southeast's development into the economic center of the country. European "contract laborers" were its first pioneers. Starting in the 1930s the grandchildren of the slaves began to move en masse into the southeast.

Even more than the governments of the 1950s, the military tech-nocrats who assumed power in 1964 adopted a North Atlantic develop-ment model. They offered foreign multinational and transnational busi-nesses a favorable investment climate. The government itself also undertook a variety of mainly infrastructural projects. Nothing seemed too farfetched, including the Transamazonica, a road straight through the immense Amazon basin; numerous power dams, among them the largest in the world at Itaipu; nuclear plants in Angra; the record time in which Brasilia, the new capital, and the capitals of several states were built; and numerous irrigation projects. The economic triangle marked off by São Paulo, Rio de Janeiro, and Belo Horizonte became one gigantic construction zone.

The successes of this industrial cycle are undeniable. The decade from 1964 to 1974 is called the period of the Brazilian "economic miracle" — and the annual economic growth rate in those years was 10.1%. Industrialization, of essential importance to a developing country, is clearly underway. Workers in industry enjoy a higher income than farm workers, and there are now social services for those not directly involved in industry. In the remotest corners of the land everyone over sixty-five can receive a pension. The *Funrural* operates in the countryside in alliance with the trade unions and has brought medical and dental care within reach of many people. Legally, at least, a minimum wage has been established for each region. The transportation network, mainly relying on buses and trucks, has been enormously expanded. Electricity is available nearly everywhere. Telephones are no longer a luxury.

But these tangible results do not spell permanent success. Brazilians have looked in vain for the multiplication effect of such initiatives that was so obvious in Europe. Not all the blame rests on government policy. External factors — the oil crisis, the rise in interest rates beginning in 1978, a world recession, which caused a drop in export revenues — have played a large role. Brazil's foreign debt is the biggest in the world, and it began to immobilize Brazil in the 1980s. Export earnings are virtually swallowed up by interest payments, and Brazilians are forced to let the International Monetary Fund put this kind of pressure on the economy. A people with less talent for improvisation would long ago have been driven to despair.

Millions of Brazilians have good reason for despair because, for all the economic miracles (called "Pharaonic works" by Helder Camara), income distribution has steadily become more skewed. This "growth with hunger" is evident from these figures, which show the progression of percentages of Brazil's total income received by four economic classes during the "economic miracle":[3]

---

3. These are nationwide figures, in which the wealthy south and the poor northeast are both represented, so they do not really represent the desperation of those in the northeast.

	Share of the total income in		
	1960	**1970**	**1976**
the poorest half of the population	17.7%	14.9%	11.8%
the next group up (30%)	27.9	22.8	21.2
the comfortable 15%	26.9	27.4	28.0
the wealthy 5%	27.7	34.9	39.0

To make the situation of the poor clearer, in 1959 a laborer had to work 65 hours to afford a monthly subsistence ration; in 1980 this was 105 hours; in 1981 it was 149 hours. Whole families must go to work, and 15.4% of the economically active population has come to be from ten to fourteen years old. There is, therefore, a direct correlation between the minimum wage and deaths and injuries of children.

Official policy proceeds from the assumption that once the problem of foreign debts is solved the remaining problems will solve themselves. Imports are restricted, and the country has to produce a surplus over the balance of payments and focus production on foreign markets. Therefore, domestic consumption is forced down, purchasing power has dropped drastically, and unemployment has spread. Because unemployment benefits are virtually unknown, people are forced to offer their work at any price.

Brazilian Politics

Broadly speaking the panorama of Brazilian politics does not differ from what exists in the rest of South America. From the 1930s to the 1950s there was a strong "populist movement," which proved unable in the end to conduct or to maintain its development policy, which was oriented to the North Atlantic economy. Next came military governments, which differed from earlier military regimes in their combination of faith in technocratic solutions with total exclusion of any "appeal to the people." Then civilian politicians were called on to repair the military-technocratic failures — while bound hand-and-foot to North Atlantic financial managers. An important background factor has always been the principle of rewards, which was described above, *clientelismo*, which is stronger than any party ties.

"Modern politics" in Brazil begins with Getulio Vargas, who came to power in the midst of the economic crisis of the 1930s. He could count on the support of "the people" and in 1934 over the opposition of the oligarchy pushed through a new, strongly autocratic constitution, which marked the beginning of the *Estado Novo*, the New State. Because of Brazil's participation in World War II on the side of the allies Vargas became morally obligated to give his populist enlightened dictatorship at least a semblance of democracy. Moreover, war revenues gave him a chance, against the wishes of the big landowners and with the support of the urban middle class, to push through a plan for industrialization.

Before the planned presidential elections of 1945 the army forced Vargas to withdraw from the race. Meanwhile three important political formations had come into existence: The PSD was Vargas's creation. He hoped, by means of its overall program, to bring together laborers, civil servants, and entrepreneurs. The PTB was a party seeking to attract urban laborers. The UDN represented the conservative coffee aristocracy, which had a strong grip on the countryside.

With General Dutra as its candidate the PSD won the elections of 1946, the year in which a new constitution went into effect. His government effected advanced labor legislation, restrictions on the power of the armed forces, and the strengthening of an independent judiciary. Although the Brazilian Communist Party remained illegal, freedom of the press was restored.

The formation of political parties and coalitions was pursued with passion. In 1950 Vargas was reelected president. But he was unhappy with the constitutional constraints on his office and even more with the sharp decline in the economy. He became disillusioned with the weak capacity for competition of nascent Brazilian industry. The UDN virtually invited the army to undertake a coup. Made powerless by all this opposition, Vargas ended his own life.

Still, the elections of 1955 and 1960 kept Brazilian politics under the spell of the PSD or of coalitions led by the PSD. President Juscelino Kubitschek pursued a policy of economic expansion referred to as "internal development" and symbolized by the construction of Brasilia. His formation of a separate socioeconomic development organization for the northeast (SUDENE) had a similar significance. His successor, President João Goulart, sought to withdraw Brazil from the exclusive guardianship of the mighty neighbor to the north, the USA. To that end he attempted to build ties with Second and Third World countries. He took over the reins of power from Janio Quadros, who, discouraged, surrendered them. Goulart, for that matter, saw his room for action firmly bounded by new constitutional amendments. By way of a strong nationalistic appeal (which had to sound anti-North American) Goulart attempted to reach what available capital did not permit him to do. A modest tax and a land-reform project finished him politically.

For twenty years successive military regimes (Castelo Branco, Costa e Silva, Médici, Geisel, Figueiredo) tried to combine an ideology of national security with technocratic planning which allowed no interference. "Leftist politicians" were eliminated or banished. Between 1968 and 1972 all this led to unheard-of repression: The initial "economic miracle" was not only paid for with an enormous foreign debt, it was especially paid for on the backs of a totally marginalized people. Figueiredo proved to have been engaged to bring about a greater degree of democracy and in 1984 the nation once again had real elections, whatever their imperfections. In Tancredo Neves the people had not only an old political pro from Minas Gerais; he also symbolized the almost inexhaustible capacity of the Brazilians to make a virtue of necessity. His death before his inauguration plunged the whole nation into mourning. What was not lost in his demise was the sense that a national solution to the problems at hand had to be borne by everyone. Of that sentiment Vice President José Sarney, with his problematic past, became the fortunate captive. Accordingly, Sarney's coalition gained a landslide in the elections of 1986. Sarney was succeeded in 1989 by Fernando Collor, who won the election by a very small margin over Lula, the candidate of the Workers Movement. The cloud of personal corruption surrounding Collor's resignation camouflaged the questionable nature of the coalition that had brought him to power.

Collor's "unimpeachably honest" successor, Itamar Franco, is conducting a zigzag policy that is threatening to destroy the Brazilian economy, making both foreign and domestic investors extremely skittish. The general economic malaise is taking its toll especially among the middle class and the poorest segments of the population. A March 1993 report from the Brazilian Institute of Statistics stated that skilled workers have lost 20% of their purchasing power since 1980; unskilled workers, who under the best of circumstances earn barely enough to live, lost 12% of theirs. At the end of October 1994 Lula was to run again for the presidency.

Religion and Church

The World's Largest Catholic Country

In Brazil, Christianity is the definitive religious factor in a multicolored religious world. In contrast with European cities, the cities of Brazil, and in particular their outer edges (the *surburbios* and *favelas*), are bursting with religious energy and creativity.

Christianity entered Brazil with the Portuguese. Their goal was "the extension of the faith and the empire." That goal, which sounds so strange today, represents a largely sacral understanding of reality. The Portuguese experience of faith was influenced less than that of Spain by the struggle with Islam. Whatever in earthly reality remained obscure to the human intellect was attributed to supernatural powers, which one had to avert or placate. On this point the Portuguese, the Indians, and the enslaved Africans understood each other perfectly. But we are speaking at this point not of the more systematic mission conducted particularly by the Jesuits but of the Christianization that occurred where unschooled Portuguese colonists passed on their religious customs and had them reflected back by Indians and Africans. To this day the wide mantle of Catholic Christianity in Brazil conceals a diverse world of Indian and African religiosity, of mediumistic religions, and of other variants of spiritism.

Among all these non-Christian forms of religion the mystical expression of the Catholic faith occupies an important place. This Catholic dimension comes not only from the Catholic faith of colonial and post-colonial Brazil, but also from the Catholic capacity for adaptation to whatever realities it finds itself presented with. In the long process of adaptation and modification out of which Brazil originated, the Catholic faith was a constant and extended its influence far beyond what we think of as the domain of religion. The whole history of Brazil has been a busy interchange of religious elements and interpretations dominated by a Catholic religious culture. The statement that "Brazil is the largest Catholic country in the world" is true only if one recognizes the multivalent character of the word "Catholic." Brazilian Catholicism has its own face. The Roman features are abundantly present but one sees a much greater diversity of forms than one would expect on the basis of Roman influence alone:

> 80% of Brazil's Catholics are adherents of "folk Catholicism." The remaining 20% is officially Catholic in accordance with Rome's formal definitions. To those within the Church there is very little that is genuinely Catholic in folk Catholicism. Folk Catholicism is the religion of the poor. It is much freer, much less rigid, without written rules, vital, and shaped completely by local customs and everyday life. This faith knows no authority that can determine what is permissible and what is not.[4]

In the nineteenth century the official Catholicism of the missionaries and bishops was drastically reformed — "Romanized," one might say. It became clerical, that is, not based on the laity, and Tridentine, hence Counter-Reformational. The Portuguese state had opposed the reforms emanating from Trent, and colonial Brazil worked, in the spirit of the

---

4. H. Groenen, *Schisma zwischen Kirche und Volk. Eine praktisch-theologische Fallstudie des Volkskatholizismus in Nordost-brasilien* (Nijmegen, 1978).

Enlightenment, at creating a submissive church of officials. In opposition to this church arose the form of Catholicism that came to be considered normative, one strongly focused on the individual and his or her interior life, with a heavy emphasis on the sacraments.

Folk Catholicism contains numerous Indian and African religious elements, but Brazil also has many cultic places in which Indian and especially African religious practices are very much alive. Indian influence is discernible in the widespread dualism of good and evil, the attention devoted to the lower spirits, which are easily equated with Catholic saints and which a person must tend to for his most immediate needs, the detachment of God, belief in reincarnated wandering souls, messianic expectations, and the kinship between the *pajé* (shaman) and the *rezador* (praying person). After the abolition of slavery African religion reorganized itself into *umbanda, macumba, candomble,* and *xangó* and in distinct African religious organizations and places of worship. In the big cities these religions were easily individualized and, in that multiracial proletarian world, were submerged in a variety of forms of folk spiritism.

From the middle of the nineteenth century on spiritism has been a staple offering in the Brazilian religious market. Kardec, the French founder of spiritism, presented his practice and his commentary on John's Gospel as "enlightened religion." It appealed to those who no longer saw anything behind the facade of Catholicism. In the same period the activity of mediums, combined with belief in a purifying reincarnation, attracted thousands of people from semi-intellectual groups.

There is no single key to unlock Brazil's multihued religious world. Any single key by itself would fail to take account of the enterprising creativity of the Brazilian people in the sphere of religion.

Since the 1940s, Protestantism, especially Pentecostalism, has also had a strong presence in the religious fermentation on the margins of all the big cities. The simple lifestyle, in which dancing, drinking, and smoking have no part, has an appeal far from characteristic of the Protestantism that came, in a strongly Congregationalist form, in the mid-nineteenth century through the Scottish Presbyterian Kalley.

The Catholic Church: Who Am I That I Should Go to Pharaoh?

Vargas sought the broadest possible support for his *Estado Novo* and felt that he had to win over the Catholic Church. From the 1930s on the church was personified by Brazil's first cardinal, Sebastiao Leme, the great builder of the "new Christianity." Fundamentally he held to a restorative ideal: Separation of church and state did not belong in the "new world," and church and state had to cooperate in the construction of society. Vargas and Leme needed each other. Beginning in 1934 the Catholic Church gained a number of rights, such as equalization of church and civil marriages, prohibition of divorce, church appointment of army chaplains, exemptions for monastics, and subsidies for Catholic schools. Leme thus saw the Church supported in its struggle against its inner weakness, which was ignorance of religion, and against its numerous external enemies: spiritism, a rising Protestantism, Marxism, and atheism. But Leme's church also remained internally divided.

The integralist movement under Gustavo Corçao found its way into the intellectual center of the army, the Higher Military School of Rio de Janeiro. The "social Christianity" movement under the leadership of Alceu Amoroso Lima inspired the Catholic action groups, an evangelistic movement that came from Europe and was intended to activate the laity under the strict leadership of the bishops. After 1948 this movement increasingly followed a French and Belgian model: Every person is an apostle in his or her own environment, which was to be judged from a perspective of Christian engagement and brought around to a changed mode of conduct. This was the basis for the youth organizations JAC for agrarian youth, JEC for students in secondary schools, JOC for workers, and JUC for university students.

In the youth organizations the Church came into contact with social and political problems as interpreted by the new middle class. A week of seminars on agrarian problems in Campanha in 1950 led to an episcopal letter from Dom Innocencio Engelke with a plea for land reform. When in 1952 the bishops organized themselves in the Brazilian Conference of Bishops (CNBB), they for the first time were able to address national problems as a group. From 1956 to 1964 the Church hierarchy strongly emphasized its possible "auxiliary" role in development. In 1959 it was actively involved in organizing SUDENE. By its agreement with the "development mentality," which under Kubitschek was given additional Christian undergirding, the Church opened itself up, permanently as it turned out, to the deepening social problems. In the first pastoral plan, the *Plano da emergencia* of 1962, and in the *Declaracao* of 1963, the CNBB described the condition of the poor and referred to capitalism as the cause for it. But socialism and Marxism were still condemned.

In 1961 the MEB (Movement for Basic Education) was set up as the Church's response to the social and political needs of the rural areas. It began as a radio school for literacy, but made reference to the whole of life, that is, also to agriculture, hygiene, community development, and folk culture. Before long the MEB got into political waters and began to occupy itself with the rural trade union movement. It thus became part of a broader radical Catholic movement, to which the JUC also belonged. This movement sought a radical reform of Brazilian society and to that end found Catholic social doctrine inadequate. The JUC increasingly involved itself in the issue of power through social and political action. Its focus shifted from a social to a political agenda, and there found allies among the Marxists. An assortment of conflicts with the Church hierarchy led to a split in the JUC and to the creation of *Ação Popular* (AP), which no longer wanted to be considered a Christian movement. Thus, a closed body of Christians opened itself to social thinking charged with development ideas inspired by Christianity, but did not want to break with the state, while their own evangelization organizations wanted to go forward.

The military coup in 1964 caused a crisis throughout the church. Out of this crisis was born a Church with a face of its own. It was to cut its umbilical cord to the state when the military dictatorship demanded all or nothing, submission or resistance. From 1964 to 1968 the Church hierarchy was racked by conflicts and hesitations while the battle between the military state, which called itself Christian, and the oppressed raged on the streets. After the coup Catholic radicals — the AP, the JUC, and a number of trade unions — were forced underground. The JOC took over the "above-ground" work of the JUC. In 1968 Bishop Padin published a sharp analysis of the "ideology of national security." In the same year the JOC squarely repudiated capitalism. The MEB had to pull in its horns, but by operating more strictly on the basis of cooperation of people within the same class than on class conflict, it survived.

But something happened on a deeper level: In all the conflicts resulting from the coup it was the oppressed, *o povo*, who consistently called on the Church for defense. The state drove those it had no need of to the Church. The Church was the only independent organization recognized by the state to which the people could go. Thus the Church was forced to make a political decision between the legitimacy of resistance by the oppressed and the legitimacy of the military-technocratic government. By isolating the radicals, winning over the ecclesiastical middle by subsidies, and deciding who was qualified to teach ethics, the state tried to shape the outcome of this decision in its favor. From 1968 to 1973, despite the very positive contribution of episcopal and theological leadership at the Latin American Bishops Conference in Medellín (1968), the majority of the hierarchy appeared to lean toward the state.

But in 1973 the other option emerged and exposed the existing injustices in clear terms. It broke into the light of day through documents written by six bishops from the midwest, "The Marginalization of a People," and by eighteen bishops and provincial superiors from the northeast, "I Have Heard the Cry of My People." The latter begins: "In the awareness of our frequent omissions and uncertainties in the course of the history of our Church in Brazil, we feel powerless and awed before such a huge task. We spontaneously repeat the question asked of Yahweh by Moses: 'Who am I that I should go to Pharaoh?' "[5]

In this way, out of internal tensions experienced in confrontation with social and political reality has come a Church that is close to the problems of the people, to their land, work, homes, consciousness, and basic communities — a Church that is breaking with the idea that its own self-preservation is more important than breaking the oppression of the people. In chapter 22 we will return to the missionary activities that have resulted from this development.

5. *Catholic Mind* 72 (November, 1974) 39-64. The statement itself is dated May 6, 1973.

PART II

World, Mission, and Church

Diversity

The preceding chapters were written to give the reader an opportunity to see global Christianity in some of its numerous varied manifestations. What is perhaps astonishing at first is that all this is still "Christianity," that people apparently find it meaningful to gather up under the heading of one religion all these divergent experiences and forms:

Christianity in the Middle East is inconceivable apart from the dominating presence of Islam and thus apart from preoccupation with the social and political survival of (usually small) Christian communities.

The history of Western Europe and therefore of Western European Christianity is colored and stamped by emancipation and secularization. Besides — and despite — a deep historical bond between culture and religion, there is much open tension and animosity. Today, against this background, Western European Christianity attempts to adapt itself to the new religious diversity of its context and to find a way to think through urgent social issues from the perspective of faith.

The history of Chinese Christianity, on the other hand, is one of penetration and adaptation from a base in Western Christianity. All the phases of China's international political and commercial relations are mirrored in the history of its relations with the West, up to and including the re-isolation of China after the 1989 suppression of the democracy movement and, more generally speaking, the new attempts to find a balance between China's identity and its links with world society.

Ghana in West Africa presents yet another story. Throughout Ghana's history one sees a struggle between powerful African religion and the technical and political superiority of Europeans. This struggle has left in its wake for Africans both feelings of inferiority and dependence on

117

European influence and a strong African self-awareness, which keeps alive ties with traditional culture and religion.

Indonesia was long dependent for its unity — for its struggle against fragmentation — on the colonial administration. In a sense *Pancasila* has come to fulfill the same function. Consequently, Christianity in Indonesia is marked by the tension between ethnicity (fragmentation) and loyalty to the country's overarching unitary structure. Christianity's relation to the majority religion of Islam is of great importance in Indonesia.

Finally, in Brazil one sees the remarkable phenomenon of a multi-hued religious world under the wide mantle of Catholicism — in a country with the greatest conceivable distance between the elite and the masses.

In these very different situations it is inevitable that very different forms of religious experience and expression arise. "Faith in Jesus Christ" cannot mean the same thing everywhere; concepts such as salvation and brokenness inevitably assume features specific to each different situation. It has become clear from the descriptions in chapters 2 through 7 that in every place what marks Christianity in the specific situation originated in the encounter with unique local cultural and religious traditions and in the attempt to deal with the problems brought on by the whole world's new situation. Each contextual form of the faith is a product of this two-sided struggle.

Unity

Use of the term "world Christianity" assumes that despite this diversity there is also a unity. How should we understand this unity? How can we put into words the relationship between that unity and the obvious diversity of Christianity? In a sense these are typically twentieth-century questions. In the process by which the different contextual forms of Christianity originated there was a formal unity furnished by church structure or mission or the common confession or an international framework of cooperation.

But in the last few decades people around the world have come to understand that from the beginning a high degree of diversity was hidden under this formal unity. Today this diversity is, as it were, coming out from under the unity and searching for new forms of expression and thus for a new legitimacy. It is especially third-world Christianity that prompts this new sense of contextuality. This is not to say that contextual diversity as such is a new phenomenon. The examples in Part I make clear enough that a local situational focus is as old as Christianity itself. But it was not until our time that it became a subject of study.

Remarkably, though, this new awareness of contextuality is coupled with a sense that, more than ever before, the various contexts of human society — and therefore of Christianity — are related to a single common global context. The issues that came up in each of the preceding chapters, that is, in each of the contexts explored there — issues bound up with tensions between Christianity and non-Christian religions, between faith and secularized culture, between local cultural identity and links with global society, between traditional and imported cultures and religions, between ethnic and national loyalties, between official religion and folk religion, between the elite and the masses — all these issues come up everywhere. They can all be linked with developments in society world-wide and in humanity as a whole into a comprehensive pattern of issues in which the future of humankind is at stake. Issues of freedom and oppression, poverty and wealth, cultural identity and change, peace and armaments, nature and technology, though they are defined in specific terms by each particular context, become visible in their real dimensions only in the global setting. More than ever, under pressure from the global problem of human survival, the many separate histories are now seen as parts of one history.

All this is true just as much of Christianity. This is the lesson of the ecumenical movement, which we are learning in our time. The motivating force for the ecumenical movement is the need for the different forms of Christian faith to give mutual acknowledgment to each other. But the complex of problems that comes to the surface as a result of this acknowledgment points beyond the churches to the greater and more comprehensive issues of unity and diversity in global society and to the necessity of reevaluating the traditions of Christianity in the context of those issues. This new way of looking at oneness-in-diversity has, of course, implications for the way in which we speak theologically of the unity of Christianity, the church's unity, and the unity of missions.

A Missiological Definition of the Problem

As was noted in the first chapter of this book, the word "mission" refers to a faith perspective and consequently to a theological concept that orders our observations of the diverse forms of the movement of Christianity in the world. In a sense, that is how the term has always been used. "Mission" referred to the overarching perspective, the golden thread running through everything: The various forms of Christianity in the world's many cultures and settings worked together to illustrate, as it were, the gospel's march of worldwide victory. In many church and mission circles this is still the prevailing view, and on careful consideration there is not much to be said against it. But it is not such a simple matter to adopt this view as a starting point for a systematic missiological definition of the problem. In this connection two considerations are important.

In the first place, the theological undergirding of the church's mission has often been intertwined with a legitimation of the superiority of Western Christianity. That is, the undergirding of missions often served to justify views and actions that in retrospect betray a denial of and contempt for contextual diversity. Therefore, it is no longer possible to formulate an overall perspective on "mission" naively from one perspective, and certainly not from a Western perspective. It will only be possible to formulate such an understanding of "mission" on the basis of theological reflection on the unity that arises in, behind, and above contextual diversity.

This unity will then have to be defined "missionarily": It will have to be defined on the basis of an understanding of the journey of Christianity in the world as a journey with a starting point (Jerusalem) and a point of reference (the kingdom of God). And it will have to be defined in terms of the "real presence" of that starting point and the focus on the common point of reference becoming visible in all the (contextual) ramifications of the journey. All the imperialistic associations linked with terms like "victory march" can then be stripped away: The point of reference is not the conquest accomplished by a specific religion, let alone one contextual form of that religion, but the completion and redemption of human existence. Of course, a missiology that takes this point of reference seriously will also be contextually conditioned. In any case the new issues and experiences surrounding unity-in-diversity will have been assimilated into this point of reference.

Secondly, in numerous reflections on the church's mission use has been made of biblical texts and creedal positions in a manner that we can characterize as naively fundamentalistic. For example, reflection on and exposition of the missionary mandate in Matthew 28 has been linked directly with recommendation of specific forms of mission action. And confession of the uniqueness of Jesus Christ has sometimes proceeded directly to condemnation of other religions. In this regard also systematic missiology will have to proceed more cautiously.

The complexity of contemporary global Christianity makes all such naive fundamentalism impossible and gives new relevance to theological "prolegomena." Hermeneutical questions, questions about revelation and experience, about gospel and religion, and about unity and plurality, push themselves in between the formulation and confession of the faith, on the one hand, and "mission," on the other. Systematic missiology will have to start with reflection on what happens as Christianity journeys through history and through human cultures. How are we to understand and order that journey, especially in view of the perspective that stands over the entire journey and gives it its direction, that of the kingdom of God? And how can we do this in such a way as to allow for critical evaluation of contextual forms and understandings of Christianity — without letting one context overshadow others?

World, Mission, and Church

What we have said so far implies an entire agenda for systematic missiology. And this makes it clear why the questions to be dealt with in the following chapters are necessary.

The first question to be raised concerns the necessity and possibility of a biblical grounding of "mission" (chapter 8). Talk about our one starting point and one point of reference does not come out of the blue. It comes, and must always be derived anew, from the testimony of Scripture. But the biblical witness gives us a multiplicity of viewpoints, which in the course of history have been used in a variety of ways. Therefore, the quest for a biblical rationale for Christian missions leads to a discussion in which decisions have to be made on different levels.

A fundamental problem that cannot be avoided in this connection is the problem of appeal to one holy Scripture as the focus of unity in a complex and diverse Christianity. As we have noted, hermeneutical questions gain a new relevance in our reflection on world, mission, and church. Therefore, chapter 9 is devoted to the subject of hermeneutics. There it becomes clear that it is no longer possible to reason from a base of supposed scriptural unity to "the world." The church possesses a plurality of interpretative contexts, which together form the network within which the search for truth and meaning is conducted.

This insight then leads us to ask how the church's being sent into the world should be interpreted in the context of current world experiences. Chapter 10 is devoted to the relationship between mission and church (*missio* and *ecclesia*). What direction is being taken by discussion of this problem in this age when missions and the ecumenical movement are being integrated? Where are the pitfalls and pressure points in this discussion, and what possibilities does it bring? We include as the last section of chapter 10 a commentary in which viewpoints differing from those in the rest of the chapter are offered and in which differing convictions plot the course. Thus the reader is offered a sample of current missiological debate.

Chapter 11 addresses the problems involved in the encounter of Christianity with non-Christian religions. This concern clearly demands priority as soon as we catch sight of the global complexity of Christianity. Discussion of this subject is of course not new, but in recent years certain clear, though still challenged, positions have emerged. Chapter 11 seeks mainly to offer information on the most recent developments.

The last chapter of Part II, chapter 12, is an attempt, in summary fashion, to speak of salvation and brokenness from within the perspective of the fundamentals of Christian faith. It is entirely in accord with what we have said above about systematic missiology that this chapter appears at the end and not at the beginning of this part of the book. It could only be written after the detour into prolegomena. It addresses the question of how we can relate the givens of Bible and tradition to the reality of the one, divided world.

Like the other chapters of Part II, chapter 12 invites discussion. The reader will note that in Part II virtually all the theological currents to be described in chapter 27 are represented. The nature of the issues confronting us come out most sharply when missiological reflection is presented as discussion among various theological points of entry. That discussion continues. Part II is thus open-ended.

CHAPTER 8

The Biblical Grounding and Orientation of Mission

M. R. SPINDLER

Why a Biblical Grounding?

The modern instinct, and this applies with respect to the Christian life as much as anything, favors spontaneity and self-development, not the solemn grounding of a subject with the aid of multisyllabic words. On the basis of this instinct, mission might perhaps claim to arise simply from the nature and character of Christians and of the Christian church. Both the World Council of Churches and the Second Vatican Council have stressed that the church is by its very nature missionary in character and that every Christian is essentially a missionary, that is, one who is sent out into the world as a witness to Christ and fellow worker with Christ.[1] Such an appeal to the Christian life as a basis for the right to engage in mission activity would make a "biblical grounding" superfluous and would allow us to break out of the hermeneutical circle.

Can missiology indeed steer clear of the problems involved in a biblical grounding of mission? Missiologists and practical theologians have sometimes answered this question in the affirmative. The first Protestant missiologist of stature, Gustav Warneck, defined mission as grounded in the church: "World mission is inherent in the nature of the church as both community of believers and salvific institution."[2] Much later the practical theologian Otto Haendler observed that "missionary drive" is inherent in the nature of the church: The church is a living organism involved in a process of shrinkage and growth, in which reproduction is inherently necessary because it is by definition an integral part

1. See *Ad Gentes* 2; N. Goodall, ed., *Missions under the Cross: Addresses and Statements of Willingen 1952* (London, 1953) 190.
2. G. Warneck, *Evangelische Missionslehre* (1892-1903) I, xv, see also 240-59.

of every vital process, both literally and figuratively.[3] Accordingly, any "biblical" grounding is of secondary importance: The essence of the church and the character of Christians are sufficient and perhaps effective legitimations of missionary enterprise.

Rightly understood, the notion of "biblical grounding" is a polemical concept designed to oppose the view of mission just outlined. It maintains that mission is *not* a natural and self-evident activity. Even when mission occurs in the form of "the spontaneous expansion of the church" (Roland Allen) it has to be judged by the standard of truth to be found in Scripture. A biblical grounding of mission is not just one among several ways to justify mission, but the justification par excellence.

With this we are referring to a classic debate: In 1944 Hans Schaerer divided missiological positions very sharply into two camps.[4] What is at issue, he said, is the relationship between nature and the supernatural in theology. When nature and the supernatural are deemed to operate synchronously and in accord, a double grounding of mission is valid. But when the coordination between nature and the supernatural is believed to function less smoothly, the double grounding runs into problems. According to this latter view, it is logical that the supernatural grounding of mission, that is, its *biblical* grounding, should have preference over a varied accumulation of natural bases for mission, namely the anthropological, social, historical, economic, and political grounds for mission often advanced by missiologists such as G. Warneck and J. Schmidlin.

Despite the general recognition of "Scriptural authority," the debate is not over. And appeal to Scripture is embattled these days, both in reaction against simplistic reasonings (sometimes dubbed "fundamentalistic use of Scripture") and in reference to deeper understandings of Scripture. For the Bible speaks of "mission" in a variety of ways, most of which do not correspond to the modern meaning(s) of "mission."

Therefore concepts of "mission" and "grounding" need to be clarified first. For example, if "mission" is understood as the sum total of all actual missionary activities in the modern period or as everything undertaken under the banner of "missions," then an honest biblical scholar can only conclude that such a concept of mission does not occur in the Bible. In an influential essay the French New Testament scholar Theo Preiss arrived at the conclusion that the term "mission," in the modern sense of organized church activity among Gentiles, is absent from the New Testament.[5]

---

3. O. Haendler, *Grundriss der praktischen Theologie* (Berlin, 1957) 60.

4. H. Schaerer, *Die Begründung der Mission in der katholischen und evangelischen Missionswissenschaft* (Zurich, 1944).

5. T. Preiss, "L'Église et la mission," in *La Lumière des nations* (Neuchâtel, 1944) 14.

It is therefore anachronistic and hence meaningless to attempt to base all modern "missionary" activities on the Bible, that is, to seek biblical precedents or literal biblical mandates for all modern missionary activities. Mission today must, rather, be seen as arising from something fundamental, from the basic movement of God's people toward the world, more precisely, toward the numerous peoples who have not (yet) accepted God's new covenant in Jesus Christ in faith, hope, and love. This movement must be understood as a way of following God, the God who sent and "gave his only Son, so that everyone who believes in him may not perish but may have eternal life" (John 3:16). The genuineness of our biblical grounding of mission stands or falls with the orientation of modern missions to this central thought. All "missionary" activities that have grown up in history must be reassessed from this perspective. Once again, a biblical grounding of mission by no means seeks to legitimate missionary activities that are actually being carried out. Its goal is, rather, evaluation of those activities in the light of the Bible.

What Is a "Biblical Grounding"?

In this ecumenical introduction it is not our intention to lay out an absolutely new foundation for mission. Numerous precedents exist and display a wide spectrum of views. For instance, the terms "biblical foundations," "point of orientation," and "biblically inspired perspective" in the titles of three Dutch church documents represent three different approaches to the Bible.[6]

6. In 1951 the Dutch Missionary Council published a report by missiologists and biblical scholars concerning "The Biblical Foundations of Mission" ("De Bijbelse grondslagen van de Zending," *De Heerbaan* 4 [1951] 197-221). In 1980 the same Council presented a report in preparation for the World Mission Conference in Melbourne entitled "The Power and the Cross" (*De macht en het kruis;* cf. *Wereld en Zending* 9 [1980] 54-99), which begins with an analysis of society and only at the end defines the biblical notion of the kingdom of God as "the point of orientation." Finally, the Council for Mission of the Dutch Hervormde Kerk prepared a policy document for the Church's 1983 synod under the title "Perspective and Reality" (*Visie en werkelijkheid. Nota van de Raad voor de Zending aangeboden aan de Generale Synode der Nederlandse Hervormde Kerk* [Oegstgeest, 1983]). Its point of departure was "a biblically inspired perspective" (pp. 11f.).

Yet another example of an approach to a biblical grounding of mission is seen in D. Senior and C. Stuhlmueller, *The Biblical Foundations of Mission* (Maryknoll, 1983), though it, too, uses the term "foundations." But here what is sought is not basic points of departure for missionary action but practical models of missionary action. Earlier André Rétif (*Initiation à la Mission* [Paris, 1960]) took this same approach with his use of biblical figures and stories as sources of missionary spirituality.

We have already noted that the concept of "biblical grounding" carries a polemical undertone in relation to other conceivable foundations for mission. Furthermore, a *biblical* grounding carries particular weight among evangelicals and to some degree among Protestants in general to the extent that it is not set alongside some other theological grounding for mission. But a biblical grounding does not carry the same theological clout among those who operate with a systematic philosophy of religion or theology alongside the Bible, for instance, some Catholic missiologists. The latter might criticize the former for using the Bible improperly as just such a book of doctrine containing a system of truths. Conversely, the former might criticize the latter for failing to do justice to the doctrinal content of the Bible and for subordinating the Bible to traditional church doctrine.

Against the background of this continuing tension among different points of view in ecumenical discussion of "church and mission," we are compelled to employ a layered concept of "biblical grounding." We can distinguish between the following three kinds of questions that must be asked in a biblical grounding of mission:

1. A biblical grounding of mission consists in giving an account of the *reasons* that, on the basis of the whole Bible, make mission both possible and necessary. An answer is sought in the Bible to the question: *Why* mission?
2. A biblical grounding of mission consists in giving an account of the *methods* of missionary action in and according to the Bible. An answer is sought in the Bible to the question: *How* must the church do mission? The key phrases we noted earlier ("biblical foundations," "point of orientation," and "biblically inspired perspective") fall into this category.
3. A biblical grounding of mission consists, finally, in giving an account of the *essence* of mission in light of the whole biblical message. An answer is sought in the Bible to the question: *What* is mission? To the degree that the biblical data are rigorously systematized one can apply the term "biblical mission theology" to the answer to this question; often the systematization is based on a central biblical theme such as "sending," "witness," or "the kingdom of God."

We will start with the last of these questions.

What Really Is Mission?

The first step in the biblical grounding of mission is, of course, to define "mission." If mission is a self-evident concept, the grounding of it can be fairly well contained. But when "mission" itself becomes problematic, then the question arises: What really is it that we are trying to give a biblical basis for? So before trying to ground the concept of mission we must define it. If the Bible is identified as the source and standard of theological reflection, then the definition of "mission" cannot be found outside the Bible. But if "mission" is given theological content on the basis of Scripture, the danger then is that the preliminary content of the concept will be automatically verified in the later evaluation. The grounding might then be nothing more than that which is grounded!

Actually, the danger of such circular reasoning is limited by the presence of recognizable options to be weighed against each other. Mission has by no means become an empty concept. It is, in fact, bursting with life! Missiology cannot restrict itself to the grounding and clarification of a "concept," an "ideal type" of "mission"; nor can its intention be to justify and promote (for the sake of the cause!) existing empirical forms of mission; nor can it play off one form or understanding against others. Missiology must be a serious attempt — without losing sight of the ideal type or, better, the eschatological promise — to make statements relevant to the concrete policies of "missionary" organizations that acknowledge the Bible as their norm or source of inspiration.

It is against this background that we must listen to the Bible in order to discover, little by little, what mission really is or ought to be.

Mission Is Being Sent Out

The pattern of "being sent out" is the first biblical idea behind the concept and reality of mission. Jesus *sent out* the twelve apostles (Matt. 10:16) and the seventy disciples (Luke 10:1f.). "Ask the Lord of the harvest to *send out* laborers into his harvest" (Luke 10:2; Matt. 9:38). "As the Father has *sent* me, so I *send* you" (John 20:21). In itself the term "apostle," like *šaliah* in the Jewish tradition, stands for the "one who is sent" or the "envoy," one who represents with authority the one who has sent. What is indicated, therefore, is the distinct authority to represent Jesus and his Father in the power of the Holy Spirit.

Christian churches are not (yet) in agreement on how it is that transmission of this authority can be valid. As a rule a missionary represents a human organization — an order, congregation, or church. That much the missionary can easily prove. But proof of having been sent by God, which would be the true "grounding" for the missionary's mission, is not of this world. Nor can this proof be furnished if "being sent" relates to the church as a whole, to the body of Christ as a missionary congregation, while no more than a few thousand individuals among all the members of the church are presented as the *special* bearers of the mission. It is easy enough for the few to understand themselves as secure participants in the corporate apostolate of the church. But the church's apostolic authority remains an article of faith (in the words of the Nicene Creed, "I believe in . . . one . . . apostolic church"). The church is no more secure a basis for missionary action than the concept of "the mission."

F. M. DuBose has based the biblical grounding of mission entirely on the concept of "sending."[7] But he goes too far beyond the horizon of this concept to be able to do justice to "mission." "Sending out" is, in my opinion, merely a formal juridical description of mission. It concerns the authority or mandate of the one being sent, even if the person in question does not know that he or she has been sent by the God of Israel (as with Cyrus: Isa. 45:1-8). The missionary's work is not materially defined by this concept.

Mission Is to Make Disciples of All Nations

"Make disciples of all nations" is part of the missionary mandate spoken by Christ in Matthew 28:19. Discussion of this passage has had two main focal points among Bible scholars and missiologists:

1. The imperative *mathēteusate*, "make disciples," suggests pedagogical action, transmission of knowledge, possibly transmission of wisdom. Emphasis on teaching, say, the precepts of Jesus, including the Sermon on the Mount, has often been labeled as the practice of mission. Actually it is more correct to stress discipleship, obedience to the living words of Jesus, listening to him. The stress in the meaning of the word as it is used here is less pedagogical than ethical: *It stresses fellowship*, that is, creation of relationship with the Lord Jesus Christ. If we understand it otherwise, the image of missions gets muddied by being combined with an assortment of pedagogical theories. When mission is conceived and practiced as the schooling of the nations, and pedagogies at the same time favor the intellectual side of schooling, the danger exists that mission will degenerate into didacticism and pedantry.

7. F. M. DuBose, *God Who Sends: A Fresh Quest for Biblical Mission* (Nashville, 1983).

2. The word *ethnē* ("nations") has occasioned an unfortunate commingling of mission with all sorts of political theories concerning the essence and nature of "people" and "nation." J. C. Hoekendijk, the well-known Reformed missiologist, has rightly protested against this confusion.[8] He labeled as "ethnopathic" the fanatical concern for national character in German missionary practice, in which ethnic units are presented as target groups that at some time in the future will act as national churches. A variation of the same theme conceived under the influence of sociological theories has made central the concept of "homogeneous units" as the target of mission (D. McGavran). In fact, in the missionary mandate the word *ethnē* is salvation-historically conditioned. It refers to the people outside the covenant — in Matthew those outside the new covenant in the blood of Jesus (Matt. 26:28) — in contrast with the people of the covenant. Mission is the universal and unrestricted opening of the new covenant. Acceptance of the covenant necessarily implies an ethical obligation.

Mission Is Deliverance, Emancipatory Action

In recent years, partly under the influence of Latin American liberation theology, mission has been understood in the terms of Isaiah 61:1f., which is cited in Luke 4:18f. as Jesus' messianic program:

> The Spirit of the Lord is upon me,
>   because he has anointed me
>   to bring good news to the poor.
> He has sent me to proclaim release to the captives
>   and recovery of sight to the blind,
>   to let the oppressed go free,
> to proclaim the year of the Lord's favor.

Jesus appears in public and acts as the Anointed of God who performs liberating deeds in the framework of a lasting, indeed an everlasting, covenant (Isa. 61:8).

The idea of the covenant, which we used a moment ago to describe the *ethnē*, is also present here. Luke 4:18f. emphasizes the proclamation of the gospel ("the good news"), and proclamation of the gospel is a definition of mission that occurs very often in the New Testament (Mark 16:15; 13:10; 14:9; Rom. 1:1; 1:16; 1 Cor. 1:17, etc.).

8. J. C. Hoekendijk, *Kerk en Volk in de Duitse zendingswetenschap* (Groningen, 1948).

Here in Luke this proclamation of the gospel is explained with two very modern-sounding qualifications: In the first place, a strong emphasis is placed upon the gospel's address *to the poor.* The gospel is for the poor. Both the Latin American Bishops Conference at Puebla (1979) and the World Missionary Conference at Melbourne (1980) regarded the missionary preferential option for the poor as central. Secondly, proclamation in word is closely linked with concrete deeds of liberation breaking through the structures of oppression and injustice that force the poor into their situation of poverty and hold them there by violence. Mission thus aims to restructure society as a whole on a global scale. It aims, that is, at the kingdom of God. It is an ambitious program, and it breaks out of the traditional separation of church and world, church and state, and spiritual and political power. It is not a specifically Christian program: In this connection mission can look for and find allies in all sorts of nonreligious and non-Christian movements that strive for and believe they have brought somewhat closer a just world order. It is not at all our wish to deal lightly with the historical disappointments of countries that have recently become independent; but it is important to realize that for the time being the kingdom of God remains an eschatological horizon and that in the Bible liberation is primarily proclaimed as deliverance from invisible powers that oppress humans *inwardly* — such as sin, unbelief, idolatry, and "flesh" (Rom. 7:24).

Mission Is Witness

The last biblical description of the concept of mission we wish to focus on is "witness." In recent ecumenical discussion this term has found strong resonance partly because in many Western circles and in former "mission fields" the concept of mission acquired an unpleasant connotation of blind triumphalism. "Witness" sounds more modest. The idea is not to perform mighty deeds but to become aware of God's mighty deeds and to testify to them.

The biblical basis for this understanding of mission is usually found in Acts 1:8: ". . . and you will be my *witnesses* in Jerusalem, in all Judea and Samaria, and to the ends of the earth." The apostles are not called to "do" but "to be." They are not to point to their own achievements. They are, rather, to ask forgiveness for the many misdeeds committed by Christians in the course of history. They are to point to God who himself and on his own effects salvation. Here we are approaching the theme of the *missio Dei* (God's mission), which is treated (critically) elsewhere in this book.

Actually the biblical concept of "witness" is less innocent than people think. When the apostles and their successors were appointed witnesses, this entailed a double risk. First, in Christ's (legal) cause, they were to witness to his true identity as the only Lord and Savior, he who possesses and mediates to his followers the power of the Holy Spirit (Acts 1:8; cf. Matt. 28:18; John 15:26f.). This is risky because Jesus' identity remains disputed: The world does not believe that he is truly sent by God.

Secondly, the witness was risky because it bears directly on the resurrection of Jesus: The apostles were primarily "witnesses to his resurrection" (Acts 1:22; 2:32). Their witness had, therefore, the same content as the kerygma. Jesus' resurrection implies the breakthrough of the kingdom of God in this world of sin and death and brings with it the new Christian economy of salvation in its totality. This horizon of eschatological expectation justifies to some degree the extremely broad spectrum of missionary activities and engagements that come under the heading of "witness" in recent ecumenical documents. Current usage assigns to "Christian" or "common" witness a strong ethical component. It denotes a manner of life and a presence. Sometimes the kerygmatic component predominates: Witness resembles somewhat a cry in the wilderness.[9]

A 1951 church report on "The Biblical Foundations of Mission" made a dialectical distinction between fulfillment and expectation.[10] Witness really occurs more on the side of fulfillment than on the side of expectation. God's work is completed! But this does not change the fact that God's work takes place in a world where "the works of darkness" seem to prevail. This world is full of agony and idols. Accordingly, witness occurs between a song of praise and a cry of pain and anger and sometimes passes into martyrdom. Here the missionary theology of witness ties in with the tradition of the suffering prophet, the suffering righteous ones, and the suffering servant people — the *'ebed Yahweh* — of the Old Testament.[11]

In the nature of the case, the presence of suffering "witnesses" in the midst of the nations and among the straying brothers and sisters of one's own people, though it lacks a triumphant aspect, does have a high polemical value over against idol-worshippers and those who cause the misfortunes of others. It is the martyr who is destined for the highest eschatological triumph.

9. See A. L. Molendijk, *Getuigen in Missionair en Oecumenisch verband. Een studie over het begrip "getuigen" in documenten van de Wereldraad van Kerken, de Rooms-katholieke Kerk en de Evangelicalen in de perioden 1948-1985* (Leiden and Utrecht, 1986).

10. "De Bijbelse grondslagen van de Zending" (see n. 6 above), 205.

11. See J. W. van Henten, *De Joodse martelaren als grondleggers van een nieuwe orde. Een studie uitgaande van 2 en 4 Makkabeeën* (Leiden, 1986).

Why Then Mission?

Proceeding from a global — not yet "purified"[12] — concept of mission, classic missiology looked for the simplest grounding of missions in the "missionary mandate" as it is summarized in Matthew 28:16-20, especially verses 18 and 19: "All authority in heaven and on earth has been given to me. Go therefore and make disciples of all nations, baptizing them in the name of the Father and of the Son and of the Holy Spirit, teaching them to obey everything that I have commanded you."

We should notice that this mission mandate is at the same time a mandate to baptize. It is viewed as the institution of baptism and therefore solemnly cited at every celebration of the sacrament of baptism.[13] No other institution of baptism exists in the Bible. The practice of baptism was never, or hardly ever, subject to controversy.

But questions *are* raised about *mission* precisely on the basis of these verses: Who are (or were) the recipients of the mandate? This was a favorite question in controversial theology from the sixteenth century on. The Protestant Reformers believed that only the apostles had received the mandate to engage in mission among the (Gentile) nations. They also believed that the apostles had no successors. Moreover, the apostles had fully discharged their missionary obligation. "All the nations" had been reached, according to a widespread opinion, held not just by the Reformers but also by many before them. Apparently, opposition to episcopal succession kept the Reformers from recognizing the permanent value and validity of the missionary command.

The Reformed and Anglican theologian Adrianus Saravia came to the conclusion that the mission mandate and episcopal succession were a unity. But this did not mean that a valid succession could only be obtained through the bishop of Rome. Anglican bishops also had a valid mandate, one that till now has not been recognized by Rome. In theory, at least, the validity of a mission mandate for churches without an episcopal office is called into question all the more by Roman Catholic and Eastern Orthodox theologians. They believe that Protestants appeal much too easily — and really incorrectly — to Matthew 28:18-20 as a basis for Protestant missions,[14] though in the debate concerning the validity of church ministries

12. With the political purges after World War II as an analogy, Swiss missiologist Hans Dürr proposed a purification of mission concepts in "Die Reinigung der Missionsmotive," *Evangelisches Missions-Magazin* 95 (1951) 2-10.

13. Cf. the Lima Report on *Baptism, Eucharist and Ministry,* on Baptism §1 (Faith and Order papers 111, 1982).

14. A. Rétif, *La mission. Eléments de théologie et de spiritualité missionnaires* (Paris, 1963) 20, where he approvingly cites Bérulle.

Protestant missions do not constitute an exception: The Roman Catholic hierarchy questions *all* non-Catholic offices and ministries.

Of course many ecumenical or bilateral dialogues concern mutual recognition of offices and ministries. The focus of such discussions is really the question of authority in the church of Christ on earth. What authority does the church have? What authority does Holy Scripture have? Is the authority of Scripture derived from that of the church or vice versa? These and other questions quickly come to the surface in connection with the authority of the mission mandate. But at that point, missiology must refer to other branches of theology.

The universal validity of Matthew 28:18-20 has been regarded as self-evident in Protestant and Roman Catholic mission circles. But it began to be undermined in the nineteenth century on the basis of critical biblical scholarship. The claim was made that the mission mandate did not contain any authentic words of Jesus but was only the product of the first-century church's theology. The historical Jesus deliberately rejected mission to the Gentiles and forbade the disciples to work outside Israel's borders (Matt. 10:5). This complex of problems occasioned far-ranging discussion among biblical scholars and missiologists. An interesting aspect of this is that some biblical scholars who made important contributions to this discussion later became leading missiologists.[15]

The tension between Jesus' *prohibition* of mission and his mission *mandate* is resolved by both the biblical-theological theme of the *oikonomia* of salvation and by Jesus' eschatology:

1. Salvation occurs in historical phases. Not until salvation was completed on the cross and at the resurrection of Jesus did the hour of mission come. The prohibition of mission was definitively lifted at Easter and Ascension.
2. The cross and resurrection are not simply historical but especially eschatological events. They ushered in the end time; only then, in the eschatological expectations of Jesus, did the movement of the Gentiles into the new people of God begin.

15. Swedish missiologist and Lutheran bishop Bengt Sundkler wrote a short dissertation on *Jésus et les païens* ("Jesus and the Pagans") for the University of Strasbourg (1936). The late David Bosch, a missiology professor at the University of South Africa at Pretoria known for his mediation between "ecumenicals" and "evangelicals," received his doctorate in 1959 under the New Testament scholar Oscar Cullmann at Basel on the topic *Die Heidenmission in der Zukunftschau Jesu* ("Gentile Mission in Jesus' View of the Future"). Joachim Jeremias offered a summary of the whole discussion in *Jesus' Promise to the Nations* (Studies in Biblical Theology 24; Naperville, 1958).

In the New Testament the motifs of *oikonomia* and eschatology are elaborated especially in Luke's Gospel and Acts and in Paul's letters. That salvation history occupies a central place in the Bible is almost universally recognized in biblical scholarship. But again the universal validity and truth-content of (salvation-)historically conditioned truths, which were always "true" and are suddenly no longer "true," has come up. How can Jesus be "the truth" (John 14:6) if his historical existence is limited? The question is not new; it already played a role in discussions between Church Fathers and Greek philosophers who fancied eternal truths. Later in church history and particularly in the period of the Enlightenment (Lessing) and more recently the problem of "truth and history" has repeatedly returned to the theological agenda. These questions are again being brought to the fore by Asian theologians, who raise fundamental questions against the salvation-historical interpretation of the Bible.

The problem, which is not new, calls for far-reaching reflection. But it would be asking too much of missiology to locate the "burden of proof" exclusively within its domain. The issue is a universal theological and philosophical problem that foundational and systematic theologians must respond to. But there is a fairly general consensus among philosophers, anthropologists, and theologians on the *historical* character of humanity and of truth in general. It is in this light that the impasse in mission theology that we have been describing, that is, the chasm between ontology and *oikonomia*, can perhaps be dealt with. The choice is unnecessary, as is any farewell to salvation history, specifically to eschatology.

From this account it is clear that the mission mandate in Matthew 28 is by no means to be viewed as an isolated "proof text." It has become fashionable to attack the so-called "biblicistic method," by which one uses a few proof texts to "ground" mission. At first this attack may seem well founded. The Bible must be read as a whole and in context. Separate texts must be interpreted in the light of their biblical contexts. But Matthew 28:18-20 is not just an isolated text. It is the formal conclusion of the First Gospel, it embodies the thrust of the entire Gospel, and it has been deliberately placed by the redactor where it is. The context in 28:18-20 can legitimately be considered and used as a core text in the search for a biblical grounding of mission. For that matter, the search for core texts is not limited to missiology. The Jewish and Christian tradition contains other deliberately chosen core texts — such as the love commandment — that need not be questioned.

But as a result of all this the question "Why Christian mission?" cannot be answered simply and formally by an appeal to the "mission mandate." We cannot just say "a command is a command," though the motif of obedience is an important part of Christian life and spirituality.

The mission mandate must be understood in a salvation-historical frame of thought in which the concrete progression of God's redemptive initiative is central. Why mission? Because now and to the end of the world the mission of Jesus Christ and the mission of the Holy Spirit provide time and space for the mission of the church.

The salvation-historical, eschatological grounding of mission on the basis of Scripture is the common property of all Christian churches today. The World Council of Churches followed this line of thought at the Evanston Assembly (1954) and in its report, edited by Johannes Blauw, on the biblical theology of mission entitled *The Missionary Nature of the Church* (1961). Emilio Castro, Secretary General of the World Council, needs to be mentioned among other ecumenical leaders for his important contribution to mission theology, in which the kingdom of God, the eschatological concept par excellence, is central.[16] And many Roman Catholic missiological contributions can be cited. In the decree on the Church's missionary activity, *Ad Gentes Divinitus* (1965), issued by the Second Vatican Council, biblical-theological patterns of thought (besides other theological arguments) are employed to ground mission: "God decided to enter into the history of mankind in a new and definitive manner, by sending his own Son in human flesh" (3). "This mission [of the church] continues and, in the course of history, unfolds the mission of Christ" (5).

Besides a salvation-historical grounding, Roman Catholic missiology also employs a biblical grounding of a foundational-theological nature. Often the following core text is cited: "God, our Savior, who desires everyone to be saved . . ." (1 Tim. 2:3f.). We are dealing here, in theological terms, with "the universal redemptive will of God." But this principle is applied somewhat ambivalently. In *Ad Gentes* the reason *(ratio)* for missionary activity — inasmuch as God's redemptive will also indicates the way of redemption — is expressly described in terms of what follows in the text just cited: God "desires everyone to be saved *and to come to the knowledge of the truth*" (cited in *Ad Gentes* 7:42). But in the Dogmatic Constitution on the Church the same verse is employed (without "to come to the knowledge of the truth") to open a way of salvation for people of good will who through no fault of their own have no knowledge of God (*Lumen Gentium* 16). The same verse serves, then, to ground both the necessity and the nonnecessity of mission. Mission becomes superfluous if God's saving will bears no relationship to human will, faith, and knowledge. But it becomes necessary if "the knowledge of the truth" — that is, faith in God — originates partly through human mediation. Mission is one form of this human mediation.

16. E. Castro, *Freedom in Mission: The Perspective of the Kingdom. An Ecumenical Inquiry* (Geneva, 1985).

How Must the Church Do Mission?

As a rule an appeal to the Bible serves to ground the choice of specific missionary methods. A biblical grounding of mission or orientation of missionary methodology to biblical models requires a good knowledge of biblical history, of the time of the Old Testament and the intertestamental period as well as the time of the New Testament. Sometimes lines have to be drawn to post–New Testament early Christian literature in order to map out more effectively biblical models of mission. Underlying this approach is the conviction that the Bible yields not only theological bases but also practical guidelines for missionary activity. Also, it is assumed that the actions of the first apostles and evangelists are worthy of imitation and *can* be imitated, that they possess, that is, a high measure of normativity.

To ground mission in the Bible often carries a polemical undertone, since it effects the formation and determination of the policies of missionary organizations. Because missionary policy has as a rule developed historically and carries the marks of a variety of social or political influences, the biblical grounding of missionary methodology often means a sharp critique of the actual policies of operating bodies and an attempt to shake off the historical burden. Brief accounts of some celebrated controversies will show this:

Mobility

In the time of Gustav Warneck a new type of Protestant missionary society arose that, appealing to the model of the Bible, developed a new method of doing mission. Older missions established fixed stations where sedentary groups of missionaries were concentrated to build up new local churches and to render a variety of services (schools, hospitals, and industries). Mission had lost its mobility and there was insufficient outreach to non-Christians. A new generation of missionaries believed that the biblical model for mission had to be applied again. They argued against sedentary missions and for mobile missions. These missionaries undertook missionary journeys of a few days and never settled permanently in the villages or cities of the "heathen" but traveled ever farther out with the good news. The parable of the sower (Matt. 13:1-9) was considered especially applicable: The sower goes out and returns; then the seed and the earth must await the outcome under God's blessing. Planting churches was not part of the design.

It is interesting to note that this direct application of biblical missionary methods did not occur just in the context of Western organizations.

Many indigenous non-Western initiatives of this kind can be identified in Indonesia, in the Pacific, and in Africa. A remarkable movement began in Madagascar in 1893 and is still active, the Disciples of the Lord *(Mpianatry ny Tompo)*. It began to send out missionaries on the model of Matthew 10 and Luke 10. Two-by-two they entered the villages, without a fixed residence, without money, dressed simply in white, to preach the gospel and to heal the sick. The work of the prophet Wade Harris (1865-1929) is well known in Africa: He travelled alone from village to village far from his place of birth, dressed in white, to preach the gospel, heal the sick, and drive out evil spirits. It would be worth investigating whether church splits and the rise of "independent churches" in Africa are not partly due to struggles over missionary methods, and not just to conflicts between whites and blacks.

To Gustav Warneck this application of a biblical model of itinerant evangelization was proof of a careless handling of Scripture. He had no good word to say about this kind of "guerilla mission." Shortly before his death he wrote a letter to the World Missionary Conference to be held in Edinburgh (1910) to warn against this sort of mission strategy, which was, he wrote, "a mistaken appeal to the apostolic model."[17] To him the imperative of the hour was patient building up of churches, leadership training, and education.

The model of the biblical and "apostolic" mission method is still operative today. In 1986 the Billy Graham Evangelistic Association organized in Amsterdam its third congress for "itinerant evangelists." Many other evangelical mission organizations continue to beat the drum of the unmet spiritual needs of "the unreached," who could be reached, they say, if, as in the apostolic age, mobility was again at the top of the mission agenda.

Moving Quickly toward Independence

Another missiological row broke out in 1912 when the Anglican missionary Roland Allen published his book *Missionary Methods: Saint Paul's or Ours?* It was first of all a thorough study of the mission practice of the apostle Paul based on the writings of Adolf Harnack.[18] Allen's comparison

---

17. G. Warneck, *Evangelische Missionslehre* II, 15. Warneck's letter was published in vol. I of the conference report, *Carrying the Gospel to All the Non-Christian World* (Edinburgh, 1910) 434ff.

18. A. Harnack, *The Expansion of Christianity in the First Three Centuries* (1904-5). Allen used the second English edition.

of Pauline mission methods with modern mission methods did not favor
the latter. In a few years, Allen stated, Paul started a wide network of
churches; modern missions still wonder whether self-government is realistic for younger churches in view of the high costs of administration and
the weak training of indigenous pastors and for other reasons. Allen pleads
for an unaltered application of the apostolic method, that is, for swift
planting of small local churches with a minimum of administrative bag-
gage and for immediate consecration of church leaders so that they will
have self-confidence and the authority to continue the mission and pastoral care on their own. Then "the euthanasia" of mission, which was the
goal of the Anglican Church Missionary Society already in 1851, can take
place and new mission fields can be opened.

Allen also asks modern mission to have the same faith in the Holy
Spirit that Paul possessed. The church lives, after all, only of and in the
power of the Spirit. At issue is not some technical innovation by which
mission will begin to score successes. Mission is for Allen a spiritual matter
and decidedly not just a question of method. We note the shift in dynamics.
Whereas in the methods opposed by Warneck mobility was the biblical
ideal, here swift planting of churches is recommended as the appropriate
"biblical method."

Allen's missiological legacy continues to have influence. The Scottish missionary Lesslie Newbigin, later a bishop in the church of South
India, followed Allen in his missionary practice and promoted the repub-
lication of his books. In his many ecumenical functions he has sought to
accelerate the movement toward independence of the "younger churches"
and has fought against a dated missionary paternalism. On this front, in
principle and in official terms, the battle has been won. But this is not due
just to the application of biblical methods.

Missionary Preaching

A third sector of mission methodology has profited from the appeal to a
biblical grounding: missionary preaching. How should the good news be
proclaimed when it is addressed to non-Christians for the first time?
Naturally preparatory contacts are indispensable in order to create and
maintain a readiness to listen. But at a given moment the Christian must
"give an account of the hope" that is in him or her. Roman Catholic mission
has favored the transmission of the content of the catechism, mainly the
creed. Protestant mission has sought to follow Jesus in telling biblical
stories and parables.

Modern biblical scholarship has attempted to analyze the missionary preaching of the apostles and to outline its main points. Comparative studies of the missionary speeches in Acts was done in the 1930s in accordance with the historical-critical method, particularly form criticism. These studies discovered or refined a distinct literary genre: the *kerygma*. C. H. Dodd's short study, *The Apostolic Preaching and its Developments* (London, 1936), was groundbreaking. Dodd and his disciples distinguished *kerygma*, the initial preaching, from *didache*, further instruction in Christian faith and conduct.

These results of biblical scholarship were processed for missiology especially by the Lutheran W. Holsten[19] and the Roman Catholic theologian A. Rétif.[20] Later the Roman Catholic missiologist A. M. Henry developed this theme in a number of books. The focus of these missiological statements has been the imperative to reach back in initial missionary preaching of the gospel to the biblical model of the *kerygma*, that is, to the central message of the resurrection of Jesus Christ our Lord.

Here again, the appeal to the Bible serves a critical and polemical function. The kerygmatic model implies that in initial contacts with non-Christians lengthy doctrinal expositions of Christian dogma or morality are not in order. The missionary or evangelist must not burden the non-Christian with subtleties; he or she must simply come to the point, which is Jesus Christ, the risen One. "The apostles gave their testimony to the resurrection of the Lord Jesus" (Acts 4:33). This is the model that must be applied if missionary preaching is to rest on a biblical foundation.

Inculturation

The fourth methodological area in which an appeal to the Bible has been especially fruitful is that of the problem of inculturation, a subject that has risen to the top of the missiological agenda since 1972, particularly in Roman Catholic circles. The Protestant term is more often "contextualization," which the World Council of Churches has employed just as long.

This theme, under either name, implies that in Latin America, Africa, Asia, and other places the new churches can and should understand and express the Christian faith in terms of their respective cultures. Even more, it means that the gospel itself receives its shape in the total

19. W. Holsten, *Das Kerygma und der Mensch. Einführung in die Religions- und Missionswissenschaft* (Munich, 1953). Holsten uses the term *kerygma* in a broader theological sense than do biblical scholars.

20. A. Rétif, *La prédication kérygmatique dans les Actes des Apôtres* (unpublished thesis, Rome, 1953), revised as *Foi au Christ et mission d'après les Actes des Apôtres* (Paris, 1953).

culture of the people among whom the church is planted and in the nation of which the church is essentially an integral part. Successful inculturation may be said to occur when the gospel and the church no longer seem to be foreign imports but are claimed in general as the property of the people. The theme of inculturation has a clear polemical thrust: Foreign Western influence and dominance in non-Western churches has to stop so that free play can be given to people's self-chosen cultural understandings of the Christian faith. But this process is not purely spontaneous, since the Bible continues to function.

Some will perhaps be astonished that the Bible of all books should be seen as the frame of reference in a process of inculturation, since it is at times seen or presented as a Western product or possession. But closer scrutiny shows that the Bible is not a Western book. Moreover, the cultures of the Bible are in many respects very close to many non-Western cultures, closer in any case than to the present Western technical-scientific culture.

And the Bible itself bears the marks of various processes of inculturation. In each such instance the faith, church order, and ethics of the people of God underwent changes in the crucible of cultures. Israel's faith enriched itself in its interaction with the cultures of Egypt, Assyria, Persia, Greece, Rome, and, of course, "Palestine" itself. But drawing from these cultures Israel in turn transformed the "foreign" elements into authentically Israelite "possessions." "People will bring into it," into the new Jerusalem, that is, "the glory and the honor of the nations" (Rev. 21:26, a text frequently cited in the literature of inculturation).

The Bible provides help with the problems of inculturation in two ways: First, the inculturation aimed at by non-Western churches finds many precedents in the Bible. In its historical pilgrimage the people of God has never existed in a cultural vacuum; it has always had to struggle with different cultures.

Second, the Bible shows how several "inculturations" have occurred. The people of God has preserved its identity as the people of the covenant through a process of falling and rising again. Choices among cultural elements have been made — in retrospect not always happy choices. Elements were transposed to different positions in the cultural constellation peculiar to every nation. Other elements were rejected or reinterpreted. In a sense a culture can experience a "conversion" — if not in the totality of historical reality, then certainly proleptically in cultural elements that are used purposefully in the formation of worship. In that case the foreign origin of worship is totally forgotten or suppressed.

A classic example of such a successful inculturation is the temple of Jerusalem, built as it was on a hill where archaeologists have found the traces of Canaanite sacrifices from long before David's time. But those older sacrificial cults left no traces in the consciousness of Israel. According to 2 Samuel 24:18-25 the hill was simply "the threshing floor of Araunah the Jebusite."

The same process occurs when the missionary church takes over fixed religious and theological terms — in the apostolic era when Aramaic was replaced by Greek, and in our own age whenever the Bible is translated into a new language. In such translations, appeals to etymologies soon become meaningless and misleading, since only an appeal to the Bible itself can clarify the Jewish and Christian concepts and names.

A Total Approach?

Finally, I wish to mention an attempt to lift the whole of a deliberate missionary policy directly from the Bible. David J. Hesselgrave bases the method of church planting on biblical precedents, which he then breaks down into operational task units in the spirit of the science of management.[21] He bases the cycle of successive actions that fall under the heading of church planting on (an analysis of) the book of Acts. He finds there ten ordinarily successive operations: commissioning of missionaries, contact with the audience, communication of the gospel, conversion of the hearers, gathering of the believers, confirmation of the faith, consecration of leaders, transference of leadership (withdrawal of the pioneers), building up of interchurch relationships, and building up of missionary participation on the base of the new sending church.

But the question arises here whether we are really dealing with a "biblical grounding" of missionary method. Hesselgrave himself speaks of biblical *precedents* in distinction from biblical principles. His construct seems contrived.

Concluding Remarks

This chapter is intended as an introduction to the broad range of problems involved in the relation between Bible and mission. It is not an exhaustive treatment of the theme. Both terms of the problem, *Bible* and *mission*, invite further and deeper reflection. In the next chapter, the hermeneutical question is examined further, particularly as it concerns the interpretation of the Bible in various contexts. In other chapters there is further reflection

21. D. J. Hesselgrave, *Planting Churches Cross-Culturally: A Guide for Home and Foreign Missions* (Grand Rapids, 1980).

on the nature and manifestation of "mission" in the present. In the narrowest terms "mission" refers to "organized mission"; more broadly it refers to missionary enthusiasm, to the missionary dimension of the entire range of Christian conduct and church activity, or even to the underside of world history conceived of as the history of salvation. The search for a biblical basis of these or other views sometimes issues in attempts to legitimate, in retrospect, decisions that are hardly open to discussion.

I have followed a different view here. The biblical grounding of mission is not, in my understanding, an attempt to define a specific form or ideal of mission. It is, rather, an effort to lay all forms and ideals of mission open to God's Word, not only initially and theoretically, in the first phase of theological construction, but during the whole process of mission. The Bible has a role to play not only in the foundations of mission but also in the whole movement of missionary thought and action — at all times and in all places. Yes, we need biblical grounding. But we also need biblical orientation and especially a disciplined return to the biblical sources, in ecumenical perspective, for all the themes that come up for discussion in missionary theology and practice.

This "ecumenical introduction to missiology" naturally furnishes several examples of appeals to the Bible, especially in this section of the book, but also elsewhere. Yes, we need biblical grounding. But not as mere lip service or devotion to the letter. The goal is to find, ever anew, the courage to make "mission" happen and to do so creatively.

After the publication of this textbook in Dutch three major contributions to the biblical theology of mission were published almost simultaneously. Father Lucien Legrand, a French biblical scholar teaching in Bangalore, India, offers an illuminating survey of the shift from the Old Testament concentration on Israel's election to the worldwide missionary project of the New Testament.[22] His assessment of the predicament of mission today focuses on diversity in mission but also, and ultimately, on the metamorphosis of mission from activism to eschatological mysticism. He emphasizes more than I do the spirituality of the kingdom of God, the "flaming centre" (J. Scherer) of mission.

Methodist bishop Walter Klaiber underlines the biblical call for "conversion" in the sense of personal decision in evangelism and discusses questions of pastoral care and ecclesiology that arise following conversion.[23] This aspect of the biblical foundation of mission is only summarily

---

22. L. Legrand, *Le Dieu qui vient. La mission dans la Bible* (Paris, 1988), translated as *Unity and Plurality: Mission in the Bible* (Maryknoll, 1990).
23. W. Klaiber, *Ruf und Antwort: Biblische Grundlagen einer Theologie der Evangelisation* (Stuttgart/Neukirchen-Vluyn, 1990).

dealt with in my own presentation under the heading "Mission Is to Make Disciples" (126).

Finally, I would like to call attention to the late Reformed missiologist David Bosch's universally acclaimed book, *Transforming Mission: Paradigm Shifts in Theology of Mission*.[24] The first part of this work is devoted to New Testament models of mission. Bosch discerns the first "shifts of paradigm" in Christian history in the New Testament, namely, those from the historical Jesus to the apostles, and from one apostle to another; in this way he identifies a variety of New Testament missionary theologies and approaches. Bosch appears to steer between the simplified biblical founding of mission offered by many fundamentalists and a modernist approach that grounds mission on purely practical motives without any reference to the Bible. He offers an excellent treatment of the biblical material that has much in common with my short presentation in this chapter. Bosch takes time to assess the textual setting of the various missionary themes in the New Testament (with the exception of the Johannine tradition), while I have limited myself to a number of topics related to certain modern debates.

24. Maryknoll, 1991.

CHAPTER 9

One Bible and Many Interpretive Contexts: Hermeneutics in Missiology

A. DE GROOT

The Bible is of crucial importance in missiology. This is so first of all because the missionary vision seeks its basis and orientation there. It is also so because — as the common inheritance of all Christians — the Bible plays a unifying role. For all sorts of reasons the church has fallen apart, but the conviction remains alive that its unity is not a lost cause as long as the Bible is opened, read, and preached in all Christian churches. A return to the Bible is always at the same time a turn toward the common future of the separated churches.

The turn toward this future, this common search, is affected by a number of developments. Always, and in all churches, there has been contention over the correct interpretation of the Bible, over what is orthodox. Now this struggle is intensified by the rise of new ways of interpreting the Bible and of doing theology.[1] These new methods are not simply academic diversions. They reflect changes that culture is undergoing and existential issues that arise from those changes.

In Western Europe and North America the Enlightenment led to a fundamental crisis in Christian faith and theology.[2] Familiar keywords for this crisis are secularization and secularism; coming of age and emancipation in the relationships among classes, races, and the sexes; the demythologizing of faith and religion; and historical critical study of the Bible. Attempts to assimilate these processes have led and still lead to a great deal of pluriformity in theology, which threatens the unity always assumed in theology.

---

1. Cf. H. Küng and J. Moltmann, ed., *Conflicting Ways of Interpreting the Bible* (Concilium; Edinburgh, 1980).

2. Cf. C. Geffré, G. Gutiérrez, and V. P. Elizondo, ed., *Different Theologies, Common Responsibility: Babel or Pentecost?* (Concilium; Edinburgh, 1984); J. B. Metz and E. Schillebeeckx, ed., *Orthodoxy and Heterodoxy* (Concilium; Edinburgh, 1987).

Besides the context of a secularized society, other contexts are making themselves felt, namely, the contexts that churches outside Europe and North America exist in. Global Christianity is becoming culturally polycentric. Many churches in the Third World have discovered the significance of their own socioeconomic, religious, and political contexts. They want to be in all respects churches involved in their own societies.[3] They are pleading for a reassessment of the importance of the local church as the meeting place of the gospel and the concrete world and are searching for new attitudes toward non-Christian religions and for prophetic postures toward all varieties of injustice. Because of all this, the church has become in our time a pluriform community in a diaspora situation, a community obligated to carry on dialogue within itself and with other religions.

Along with Western secularization and the self-discovery of Third World churches, the challenging character of the gospel message — summed up in the words "the liberation of the poor"[4] — is also being rediscovered. In keeping with this discovery, it is being realized that the universalism of the church does not consist in having the largest possible number of Christians but in the integral liberation of people. According to this insight, redemption is actualized in two perspectives: the eschatological perspective in which the ultimate destiny of humankind in God is central and the historical perspective, which concerns the concrete development of humanity and society, the construction of a viable, just, and peaceful world community embracing all human beings. Many Christians are coming to the insight that the poor person constitutes a *locus theologicus*, that is, that one can understand the gospel better from the viewpoint of the poor.

All these developments and questions influence the place the Bible occupies in the Christianity of our time. The a priori character of biblical authority is gone. Those who have been shaped by the Enlightenment read the Bible from critical distance and only give in when the Bible proves to have a relevant message even in the context of a secularized understanding of life. Experiences and expectations that play a role in specific sociocultural contexts or among certain groups of people defined by race, class, or gender influence the reading, understanding, and interpretation of the Bible. For many Christians the vision of the liberation of the poor has become the key in reading the Bible and therefore also in analyzing and understanding their own situations.

3. J. Pereira Ramalho, ed., *Sign of Hope and Justice* (Geneva, 1980).
4. G. Gutiérrez, "Het Recht om te Denken. Bevrijdingtheologie als zelfverstaan van uitgebuite gelovigen," *Tijdschrift voor Theologie* (1979) 147-63.

Thus in a variety of ways the Bible itself has again become the subject of discussion. When people allow the real situation of global Christianity to come home to them and when they look more closely at the appeal to Scripture that Christianity continues to make, then hermeneutical questions gain new relevance and new urgency. The one Bible disintegrates contextually. Just what are the implications of this for missiological reflection?

Examples of Contextual Use of Scripture

Asia: A. J. Appasamy

Hindu — and for that matter also Buddhist and Jainist — India has long been preoccupied with salvation in the sense of individual liberation from the necessity of being born to yet another earthly life, from the "endless chain of existences." This liberation "is possible if one succeeds in totally destroying karma."[5] *Karma* is the moral credit that determines a person's next existence: One can ascend to God or descend to the lowest animal existence. Salvation *(moksa)* is the ending of this line of continuation and the misery associated with it.

It is against this background that we must understand the attempts of A. J. Appasamy (1891-1971) to explain the Gospel of John. He sought to make John's Gospel come alive in India with the aid of important concepts from Hinduism, specifically from the *bhakti* tradition, which has the character of a folk religion (in contrast to the more elitist *advaita* tradition).[6] Appasamy unhesitatingly used the idea of *moksa* as pivotal, understanding it as eternal life and liberation from ignorance and the power of darkness. But he gave this concept a twist, stressing the role of the unique mediator, Jesus Christ, with whom one enjoys a personal bond of love. This bond has far-reaching ethical consequences, especially love of neighbor. *Moksa* is thus

> a continuous contact with Reality, personal, conscious and radiant with joy. It is like the life of Jesus with God. It is not the realization of identity but the experience of a moral harmony with the holy and righteous Father. It is a personal experience which, however, in its higher reaches

5. J. Gonda, *De Indische Godsdiensten* (Wassenaar, 1947³) 69.
6. Cf. the following works by A. J. Appasamy: *The Mysticism of the Fourth Gospel in its Relation to Hindu Bhakti Literature* (unpublished dissertation, Oxford, 1922); *What is Moksa?* (Madras, 1931); *Temple Bells* (Calcutta, 1930); *What Shall We Believe? A Study in Christian Pramanas* (Madras, 1971).

transcends the personal. It is a corporate experience, man mingling with his fellowmen in order to attain the heights of God's love. It begins even in this life and does not wait for an indefinite future.[7]

It is clear that this interpretation of *moksa* both employs elements from Hinduism and also is set some distance from Hinduism. Appasamy distances himself from the traditional impersonal understanding of the word. Striking also is his use of the word "experience." In it resonates the Hindu theory of the three *pramanas* (standards of authority and truth): *sruti* (scripture), *anubhava* (experience), and *anumana* (logical inference or deduction). For Appasamy "experience" is encounter with Jesus Christ. Interpretation of the Bible, for him as for other Indian theologians, is oriented to the Christian life, to spirituality. In general these thinkers reject a purely scholarly handling of the Bible as a perverse Western luxury and a failure to recognize the Bible's true nature.[8]

Africa: Patrick Kalilombe

African Christians who have not been Westernized by their education and who are thus not estranged from their own cultural context often approach the Bible with questions and experiences that Western theologians find hard to understand. Something that usually plays a strong role in the approach of such Africans to the Bible is a strong feeling of attachment to their ancestors and to nature. Communion with one's ancestors is an important religious given, as is unity with the cosmic whole of creation, in which we have been placed. When Western Christianity comes in, it is often experienced as an assault on these original forms of communion. From this arises the need, when one takes the Bible in hand, to emphasize those aspects of it that resist this assault. So what is sought in the Bible is a God who accepts and confirms the African's experience of life and the world.

This produces, in the first place, a strong sense of kinship to the Old Testament. For many African independent churches the Old Testa-

---

7. *What is Moksa?* 6, cited by R. Boyd, *An Introduction to Indian Christian Theology* (Madras, 1975²) 123.

8. J. Pathrapankal, "Gottes Wort in der Begegnung mit Gottes Welt. Über die Aufgabe der Exegeten von Heute," *Zeitschrift für Missionswissenschaft und Religionswissenschaft* 66 (1982) 1-7; M. R. Spindler, "Recent Indian Studies of the Gospel of John: Puzzling Contextualisation," *Exchange* 27 (1980) 1-55; G. M. Soares-Prabhu, ed., *Wir werden bei ihm wohnen. Das Johannesevangelium in Indischer Deutung* (Freiburg im Breisgau, 1984).

ment is the only Bible. Sometimes this affinity is interpreted as both a preoccupation with dramas of origin and also a kinship with the notion of "corporate personality."[9] In any case many social structures seen in the Old Testament can be immediately identified with structures in African society.

This concern for finding in the Bible what relates to the African experience of life also leads to a heavy emphasis on creation as the original covenant that God made with all people, the covenant that underlies all other covenants (both "old" and "new") mentioned in Scripture. This accent on the covenant of creation is then used as a weapon against readings of the Bible that stress the exclusiveness of Israel and the church at the expense of other — "heathen" — traditional religions.

Patrick Kalilombe typifies this approach.[10] He resists a "missionary" reading of the Bible, in which paganism is assumed to be the enemy and in which a one-sided selection of texts is made, say, from deutero-Isaiah, in order to picture the Jewish people as withdrawn into a hard attitude toward unbelievers. Bible books like Ruth and Jonah emphasize entirely different perspectives, which, says Kalilombe, are further developed in the New Testament. Here is the evidence that God's love for his chosen nation does not exclude his love for other nations. Consequently, Israel and the church must be viewed as components of an all-embracing divine plan of salvation rooted in the original covenant of creation. Israel's election does not mean that this original covenant has been abolished. It points, rather, to an impulse to ensure that justice is done to that original covenant.

Kalilombe stresses that negative judgments concerning African traditional religions are often based on biblical studies as done by non-Africans. When Africans themselves undertake the study of the Bible they reject these frequently simplistic judgments as fundamentally at odds with one's relationship to one's ancestors, for whom the religion in question was a sacred matter. Just as Paul felt a close kinship with the Jews who rejected the gospel, and on account of that painful experience felt compelled to write a new "midrash" of Scripture, so the kinship of an African

9. B. Sundkler, *The Christian Ministry in Africa* (London, 1960) 284; B. Gaba, "Corporate Personality, Ancient Israel and Africa," in B. Moore, ed., *Black Theology: The South African Voice* (London, 1973) 65-73. See also E. Jansen Schoonhoven, "The Bible in Africa," *Exchange* 25 (1980) 1-48. Sometimes discontinuity is stressed: K. Dickson, "Continuity and Discontinuity between the Old Testament and African Life and Thought," in K. Appiah-Kubi and S. Torres, ed., *African Theology en Route* (Maryknoll, 1979) 95-108.

10. P. Kalilombe, "The Salvific Value of African Religions," *Afer* 21 (1979) 143-57, a lecture given during the first congress of African Old and New Testament scholars at Kinshasa, 1978.

Christian with his or her own tradition will shape his or her Bible exposition. The African Christian will assume that God was present as a benefactor in the faith and religious understanding of those ancestors. To be sure, this faith and understanding, too, remain subject to the judgment of God, but that is just as true of Judaism and Christianity. Only a point of view that takes account both of God's special choices and elections as well as his relationship with humankind as a whole can do justice to the whole of Scripture. Sometimes such a point of view has to be won back through the detour of partiality.

Latin America: Carlos Mesters

In our time the church in Latin America is not conceivable without the base Christian communities. The terrain of these communities is the countryside and the urban working class districts and slums. Their social base is that of common people. Their members are poor. Through the base communities the gospel reaches environments not accessible to the church in the past. These communities have thus become a sign of an alternative society, one in which an impersonal mass becomes a people and non-humans become persons.

The Bible has gained great importance in the base communities because in them people develop a dialogue between the word of God and their own life situations. In this "popular Bible movement" Carlos Mesters fulfills a pioneering role. He is a Carmelite trained as an exegete in Rome and Jerusalem and active in the archdiocese of Belo Horizonte in Brazil. He makes clear what is going on in the base communities in the following parable:[11]

> The Bible was a building where people went in and out every day and felt at home. On a certain day, however, learned people arrived who had heard of its beauty and antiquity. They received permission to investigate and made any number of discoveries of which the people knew nothing. As the building became famous and known all over the world, the people felt less at home in it. The building became a workshop for scholars and the people began to forget it. The entry became overgrown with weeds and was soon impossible to find. Only the side door was sometimes still used. After some time, however, an old beggar

11. H. Brandt, ed., *Die Glut kommt von Unten. Texte einer Theologie aus der Erde (Brasilien)* (Neukirchen, 1981) 9-15, quoted in J. T. Witvliet, "De Hebreeuwse Bijbel in Latijns Amerika. Het voorbeeld van Carlos Mesters," in K. A. Deurloo and F. J. Hoogewoud, ed., *Beginnen bij de letter Beth* (Kampen, 1985) 171-80.

looking for shelter stumbled on the closed main entry. He entered the building and was so surprised at what he saw that he told his friends of his discovery. The people came in droves, recognized the house as their own, and began, without paying an admission fee, to celebrate inside for days and nights at a time.

Mesters stresses Bible reading *of the people*. Such a reading has these characteristics:[12] The Bible is being discovered as the book of the community: People recognize themselves in the common life of the first Christians described in Acts, with all the positive and negative aspects of that experience. By way of this discovery they hear the word of God also in their own world. The shock of recognition occurs: "*We* are Abraham" or "This is *our own* land." Bible study becomes the means by which the transforming presence of God's Spirit is discovered in the reality of today. A sensitivity to the symbolic value of the stories told in the Bible — a sensitivity that North Atlantic people, in their estrangement from themselves in their contexts, have largely lost — is an important source of help here.

Mesters compares the method of interpretation that arises in this way with that of the Alexandrian church fathers, who searched for the allegorical sense of Scripture. For the "people's reading of Scripture" this means that their way of reading can no longer be neutral: The Bible receives its critical meaning from an original act of linking the suffering of one's own people to the suffering of the people of God. God is no longer the guarantor of the existing order but the liberator.[13] Consequently this use of the Bible is inseparably linked with practical orthodoxy, that is, with orthopraxy. This is a risky step because solidarity with the suffering entails the risk of martyrdom.

A final characteristic of this manner of reading described by Mesters is the link between it and spirituality, liturgy, and prayer. This unique way of handling Scripture is expressed in prayers, poems, songs, and liturgical texts. However ambivalent and disturbing "folk religiosity" in Latin America may be at times, it remains an important constituent in the "people's reading of Scripture."

12. C. Mesters, "How the Bible Is Interpreted in Some Basic Christian Communities in Brazil," in Küng and Moltmann, ed., *Conflicting Ways*, 41-46; *idem*, "The Use of the Bible in Christian Communities of the Common People," in S. Torres and J. Eagleson, ed., *The Challenge of Basic Christian Communities* (Maryknoll, 1981) 197-210; J. van den Berg, "De bijbel waarin armen zich herkennen," *Wereld en Zending* 16 (1987) 115-23; J. van Nieuwenhove, "Kerkelijke basisgemeenschappen in Brazillië," in J. van Lin, ed., *Parochie en Gemeenschap* (Hilversum, 1987) 74-97.

13. J. Severino-Croatto, *Exodus: A Hermeneutics of Freedom* (Maryknoll, 1981); T. D. Hanks, *God So Loved the Third World: The Bible, the Reformation and Liberation Theologies* (Maryknoll, 1983).

A clear example of this can be found in Mesters's treatment of the four songs of the suffering Servant in deutero-Isaiah. Consciously starting from the experience of Brazil's suffering people, Mesters has us read these four songs as descriptions of the mission of these people: "As Abraham, Moses, Sarai, and especially Jeremiah in their time were servants of God for the people, so now the people of bondage will be the servant of God, and not only for the survivors of Israel but for the whole of humanity."[14] Here again the experience of God's presence in one's own situation becomes the key in reading the Bible. This is a reversal of traditional hermeneutics.

Catholicity and Context

The Hermeneutical Problem

Hermeneutics is the attempt to bridge the gap between past and present from the perspective of understanding and interpretation.[15] One could perhaps describe this gap as the reflective relationship between one's own subjectivity and an alien subjectivity (one of the past). The issue is not only whether one can understand the alien subjectivity but especially whether — and if so, how — knowledge of truth then and knowledge of truth now are connected.[16]

The truth of salvation and deliverance does not come "straight down from above." It comes, rather, through the interpretive responses of the Old and New Testaments. Therefore, every reference to the "God of salvation" has had, from the beginning, a historical context, a *Sitz im Leben*.[17] Furthermore, a long period of time passed between the oral interpretive witness and the final written redaction. So the context of the witness also changed, and repeatedly, before the witness came into the written form that we possess. For the New Testament that means that we know Jesus only by way of the redemptive experience of his believing church.[18] And the New Testament preserves the recollection of Jesus from

14. C. Mesters, *Die Botschaft des Leidenden Volkes* (Neukirchen, 1982) 87, quoted in J. T. Witvliet, *op. cit.*, 175.

15. E. Schillebeeckx, *Geloofsverstaan. Interpretatie en Kritiek* (Bloemendaal, 1972; partially translated as *The Understanding of Faith: Interpretation and Criticism* [New York, 1974]); T. S. van Bavel, "Hermeneutische Knelpunten in een Theologisch Dispuut," *Tijdschrift voor Theologie* 20 (1980) 340-60.

16. Schillebeeckx, *op. cit.*, 17.

17. *Ibid.*, 13.

18. H. Berkhof, "Jezus Zelf en de Christelijke Gemeente als Criteria," in *Meedenken met Edward Schillebeeckx* (Baarn, 1983) 142 (133-45).

within different early church traditions: the Synoptic, Pauline, and Johannine traditions.

Therefore in this "preservation" of the witness the hermeneutical problem is already fully present. But one must also say that this preservation is itself the guarantee that the story of Jesus does not dissipate but is kept in its resistance to all our projections.

This process of preservation continues into every age and every situation, and with it all kinds of contextual data enter the interpretive witness. This is necessary if the text is to be intelligible and is to function as a new response of faith.

Community and Praxis

Once the hermeneutical problem has been formulated in this way, it becomes clear that in order for this historical process of interpretation to continue, a community is needed that fully shares in and remains constructively involved in a specific contextually conditioned experience of the world, while it preserves the recollection of Jesus. The church has always understood itself thus, though strictly speaking it is not the church itself that preserves the recollection but the "lifegiving (Holy) Spirit" who keeps the church centered on that recollection. The church celebrates the living presence of the remembered Jesus; recollection and confrontation with the living Word now together form a single activity.

But how is the church to do this? How can it be the direction-giving framework for the hermeneutical process? This question has been answered in different ways in history and has therefore occasioned considerable conflict. The churches of the Reformation have always asserted that the only thing the church can and may do is refer back to the authority of the one living and infallible Word contained in the books of the Old and the New Testaments. The Roman Catholic Church speaks in this connection of the necessary function of a teaching authority that can bind believers to certain interpretations. But neither of these "classical" responses makes the hermeneutical process superfluous. Both responses provide a way in which direction is given within the particular communion, which in one way or another will itself have to do the work of remembering and appropriation.

By saying this we have at the same time touched on the issue of "orthopraxy," that is, right conduct in addition to right belief. To cling to a recollection is also to follow a way. The truth, says John's Gospel, has to be done. In the message of the kingdom of God the goal is a new mode of human existence, a new community in which love, peace, righteousness, reconciliation, and deliverance from all the powers that hold people in spiritual and physical bondage take shape. Action, too, has a hermeneutical function, and sometimes concrete discipleship precedes understanding and interpretation.

Hermeneutics and Missiology

The functioning of the one Bible in many different contexts is a challenge to the catholic cohesiveness of the church. In a sense this state of affairs is not new, for the church has always been pluriform, even when it was under the dominance of Western culture. But the global pluralism of today poses a new challenge to theological reflection[19] in that now broader inferences have to be drawn from the idea that the Word of God is real only in the diversity of its reception. The result of "inculturation" is that the plurality of historical realities comes to stand in a relationship of tension with the direction-giving Word. This tension is intrinsic to the preaching of the gospel itself, as is evident from the New Testament. The gospel cannot and may not be presented as "dogmatic canned goods" but must be dealt with in the uniqueness of each human situation in such a way that an authentic response can follow. For that reason no single cultural context — Western or otherwise — can demand a monopoly in interpreting the gospel.

Therefore, the hermeneutical problem in missiology is that in the course of history a large number of different communities have arisen that — as they remember, celebrate, interpret, follow Christ, and act — all seek to do service to the ongoing proclamation of the one Word. In each of these communities the process of interpretation enshrined in Scripture itself is continued in a process of interpretation peculiar to that community: One recognizes the one process in the other. Usually that recognition is one-sided or shallow — but who can point out a process of interpretation anywhere in the history of the church or in contemporary Christianity where that is not the case? Corrections, additions, and deeper construals are always added in time.

Every individual process of interpretation thus issues in one ongoing living process of recollection and proclamation, even when the unity of recollection and proclamation is not explicitly recognized. In no case can the unity be imposed from the perspective of a single interpretation.

19. Cf. the twelfth of the fifteen theses of the international theological commission concerning the unity of the faith and the diversity of theology, *Archief van de Kerken* 28 (1973).

On the contrary, unity has become dependent on the possibility of effecting joint deliberation among all the different communities and their processes of interpretation, a conversation that is critical and enriching in all directions.

How such joint deliberation could function can be illustrated to some degree with the aid of two points from the examples given earlier in this chapter:

First, in the interpretation of the Bible, how does one deal with Israel?[20] How, and within what limits, do we identify ourselves with the people of the covenant? On this point the examples from Africa and Latin America that we have discussed show differing approaches, and they lead very concretely to different accents in the exegesis of deutero-Isaiah. How does one fit the stubborn fact of Israel into one's own history? Is Israel the beginning of a line of election on which first a specific nation, then "the suffering" in general, are accorded a special place? Or does Israel point to the breadth of God's concern for all people? What does it mean that Jesus belonged to Israel historically? What follows from an interpretation of, for instance, the Gospel of John, in which Jesus' identity as an Israelite is left out of consideration? To what degree does one thereby detach oneself from a concrete history of salvation?[21]

Second, what image of Christ is decisive when one practices "living recollection"? Is it the risen, exalted Lord or the historic, militant, and suffering Jesus? It makes a substantial difference where one chooses to begin. The history of Western Christian doctrine, by its use of a number of abstract Greek categories, has perhaps suppressed essential aspects of that recollection, aspects that are now being rediscovered elsewhere.[22] How are the Christ of mystical encounter, the Christ of neighborly love, and the Christ of the liberation of the poor related? Within what limits can one see "redemption" overlapping with "liberation"?

None of these questions is new in the history of Christianity. What is new is that now they are being posed within a global hermeneutical process. Interpretation of the Bible is no longer just a matter of a community dealing with the Word in its own context. It is now a matter of deliberation among communities listening to one another and correcting

20. Choan-Seng Song, "From Israel to Asia," in G. H. Anderson and T. F. Stransky, ed., *Mission Trends No. 3: Third World Theologies* (New York and Grand Rapids, 1976) 211-22; *idem, Third-Eye Theology: Theology in Formation in Asian Settings* (Maryknoll, 1979).

21. See A. Honig, "Reactie tegen heilshistorische theologie in Azië," *In de Waagschaal* 12 (1983) 297-304.

22. See especially J. Sobrino, *Christology at the Crossroads* (Maryknoll, 1978), chapters 10 and 11, and passim; A. Wessels, *Images of Jesus: How Jesus Is Perceived and Portrayed in Non-European Cultures* (Grand Rapids, 1990).

one another. More than ever before, hearing the Word and listening to each other are intertwined. In other words, the unity of Scripture is not available separately but must be linked to the unity of the church as a gift and a command. And in that linking of Scripture's unity with the church's unity it becomes apparent how tightly each different doctrinal emphasis applied in interpretation of Scripture is interwoven with the preoccupations of the interpretive context out of which it comes.

Unity of Scripture and Diversity of Interpretations

The last-mentioned point raises two questions, one concerning the relationship between biblical studies and contextual interpretation of the Bible, the other concerning the relationship between objective truth and subjective interpretation. These questions, too, are old, though they acquire a new profile in a missiological framework.

The examples of contextual use of Scripture cited above show clearly the tension between such use of Scripture and the work of professional exegetes. Biblical scholarship has developed, by means of historical and literary criticism, an impressive body of knowledge and methods, by means of which it would be compelled to make innumerable critical comments regarding ways of reading the Bible that posit intuitive connections between Scripture and the reader's context.

But from another perspective, Western biblical scholarship has been called a "perverse luxury," one that alienates common people from Scripture. This tension, which comes sharply to the fore in Mesters's parable, is a real problem. The Bible is and has always and everywhere been used as a "sacred book," as a source of wisdom, as a means of comfort and protection, as a mirror of daily joys and cares, and as a collection of useful maxims. Scholarly study of the origin of the Bible, of the different traditions and contexts that speak in it, of the literary structure of its texts and books, cannot be used as criteria by which to judge or restrict this multiform use of the Bible. What scholarship *can* do is make available and visible connections, backgrounds, and forgotten details and thus stimulate an open and inquiring attitude in reading Scripture. Scholarly discussion will certainly continue to have a place in the global conversation being carried on by Bible-interpreting communities, but not a place of central authority.

An approach sometimes taken to escape the confusion and the relativizing effect of a multiplicity of Bible interpretations is that of rigorously distinguishing between the truth objectively given in Scripture and the subjective coloring of that truth. This approach, though attractive, is not in the end one that will work. Basic to it is the idea of the Bible as a storage house of truth, which fails to do justice to the dynamics of the process of interpretation to which the Bible itself bears witness. Moreover, the line of demarcation between objective truth and subjective coloring can only be drawn as a line between one "subjective coloring" and another; to draw the line would therefore be to impose a single opinion.

Nonetheless, there is concealed here a correct intuition — the intuition that in the end the truth, authority, and inspiration of Scripture will triumph over the contextual gropings of human beings. Were that not the case, the search for unity and fellowship among all the world's Bible-readers, a search carried on in the perspective of a divine promise extending to the ends of the earth, would have no meaning at all. But how Scripture triumphs cannot be charted or canonized in advance. That victory is hidden in a history in which the divine word and human speech are intertwined.

We have thus come back to where this chapter began. The connection between the Bible as the central point of reference and the unity of the church — which in a sense served as the basis of our considerations and which seemed at first to disappear in the plurality of Bible-interpreting communities — returns at a higher level of complexity. We have found it again in an emphasis on the essential role of the community that deals with the gospel in interpretation and action and of conversation among communities in which augmentation and correction of individual interpretations can take place.

Only in such handling of Scripture is justice done to the fact that we are dealing with a historical word that enters human history and in that way keeps alive the hope that prompts Christians to keep moving "to the ends of the earth." These are essential perspectives for missiology.

CHAPTER 10

The People of God and the Ends of the Earth

L. A. HOEDEMAKER

Missio and Ecclesia: A New Link?

That the church is related to the whole world, that its origin has to do with a vision for the whole of humankind, in short that the church is "sent," is one of the fundamental givens of the Christian faith. In the church and in theology "mission" is a key word, and that has always been the case.

But that does not alter the fact that in the course of history the tension of origin and vision has been experienced in a great variety of ways, depending — of course — on the empirical reality of the church. When the church is a minority in a non-Christian or even anti-Christian environment, mission has a different look to it than when the church occupies a dominant place in a supportive culture.

It is at least premature, therefore, to link the key word "mission" closely to the idea of the expansion of Christianity's sphere of influence and number of adherents. This link is what the modern onlooker thinks of immediately, to be sure, but it can never be the point of departure for a principled perspective. There are many ways of relating to the world and to humanity that are not covered by the general characterization of mission as expansion. That there are only underscores the fact that the content and meaning of origin-as-mandate cannot be expressed in terms meant to be applicable to all times and situations. For that reason the usual linkage of mission to the sphere of expansion, discovery, conquest, and recruitment has to be regarded with suspicion, however little help the older standard works on mission history afford us in that respect.[1]

---

1. K. S. Latourette, *A History of the Expansion of Christianity* (7 vols.; New York, 1937-45); S. C. Neill, *A History of Christian Missions* (London, 1964).

It is true that the European discovery of the non-Western world and the associated movements of expansion have for centuries been the framework within which Christianity learned again to understand the fundamental world-relatedness of the church. Moreover, the context of that relearning has produced a large number of essential insights and experiences, which we cannot dispense with in our reflection on mission. But it would be shortsighted to equate that framework of expansion with mission. In a new experience of the world a fresh return to the origin of the church has to take place.

The twentieth century's radical changes in global relationships make such a return necessary. In this connection we are not surprised to learn that missiology as systematic scholarly reflection on mission got off the ground only at the beginning of the twentieth century.[2] The rise of missiological reflection has to do with two different experiences focused on the *world:*

- One has been the rise of global Christianity, that is, the expansion of Christianity particularly in non-Western cultures, with all the associated questions of cultural diversity and adaptation.
- The other has been the drift of Christianity into a network of global processes, namely, industrialization, relationships of economic dominance and dependence, cultural interchange, and the rise of non-Christian religions and non-religious ideologies.

At the cutting edge of these world experiences the word "world" must be almost immediately qualified, even beyond "non-Christian" and "non-Western" — which already represent considerable change from before the twentieth century.

But even mission itself, specifically the relationship between mission and church, becomes a problem. The modern missionary movement in a sense left the church undisturbed. Among Protestants the missionary movement was borne mainly by individuals or voluntary mission societies. Among Catholics it was borne by orders and congregations that opted especially for mission. Naturally, this situation could not simply continue. On the one hand, new churches arose on the mission field, churches that aspire toward equal partnership with the older churches. On the other hand, as a result of pressures from the new experiences of the world, a rediscovery of the church occurred within the older Christianity. This rediscovery implied new questions concerning the missionary relatedness of the church to its own environment.

---

2. G. Warneck, *Evangelische Missionslehre* (5 vols.; Gotha, 1892-1903); J. Schmidlin, *Katholische Missionslehre im Grundriss* (Münster, 1923[2]).

In our age this new complex of questions determines the agenda of the ecumenical movement. This movement arose not only from desire for the reconciliation of separated traditions or for a new social relevance of Christianity in a swiftly changing world. It was also nurtured by the modern missionary movement, with all the fresh insights, experiences, and problems that belong to it. Therefore, the ancient question of the relationship of mission and church comes back to us in the form of questions concerning the integration of mission and ecumenicity. These questions extend beyond the organizational problems involving the integration of the International Missionary Council with the World Council of Churches in 1961,[3] though these, too, were questions of fundamental principle.

We are dealing — as ecumenical development since the 1960s teaches us — with issues such as:

- the special identity of non-Western Christianity and non-Western theologies,
- the relationship between missionary and diaconal endeavors,
- dialogue with persons of other faiths,
- the need to stake out positions in questions of racism, poverty, and armament, and
- the question of how the legacy of the modern missionary movement can become fruitful in regard to each of these issues.

We are struggling, in short, to gain a new view of the relationship between the globalization of Christianity and the world-relatedness of the church.

In this connection just what do we envisage? A strong Christianity that can be a clear beacon in a chaotic world? Or a multiform Christianity that will be a sign of continuing "mission" precisely in its mobility? An evangelization movement with worldwide support? Or a process of communication in which global problems are made visible and processed in the light of the gospel? Clearly, broad and fundamental reflection is called for by these questions, and the local contextualization of mission and church is very much at stake in them.

In this ecumenical crucible the concept of mission is subjected to unheard-of expansion, so much so that according to some its content has become unrecognizable. It has been pulled out of the sphere of ethics, practical theology, and church order and into that of ecclesiology, from

---

3. M. Warren, "The Fusion of I.M.C. and W.C.C. at New Delhi," in *Zending op weg naar de toekomst. Essays aangeboden aan J. Verkuyl* (Kampen, 1978) 190-202; L. Newbigin, *Unfinished Agenda* (Grand Rapids, 1985).

the sphere of application to that of fundamental theology, so that the question concerning the foundation and substance of mission is posed much more radically than it was before. The same thing is happening with the idea of "church." The question "What is the church in the framework of God's total plan of salvation?" is raised because in the new experience of the world the church is no longer a self-evident part of one's own context. And this question takes us farther than simple definitions that have "the gathering of believers" or "the hierarchy" as their point of reference. Missiology and ecclesiology are being pulled toward each other.

Illustrations of this convergence in the twentieth century are not hard to come by. The Catholic missiologist Joseph Amstutz attempts to ground mission more deeply than did the classic view, which defined mission as the expansion of or planting of the hierarchical church in areas where it was not present before. That the church engages in mission flows from, Amstutz says, God's redemptive action in Christ, which is directed to all humankind and therefore calls for universal expression. Mission is the church's becoming present on its way toward that universal expression.[4] Conversely, in the ecclesiology of Hans Küng we encounter a strong accent on the idea that the church is not an end in itself, but, as the body of Christ, is caught up in a movement of the Holy Spirit that extends through all history and all humanity.[5] And Karl Rahner deduces the church and mission from "the incarnational dynamic of grace," which by definition ties in with questions concerning the salvation of all humanity — and the church is the forerunner and sacrament of that all-embracing process.[6]

On the Protestant side things seem at first even more complicated, since one cannot speak as freely of the continuity between church and humanity. But here, too, there is an undeniable convergence between missiology and ecclesiology. Missiologist Hans Werner Gensichen attempts in his work to subject the common Protestant reality of a non-missionary church alongside a non-ecclesiastical mission to a fundamental critique. In his work the dynamism of mission, though primary, cannot do without the church, precisely because the world shuts itself off from God's salvific will.[7] And the church cannot exist without mission because mission lifts the marks of the church above its own limitations. Karl Barth begins his great essay on the calling of the Christian commu-

---

4. J. Amstutz, *Kirche der Völker* (Freiburg, 1972) 95.
5. H. Küng, *The Church* (London, 1967).
6. K. Rahner, *Theological Investigations* X (New York, 1973) 3-49.
7. H. W. Gensichen, *Glaube für die Welt* (Gütersloh, 1971) 129-62.

nity[8] with a fundamental consideration of "the people of God in world history." Here he indicates that neither mission nor church is a starting point in theology: What is at issue is the structure of God's witness concerning himself. The Christian community is a provisional form of a calling that is extended to all of humanity.

It was especially the Second Vatican Council that gave authority and influence to these attempts to define church and mission anew in their mutual relatedness. The Dogmatic Constitution on the Church (*Lumen Gentium*) immediately introduces the issues of Christ and the nations and of the church as the sacrament of the unity of humankind. The decree on the church's missionary activity says that the church is missionary by its very nature because it has its origin in the sending of the Son and the Holy Spirit. Also significant are later documents based on these decrees, such as the apostolic exhortation *Evangelii Nuntiandi* (1975) and the report of the Latin American Bishops' Conference at Puebla (1979), which even more explicitly reflects the actual and fundamental involvement of the church in the problems of humanity.

On the Protestant side one can refer to the world mission conferences of the International Missionary Council and the World Council of Churches, especially those at Willingen (1952) and Melbourne (1980) — and to their evangelical counterparts at Lausanne (1974) and Pattaya (1980). In these conferences, too, we see evidence of how powerfully the fundamental intertwining of church and mission leads to new and concrete insights into the church's involvement in the world.

After all this one would expect a broad ecumenical consensus on the new connectedness of *missio* and *ecclesia*. The usual contemporary division of missionary theology into "Catholic," "ecumenical," and "evangelical"[9] shows, however, that the pressure of a common definition of the problem proves unable to raise our sights above the old dilemmas of fundamental theology. It is apparently no simple matter to link the total involvement of the church in world history and a global complex of problems to the idea that the church's mission is to involve people in God's history with the world. Here fundamental perspectives on salvation, world, and history are at stake.[10]

How then should the church today interpret the vision given with its origin? How is the church a missionary body?

---

8. K. Barth, *Church Dogmatics* IV/3/2 (Edinburgh, 1962) 681ff.

9. R. C. Bassham, *Mission Theology 1948-1975* (Pasadena, 1979); A. F. Glasser and D. A. McGavran, *Contemporary Theologies of Mission* (Grand Rapids, 1983).

10. T. Kramm, *Analyse und Bewährung theologischer Modelle zur Begründung der Mission* (Aachen, 1979).

- If it is and does so by defining itself in and over against the world as the bearer of a message of redemption and of a call to conversion, then one can focus on:
  - the church as a segment of the realized rule of God, which seeks expansion in the world,
  - or on mission as the act of raising the issue of the relation of judgment and grace between God and humankind, a process in which the church then emerges as a collection of converts.
- But if the church is missionary by showing in word and deed, in and on behalf of the world, what is at issue between God and humankind, then one can focus on
  - the church as an instance of the contextual assimilation of the problems of humankind and the world in the light of the gospel, which expresses itself in prophetic speech and diaconal demonstration,
  - or on mission as an active contribution to the humanization of the world, with the church as the basis of awakening and action.

One can trace all these accents in current missiological discussion. It is often suggested that they exclude each other because the answers to the search for a new link between church and mission that resonate in these emphases are fundamentally divergent. But must it be so? In many Third World theologies the possibility of combining these different perspectives is provisionally assumed. However this may be, the intensity that sometimes marks the discussion illustrates that no convincing formula for the integration of "mission" and "church" has as yet been found. Or perhaps we must use stronger words and say that the process of integration has become stuck.

The Concept of *Missio Dei:* Is It Helpful or Confusing?

God is the one who sends; church and mission do not have their origin in themselves or in each other but in God's "missionary" relatedness to the world and humankind. One finds this idea in all the positions sketched above. It serves to bring out sharply the convergence of missiology and ecclesiology, and it has great ecumenical value.

It is certain that in numerous difficult discussions on *missio* and *ecclesia* the term *missio Dei* has made possible a liberation from obsolete conceptual models and a deepening reflection on the world-relatedness of the church. But this does not alter the fact that it is an artificial device: A generally current concept (mission) is linked retrospectively with a dogmatic term *(missio)* that belongs to the theology of the trinity and is used primarily in a passive sense to refer to the "sentness" of the Son and the Spirit.[11] What is gained by this retrospective linkage is not immediately clear. If the purpose is to stress the sovereignty and independence of God's work of redemption, the linking of two heterogeneous notions of *missio* is confusing.

The cradle of the *missio Dei* concept is sometimes identified as the world mission conference of Willingen (1952). But it was not used there.[12] It does occur in a commentary on Willingen by the German missiologist Karl Hartenstein.[13] But he had used the term already in 1934, apparently under the influence of Karl Barth, who in a lecture on mission in 1928 had connected mission with the doctrine of the trinity.[14] Barth and Hartenstein want to make clear that mission is grounded in an intratrinitarian movement of God himself and that it expresses the power of God over history, to which the only appropriate response is obedience. The reference to the theology of the trinity apparently functions as an instance of the crisis motif in early dialectical theology: Over against God as the real subject of history human activity has no leg of its own on which to stand.

The trail that leads to Hartenstein's theology takes us next to European biblical-theological discussions of salvation history and eschatology, in which Oscar Cullmann played an especially important role.[15] In these discussions mission becomes an aspect of the coming of the kingdom of God rather than an aspect of the expansion of the church. Mission is situated in the "interim" between the first and second comings of Christ. In salvation-historical terms mission and church stand together between Israel and the *parousia*. In this perspective *missio Dei* means that God himself actualizes the coming of his kingdom. Mission consists in waiting and possibly preparing for that coming.

These ideas were by no means dominant at Willingen. One has to conclude that Hartenstein too quickly identified the references at Willin-

---

11. H. H. Rosin and G. van Winsen, *Missio Dei, term en functie in de zendingstheologische discussie* (Leiden, 1971).

12. N. Goodall, ed., *Missions under the Cross: Addresses and Statements of Willingen 1952* (London, 1953).

13. K. Hartenstein, "Theologische Besinnung," in W. Freytag, ed., *Mission zwischen Gestern und Morgen* (Stuttgart, 1952).

14. G. Schwarz, *Mission, Gemeinde und Oekumene in der Theologie Karl Hartensteins* (Stuttgart, 1980) 130; K. Barth, "Die Theologie und die Mission in der Gegenwart," *Zwischen den Zeiten* 10 (1932) 204 (189-215).

15. O. Cullmann, *Christ and Time* (Philadelphia, 1950); see in general L. Wiedenmann, *Mission und Eschatologie, eine Analyse der neueren deutschen evangelischen Missionstheologie* (Paderborn, 1965).

gen to "God's mission" (via the *missio Dei* concept) with the European theological background. Later, when the concept gained general currency in missiology, especially as a result of G. F. Vicedom's book,[16] this identification again disappeared. What survived was a general formula that symbolizes the fact that precritical and in a sense pretheological discourse on mission (in what is called "the Warneck era") is past. And in fact the boundary line *was* marked by Willingen.

The concept of *missio Dei* has had salutary effects on systematic missiology at two points. In the first place, over against all ambivalent and depressed historical forms of mission it stresses that church and mission are rooted in being sent, that ultimately the issue is not the defense, extension, and expansion of "the church" or "Christianity" but participation in the world-relatedness of God himself, in which all historical forms are merely instrumental.[17] Admittedly, such a statement must immediately be qualified by our saying that the word *missio* thus suffers some loss of substance. It could easily be linked with an assortment of historical movements, such as "humanization" or "revolution" in the 1960s or "liberation" in the 1970s, or it could become the designation of a generalized relationship between God and humanity that makes specific mission work virtually superfluous. In both instances, continuity with the concrete history of the church's world-relatedness becomes vague.

Add to this that in the course of years the flag of *missio Dei* has been flown on ships carrying a broad range of cargoes. We have already mentioned the radical eschatological school of Hartenstein and Cullmann. There, in an attenuated and derived sense, *missio Dei* becomes a synonym for the continuing salvation history of God's election-to-mission from Abraham up to and including the church.[18] But the concept can also refer to a dynamic relatedness of the kingdom of God to the world in which the church is no more than a function of apostolate and a self-emptying messenger of shalom.[19] In the thinking of others, including evangelicals, it refers to a fundamental distinction between salvation history and world history.[20] Diametrically opposed to this is, for instance, the American preparatory report for the Willingen conference,[21] in which we are told

16. G. F. Vicedom, *Missio Dei, Einführung in eine Theologie der Mission* (Munich, 1958).

17. J. C. Hoekendijk, "Notes on the Meaning of Mission(ary)," in T. Wieser, ed., *Planning for Mission* (New York, 1966) 37-48.

18. J. Blauw, *Gottes Werk in dieser Welt* (Munich, 1961).

19. J. C. Hoekendijk, "Zur Frage einer missionarischen Existenz," appendix in *Kirche und Volk in der deutschen Missionswissenschaft* (Munich, 1967) 297-354.

20. G. Sautter, *Heilsgeschichte und Mission* (Giessen, 1985) 159.

21. See the summary in P. L. Lehmann, "The Missionary Obligation of the

that "God's mission" is to be observed in world history. Finally, the Catholic idea that the church is the sacrament of the unity of humankind is also sometimes linked with the concept of *missio Dei*. In other words, the confusion is complete.

The second salutary effect of the *missio Dei* concept lies in the attempt to provide mission with a broader theological basis, specifically a trinitarian foundation. This effect is free from any direct connection of the term with the theology of the trinity. It arises especially from the fact that in *missio Dei* one hears more notes than in a christological or ecclesiological narrowing of mission: Notes from creation theology and pneumatology are included. Mission thus comes to be more clearly linked with the entire horizon of created reality and with the renewing power of the Spirit, who works in people as well as in historic movements. In this regard the Willingen conference did give missiology some movement forward — though it must immediately be added that the trinitarian terminology of the official Willingen report conceals a contrast between the approach of the American preparatory report (mission is the response to what the triune God is doing in the world) and more classic salvation-historical approaches. The conclusion that here we have reached a balanced relationship between mission and church seems, in any case, premature.[22]

All in all, the harvest has been poor. The formula *missio Dei* marks a transition toward a new discussion, toward an attempt to bring mission and church together in a new theological connection. But it is too open in all directions to be fruitful for a treatment of the problems described in the first section of this chapter. The polarization of "ecumenical" and "evangelical" shows that. On the one hand, continuity with the missionary movement evaporates because everything God does in the world is called mission. Organized "mission" remains then as a relic amidst involvement with diaconate, development, liberation, and dialogue. On the other hand, the peculiar content of mission is so anxiously protected against the implications of recent world events that the whole problem of integration actually remains untouched.

In order to rescue the salutary effects of the concept of *missio Dei* with a view to that integration, we will have to attempt to make further progress with a number of the questions referred to above, questions that are hidden behind the general discussion of *missio Dei*. We are concerned here specifically with questions concerning the relationship between sal-

---

Church," *Theology Today* 9 (1952) 20-38. For the opposite position, see Sautter, *op. cit.*, 137, 139f.

22. W. Andersen, *Towards a Theology of Mission* (London, 1955).

vation history and concrete human history, church and Israel, and kingdom of God and humanity. Unless we address these questions, the new
link between *missio* and *ecclesia* will remain vague.

Israel and the Nations

The development of the church's experience of the world, which was
referred to in the first part of this chapter, has not stood still. Much more
than when the International Missionary Council and the World Council
of Churches were being united and when the Second Vatican Council was
occurring, the ecumenical movement has become the instrument that reg-
isters that experience of the world and makes it possible for the churches
to understand it. In the ecumenical movement the church itself assumes
a global form. In that global form — a network of communication among
Christians and churches that, each in its own situation, give shape to their
world-relatedness — the world is made present to the church in a manner
that did not exist until now. This globalism of the church is the context in
which new life is being breathed into the process of integration of mission
and ecumenicity, which had slowed down. Then the question will no
longer be: How can the missionary movement and the ecumenical movement be integrated? It will be, rather: Under what conditions can the global
church be viewed as a missionary church?

It is especially the emancipation of Third-World Christianity and
Third-World theology, with their incisive questions about history and
about the ideological biases of Western Christianity, that completes and
shapes the globalism of Christianity and thus makes inevitable the end of
the mindset of expansion.[23] The "ends of the earth" are no longer beyond
the horizon. Nor are they what is sought in a journey of discovery: As
vision and mandate they are made present in the global reality of the
church. Of course, in a sense "the world church" is a fiction, as is "the
unity of humankind." But both fictions are needed to do justice to the
church's new experience of the world and to link the eschatological tension
belonging to the legacy of the missionary movement with that experience.
Without that tension, the church's global existence would fade into a
universal human datum. Global existence must be seen in the light of a
promise of unity and blessing, which is linked, biblically speaking, with

---

23. Cf. especially the EATWOT publications mentioned elsewhere in this book.
On mission and ecumenicity see C.-S. Song, *Christian Mission in Reconstruction* (Madras,
1975), and J. Míguez Bonino, "A 'Third World' Perspective on the Ecumenical Movement," *Ecumenical Review* 34 (1982) 115-23.

the relationship between God and his people, which involves judgment and faithfulness.

In this reordering of tradition and experience, is it possible to raise again the question of the connection between mission and church? To do so would imply that attention is needed again to the rootedness of the church in God's covenant with Israel and in the tension between that *particular* covenant and "all nations." The implication is not that the church ushers in a new phase that leaves "the Israel phase" behind but that the church becomes the expression of the tension between the particular covenant and the universal kingdom and is in that way, by definition, "mission." It is specifically in the church's global form that it can evoke that tension and that it can, with regard to every local form of world-relatedness, heighten awareness of what is actually going on with humanity. In other words, global communication is necessary for the church's world-relatedness, which can, however, only be embodied locally.

Remarkably enough, recent discussions concerning the theological significance of Israel have barely penetrated systematic missiology.[24] Still, the growing consensus rejecting the "replacement" theory, according to which the church "replaces" Israel as the bearer of the covenant, is of paramount importance for the discussion of the relation between church and mission. The issue is, after all, the interpretation of the manner in which "the nations" come into view in the New Testament. Is this opening toward the Gentiles a consequence of Israel's turning away? Or does the question concerning this opening have to be raised *within* Israel and thus be seen as a problem of the identity of the covenant people in the context of and relation to the great whole of humankind? Viewed thus, the problem is old as well as new: It is old because it is a theme seen especially in the prophets in their endeavor to make the covenant between Israel and its God relevant and effective. It is new because it undergoes an unprecedented radicalization in the ministry and history of Jesus. Whether the covenant can genuinely and consistently be lived, whether *shalom* can be genuinely realized, is a question that comes up, in the way of Jesus, as a radical question concerning the very foundations of humanness, as a question of lostness and faith, of guilt and forgiveness, of death and

---

24. A. G. Honig, *What Is Mission? The Meaning of the Rootedness of the Church in Israel for a Correct Concept of Mission* (Kampen, 1982). For a sampling of the literature in systematic theology see M. Stöhr, ed., *Jüdische Existenz und die Erneuerung der christlichen Theologie* (Munich, 1981); P. von der Osten-Sacken, *Grundzüge einer theologie im christlich-jüdischen Gespräch* (Munich, 1982); C. Thoma, *Die theologischen Beziehungen zwischen Christentum und Judentum* (Darmstadt, 1982); P. M. van Buren, *Discerning the Way* (New York, 1980); *idem, A Christian Theology of the People of Israel* (New York, 1983).

resurrection. It is also thus a question in which the limits of the usual religious and national systems are "automatically" exceeded. The final question concerning humanity and world has been posed, and in that sense the kingdom of God has come very near.

On that line, the point of contact between covenant and the kingdom of God, the church appears as the beginning of a learning process in which — how could it be otherwise? — all nations are involved. Israel remains, as Paul asserts at length in the letter to the Romans; it is not discarded. On the contrary, the way of Israel, the way of the covenant, is laid down as a question and a claim before and in the midst of all nations. *That* is mission.

This does not mean that Christians have an answer where Israel was left with an open question. It means that the question posed within Israel is for the church the starting point for continual conversion and for an expectation that reaches to the ends of the earth. By saying that, we are by no means losing sight of the fact that alongside the church Israel has continued to travel a road of its own, on which it deals with the question and the promise of the covenant in its own way. The appearance of the church does not stamp the way of Israel as an obsolete or dead-end road. The two roads, in virtue of their content and direction, remain related.

We cannot answer in this chapter every question evoked by this train of thought. The most important point here is that the church not only has its start geographically and historically in Israel but is also rooted materially in the question and promise of the covenant. The advantage of this approach is that in the world-relatedness of the church we are not so much dealing with a new religious way but with the concrete claim of the covenant, that is, with exodus from slavery, with conflict with the gods who seek to redomesticate existence, with distrust toward concentrations of power, and with consistent care for the widow, the orphan, and the stranger. The church does not start at square one. When the the Holy Spirit was poured out, the apostles immediately referred back to the prophets of Israel. The church keeps alive and reproduces God's controversy with his people in the midst of and with a view to "all nations" from the perspective of the end that has come near, the imminent rule of God. In the convergence of these lines in the birth of the church and subsequently in numerous historical situations where "faith" begins or is revived, one discovers what "Holy Spirit" means: It is the actualization of the judgment, the faithfulness, and the dawning rule of the God of the covenant.

The fact that the church is situated in the midst of all peoples, cultures, nations, and religions comes to expression precisely in its global form. For this form is its best defensive and offensive weapon in the fight against being identified with particular peoples, cultures, nations, religions, classes, or races. In other words, the global existence of the church is what enables the church to keep alive the expectation of the unity of humankind from within the covenant.

The unity of humankind is not a natural or historical datum. For the time being we know only negative manifestations of this unity: world wars, balances of terror, economic domination, and the networks of the drug trade. Besides, the term "unity" evokes associations with ideologies in which this unity is viewed as the end result of a specific historical struggle or is equated with uniformity in accordance with certain principles. But still we cannot forget that the unity of humankind is also a promise and an expectation given with the covenant between God and his people. In the light of this truth the global church is called to hold before the world the promise of the covenant, the judgment and faithfulness of God, precisely where the conflict between reality and the promise is most acute, that is, where people suffer because of humankind's *dis*unity. *That* is mission.

The church's world-relatedness implies that God's judgment, faithfulness, and future are explained to people amid the concrete tensions between human reality and the promised unity of humankind, amid, that is, the tensions in which people live. This explanation does not arise from superior knowledge but from a process of conversion, a process in which God's judgment, faithfulness, and future are observed and assimilated anew. And this takes place very emphatically within global communication. To speak of mission as "communication of the message of the gospel" is justified if that definition is combined with this broader process. When we communicate the gospel we are not simply transmitting information: The objective is to reproduce the covenant question concerning the unity of humankind and therefore to maintain a learning process in which all the partners are fully involved and which can take any number of forms. Missionaries both Protestant and Catholic have understood and practiced this through the centuries, even though we have not dealt with it much in theological reflection.

The idea that pneumatology, the doctrine of the Holy Spirit, can play an important role in that reflection has already been suggested. According to the biblical witness, the lines of the covenant question (as it is radicalized by Jesus), of the dawning rule of God, and of the groaning of all creation come together in the Holy Spirit.[25] In other words, when we

---

25. A. A. van Ruler, *Theologie van het apostolaat* (Nijkerk, 1954), especially ch. 3; J. V. Taylor, *The Go-Between God: The Holy Spirit and the Christian Mission* (London, 1972); A. M. Aagaard, "Missio Dei in katholischer Sicht," *Evangelische Theologie* 34 (1974) 420-33; C. Schütz, *Einführung in die Pneumatologie* (Darmstadt, 1985) 24, 30f., 254f.

call the church "the communion of the Holy Spirit," we are touching the core of its missionary identity. Whenever the church makes a connection between its concrete experiences and analyses of the world, on the one hand, and the judgment and future of God, on the other, the process of conversion, which is the golden thread connecting church and mission, is activated. This may involve very personal experiences of guilt and forgiveness, death, and life or weighty global realities of poverty and violence. But at every point we are dealing with a humanity over which the promise of unity has been pronounced and a church called to link that humanity with the memory of the covenant and the expectation of the kingdom of God.

The "communication of the gospel" was described above as taking place first in the church itself, both locally and globally, which thus bears witness. That is not to say that communication with "others," with the innumerable people who do not know the gospel, disappears from view. On the contrary, the two forms of communication — if we need to distinguish them — presuppose each other. The world-relatedness of the church embraces, by definition, the process of adding links to a continuing chain, of broadening the field, of involving more experiences and more situations and hence more people in the web of communication. For the church it is essential that that movement continue, drawing ever wider circles.

In the light of everything that has been said above, one could distinguish two aspects in that continuing process of communication. In the first place we are dealing with a dialogical openness toward others and an acceptance of others that presupposes and reflects the faithfulness of God and draws already on a "unity of humankind" in which all barriers have been cleared away. And in the second place, when we speak of our encounter with others, we are dealing with our own conversion, a conversion that presupposes and mirrors the judgment of God and the critical questions of the covenant and already draws on a "unity of humankind" in which justice and peace go together. The first of these two aspects of this communication — openness and acceptance — is a hopeful anticipation of the possibility that in other situations and among other people the conversion process will begin and that thus the circle of communication will be extended. The second aspect — one's own conversion — is a hopeful anticipation of real openness and acceptance on the part of the other.

These distinctions are necessary in order to modify an overly simple idea of mission, one that has not gone through the learning process of the ecumenical movement, and in order to link an overly simple idea of church and ecumenicity, one that neglects the legacy of the missionary movement, with the essential eschatological perspective of that legacy.

Communication between Christians and non-Christians is never "pure." Religious, cultural, social, and political understandings of what constitutes "humanity" always play a part, and we cannot speak in isolation from them. It would not even be good to try. For it is precisely in those understandings that we are dealing with the tension between the world and the kingdom of God.

Missio Ecclesiae: **A Postscript**

In this chapter I have attempted to describe the impact of the globalization of Christianity upon our understanding of mission and our understanding of the relationship between mission and church. And I have attempted to advance the discussion — at least on a few points — that is being conducted in line with this development. In this connection I have assumed that it is no longer possible to speak of mission without taking account of the ecumenical movement and that, conversely, an ecumenical movement that fails to integrate consciously the legacy of the missionary movement remains incomplete. Although I have of course made use of elements from earlier theological discussions — especially those associated with and occasioned by the world missionary conference of Willingen — I have come to the conclusion that the term *missio Dei,* which has usually been pivotal in the discussions that have happened, does not really help us. And I have pleaded for a more historical approach with the aid of ideas like covenant judgment and covenant faithfulness, the rule of God, and Holy Spirit and for inquiry into the manner in which the new experience of the church's global reality can bring these biblical ideas into a new coherence and confer new relevance on them.

That in the process the concept of *missio* has somewhat receded into the background, or at least no longer occupies a key position, does not imply a denial of the basic perspective that the church is "sent." On the contrary: That the church is sent means that the inner dynamic of being a church and the world-relatedness of the church coincide. That is to say at the very minimum that it is impossible to view "mission" as one of the many activities of the church grounded along with other activities in a comprehensive ecclesiology defined apart from the church's world-relatedness. It is equally impossible to regard the church as a secondary datum by comparison with the ongoing movement of mission and evangelization. For the process of conversion, which the missionary vision of the ends of the earth evokes from within the covenant between God and his people, constitutes the very content of what it is to be the church.

CHAPTER 11

Standing under the Missionary Mandate

R. H. Matzken

This short chapter is a commentary on the preceding chapter. Here I wish to present an alternative theological interpretation, one that does not separate mission from the divine mandate and does not isolate and alienate Western missiology from the fulfillment of the missionary mandate on six continents.

Beginning in Willingen (1952) and Ghana (1958) an attempt has been made to transform the concept of "realized eschatology" (which is akin to "the theology of hope") into that of "realized evangelism." "Realized evangelism" is understood as the recognition that the "full and perfect atonement" of Christ has already saved Christians and non-Christians alike.[1] Peters calls this concept "neo-universalism" and observes that this salvation of all humankind is included in the *missio Dei* in and with the world.[2]

How is it that concepts like "being saved," "being lost," and "eternal life" have become so problematic — first in theology and then in missiology? This has come about from the idea of the church as a universal salvific institution and from the "replacement" theory, that is, the idea that the church stands now in the place of Israel. But these ideas have no basis in the Bible: There the uniqueness of Christ's church and its distinction from Israel in past, present, and future are made clear (e.g., in Romans 9–11).

The basis of this thinking lies, rather, in the work of the early church Fathers, in Augustine and Aquinas, and in the Reformers Luther and Calvin. It proceeds from concepts against which there is today extreme reaction, such as the concept *katholikos*. The original meaning of this word is "universal," "for all." It was first used of the church by Ignatius of Antioch. This term implies, in fact, that beside the universal church there

---

1. A. Johnston, *The Battle for World Evangelism* (Wheaton, 1978) 84-88.
2. G. Peters, *A Biblical Theology of Missions* (Chicago, 1972) 336-39.

cannot be anything else. Otherwise, the church would not be universal! Accordingly, in its deepest meaning the term is "absolute" and therefore intolerant: By definition nothing else can exist for God but "the catholic church," and so all Christians outside that church, however "puritan" or "cathar" (both words imply purity) they might be, are declared apostate and heretical.[3]

Naturally, in this time of ecumenical and global awakening, such a concept, which led with historical necessity to ecclesiastical imperialism, can no longer be used. The evangelical "low church" alternative has always been the starting point for Protestant missions. In the missionary consultation that has been held for years in Gunterstein (Breukelen) this difference in starting point comes clearly to the fore. Mission and evangelization is a matter of "saving people" "out of the sea of the world into the ark of salvation" (I. H. Enklaar, past rector of the Hendrik Kraemer Institute at Oegstgeest).

But others have a much broader view of mission: They see it as "the reclamation of the sea of the world," hence not as an exclusive but as an inclusive process.

There are, therefore, many views of mission. This comes to the fore in, for instance, the Seoul Declaration of the Asian Theological Association.[4] We can distinguish:

missio ecclesiae: the expansion of the church as a unique salvific institution, Catholic, high church, and anti-ecumenical,

missio Christi: the proclamation of the saving death and justifying resurrection of Christ, which he commanded his disciples to give (Matt. 28:16-20), as in the Lausanne Covenant of 1974 and the Seoul Declaration of 1975, and

missio Dei: God's "missionary" relatedness to the world and humanity, which was later implied in the ideas of neo-universalism (Peters), "realized evangelism," and "wholism" (Johnston).

Among evangelicals the *missio Christi* is seen as the only biblically legitimate form of mission, based as it is on the missionary mandate that

3. E. H. Broadbent, *The Pilgrim Church* (London, 1931) 15, 62, 85, 89, 97; cf. R. H. Matzken, *Handelingen der Gemeente* (2 vols.; Kampen, 1985-86) I, 54.
4. Matzken, *Handelingen* II, 145-47; cf. Bong-Rin Ro and R. Eshenauer, ed., *The Bible and Theology in Asian Contexts* (Taichung, 1984) 21-27.

Christ extended to the apostles and hence to the church. By assuming this position evangelicals have always been opposed to all forms of *missio ecclesiae*, in which an identification with the church as salvific institution was both the goal and the starting point of mission.[5]

"Evangelical" in this connection is not the name of a new fundamentalist sect but a word that describes that in which Christians and missionaries of all kinds of churches will recognize themselves once they know and understand its essence. It means, first of all, that the Bible is expressly recognized as God's infallible Word ("inerrancy"). While this position is under assault from all directions, it means that its adherents reflect with thoroughness not only on the Bible itself but also on the instruments that exist to interpret the Bible, such as the original languages and scholarly hermeneutics. Besides this, but with no less emphasis, evangelicals lay stress on the individual's personal relationship to the Lord Jesus Christ, in whom alone there is salvation, and on the necessity that before the return of Christ Christians take the gospel into the whole world.[6]

Christians and churches from the Third World (the former mission fields) have pointed out to us the one-sidedness of Western theology, that it is too rationalistic, too secularized, and too individualistic.[7] They have shown us the failures and errors of the churches and their missionary methods. The question is now how we are respond to this. Is the response to be a humbling of self and a catharsis so that we can proceed jointly on the basis of a new partnership (as in the Asian Theological Association) — or a moratorium and *kenosis* of institutional mission as such, a decision in which not only Western but also biblical thinking is discarded, as for example, in Chinese theology, in the movement of dialogue with world religions, and in "post-Holocaust theology."

In the view represented in the preceding chapter by L. A. Hoedemaker and expressed also in Vatican II, we encounter a response to the present untenability of the *missio ecclesiae*, but with no break with the "neo-katholikos" thinking that views humankind as a unity. "Neo-katholikos" obviously requires further explanation: *Katholikos* assumes that humanity belongs to the *massa perditionis*, the mass of the lost (Thomas Aquinas, the Council of Florence), until it has gained access to the sacrament, which can only be administered by the priests of the Catholic Church as an expression of Christ's ministry on earth. The church's aim

---

5. This important theme comes to expression in Broadbent (see especially the preface by F. F. Bruce) and in Matzken, *Handelingen* I.

6. From the prospectus of Tyndale Theological Seminary at Badhoevedorp.

7. Ro and Eshenauer.

is, therefore, conversion of the mass of humankind. *Neokatholikos* recognizes that this view no longer fits in today's worldview, that the concepts "church" and "Christianity" are historically conditioned and fail to take account of the results of the modern science of religion as they have emerged in, for instance, dialogue with other living world religions (so Panikkar, Rahner, and many others). The old concept of mission as *missio ecclesiae* is now, therefore, elevated to a higher level: that of *missio Dei*, becoming thus a mission for all humankind.

In this, developments in theology run parallel to developments in sociology and the political sciences and are seen in, for instance, the books of Peter Beyerhaus[8] and in an idea that has not yet been dealt with in the present book, that of *One World–One Religion?* (the theme of the International Confessional Congress at Zurich, September, 1987), that is, the syncretistic threat to our faith known as "New Age" religion. For this reason leading evangelical theologians and missiologists reject *missio Dei* as an understanding of mission and stress the *missio Christi* concept, which is rooted in the missionary command (Matt. 28:16-20; Mark 16:14-18; Luke 24:46-49; John 20:21-23; Acts 1:6-8).

We refer to a tendency among some Christians who think that they alone possess the truth, that they are on their way to heaven, and that they constitute the only true church. Often this posture is marked by a settledness that is averse to the dynamism and confusion of "the evil world" and by an emphasis on inwardness and liturgy. Examples of this are some Orthodox churches, such as the Greek Orthodox Church and parts of the Coptic Church, but this mentality also occurs in Western Europe and North America. With the title chosen for his chapter, "The People of God and the Ends of the Earth," Hoedemaker has emphatically — and correctly — placed us into this tension, though perhaps he could have linked "the eschaton (ends) of the earth" more closely with "the eschaton of time" as in Acts and thus given sharper focus to his quotations from Cullmann and his view of Israel.

The evangelical movement operates in the same tension. In fact, being in this tension is inherent in the whole notion of evangelicalism. The Salvation Army adopted the slogan "saved to save," and Paul wrote that we are "reconciled in order to reconcile" (2 Cor. 5). Evangelical Christians are strongly oriented to and involved in mission and evangelization. Their focus, as always, is the *missio Christi*, which calls people to Christ from an antithetical position. Mission is therefore a calling out, which proceeds

---

8. *Bangkok '73: The Beginning or End of World Mission?* (Grand Rapids, 1974); *Reich Gottes oder Weltgemeinschaft?* (1975); *Ideologien. Herausforderung an den Glauben* (1979).

from the divine mandate, of people to the one who is Lord and Savior. This is a matter not of choice, as Hoedemaker posits (it is clear where his choice lies), but of obedience to the intelligible Word of God.

Nor is standing under this missionary mandate a matter of a "realized rule of God" — neither "realized eschatology" nor even "realized evangelization." It is a matter of "working while it is day," until Christ returns, until the ends of the earth as well as until the end of time. To illustrate this movement we can quote the concluding article of the Lausanne Covenant, which was formulated in 1974 by three thousand evangelical leaders:

> We believe that Jesus Christ will return personally and visibly, in power and glory, to consummate his salvation and his judgment. This promise of his coming is a further spur to our evangelism, for we remember his words that the Gospel must first be preached to all nations. We believe that the interim period between Christ's ascension and return is to be filled with the mission of the people of God, who have no liberty to stop before the End. We also remember his warning that false Christs and false prophets will arise as precursors of the final Antichrist. We therefore reject as a proud, self-confident dream the notion that man can ever build a utopia on earth. Our Christian confidence is that God will perfect his kingdom, and we look forward with eager anticipation to that day, and to the new heaven and earth in which righteousness will dwell and God will reign forever. Meanwhile, we rededicate ourselves to the service of Christ and of men in joyful submission to his authority over the whole of our lives.[9]

9. John Stott, *The Lausanne Covenant: Exposition and Commentary* (Minneapolis, 1975) 56.

CHAPTER 12

Models for a Theology of Religions

J. van Lin

Christians and People of Other Faiths

The central concern of a "theology of religions" is to formulate, theoretically as well as practically, general and specific foundational ideas on the basis of which, in divergent contexts, Christians can determine their relationship to people of other living faiths. Here our concern is mainly with three foundational ideas that now play the most important roles in determining this relationship and in defining the missionary mandate that Christians have to fulfill in relation to these people.[1] In elaborating these ideas, two questions are of central importance: How, on the basis of faith

---

1. See, e.g., J. van Lin, *Protestantse Theologie van de Godsdienten. Van Edinburgh naar Tambaram 1910-1937* (Assen, 1974); G. Vallée, *Mouvement oecuménique et religions non chrétiennes. Un débat oecuménique sur la rencontre interreligieuze. De Tambaram à Uppsala 1938-1968* (Tournai, 1975); D. Amalorpavadass, *Research Seminar on Non-Biblical Scriptures* (Bangalore, 1975); D. G. Dawe and J. B. Carman, ed., *Christian Faith in a Religiously Plural World* (New York, 1978); T. Emprayil, *The Emerging Theology of Religions: The Contribution of the Catholic Church in India* (Padra, 1980); P. Rossano, "Christ's Lordship and Religious Pluralism," in *Mission Trends No. 5: Faith Meets Faith*, ed. G. H. Anderson and T. F. Stransky (New York and Grand Rapids, 1981) 20-35; A. Race, *Christians and Religious Pluralism* (London, 1983); H. Coward, *Pluralism: Challenge to World Religions* (New York, 1985); P. F. Knitter, *No Other Name? A Critical Survey of Christian Attitudes Toward the World Religions* (Maryknoll, 1985); W. Ariarajah, *The Bible and People of Other Faiths* (Geneva, 1985); G. D'Costa, *Theology and Religious Pluralism* (Oxford, 1986); A. Camps, *Partners in Dialogue: Christianity and Other Religions* (Maryknoll, 1983); L. Swidler, ed., *Toward a Universal Theology of Religion* (New York, 1987); L. Swidler, J. B. Cobb, P. F. Knitter, and M. Hellwig, ed., *Death or Dialogue? From the Age of Monologue to the Age of Dialogue* (New York, 1990); J. Sanders, *No Other Name: An Investigation into the Destiny of the Unevangelized* (Grand Rapids, 1992); F. A Sullivan, *Salvation outside the Church? Tracing the History of the Catholic Response* (London, 1920); J. H. Pranger, *The World Council of Churches and the Challenge of Religious Plurality between 1967 and 1979* (Utrecht and Leiden, 1994).

in the good news of Jesus of Nazareth — confessed by his followers to be the Christ — should, according to these three approaches, the relationships between Christians and people of other faiths be characterized? And what then are the consequences, in both content and method, for the definition and realization of the Christian missionary mandate?

We will let three main models for answering these questions speak for themselves. As we do so, it will become clear that christology is of greatest importance in all three. Whenever in the theology of religions one advocates either a trinitarian starting point or a central place for knowledge on the basis of the Holy Spirit, then it becomes clear that the outworking thereof is always decisively guided by one's unspoken but underlying understanding of Jesus of Nazareth, the Son of God, the Christ.

A Christocentric Exclusive Approach[2]

Human Sinfulness

The Bible opens with the story of creation, in which God is spoken of as the creator of heaven and earth. He creates humans in his own image, male and female. And he blesses them and says to them: "Be fruitful and multiply, and fill the earth and subdue it . . ." (Gen. 1:28). But the story of creation has barely begun when the story of human sinfulness begins. Humans transgress God's commandment. They sin. "This sin is guilt . . . . Sin affects the whole of humankind, every person, all peoples, the whole. The world was created by God and is fallen because of us humans."[3]

On the basis of this understanding of humankind Christians have

---

2. In addition to the literature cited in n. 1 see also for this viewpoint P. Beyerhaus, *Missions: Which Way? Humanization or Redemption* (Grand Rapids 1971); *idem*, "Mission and Humanization," in G. H. Anderson and T. F. Stransky, ed., *Mission Trends No. 1: Critical Issues in Mission Today* (New York and Grand Rapids, 1974) 231-45; "Lausanne Covenant," in G. H. Anderson and T. F. Stransky, ed., *Mission Trends No. 2: Evangelization* (New York and Grand Rapids, 1975) 239-48; C. E. Braaten, "The Uniqueness and Universality of Jesus Christ"; J. R. Stott, "Dialogue, Encounter, Even Confrontation," and D. J. Hesselgrave, "Evangelicals and Interreligious Dialogue," in Anderson and Stransky, *Mission Trends 5*, 69-89, 156-72, 123-27; the following numbers of the *Lausanne Occasional Papers*: 2: *The Willowbank Report — Gospel and Culture*, 4: *The Glen Eyrie Report — Muslim Evangelization*, 5: *Thailand (Pattaya) Reports* 11, 13f.: "Christian Witness to the Chinese People," "Christian Witness to New Religious Movements," "Christian Witness to Muslims," and "Christian Witness to Hindus"; W. Scott, " 'No Other Name' — An Evangelical Conviction," in Anderson and Stransky, *Mission Trends* 5, 58-74; *Laat doorgaan! 50 jaar IZB* (1935-1985).

3. *Laat doorgaan!* 27.

had no choice but to cling to the conviction that from general revelation in nature all humans have some knowledge of God. God is continually at work and present in their lives. He has not left himself without a witness. "For what can be known about God is plain to them, because God has shown it to them" (Rom. 1:19). But people are caught up in sin and so reject what they can know of God. They use their religiosity to elude God. Fallen into sin and unrighteousness, humans are totally turned in on themselves and away from God. All humans are the objects of God's wrath, dead through trespasses and sins (cf. Eph. 2:1-3), alienated from the life of God because of the ignorance that is in them and because of the hardness of their hearts (cf. Eph. 4:18), and blinded in unbelief by the god of this world (cf. 2 Cor. 4:4).

Salvation in Jesus Christ Alone

Humans cannot save themselves from this situation of sinfulness even though they have some knowledge of God. There is no other name by which humans can be saved than by the name of Jesus Christ. He alone is the Savior. He is the only mediator of God's reconciling and justifying grace for humans and the world. "There is salvation in no one else, for there is no other name under heaven given among mortals by which we must be saved" (Acts 4:12).

Salvation in Jesus Christ is of unique, exclusive, and universal significance. This conviction of faith is nonnegotiable. Jesus is the only person in whom God became human. He is the Son of God *and* the Son of man. He is fully God and fully human, God's only Son, our Lord. God raised him from the dead and thereby designated him as God's Son. Confirmation of this confession can be found in Paul's words in the synagogue at Antioch: "And we bring you the good news that what God promised to our ancestors he has fulfilled for us, their children, by raising Jesus; as also it is written in the second psalm, 'You are my Son; today I have begotten you'" (Acts 13:32f.).

All this is intended in the confession of *sola gratia, sola fide,* and *sola scriptura:* Salvation is received *by grace alone,* on the basis of the merits of Jesus Christ; this salvation is received only in the act of surrendering in *faith* by the power of the Holy Spirit; and this salvation in Christ is revealed to us only in *the Bible.*

The Christian religion itself can make no claims to being of unique, exclusive, and universal significance for the salvation of humans from their guilt and sin. As a religion Christianity is a historical phenomenon: It is joined to human ideas and institutions, and it is sinful and impermanent.

The difference between Christianity and other religions is that

Christianity proceeds from the revelation of God in the person of Jesus Christ. In him is the foundation of Christianity and of the church. The claim of Christians that their religion possesses the absolute truth is based on him. That which distinguishes Christianity from other religions is the person of Jesus Christ. In him lies the unique, exclusive, and universal significance of Christianity. Christianity itself is not absolute, but the revelation of God in Jesus Christ that comes to expression in it is.

Mission and Dialogue

The good news must be spread to the more than two-thirds of humankind that has not yet been confronted with it. The followers of Jesus Christ are called to proclaim to these people the gospel of reconciliation. Without reconciliation with God through faith in Jesus Christ no salvation is possible for any person. Haste is imperative. After all, those who have not yet heard of Jesus Christ are threatened with being lost forever, for only through faith in him is there eternal life for them. He must be preached to these people as the Way, the Truth, and the Life. The message that God's righteousness in grace is granted to those who believe in Jesus Christ implies that the invitation to let oneself be reconciled with God, to cease one's attempts at coming to God by way of self-realization, self-justification, and self-redemption has been given.

It is clear that in the proclamation of the good news one must decisively hold on to the unique, exclusive, and universal significance of the crucified Jesus, who died for all for the expiation of their sins, who rose to new life for all, and who is confessed as the Christ. Within this firmly held conviction there can be no question of a dialogue that does violence to this biblical witness by discounting its unique and exclusive character. A dialogue presupposing the syncretistic notion that Jesus Christ speaks equally through all religions detracts from the decisive significance that in God's redemptive history has to be accorded to him and to the gospel. In this view dialogue and syncretism are unacceptable.

Admittedly, dialogue formed a part of Paul's preaching of the gospel, but it remained subordinate to that preaching and served it. Faith in Jesus Christ was always central in this dialogue. What always came through in it was the call to repent and to turn to him.[4] Dialogue can only be accepted when its aim is to learn to know other people. In preaching one must take account, after all, of the people to whom the good news is addressed; they need to be approached with understanding, love, and appreciation. Then dialogue serves as the way by which people of other

---

4. Cf. Stott, "Dialogue," 159-61.

faiths are led to accept God's revelation in Jesus Christ. Christ must be preached. Precisely with this in mind it is of great importance for Christians to get to know their fellow people.

Any form of syncretism is utterly unacceptable to Christians because it robs Scripture of its very core: God has once and for all time revealed himself in Jesus Christ. People are called by God to respond to this reality. Christians are not free to let Christianity become part of a world religion composed of elements of different religions. For Christians there can be no plurality of revelations, none of which could be decisive. To classify Christianity as one of several expressions of the general phenomenon of "religion" is at cross purposes with what this religion is originally: the definitive revelation of God.

A Christocentric Inclusive Approach[5]

Salvation History Centered in Jesus Christ

Paul calls Jesus Christ the image of the invisible God. Christ is "the firstborn of all creation; for in him all things . . . were created. . . . He himself is before all things, and in him all things hold together. . . . For in him all the fullness of God was pleased to dwell," so that God might thus "reconcile to himself all things, whether on earth or in heaven" (Col. 1:15-17, 19-20; cf. 1 Tim. 2:5; Eph. 1:3-10). Faith recognizes that the Word of God, which in Jesus became a man, was central in God's plan of salvation from creation on. The New Testament is suffused with belief in the central place occupied by God's revelation and redemption in Jesus Christ in the history of humankind. He is the center of God's salvation history.

5. Besides the literature cited in nn. 1 and 2, see also: P. Rossano, "Interfaith: Its Importance and Implications: An Analytical Study from a Catholic Point of View," *Bulletin* 13 (1978) 29-39; *idem,* "Gospel and Culture at Ephesus and in the Province of Asia at the Time of St. Paul and St. John," *Bulletin* 15 (1980) 282-96; *idem,* "Christ's Lordship and Religious Pluralism"; S. J. Samartha, ed., *Living Faiths and the Ecumenical Movement* (Geneva, 1971); *idem, Faith in the Midst of Faiths: Reflections on Dialogue in Community* (Geneva, 1977); *idem, Courage for Dialogue: Ecumenical Issues in Interreligious Relationship* (Geneva, 1981); *The Evangelical-Roman Catholic Dialogue on Mission 1977-1984,* ed. B. Meeking and J. Stott (Grand Rapids, 1986); M. M. Thomas, *Risking Christ for Christ's Sake: Towards an Ecumenical Theology of Pluralism* (Geneva, 1987); E. Hillman, *Many Paths: A Catholic Approach to Religious Pluralism* (New York, 1989); J. Tomko, *Missionary Challenges to the Theology of Salvation* (FABC Papers 1988, no. 50); J. Dupuis, *Jesus Christ and the Encounter of World Religions* (New York, 1991); J. Kirk, *Loosing the Chains: Religion as Opium and Liberation* (London, 1992); J. Zehner, *Der notwendige Dialog: Die Weltreligionen in katholischer und evangelischer Sicht* (Gütersloh, 1992).

The Word of God, creating and illuminating, is present at the origin of the creation of the world and of humankind and sustains the history of the world and of humankind. Because the Word is actively present in that history, humanity was prepared for the incarnation of the Word in Jesus Christ, in whom God has been fully revealed. The adherents of the preparatory traditions are moved by God to seek Christ. All of salvation history is directed toward Christ and is completely "christocentric" in nature. From creation on humankind has been called by God to redemption in Jesus Christ.

When seen from the perspective of the New Testament, God's history of salvation for the whole world and all humans proves to have been led by and oriented to the Word of God that became man in Jesus Christ. This is the basis of the Christian conviction that God's revelation and salvation in Jesus Christ is of unique and universal significance.[6]

Jesus Christ, Unique and Universal

The first followers of Jesus left no doubt that they believed that Jesus was the Messiah announced by Isaiah (Isa. 35:4-6; 61:1-3) and anticipated by Israel. In the oldest testimonies of faith the disciples of Jesus confess that he is "the Messiah, the Son of the living God" (Matt. 16:16; cf. Mk. 8:27). This confession of Jesus as Messiah and Son of God originated in the experience of the resurrection of the crucified Jesus. He who in his death on the cross redeemed every human being and all of humanity from sin was in his resurrection set by God as Lord over all. Jesus was given by God not as a son of God but as *the* Son of God, not as a lord but as *the* Lord, not as a savior but as *the* Savior.

Jesus occupies a unique place in salvation history as Savior of all the world. Of all humanity he alone is of universal significance. Only in him is there redemption; he alone is the way to salvation. There is no other salvation and no other way to salvation. By him alone the world and humanity are reconciled to God. "For as all die in Adam, so all will be made alive in Christ" (1 Cor. 15:22).

> He is the one and only Christ, or he is not the Christ at all. He is the one and only Son of God, or he is not God's Son at all. He is the one and only Savior or he is no Savior at all. The exclusive claim is not a footnote to the gospel; it is the gospel itself. Not part of the husk, it is the kernel itself.[7]

---

6. Cf. Rossano, "Interfaith," 37; *Evangelical-Roman Catholic Dialogue*, 2.
7. Braaten, *op. cit.*, 75.

The Christian community's claim to the uniqueness of the Christian faith is rooted in Jesus Christ as the head of the church. In him also lies the significance of that community's message. What Christians are entitled to claim is that they accept in faith that in Jesus Christ God decisively and irreversibly revealed himself in history and redeemed humanity.

But the claim to uniqueness and exclusivity, to the universality and absoluteness of the Christian faith, cannot mean that only Christians — to the exclusion of others — are the recipients of God's saving grace and thus alone know him in the fullness of his truth. It is not true that only the people with whom the new covenant was made may view themselves as saved and that, though there is revelation outside the church, there is no salvation from God outside the church.[8]

> As Christians we do not claim any monopoly on God's love nor do we regard ourselves as the exclusive agents of God's love in the world. On the contrary, we believe that God has been and is creatively and redemptively at work among all human beings. Or, to put it another way, while as Christians we feel we are possessed by God's love, we recognize that God's love is not an exclusive possession of Christians.[9]

Revelation and salvation in Jesus Christ reach the whole creation, every human being, and all of humanity, and are thus of universal significance.

It is the deepest Christian conviction that all people without exception are saved by Christ and that Christ is united with humankind, with every person without exception, even those who are unaware of this: "Christ, who died and was raised up for all, provides man — each man and every man — with the light and the strength to measure up to his supreme calling."[10]

A Responsible Mandate

The church of Jesus Christ has the mandate to represent this new covenant in the history of humankind and the world and to cause its presence to be illumined and discovered outside the church. The risen Lord is active as revealer and redeemer in the life of non-Christians and in their religious traditions. The salvation that God accomplishes in Jesus Christ is not

8. D. Paton, ed., *Breaking Barriers* (Nairobi, 1975, and Geneva, 1976) 76.

9. "Conference Statement and Central Committee Recommendations to Churches," in *Christian Presence and Witness in Relation to Muslim Neighbours: A Conference* (Mombasa, 1979, and Geneva, 1981) 71.

10. John Paul II, *Redemptio Hominis* III, §14, 42.

confined to the church but touches all humanity. Christians are summoned to witness to this presence of God in the (religious) lives of others.[11] "So although in ways known to himself God can lead those who, through no fault of their own, are ignorant of the Gospel to that faith without which it is impossible to please him (Heb. 11:6), the Church, nevertheless, still has the obligation [cf. 1 Cor. 9:16] and also the sacred right to evangelize" (*Ad Gentes* 7).

As they carry out this mandate, Christians themselves face the challenge of accepting Jesus Christ as he reveals himself to them in the convictions and lives of adherents of other faiths.[12] If Christians thus open themselves before the religious convictions of people of other faiths, then perhaps they will be better able to understand what God has to say to them in Jesus Christ. It is not at all the case that in this approach an assured faith in Jesus Christ as Lord and Redeemer is given up, and therefore it is not correct to say that this view simply ends in syncretism.[13] Faith in the unique character of the birth, life, death, and resurrection of Jesus remains the unaltered content of the witness rendered to people of other faiths.

Dialogue as Mutual Witness

The diversity of content, method, and form in dialogues with people of other faiths is too great for the term "dialogue" to be defined in a single formulation to the satisfaction of all. In the encounter between Christians and people of other faiths the term "dialogue" especially denotes a certain way of relating to others. What is at stake is mutual trust, respect for each person's uniqueness, openness to each other's views, and a readiness on both sides to express what motivates one at the deepest (religious) levels, to listen to each other, and to examine jointly what each one's view of ultimate reality is.

Christians face the call to share with people of other faiths their experiences with Jesus the risen Christ and to discover in the process what God has brought about in their lives and religious traditions in the way of revelation and salvation in Jesus Christ. In this way, both to people of other faiths and to Christians themselves, it may become evident where and how in the religious traditions of non-Christians elements of truth,

11. Cf. C. Geffré, "Theological Reflections on a New Age of Mission," *International Review of Missions* 71 (1982) 483-85.

12. Cf. Samartha, *Living Faiths*, 36f.

13. Cf. "Mission as Seen from Geneva: A Conversation with Eugene R. Stockwell," *International Bulletin of Missionary Research* 11 (1987) 116.

goodness, and grace are present.[14] In the same way it may also become clear to both partners in dialogue where and how God's presence among people is obscured, where and how they fail to apprehend the salvation given in Jesus Christ, and where conversion to him is necessary.[15]

In this manner Christians are called to witness in dialogue to the good news of God's saving love and to the kingdom of God both present and to come as it has been revealed in Jesus Christ. If Christians enter into dialogue in this spirit and manner, renewed opportunities for witness will continue to arise. In dialogue Christians confess their faith in Jesus Christ.[16]

> In the context of dialogue with men of other faiths, which demands genuine openness on both sides, the Christian is free to bear witness to the risen Christ, just as his partner of another faith is free to witness to what is most important in his own existence. It thus repudiates not mission as such, but merely certain one-way patterns of mission.[17]

Dialogue cannot be a secret weapon in the hands of aggressive Christians. It is not a new means of continuing earlier forms of mission in which feelings of dominance prevailed. Participants in dialogue cannot have in mind an attempt to convert people in which one's partner in dialogue is not really taken seriously. There is no room for a contrast between witness and dialogue. Dialogue and mission cannot be had separately. In fact, they are always essentially bound together. To play one off against the other is to set up false alternatives.

A Theocentric Pluralistic Approach[18]

In every Christian study of the relationship between Christians and people of other faiths the understanding of Jesus Christ is of central significance. Is

---

14. Cf. Braaten, *op. cit.*, 85f.

15. Cf. Paton, *op. cit.*, 76, 79.

16. "Christians in Dialogue with Men of Other Faiths: Statement Made by the Protestant/Orthodox/Catholic Consultation on Dialogue with Men of Other Faiths, Kandy, Ceylon, February 27 to March 6, 1967," *International Review of Missions* 56 (1967) 342; cf. "Conference Statement and Central Committee Recommendations to Churches," 81.

17. Samartha, *op. cit.*, 34.

18. Besides the literature already cited, see also: W. C. Smith, *Towards a World Theology: Faith and the Comparative History of Religion* (London, 1981); E. J. Highes, *Wilfred Cantwell Smith: A Theology for the World* (London, 1986); J. Hick, *God and the Universe of Faiths: Essays in the Philosophy of Religion* (London, 1973); *idem*, ed., *The Myth of God*

there no salvation outside Jesus Christ and his church? Is there no salvation without him and his church? Can an answer be given to these questions that opens new and hitherto undreamed-of perspectives for further development in the theology of religions and that can meet the test of critical evaluation in the light of theological tradition and Holy Scripture?

Jesus Christ, Salvation from God

Throughout the centuries the christological confessions of the councils of Nicea (321), Ephesus (431), Constantinople (381), and Chalcedon (451) have served as the basis of Christian understanding of Jesus Christ. That is still true today. But in order to understand these confessions properly we must realize that the primary intent of the councils was to preserve the fundamental New Testament inspiration concerning Jesus, which was: salvation-in-Jesus from God. The intent of the councils was to establish how the Bible should be read where it speaks of Jesus.

The name of Jesus Christ embraces the confession of the earliest Jerusalem community, namely that the crucified Jesus is the promised

---

Incarnate (London, 1977); *idem, The Center of Christianity* (New York, 1978); *idem,* "Is There Only One Way to God?" *Theology* 85 (1982) 4-7; *idem,* "The Theology of Religious Pluralism," *Theology* 86 (1983) 335-40; *idem, Problems of Religious Pluralism* (London, 1985); *idem, The Metaphor of God Incarnate* (London, 1993); P. Knitter, "Catholic Theology of Religions at a Crossroads," in *Christianity among World Religions,* ed. H. Küng and J. Moltmann (Concilium; Edinburgh, 1986) 99-107; S. Samartha, *One Christ — Many Religions: Toward a Revised Christology* (New York, 1991); *idem,* "De Jordaan oversteken. Naar een christelijke theologie der religies," *Wereld en Zending,* 15 (1986), 126-30; E. Klootwij, *Commitment and Openness: The Interreligious Dialogue and Theology of Religions in the Work of Stanley J. Samartha* (Zoetermeer, 1992); J. Schineller, "Christ and Church: A Spectrum of Views," *Theological Studies* 37 (1976) 545-66; E. Schillebeeckx, *Jesus: An Experiment in Christology* (New York, 1979); *idem, Christ: The Experience of Jesus as Lord* (New York, 1981); *idem, Interim Report on the Books Jesus and Christ* (New York, 1981); *idem, Jesus in our Western Culture* (London, 1987); J. Bowden, *Edward Schillebeeckx: In Search of the Kingdom of God* (New York, 1983); H. Berkhof, *Christian Faith* (revised ed., Grand Rapids, 1986); H. Küng, *On Being a Christian* (Garden City, 1976); *idem,* "Toward an Ecumenical Theology of Religions: Some Theses for Clarification," in Küng and Moltmann, ed., *Christianity among World Religions,* 119-25; *idem,* "The World Religions in God's Plan of Salvation," in J. Neuner, ed., *Christian Revelation and World Religion* (London, 1967) 25-66; J. A. Fitzmyer, *Scripture and Christology: A Statement of the Biblical Commission with a Commentary* (London, 1986); Leonard Swidler, ed., *Toward a Universal Theology of Religion* (Maryknoll, 1987); J. Hick and P. F. Knitter, ed., *The Myth of Christian Uniqueness: Toward a Pluralistic Theology of Religions* (Maryknoll, 1987); G. D'Costa, ed., *Christian Uniqueness Reconsidered: The Myth of a Pluralistic Theology of Religions* (New York, 1990); R. Bernhardt, *Horizont Überschreitung. Die pluralistische Theologie der Religionen* (Gütersloh, 1991); C. Gillis, *Pluralism: A New Paradigm for Theology* (Louvain, 1993).

Messiah, the eschatological anointed of the Lord (cf. Acts 2:36; Rom. 1:3, 4).[19] In the encounter with Jesus the disciples experienced an encounter with God. Jesus acts as God does; God acts like Jesus. In Jesus they encountered salvation-from-God.

Jesus' disciples and the first Christians after them, in the light of their experience of his resurrection, experienced in him the presence of God. This encounter with God filled their whole existence. In Jesus God's saving power became visible and tangible to them. For them Jesus was God's image, "so fully God's agent, so completely conscious of living in God's presence and serving God's love, that the divine reality was mediated through him to others."[20] Expressions like "Son of God," "God the Son," "incarnate God," and "God-man" were used to articulate this experience. Characterizations of Jesus as the Messiah and as the anointed of God, the Christ, are to be understood in the same way. These expressions, which are not to be taken literally, indicate the religious significance that Jesus had for the disciples and for early Christians.

> Christians believe that in Jesus Christ God revealed himself/herself in such a way that thereby his/her love for the whole world became visible and a way of salvation was made available to all humans. . . . To be touched by the person of Jesus of Nazareth, his life, his work and instruction, and his death and resurrection is to experience salvation — from God. To be saved in Jesus Christ signifies reconciliation with God and fellow humans.[21]

Through the centuries this conviction remained the core of the faith held by communities of Christians. It belongs to the heart of their "credo." For Christians Jesus is a translator — rather *the* translator — of the salvation God promised to humankind and the world from the time of creation.

> For Christians Jesus (a) is therefore the decisive and definitive revelation of God and (b) precisely through this at the same time shows us what and how we human beings can, need to and really may be. Therefore any definition of the man Jesus in fact has to do with the being of God. In Jesus God reveals his own being by wanting to be salvation of and for human beings in him.[22]

Jesus stands for God. His relationship to God is of such a nature and so defines his life that he addresses God as "Father." The experience

19. Schillebeeckx, *Jesus in our Western Culture*, 15.
20. Hick, *God and the Universe of Faiths*, 177.
21. Samartha, "De Jordaan oversteken," 129.
22. Cf. Schillebeeckx, *op. cit.*, 17.

of this existential relationship to God was the sustaining ground of Jesus' existence. It was this that led his followers to confess him as "Son of God," as "only begotten Son of God," as the Christian "credo" formulates this faith.

The Normative Significance of Jesus

Does this understanding of Christian faith make possible a new and radical development in the theology of the relationship between Christians and people of other faiths? Not necessarily. This is so because, according to some, even in a theocentric christology it is still of existential importance to retain the unique, normative, and universal significance of Jesus the Christ. For Christians Christ remains both norm and goal.

> Any theologian who is not prepared to give up this normativity and finality of Christ does so . . . because otherwise he or she would be abandoning the central declaration of the Scriptures that go to make up the New Testament. For the whole of the New Testament — like it or not — Jesus is normative and definitive: he alone is the Christ of God (the oldest as well as the briefest confession of faith in the New Testament is just this: *Iēsous Kyrios)*, he is "the way, the truth and the life."[23]

On the basis of these considerations Christians, in meeting with people of other faiths, are not free to abandon the normative character of Jesus Christ. He cannot be put on a par with other prophets and saviors. To do so is, according to this view, non-Christian.[24]

What God did in Christ was done not only for the church but for all people irrevocably. The mission of the church, in this view, is to adopt a posture of service to people of other faiths.[25] The church may not forget for a single moment that it can and must live as the representative of what God in Jesus Christ promised to all the people of the world religions who know nothing of what God has done for them.[26] To engage in mission is therefore to engage in dialogue with people of other faiths, a dialogue in which both sides introduce their deepest convictions and in which Christians do not in the process reduce their confession of faith to a list of general truths. Through Jesus Christ Christians know what, as far as God is concerned, the situation of people of other faiths is and where their

---

23. Küng, "Towards an Ecumenical Theology of Religions," 122.
24. Cf. *ibid.,* 123.
25. Cf. Küng, *On Being a Christian,* 111f.
26. Cf. *ibid.,* 64.

salvation lies. In this sense people of other faiths, whether they know it or not, need the help of Christians.[27]

Jesus Is Normative for Christians

Is it really possible to speak responsibly of several "incarnations" of God? Why should we say that God's complete and irrevocable offer of grace can be made only once? Did Jesus "mediate the presence and saving power of God in a unique sense in which no other religious figure has ever mediated it or ever could?"[28] Is the rejection of a theocentric christology, together with a theology of religions developed consistently in terms of such a christology, not grounded in the dogmatic assertion that the believing confession of Jesus has to be understood literally?[29] But if another understanding of the confession of Jesus is possible, then what? Does not this other understanding force Christians to speak in a new and very different way about the normativity of God's revelation in Jesus?

Opposition to the idea that though Jesus must be understood as unique he need not be understood as normative rests on a central datum of the Christian faith: the resurrection of Jesus. "Does not the resurrection establish not only an inclusive but exclusive uniqueness for the man from Nazareth?"[30] That is the question. The resurrection and the Easter faith based on it are, of course, of central importance in the Christian faith. But in a theocentric christology this need not automatically lead to the view of the uniqueness of Jesus that we have described and to an interpretation of New Testament texts that characterizes Jesus as the one and only Savior of humankind.[31]

To speak of Jesus as unique is to speak the language of faith. In such a confession the overpowering experience of Easter clearly comes through. The first Christians were so "possessed" by this Jesus that expressions like "one mediator between God and humankind" (1 Tim. 2:5), God's "only Son" (John 3:16), "no one comes to the Father except through me" (John 14:6), "as all die in Adam, so all will be made alive in Christ" (1 Cor. 15:22), and "he entered once for all . . ." (Heb. 9:12) were "symbols" needed to express what was happening inside Christians after Jesus' death and resurrection.[32] These confessions describe Jesus' uniqueness for the first Christians and for the entire community of Christians through sub-

---

27. Cf. *ibid.*, 61.
28. Cf. Hick, *God and the Universe of Faiths*, 177.
29. Cf. Hick, *Center of Christianity*, 70ff.; idem, *God and the Universe of Faiths*, 177-79.
30. Knitter, *No Other Name*, 197; cf. Hick, *God and the Universe of Faiths*, 170.
31. Cf. Knitter, *op. cit.*, 182.
32. Cf. *ibid.*, 182, 151.

sequent centuries. But exclusive uniqueness was not the intent of this language of faith.

This also applies to the understanding of Jesus' resurrection: It does not necessarily imply that Jesus is the only way of salvation or the only God-given mediator for all humans. That which took place in Jesus and which the first Christians experienced of God's involvement in human lives in him can possibly happen also in other saviors and in the experience of their followers. Openness to the possibility that besides Jesus there are other persons in whose lives God has been present with revelation and salvation need not diminish in Christians their full commitment to Jesus,[33] in whom, for them, "the interior side" of God came to expression. In the coming of the kingdom of God Jesus remains for Christians of constitutive importance.[34] For Christians Jesus is God's decisive and definitive revelation.[35]

> While as Christians we can and may make Jesus the Christ the center of history for ourselves, we are not at the same time in a position to argue that the historical revelation of salvation from God in Jesus Christ exhausts the question of God, nor do we need to. Although we cannot attain Jesus in his fullness unless at the same time we also take into account his unique relationship with God which has a special nature of its own, this does not of itself mean that Jesus' unique way of life is the only way to God. For even Jesus not only reveals God but also conceals him.[36]

Jesus cannot reveal God in his fullness. However unique the relationship was between Jesus and God, Jesus remains only a contingent phenomenon. The historical Jesus-event does not close off other roads to God and therefore cannot be absolutized as the sole divine norm for human conduct, including religious conduct.[37]

This is all the more the case because God's history of salvation has been in process from creation on. The creation of humanity and human history, which is a history of salvation and non-salvation, is where God acts redemptively to save and to judge. God's self revelation in Jesus Christ was neither exhaustive nor exclusive. No human person and no religion can reserve the divine self-revelation exclusively for himself, herself, or itself. The history of salvation cannot be reduced to the history of Judaism and Christianity.[38]

---

33. Cf. *ibid.*, 200f.
34. Cf. Schillebeeckx, *Jesus in Our Western Culture*, 19.
35. Cf. *ibid.*, 17.
36. *Ibid.*, 2.
37. Cf. *ibid.*, 2f.
38. Cf. *ibid.*, 7.

On the basis of all this, we Christians are faithful to the revelation of God's limitless love in Jesus when they see Jesus as constituting a particular disclosure of a universal reality. And they thus take the universal reality of God's love seriously. For God's love would not be effectively universal if it could be received and responded to only within one limited strand of human history.[39] God can and does meet people outside the revelation in Jesus. For all these reasons non-Christian faiths can be viewed as ways of salvation just as the Christian faith is a way of salvation, since in such traditions people are attempting, each in his or her own way, to respond to God's active presence among them.

Living Reminders of God

Being persuaded in faith that Jesus, as the sacrament of divine encounter, is of universal significance, Christians will want to share this conviction of faith with people of other faiths. Conversely, this is also true of the "others," those who have had their own experiences with God in their own special revelations.[40] Christians and people of other faiths are called, from within their convictions, to bear mutual witness to the salvation from God that they have experienced. They must testify to each other regarding this salvation, but they are not themselves this salvation. Christian and other religious traditions are signs or sacraments of salvation.

> Religions, churches are the *anamnesis*, i.e. the living recollection among us, of this universal, "tacit" but effective will to salvation and the absolute saving presence of God in the history of our world. By virtue of their religious word, their sacrament or ritual and their life-style, religions — synagogues and pagodas, mosques and churches — prevent the universal saving presence from being forgotten.[41]

Whenever this happens, adherents of different religions are making evident God's creative action in history for the salvation of humans and are allowing the Word of God to be heard in faith languages of their own.[42] Given this reality, Christians and people of other faiths, like pilgrims, are journeying together toward God and are telling each other of the experiences each of them has had with God.

In this view, mission and dialogue imply mutual witness. On this journey Christians will bear witness to Jesus because for them God's

---

39. Hick, *The Center of Christianity*, 79.
40. Cf. J. Hick in *idem*, ed., *Myth of God Incarnate*, 180.
41. Schillebeeckx, *Jesus in Our Western World*, 32f.
42. Cf. *ibid.*, 33f.

history of salvation cannot even be thought of without Jesus in his uniqueness. What God revealed of himself in the life, death, and resurrection of Jesus Christians experience as possessing such decisive significance for the salvation of human beings. This is why they want to tell and show precisely this to people of other faiths.

Encounter in Context[43]

For some decades now renewed and very careful attention has been given in wide Christian circles to encounter between Christians and people of other faiths. This interreligious encounter has been built on the awareness, from experience, that the countless concrete contexts in which people of

43. Besides the literature cited above see also: A. van der Bent, *Six Hundred Ecumenical Consultations (1948-1982)* (Geneva, 1983); the journal *Bulletin* van het Secretariat voor de niet-christenen; the issue of *International Review of Missions* on "Gospel and Culture" (74 [1985]); J. S. Mbiti, *African Religions and Philosophy* (London, 1969); R. H. Drummond, *Gautama the Buddha: An Essay in Religious Understanding* (Grand Rapids, 1974); T. A. Aykara, *Meeting of Religions: New Orientations and Perspectives* (Bangalore, 1978); G. Gispert-Sauch, *God's Word Among Men* (Delhi, 1973); I. Jesudasan, *A Ghandian Theology of Liberation* (Maryknoll, 1984); W. Bühlmann, *All Have the Same God* (Slough, 1979); K. Cragg, *The Call of the Minaret* (London, 1986); idem, *Mohammed and the Christian: A Question of Response* (Maryknoll, 1984); idem, *Jesus and the Muslim: An Exploration* (London, 1985); *A Working Party of the Churches' Committee on Migrant Workers in Europe* (London, 1984); K. Cracknell, *Towards a New Relationship: Christians and People of Other Faith* (London, 1986); J. B. Cobb, *Beyond Dialogue: Toward a Mutual Transformation of Christianity and Buddhism* (Philadelphia, 1982); G. Parrinder, *Encountering World Religions* (Edinburgh, 1987); R. Viladesau, *Answering for Faith: Christ and the Human Search for Salvation* (New York, 1987); A. Pieris, *An Asian Theology of Liberation* (New York, 1988); H. Coward, *Hindu-Christian Dialogue: Perspectives and Encounters* (New York, 1989); P. J. Griffiths, *Christianity through Non-Christian Eyes* (New York, 1990); W. Ariarajah, *Hindus and Christians: A Century of Protestant Ecumenical Thought* (Amsterdam and Grand Rapids, 1991); D. J. Krieger, *The New Universalism: Foundations for a Global Theology* (New York, 1991); L. N. Mercado, *Non-Biblical Revelation: Filipino Religious Experience* (Manila, 1992); idem, "Within God's Gracious Purposes: Interfaith Dialogue in Britain," *ER* 37 (1985) 452-61; A. G. Hunter, *Christianity and Other Faiths in Britain* (London, 1985); *Segundo Congreso Misionaro Latino-americano. Comisión Episcopal de Missiones y Dirección Nacional de OMPE* (Mexico City, 1983); J. Berthrong, "Interfaith Dialogue in Canada," *ER* 37 (1985) 462-70; *My Neighbour's Faith — and Mine: Theological Discoveries through Interfaith Dialogue. A Study Guide* (Geneva, 1986).

On the place of the theology of religions in the theological curriculum see: R. H. Drummond, *Toward a New Age in Christian Theology* (New York, 1985); K. Cracknell and C. Lamb, *Theology on Full Alert* (London, 1986); S. Amirtham and S. W. Ariarajah, ed., *Ministerial Formation in a Multifaith Milieu: Implications of Interfaith Dialogue for Theological Education* (Geneva, 1986).

different religious traditions live and work together in everyday life are of fundamental significance for this encounter. Such concrete situations are the primary laboratory in which we work out a theology of religions. The initial authors of this theology are those who are directly involved in interreligious encounter. They have furnished the basic material on which systematic religious and theological structures must arise. The theology of religions is essentially *contextual* theology, and those who have articulated the theology of religions have increasingly shown that they have understood this. They have become thoroughly aware that assessment of the "truth-content" of Christian religious and theological ideas that happen to be in vogue will have to take account of repeated concrete encounters with Hindus, Buddhists, Muslims, and people with other, less widespread, faiths.

This growing awareness has been accompanied by increasing numbers of worldwide meetings between Christians and people of other faiths. The participants and topics of discussion in these meetings have been varied, but all have been directed toward intensifying, clarifying, and promoting interreligious relationships.

There have also been increasing numbers of gatherings in which Christians and persons of other faiths have prayed or meditated in each other's presence. These encounters have constituted a second level of contexts in which the theology of religions assumes form and cooperates in the creation of religiously responsible, concrete, and viable relationships between Christians and persons of other faiths.

The contextual theology of religions is constantly in ferment. Changes and new developments occur all the time. The development of this theology in continual dialogue with persons of other faiths is the responsibility of the whole Christian community and every Christian. This confronts the leadership of the church — pastors, theologians, and theological training schools — with the challenge of validating their pastoral and academic responsibility also in this area. It is of existential importance to all Christian communities to take up this responsibility in the coming years.

CHAPTER 13

Human Distress, Salvation,
and Mediation of Salvation

J. D. Gort

A number of questions arise for systematic missiology from the relation between the one gospel and the world, the latter being marked by various experiences of distress and varied expectations of salvation. All these questions point to the basic question of the missionary mediation of salvation: How should we describe the content of the church's mission? The present chapter's biblical and theological examination is intended to stimulate discussion of this fundamental question.

Introduction

The Motif of Soteriology

Always and everywhere people have sought to be rescued from the distress and suffering of human existence, an existence which they experience "in their deepest dreams as being destined for happiness."[1] The basic question of humanity concerns this sense of a destiny of salvation in the midst of an earthly life suffused with distress. Every human philosophy and religion is "fundamentally and principially preoccupied" with this question.[2] In other words, all authentic world-and-life views and religious traditions are soteriologically oriented.[3]

---

1. W. Beinert, "Jesus Christus der Erlöser von Sünde und Tod: Überblick über die abendländischen Soteriologie," in K. J. Rivinius, ed., *Schuld, Sühne und Erlösung in Zentralafrika (Zaïre) und in der christlichen Theologie Europas* (Sankt Augustin, 1983) 197.
2. *Ibid.*
3. On this orientation in other religions, see, e.g., B. Mensen, ed., *Schuld und Versöhnung in verschiedenen Religionen* (Sankt Augustin, 1986); David J. Krieger, "Zur

194

In the Christian faith as well the proclamation of salvation is of central significance. Soteriology must not be thought of, says W. Beinert, as one of the "themes of theology" (*capita theologiae*). It is, rather, the theme of the whole teaching of the faith.[4] In short, in the whole of theology the subject is God and the mediation of his saving acts to human beings in their world (J. Firet).

The motif of soteriology is also the beating heart of the study of mission. The concern of missiology is to reflect on the mediation by the community of believers of God's salvific coming in Jesus Christ to humans in all sorts of situations of distress — people who have never experienced this salvation or who no longer experience it. It is these three core concepts that we want to explore in what follows: What is this human distress? What is salvation? At what point does distress give way to salvation? Is salvation primarily related to individuals or does it relate also to the common life of human beings and to the whole creation? In what does mediation consist? That is, what is the purpose of mission? What is it that mission must say and do?

A Note on Method

These questions cannot be answered on the basis of texts or doctrinal materials alone: We are dealing with concretely experienced realities. The one salvation that comes from God assumes specific form within various and sometimes very different human situations. "The question of salvation is unavoidably bound up with the interpretation of a specific situation."[5] Therefore, in all legitimate reflection on mission — that is, on the relationships among God's salvation, the world's distress, and the mediatory task of the church — both text and context have to be consulted.

Textual discourse is not truly intelligible apart from knowledge of contextual reality. We can read a text only when we make use of the context as explanatory dictionary. The context reveals the specific forms of human distress, shows the full dimensions of salvation and the scope of liberation needed, and specifies the forms of missionary mediation called for in a given situation.

Heilslehre in Hinduismus und Christentum," in H. J. Braun, *Indische Religionen und das Christentum im Dialog* (Zurich, 1986) 59-73; J. Verkuyl, *Met moslims in gesprek over het evangelie* (Kampen, 1985); P. M. Starkey, *Salvation as a Problem in Christian Theology of Religions* (New York, 1978); A. Wessels, *De moslimse naaste. Op weg naar een theologie van de Islam* (Kampen, 1978); S. G. F. Brandon, ed., *The Saviour God: Comparative Studies in the Concept of Salvation* (Manchester, 1963).

4. Beinert, *op. cit.*, 208.

5. *Ibid.*, 199.

On the other hand, not everything can be inferred from experience or empirical observation: We are dealing with a Word that has made itself heard from the beginning of the human world and continues to call for attention in that world. Without knowledge of the gospel one cannot plumb the depths of contextual reality. According to Christian conviction, a clear view of earthly reality — of the real significance and meaning of human history — can ultimately be gained only when we look at it through the lens of the biblical text and historical reflection on that text.

In order to understand the context hermeneutically one must read the text exegetically, and in order to understand the text hermeneutically one must read the context exegetically. In other words, in missiological reflection a *continual correlation* of text and context is required. This interaction is already found, for that matter, in Scripture itself, where documents of human life and experience are interwoven with revelations of and witnesses to God. Adequate missiological reflection seeks to take full account of this continuing dynamic relationship. The World Missionary Conference at Melbourne spoke strikingly in this connection of "a reading of the Bible that goes hand in hand with a reading of human history."[6]

The question facing every new generation of the missionary church is: How can the gospel be related to human culture in a truly effective way? How can the path that the good news takes through the world be understood both in terms of the content of the message and against the background of the dominant situation? In every period the church is summoned anew to develop a soteriology that has something meaningful to say to its own time but that also adheres to the essence of the biblical witness concerning God's redemption in Jesus Christ and respects and preserves the valuable elements of the church's faith traditions.[7]

This chapter can offer only an exploratory model to serve as a point of departure for further reflection. In doing so, it will move from text to

---

6. A number of examples of this simultaneous reading of text and context from different continents are in a special issue of *Voices From the Third World*, EATWOT (10/2, June, 1987) entitled "On Interpreting the Bible." For Asia see the thorough study by A. A. Yewangoe, *Theologia Crucis in Asia: Asian Christian Views on Suffering in the Face of Overwhelming Poverty and Multifaceted Religiosity in Asia* (dissertation, Amsterdam, 1987).

7. We receive the biblical witness and learn to understand it also through the reflection and practice of the historical church. But in the framework of this chapter we cannot deal with this church tradition separately; our section on the textual witness presupposes various insights from this tradition. For a superb overview of Western soteriology, see Beinert's essay (cited in n. 1 above), which D. Bosch has rightly characterized as "perhaps the best existing overview of the history of Western soteriological reflection" (*Missionalia* 14 [1986] 146).

context. First, we will attempt to summarize the key points of the Christian message by describing God's offer of salvation to humankind and to the world in terms of the Apostles' Creed. Then we will seek to clarify the three concepts of human distress, salvation, and mediation by relating the textual message laid out in the first part of the chapter to the present world context.

The Witness of the Text: God for Us

The fundamental word underlying all the derivative words of the church, the absolute foundation of the Christian faith and confession, is the Scriptural message concerning the disastrous and death-dealing disturbance of the relationship between heaven and earth and the salutary and life-giving restoration of that relationship. The Bible's pivotal concern is the kingdom of God *(basileia tou theou)*. The goal of this kingdom is the consummation of the total rule of the King in the whole world, the total subordination of all people, all earthly structures, and all cosmic powers to his kingship, so that he may rule in glory and his will may be done "on earth as it is in heaven" (cf. Isa. 65:17-25). This kingdom is established by the saving action of the triune God, Father, Son, and Holy Spirit. Human redemption comes exclusively from this God, "the ultimate and boundless salvation of us all."[8]

Redemptive Creation

I believe in God the Creator, who in the beginning as *the Almighty* made *heaven and earth* from chaotic nothingness by his Word and Spirit and who as the *Father* formed human children after his image and in his likeness, and did so simply out of love.

He placed his children, his crowning work, in paradise at the center of creation. But the man and the woman came to be dissatisfied with this state of well-being and wholeness. They allowed themselves to be tempted to desire something more. But the "something more" they desired led directly to a state in which nothing remained. The moment they ate of the tree, they discovered that they were naked. That is, they became vulnerable and afraid of each other and of God. When they said farewell to innocence they lost the likeness of God and, thereby, paradise.

But God did not abandon his human children. He made a covenant

---

8. Beinert, *op. cit.,* 220.

with them whereby he promised to stay with them and to hold them in his hand for all eternity and at the same time demanded of them that they always remain close to him. The realization, experience, and preservation of human salvation, of true humanity, is anchored in this covenant. The primeval stories in the Bible and the *pars pro toto* history of Israel show this clearly. Though the people of Israel, the people whom God had called and had chosen, constantly proved unfaithful, God never broke his promise. He never abandoned his creation, but upheld it with unfailing faithfulness. Though nature was subject to a curse because of human disobedience, God persistently caused it to bear fruit and to bring forth life. Over and over he raised up signs of his kingdom (cf. Isa. 40:3; 57:14; 62:10). Again and again he resumed the interrupted dialogue with his people and summoned them to listen to him: "Turn to me and be saved" (Isa. 45:22).

Creative Redemption

I believe in Jesus Christ, God's only Son, our Lord, the Mediator in whom God's love for the work of his hands took definitive shape.

Christology is the focal point of soteriology. In God's plan for the redemption of the world Christ occupies the center. "He is the final and highest response of God to the human need for redemption."[9] In his person the reality of heaven and the reality of earth are brought together in a uniquely salvific way. As the Mediator he embodies the whole of salvation history, makes that history possible with power that works in all directions: backward, forward, and sideward, and fills that history with its content and meaning. He is the Alpha and the Omega, the first and the last, the beginning and the end, the one who has so decisively effected the salvation of the world that ever since it is possible to speak of the conclusive victory of the kingdom of light over the kingdom of darkness in him for all time. In him the kingdom of God is at hand (Matt. 4:17).

By his obedience the likeness of God has been restored in human beings: God "made him to be sin who knew no sin, so that in him we might become the righteousness of God" (2 Cor. 5:21). Christ's assumption of our human nature issues in the universal redemption to which Scripture witnesses. The same thing is stated negatively in the classical formulation *Quod non assumptum, non sanatum.*[10] The solution to human distress that God has provided in Christ is "entirely human and acceptable

9. *Ibid.,* 219.
10. "That which has not been assumed in Christ is not saved."

to humans" because Jesus stands "in history as a human being," and is "truly redemptive, because this human being is at the same time God."[11]

The pivotal concern of revelation is not the beginning or even the end of Jesus' appearance on earth, but on the contrary, the entire indivisible life and praxis of the Lord, *acta et dicta et passa tota Jesu Christi in carne.*[12] All the elements and moments of his life and work are essential components of the universal comprehensive salvation that has been, is, and will be given to the world by the Father in the Son.

The Bible makes unambiguously clear that God seeks to encounter all human beings with the life and work of the Messiah. But Scripture also teaches that God cares in a special way about people in whose lives salvation is most deeply lacking. The Redeemer can be found most clearly in his saving action where the need for salvation is most poignant, that is, in the lives of those who have never, or only scarcely, experienced deliverance. God chooses to be present especially where the promises of his kingdom are frustrated or blocked by demonic and human powers, where those obstructive powers have been at their worst. The more urgent the distress, the more intense his care and his empathic and sympathizing presence. The greater the scope of the lostness, the more intensive is his seeking.

One category of people that must certainly be mentioned in this connection is God's little ones: the poor and the oppressed, the widow and the orphan, the prisoner and the beggar, the weak, the wounded, those who have gone astray, those who have no real choices, all those to whom no one gives an accounting and from whom no one demands an accounting. Among these little ones are those who are ruled with "force and harshness" (Ezek. 34:4). God takes up the cause of the helpless who have no helper, the voiceless whose cause no one defends, the scattered, victimized sheep for whom no one searches, and about whom no one inquires (cf. Ezek. 34:1-16). The poor have a special place in the heart of God's Son, who from his position in the center can always be found outside the gate, at the fringes of human life where the underprivileged and the marginalized are to be found. He is present among them, he takes his stand alongside them, and he walks in their company.

God's kingdom came in Jesus the Messiah not only in a formal and qualitative sense but also in reality. Divine salvation does not float out of reach as a vague promise in the sky but concerns a very concrete reality within human history. Jesus demonstrated that the gospel of the kingdom does not merely consist of intentions but is the catalyst of the transforma-

---

11. Beinert, *op. cit.,* 219.
12. "The whole of the acts, words, and suffering of Jesus Christ in the flesh."

tion of human life and interhuman relationships at both the personal and communal levels. He clearly showed that the good news is the means of liberation from all forms of human bondage and that it is creative of situations of tangible peace, justice, love, joy, forgiveness, comfort, hope, happiness, and new, eternal life.

Nonetheless, human distress has clearly continued to spread in the experience of this world. In a material sense the mediation of salvation is not yet complete; viewed quantitatively salvation has been only partially realized. The kingdom of God that has already come in the Son is also yet to appear. When we speak of the historical effectuation of human deliverance, we are compelled to speak in terms of an eschatological reserve.

Jesus left his human followers and returned to his Father, from whom he had gone forth when he came into the world (John 16:28). But his disciples were not to allow themselves to be led into temptation, despair, and disillusionment by his departure. Without him they would have much to endure in the world, but they were called to be of good courage, knowing that he had overcome the world (v. 33). From his place on the heavenly throne he would be able to meet all the expectations of his followers and fulfill all their hopes: "I will do whatever you ask in my name" (John 14:13). He promised that he would return soon and that he and his own would never again be separated.

Redemptive Animation of Creation

I believe in the Holy Spirit, who in the time between the times, in the period between the Ascension and Second Coming, mediates the continuing salvific presence of Jesus Christ on earth in accordance with God's universal will to salvation. The liberation wrought by Christ would be available not only in Palestine to a limited number of people but everywhere, to the ends of the earth.

I believe in the holy and universal Christian church, the communion of saints. On the day of Pentecost Christ by his Spirit created the new community. He thus fulfilled the promise that he would not leave his disciples desolate. From the beginning the "other Advocate" (John 14:16) animated this body of Christ. Always he would show it the way to go, teach it all things and bring to its remembrance all that Jesus had said (cf. v. 26). He was to remind believers consistently of Jesus' new commandment: "that you love one another. Just as I have loved you, you also should love one another" (13:34). This common life was bound to appeal to others: "By this everyone will know that you are my disciples, if you have love for one another" (v. 35). That, ultimately, was what Jesus was after. In creating his church he had in mind the whole of humanity. It was also from within this universal orientation that he prayed for his followers, "that they may all be one. As you, Father, are in me and I am in you, may they also be in us, so that the world may believe that you have sent me" (17:21).

Jesus summoned his disciples to go into the world to disciple all nations, baptizing them in the name of the triune God and teaching them to observe all that he had commanded (Matt. 28:19). Just as he had made this clear when he sent out the first twelve disciples (cf. 10:9-14), so also the church's missionary service was never to be carried out aggressively or with any display of earthly power. Jesus expected of his disciples that they would follow him and that, denying themselves and carrying the cross, they would walk in his footsteps (cf. Mark 8:34). The mission of the new community was to be analogous to God's mission: "As the Father has sent me, so I send you" (John 20:21).

I believe in the forgiveness of sins, the resurrection of the body, and eternal life. If Christ's followers would keep his commandments, all his promises, too, would be theirs. Then they would be enabled by the Spirit to continue his work in the world. As they followed him as his disciples they would be restored to the paradise of living communion with God, who enables human beings to deal with each other salvifically and to live together in peace and harmony. On the basis of its obedience the church would be continually blessed with the glory of the Lord. But even if it allowed itself to be seduced into unfaithfulness, Christ would always remain faithful: "And remember, I am with you always, to the end of the age" (Matt. 28:20).

Distress, Salvation, and Mediation in Context

We can give substance to the idea of mission with the aid of the three concepts of *human distress, salvation,* and *mediation.* We have already attempted to explain these concepts in terms of the basic message of the Bible. At the beginning of this chapter, however, we warned that what we are speaking of cannot be described adequately on the basis of the text alone but can only be clarified if text and context are taken together. Mission is involvement in the continuing dialogue between God, who offers salvation, and the world, which longs for that salvation and is entangled in all sorts of evil and woe. The missionary task requires us to identify the distress present in our world and to articulate and give form to the salvation offered by Christ.

The contexts in which we do this are numerous and diverse, but they also have much in common. They share, of course, the same theological and anthropological floor. But even beyond that there is an increasing measure of uniformity among human contexts. The unity of humankind is beginning to take shape in the form of a worldwide civilization that is being promoted and spread throughout the world "through the university and technical training network, the multinational corporations and the media."[13] Our further discussion of human need, salvation, and mediation in terms of context will be concerned with this present and developing world context.

Human Distress

We are living in a world full of distress. What we are calling "distress" exists wherever a genuinely human existence is in any way or for whatever reason threatened or made problematic or impossible.

There is a broad spectrum of forms of human trouble and need: The demonic forces binding people are legion. Some of this distress occurs without demonstrable cause. Millions of people experience the suffering of Job, his story of inexplicable adversity continues in our own history, and we share his experience of unforeseen evil. We are still very much in his company. Everywhere there are people who suffer hideous diseases, who are struck by personal tragedy and misfortune, or who are victims of natural disasters. Very often people are "threatened and challenged by nature. Nature is ambiguous . . . . Hers are the hurricanes, the floods, the droughts, the earthquakes, the famines"; nature "can swallow and suffocate" human beings.[14] But much distress comes, too, as part of global civilization. Along with Toynbee, Verkuyl points to the dangers of that civilization and states that "the religious and ethical problems which it poses" call for continued missiological attention.[15]

Most of the world's distress can be attributed to human disobedience. As a result of humanity's continuing fall into sin and the guilt that comes from the fall, the chasm between humankind and its Creator has persisted. As a result, we are also profoundly estranged from ourselves, from each other, and from the rest of creation. All these relationships — between the human individual and God, among people, and between

---

13. L. Newbigin, *Foolishness to the Greeks: The Gospel and Western Culture* (Grand Rapids, 1986) 1.

14. *New Directions in Faith and Order: Bristol 1967* (Geneva, 1968) 17, 18. For a lucid theological analysis of the problem of evil, see J. Gründel, "Sünde als Verneinung des Willen Gottes: Zur Frage nach dem Ursprung von Leid, Uebel und Bösem," in Rivinius, *op. cit.*, 105-25.

15. J. Verkuyl, *Contemporary Missiology: An Introduction* (Grand Rapids, 1978) 172.

humanity and nature — are closely interwoven. When God is banished from the public life of society, people oppress and exploit each other.[16] When humans cease serving God, they become incapable of serving one another or of relating lovingly and respectfully to their "mother" and "sister," nature. As a result of our rebellion against God, we turn into wolves who prey upon each other *(homo homini lupus)*, and our relation to nature becomes hopelessly disjointed.

We can point to three broad ways in which this evil is experienced. First, many people in our time have become trapped in what may perhaps best be called psychospiritual distress. They have lost their bearings and no longer know how to cope. Every day brings renewed feelings of purposelessness and meaninglessness with respect to their own lives and of disillusionment and depression on account of the state of the world. They exhaust themselves in a constant search for rest and become discouraged because they never find it. This crippling condition is present everywhere in the world. But it is striking that it is often the rich who, despite — or, more likely, because of — their material abundance, are particularly afflicted with this mental and spiritual fatigue. Ever increasing material consumption among affluent people and communities is proving unable to meet their deepest and most essential needs.

Second, vast numbers of people are trapped in acute physical and material distress. Many of our fellow human beings suffer hunger and thirst and are poor and homeless. Many parents lack the means to feed and to care for their children. Millions of refugees, driven from their homes and countries, have no reason to place any hope in the future. Many millions of people in our day are plunged into great distress and misery, not because they have sinned and are guilty, but only because they live with Lazarus outside the rich man's gate (Luke 16:19-31). They are those who suffer for the sins of others, those who are sinned against.

Such structural evil, i.e., the evil caused by unjust economic, political, cultural, and social systems, exists on a small scale, e.g., in villages, but also in larger, national, regional, and global contexts. This evil occurs most clearly and on the largest scale in the Two-Thirds World. The reason for this is simple: The present geopolitical and economic structures are arranged by the most powerful party, the North Atlantic bloc, in such a way that they work to the advantage of the northern hemisphere and to the disadvantage of the southern hemisphere.

But such conditions of misery and destitution also exist in prosperous nations. In the most industrialized regions, "affluent" America and

---

16. On the banishment of God from the public life of modern post-Enlightenment society see the fascinating book by Newbigin *(op. cit.)*.

the European Community, "often called a 'Rich Man's Club,' "[17] exists an ever expanding Fourth World in which poverty is present on a large scale. In the words of a European Community Commission report: "Around the mid nineteen-seventies there were at least 30 million people in poverty in the countries which now comprise the Community (excluding Greece)."[18] In this connection the report mentions specifically immigrants, unskilled workers, single-parent families, large families, drifters, alcoholics, and drug addicts, and reports that in 1978, by conservative estimates, no fewer than five million European households were totally dependent on social welfare.[19] In the same year some one-and-a-half million people in Europe were homeless or lived in hostels, shacks, and shanty towns under extremely unhealthy conditions, and at least four million people in Europe were illiterate.[20] Many were victims of structural unemployment and are condemned to "perpetual poverty as second-class citizens."[21]

And research shows that this situation has become dramatically worse in recent years. The adage of the well-known sociologist, the late Gunnar Myrdal, is still being confirmed: "Poverty in the Western world is the tragic counterpart of prosperity." If European societies were measured by the Just, Participatory, and Sustainable Society (JPSS) criteria formulated at the 1975 fifth assembly of the World Council of Churches in Nairobi, one would discover in Europe a huge number of poor, that is, culturally and socially isolated or marginalized people.

Finally, one needs to describe as a form of evil what is happening in our time to nature. We arise from nature. Our lives, the whole of our human existence, is rooted in nature and cannot possibly be detached from it. It has become abundantly clear, however, that we have come to regard nature as an object of exploitation, as a maidservant ever at our disposal, rather than as a sister to be treated with decency or a mother to whom we should relate with love and gratitude. We are living in a time in which vast rain forests, the lungs of this good earth, are being cut down purely for profit. Large parts of the inhabitable world are being poisoned and changed into dead moonscapes, uninhabitable areas where neither plant, animal, nor human can flourish. In short, thanks to the insane behavior of humankind the environment is being hopelessly polluted and defiled.

17. L. Hamilton and W. D. Just, *Poverty and Dependence in the European Community: An Ethical Perspective* (Rotterdam, 1983) 9.

18. Cited in Hamilton and Just, *ibid.*

19. *Idem.*

20. *Ibid.*, 9.

21. *Ibid.*, 12.

Salvation

But this is not the whole story. There is more to be said about this world than that it is severely fragmented and broken. It is and remains God's creation. That is, it continues to be the permanent object of his inexhaustible love, care, and concern. He maintains his creation and has compassion for it. In the New Testament the concept of *ktisis* (creation) contains the idea of the whole of created reality. This means that God's salvation has cosmic, social, and personal dimensions.

In the first place, heaven, earth, nature, and all living beings — the universe, all things *(ta panta)* — will be redeemed. The whole creation in all its parts "will be set free from its bondage to decay and will obtain the freedom of the glory of the children of God" (Rom. 8:21).

Secondly, God's salvific action is directed to the life of humankind. As one of the preparatory documents (Issue Paper I) of the Vancouver Assembly of the World Council of Churches put it: The whole of human history — at all possible levels, times, and places, with all its social, cultural, and religious traditions, classes, and peoples, all its dark or glorious, destructive or creative aspects — is "the *theatrum Dei*, the arena" of the action of the triune God.

Thirdly, all people as such are the special objects of God's redeeming mercy. Despite everything, the human person still bears God's image and consequently retains the capacity for receiving what D. C. Mulder has called "salvation at the deeper level" and for relating salvifically to his or her neighbor and to the rest of creation. Beyond that, nature remains, by the grace of the Creator, a source of "proximate salvation."[22] Nature nurtures us in all sorts of ways: It furnishes us with food, affords us "esthetic delight" and opportunity for healing meditation, offers us "companionship . . . , consolation, and inspiration," and enables us to come to ourselves "in times of inner crisis."[23]

To quote the Indian theologian Stanley Samartha: "Humankind still lives fully under the rainbow of the Noachic covenant."[24] It is as true now as it was in the past that the Lord of heaven and earth does not will to abandon his people. Today, too, in the history of our present world, his kingdom is coming. In the life and work of Jesus Christ, God the Redeemer provides the full solution to the needs of people whose existence is threat-

22. The terms "deeper" and "proximate" in relation to salvation are from D. C. Mulder, "Over onheil en heil," in D. J. Hoens, et al., *Inleiding tot de studie van godsdiensten* (Kampen, 1985) 78.

23. *New Directions in Faith and Order*, 17.

24. From an unpublished lecture presented by Samartha to the theological faculty of the Free University in Amsterdam, October 6, 1987.

ened in whatever way. God does not leave people in their misery and sin; he is present in "their immediate concerns for food, security, and health" and their striving for "deeper-lying, ultimate salvation."[25] In Christ he comes to them in order to effect complete redemption among them. "The core of the messianic confession remains resurrection from the (multiform) powers of death, with Jesus of Nazareth in the fore, profoundly humiliated, surpassingly exalted."[26] The salvation that is definitively offered to all in the Messiah is intended for all situations of human want. It includes the mending of divisions, the restoration of disturbed relationships, the healing of brokenness, and holistic liberation from all forms of human captivity.

The news of "the manifold grace of God" (1 Pet. 4:10), the gospel of redemption, corresponds directly to the manifold forms of human need. It comprises the liberation of the whole person, not merely of the body or of the soul. The gospel message of salvation knows no such distinction. There is nothing corporeal that does not immediately affect the spirit and nothing spiritual that does not also have to do with the body. The fundamental biblical idea of the kingdom permits no dichotomies and excludes all false dilemmas, whether they be between the spiritual and the material, the transcendent and the immanent, the internal and the external, the personal and the communal, the individual and the social, the "already" and the "not yet," "here" and "there," the present and the hereafter. God's salvation must be conceived comprehensively. In the gospel of the kingdom there can be no doubt that in Christ God desires to come to all, to the publican, to Lazarus, and to Job, to the sinner as well as to those sinned against, and to those who suffer for no understandable reason.

But this does not mean that heaven and earth, salvation and well-being, simply coincide. The view that the two are identical leads to a number of unacceptable conclusions. If well-being cannot be distinguished from salvation, then human happiness lies solely in salvation. But that would mean, first, that unbelievers cannot experience happiness, which is obvious nonsense, and, second, that *earthly* well-being could in no way be associated with salvation, which is biblically-theologically untenable. Conversely, if salvation consists entirely in earthly well-being, it would mean that "every mishap would have to be viewed as lack of salvation, as that which cuts off the victim from fellowship with God."[27] But this is an utterly inhuman idea. Furthermore, this would mean that conversion

25. Mulder, *op. cit.*, 78.

26. N. A. Schuman, "Notities bij een signalement," *Voorlopig* 18 (1986) 90.

27. J. Wiebering, "Auf der Suche nach einem geglückten Leben," *Theologische Literaturzeitung* 112/1 (1987) 9.

to and union with God, forgiveness of sin and guilt, personal relationship with Christ, and eternal life fall outside the terms of salvation-reality, which is a thoroughly blasphemous concept. Salvation and well-being may not be fused. Here, too, the notion of "eschatological reserve" must be maintained. But earthly happiness does belong to the salvation that comes with God's kingdom. Though these two realities must always be distinguished, they "may not be isolated from each other," at least not if we are concerned to uphold the biblical idea "of the whole person or of humanity as a whole."[28]

Mediation

Since Pentecost the new community of Jesus Christ has extended itself throughout humanity. From that first day in Jerusalem people "from every nation under heaven" (Acts 2:5) have been able to hear the news of the *magnalia Dei*, the mighty acts of God. Since then it has become possible for all human families, east and west, south and north, to encounter the living Lord and to participate in the salvation that God offers in Jesus Christ.

But the *imitatio Christi* is essential to this salvation. As a means of preserving its own spiritual health and identity, the new community is summoned to discipleship in humble service of a humankind in desperate need of healing. Material realization of salvation depends in part on the participation of the Spirit-animated, ever-repenting community of believers in the suffering and salvific work of Christ in this world until he comes again. In this process the church must not succumb to disillusionment in the face of world conditions. In the tension between the "already" and the "not yet" lies the new community's opportunity for and summons to mediation of salvation: Both of these eschatological poles act as spurs to prompt the community to carry out its missionary task. The salvific imperative thus arises from the tension between the salvific indicative and subjunctive: The *possibility* of the church's mediation is grounded in the redemption in Jesus Christ, which is complete in principle; the *necessity* of this mediation is rooted in the material incompleteness of salvation in the world.

But the new community cannot allow itself to be led into confusion or temptation by this possibility and necessity. When God comes to people, the community plays only a participatory role. The salvific action of the church never stands by itself, *sui generis*. It is always an outflow of God's

28. *Ibid.*

saving activity. The new community needs to recall again and again that the imperative of its mediation is derived exclusively from the salvific indicative of God. It is only on the basis of that awareness that it can protect itself against inclinations toward a "chiliastic and gnostic anticipation of that which belongs to God alone."[29] God is working to realize the purpose of his kingdom here and now. On that account the new community can, may, and must be involved in that work. But it is God alone who establishes the kingdom; the new community can only direct its energies toward that end. What God brings to pass, the community of faith has the privilege of promoting.

Against this background we can now flesh out the contours of the Christian mediation of salvation. "The church is called to proclaim the gospel to all the world in words and by life, walking the way of the cross."[30] But in order to fulfill this task properly the new community needs to assume a posture of attentiveness with the intention of receiving important corrective messages from a divided world and a suffering humanity, knowing that all too often it has not remained faithful to its calling. It must insure that its witness is not shaped wrongly, in such a way that it hinders God's action and blocks the kingdom. Looking at the practice of the past one is struck by the fact that the church has frequently given its witness to the gospel "with might and main," exhibiting a crusading rather than a crucified mind. And in many situations this remains true even now.

Coercive witness is not consistent with the essential nature of salvation history and certainly does not accord with truly effective Christian testimony. Throughout the whole history of the witnessing community it has been, in fact, the weak, the little ones, and the oppressed who have most rapidly and spontaneously accepted and passed on the gospel. Men, especially powerful men, often rely on their own abilities and knowledge to save them. Not so the little ones: the poor, many women, and children. In their marginal positions they usually have only one option, which is to place their trust solely in God and to expect deliverance from him alone. Often they experience the deepest intent and meaning of the gospel more authentically than others. They sense more truly what the good news is all about. For that reason the witnessing and mediating community may never fail to give ear to *their* witness.

The church must measure its mediation by the kingdom of God. The goal toward which the Christian community needs to strive is, stating

29. D. J. Krieger, "Zur Heilslehre in Hinduismus und Christentum," in Braun, *Indische Religionen,* 68.

30. W. H. Lazareth, ed., *The Lord of Life: Theological Explorations of the Theme "Jesus Christ, the Life of the World"* (Geneva, 1983) xv.

it briefly, a society shaped in accordance with the features and categories of the kingdom, a society that exhibits shalom. And because such a society can only be formed, populated, and inhabited by liberated human beings, the church's task of mediation is the promotion of the holistic liberation of men, women, and children everywhere by words and deeds, speech and action, proclamation and the practice of solidarity, and by modeling the faith.

The church's mediatory mandate thus consists of a number of facets that together constitute a single indivisible whole.

Proclamation. People must be summoned to faith and repentance, to reconciliation with their Creator and their fellow creatures — including their "mother" and "sister," nature. They must become acquainted with the good news of acquittal, of forgiveness of sin and guilt, and of the new life that begins in the present and continues beyond the grave with Jesus Christ in the New Jerusalem, where "he will wipe away every tear from their eyes," "death will be no more," and "mourning and crying and pain will be no more" (Rev. 21:4).

Community. People who are lonely and estranged, who have no purpose for living and no longer understand the meaning of their own existence, need to be told and especially shown the good news that in Christ the dividing walls have been broken down. They must be invited to join the new community of those who have devoted themselves to the King and his kingdom and who live in joyful expectation of its coming.

The ministry of mercy. Part of the task of the mediating community is the extension of help and assistance to all who are in deep physical or material distress. The bearers of the gospel of liberation, the followers of Jesus Christ, who are called to share in his suffering in the world and who indicate their readiness for such suffering by drinking the wine and eating the broken bread of his eucharistic meal, can never forget or ignore the personal suffering and distress of even the least among his brothers and sisters.

The ministry of justice. The gospel of the kingdom is just as directly applicable to the macrostructural enslavement of people as to any other form of human captivity, evil, or distress. Therefore, the search for liberation on the structural level also directly and inseparably belongs to the church's missionary task of mediation. The church is called to advance the liberation of the poor and oppressed by doing everything it can to bring about a social, political, and economic order that is as just as possible, both close at hand and far away.

Though all people are called to salvation, many live in a human hell. The church, as the healing community, is called vigorously to oppose all things that lead to situations of evil and the frustration of salvation and to do its utmost to promote human liberation and wholeness. For human beings individually and humankind as a whole are called in Jesus' name to fullness of life, life in abundance (John 10:10).[31]

---

31. F. J. Verstraelen, "De kerk als helende gemeenschap," in A. Houtepen, ed., *Gerechtigheid, eenheid en vrede* (Amersfoort, 1982) 89.

PART III

The Missionary Movement in History

In this section four authors discuss the changes and lines of continuity that have existed in the Protestant and Roman Catholic missionary movements through the course of history. The focus is on mission as movement: What points of view and perspectives have been held successively in that history? The aim is not to chart the history of mission or of the theory or theology of Roman Catholic or Protestant missions. Both of those tasks have been carried out before.[1] But until now relatively little attention has been given to the history of the *motivating forces* of mission.[2] So here the aim is to steer a middle course between a history of missions and a history of mission theory and theology and to describe the dynamics of the different missionary movements.

The authors begin with the great changes that occurred toward the end of the fifteenth century with Columbus's first landing in what is now called Latin America (1492) and Vasco da Gama's discovery of a sea route to Asia, which made possible the rise of global Christianity. 1789 was a watershed year: The French Revolution had a profound effect on the dynamics of mission. Moreover, in 1792 the first Protestant mission society came into being. The chapters in this section discuss Catholic and Protestant missions up to 1789 (chapters 14 and 15) and then to the early 1960s (chapters 16 and 17), when the International Mission Council was integrated with the World Council of Churches and when the Second Vatican Council, attended by many non-Western bishops, ushered the Roman Catholic Church into a new era. The relativizing of the missionary spirit by the philosophy of the Enlightenment is treated in connection with Protestant missions before 1789 (in chapter 15). Not as an appendix to

---

1. J. A. B. Jongeneel, *Missiologie* I: *Zendingswetenschap* (The Hague, 1986) 132-59, offers a summary and analysis of mission histories published up to the mid-1980s.
2. *Ibid.*, 54-99, offers a list and an evaluation of the principal works in this area.

these four chapters, but as the reverse side of their Western view of mission history a fifth chapter appraises the history of the missionary movement from the perspective of the Third World (chapter 18). Later sections of the book (beginning with chapter 19) deal with the years since the early 1960s.

The mission historian employs the historical method and draws on both primary and secondary sources. These sources include not just materials in archives, the innumerable reports of mission conferences, the hundreds of mission periodicals, and a larger number of other written sources, but also oral history, which is especially important in the history of missionary movements from a Third World perspective.

3. New directions are explored in J. Glazik, N.-P. Moritzen, et al., *Warum Mission? Theologische Motive in der Missionsgeschichte der Neuzeit* (Kirche und Religionen — Begegnung und Dialog III/1-2; Munich, 1984).

CHAPTER 14

The Catholic Missionary Movement from 1492 to 1789

A. CAMPS

The Christian faith experienced worldwide expansion for the first time in the period from the late fifteenth to the late eighteenth centuries.[1] Before then Christianity had sent down firm roots mainly in Europe, Asia Minor, and North Africa, with side shoots to southern India, Central Asia, and China. But during the period we are considering the faith went to all the world's continents, though not to all parts of all the continents.[2] Here our task is to describe the missionary movement in terms of its missionary points of view and perspectives.[3]

The missionary movement took off in two directions: into Asia and Latin America. The Spanish conquest of most of South and Central America and part of North America began when Columbus landed on Hispani-

1. T. Ohm, *Wichtige Daten der Missionsgeschichte. Ein Zeittafel* (Münster, 1961[2]).
2. S. Neill, *A History of Christian Missions* (Harmondsworth, 1986[2]). See also H. Jedin and J. Dolan, *History of the Church* (New York, 1965-81) V, 575-614; VI, 232-325; VII, 189-205; VIII, 175-207; IX, 527-75; X, 672-804; A. Mulders, *Missiegeschiedenis* (Bussum, 1957). For further literature see *Bibliotheca Missionum* 1-30 (Münster, 1916-75) and *Bibliografia Missionaria* (Rome, 1933-).
3. See G. Goyau, *Missions et missionnaires* (Paris, 1931); F. Rousseau, *L'idée missionnaire aux XVIe et XVIIe siècles* (Paris, 1930); *Les réveils missionnaires en France du Moyen-Âge à nos jours (XIIe-XXe siècles)* (Paris, 1984); J. Beckmann, "Utopien als missionarischer Stosskraft," in *Vermittlung zwischenkirchlicher Gemeinschaft,* ed. J. Baumgartner (Schöneck-Beckenried, 1971) 361-407; U. Bitterli, *Die "Wilden" und die "Zivilisierten." Grundzüge einer Geistes- und Kulturgeschichte der europäisch-überseeischen Begegnung* (Munich, 1976); idem, *Alte Welt — Neue Welt. Formen des europäische-überseeischen Kulturkontakts (15.-18. Jahrhundert)* (Munich, 1986); C. R. Boxer, *The Church Militant and Iberian Expansion 1440-1770* (Baltimore, 1978); *Expansion and Reaction,* ed. H. L. Wesseling (Leiden, 1978); *The Expansion of the International Society,* ed. H. Bull and A. Watson (Oxford, 1985); *Dokumente zur Geschichte der europäischen Expansion,* ed. C. Verlinden and E. Schmitt (7 vols.; Munich, 1986).

ola in 1492. In 1498 Vasco da Gama landed on the coast of Malabar in South India and with that event Portugal's influence in Asia began. Spanish expansion was therefore primarily in America and Portuguese expansion was primarily in Asia, except for the Philippines, which were colonized by Spain from its South American base, and Brazil, which was accidentally "discovered" in 1500 by Pedro Cabral and thus fell under Portuguese control.

These two movements of conquest were very different in character. Spain saw its *conquista* as the sequel to the *reconquista*, that is, to the expulsion of Islamic rule from Spain itself. Granada, the last Islamic city in Spain, was conquered in 1492. This background in the *reconquista* explains why in the Americas Spain strove to take possession of the whole continent.

Portugal, after a long period of searching for a sea route around Africa, found the way to Asia around the Cape of Good Hope. Its purposes were to attack the Islamic countries of the Middle East from another direction, which failed, and to take over the business of the Islamic traders, at which it succeeded. Therefore, Portugal conquered no territories in Asia and was satisfied to establish trading posts and forts on Asian coasts.

These different approaches to conquest had far-reaching consequences for the development of America and Asia. In America, the whole process of conquest, colonization, and liberation had approached the end of its course by the beginning of the nineteenth century, and new states had begun to be formed by mainly European populations. In Asia, indigenous powers remained in place and Western influence remained weak. This was to change only in the nineteenth century when the power of the new capitalism was felt.[4] Because of these differences, differences in missionary perspectives were inevitable.

Pope Alexander VI issued three Bulls in 1493 that divided the world according to rights of patronage between Spain and Portugal. He charged both nations with spreading the Christian faith and planting churches in their respective domains. In time the disadvantages of this division of realms became clear. In 1622 Pope Gregory XV attempted to give a different orientation to missionary activity by creating the congregation of the *Propaganda Fide,* the first secretary of which, Francisco Ingoli, was a wise man with considerable foresight. The two systems of patronage and *Propaganda* were not compatible. The *Propaganda* was limited to areas where neither Spain nor Portugal had strong influence on missionary activity, but its missionary guidelines — very modern for the times — extended into the Spanish and Portuguese realms. But it was not until after World

4. H. L. Wesseling, Introduction, in *Expansion and Reaction,* 4f.

War II that the patronage system completely disappeared. Along with the patronage system and the *Propaganda Fide*, from the seventeenth century on France began to exert influence in the non-Western world and French missionaries began to take a noteworthy part in missionary work.

This chapter will discuss in order the missionary perspectives of Spanish patronage, Portuguese patronage, the *Propaganda Fide*, and the French missions.

The Mission under Spanish Patronage

Bitterli distinguishes four stages in the encounter between Spain and the inhabitants of America. When the two cultures first met there was astonishment on the part of the Spanish and terror on the part of the natives. The Spanish overcame their own timidity by using cannons. They did not come to any understanding of the strangeness of the native cultures and were more concerned with trade, that is, with greed. Hospitality on the part of members of the indigenous cultures was answered with hostility. So relations remained tenuous and fragile.

Unsurprisingly, the second stage, that of cultural contact, did not go well. Spain was overpopulated. Emigrants to America settled in accessible and fertile regions. The highly organized native cultures lacked the capacity to adapt to this invasion. Indigenous people who did not wish to die young in goldmines and on plantations had to retreat to remote areas. But their mortality rates were very high. In 1492 there were about one million people living in Hispaniola. In 1510 the indigenous population there was only fifty thousand.

The church's mission was not devoid of responsibility for the death of the native populations, but there was a strong countermovement among Franciscans and Jesuits in favor of the native people. Bartholomé de las Casas, a secular priest who became a Dominican, fiercely defended the rights of the native people, but then he was the one who came up with the idea of using African slaves to replace the natives as workers.[5] In the first century of the Spanish conquest the Franciscans tried to found a native — not Spanish — church and were able to maintain it for a century.[6] This was the origin of the "reservations" ("*aldeias*" in Portuguese), protected

---

5. J. Höffner, *Kolonialismus und Evangelium. Spanische Kolonialethik im goldenen Zeitalter* (Trier, 1972³); *Bartolomé de Las Casas: A Selection of His Writings*, tr. and ed. G. Sanderlin (New York, 1971) 100-102.

6. E.g., J. de Mendieta, OFM (1525-1604), *Historia ecclesiástica indiana* I-IV (Mexico, 1945); *Motolinia's History of the Indians of New Spain*, tr. and annotated Fr. Borgia Steck, OFM (Washington, 1951; the Spanish work was written between 1536 and 1641).

areas where native people could live under the leadership of Franciscans and Jesuits. Many learned missionaries studied and recorded the native cultures.[7]

The third stage was that of the clash of cultures, which actually began during the preceding stages. The military superiority of the Europeans was used to exterminate native Americans, to drive them into unlivable areas, or to deprive them of their cultures. Already during Columbus's second stay on Hispaniola there was a battle between the Europeans and the indigenous people. Such bloody incidents have cast a shadow over the history of Europeans in America, as has, even more, the importation of slaves from Africa.[8] At the root of all this were not only the quest for gold and the desire for fertile land but also the superior self-image of the Europeans and the negative attitude of Christians toward the religious and moral convictions of the native peoples. Again, many missionaries advocated a more humane approach. But because the church had become institutionalized, its legislation and the influence of its local councils left no freedom for any approach to indigenous people that took account of the context.[9]

The fourth phase — also not strictly chronological — was that of acculturation and cultural interpenetration. People did become aware of the need for cooperation, but that took more than one generation. One can discern this process most among the "mestizos" and among people of African ancestry.

Disputes arose in the church with regard to the degree of cultural accommodation or interpenetration. For example, some identified the Aztec deity Quetzalcoatl with the apostle Thomas, who was said to have preached the gospel in Mexico and who was expected to return. Cortés, the Spanish conqueror, exploited this expectation, saying that he himself was Thomas. The Franciscans, who wanted to build up a native church, vehemently denied this. Those supporting Cortés took up this identification partly in order to identify the native people as apostate Christians, who could therefore be enslaved. But their opponents wanted nothing to do with such assumptions. Without referring to any earlier missionizing, they stressed the good qualities of the Indians, qualities that made it possible for them to become Christians — in their own way.

Great Franciscan authors such as Motolinia, de Mendieta, and de

---

7. H. Wismann, *Sind doch die Götter auch gestorben. Das Religionsgespräch der Franziskaner mit den Azteken von 1524* (Gütersloh, 1981); J. G. Durán, *Monumenta Catechetica Hispano-americana* I (siglo XVI) (Buenos Aires, 1984) 285-353.

8. A. de Kom, *Wij slaven van Suriname* (The Hague, 1984[4]).

9. W. Henkel, *Die Konzilien in Lateinamerika* I: *Mexiko 1555-1897* (Paderborn, 1984).

Sahagun and Dominicans such as de las Casas and Duran fostered and recorded the growth of the native church as a counterpart to the state church. But the state church was too powerful. It suppressed both the ideas and the writings of these men. The Third Council of Lima (1567-68) prohibited the consecration of native Americans as priests. The Spanish state party in the church prescribed that the good name of the conquest had to be propagated, that information concerning conflicts between the mission and the state had to be suppressed, and that the native peoples had to be regarded as inferior human beings with no culture. A century after the conquest the struggle between the pro-Spanish and pro-Indian parties in the church was thus settled in favor of the former.

The pro-Indian party was propelled by four utopian motives: They wanted to reform the church by returning to its primitive era; they emphasized pastoral care and imitation of Jesus in humility and poverty; they sought to establish a mission church, not a state church, and to do so without violence; and they sought to gather the Indians into larger units in the "reservations" with the aim of accomplishing what had failed in Europe, the establishment of a millennial Christian kingdom. The Franciscans understood that before the arrival of the Spanish the Incas in Peru had enjoyed a genuine community with a high degree of civilization. That was their model.[10]

The pro-Spanish party acted from a very different set of motives. Its members included the Dominicans in Mexico who opposed the sacramental practices of the Franciscans, who regarded the native people positively and admitted them to the Eucharist. The pro-Spanish party sought above all else to establish a church like the church in Spain, an orderly church with rules and structures laid down by synods and councils.[11]

10. J. L. Phelan, *The Millennial Kingdom of the Franciscans in the New World* (Berkeley, 1970[2]), E. E. Sylvest, *Motifs of Franciscan Mission Theory in Sixteenth-Century New Spain* (Washington, 1975); Beckmann, *op. cit.*, 373-85; Bitterli, *op. cit.*, 81-179; A. Camps, "Das Franziskanische Missionsverständnis im Laufe der Jahrhunderte," in A. Camps and G. H. Hunold, *Erschaffe mir ein neues Volk. Franziskanische Kirchlichkeit und missionarische Kirche* (Mettingen, 1982) 30-43; H.-J. Prien, *Die Geschichte des Christentums in Lateinamerika* (Göttingen, 1978) 79-326; T. Lemaire, *De Indiaan in ons bewustzijn. De ontmoeting van de Oude met de Nieuwe Wereld* (Baarn, 1986); A. Camps, "Begegnung mit indianischen Religionen," in M. Sievernich, ed., *Conquista und Evangelisation* (Mainz, 1992) 348-72.

11. J. Specker, *Die Missionsmethode in Spanisch-Amerika im 16. Jahrhundert mit besonderer Berüksichtigung der Konzilien und Synoden* (Schöneck-Beckenried, 1953).

The Mission under Portuguese Patronage

Where Portugal took power — in Brazil, in coastal settlements on the African continent, and at trading posts and forts in Asia — there was usually not the kind of extensive contact with large parts of the indigenous population that occurred in Spanish America. Portugal was not out to conquer but to increase trade and to gain control of sea routes. Moreover, under Portuguese patronage there was a strong emphasis on the concurrence of the temporal and spiritual powers (the two swords). Use of weapons was permitted only because the patron had granted the right to preach, and preaching served its purpose only when it was accompanied and protected by weapons. Spiritual conquest and worldly conquest went hand in hand. The kings of Portugal viewed themselves, independently of Rome, as the rulers over bishops, over provincials of orders, and over individual missionaries. Royal consent was required in all matters. Portugal viewed itself as the missionary nation par excellence. This self-understanding prevailed among both Portuguese missionaries and the Portuguese authorities into the twentieth century. In 1774 Pombal wrote to the newly appointed archbishop of Goa that the king of Portugal, as the highest authority in the Order of Christ, was the spiritual prelate, with jurisdiction over all dioceses from Brazil to Japan.

This understanding of Portuguese power was the most conspicuous motive for Portuguese missionary activity. But it produced difficulties. The Spanish mendicant orders, which had established themselves on the Philippines from their base in South America, did not accept the Portuguese arrangement. They attempted to enter Japan and China, which had been entrusted to the Jesuits, and after considerable struggle succeeded.

Furthermore, there were always missionaries who were dissatisfied with the normal practice of the Portuguese and who wanted to leave the Portuguese enclaves and go to the *real* India, the real China, or the real Japan. The Jesuits, for example, Jerome Xavier in the Mogul Empire in North India, Matteo Ricci in China, Francis Xavier in Japan, and Roberto de Nobili in South India, were especially prominent in this endeavor. The great thinker behind these ventures was Alessandro Valignano (1539-1606). In him we find an approach very different from the usual Portuguese pattern: He studied the uniqueness of other peoples, he adapted to their customs and convictions, and he used persuasion in place of force, patience instead of haste, and depth instead of superficiality. With these men an approach to mission originated that sought to operate independently of Portuguese power.

Of course this approach occasioned friction with Portugal and with other orders. The Rites controversy in India and China over the legitimacy of their adaptations and the agelong persecution of Christians in Japan, Vietnam, and China was among the results. For centuries all this hindered the expansion of Christianity in Asia. It remained "a stranger in the land." That these Jesuits were not Portuguese is noteworthy: Their theological and cultural training was very different from that of the Portuguese. Of course, they did not advocate what we would call interreligious dialogue today, but the Portuguese manner for converting people was foreign to them.[12]

The *Propaganda Fide*

The full name of the *Propaganda Fide* is *Sacra Congregatio de Propaganda Fide*. This department of the Roman Curia was established in 1622. Attempts had been made from the time of Raymond Lull (at the beginning of the fourteenth century) to centralize the church's missionary work. One must not misunderstand the word "propaganda." The word "mission" did not exist yet, so a medieval term was used.

Many motives played a role in the creation of the Congregation of the *Propaganda Fide*. Among these were the spirit of the Counter-Reformation, that is, the consciousness of a tragic split in the church; the realization that turning the expansion of Christianity over to the patronage of Spain and Portugal was a mistake, one that badly muddied the religious motivations of mission; changes in the political, economic, social, and cultural context with the appearance of England, the Netherlands, and France on the international scene beside Spain and Portugal; and the growing conviction that mission is universal and that all non-Christians have a right to hear the gospel. The issue at stake was the unity of the church, Catholic, Protestant, and Orthodox, and the conversion of all non-Christians.[13]

---

12. C. R. Boxer, *The Portuguese Seaborne Empire 1415-1825* (London, 1969); *idem, Portuguese Conquest and Commerce in Southern Asia, 1500-1750* (London, 1985); A. Jann, *Die katholische Missionen in Indien, China und Japan. Ihre Organisation und das portugiesische Patronat vom 15. bis ins 18. Jahrhundert* (Paderborn, 1915); F. A. Plattner, *Pfeffer und Seelen. Die Entdeckung des See- und Landweges nach Asien* (Einsiedeln, 1955²); J. F. Schütte, *Valignano's Mission Principles for Japan* I-II (St. Louis, 1980, 1985); A. Camps, *Jerome Xavier S.J. and the Muslims of the Mogul Empire* (Schöneck-Beckenried, 1957); S. Rajamanickam, *The First Oriental Scholar: Robert de Nobili* (Tirunelveli, 1972); on M. Ricci see chapter 4 above; also G. Minamiki, *The Chinese Rites Controversy from Its Beginnings to Modern Times* (Chicago, 1985).

13. Thomas a Jesu, OCD, *De procuranda salute omnium gentium* (1613). Cf. P. Rovenius, *Tractatus de missionibus ad propagandam fidem et conversionem infidelium et haereticorum instituendis* (Louvain, 1626); the author has a very broad concept of missions. The word "mission" was used the first time with reference to the Jesuits and their activities in northern Germany.

The establishment of the Congregation was a milepost in the history of the church. It arose from the personal initiative of Pope Gregory XV, who appointed an expert staff to guide the Congregation. The first secretary (from 1622 to 1649), Francesco Ingoli, shaped both the content and the form of the work. He took stock of the church's condition and built up what eventually became the comprehensive archive of the Congregation. The archive has been almost completely preserved, though during the Napoleonic era some volumes were lost when the entire archive was taken to Paris.

Perhaps the instruction of 1659, sent by the Congregation to the apostolic vicars of Indochina, best reflects the program of the Congregation. It states that the church must distance itself from colonialism to give the missions a purely spiritual character, that missionaries must abstain from politics and trade, that they are to receive adequate spiritual and academic formation, that an indigenous clergy is to be trained, that Europe is not to be exported to the mission field, and that other cultures and local customs are to be respected. The criticism here of certain approaches implies a new motivation and orientation. This program could not be implemented everywhere immediately. The opposition of the patronage countries was strong and the scope of the work was enormous. But with stubborn tenacity the Congregation managed in the course of centuries to give credibility to its task.[14]

The Influence of France in the Seventeenth and Eighteenth Centuries

Unlike the Hapsburg monarchy, which in this period tried in vain to influence Catholic missions, French missionaries exerted increasing influence. As a result France viewed itself as a Catholic nation *par excellence* with a special responsibility for Catholic mission.

A number of phenomena pointed in this direction already in the seventeenth century and persisted into the eighteenth century. The word "mission" was used often and took on specific content, namely, the reuni-

14. *Sacrae Congregationis de Propaganda Fide Memoria Rerum, 350 Anni a servizio delle missioni, 1622-1972* (4 vols.; Rome, 1971-1976); N. Kowalsky and J. Metzler, *Inventory of the Historical Archives of the Sacred Congregation for the Evangelization of People or "Propaganda Fide"* (Rome, 1983); J. Beckmann, *La congrégation de la Propagation de la Foi face à la politique internationale* (Schöneck-Beckenried, 1963); M. Muskens, *Friezen — Franken — Nederlanders op bedevaart, voor studie, voor overleg in Rome. Een geschiedenis — een uitnodiging* (Rome, 1988[2]) 209-27: This last volume contains much information on the establishment of the *Propaganda Fide*.

fication of Protestants with the Catholic Church, the conversion of unbelievers, the reconquest of Jerusalem, and the destruction of the Turkish Empire. Missionaries were sent to the Middle East, Canada, India, Indochina, China, and other places. A variety of institutions for internal missions arose, like the Lazarists, who worked in rural Catholic areas. Remarkably, Jesuits began to focus less on China and more on the French countryside, and the new institutions began to focus more on "distant missions." Of influence in these developments was the establishment of the *Propaganda Fide* and the canonization of Francis Xavier — both in 1622. The Roman congregation wanted to lodge greater responsibility for mission with bishops and to gain more control over the missionary activities of the religious. This became clear in France. The Capuchins became especially active in mission work, and various institutions such as the Lazarists and Oratorians gave non-religious priests a chance to go to "distant" missions. Also striking was the involvement of lay persons both at home and abroad.

In searching for the motivation of this movement one may not exclude political, colonial, and commercial considerations. But along with this was a new theology of mission (Bérulle: the mission of the incarnate Word), a linking of mission to martyrdom, and the conviction that Catholicism in Europe was moribund and that now the church was in the process of moving from the old lands to new lands. Some believed that the "heathen" were lost and had to be converted, while others expressed a milder view: Sincere non-Christians could obtain salvation. This turns out to have been a prelude to later discussion.[15]

15. *Les réveils missionnaires* (n. 3 above), 81-198.

CHAPTER 15

The Protestant Missionary Movement
up to 1789

J. A. B. JONGENEEL

Between the "discovery" of America by Columbus in 1492 and the establishment of the first Protestant mission society in England in 1792 lie three centuries of European expansion. In that period Protestantism not only spread from Germany and Switzerland over large parts of Northern, Central, and Western Europe and North America, but also grew into a true mission movement *in nuce*. In this historical survey we can label the sixteenth century as the century of the *initial unfolding*, the seventeenth century as the century of the *initial shaping*, and the eighteenth century as the century of the *further definition* of Protestant mission as a movement in process of development.

The Initial Unfolding of the Missionary Perspective
in the Sixteenth Century

Luther, Calvin, and Zwingli never set foot outside Europe. They considered it their mission to reform the Western European Catholic Church. In their writings there are scattered comments on mission, to be sure, but more important than collecting and systematizing these comments is the task of investigating whether — and if so, how — their Reformation starting point has been made fruitful for mission.

Luther preached the message of justification "by faith alone" (*sola fide*) and "by grace alone" (*sola gratia*) out of "Scripture alone" (*sola scriptura*), which meant not "the Vulgate (the Roman Church's Latin translation) alone" but "the Old and New Testaments (in or translated out of their original languages) alone." He translated the Bible from the original languages into German so that God's Word could be read and understood not

222

only by the clergy but also by common church people. Since then translation of Scripture from the original languages into vernacular languages and distribution of those translations among believers have been essential characteristics of all Protestant mission work. The nineteenth-century creation of Bible societies to translate and distribute the Bible was a logical consequence of the Reformation's doctrine of *sola scriptura.* Though one could draw many other lines of continuity from the Reformation to Protestant missions of later periods, this one example makes it clear enough that the terms "Reformation" and "mission" are not foreign to each other. In its essence the Reformation of the sixteenth century had missionary potential.

The central ideas of Luther, Calvin, and Zwingli, as well as Bucer and Bibliander, constituted a working outline for later Protestant mission. But they also sometimes put obstacles in its way. One of the main barriers was probably their understanding of the missionary mandate of Matthew 28:16-20. In their opinion this commandment was given only to the apostles and not to the apostles' successors, that is, to the bishops. Consequently this passage was stripped of its meaning for the present. The first Protestant theologian to break with this exegesis and to plead for the view that Jesus' missionary command still applies fully here and now was Hadrian Saravia (1531-1613), who was born of a Spanish father and a Flemish mother.[1] Theodore Beza, Calvin's successor at Geneva, vigorously opposed Saravia's opinion on the subject. But Protestantism gained from Saravia theological space to base the duty to engage in mission here and now on Matthew 28.

Given the life-and-death struggle between Rome and the Reformation in the sixteenth century, it is not surprising that the Protestantism of that time was only marginally active in mission. In the North, King Gustavus Vasa of Sweden initiated mission work among the Lapps on the basis of the rule *cuius regio eius religio* (the ruler of a domain decides its religion). In the West, The Huguenot Gaspard de Châtillon (Admiral de Coligny), supported by Calvin, launched an expedition to Brazil, but for a variety of internal and external reasons this first overseas Protestant mission effort failed. In the South, Valentin Clesz planned to visit the coast of northern Africa, but never managed to implement his plans. And in the East, Wenzel Budowetz of Budowa and some others ventured to do mission work among the Muslims in Constantinople.[2] In sum, all four points of the compass were considered, but sixteenth-century Protestant work

1. On Saravia see L. B. Smith, *The Contribution of Hadrian à Saravia (1531-1613) to the Doctrine of the Nature of the Church and Its Mission: An Examination of His Doctrine as Related to That of His Anglican Contemporaries* (dissertation, Edinburgh, 1965).

2. These mission efforts are mentioned in H.-W. Gensichen, *Missionsgeschichte der neueren Zeit* (Göttingen, 1976) 5-13.

never amounted to more than the initial unfolding of a few missionary vistas and perspectives.

The Initial Shaping of the Missionary Perspective in the Seventeenth Century

In the seventeenth century the Netherlands, England, and Denmark became important sea powers. This opened possibilities for Protestant mission work overseas, just as earlier Spain and Portugal had accomplished this for Roman Catholic mission work.

In its "Golden Age" the Netherlands played a prominent role in missions both at home and overseas. Even before the founding of the United East Indies Company in 1602 Peter Plancius (1552-1622) was a zealous advocate of mission. Later Justus Heurnius (1587-1652), William Teellinck (1579-1629), Gysbert Voetius (1589-1676), Godfrey Cornelius Udemans (1580-1649), John Hoornbeek (1617-66), and Jodocus of Lodenstein (1620-77) were the earliest Protestant theologians to lay the foundation of an advanced theory of mission, which did not shrink — be it noted — from intensive use of Roman Catholic missionary insights.[3] In 1618-19 the national synod of Dordt not only composed the Five Articles against the Remonstrants but also considered the problem of the administration of baptism overseas. And in 1622, the year that saw the founding of the *Congregatio de Propaganda Fide,* the first Protestant mission seminary, the Seminarium Indicum, was founded with the approval and support of the East Indies Company at the home of professor Anthony Walaeus (1573-1639) of Leiden. In the eleven years of the seminary's existence twelve students were trained for ministry overseas.

Seventeenth-century Dutch Reformed Protestantism combined the Calvinistic doctrine of election with missionary élan. The theology of Arminius and the Remonstrants, on the other hand, "would seemingly lead to a theology of missions, but Arminius did not move on to make such an application explicit. Oddly, it was Plancius, the predestinarian Calvinist in Amsterdam, who proposed Christian missions as one of the purposes of the East Indian trade."[4] But Remonstrantism did prove to be

---

3. Cf. the study by M. Galm, *Das Erwachen des Missionsgedankens im Protestantismus der Niederlande* (St. Ottilien, 1915), which overemphasizes the degree to which these Dutch authors relied on Roman Catholic theories of mission. Cf. J. A. B. Jongeneel, "The Missiology of Gisbertus Voetius: The First Comprehensive Protestant Theology of Missions," *Calvin Theological Journal* 26 (1991) 47-79.

4. Carl Bangs, *Arminius: A Study in the Dutch Reformation* (second ed., Grand Rapids, 1985) 258.

serviceable to mission. Hugo Grotius (1583-1645) wrote *The Truth of the Christian Religion* (1622), which was translated into many European languages and into Arabic and Malay. It inspired the German jurist Peter Heyling to go to Ethiopia.[5]

In seventeenth-century Europe there were centers of Protestant missionary enthusiasism also in Germany and England, for instance in German university cities like Kiel, where professors Wasmuth and Rave wanted to establish an institute for oriental languages,[6] and Halle, where August Hermann Francke, working in the spirit of Philipp Jacob Spener, created a Pietist mission climate. But with Francke and his pupils Bartholomew Ziegenbalg and Henry Plütschau, who went to India, we have already arrived at the transition to the eighteenth century. In England we note here only Oliver Cromwell's plans for a kind of Protestant *Congregatio de Propaganda Fide* and the formation of the New England Company in 1649, the Society for Promoting Christian Knowledge in 1698-99, and similar institutions later in the eighteenth century.

Seventeenth-century mission work was usually carried out in the wake of trade. "The religion of truth" accompanied "the religion of trade." Dutch missionaries came with the East Indies Company to the Gold Coast in Africa, to southern Africa, to Ceylon, to Malacca, to the Dutch East Indies, and to Taiwan, where missionaries Anthony Hambroek, Arnold Winsheim, Peter Mus, and Jacobus Ampzingius were killed in 1661. As a rule Dutch missionaries followed the dictates of the East Indies Company, but at times they emphatically opposed the company. They criticized, for instance, the Company's Japan Edict of 1648, which forbade the Dutch to display in Japan any sign whatever that they were Christians.

Several Dutch Reformed missionaries went to the New World, to Brazil and to the vicinity of New York. A number of Dutch Labadists went to America to establish house churches.[7] The German Justinian von Welz traveled via the Netherlands to Suriname, but died shortly after his arrival. One of the most important Protestant missionary figures of the seventeenth century was John Eliot, who beginning in 1632 worked among native Americans of North America, baptized thousands of them, and, when they were admitted to the settlements, had them make this vow: "The grace of Christ helping us, we do give ourselves and our children to God to be his people. He shall rule us in all our affairs, not only in our

5. Cf. O. Zöckler, *Geschichte der Apologie des Christentums* (Gütersloh, 1907) 319-24, where Heyling is not, however, mentioned.

6. Gensichen, *op. cit.*, 12.

7. W. Goeters, *Die Vorbereitung des Pietismus in der Reformierten Kirche der Niederlande bis zur Labadistischen Krisis, 1670* (Leipzig, 1911) 286.

religion and the affairs of the Church, but also in all our works and affairs in this world."[8]

In sum, for lack of an infrastructure of their own, seventeenth-century Protestant missions were bound to the trading companies. They did conceive structures of their own on occasion (e.g., Heurnius), but did not have sufficient scope to bring them to realization. Wherever they could operate with relative freedom from the embrace of the traders, they were more successful. Looking back on his lifework, Eliot commented: "Prayer and pains, through faith in Christ Jesus, will do anything."[9]

Further Definition of the Missionary Perspective in the Eighteenth Century

It was not just because of increasing activities overseas, but also and *especially* because of the changing spiritual climate in Europe itself that Protestant mission took on a very different look in the eighteenth century. We have in mind especially the influence in the West of the Enlightenment, which regarded natural religion as the standard for revealed religion. The philosopher Leibniz fell under the influence of Jesuit-written material on the religion and culture of China, which was far from savage. Jesus was no longer compared just with Moses and the prophets of Israel but also with Socrates and Confucius.[10] The question concerning the salvation of pagans was expressly posed and answered: Virtuous pagans enter heaven, it was said, apart from the merits of Christ's cross, solely on the basis of God's mercy.[11] This repudiation of the normative christology and soteriology naturally called into question the necessity of mission. Whereas in the seventeenth century some Remonstrants deemed mission superfluous because pagan nations were unworthy of the gospel,[12] in the eighteenth century the necessity of mission was called into question because the gospel to be preached to people overseas was deemed irrelevant. After all, they could all be saved in their own ways.

Eighteenth-century Christians tried in a number of ways to give an

---

8. Cited in S. Neill, *A History of Christian Missions* (revised edition by O. Chadwick; London, 1986) 192.

9. Quoted in *ibid.*

10. J. A. B. Jongeneel, *Het redelijke geloof in Jezus Christus. Een studie over de wijsbegeerte van de Verlichting* (Wageningen, 1971) 185ff.: "De plaats van Jezus in de geschiedenis."

11. Cf. *ibid.* 96-99: "Het heil der heidenen."

12. Cf. A. T. van Deursen, *Bavarianen en slijkgeuzen; kerk en kerkvolk ten tijde van Maurits en Oldebarnevelt* (Assen, 1974) 149ff.

appropriate answer to the challenge of the Enlightenment.[13] Some went to great lengths in adapting to the spirit of the times. Others began to think and preach in even more christocentric and soteriocentric ways. Count N. L. von Zinzendorf and the Moravian Church of the Brethren at Herrnhut made their missionary goal "to win souls for the Lamb," but consciously chose no longer to assume the *corpus Christianum* as the context of modern mission. Consequently, they came into conflict with government-sponsored and trading company-sponsored missions that still worked within that context. In the English-speaking world the Methodism of John Wesley ("The world is my parish") also engaged in a missionary reaction to the Enlightenment and its relativizing of the gospel, the Christian faith, the church, and mission.

In the eighteenth century, whether influenced by the Enlightenment or not, Christians carried on their mission work. Ziegenbalg and Plütschau worked enthusiastically in India and were succeeded by C. F. Schwartz and J. P. Fabricius. Their aim was to establish an Indian church. The first Indian pastor, Aaron, was ordained in 1733. In 1721 Hans Egede went to Greenland to labor among the indigenous people there. Von Zinzendorf's Herrnhut church sent out missionaries in all directions: to Greenland, western India, Suriname, the Gold Coast, Ceylon, Australia, and other places. Thomas Thompson also went to the Gold Coast and from there sent the African Philip Quaque to England to study; as the first African ordained in the Anglican Church (1765), Quaque returned home to serve until his death in 1816 as a school administrator and catechist.[14]

The expansion of missionary vision in the eighteenth century also led to the first clashes among Protestant missionaries. In Greenland

> the Moravians were very critical of Egede as a "colonializer," a stiff orthodox churchman, possessed (in their judgement) of very little real Gospel light; while Egede found that the Moravians preached an intolerably sentimental Gospel and had little idea of the moral conflict involved in the attempt to change the whole way of life of the Greenlanders.[15]

"The eighteenth century was a time of renewed awareness and of small and tentative beginnings."[16] Though since that century church and

---

13. Cf. Jongeneel, *op. cit.*, 213-24.

14. Neill, *op. cit.*, 203. Cf. David N. A. Kpobi, *Mission in Chains: The Life, Theology and Ministry of the Ex-Slave Jacobus E. J. Capitein (1717-1747) with a Translation of his Major Publications* (Zoetermeer, 1993).

15. Neill, *op. cit.*, 202.

16. *Ibid.*, 204.

mission had been forced into a defensive posture in Europe, elsewhere they were on the offensive. Hume, Voltaire, Rousseau, Lessing, and other Enlightenment philosophers never went to the icy polar regions and steamy tropics of the world, but that is what Reformed, Lutheran, Methodist, Baptist, and Anglican missionaries — and, in large numbers, the members of the Herrnhut church — did. When Egede could no longer do his pioneering work in Greenland alone, his son came out to help him, to write a grammar of the natives' language, and to translate the New Testament for them. Eliot, "the apostle to the Indians" in North America, had a worthy successor in David Brainerd, who left a diary that decades later inspired William Carey, the father of nineteenth-century mission societies, Henry Martyn, and others to engage in mission work. When Brainerd lay on his deathbed he transferred responsibility for his mission work to his brother John. Far from the salons of Enlightenment Europe missionaries both Protestant and Catholic shared fish, corn, or rice with those who in "civilized" literature were described as "savages." Does not mission, for all its mistakes, thus furnish "practical proof for the existence of God" (Kant)?

The oldest Protestant mission hymn gives us insight into the connection between the "Spirit-enlightened" revival movement of the eighteenth century — of Francke, Von Zinzendorf, Wesley, Edwards, and others — and mission:[17]

> Awake, thou Spirit of the martyrs,
>   Thy faithful watchmen who thy walls defend;
> Ne'er silent night and day as watchers,
>   But who in faith against the foe contend;
> Yea, their triumph cry the world has known,
>   And countless peoples they to Thee have won!

---

17. Composed in 1750 by the Hungarian Pietist Karl Heinrich von Bogatzky and translated by John J. Overholt in 1969 (*The Christian Hymnary* [Sarasota, 1972] number 404). Cf. J. A. B. Jongeneel, "Opwekking en zending," *Kerk en theologie* 34 (1983) 1-11.

CHAPTER 16

The Catholic Missionary Movement
from 1789 to 1962

A. CAMPS

Toward the end of the eighteenth century the Catholic missionary movement experienced a low point. Other than in the Philippines and among
Spanish and Portuguese-speaking people of Latin America, there were at
the time one and a half to two million Catholics in Asia, Africa, and Latin
America. Mission personnel had shrunk to a minimum.

     The causes of this were many and various. Philip II of Spain wanted
the Latin American church to be more or less independent of Rome.
Regalism in the form of two systems of patronage was extended. Deliberate
abolition of the indigenous church was coupled with persistence in building up a Spanish church. The native people of America were looked down
on and seen as cultureless, and the conquest was glorified. The Enlightenment had its influence among the European settlers in Latin America, from
whose ranks the clergy were recruited, who in their contempt for the native
peoples applied Enlightenment ideas only to themselves.

     The religious were forced to live in large monasteries far from
mission posts among the native people. The centralizing thrust of the
Council of Trent was allowed full sway, greatly increasing the power of
the bishops at the expense of the religious. There was continual conflict
between the Portuguese and Spanish slave traders, on the one hand, and
the religious, especially Franciscans and Jesuits on the reservations, on the
other.

     The struggle of Protestant nations against Portuguese rights of pa-
tronage in Brazil and Asia also played a role in the decline of Catholic
mission. The rites controversy in the Catholic church in China, India, and
Indochina and the conflict between "the church from above" of the Portuguese and "the church from below" of the Congregation for the Propagation of the Faith in Rome also hindered the progress of mission.

229

Yet further causes of the decline were the suspension of the Jesuit order, the Napoleonic wars, which made impossible any contact with other continents, and Napoleon's policy of assigning to France protection over all the missions. Pope Pius VII took exception to this policy, with the result that he, together with the entire Congregation for the Propagation of the Faith, was taken captive and brought to France.[1]

But at the beginning of the nineteenth century Catholic mission was revived. This, too, was a tumultuous period with high points and low points. We will consider here some of this period's most important movements.

Steps in Renewal

From his base in England the exiled priest Denis Chaumont succeeded in reawakening missionary interest in France. In 1805 the Parisian mission seminary and the seminary of the Fathers of the Holy Spirit were allowed to reopen. René de Chateaubriand's book *Le Génie du Christianisme* (1802), in which mission — especially mission in America — played a large role, had great influence. This was an early attempt at overcoming the rationalistic and anti-Christian forces in France.

Moreover, new orders and congregations with a missionary purpose arose: the Congregation of the Holy Hearts of Jesus and Mary (1805), the Sisters of St. Joseph of Cluny (1807), the Oblates of the Immaculate Virgin Mary (1816), and the Marists (1824). In Lyon Marie-Pauline Jaricot founded the Society for the Propagation of the Faith (1822), which was initially directed toward France but soon became international. Beginning in 1824, the *Annales de la Propagation de la Foi* came out in nineteen languages. After the *Congregatio de Propaganda Fide* had twice been plundered during the French Revolution and under Napoleon, Jaricot's society became the main source of financial aid to mission. In Germany there was no desire to link up with this French initiative, so other institutions arose: the Leopoldinen-Stiftung, based in Austria, the Xaverius-Verein, and the Ludwig-Missions-verein.

Another important factor at this time was the reestablishment of the Jesuit order by Pius VII in 1814 — after he had confirmed the continuation of the order in Russia under Catherine II in 1800. On other continents it was the church in China that despite persecutions still gave an impression of vitality: In 1815 there were eighty-nine Chinese priests and eighty

1. S. Delacroix, ed., *Histoire Universelle des Missions Catholiques* II (Paris, 1957) 321-94; H. Jedin and J. Dolan, *History of the Church* (New York, 1965-81) VI, 232-325.

European priests and 210,000 believers. Pius VII supported them and thus prepared the church for a restoration.[2]

The Restoration of Mission under Gregory XVI (1831-46)

The first thing Gregory XVI did was to depict clearly to the church of the West its task in regard to the propagation of the faith, which until that time had been carried out mainly by the patronage powers of Portugal and Spain. This he did in the first papal mission encyclical, *Probe Nostis* (1840). He supported the existing mission societies in France, Germany, and Austria and sought to place them under the direction of the society in Lyon. He also subscribed to the goals of the Mission Work of Infancy, the papal mission work for children that Bishop Forbin-Janson of Nancy founded in 1843.

All orders and religious communities were abolished in the midst of persecutions in Spain and Portugal in 1834 and 1836. Gregory sought to combat the consequences of this on recruitment of missionary personnel by attracting new workers from the revived Jesuit order. In this regard he received much cooperation from the Dutch General Superior, John Philip Roothaan. This was the origin of the system that followed until well into the twentieth century: Mission districts were marked off and turned over to the different orders and congregations, which were to furnish the bishops for the districts. Besides the Jesuits the members of the Paris mission seminary also followed this system.

In 1841 the Jewish convert Francois-Marie Libermann founded the Society of Missionaries of the Holy Heart of Mary, which in 1848 joined the society of the Holy Spirit, which had been founded in 1703. This French organization devoted its energies entirely to Africa and aimed at establishing indigenous churches there. Mére Anne-Marie Javouhey, founder of the St. Joseph Sisters of Cluny and of the Work of the Propagation of the Faith in Africa, did trailblazing work in Africa and among African-Americans.

Gregory gave Portugal a choice: either meet the obligations of patronage or give them up. When Portugal did not respond, the pope himself took in hand the reordering of ecclesiastical relations in Asia. He appointed vicars apostolic for India, Ceylon, Further India, China, Korea, Mongolia, and Africa. Conflicts arose over this with England and especially with Portugal in regard to India. The direction of mission districts was increas-

---

2. Delacroix, ed., III (1958) 27-51; VII, 189-205; *Les réveils missionnaires en France du Moyen-Âge à nos jours (XIIe-XXe siècles)* (Paris, 1984) 201-362.

ingly concentrated in the mission department at Rome. Gregory established forty-four new vicariates apostolic, a process that continued under
his successors. A new structure had come into being. As a result of close
ties with the orders, congregations, and religious institutions to which the
districts were entrusted, the earlier tension between the hierarchy and the
religious disappeared, new lay involvement was made possible, and a new
missionary spirituality developed. The restructuring also brought with it
certain disadvantages: Active missionizing was in the hands of the religious but centralized direction in Rome came mainly from secular priests
who had no field experience. Furthermore, political reorientation to the
colonial powers of France and England, in keeping with the spirit of the
time, was not an unmixed blessing.[3]

New Missionary Initiatives under Pope Pius IX (1846-78)

The restoration begun under Gregory XVI continued at an accelerated rate
under Pius IX, under whom thirty-three vicariates, fifteen prefectures, and
three delegatures came into being. Many missionary institutions were
established: in Italy the mission seminary of Milan, the Salesians, and the
Combonians; in France the Missionaries of the Sacred Heart, the Society
for African Missions, the White Fathers, and the Community of St. Francis
de Sales; in Belgium the Missionaries of Scheut; and in England the missionaries of Mill Hill. In many Western nations orders and communities
for women were formed under the inspiration of the ideals of St. Francis
of Assisi. Soon they, too, became active in mission. The old missionary
orders, such as the Franciscans, Capuchins, and Dominicans, experienced
a revival, stressing education and charity alongside preaching. Some
orders, congregations, and institutions specialized, particularly favoring
Africa, Oceania, eastern Asia, and people of African ancestry in South
America. Moreover, as appears from innumerable annals, periodicals, and
books,[4] a high degree of mission-mindedness was achieved among both
missionaries and those who stayed at home.

A clear need of the time was a new political initiative. The Por-

---

3. Delacroix, ed., III, 52-71; Jedin and Dolan, ed., VII, 195-205; J. Guennou,
Missions Etrangères de Paris (Paris, 1986); H. J. Koren, *To the Ends of the Earth: A General
History of the Congregation of the Holy Ghost* (Pittsburgh, 1983); C. J. Ligthart, *De Neder-
landse jezuïetengeneraal Jan Philip Roothaan* (Nijmegen, 1972); B. Arens, *Die katholische
Missionsvereine* (Freiburg, 1922); O. Stoffel, *Die katholische Missionsgesellschaften* (Im-
mensee, 1984).

4. L. Iriarte, *Der Franziskusorden* (Handbuch der franziskanischen Ordens-
geschichte; Altötting, 1984) 363-73; Jedin and Dolan, ed., VIII, 175-207.

tuguese, defending their rights of patronage in mission, especially in India, continued to resist the centralization of mission work at Rome in the Congregation for the Propagation of the Faith. In 1857 a concordat between the Vatican and Portugal was achieved. It worked well in China because only Macao remained under Portugal. But in India the concordat's effect was less favorable because important dioceses remained under Portuguese jurisdiction, though enough vicariates apostolic had been established to form a counterweight to Portugal there, and the prudent attitude of the vicars apostolic toward the Catholics from Goa who lived in their districts prevented major difficulties.

The global political influence of the Western powers was increasing, and this was especially clear in China and Indochina. The unequal treaties forced on China humiliated the country. From 1844 on this semicolonialism expanded rapidly. A result was a French protectorate over Catholic missions in China. Chinese hatred of foreigners was directed against the missionaries and the Christians, who were protected by these treaties. "Missionary incidents" evoked reprisals, especially from the French military. In the coming decades this state of affairs was to prove fatal.[5]

In this period a strong emphasis was placed on the training of indigenous clergy. The Congregation for the Propagation of the Faith continued to insist on this point. Especially in Indochina but also elsewhere this concern was taken solidly in hand by the founding of seminaries. Participation of the laity in the work of the church was promoted in new ways.[6]

Contrasting sharply with this renewal was the treatment of mission activity at the First Vatican Council (1869-70). Conflicts arose over whether the vicars apostolic who administered districts on behalf of the pope were entitled, like bishops, to participate in the Council. They were admitted, but during the Council meetings their position continued to be questioned.

Even more disappointing for mission representatives was that in the preparatory commission "For the Eastern Church and for Mission" no mission representative had a seat, and the commission devoted all its attention to the Eastern Church Mission, seeming to favor the Latinization of all the eastern churches. During the Council, proposals for the support of mission work were submitted, but even the third draft of a decree was so one-sidedly focused on the eastern churches that mission representatives had no use for it.

---

5. See chapter 5 above on China.
6. J. Beckmann, ed., *Der einheimische Klerus in Geschichte und Gegenwart* (Schöneck-Beckenried, 1950); J. Specker and W. Buehlmann, ed., *Das Laienapostolat in den Missionen* (Schöneck-Beckenried, 1961); J. Beckmann, ed., *Die Heilige Schrift in den katholischen Missionen* (Schöneck-Beckenried, 1966).

Furthermore, a strong centralist tendency emerged at the Council that favored the vicars apostolic and bishops at the expense of the superiors of orders, congregations, and institutions. In defense, the representatives of China and India formed separate groups that sought to counter the prevailing emphasis. In the end no decree was adopted because mission remained marginal. But the opinions (the "*vota*") submitted were used by later popes in their mission encyclicals.[7]

1878 to 1914: Mission and Imperialism

Other colonial powers besides France and England came on the scene, including united Germany, the Netherlands, Russia, the United States of America, and Belgium. Catholic mission derived some benefit from this as it gained global dimensions, but it also suffered the disadvantage of being viewed by the non-Western world as an extension of the imperialist powers and therefore as a foreign element.

Missionaries, being subject to the imperialist powers, had no real freedom to preach. In Further India this sometimes led to bloody persecutions by native authorities. In China it led to conversions based on material motives, to hatred on the part of mandarins and scholars, and to explosive uprisings (the Boxer Rebellion in 1900). In Korea, where the missionaries of Paris had tried from the beginning of the nineteenth century, despite repeated persecutions, to come to the aid of the lay church, there was peace from 1887 on, thanks to treaties between France and Japan. In Japan, under pressure of treaties with European powers, freedom of religion came about in 1889. At first this led to a brief period of vitality in the church, but then it led to stagnation, partly because Christianity remained a stranger in the land. In the Philippines, which had a Catholic majority, the church came close to destruction as a result of the political-ecclesiastical attitude of Spain and later as a result of American intervention. In the Dutch East Indies the government was tolerant, and the Catholic Church, which had been refounded at the beginning of the nineteenth century, was able to surge forward. Oceania was completely divided among the Western powers. Among them France and England especially opposed one another, and the missionaries from those two countries remained rivals until very recently. Africa was almost totally divided between the Western colonial powers, who experienced little resistance except in Uganda.[8]

7. Jedin and Dolan, ed., VIII, 199-207.
8. Delacroix, ed., III, 90-125; T. Christensen and W. R. Hutchison, ed., *Missionary Ideologies in the Imperialist Era: 1880-1920* (Arhus, 1982).

Notwithstanding all this, flourishing Catholic communities some-times came into being in China, Vietnam, Korea, and Africa. In Africa much energy was devoted to the abolition of slavery. In Japan, India, and China the focus was on university education. Catechists played important roles as lay leaders, and new pastoral and missionary methods were tested. The increase in the number of mission districts was explosive and the church became worldwide. Large numbers of new missionary orders, congregations, and institutions came to help. But penetration into the social, religious, and cultural context was frequently missing, especially in Africa, Japan, and China, as was sufficient courage to admit the numer-ous native priests and religious to higher ministries.

In Rome there was a shift in focus from the eastern churches to non-Christian countries during the papacies of Leo XIII (1878-1903) and Pius X (1903-14). In 1908 five Western European countries, the USA, and Canada were detached from the *Congregatio de Propaganda Fide;* in 1917 the eastern churches were detached. New missionary societies for material aid, including charitable work for native clergy, were organized. The Missionaries of the Divine Word (formed at Steyl, the Netherlands), the Marianhillers, the Benedictines of St. Ottillien, and the Missionaries of Parma and of de Con-solata were new institutions seeking to supply the now open world with missionaries.[9] Great missionary figures included Cardinal Lavigerie in Africa, the Jesuit Lievens in India, Lebbe in China, Pfanner in southern Africa, the Jesuit Van Lith in Indonesia, Deveuster in Oceania, and Zaleski in India.[10]

1914 to 1962: From Mission District to Local Church

Our emphasis to this point has been on the revival of the church's mis-sionary activity from the beginning of the nineteenth century *from within the Western Catholic Church*. This origin of missionary activity was natural in the context of the time. But World War I constitutes a clear transition. From this point on the missionary movement assumed new forms.

9. Delacroix, ed., III, 169-414; Jedin and Dolan, ed., IX, 527-75; Stoffel, *op. cit.*

10. K. J. Rivinius, "Wettlauf nach Afrika. Dargestellt am Leben und Werk Lavigeries," in *Warum Mission?* I (Munich, 1984) 261; F. Rauscher, *Die Mitarbeit der einheimischen Laien am Apostolat in den Missionen der Weissen Väter* (Münster, 1953); F. Renault, *Le Cardinal Lavigerie 1825-1892* (Paris, 1992); O. Tanghe, *Gods Adem. Pioniers en profeten in India* (Brussels, 1984); J. Leclercq, *Vie du Père Lebbe* (Paris, 1955); P. J. Dahm, *Mariannhill* (Natal, 1950); L. van Rijckevorsel, *Pastoor F. van Lith S.J., de stichter van de Missie in Midden-Java, 1863-1926* (Nijmegen, 1952); "Damiaan de Veuster 1840-1889, melaats onder de melaatsen," in J. Winkler, *In Gods Naam* (Amsterdam, 1960) 129-62; G. Daws, *Holy Man, Father Damien of Molokai* (Honolulu, 1973).

Under Benedict XV (1914-22) and Pius XI (1922-39) the endeavor to depoliticize mission and to emancipate the mission districts to become young churches began. Pius XII (1939-58) firmly continued this development. Well-known mission encyclicals from these popes contained courageous criticism and clear solutions. The popes were supported in their efforts by the Dutch cardinal and prefect of the *Congregatio de Propaganda Fide*, Willem van Rossum, a Redemptorist, and by the Catholic missiology arising at the beginning of twentieth century in Rome, Münster, and Louvain. Mission again became a function of the essence of the church. It was to be carried on in such a way that it would validate the church's supranational character. People of other faiths were valued more positively and space was made for the differences of peoples and cultures. Local churches could no longer be copies of Western churches and were to be led by their own people, even at the episcopal level. Pius XII conducted this policy with firmness, consecrating Chinese, Indian, and Vietnamese bishops.

Even before the Second Vatican Council opened up possibilities in large ways, the spiritual wealth of the peoples of Asia and Africa was incorporated into the liturgy. The rites controversy finally came to an end. The first steps in the direction of indigenous theologies were taken. None of this came easily, but change was inescapable. Local churches were able to develop and increased in number and depth. The histories of these churches speak for themselves. One can only understand the influence of Vatican II (1962-65) by keeping in mind its main goal, which was to move from monologue to dialogue with the world, cultures, religions, and local churches.[11]

---

11. Jedin and Dolan, ed., X, 672-804; Delacroix, ed., IV (1959); E. Marmy and I. Auf der Maur, ed., *Geht hin in alle Welt. Die Missionsenzykliken der Päpste Benedikt XV., Pius XI., Pius XII. und Johannes XXIII.* (Freiburg, Switzerland, 1961); J. O. Smit, *W. M. Kardinaal van Rossum* (Roermond, 1955).

CHAPTER 17

The Protestant Missionary Movement from 1789 to 1963

A. WIND

The swift expansion of Christianity in the nineteenth century, which has been called "the Great Century of Mission,"[1] was due in part to the work of many Western Protestant mission societies representing the Evangelical Awakening. Of decisive importance were the mission efforts of Protestants working on their own initiative, both locally and outside their own communities.

Protestant mission work in the nineteenth century can be characterized as "ecumenical": There were increasing contacts and common agreements, first on the mission fields and then at the level of the sending bodies. This process culminated at the World Mission Conference of Edinburgh in 1910. But it did not touch relations between Roman Catholic and Protestant missions or relations with a number of Protestant mission organizations that were very strictly defined by confessional limits.

The Nineteenth Century:
The Great Century of Protestant Mission

The Evangelical Awakening brought fresh missionary enthusiasm.[2] The resistance to Enlightenment rationalism and modernism was pivotal, as

---

1. So K. S. Latourette, who devoted three of the seven volumes of *A History of the Expansion of Christianity* (New York, 1927-45), to the nineteenth century. See also A. Wind, *Zending en Oecumene in de Twintigste Eeuw. I: Van Edinburgh in 1910 tot en met Evanston 1954* (Kampen, 1984) 8ff., 28ff.

2. On the revival movement, see J. van den Berg, *Constrained by Jesus' Love: An Inquiry into the Motives of the Missionary Awakening in Great Britain in the Period between 1698 and 1815* (Kampen, 1956); W. R. Hogg, *Ecumenical Foundations. A History of the IMC and its Nineteenth-Century Background* (New York, 1952) 4ff.; R. Rouse and S. C. Neill, *A History of the Ecumenical Movement, 1517-1869* (London, 1967²) 309ff.

was reaction against moribund ecclesiastical orthodoxy. The evangelical movement emphasized personal conversion, a devout regenerate life, new enthusiasm for witness to God's saving love in Christ, and social concern. External factors, such as colonial expansion, also played a role in the surge of mission activity.

From the end of the eighteenth century on, dozens of new mission organizations were formed in the North Atlantic world. They were mainly independent mission societies, but ecclesiastical mission work was not totally lacking. This included the churches of the Brethren, the Church of Scotland, the Scottish Free Church, and the Lutheran State Church of Sweden. In the Netherlands the Reformed churches viewed mission as a task of the church from the beginning. But the dominant form of organization was that of the independent mission society.[3]

The first such society was the Baptist Missionary Society, founded by William Carey in 1792. This organization was characterized by a global and ecumenical outlook. 1795 saw the founding of the first interdenominational society, the London Missionary Society. Its goal was not to propagate any particular form of church government, but simply to spread the gospel. By the end of the nineteenth century more missionaries were being sent from the USA than from any other country, which is a testimony to missionary enthusiasm especially among Congregationalists, Presbyterians, and Baptists. In 1810 Congregationalists had founded the American Board of Commissioners for Foreign Missions, which for a time served also as the mission board of the Presbyterian and Reformed churches.[4]

On the European continent the new élan of the Evangelical Awakening spread from a base in Basel through J. A. Urlsperger's founding in 1780 of the *Deutsche Christenthum Gesellschaft* and its offshoot, the *Basler Mission,* in which Lutherans and Calvinists worked together. The *Basler Mission,* the LMS, and the Brethren in Zeist stimulated the founding of the first mission society in the Netherlands, the Nederlandsch Zendeling Genootschap, in 1797. It was begun at the initiative of J. T. van der Kemp, who was later a missionary in southern Africa.

In Germany, Johann Jänicke founded a mission school at Berlin in 1800, which in its twenty-seven years of existence produced some eighty missionaries serving a number of mission societies. In 1828 the Rheinische Missions Gesellschaft was founded. Because of the theological training being given to its missionaries, Johan Goszner broke with the *Berliner*

---

3. See the overview in G. Warneck, *Abriß einer Geschichte d. Prot. Missionen von d. Reformation bis auf d. Gegenwart* (Berlin, 1913); Latourette, *op. cit.,* IV; Hogg, *op. cit.;* van den Berg, *op. cit.;* Rouse and Neill, *op. cit.*

4. Cf. W. E. Strong, *The Story of the American Board: An Account of the First Hundred Years* (Boston, 1910).

Mission (founded in 1824) and started the *Goszner Mission* in order to send out self-supporting tentmaker-missionaries. In the Netherlands O. G. Heldring adopted this idea. Theological training was also the difference between the two strictly Lutheran societies, the *Lutherische Mission Gesellschaft* in Leipzig and the *Hermannsburger Mission*, the "farmers' mission" of Ludwig Harms (1849).[5]

Missionary interest in Jews also grew in Western Europe. The Dutch Mission Society began to work among Jews in 1807. In England and Germany organizations were started in the course of the nineteenth century with the goal of mission among Jews. In 1906 there were fifty-eight such societies in Western Europe. Generally people viewed the church as having taken the place of Israel as God's covenant partner, and there were occasional signs of anti-Semitism, as in Adolf Stoecker and to a lesser degree in Theodor Christlieb in Germany.[6]

Missionary Motives and Goals

Motives and goals in mission are closely bound up with and strongly affected by their social, political, religious, and cultural context. As a result of developments such as the French Revolution, industrialization, the abolition of the slave trade and the opium trade, and colonial expansion, the Protestant missionary movement had to confront the question of its posture toward the ideal of civic liberty and colonial politics.

The religious and cultural background of the Protestant missionary movement includes on the one hand the Enlightenment, liberalism, and cultural optimism and on the other hand Pietism and Neopietism, that is, the "free" churches and the evangelical revival within the established churches. In Germany the relation between mission and church and the place of the study of mission in theology played important roles. By way of the kingdom theology of J. A. Bengel and his school, which constructed a bridge between new interest in God's mighty acts in history and the strong eschatological focus of Neopietism, mission received a place between "Orthodoxy" and "Enlightenment." In this connection Lutheran confessionalism, while it secured the legitimacy of mission within the church, also involved it in ecclesiastical party struggles.

At this point we shall restrict ourselves to England and Germany. We will not offer assessments concerning pure or impure motives and

5. On the Rheinische Mission see A. Bonse, *Hundert Jahre Rheinische Mission* (Barmen, 1928).

6. See Latourette, *op. cit.*, IV, 110-18.

goals, but will attempt rather to let insights be based simply on description.[7] Germans have occasionally taken exception to a supposed tendency of English-speaking people to mix mission with Western cultural propaganda. This tendency, it is said, began with the sending of missionaries and ended in national propaganda and world domination (H. Frick). Germany, on the other hand, started with mission schools and ended with the science of mission.

But in actual fact it was in Germany that the real task of mission was soon exchanged for German national and colonial cultural propaganda as a result of the goal and praxis of "national Christianization."[8] Although mission has been called "the hunting dog of imperialism," British empire-builders sometimes viewed mission as a threat to colonial politics. J. van den Berg has demonstrated that political and cultural-humanitarian motives did not play a dominant role in the missionary motives of Protestant English-speaking revivalism: The goal was not the glory of the British Empire but the glory of God's kingdom.

For many, other motives that were more romantic (e.g., the "noble savages" of Tahiti) or were based on appreciation for natural theology (e.g., elements of truth in Hinduism, Jesus as Avatar) were balanced by the Calvinistic doctrine of the radical corruption of humanity. Even in mission circles of the Victorian era many were persuaded of the duty to bring to "barbarians" and "pagans" the blessings of a superior and orderly Western Christian civilization. This "white man's burden" (Kipling) was clearly present as a motive at the 1910 Edinburgh mission conference. Over against this approach we also encounter the awareness that the Christian West was obligated to compensate by mission for its many mistakes and its large debt toward the colonies.[9]

J. van den Berg distinguished five religious motives for missionary enthusiasm in the nineteenth-century English-speaking world, and we can find the same motives elsewhere:

- a theocentric motive: the *gloria Dei,*
- the motive of love and compassion, that is,

7. This in contrast to Verkuyl, *Contemporary Missiology* (Grand Rapids, 1978); from the Catholic side cf. M. C. Reilly, *Spirituality for Mission* (New York, 1978) 161-81.

8. Cf. H. W. Gensichen, "Missionsgeschichte d. neueren Zeit," in K. D. Schmidt, et al., ed., *Die Kirche in ihrer Geschichte* IV (Göttingen, 1976) 44. On the political, religious, and cultural context and mission motives, cf. van den Berg, *op. cit.,* 106-65; J. C. Hoekendijk, *Kerk en Volk in de Duitse Zendingswetenschap* (Utrecht, 1948) 13-16, 52-107.

9. On the "white man's burden," cf. P. Potter, "From Edinburgh to Melbourne," in *Your Kingdom Come: Mission Perspectives. Report on the World Conference on Mission and Evangelism, Melbourne, Australia, 12-25 May 1980* (Geneva, 1980).

- imitation of Jesus' love and
- soteriological concern for the eternal lostness of millions of people without Christ,
- an ecclesiological motive: the planting of churches,
- a salvation-historical, eschatological motive, that is,
  - expectation of the imminent arrival of the millennial kingdom, Christ's spiritual rule on earth,
  - expectation of great things from God (William Carey),
  - a sense of historical crisis focusing on the decline of pagan cultures and religions, and
  - desire for conversion of the Jews and hence the urgency of mission, and, finally,
- the motive of obedience to Christ's missionary command.

It is clear that in the English-speaking world, despite some shifts of emphasis toward cultural motives, the essential motivations of Pietism persisted: love for Christ and one's neighbor, desire for the salvation of non-Christians, and the sense that it is the duty of all converted Christians, in the light of the coming of Christ's kingdom, to pass on to others redemption in Christ.

The shift in missionary goals in Germany, on the other hand, was notable. In Pietism the central focus was the conversion of individuals, understood as the firstfruits of a lost world (though a theological missiology like that later developed by Gustav Warneck, Theodor Christlieb, and others was lacking). Then we observe a shift in the direction of "national Christianization" in, for example, F. Ehrenfeuchter, K. Graul, L. Harms, and W. Löhe and toward "nationally-oriented pedagogy" on the model of the Christian German people in Ernst Buss. This shift cleared the way for the functional subordination of mission to German colonialism and German national cultural propaganda. These nineteenth-century shifts in missionary motives and goals must be understood within the wider context of thinking focused on the *corpus Christianum* and of the close link implied by such thinking between Christianity and culture. This way of thinking was fundamentally affected in the same period by the ideas of the French Revolution and the rise of secularization.[10]

Growth in Cooperation and Ecumenicity

The ecumenical openness and growing interdenominational cooperation of the nineteenth-century missionary movement made mission the most

---

10. Cf. Wind, *op. cit.*, 39f.

important catalyst for the twentieth-century ecumenical movement. The pioneer of the Baptist Missionary Society, William Carey, was far ahead of his time: Already in 1806 he proposed that once every ten years an inter-denominational and international mission conference be held, beginning in 1810 at the Cape of Good Hope.[11]

In the course of the nineteenth century the sense of common membership in the circle of mission and the sense of a need for greater unity for the sake of the gospel testimony grew, especially among mission-minded youth and students. The need for "ecumenizing" in mission first became evident on the mission fields. Missionaries often confronted the same problems. Therefore, many consultations and conferences were held in Asia, Africa, and Latin America, of which some were useful "finger exercises" for the later world mission conferences and some culminated in the establishment of permanent organs of cooperation.[12] From these conferences pressure was naturally brought to bear on the home front for increased cooperation.

But the strongest stimulus to ecumenical missionary cooperation came from the ecumenical youth and student movements, which also produced the pioneers of the twentieth-century ecumenical movement, people like John R. Mott, J. H. Oldham, and W. A. Visser 't Hooft. We have in mind here especially the Student Volunteer Movement for Foreign Mission (SVM), founded in 1888 under the leadership of Mott with the watchword "the evangelization of the world in this generation," and the World's Student Christian Federation (WSCF), founded in 1895. According to Ruth Rouse, the ecumenical influence of the WSCF was rooted in its international character, its efficient meeting techniques, the training of church leaders in Africa and Asia, and the strategic importance of the student world.[13]

Ecumenical cooperation among mission boards on the home front began with the Association for Mutual Counsel and Fellowship, which was initiated in 1819 by four secretaries of mission organizations in London. International mission conferences were held regularly in Europe from 1866 on. In 1885, at the initiative of Gustav Warneck, the first permanent organ of cooperation in the North Atlantic region came into being: the

11. See R. Rouse, "William Carey's Pleasing Dream," *International Review of Missions* 38 (1949) 181-92.

12. Overviews of these conferences are in Hogg, *op. cit.*, 16-35; Wind, *op. cit.*, 18-22.

13. On the youth and student movements, see Latourette, *op. cit.*, IV, 30-39, 95-103; Hogg, *op. cit.*, 81-97; D. P. Gaines, *The World Council of Churches: A Study of its Background and History* (Petersborough, 1966) 14f.; Rouse and Neill, *op. cit.*, 327-45; Wind, *op. cit.*, 14-18.

Select Committee of German Evangelical Missions. Its example was followed in England and the USA.

In 1846, at a conference in London of some eight hundred church and mission leaders from fifty-two denominations, an important initiative was undertaken: the establishment of the Evangelical Alliance. From 1854 on the Alliance organized numerous national and international conferences that may be called direct forerunners of the 1910 Edinburgh conference. The largest Evangelical Alliance conference was the Ecumenical Conference on Foreign Missions held in New York in 1900.[14] Important roles were played by missiologists Rufus Anderson of the USA and Theodor Christlieb and Gustav Warneck of Germany.[15] The Evangelical Alliance conferences were meetings of like-minded evangelicals from various churches and countries who were involved in mission work. The idea of a conference of delegates from churches and mission societies was rejected in 1873. The Evangelical Alliance lacked continuity of leadership and planning.

The World Mission Conference of Edinburgh in 1910

The 1910 conference, generally known as the cradle of Protestant world mission and ecumenism in the twentieth century, marked the transition of the missionary movement from the nineteenth to the twentieth century.[16] A number of metaphors have been used to describe it: "landmark," "watershed," "lens," "prism." Cultural optimism, the West's sense of superiority, and the expectation of a speedy Christianization of the whole world still prevailed. But the end of the Vasco da Gama era had already announced itself with Japan's victory over Russia in 1905. An era of awakening nationalism, of the renaissance of non-Christian world religions, and of growing secularization had been entered.

It is remarkable that — at the very moment when the Western powers, in their struggles for worldwide political and economic expansion, were steering directly toward worldwide conflict — in the ecumenical movement Christian churches were beginning to grow toward unity and fellowship. After Edinburgh and especially after World War II a new

14. Cf. Wind, *op. cit.*, 22-25.

15. Cooperation in missiology among Americans and Germans (R. Anderson and T. Christlieb) began with the Evangelical Alliance conference in New York in 1873. See Rouse and Neill, *op. cit.*, 318-24, 329-33.

16. For bibliography see Hogg, *op. cit.*, 98-142; I. P. C. van't Hof, *Op zoek naar het geheim van de Zending. In dialoog met de wereldzendingsconferenties 1910-1963* (Wageningen, 1973) 12-62; Wind, *op. cit.*, 6-44.

phase in the Protestant missionary movement began, which lasted well into the 1960s. What took place thereafter was not only the integration of world mission and the ecumenical movement but also the expression of a variety of new missiological views and the emergence of conflicts that continue to occupy missiologists today.

Here we are concerned with three aspects of the Edinburgh conference and of the developments up to the 1960s: the ecumenical aspect, the aspect of mission theology, and the aspect of mission strategy.

The Ecumenical Aspect: Permanent Cooperation

The decision of Edinburgh to work through a "Continuation Committee" toward permanent cooperation among mission organizations has been called "an ecumenical direct hit."[17] In 1921 the Continuation Committee was transformed into the International Missionary Council (IMC).

And not only did interdenominational missionary cooperation get its start at Edinburgh in 1910; so also did the history of the ecumenical movement. The work of the pioneers of the Movement for Practical Christianity (Life and Work), especially Nathan Söderblom, and of the Movement for Faith and Order, specifically Charles H. Brent, led to the founding of the World Council of Churches (WCC) in Amsterdam in 1948.[18]

The Theology of Mission

The main theme of the Edinburgh conference was "Carrying the Gospel to All the Non-Christian World." The world was divided into the civilized Christian West and the non-Christian rest. To the latter, with urgency — the *kairos* was present — the gospel had to be brought in accordance with the mission mandate of Matthew 28. Edinburgh was clearly based on a trinitarian foundation of mission: Mission is the work of God. God the Father, the Creator, has a just claim on all and uses his power to make all *de facto* his own. God the Son is King Christ, for whom the world must be conquered. The spirit of the conference reports was militant. God the Holy Spirit converts individuals, nations, and their cultures and guarantees the success of mission.

The goal of mission, so the reports stated, is the Christianization of

17. Van't Hof, *op. cit.*, 60; Cf. J. R. Mott, "The Continuation Committee," *International Review of Missions* 1 (1912) 62-78.
18. Cf. Rouse and Neill, *op. cit.*, 362-402; Wind, *op. cit.*, 82-115, 175-211.

the entire non-Christian world, with Western culture and the Western church as the model. The conference participants thought in ecclesiocentric terms: Their goal was to plant the one undivided church of Christ in non-Christian lands. They criticized the laxity of many churches with regard to mission. Missionary societies were considered legitimate means for mission, especially for churches that were not engaged in mission. But it was also said that every church should be a mission society. The conference participants saw mission as the expansion of the Western Christian church and expected God's kingdom to come soon. They thus created the impression that the church was identical to the kingdom. And on this basis they emphasized planning, mission strategy, and efficient communication of the gospel.

Edinburgh was still caught up in thinking focused on the *corpus Christianum*. The participants wanted to establish new *corpora Christiana* everywhere on the Western model. They still thought of Christendom in religious terms and sought by heightened mission activity to gain an advantage over rising secularization. They were blind to political distress in colonized areas and at most criticized the unchristian manner of life of some colonists.

But they did have a great deal of interest in non-Christian religions. They clung to the absoluteness of Christianity, but also had an eye for elements of truth in other religions and argued for a sympathetic approach. A difference emerged in Edinburgh between English-speaking and continental theologians. The former assumed a continuing nurturing revelational activity of the Word (John 1) in history as the source of the true and the good in other religions and spoke in terms of the "fulfillment" of these aspects of other religions by Christ in analogy with his fulfillment of the Torah (Matt. 5:17). Continental theologians viewed these elements of truth as remnants of a primeval revelation and therefore as points of contact for a gospel message calling for conversion, for a break with the hearers' religious past. Discussion of the theology of the religions had thus already begun in 1910.[19]

Mission Strategy: Relationships with Young Churches on the Mission Fields

Although Edinburgh laid heavy stress on the necessity of indigenous churches, the conference participants' thinking about the newer churches

---

19. Cf. J. J. E. van Lin, *Protest. Theologie van de Godsdiensten, Van Edinburgh naar Tambaram (1910-1938)* (Assen, 1974) 1-35.

was still very paternalistic. They sought missionary structures for these churches modeled on Western churches and mission societies. The role assigned to these churches was that of being the most important mission-ary instrument of Western mission. For that reason, the few Asiatic Chris-tians who attended the conference, such as V. S. Azariah from India and Cheng Ching Yi from China, pleaded for genuine love and friendship in place of guardianship.

Mission Perspectives from 1910 (Edinburgh) to 1963 (Mexico City): The Ecumenical Movement

In 1910 the climate of missiological thought still belonged very much to the nineteenth century. After World War I this was to change radically. The Continuation Committee had met five times when the war broke out in 1914, making the committee's work virtually impossible. Before the end of the war the Emergency Committee of Co-operating Missions was formed to provide aid to "orphaned" — mostly German — mission fields. A crisis of confidence between the German mission and Mott lasted into the 1920s. In 1920 a meeting of the Continuation Committee was held in Crans near Geneva. There J. H. Oldham submitted the blueprint for the International Missionary Council (IMC).[20]

The Origin and Work of the International Missionary Council

The IMC was started in 1921 in Lake Mohonk, New York, by delegates of seventy mission organizations based in Western Europe, North America, southern Africa, and Australia. Only seven delegates came from the newer churches.[21] The council was not authorized to set mission strategy or make pronouncements on controversial questions of faith and church order. A consensus was reached in 1923 with regard to the degree of doctrinal agreement necessary for missionary cooperation.

The IMC's tasks were to stimulate missiological reflection, to coordinate mission activities, to seek common perspectives on freedom of religion and conscience and on the freedom to do mission work, to com-bine Christian forces for justice in international and interracial relations,

20. On the period of the Continuation Committee and problems between Mott and the Germans, see Hogg, *op. cit.*, 143-201; Wind, *op. cit.*, 45-49.
21. Cf. *Minutes of the IMC, Lake Mohonk, New York, Oct. 1-6, 1921* (London, 1921); Hogg, *op. cit.*, 202-26; Wind, *op. cit.*, 50-56.

and to organize world mission conferences. Before the integration of the IMC into the World Council of Churches (WCC) in New Delhi in 1961, the IMC held five conferences: in Jerusalem (on the Mount of Olives) in 1928, in Tambaram, Madras, India, in 1938, in Whitby, Ontario, in 1947, in Willingen, Germany, in 1952, and in Achimota, Ghana, in 1957-58.[22]

The Relation between the IMC and the WCC: From "Association" to "Integration"

Although the mission movement gave the first impetus to the ecumenical movement, in Tambaram the IMC did not go along with the Movements for Practical Christianity and for Faith and Order, which had decided jointly at Utrecht in 1938 to form a World Council of Churches. The IMC did agree to close cooperation as expressed in the formula: "the IMC in association with the WCC and the WCC in association with the IMC," which was officially accepted by the IMC in 1947 and by the WCC in Amsterdam in 1948. From the beginning there were objections to a fusion of the two councils on the basis of their structural differences (the members of IMC were national or regional councils; the members of the WCC were churches), because a number of IMC-affiliated churches were too small for the WCC or did not wish to join, and because the IMC was a functional organization designed for mission work while the WCC was much broader in scope.

Cooperation between the two councils took shape as a result of the work of the Joint Committee (JC) of the WCC and the IMC, which was established in 1939, though war prevented its work from beginning until February, 1946. During the 1950s the work of the two world councils increasingly overlapped. The JC sought permission in 1956 to consider the possibility of integration. An attempt was made to resolve the structural differences and to meet the objections existing on both sides, for example, from the Orthodox churches, which were fearful, among other things, of proselytism on the part of IMC-related mission organizations.

Following intense discussions, the WCC Central Committee (in New Haven in 1957) and the IMC (in Achimota in 1957-58) made fundamentally favorable decisions with regard to the "marriage" of the two

---

22. For literature see the sources (minutes, reports, and findings) and Hogg, *op. cit.*; Rouse and Neill, *op. cit.*; Van't Hof, *op. cit.*; van Lin, *op. cit.*; Wind, *op. cit.*; H. E. Fey, ed., *The Ecumenical Advance: A History of the Ecumenical Movement II: 1948-1968* (Geneva, 1986); and articles in *International Review of Missions*, especially in the issue on "Edinburgh to Melbourne," 67 (July, 1978).

organizations, though some, especially in the IMC, called it "the funeral of mission." At the third assembly of the WCC in New Delhi, 1961, the chairman of the plenary meeting, Archbishop Iakovos, solemnly declared in the name of the triune God that the union of the two councils into one body, the WCC, had been accomplished.

The IMC became the Commission on World Mission and Evangelism (CWME) of the WCC. Its executive committee, until 1971 called the Division on World Mission and Evangelism (DWME), organized mission conferences that met in Mexico City in 1963, in Bangkok in 1972-73, in Melbourne in 1980, and in San Antonio, Texas, in 1989. Thus mission, in Achimota considered the heart of the Christian church, became the heart of ecumenism. Integration facilitated contributions to missionary reflection from Asian, African, and Latin American churches and from the large Orthodox churches that joined the WCC in 1961. This broadened dialogue has been one of the most important factors in the development of the Protestant missionary movement since the 1960s.

Mission Perspectives from 1910 to 1963:
The Theology of Mission

The Basis, Essence, and Goal of Mission

The theocentric-christocentric basis given to mission in Edinburgh remained characteristic, apart from shifts of emphasis in christology, in the mission conferences of Jerusalem and Tambaran. The focus was on the church and its essential task of carrying the Christian message. Before World War II there was also concern for religion itself. The Jerusalem conference saw secularism as the great enemy of Christianity. This emphasis on religion ended only at Whitby (1947), where a political emphasis came to the fore, namely, the revolutionary church and world. But this was combined with a sense of the urgent necessity of mission and a sense that great things were to be expected.

At both the Willingen and the Achimota conferences (1952 and 1957-58), the central focus continued to be the church and its duty to engage in mission. But already at Willingen J. C. Hoekendijk had launched an attack on ecclesiocentric thinking, positing that what was at stake was the *missio dei*, God's redemptive action toward the world.[23]

23. Cf. J. C. Hoekendijk, "The Call to Evangelism," *International Review of Missions* 39 (1950) 162-75; *idem*, "The Church in Missionary Thinking," *International Review of Missions* 41 (1952) 324-36; van't Hof, *op. cit.*, 157-73; Wind, *op. cit.*, 219-26.

The focus was clearly changed in New Delhi in 1961. Alongside a strong emphasis on "witness," there was much interest in the cosmic significance and universality of Christ's work of reconciliation and his resurrection as articulated in texts like Eph. 1:7-12 and Col. 1:15-20. It was asserted that in Christ humanity is reconciled with God and that a new humanity has arisen. By his Spirit, it was said, Christ works in the whole world and in all of history, even among people of other faiths and of no faith. The task of the missionary movement is to discover God's liberating hand in history and to participate in his work. Consequently, there were great changes in the theology of religions. There was strong resistance to the tendency toward redemptive universalism, but the main emphasis was no longer on proclamation of the gospel summoning people to personal conversion and faith. Two opposing missionary movements thus came into being, with the designations "ecumenical" and "evangelical."

In Mexico City (1963) the world began to set the agenda for the missionary church, and there was some sympathy for the positive side of the process of secularization. It was asked what God is doing in the religious, secular, and sociopolitical world. It was no longer the church but the world that was central in missiological reflection. "God-church-world" had become "God-world-church."

Missiological Reflection on the Theology of Religions

The differences in theology between English-speaking and continental Europeans at Edinburgh deepened in the period leading up to World War II. What was at issue was the choice between emphasizing the continuity between the Christian faith and non-Christian religions (the fulfillment model) or emphasizing discontinuity and the necessity that believers make a radical break with their religious past (the conversion model). H. Kraemer's emphasis on discontinuity, based on his "biblical realism," encountered much resistance in Tambaran from English-speaking theologians and from representatives from India.

After Evanston (1954) and at the insistence of the Asian representatives, specifically D. T. Niles, discussion of the theology of religions was reopened at a consultation in Davos in 1955 on "Christianity and non-Christian Religions." The background for this meeting was the changed position of churches and Christians in Asia after the war in the new period of nationalism and decolonization. Asian Christians wanted to escape the odium of being "foreign" by becoming involved, along with people of other faiths, in the struggles for independence and in building up the new states.

This new reflection on the theology of religions was chan-
nelled into a study project on "The Word of God and the Living Faiths
of Men."[24] The focus had shifted from religious systems to *people* of
other faiths. Study centers established by the IMC in places where non-
Christian religions were dominant began to play an increasingly large
role. At the New Delhi conference it was decided to assign the entire
study project to these study centers. There people began hesitantly to
engage in interreligious dialogue, for which New Delhi had provided a
basis by asserting that Christ can address Christians even through people
of other faiths.[25]

Social Concern in Missionary Reflection and Praxis

In contrast to Edinburgh, Jerusalem devoted considerable attention to
social and racial issues, specifically to the consequences of industrialization in Asia, which were studied by the Bureau of Social and Economic
Research and Information of the IMC under the leadership of J. Merle
Davis. Social involvement also received much attention in Tambaram.
There already the choice between striving for personal conversion and for
social-structural changes was dismissed as a false dilemma. It became
increasingly clear that witness and service are inseparable. On this basis
attention to the social aspects of the church's ministry to the world grew
increasingly stronger in the 1960s, especially at the fourth WCC assembly
at Uppsala in 1968.

Mission to the Jews and the Relationship
between the Church and Israel

In 1930, at Mott's initiative, the IMC's Committee on the Christian Approach to the Jews (IMC-CCAJ) was formed. Initially it was led by Conrad
Hoffmann, later by G. Hedenquist. After World War II, many Christian
people began to understand the brutality and scope of the Nazi destruction

24. Cf. *Rethinking Missions: A Layman's Inquiry after One Hundred Years* by the
Commission of Appraisal, Chairman William E. Hocking (New York, 1932); H. Kraemer, *The
Christian Message in a Non-Christian World* (New York, 1938); van Lin, *op. cit.*, 36-371;
Wind, *op. cit.*, 58-67, 71-74, 118-31, 135-48 and the literature cited there.

25. Cf. G. Valée, *Mouvement oecuménique et Religions non-chrétiennes. Un débat
oecuménique sur la Rencontre interreligieuse. De Tambaram à Uppsala (1938-1968)* (Montreal,
1975). On a variety of study projects of missionary interest both for the IMC and the WCC,
cf. A. J. van den Bent, *Major Studies and Themes in the Ecumenical Movement* (Geneva, 1981).

of the Jews, but they generally continued to view Jewish mission as a duty of the church. This only changed in the course of the 1950s.[26]

The first WCC assembly (Amsterdam, 1948) did not yet dare to say anything about the creation of the state of Israel. But in Evanston (1954) there was intense discussion of the subject.[27] Many people continued to view Zionism solely as a political movement, not as a Jewish religious movement. But there was increasing dialogue between Christians and Jews. After the New Delhi meeting, the Committee on the Church and the Jewish People (CCJP), sponsored by the CWME, was formed.

Mission Perspectives from 1910 to 1963: Mission Strategy

Edinburgh's North Atlantic paternalism decreased more and more after World War I. This was apparent at the creation of the IMC in 1921 from suggestions to let the leaders of young churches codetermine mission strategy and at Jerusalem and Tambaram from the changing relations between "sending" (i.e., older) churches and "receiving" (i.e., younger) churches.

Only after the younger churches had been abruptly cut off from North Atlantic resources by World War II and had for that reason come to stronger national and ecclesiastical self-awareness did relations become decisively different. The term was now "partners in obedience" (Whitby, 1947). Representatives of the younger churches began to experience these relationships as those between older and younger brothers and sisters. The whole world came to be seen as a single mission field for the whole church: "Mission in unity" (Willingen).[28]

On this basis, reflection on mission strategy changed. Initially some churches, basing themselves on Whitby in 1947, could still say that they had as much responsibility for mission strategy in colonial lands as their partners. But increasingly the view prevailed that every church, as part of the one world church, bears primary responsibility for mission strategy in its own environment and can ask for assistance in implementing that

26. This was evident at conferences of the IMC-CCAJ in Bossey 1956: "Christian Convictions and Attitudes in Relation to the Jewish People," *Ecumenical Review* 9 (1956-57) 303-20; cf. Fey, *op. cit.*, 195f.; *The Church and the Jewish People* (Faith and Order Studies 1964-67; Geneva, 1968) 69-80; articles in *International Review of Missions* 37, 38, 40, 45-47, and 49 (1948-49, 1951, 1956-58, and 1960).

27. See Wind, *op. cit.*, 279f.; *Ecumenical Review* 7 (April, 1955).

28. On these developments see E. Jansen-Schoonhoven, *Wederkerige assistentie van kerken in missionair perspectief* (Leiden, 1977).

strategy from one or more churches or mission organizations. Multilateral cooperation, that is, joint action for mission, was able to break the oppressive relationships of dependence, which had originated in the aid extended by rich churches to poor churches.[29] In bilateral relationships the ideal is two-way traffic, mutual assistance.

But it is not always a simple matter to arrive at such "mature" relationships. This became evident in the 1970s when African representatives at Bangkok (1972-73) and Lusaka (1974) asked for "moratorium," a suspension of all missionary support from abroad.[30]

The problems associated with Western mission strategy and the position of the Western mission worker received a great deal of attention especially at Achimota (1957-58). At that meeting a jointly supported independent missionary project, the "Theological Education Fund," was begun. In Mexico City this was followed by a second such project, the "Christian Literature Fund."

After New Delhi the churches of the Third World began to play a dominant role in world mission, so that the trend of Willingen and Ghana was reinforced. It became apparent that the entire world, including the North Atlantic countries, is a mission field. As a result, in Mexico City home and foreign mission representatives sat down together for the first time. The slogan became: "Mission on six continents."

It is clear that from the end of the eighteenth century to the 1960s a number of important changes occurred in the Protestant missionary movement: the shift from independent mission organizations to ecumenical cooperation; fundamental changes in thinking concerning the basis, essence, and goal of mission; changes in the theology of religions; and finally growth toward mature relationships among churches on all continents, all involved together in carrying out the one mission mandate for the one church of Jesus Christ in the whole world.

29. On dependence relationships see P. Quarles van Ufford, *Grenzen van intern, hulpverlening. Een onderzoek naar de samenhang van de aard en effecten van de hulprelatie tussen de Javaanse kerk van M. Java en de zending van de GKN* (Assen, 1980) (cf. A. Wind, "A Case Study in Aid Relationships," *International Review of Missions* 73 [1984] 246-49); Verkuyl, *op. cit.*, 309-40; *Wereld en Zending* 2.1 (1973) and 6.2 (1977).

30. On the discussion of moratorium, see pp. 111-13 of the Bangkok Report; *International Review of Missions* 64.254 (1975); *Wereld en Zending* 4.6 (1974); Verkuyl, *op. cit.*, 334-38.

CHAPTER 18

The History of the Missionary Movement from the Perspective of the Third World

G. M. Verstraelen-Gilhuis

Christianity's center of gravity is shifting from the northern hemisphere to the southern hemisphere. Nonetheless, though the history of the Christian missionary movement has often been written, it has not yet been written as a whole from a consistent Third World perspective. This history, which in large part ran parallel to the history of European colonial expansion, is normally depicted as a movement from the European Christian "center" to the pagan "periphery" of Africa, Asia, and Latin America. America was "discovered," we say, but when people in a base community in north-eastern Brazil saw the record of this "discovery" in print, their spontaneous reaction was: "That was the beginning of the *invasion* of our America."[1]

EATWOT: Toward a History of the Church in the Third World

A plan for writing a concise three-volume church history of the Third World was originated by EATWOT, the Ecumenical Association of Third World Theologians. The idea was launched in Accra (1977) by E. Dussel, the leader of the related CEHILA project in Latin America. During an international ecumenical consultation in Basel in 1981 a fruitful exchange of ideas occurred among third-world theologians interested in history. Two years later the sixth EATWOT conference, meeting in Geneva (1983), appointed a Working Commission on Church History. Among its members were Sr. Mary John Mananzan of the Philippines (secretary), Dussel of Mexico (coordinator), M. D. David of India, Engelbert Mveng of

---

1. E. Dussel, "Towards a History of the Church in the World Periphery," in Lukas Vischer, ed., *Towards a History of the Church in the Third World* (Bern, 1985) 112, 127.

Cameroon, and Ogbu U. Kalu of Nigeria (contact person for French and English-speaking Africa).

The first consultation of the working commission took place in July, 1983 in Geneva and was devoted to questions surrounding periodization. Regional consultations were held in Bombay (1984, focusing on Asia) and Nairobi (1986, focusing on Africa). The reports of the consultations in Basel and Geneva have been published in two small books: *Church History in an Ecumenical Perspective* and *Towards a History of the Church in the Third World*.[2]

Besides a provisional scheme for the periodization of church history, which is to be adapted to the particular situations of different countries and churches, a number of goals and guidelines were adopted in Geneva. The aim was "a new church history," one that would do justice to the reality and experience of the Third World and would be written by Third World church historians, a history that deepens "the self-understanding of the church in these lands and stimulates the process of developing a theology of its own." The church history of the Third World should be not the familiar missionary story but the account of "the creative reception and incarnation of the gospel in the different regions and cultures." "It should be written from the viewpoint of the suffering and oppressed peoples of the Third World and the emancipation of women and other oppressed groups . . . needs to be related to it." By way of social analysis the poor and oppressed in the different contexts need to be identified.

In the last-mentioned guideline one detects strong input from Latin America. Whereas at the Basel symposium Asians and Africans spoke of a "people's history," a history from below, not so much in terms of church institutions but of the experience of ordinary people, Latin American liberation theologians referred more expressly to the theological locus of the "poor" (Luke 4) as the hermeneutical key for a church history from a Third World perspective.[3] A representative of the Pacific said that to him the provisional decision for a "people's history" and a "history of the poor and oppressed" was not altogether satisfactory: It was a fruitful perspective, but not the only one. For the Pacific the word "exploitation" seemed more appropriate than "oppression." Furthermore, the missionary movement in his isolated part of the world had been primarily a movement of the islanders themselves. The chapel of the Pacific Theological College at Fiji commemorates the names of 1200 Protestant and Catholic islander

---

2. Lukas Vischer, ed., *Church History in Ecumenical Perspective: Papers and Reports of an International Ecumenical Consultation held in Basle October 12-17, 1981* (Bern, 1982). See n. 1 above on the second volume named.

3. Vischer, ed., *Church History*, 108.

families; voluntary missionary migrations of these people carried the gospel from the east to the west of the Pacific. By way of family documents and oral information these micro-histories have been reconstructed.[4]

The desired goal was a history written out of clear engagement. Several participants in the conference were opposed to the idea of an "objective" history, since too often a European story had been written under the banner of objectivity. Every age (and place!) interprets the evidence "in such a way that the past can speak to the needs of the present," says Ogbu Kalu.[5]

Besides the "scholarly" goal, there is a "pastoral" goal. What is needed in the current phase is a strengthening of self-awareness and of group identity. If one were to wait until specialized studies had been made of all the subsections, the opportune time could pass away. This is not to say that a historiography that is conscious of the context out of which it writes is not open to the method of historical criticism. "If we want to be sure of not exchanging one myth for another, we must see that historical truth . . . is strictly tested and substantiated," writes J. Ki-Zerbo of Upper Volta in the methodological section of a new *General History of Africa* written from an African perspective.[6]

The history in view must also be written from within "an ecumenical viewpoint which takes account of the special situation of the different Christian groups." Most areas in the Third World have been evangelized along strict confessional lines, not without a "cold war" between Rome and the Reformation. But to a Latin American historian like Dussel, the Reformation and Counter-Reformation are of interest only in regard to *European* church history. From a global perspective the Spanish and Portuguese expansion, the "decloistering" of Europe, was a much more radical interruption, as a result of which the Christian religion changed from a regional phenomenon on the periphery of the Arab world to the first world religion, extending across Eurasia, America, and Africa.[7] The goal of the project is to rewrite the history of the church in the Third World, but in doing this it intends to make a contribution to a *universal* church history in ecumenical perspective.

4. John Garrett, "A History of the Church in Oceania," in Vischer, ed., *Towards a History of the Church*, 30-32; Vischer, ed., *Church History*, 52f.

5. Ogbu U. Kalu (Nigeria) in Vischer, ed., *Church History*, 78; cf. M. D. David (India) in Vischer, ed., *Towards a History of the Church*, 8f., and E. Dussel, "Reflections on Methodology" (inaugural address of CEHILA in 1973), in *idem, A History of the Church in Latin America: Colonialism to Liberation (1492-1979)* (Grand Rapids, 1981) 301ff.

6. Vol. I: *Methodology and African Prehistory* (London, 1981) 3; cf. also Vischer, ed., *Church History*, 106.

7. Dussel, *art. cit.*, in Vischer, ed., *Towards a History of the Church*, 118.

Latin America: History from the Perspective of the Poor

To a significant degree the model for the project of a Third World church history presented in the 1980s was the CEHILA, the *Comisión de Estudios de Historia de la Iglesia en América Latina,* which was formally launched in January, 1973 in Quito, Ecuador. Since then more than one hundred voluntary researchers, both Catholic and Protestant, have worked in different regions to gather material for this new eleven-volume church history of Latin America. This history will reveal the connections of church history with the political and economic history of the continent and will break with the tradition that "we are merely the object of history," as coworker José Oscar Beozzo of Brazil puts it. Volumes on Brazil, on Colombia and Venezuela, and on Mexico have already been published in Spanish or Portuguese, as has the methodological introduction written by Dussel. Almost every year symposia on important themes (e.g., Bartholomé de las Casas in 1974, the position of women in Latin American church history in 1984) have been held, the results of which have been published.[8]

The goal is a history "of, for, and — ideally — by the poor," according to Dussel, CEHILA's initiator and president. The idea for a history from the perspective of the poor came to Dussel during a discussion in 1959 in Nazareth. The hermeneutical keys to this history are both the "poor" and "Christianity" — to Dussel the institutionalized model of the church, which was bound to political and economic power. Despite the oppressive structures within which missionizing usually took place, an authentic "reception" — by a miracle of the Holy Spirit — nevertheless took place. The components of the "popular church," the church of the people, have to be "torn," as it were, from the oppressive straitjacket of "Christianity." In the entire seventeenth century not a year passed in which there was not an uprising somewhere on the continent, for example, the Indian revolt against new taxes during Easter week in Tehuantapec.[9] Dussel draws clear lines of continuity from the past to the present. His own concise Latin American church history (a rehearsal for CEHILA) is dedicated to a bishop and a priest who died martyrs' deaths in Nicaragua and Brazil in the sixteenth and twentieth centuries, both of them victims of oppressive violence.[10]

8. J. O. Beozzo, "The Project of CEHILA," *Paper Workshop VI, IVth IAMS Conference* (Maryknoll, 1978) 7. For a list of CEHILA publications, see *Mission Studies, Journal of the IAMS* 3 (1986) 93.

9. Dussel in Vischer, ed., *Church History,* 30, 36; "by the poor" was somewhat realized in "historico-popular production workshops," *ibid.,* 50.

10. Dussel, *History of the Church in Latin America* (apart from some details based on the third Spanish edition, 1971), viii.

CEHILA has not been spared criticism and even severe reactions. Before a word of it had been published, the results of its research were already being branded as falsifications of the truth in, for example, circles around CELAM (the Latin American bishops' conference). CEHILA co-worker Josep M. Barnadas of Bolivia parried the charge of "unscholarli-ness" that reviewers applied to the volume on Brazil by saying that, instead of proposing corrections on specific points, they were rejecting the prophetic perspective of the book. To his mind the conflict surrounding CEHILA was not historiographical but theological. Critics were annoyed at the social analysis that was deliberately integrated into CEHILA research, but did not realize that existing standard works (unconsciously) proceeded from an image of society in which the West was the center of the world. Barnadas also wrote that CEHILA had to earn its credibility on the basis of its scholarly results, though no one should be so naive as to think that scholarly seriousness is the same as supposed impartiality.[11]

India: Toward an Ecumenical and Contextual History

In Asia as well various church history projects have begun. We mention India in particular because there — stimulated by a church history delegation of the IMC that made a tour of the East — an Indian church history society was founded already in 1935. At first this society included Burma and Ceylon as well. Under the influence of the ecumenical movement and plans for church union in northern and southern India, there was strong historical interest among Indian theologians like A. J. Appasamy and C. E. Abraham. The society published a *Bulletin* (1936-1941, 1961-1966), later continued as the *Indian Church History Review,* the periodical of the Church History Association of India (CHAI).[12] From the beginning the ecumenical aspect was present, and from the mid-1960s on, when Catholic historians began to participate fully, it was considerably reinforced. The contextual aspect came into view only after India's independence (1947). In the 1950s Rajaiah D. Paul and P. Thomas published a concise church history from a nationalist perspective. The same period saw the appearance of the work of the well-known Indian historian K. M. Panikkar, *Asia and Western Dominance* (1953), the first sharp critique of Western expansion in the Vasco da

11. J. M. Barnadas and R. M. K. van der Grijp, "Kerkgeschiedenis schrijven in Latijns Amerika," *Wereld en Zending* 12 (1983) 48-54; cf. also Van der Grijp in *Wereld en Zending* 4 (1975) 332-40, and in *Exchange* 19 (1978).

12. H. S. Wilson, "The Church History Association of India: An Ecumenical Experiment," in Vischer, ed., *Church History* 65-76; C. E. Abraham, "The Study of Church History in India," *International Review of Missions* 25 (1936) 461-69.

Gama era — including missionary expansion — from within the Third World.[13]

In 1974 CHAI, which is, like CEHILA, affiliated with the International Committee for Comparative Church History, undertook to write a six-volume "History of Christianity in India." It was intended that this history would be ecumenical and contextual and that it would do justice to the history of the Christian *people*, in agreement with the growing interest among secular historians in history "from below," history of peasant movements, and the like.[14] This Indian church history will not be focused on a few prominent missionaries or Indian figures but on the people's experience, both the Christians and their non-Christian environment. Thus in the second volume one encounters a scene of women in Tamil Nadu in 1585 who by their loud complaints forced the Jesuit missionaries to give them communion, which had been denied them because of their formal ignorance of the Christian faith.[15] The editors of this history, including Mar Thoma, Catholic, and Protestant historians, describe the new perspective in this way:

> The history of Christianity in India is viewed as an integral part of the socio-cultural history of the Indian people rather than as separate from it. The history will, therefore, focus attention upon the Christian people in India; upon who they were and how they understood themselves; upon their social, religious, cultural and political encounters, upon the changes which these encounters produced in them and in the appropriation of the Christian gospel, as well as in the Indian culture and society of which they themselves were a part.[16]

Africa: Attention to its Own Missionary Initiative

Under the stimulus of the movement toward political independence in the 1950s and 60s, the perspective of African historiography has changed

13. K. M. Panikkar, *Asia and Western Dominance: A Survey of the Vasco Da Gama Epoch of Asian History* (London, 1953) 375-460 (on Christian Missions). On Panikkar cf. S. J. Samartha, "The Modern Hindu View of History," *Religion and Society* VI/3 (1959) 24-40.

14. M. D. David, in Vischer, ed., *Towards a History of the Church*, 7; cf. S. I. David, "History of Christianity in India: Changing Perspectives," *Indian Church History Review* 20 (1986) 5-12.

15. J. Thekkadath, *History of Christianity in India* II (Bangalore, 1982) 267. Vol. I by A. M. Mundadan appeared in 1984. On the progress of the project see *Indian Church History Review* 19 (1985) 5-7, 88-90.

16. *History of Christianity in India* II, vi (Foreword by general editor D. V. Singh).

dramatically. This holds true for church history as well.[17] For a long time already the external perspective of C. P. Groves's four-volume *The Planting*(!) *of Christianity in Africa* (1948-1958) has left much to be desired. The focus of interest was "from the perspective of those who invaded Africa (whatever their motives have been), rather than from that of the Africans who responded (negatively, positively, or indifferently) to the new religion and culture," according to J. N. K. Mugambi of Kenya.[18]

While only an initial plan for writing a continent-wide African church history was formulated at the consultation in Nairobi in 1986 (organized by the EATWOT Working Commission),[19] in the past decades a large number of studies that are serviceable for this project have been completed. Its editors have also, in many respects, profited from the results and methodology of the general historiography of Africa as laid down, for example, in the new *General History of Africa* (UNESCO, 1981), itself written "from the inside."

This concerns specifically the use of oral sources: oral history (personal memories) and oral tradition (material handed down from generation to generation). In the period in which Kwame Nkrumah challenged Africanists to explode the myth that Africa had no history, Jan Vansina published *De la Tradition Orale* (1961), in which the instruments for distinguishing the oral traditions of African cultures were made available. Furthermore, the process of gathering and interpreting more recent oral history requires special knowledge and attention. The same is true of the process of interaction between the various oral and written sources.[20]

Often African church historians feel handicapped by the poor accessibility of widely scattered missionary archival material. Their plea is that microfilmed documents be made available to documentation centers

17. Cf. "Recovering the African Perspective of Mission History," in G. Verstraelen-Gilhuis, *From Dutch Mission Church to Reformed Church in Zambia: The Scope for African Leadership and Initiative in the History of a Zambian Mission Church* (Franeker, 1982) 13-18.

18. J. N. K. Mugambi, "A History of the Church in East Africa, " in Vischer, ed., *Towards a History of the Church* 40.

19. Cf. *Voices of the Third World*, 9-3, Sept. 1986, 128. The papers from Nairobi are in Ogbu U. Kalu, *African Church Historiography: An Ecumenical Perspective* (Bern, 1988).

20. See Verstraelen-Gilhuis, *op. cit.*, 18-21: "Written and Oral Sources." Vansina's pioneering study of 1961 has been superseded by his *Oral Tradition as History* (London, 1985), which embodies the continuing discussion. See also M. Schoffeleers, "Oral History and the Retrieval of the Distant Past: On the Use of Legendary Chronicles as Sources of Historical Information," in W. van Binsbergen and M. Schoffeleers, *Theoretical Exploration in African Religion* (London, 1985). For those mainly occupied with more recent history a very practical guide is D. Hennige, *Oral Historiography* (London, 1982).

in Africa or that the archives, which they want to "plunder" from an African perspective, be made more accessible in some other way.[21]

Ogbu U. Kalu of Nigeria says in "Doing Church History in Africa Today," a paper delivered before the ecumenical consultation in Basel (1981), that African church historiography has now reached a mature phase. The time of the defensive nationalistic historiography of the 1960s is past. That was an exciting time in which many initiatives were undertaken, such as, for example, the publication of *The Bulletin of the Society for African Church History* (1965-1970; it ceased publication as a result of the civil war in Nigeria). Critical studies were written on the political and social effects of the missionary movement, as for example E. A. Ayandele's *The Missionary Impact on Modern Nigeria* (1966). These and other publications in the "Ibadan History Series" furnished fresh stimuli, even though Ayandele's thesis concerning the role of mission as the forerunner of imperialism was later strongly qualified by a younger generation of scholars (Afigbo and others). But it is no longer a debate between white and black: "The debates have not been between blacks and whites but between us and about us."[22]

In the early 1970s the focus shifted to African religious initiatives. This development began for western Africa in 1969 with the well-known article by J. F. Ade Ajayi and E. A. Ayandele (in the Festschrift for Bengt Sundkler) on the absence of African people from missionary and ecclesiastical historiography. The shift of focus to African religious initiatives began for eastern Africa with T. O. Ranger's inaugural address in Dar es Salaam, "The Recovery of African Initiative in Tanzanian History."[24] Here the primary concern was traditional religion and the changes it underwent in the course of interactions with Christianity and Islam. There is a strong sense here that the religious history of Africa does not begin with the arrival of the first missionary — and a strong opposition to the light-darkness scheme (a derivative of the Reformation *post tenebras lux* scheme?) of numerous missionary history books with "dawn" or "daybreak" in their titles.[25] In the plan

21. Cf. E. Mveng, speaking at the IAMS Conference of 1985, *Mission Studies* II/1 (1985) 127. For the published materials of Dutch mission archives, see T. van den End, *De Gereformeerde Zendingsbond 1901-1962. Nederland-Tanah Toraja* (1985); *Gereformeerde Zending op Sumba 1859-1972* (1987).

22. O. U. Kalu, *art. cit.*, in Vischer, ed., *Church History*, 85.

23. "Writing African Church History," in *The Church Crossing Frontiers* (Uppsala, 1969) 90-108.

24. Inaugural Lectures Series No. 2, University College Dar es Salaam, March 1969.

25. See T. O. Ranger and I. Kimambo, ed., *The Historical Study of African Religion with Special Reference to East and Central Africa* (London, 1972); D. B. Barrett, ed., *African Initiatives in Religion* (Nairobi, 1971). For the dawn image, see, e.g., J. W. Jack, *Daybreak in Livingstonia* (Edinburgh, 1901); J. M. Cronjé, *En daar was Lig* (Bloemfontein, 1948).

adopted in Nairobi for a continental African church history, the field of study first listed is that of religious developments *before* the encounter with Christianity.

Another subject that has provided much material for discussion and study has been the role of the African evangelist-catechist in mission-based churches. Both quantitatively and qualitatively this role was much larger than was generally assumed before. In his compact regional history of Christianity in western Africa published in 1983, Lamin Sanneh of Gambia pointed to the great importance of the African missionary messenger, whose significance far exceeded the Western missionary contribution. After the "failure" of the period from the sixteenth to the eighteenth centuries came the "success" of the nineteenth century when "the Sierra Leoners" — West African former slaves, among them the later bishop Samuel Adjayi Crowther — became involved in mission.[26]

For eastern and southern Africa as well there have been various studies that, drawing on oral sources, highlight the crucial role of men and women who did not follow their missionaries but who literally preceded them.[27] In the article referred to above, Kalu concludes: "In the long run, Africans evangelized Africans."[28]

All this applies even more to the alternative tradition of the "independent churches," which almost from the beginning accompanied the Western missionary movement, for example, the religious initiative of the Congolese prophetess Kimpa Vita in 1700.[29] Sanneh mentions the actions of the western African prophets William Wadé Harris (1913, Ivory Coast) and Garrick Braide (1915, Nigeria), who in just a few months persuaded 100,000 people to undergo baptism. The same can be said of the Zambian prophetess Alice Lenshina Mulenga (1950s, Chinsali) who, in an area that for years had been worked by missions with little success, won a large following in a short period of time.[30] The trek to the mines made necessary

---

26. L. Sanneh, *West African Christianity: The Religious Impact* (London, 1983), xiiff.

27. On Uganda see, e.g., M. L. Pirouet, *Black Evangelists: The Spread of Christianity in Uganda 1891-1914* (London, 1978); on Zambia see Verstraelen-Gilhuis, *op. cit.*, 41, 55 ("Preparation through Singing Migrants"); on the trek of Tsonga evangelists to Mozambique see J. van Butselaar, *Africains, Missionnaires et Colonialistes. Les Origines de l'Église Presbytérienne de Mozambique, 1880-1896* (Leiden, 1984).

28. O. U. Kalu, *art. cit.*, in Vischer, ed., *Church History*, 84.

29. Cf. M. L. Martin, *Kimbangu: An African Prophet and His Church* (Grand Rapids, 1975) 14-19; D. Sweetman, *Women Leaders in African History* (London, 1984) 48-54.

30. Sanneh, *op. cit.*, xiii and passim; D. A. Shank, "The Legacy of William Wadé Harris," *International Bulletin of Missionary Research* 10 (1986) 170-76; G. O. M. Tasie, *Christian Missionary Enterprise in the Niger Delta 1864-1915* (Leiden, 1978) 166-201, on

by the new money economy and the attendant migratory labor was the channel by which independent churches from southern Africa expanded northward to Zimbabwe, Zambia, and Malawi. A few of these churches have roots even farther away and go back to the visits of African-American bishops to southern Africa in 1898 and to western Africa in 1887. Little study has as yet been made of the missionary influence of Black America in Africa,[31] which, despite the restrictions imposed by colonial governments after the uprising of John Chilembwe (1915, Nyasaland), continued in other ways.

The perspective conveyed to us from the Third World also challenges Western church historians to look at missionary history in another way — with more attention to the political, economic, social, and religious structures within which the missionary drama was enacted and with one's searchlight directed toward *all* the players.

---

the G. Braide movement; on Lenshina see A. D. Roberts, *The Lumpa Church of Alice Lenshina* (Lusaka, 1972); H. F. Hinfelaar, *Bemba-Speaking Women of Zambia in a Century of Religious Change (1892-1992)* (Leiden, 1994).

31. See G. S. Wilmore, "Black Americans in Mission: Setting the Record Straight," *International Bulletin of Missionary Research* 10 (1986) 90-103.

PART IV

Missionary Vitality
in Contemporary Christianity

Part IV offers a sketch of new missionary forms and theologies. Further reflection on this material is presented in Part V. Here the authors sketch out reflections on and applications of the gospel message that originate and emerge from different contexts. In what way is Jesus' gospel of the nearness of the kingdom a liberating experience for people of our time and therefore worthy of being disseminated? A consequence of history has been that people have had to wait and wait for the time in which they could break free from the dominance of Western Christianity. A Copernican revolution has occurred; we have arrived at a turning point. Questions remain concerning the universality and particularity of the church and of theological reflection, but these questions can only be considered when the pole of particularity gets a chance to encounter the pole of universality on a legitimate basis.

Africa: Africanization and Liberation
of Church and Theology

The vitality of Christianity in Africa has manifested itself quantitatively in enormous numerical growth and qualitatively in a process of Africanization and liberation. In chapters 19 and 20 we examine the place and role of church and theology in contemporary Africa. In the context of independent Africa the emphasis is primarily on the rootedness of church and theology in African culture (chapter 19). In the context of the Africa that is still colonial the emphasis is primarily on the effort devoted by church and theology to liberation from injustice and dehumanization (chapter 20). Therefore, we must deal with two different ecclesiastical and theological orientations.

There are also convergent developments. In independent Africa people are often the victim of neocolonial economic dependence and the associated mismanagement by their own political leaders. In this context, therefore, church and theology have to find their way "between cultural rootedness and liberation" (chapter 19). In the Africa that is still colonial, that is, South Africa, church and theology are moved by the cry of the oppressed to exert themselves on behalf of justice and the dignity of all. The issue is not just socioeconomic and political liberation. Just as necessary is liberation of the oppressed black culture. Because in the black church and in black theology the issue is ultimately one of the integral development of the people, an attempt is made here to keep this double liberation in view (chapter 20).

CHAPTER 19

Africa: Between Cultural Rootedness and Liberation

J. P. HEIJKE

In the year 2000 the population of the African continent will be more than 32 percent Christian. Half of these African Christians will live in cities. Of every five Christians in the world one will be African and one European. Thirty percent of the catechumens in Africa who receive baptism will be adults. These figures convey the importance of African Christianity, a Christianity that continues to distinguish itself by its freshness. It is the church of the dance and of the joy of living, despite all oppression.

Nevertheless, it remains difficult to assess the churches' actual circle of influence in Africa's swiftly growing cities. Full and lively Sunday services say nothing about those who stay at home. Besides the usual statistics, in which the available 100 percent is divided among the various religions and denominations, one also encounters surveys reporting, for instance, that "100 percent of the country is animist, and of those 33% have been Muslimized and 11% Christianized."

Africa's Churches

A number of phenomena distinguish African churches from Christian communities elsewhere in the world, and two are of special significance for the particular nature of African Christianity. The first of these is that the churches of Africa have as one objective the integration of human development. Amid coups, uncertainty, and poverty, the larger churches have been the only independent organizations of any importance, and they have usually been efficient and reliable. Often they have offered the only recognizable alternative structure, possessing both a fairly objective information network and leaders of regional and national significance.

265

The churches have been almost a "total society," and this social importance has increased their political responsibility.

The second distinction of African churches that bears particular importance in defining them is the continuous demand for recourse to traditional religious convictions as a source of guidance. We will return to this in our discussion of African theology.

There are other distinctives: In all the large African churches the tremendous numerical growth has created numerous pastoral problems. In the Catholic Church, for example, the shortage of priests has resulted in church communities that manage without official ministers and their services — to lay churches without sacraments — in which charisma, prayer, and song play increasingly prominent roles. Almost as a matter of course the few officeholders who have finished their training end up as staff members in the Church's headquarters.[1] A Christianity without sacraments is also encouraged by the failure of official church marriage:[2] In some African countries 80 to 90 percent of the baptized Catholic adults are excluded from the sacraments because of the irregularity of their marriage situations.

There are many independent churches in Africa, and they have large numbers of members. Originally these churches were oriented toward emancipation and were often prominent in the fight against colonial oppression. They have always taken tribal reality seriously, believing that the coming of Christ touches the ethnic group as a whole. The founders of such churches are regarded not merely as witnesses but as persons with authority.

The paschal mystery is at the center of the life of the independent churches. In their healing services they seek to make clear that Christ has overcome the powers of death. New members begin by renouncing witchcraft as a violation of life. The dialogue between the biblical life-view and the ancient African traditions takes place above all in the independent churches. Indeed, that dialogue occurs experientially in the lives of the members of these churches.

It is easy to get the impression that the independent churches have lost some of their resistance to oppression. They tend to overlook the distance in time between today and the Old Testament, they lapse easily into legalism, they exhaust themselves in offering consolation amid hopeless poverty and uprootedness without protesting against social condi-

---

1. See A. Hastings, *A History of African Christianity 1950-1975* (Cambridge, 1979) 265ff.

2. See J. Heijke, *Marriage in Africa* (Pro Mundi Vita, Africa Dossier 36; Brussels, 1986).

tions, or they seek recognition and government subsidies, which end up muzzling them. But because they are independent they have the latitude to bring to light dimensions of the gospel not explored elsewhere. They may very well force Western exegetes to deal with the healing pericopes of the Gospels.

A new wave of evangelization has washed over Africa, coming from fundamentalists who usually receive support from the USA. On street corners, in squares, and in long-distance busses the gospel is rousingly preached and revival hymns are sung vigorously. Alongside the lure of Islam and, increasingly, of Asiatic religions, this form of Christianity is a factor that will be of inestimable importance for the religious nature of the continent.

Two other factors that affect African theology are the issue of Christianity's social relevance in Africa and the significance for Christian faith of the growing awareness of cultural identity.

African Theology

Just as one must speak of "biblical theology" cautiously because the Bible has as many theologies as it has authors, so also it is risky to speak of one "African theology." To Africans themselves it is not a foregone conclusion that, just as there is an Eastern Orthodox theology, so there is an African theology. Already in the 1960s African theologians were beginning to make themselves heard. Among Protestants Bolaji Idowu of Nigeria, John S. Mbiti of Uganda, and Harry Sawyerr of Sierra Leone have been of particular importance.[3]

"Theology" and "African Theology"

A discussion arose around 1960 at the Catholic theological faculty of Kinshasa between a student, Tshibangu, and the dean of the faculty, Vanneste. According to Vanneste, attention had to be given to "real" theology before any African experiments. By "real" theology he meant the prevailing academic theology conceived in the North Atlantic world, which could subsequently be made relevant for local use. But Tshibangu pleaded for a

---

3. See B. Idowu, *Olodumare: God in Yoruba Belief* (London, 1962); *idem, Towards an Indigenous Church* (London, 1965); J. S. Mbiti, *African Religions and Philosophy* (London, 1969); H. Sawyerr, *Creative Evangelism: Towards a New Christian Encounter with Africa* (London, 1968).

nonuniversal theology. For him authentic theological truth possessed "local color." "Real" theology, he believed, makes regular local landings or, rather, stays constantly on the ground. Later Tshibangu said that African thought has an epistemology of its own and that authentic African theology cannot ignore the traditional religions.

People like Tshibangu were not comfortable with the periodical called *Revue AFRICAINE de Théologie* (published in Kinshasa), in which Africans can prove their competence in matters of general theology. They were to start a periodical for *African* theology (also published in Kinshasa).

But for someone like the Mozambican P. Couto, there is nothing African that cannot be found among other peoples. What is identified as "typically African" is like a fashionable suit of clothes that will before long be put away as preindustrial and pretechnical. Couto is not alone. At the EATWOT conference at Accra in 1977 George Bebawi of Egypt began his address by saying: "It is to be hoped that the expression 'African Theology' will fade away as a fad."[4]

The rejection or at least fear of something like an African theology can be based on two grounds. First, as with Couto,[5] it can be based on scepticism with regard to any enduring African ethnocultural identity. And this scepticism may in turn be inspired by either empirical observation ("you can see what is uniquely African disappearing") or a concern that dwelling on the cultural genius of the different peoples of Africa may lead to a dangerous delay in the urgent task of addressing the crippling economic marginalization of the continent and its population. Second, there can be confessional objections to particular ways of linking "theology" with the adjective "African." To African evangelicals (e.g., Byang H. Kato, Tite Tiénou, and Adeyemo Tokunboh)[6] all religion, including African religion, falls under Karl Barth's verdict of "No." There is no continuity between the unique and transcendent God of revelation and the religions and religious approaches of human societies.

Couto's position is extreme. It is opposed by the vast majority of Africans and is refuted by the "soul" of the black population of America.

---

4. As a rule Coptic theology is ignored when African theology is discussed. Studies like those of M. Bilolo, "Die Begriffe 'Heiliger Geist' und 'Dreifaltigkeit Gottes' angesichts der afrikanischen religiösen Ueberlieferung," *ZMR* 68 (1984) 1-23, are rare. Sunmer, *Africa Philosophy,* has pointed to the learned Ethiopian king-theologian Zara Yakole of the fourteenth century as an important point of reference for the history of African theology.

5. F. J. Couto, in T. Sundermeier, *Zwischen Kultur und Politik. Texte zur Afrikanischen und zur Schwarzen Theologie* (Hamburg, 1978) 110-41.

6. B. H. Kato, *Theological Pitfalls in Africa* (Kisumu, 1975); T. Tiénou, *The Problem of Methodology in African Christian Theologies* (Ann Arbor, 1986); A. Tokunboh, *Salvation in African Tradition* (Nairobi, 1979).

Despite the uprooting of Africans by mass deportation to the "new world," the breaking apart of ties of family and kinship, slavery on the plantations, and white attempts at indoctrination over two hundred years or more, African Americans managed to maintain a distinctive religious and cultural identity. They also made recognized contributions to Western culture, such as the blues, jazz, and a special relationship to one's own body[7] — and a distinctly Christian contribution: the spirituals.

But two words of warning must be addressed to those who seek to rehabilitate the traditional African religious inheritance: They must first guard against continent-wide generalizations, as though without careful research in specific areas one could speak of *the* African concept of God or of "African eschatology."[8] Secondly, to chart traditional African religion is not to do (African) theology. Description of a worldview is not the same as reflection on that worldview. Reflection requires critical distance from the modes of thought and behavior being presented and critical demonstrations of the claims made about them. Whether one speaks of African modes of thinking or of the viewpoints of the average Nebraskan, one cannot abolish the distinction between what is *de facto* and what is *de jure*.[9]

7. Cf. Charles Reich, *The Greening of America* (New York, 1971) 241ff.

8. Alongside African religions of small communities (farmers, hunters, and cattle keepers) Africa also has religions centered on founders of particular cities and kingdoms making claims of absoluteness, being initially critical, despotic later — hence schisms and heresies. It makes a difference whether an African Christian theologian refers to the first or to the second category. Bimwenyi with his study of the life view of the Luo Kete is an example of the first; Adoukonou with his reflection on Voodoo in Bénin of the second (B. Adoukonou, *Jalons pour une théologie africaine. Essai d'une herméneutique chrétienne du Vodun dahoméen* [2 vols.; Paris, 1980]).

9. The term "African theology" by rights also includes work by adherents of traditional African religions and of African Islam. On traditional African religion see, e.g., M. Griaule, *Conversations with Ogotemmêli: An Introduction to Dogon Religious Ideas* (Oxford, 1975); D. Zahan, *Religion, Spirituality and Thoughts of Traditional Africa* (Chicago, 1979); A. Wande, *Sixteen Great Poems of Ifa* (New York, 1975). On African Islam see A. H. Bâ, *Vie et enseignement de Tierno Bokar. Le sage de Bandiagara* (Paris, 1980); L. Brenner, *West African Sufi: The Religious Heritage and Spiritual Search of Cerno Bokar Saalif Taal* (London, 1984).

Conversation — even if only argument — between Christian theologians and defenders of traditional African religions or of African Islam has yet to begin. An apologetic publication of non-Christian African provenance like M. Balibutsa, *Les Sacrifices humains antiques et le mythe christologique* (Kigali, Rwanda, 1983) is an exception, as is the sagacious dialogue with Western Christianity of the Senegalese Muslim, C. H. Kane, in *Ambiguous Adventure* (London, 1972).

Contacts with the Diaspora

In Dar es Salaam in 1971, African American and African theologians met in a "Conference of Black Churchmen." The initiative came from the Americans, who went to Africa out of a desire to get closer to their African roots. The contact took an unexpected turn. The Africans felt uncomfortable with the heavy emphasis that their partners in dialogue placed on political and economic liberation. But they did sign a document stating that with regard to liberation they could learn something from African American theology of use especially in the newly independent countries where Africans oppressed Africans and where political power was maintained by brute force against the will of the people. In 1972 another encounter with African Americans took place in Uganda. There it was said that African theology may be starting from a mistaken base if it views the agrarian past of Africa as its frame of reference.

In 1973 the Americans again organized a meeting, this time at Union Theological Seminary in New York, where the well-known African American theologian James Cone was teaching. Because English was used, the African delegation, as at the preceding meetings, consisted mainly of English-speaking theologians, most of them Protestant. French-speaking Catholic theologians have been much less influenced by African American theology. But the English-speaking Africans have not simply given in to the American point of view with its heavy emphasis on liberation. Yet another encounter, at Accra in 1974, bore the title: "Africans and Black Theology: Soul Mates or Antagonists?" John Mbiti of eastern Africa issued an irritated repudiation of this meeting, while Bishop Desmond Tutu, who could not be present in person, submitted a conciliatory essay.[10]

Organizational Initiatives

The need for Third World theologians to see themselves distinctly over against the dominant and omnipresent North Atlantic and white theology has been embodied in important African initiatives.

---

10. D. M. Tutu, "Black Theology: Soul Mates or Antagonists?" in G. S. Wilmore and J. H. Cone, ed., *Black Theology: A Documentary History, 1966-1979* (Maryknoll, 1979) 483-91.

The Ecumenical Association of Third World Theologians (EATWOT)

A young Zairian theology student at Louvain, Oscar Bimwenyi-Kweshi, came to the conclusion that the different situations of the Third World have enough in common that close cooperation among its theologians should be strongly desired. Together with an Asian student he issued a call in 1974 to a number of theologians, asking them for substantive suggestions.[11] The result of this preliminary work was the first conference of Third World theologians in Dar es Salaam in 1976 and then the creation of EATWOT (The Ecumenical Association of Third World Theologians) at this conference. Tanzania was deliberately chosen as the meeting place because of the specific orientation of that country, that is, the Ujamaa socialism of Julius Nyerere. All Catholic and Protestant African participants endorsed the final communication of this first EATWOT assembly and accordingly subscribed to a theology that views the struggle for a just society as an important mandate.

Still, a number of African contributions to the Dar es Salaam conference ascribed a "surplus value" to cultural context as frame of reference for an authentic African theology. Looking back, E. W. Fasholé Luke wrote: "Honesty requires us to say that the Dar es Salaam assembly was dominated by the Latin Americans."[12] Also E. Mveng complained about the misunderstanding that EATWOT represented the institutionalization of Latin American liberation theology. During the first five years of EATWOT, Africans repeatedly felt excluded or reduced to the role of listeners. Even in EATWOT Africa thus proved the eternally marginalized and forgotten continent. Mveng therefore warned against a new form of paternalism that would place Africa under a new guardianship: "People must stop lecturing us."

The transition from "universal" to "contextual" theology cannot be limited to a single event. The participants in the Dar es Salaam conference agreed that in the coming years they would organize continental working conferences. This led to a colloquium of African theologians at Accra in 1977. The eighteen papers of that meeting have been published in both French and English, the latter under the title *African Theology En Route* (Maryknoll, 1979). The participants came from Botswana, Angola, Uganda,

---

11. On the history of EATWOT's beginnings see O. Bimwenyi-Kweshi, "Déplacements. A l'origine de l'Association oecuménique des Théologiens du Tiers Monde," *BTA* 3 (1980) 41-54 (summarized in *idem*, "The Origins of EATWOT," *Voices from the Third World* 4 [1981] 19-26).

12. E. W. Fasholé-Luke, "Footpaths and Signposts to African Christian Theologies," *BTA* 3 (1981) 30.

Nigeria, Malawi, Kenya, Zaire, Cameroon, Ghana, Lesotho, and South Africa. Two female African theologians were present. James Cone of the USA also gave a lecture.

The principal themes of the Accra colloquium were: adaptation versus liberation, currents of liberation, and sources for an African theology. A closing document was signed by all the participants. In it one reads of solidarity with the rest of the Third World, of oppression of Africans by Africans, of the gap between church leaders and the realities of rural village life, and of the intention to contextualize the gospel — though under the heading "Context" the document speaks of the vitality of African culture and a key sentence reads: "Contextualization will mean that theology will deal with the liberation of our people from cultural captivity." The participating theologians also spoke out in favor of the ultilization of African drama, novels, and poetry.[13] Finally, the document speaks of oppressive economic and political structures.

The Ecumenical Association of African Theologians (EAAT)

However, more important than the final document of the meeting in Accra was the formation there of the Ecumenical Association of African Theologians (EAAT), in which Catholic as well as English-, French-, and Portuguese-speaking Protestant theologians participate. There now thus exists a work group with a program, a structure uniting widely separated efforts, a means for breaking through communication barriers. Its members are jointly establishing a Bible center at Jerusalem, formulating research topics, and pleading (as they did in 1980 through the EAAT secretary, Professor E. Mveng of Cameroon) for the convening of an African Council. But the attempt to combine and direct the energies of participants is proving to be difficult. In a review of the first three years of the EAAT, Mveng complains of a lack of interest on the part of his colleagues and of financial difficulties.

From 1979 to 1985 the theologians of the EAAT published the semiannual *Bulletin de Théologie Africaine/African Bulletin of Theology (BTA)*. The *Bulletin* had a strongly French-speaking, Catholic, and Zairian bent. In its first issue it positioned itself alongside existing African theological periodicals as the official multilingual, ecumenical, and pan-African organ of the EAAT. In reality, it was not able to realize this goal. Culture, not political, economic, or social problems, was by far the most significant frame of reference for the theologians who wrote in the *Bulletin*.

---

13. See J. Heijke, "Afrikaanse romans: missiologische lectuur?" *Wereld en Zending* 12 (1983) 201-9; *African Theology En Route* 126-36, 194.

In 1988 a new theological journal began publication in Nigeria entitled *Bulletin of Ecumenical Theology;* it is published by the Ecumenical Association of Nigerian Theologians. The Catholic theological journal of the Ivory Coast, *Savanes et Forêts,* was replaced in 1992 by *Revue de l'Institut Catholique de l'Afrique de l'Ouest.*

The Lutheran *Africa Theological Journal* (published three times a year in Tanzania since 1968) reflects a strongly pan-African or international character, not just in its statement of intent but in reality. All its articles are written in English, but in terms of geographical origins it represents a considerable part of Africa, and there are contributions by Catholic authors. A relatively large amount of space is devoted to the theological relevance of Tanzanian socialism, to rural development, to Luther, to Muslim-Christian relations, and to the relationship of Islam and Christianity to traditional African religions. One also finds topics like evil spirits *(kindoki),* glossolalia, angelology, demon possession and exorcism, oaths, divination, proverbs, and mourning, and of course attention is paid to theological training, hermeneutical issues, oral theology, the question of Jesus, revelation and African religion, ministry, liberation, Marxism, war and peace, women, and theological libraries. The journal's editorial policy manages to combine practical issues and theology in a balanced manner. In other African theological journals,[14] the main focus is, again, on the incorporation of the African cultural inheritance, not on the *socioeconomic situation of present-day Africa.*

Theological Work

In 1983 the Zimbabwean theologian Ambrose Mavingire Moyo wrote as follows:

> The need for African Christian Theology or for indigenous expressions of the Christian faith has long been felt, and indeed it has been the subject of discussion in many books and journals of theology and religious studies. Much interest and enthusiasm have been expressed on the subject by Christian theologians in both Europe and Africa. And yet . . . very little theology of real significance has come forth. Most of the efforts have so far concentrated on criticizing the work of early missionaries, as pointed out by John Pobee (*Toward an African Theology,*

14. Such as *Savanes et Forêts* (Abidjan), *Telema* (Kinshasa), *Afer* (eastern Africa), *Cahiers des Religions Africaines* (Kinshasa), *Revue Africaine de Théologie* (Kinshasa), *Flambeau* (Cameroon), and *Orita* (Nigeria).

1979, p. 9), and it is mostly talk about doing such a theology. The actual work of such a theology is still a work of the future.[15]

This is a strong statement and it fails to do justice to the work of many individuals who can appeal to a large number of publications justifying or setting the parameters of an African theology. Not long ago Mercy Amba Oduyoye repeated the complaint: Let us begin — at last! As for the individuals concerned, one can divide them into teachers of theology in university departments and other theologians.

Teachers of Theology

Instructors in African theological institutions face a heavy task. Their work loads are heavy; there are considerable demands on their time. Often communication with their African colleagues is difficult. French-speaking theologians barely know what their English-speaking counterparts are publishing and vice versa. Transportation is costly. Conferences provide a chance to meet, but there is often not much opportunity for regular national or international exchanges, say, in the context of work groups or editorial boards.

Still, African teachers of theology determine to a large extent the shape and image of African theology. They are close to the libraries, they write reviews, sometimes they serve as ghostwriters for church leaders, they represent their countries at academic conferences, they publish their findings in journals and books, and they are constantly challenged and stimulated by their students. Their own backgrounds and the structures of the institutions with which they are connected tend to color the character of their work, whether it is pastorally oriented or highly academic, whether it is British and pragmatic or French and speculative.

One can say that academic theology in Africa accords priority to a theology searching for a reflexive, authentically African expression of the Christian faith. Questions surrounding African identity or personality are central. In that respect an East African theologian like John Mbiti and a Zairian theologian like Ngindu Mushete are alike. The notion that a specifically African identity is doomed to disappear to make way for the new person of urban and technical civilization is resolutely rejected.

The work of these teachers and the students stimulated by them undoubtedly spreads and deepens knowledge of traditional African values and convictions. The gospel, it is said, must be seen as linked with

---

15. A. M. Moyo, "The Quest for African Christian Theology," *Africa Theological Journal* 12 (1983) 95.

these values and convictions. Partly as a result of the formative work of the African teachers of theology, Christian Africa is going through a new conversion — a conversion to the best of the millennium-old religious traditions of the continent.[16]

Though one cannot in a few lines do justice to the outlook of teachers who have published a variety of articles and books, I will introduce a few who, without necessarily being "the best," represent somewhat the range of current thought:

"Long ago God spoke to our ancestors in many and various ways. . . ." These words from Hebrews 1:1 are a motto for the work of **Oscar Bimwenyi-Kweshi** of Zaire.[17] Through hard "field work" Bimwenyi wants to cultivate his theology in the soil of the oral culture of the Luba-Kete region in the Kassai. His culture attributes a high value to a quality of inner hospitality, translated by Bimwenyi as "receptivity to the unexpected and improbable." By a careful "textual reading" in oral tradition Bimwenyi discerns the deeper connections in the fragments. Joining them together, he draws the outline of the God-image: God, the first Voice, that which precedes all human speech; God's word, which is always too big for any human mouth; God, who is always in the lead, by contrast with humankind, who is always behind: "Where God is the cook there is no smoke; all of a sudden the dish is before you." Humans are incorrigibly of the opinion that it is they who see, but they often overlook the fact that to be seen is part of being human. Therefore, the God of Israel manifests himself in the burning thornbush of initiation into Luba-Kete society. He also leaves the bush intact: He lets himself be approached in it.

Tite Tiénou is from Mali and works now in Burkina Faso with the Association of Evangelicals of Africa and Madagascar (AEAM).[18] He advocates a contextual theology carried not only by well-equipped researchers but also by the people of the church. He considers a great deal of African theology much too professorial and insufficiently pastoral. Most of what has been produced so far has barely influenced the actual life of

---

16. In 1980 *Savanes et Forêts* published a list of theses that had been submitted to the Institut Catholique de l'Afrique de l'Ouest in Abidjan. The vast majority of the themes came from the field of cultural anthropology. One may with some justification draw the conclusion that both the Abidjan Institut and the journal attach great value to the cultivation of cultural inheritance and have little to do with matters like social analysis.

17. O. Bimwenyi-Kweshi, *Discours théologique négro-africain. Problème des fondements* (Paris, 1981); abridged German edition: *Alle Dinge erzählen von Gott. Grundlegung afrikanischer Theologie* (Freiburg, 1982). See also J. Heijke, "Theologie in Zaire," *In de Waagschaal* 12 (1983) 137-41, 172-77.

18. See note 6 above and *Tâche théologique de l'Église* (Abidjan, 1980).

the church. A theologian, an African theologian as well, must begin by understanding a concrete church existing in a specific non-Christian religious and cultural environment. Into that complex the theologian must introduce the corrective message of Holy Scripture. Tiénou speaks of a prescriptive theology which, like a physician, gives prescriptions: The physician must take serious account of who his patients are, must know them well, must approach them as serious cases, and must help them get rid of their disorders. The study of the traditional African cultural and religious world is necessary in order to arrive at a concrete and correct diagnosis and to focus the therapy of the gospel correctly. In that sense theology in Africa and elsewhere must be contextual: It must have a real feel for the local situation.

Mercy Amba Oduyoye is a member of the Methodist Church, is active in EATWOT, and is vice president of EAAT.[19] She observes with approval that around the world theologians are aligning their discipline to life issues. She is opposed to a church that avoids conflict and wants to become prominent, respectable, and established. Fortunately the academic world in Africa is beginning to turn to the "underside" of Africa's history and to recognize the "rural-oral" as a valid source of knowledge and wisdom. Nevertheless, emerging African liberation theology must address itself not only to combatting (neo-)colonialism but also to the burden that traditional social structures are on people. If God made himself known as the liberator of slaves forced to build pyramids for an Egyptian pharaoh, then he is also the liberator of starving Africans forced to grow cocoa and coffee. The answer to the question "Is anyone in charge here?" — in this chaotic world — is Yes. History as interpreted by Holy Scripture points to that one who is in charge.

Amba Oduyoye, a Ghanian teaching in Ibadan, Nigeria, pays ample attention to African evangelical theology, but rejects it. Sin, she says, is not the only form of misery from which God delivers people. One of the unique contributions of Christianity is the doctrine of the suffering Messiah, the image of the suffering God. Christianity claims to be a movement of healing in this chaotic world. Baptism in the name of the triune God — a model for and source of human relationships — motivates us not to support hierarchies or monarchies but to participation, to sharing of power

19. M. A. Oduyoye, *Hearing and Knowing: Theological Reflections on Christianity in Africa* (Maryknoll, 1986); "Church-Women and the Church's Mission in Contemporary Times: A Study of Sacrifice in Mission," *BTA* 6 (1984) 259-72; "Feminism: A Pre-Condition for a Christian Anthropology," *Africa Theological Journal* 11 (1982) 193-208; "The Doctrine of the Trinity: Is It Relevant for Contemporary Christian Theology?" *Orita* 14 (1982) 43-54; "Naming the Woman: The Words of the Akan and the Words of the Bible," *BTA* 3 (1981) 81-95.

and responsibility. Amba Oduyoye relates this viewpoint of faith to the position of African women.

Rural African Theologians

A few African theologians write not in cities or in studies, but in the countryside, "under a tree," though before they began to write, or in the course of writing, they spent a fair amount of time reading — often in difficult material circumstances. I will introduce two of these theologians, both of them from Cameroon.

For **Jean-Marc Ela** it is of decisive importance that he left his own tribal area and began to work as missionary among people totally foreign to him, the so-called Kirdi in the north near the border of Cameroon and Nigeria. He thus demonstrated existentially his willingness to relativize his own ethnic identity, subordinating it to the challenge of the gospel.[20] He believes that inculturation is fine and necessary but also usually functions as an alibi for eluding the mandate of the gospel in the African situation. Ela writes about dreams, ancestors, witchcraft, and traditional notions of sickness and health: the actual problems of ordinary people. But Africa is for him above all an oppressed and exploited continent whose rural populations bleed for the sake of the few well-to-do people in the capital cities.

The economy that controls Africa, says Ela, serves the interests of the North Atlantic world. Most African people can only expect a premature and unnatural death. This situation exists in flagrant contradiction to the kingdom that God wills to realize by his Spirit. To lose oneself in medical missionary activity without combating the causes of premature death or to exhaust oneself in educational endeavors that are really designed to keep the deadly system functioning is to shrink from the real challenge. To revel in the Africanization of the liturgy without actively standing up for the dispossessed African is unconscious idolatry. Ela searches for indigenous African forms of consciousness-raising for both the exploited and deceived rural population and for the young people studying in the

---

20. Twice Jean-Marc Ela interrupted his stay among the marginalized mountain-dwellers in this Muslim-dominated area: In 1969 he wrote a dissertation at the University of Strasbourg on Luther, *La Transcendance de Dieu . . Essai d'introduction à la logique d'une théologie*. These two volumes total 1110 pages but contain not a single reference to Africa. In 1978 he wrote a second dissertation, this time at the Sorbonne, in the social sciences on the condition and perspectives of the people among whom he worked: *Structures sociales traditionnelles et changements économiques chez les Montagnards du Nord-Cameroun*. In his later publications I encountered no references to his first dissertation and many to the second.

cities, the leaders of tomorrow. He seeks direction from traditional Africa so that the kingdom of God may break through and so that a society corresponding to God's intentions may be established. Did not Jesus identify himself with the hungry, the sick, the imprisoned, and the strangers or refugees?[21]

Fabien Eboussi Boulaga is a former Jesuit, well-read and fluent, probably one of the most sagacious and original theologians of contemporary Africa. His books[22] contain virtually no footnotes or quotations, which is an exception in African theological literature. Their purpose is no less than a total rethinking of Christianity. Christianity as it has been introduced into Africa is a "custom religion" fused with a technical civilization and an ideological atmosphere in which atheists and believers share the same basic convictions. It is accustomed to speaking in the name of the whole of humanity. Carried into a non-Western universe, it is not capable of exchange, only of dictation and domination. Prevailing Christianity stumbles under the weight of its own certainties about God. According to Eboussi, to localize the Inviolable in this way is fetishism. He considers *theologia negativa* the only authentic form of theology. One must become a Christian in order to find out what God is not. Accordingly, Christianity must adopt myths instead of rejecting them. Truth does not come down: It must be sought out by an arduous ascent. Relations with the True and Inviolable operate through people, who are, in fact, united by ties of blood and sustained by a (local) culture. Birth and death furnish the framework for and the experience of the sacral and sovereign immanence of God for which we are searching.

Eboussi reserves numerous pages for the description of what he calls the Christ-model. He stresses that Jesus restricted himself to his own Jewish tradition, finding it adequate. It is not for nothing that the gospel begins with a genealogy. The early churches defined themselves as the "way" within Judaism. There is room also for Gentile churches. Each maintains its own ethnic solidarity, at the same time relativizing it. Unfortunately, Jewish Christians were eventually asked to "dejudaize" themselves to become individualized, uprooted souls. One could no longer be both Jewish and Christian. The tendency to regard all cultural differences as illegitimate took root in Christianity. It will be a long time before a Jew,

21. Besides the two unpublished dissertations and a number of articles, Ela has written, among other things, *The Cry of African Man* (Maryknoll, 1986), *My Faith as an African* (Maryknoll, 1988), and, with R. Luneau, *Voici le temps des héritiers. Églises d'Afrique et voies nouvelles* (Paris, 1981).

22. F. E. Boulaga, *La Crise du Muntu. Authenticité africaine et philosophie* (Paris, 1977); *Christianity Without Fetishes: An African Critique and Recapture of Christianity* (Maryknoll, 1984).

a Taoist, a Buddhist, a Hindu, or an animist will be allowed to be a Christian.

The African Independent Churches

The systematization of the views of the African independent churches has so far been the work of outsiders. Similarly, the input of white instructors in the theological faculty of the Kimbanguists at Kinshasa has from the beginning been very substantial. In some regions, thanks to stimulating initiatives of outsiders, these churches have decided to set up joint facilities for theological training where the future leadership can learn modern Bible scholarship. At the same time, because after their schooling many students play leadership roles in the villages, courses in agrarian science are also offered. It is still too early to sketch a profile of African people's theology or "peasant" theology. It is to be hoped that there will be mutual — and balanced — influence between the future theologians of the African independent churches and other African theologians.

Conclusion

On reading Lloyd Timberlake's *Africa in Crisis*,[23] one can no longer as an American or European set oneself to work at a critical presentation of African theology. In virtually all sectors experts on Africa have failed — not for lack of technical knowledge, but because they proved incapable of giving due weight to the African situation and especially to the African people themselves. Therefore, it is foolhardy to assume that a non-African evaluation of African theology can be pulled off with aplomb. "Rule the country as if there were no inhabitants" was the slogan of occupying colonial governments, and this watchword seems still to apply to foreign experts seeking to serve Africa with advice. Could theology be the only discipline to escape this misunderstanding? Would the validating norms with which the white missiologist addresses church and theology in Africa enable him or her to elude — in virtue of an appeal to divine revelation

23. L. Timberlake, *Africa in Crisis* (Philadelphia, 1986). For African perspectives on African theology see G. H. Muzorewa, *The Origins and Development of African Theology* (Maryknoll, 1985); K. A. Dickson, *Theology in Africa* (London, 1984). See also B. Bujo, *Afrikanische Theologie in ihrem gesellschaftlichen Kontext* (Düsseldorf, 1986). For European perspectives see A. Shorter, *African Christian Theology: Adaptation or Incarnation?* (London, 1975); T. Witvliet, *A Place in the Sun: An Introduction to Liberation Theology in the Third World* (Maryknoll, 1985) 104-17.

— the danger of gross miscalculation that clearly threatens nontheologians who regard themselves as Africanists?

It is risky to offer prognoses as though, after all, we did possess universal insight. But we may perhaps stress one point in conclusion: A consensus exists with regard to the distinction between the African and the North Atlantic understandings of personhood. In the African view the human person is not a point of origin, one who has to validate himself or herself by new ideas, original behavior, or fresh contributions to culture, not an individual who has to fight for himself or herself and somehow make it on his or her own as an orphan. In the African view a person is a point of convergence where many lines from the past come together. It is of a person's essence, first of all, to *receive*. Apart from the social fabric of which he or she is a part, a human being is nothing. The sense of being supported on every side by the past is much stronger than the invitation to add something new. Language, interpretations, skills, insights, and security all await the African at birth. That which the African has received is infinitely more important than what he or she can bring about.

This rootedness in kinship, this priority of gratitude over any drive to achieve, constitutes a sounding board for the gospel and for theological and pastoral reflection, one to which we of the North Atlantic world are not accustomed. The fruitfulness of an authentic African way of doing theology will, hopefully, be brought into an ecumenical, intercultural dialogue and contribute to the healing of our one-sidedness. When this happens, the cultural and economic spheres will presumably intersect.

CHAPTER 20

Church Conflict and Black Theology in South Africa

G. M. VERSTRAELEN-GILHUIS

Some very significant impulses for the liberation of church and theology in Africa are arising from the shackled feet of the continent. Whatever happens in church and theology in South Africa resonates around the world. South Africa is a microcosm. World problems that can be kept at a greater distance elsewhere are intensely concentrated here: poverty and riches, exploitation and domination, a dominant white minority over a marginalized black majority.

As a result South Africa is also a test case for the credibility of the global claims of the Christian faith. This is all the more pressing because South Africa is a "very Christian" land. At least 77% of the population belongs to the Christian churches.[1] But the churches in South Africa are divided, not so much because there are some four thousand denominations but because in every church there are two churches: a "white" church appealing to its faith in the interest of maintaining the status quo and a "black" church that pleads for change on the basis of the same gospel. There are Christians on both sides of the conflict — and the line separating them does not necessarily follow color lines. "There we sit in the same Church while outside Christian policemen and soldiers are beating up and killing Christian children or torturing Christian prisoners to death while yet other Christians stand by and weakly plead for peace," as the *Kairos Document* sketched the situation (1985). The ongoing struggle concerns the correct understanding of the Christian faith — not in academic discussion but in the context of life-and-death questions.

Following a few historical notes on the development of political

---

1. The 77% is based on an analysis of the 1980 census. Cf. J. J. Kritzinger, *Statistische beschrijving van de bevolking van Zuid-Afrika* (Pretoria, 1985).

and ecclesiastical relationships, this chapter will address "the struggle for a confessing and prophetic church" and the rise and significance of black theology in this context.

Historical Background

The history of Southern Africa has taken a different course than the history of other parts of Africa because of the permanent settlement of white colonists since 1652 and the discovery of diamonds and gold in Kimberley (1867) and Witwatersrand (1886). The Boers took the land away from the black population, and the British saw to it that the gold of that land would be exploited under their direction. After the Anglo-Boer War (1899-1902), which severely traumatized the Boers, the white Union of South Africa (1900) came into being, followed by the Natives Land Act (1913), which legalized the expropriation of the land and assigned a mere 7% (later 13%) to the black population. Colonial conquest was now a fact. The black population had been reduced to a labor pool for the mines and farms of the whites.

In reaction to the white Union, black political organizations united in 1912 and formed the South African Native African Congress, which in 1925 became the African National Congress (ANC). In the same year the Congress adopted the national song *Nkosi Sikelel'i Afrika* ("God Bless Africa") and the black, green, and yellow flag, which symbolizes the African people, land, and gold.[2] In vain the Congress leaders, black ministers among them, pleaded in London for the extension to the rest of the Union of the limited black franchise in force at the Cape. For the British the protection of black rights had apparently not been the issue over which the Boer War had been fought after all. The regulation of native affairs was left entirely to the white colonists.

This led to an ever-tightening demarcation of the color bar. In 1926 the industrial color bar became a reality in the mines. In the 1930s the whites, including "poor whites" and women, were given universal suffrage, but the 16,000 members of the black elite of the Cape were deleted from the voters' rolls. Following the electoral victory of Afrikaner nationalists in 1948, the segregation policy of the preceding decades was expanded into the much more systematic policy of "separate development" or "apartheid." The earlier policy had established a limited separation of white and black in a sort of multiracial caste society. But apartheid aimed

---

2. P. Walshe, *The Rise of African Nationalism in South Africa: The African National Congress 1912-1952* (Los Angeles, 1970, reprint 1982) 204.

from the beginning for total separation of white and black, including the resettlement of people by ethnic categories in supposedly independent "Bantu homelands."[3]

Afrikaner Churches and Apartheid Theology

Shortly after the introduction of apartheid, a congress of white Dutch Reformed churches, meeting in Bloemfontein (1950), declared that "it was the Afrikaner churches themselves that laid the foundation for the policy of separate development."[4] The Afrikaner (or Boer) churches have, indeed, played an important role in the formation of the policy of apartheid and in theological justification of apartheid.

This has been especially true of the influential Nederduitse Gereformeerde Kerk (NGK).[5] Four times in the 1930s and 1940s — the incubation phase of apartheid — this church petitioned the government to outlaw racially mixed marriages. Its mission secretary, J. G. Strydom, speaking at a mission congress in Bloemfontein in 1938, called apartheid "an issue of faith." He was thus one of the first to promote the use of the term "apartheid" along with the implications that the term carries.[6]

The first steps down the slippery slope that was to end in the formation of separate churches were taken by the NGK synod of 1857. Confronted with problems in various congregations relating to communion between "born Christians" and "members from among the heathen," the synod declared that it was "desirable and in accord with Holy Scripture" that new black Christians be accepted and initiated into existing congregations. But where "on account of the weakness of some," that is, of white members, this was not possible, arrangements could be made for black Christians to meet in separate buildings. Separate services and separate church buildings paved the way for the formation of separate churches: In 1881 the NG Sendingskerk (i.e., "Mission Church," the NGSK)

---

3. Cf. N. J. Rhoodie and A. J. Venter, *Apartheid and Partnership* (Pretoria, 1966) 148.

4. *Die Naturellevraagstuk* (Bloemfontein, 1950) 123.

5. Cf. J. C. Adonis, *Die Afgebreekte skeidsmuur weer opgebou. Die verstrengeling van die sendingbeleid van die NG Kerk met die praktyk en ideologie van die Apartheid* (Amsterdam, 1982); J. Kinghorn, ed., *Die NG Kerk en Apartheid* (Johannesburg, 1986). The latter is a collection of studies by NG theologians seeking to help free their church from the "ideological enslavement" of apartheid theology. It includes a chapter on "Criticism from the Ecumenical Church," but pays little or no attention to the Belhar Confession or to the criticism of black Reformed theologians.

6. G. Verstraelen-Gilhuis, *From Dutch Mission Church to Reformed Church in Zambia* (Franeker, 1982) 201, 205f., 216.

was founded for "coloreds," followed by the NG Kerk in Afrika (NGKA) for "blacks" and the Indian Reformed Church for Indians.

"Instead of the church committing itself to overcome the sin of racial pride, black people were asked to be the least and to leave the church."[7] The opinion (expressed in the official NG mission history of D. Crafford [1982] and the more recent policy statement "Church and Society") that it was merely "cultural differences" and "administrative needs" that shaped these decisions has been refuted in studies by Adonis, Loff, Borchardt, and Bosch.[8]

The compromise of 1857 was motivated by practical concerns. What came to be the fundamental rationale was not stated until after 1930 as increasingly close ties between church and people were forged and the civil religion of "Afrikanerdom" came into being.[9] The mission policy adopted in 1935[10] straightforwardly opposed "racial mixing" and "social equality." "Evangelization without denationalization" was the slogan (one that was not unknown in the international mission circles of that time).[11] The evangelical-pietistic Murray tradition — which in missionary praxis had often been a counterweight offsetting racial prejudice — was outflanked by Kuyperian neo-Calvinism. With the aid of a South African variant of this Kuyperian Calvinism, an apartheid theology was developed on the basis of a rooting of the diversity of peoples in creation ordinances. In this South African variant, developed by H. G. Stoker and others, "peoples" as ethnic units were allotted "sphere sovereignty."[12] Subse-

---

7. So C. Loff, who has rewritten the history of the NGSK from a black perspective ("The History of a Heresy," in J. de Gruchy and C. Villa-Vicencio, ed., *Apartheid Is a Heresy* [Capetown and Grand Rapids, 1983] 22).

8. D. Crafford, *Aan God die Dank. Geskiedenis van die Sending van die Ned. Geref. Kerk* I (Pretoria, 1982) 42; *Kerk en Samelewing* (1986) 25, 252; Adonis, *op. cit.*, 44, 56; C. Borchardt in Kinghorn, *op. cit.*, 70-85; D. J. Bosch, "Eenheid binne die 'Familie' van NG Kerke-waarheen?" in *Die Eenheid van die Kerk* (Pretoria, 1987) 45-73.

9. T. D. Moodie, *The Rise of Afrikanerdom: Power, Apartheid and the Afrikaner Civil Religion* (Los Angeles, 1975). More recent research by Afrikaner historians has shown that Moodie has mistakenly projected his "Calvinistic model" back into earlier times: The idea of an "elect people" first emerged at the end of the nineteenth century in response to British imperialism. Cf. D. J. Bosch, "The Roots and Fruits of Afrikaner Civil Religion," in J. S. Hofmeyr and W. S. Vorster, ed., *New Faces of Africa* (Pretoria, 1984) 14-35.

10. "Die Sendingbeleid van die Gefedereerde Ned. Gereformeerde Kerke," in *'n Eeu van Sendingwerk* (Kroonstad, 1938) 168-72; cf. Verstraelen-Gilhuis, *op. cit.*, 206f.

11. For this see the IMC conference of Le Zoute (1926); cf. my "African Education as Seen from Le Zoute, 1926," in G. Verstraelen-Gilhuis, *A New Look at Christianity in Africa* (Gweru, 1992) 37-61; Verstraelen-Gilhuis, *op. cit.*, 333, 206-9. In German missiology there were more points of contact; cf. Bosch, *art. cit.* (note 8) 56.

12. Moodie, *op. cit.*, 61, 65ff. See also the study by L. R. L. Ntoane, *A Cry for Life: An Interpretation of "Calvinism" and Calvin* (Kampen, 1983).

quently, in the 1940s and 1950s, exegetical studies (by Groenewald and others) reinforced this biblical rationale for apartheid.[13] All this was summed up in *Ras, Volk en Nasie en Volkereverhoudinge in die Lig van die Skrif* (Race, People, and Nation, and Relations among Peoples in the Light of Scripture), the widely distributed synodical policy statement issued in 1974.

The Ambivalence of the English-Speaking Churches

The English-speaking churches are often viewed as the opposite of the Afrikaner churches. These churches of British origin — Anglicans, Congregationalists, Methodists, Presbyterians, and others — work together in the South African Council of Churches, the membership of which also includes Lutherans, black Dutch Reformed churches, and — as an observer — the Roman Catholic Church.

It is said that historically these churches assumed an increasingly critical position with regard to racial discrimination. One can, indeed, point to a missionary tradition that regarded the defense of the rights of the black population as an essential component of the gospel. The first missionary at the Cape, J. T. van der Kemp of the Netherlands, who arrived in 1799 under the auspices of the London Missionary Society, refused to preach in church services where "Christians from the heathen" were not welcome. He became the great advocate of the rights of the Khoikhoi before the colonial administrators.[14] Van der Kemp and others following his policies were a great annoyance to the Dutch Boers — and also to the British colonists and their clergy. Here, too, the conflict between "the church of the colonists" and "the mission church" was never really resolved.

At the end of the nineteenth century most English-speaking churches were, in fact, divided along ethnic lines, though, unlike the Afrikaner churches, under common synods or bishops and within the same denominational structures.[15] The multiracial organization of these churches was at the top rather than the base of the life of these churches — a tendency merely reinforced by the introduction of the *Groups Area Act* (1950) under the apartheid regime. On various occasions, for example,

13. See the discussion in Adonis, *op. cit.*, 87-92, 199-205.

14. I. H. Enklaar, *Life and Work of Dr. J. Th. van der Kemp, 1741-1811: Missionary Pioneer and Protagonist of Racial Equality in South Africa* (Cape Town, 1988) 113, 208.

15. J. W. de Gruchy, *The Church Struggle in South Africa* (Grand Rapids, 1979) 12f., 18.

when the expropriation of the land was established in law (1913), sharp verbal protests came from the top leadership of these churches. In his study of the Anglican and Methodist churches from 1903 to 1930, J. R. Cochrane concluded that despite their criticism of the segregation laws they remained "servants of power." There was no interest in economic questions or the problems of black laborers since, says Cochrane, South African realities were viewed from a predominantly white British perspective.[16]

The English-speaking churches have increasingly made public declarations against apartheid since its introduction in 1948. While they have had no use for the apartheid theology of the Afrikaner churches, the lifestyle and the social and political values and practice of their white members have differed little from those of the Afrikaner churches. Sound doctrine has not enabled them to escape the practice of heresy.[17]

The African Independent Churches

Of the black population, a little less than 30% belongs to one of the African independent churches and 45% belongs to the mainline or historical churches. In 1980 there were about 3500 independent churches. Most of their members belong to the very poorest part of the population. Usually these churches restrict themselves to a narrow world: They focus on healing the sick and driving out spirits and leave the exorcism of evil from society to the much better educated black leaders of the historic churches.

It has not always been that way. Just as the history of Afrikaner nationalism has been bound up with that of the Afrikaner churches, so the history of the black nationalist movement is rooted in the black churches, particularly in the Ethiopian movement. At the organizational meeting of the ANC in 1912 the opening prayer was delivered by Rev. Henry Ngcayiya, president of the "Ethiopian Church." He was also a member of the black delegation sent to London to protest the adoption of the Natives Land Act.

The Ethiopian movement, out of which the independent churches in South Africa first grew, unfolded in 1872 to 1912.[18] At one after another mission station well-trained black Christians broke away from oppressive

16. J. R. Cochrane, *Servants of Power: The Role of English-speaking Churches in South Africa, 1903-1930* (Johannesburg, 1987) 89. Cf. also De Gruchy, *op. cit.,* 37f.

17. C. Villa-Vicencio, "An All-Pervading Heresy: Racism and the English-speaking Churches," in *Apartheid Is a Heresy,* 61, 67.

18. Cf. for this E. Kamphausen, *Anfänge der kirchlichen Unabhängigkeitsbewegung in Südafrika. Geschichte und Theologie der Äthiopischen Bewegung 1872-1912* (Bern, 1976).

missionary structures and started "Ethiopian churches," where, freed from white domination, they could develop their own gifts for leadership, though their new churches otherwise differed little from the model provided by the missionary churches. Charlotte Manye Maxeke (who later organized the ANC women's movement) was a student in the USA at the time, and through her contact was made between the Ethiopian churches of South Africa and the pan-Africanist movement and the African Methodist Episcopal (AME) Church in America. The visit of the Bishop Henry M. Turner of the AME Church to South Africa in 1898 gave great impetus to the Ethiopian churches. In 1910 there were already about seventy such "sanctuaries" where black Christians — crossing tribal boundaries — could meet to encourage each other. The Ethiopian movement — the name is derived from Ps. 68:31b: "Let Ethiopia hasten to stretch out its hands to God" — was broader than the Ethiopian churches. It was also a sociopolitical movement of emancipation. It can be viewed as the first black nationalist movement and as such a forerunner and supporting force of the political organizations united in the ANC in 1912.

While the political force of the Ethiopian movement was taken over by the ANC, the Ethiopian churches were inundated religiously in 1920 by the larger wave of the Zionist churches. Over against the pan-African ideals of the Ethiopians stood the more tribal orientation of the Zionists. Their leaders, raised up from among the common people, were closer to the traditional inheritance. They were called by a vision to establish a holy city, Zion, and to heal the sick. These churches — also called spiritual churches on account of their emphasis on the lifegiving power of the Holy Spirit — became immensely popular. But they were ignored by the historic churches and had a hard time gaining legal recognition. But since the mid-1960s friendly relations have developed between the leaders of the Zion Christian Church — which grew to be the largest independent church in South Africa — and the South African government. In exchange for loyalty to the government these churches have received land and other favors. Obedience to parents, chiefs, pastors, and bishops is run together in the preaching of these churches with obedience to the law and to the government. A fundamentalist exegesis of Romans 13 and traditional legalism tend to reinforce each other.

In the past few years a small but growing segment of the independent churches has come into contact with the ecumenical movement, that is, with the South African Council of Churches (SACC) and the Institute for Contextual Theology. These churches published a brochure entitled *Speaking for Ourselves* in 1985. There they presented themselves as "churches of the people." It was their aim, they said, to study their own history and theology, and they were critical of many things written about them by outsiders. On the question of their political posture they said: "Our people, therefore, know what it means to be oppressed, exploited and crushed. Our Churches are not powerful institutions that can make statements to influence the government or the struggle. The 'Churches of the People' and the political organisations have different roles to play. It is often the same people who belong to both."[19]

The Struggle for a Confessing and Prophetic Church

In the pursuit of the church's liberation from servitude to powers alien to the gospel, people in South Africa speak of the struggle for a "confessing church." Their concern is not to add still another denomination to the many already existing but to forge ecumenical ties between Christians and groups of Christians who believe that the credibility of the church stands or falls with the manner in which it fights against apartheid and works for liberation and political and economic justice.[20]

The Christian Institute, the Council of Churches, and the Bishops' Conference

The statement that "the time for a confessing church" had come in South Africa was made for the first time in 1965 by C. F. Beyers Naudé in an article in *Pro Veritate*, the official organ of the Christian Institute. Here the struggle of the Confessing Church in Germany against the "German Christians" and against Nazi ideology was presented as a model for the "church struggle" in South Africa. Despite differences, there were, after all, striking resemblances, such as a false unity between church and people, the silence of the official church, and state intimidation of dissident groups.

Beyers Naudé wrote his article shortly after security police had searched the offices of the Christian Institute (CI). The CI was founded in the wake of Cottesloe (1960), the WCC-initiated consultation of South African churches after the bloodbath of Sharpeville. The Cottesloe Declaration, which contained moderate criticism of aspects of apartheid, was

19. *Speaking for Ourselves* (Braamfontein, 1985) 30f.
20. Cf. C. F. Beyers Naudé, "Op weg naar een belijdende kerk," and S. Govender, "Een belijdende kerk in Zuid-Afrika?" in *Met de moed der hoop* (Baarn, 1985) 167-79 and 94-102; J. de Gruchy, "Toward a Confessing Church," in *Apartheid Is a Heresy*, 75-93; *idem, The Road Ahead: Documentation on the Confessing Church Debate* (Cape Town, 1987); *idem*, "Strijd voor een belijdende kerk," *Wereld en Zending* 13 (1984) 97-174.

signed by the NGK's delegates, but after intervention by Prime Minister Verwoerd it was rejected by the NGK synods. About 280 people attended the organizational meeting, few of them black, most of them white. They included officials in the English-speaking churches, a small group of Dutch Reformed ministers — their numbers sharply reduced after Cottesloe and about twenty socially involved Roman Catholic priests and laypeople. The intention of the CI was to continue the dialogue begun in Cottesloe. To that end it organized Bible studies and other activities, bringing together Christians from all denominations who were prepared to engage in the struggle for racial justice.

Although the CI still had a long way to go before it learned to look at South African society through black eyes, its very founding was something new: The contours of a prophetic ecumenical movement were beginning to emerge.[21] From the beginning the CI emphasized becoming a critical ferment within the white Afrikaner churches. In the 1970s this orientation made way for increasing involvement in the struggle of black liberation. Listening to voices of the Black Consciousness movement and of emerging black theology, CI leaders devised study programs that were more action-oriented. As more radical positions were taken, the CI was first declared an "affected" organization and then was hit by a banning order, along with sixteen Black Consciousness organizations, in October 1977.

The CI had an important part in producing *A Message to the People of South Africa,* which was issued by SACC in 1968. This message said — for the first time in an ecclesiastical policy statement — that apartheid was directly in conflict with the central content of the Christian gospel. Believers were called on to "distinguish this false alien gospel from the true eternal gospel of Jesus Christ."

The end of CI was cushioned by other agencies. SACC, of which Bishop Desmond Tutu became secretary in 1978, developed into an outspoken exponent of ecclesiastical resistance to apartheid. This prompted the state to appoint the Eloff Commission to investigate SACC's theology.[22] In this context SACC worked hand-in-hand with the South African Catholic Bishops' Conference (SACBC). Together in 1983 the two organizations published a report on the forced resettlements in the black homelands.

Within the SACBC itself a process of radicalization had taken place under the influence of Vatican II, Latin American liberation theology, and

21. P. Walshe, *Church versus State in South Africa: The Case of the Christian Institute* (London, 1983) 35.

22. *Bekenntnis und Widerstand. Kirchen Südafrikas im Konflikt mit dem Staat* (Hamburg, 1983); *Wereld en Zending* 13 (1984) 116-23, 152.

especially the South African Black Consciousness movement. In 1957 the bishops called apartheid a "fundamental evil" that must be removed step by step. Twenty years later, when the uprising of black youth in Soweto had opened the eyes of the people, the bishops declared themselves to be "on the side of the oppressed" and stated that "the only solution of our racial tensions consists in conceding full citizen and human rights to all persons in the Republic, not on the false grounds of colour, but on the grounds of the common humanity of all men, taught by our Lord Jesus Christ."[23]

Belhar: Status Confessionis for the Dutch Reformed Churches

After the banning of Pro Veritate, the CI journal Dunamis, a publication of the ministers' Broederkring (BK), began publishing. It had the subtitle Witness for the Struggle for a Relevant Church. In the foreword of the first issue we read: "It is our intention to make audible in the church those voices that are sometimes never heard. It is our conviction that Christian participation in the struggle for justice, human dignity, and reconciliation can and may not be missing in South Africa."

The Broederkring, which originated in 1974, was a group of ministers and evangelists in the racially separated Dutch Reformed churches whose goal was to restore unity in its divided family of churches and to take seriously the prophetic and priestly task of the church in regard to oppressive apartheid legislation and its victims. In 1983 its name was changed to Belydende Kring (BK) or "Confessing Circle" of the Dutch Reformed churches, a name that was more clearly expressive of its goals and also sought to overcome the clergy and male orientations of the group.[24]

With bewilderment and pain the members of the BK became aware of the background of the racial division of the white, "colored," black, and Indian Reformed churches in South Africa. This bewilderment became even greater when through their own studies and other publications the role that the white NGK had played in the formation and theological justification of apartheid was laid bare.

The discovery of this Christian legitimation of apartheid did not, however, lead to the abandonment of the Christian faith. On the contrary, it served to stimulate an intensive study of the Bible and of the version of the Reformed tradition handed down to them within the black experience. An initial joint product of this study was the Theological Declaration of

---

23. A. Prior, ed., Catholics in Apartheid Society (Cape Town, 1982) 171, 187.
24. Belydende Kring Bulletin, 1/8 (October, 1983).

the BK (September, 1979). Ideas that were later elaborated in the Belhar Confession of the NGSK — the church as the undivided body of Christ, God as the champion of justice and as the one who stands on the side of the victims of injustice, and the obligation to be more obedient to Christ than to earthly governments, powers, and ideologies — were already present in this declaration.[25]

In ABRECSA (the Association of Black Reformed Christians in South Africa) as well, black South African members of churches belonging to WARC (the World Alliance of Reformed Churches) were drawn into the search for the roots of the Reformed tradition. In the theological basis of ABRECSA, adopted in October, 1981, in Hammanskraal, it was stated that "apartheid is a sin and its theological justification a betrayal of the Reformed tradition and a heresy," a verdict that a year later, under the influence of black South Africans, was adopted also by the WARC assembly in Ottawa. "The Reformed tradition has a future in this country only if black Reformed Christians are willing to take it up, make it truly their own, and let this tradition once again become what it once was: a champion of the cause of the poor and the oppressed. . . . Black Christians should formulate a Reformed confession for our time and situation in our own words." Dr. Allan Boesak, a minister of the NGSK and from 1982 president of WARC, spoke these words to the ABRECSA conference at Hammanskraal.[26]

At the synod of the NGSK in October 1982, convened soon after the Ottawa assembly, this wish was realized. Here an early draft of the Belhar Confession, which was to be adopted as an official Confession in 1986, was born. A resolution stated the reason for adopting a new confession:

> Because the secular Gospel of apartheid threatens in the deepest possible way the witness of reconciliation in Jesus Christ and the unity of the Church of Jesus Christ in its very essence, the NG Mission Church in South Africa declares that this constitutes a *status confessionis* for the Church of Jesus Christ. (A *status confessionis* means that we regard this matter as a concern about which it is impossible to differ without it affecting the integrity of our communal confession as Reformed Churches.)

This contextual confession puts its finger on a subject that was very sensitive in South Africa, that of the unity of the church (art. 2). It addresses

25. Adonis, *op. cit.*, 218.
26. A. Boesak, *Black and Reformed: Apartheid, Liberation and the Calvinist Tradition* (Maryknoll, 1984) 95.

the message of reconciliation that the church is called to carry out in society, a task that entails rejection of "enforced separation of people on a racial basis" (art. 3). It refers to God as the one who is "in a special way the God of the destitute, the poor and the wronged" (art. 4) and to the fact that the church is called in obedience to Jesus Christ to confess all this "even though authorities and laws forbid them, and even though punishment and suffering be the consequence" (art. 5).[27]

Shortly after accepting this draft the NGSK presented its confession to the white NG church, in relation to which it saw itself in the role of "prophet and priest." The NGK synod of 1982 refused to consider an open letter signed by one hundred twenty-three of its own ministers that contained radical criticism of the church's policy with regard to apartheid, and it only formally received the NGSK confession.

After a year and a half of study the NGK's board of moderators issued a very critical commentary on the confession. In its view there was no question of a *status confessionis*. "Between us and you there is clearly a radical difference of judgment in regard to the situation."[28]

That difference surfaced again in October 1986 when the NGK adopted a new policy statement entitled *Church and Society: A Testimony of the Dutch Reformed Church*. From a white perspective and by comparison with *Ras, Volk en Nasie* (1974) there were significant changes, but to the synodical committee of the NGSK, which evaluated the document "from a situation of oppression" in 1987, nothing fundamental had changed.[29] Worthwhile explanations of biblical concepts such as justice, unity, and church continued to function in the framework of a social analysis in which race, ethnicity, and culture were decisive factors (chapter 1 of the statement). *Church and Society* employs a dual notion of church. Faith is the only criterion for church membership but, by contrast with the Belhar Confession, this does not lead to a rejection of separate churches. The moment practical application of the statement's principles comes into view, there turns out to be a very close bond between church and *Volk*.

Church and Society rejects the theology of apartheid: Past attempts to justify this system on the basis of Scripture were mistaken. But it does not reject apartheid itself. Theological justification is no longer needed. The structure is now a reality. The church proclaims "love, justice, and

27. *Apartheid Is a Heresy*, 178-81. On Belhar, cf. G. D. Cloete and D. J. Smith, ed., *A Moment of Truth: The Confession of the Dutch Reformed Mission Church* (Grand Rapids, 1984).

28. Published in *Die Burger* (full page), April 18, 1984; for the open letter, see D. J. Bosch, et al., *Perspektief op die Ope Brief* (Kaapstad, 1982).

29. *Kerk en Samelewing:* Kommentaar deur die Sinodale Kommissie vir Eku-menische Sake van die NG Sendingkerk (1987).

human dignity," but cannot make pronouncements "on any political model or policy." Consequently it cannot cooperate in breaking down the structure that was created with its help. The statement forcefully insists on obedience to government. It acknowledges the theoretical possibility that an illegitimate government might need to be replaced. But this does not apply to the South African situation. The church must go the way of gradual reform: Nonviolent resistance and civil disobedience cannot be supported.

The NGSK concluded that the NGK still supported the policy of apartheid: The new statement was "a theological and biblical justification of the reform policy of the present government" and contained "no hope and no gospel for millions of Christians in our country." This difference in outlook between the leadership of the "colored" and white NG churches came to painful expression when NGSK moderator Boesak — after eighteen black political organizations had been politically silenced (February 1988) — took part, together with Bishop Tutu, in a peaceful protest march against arrests made without charges. In a public statement the NGK announced that Boesak's action was in conflict with Scripture and the laws of the land. However, the NGKA, the black Reformed church, parried the attack: Boesak and Tutu are "church leaders fulfilling their prophetic calling."[30]

The Kairos Document *and* Evangelical Witness

Whereas the Belhar Confession functioned especially within the Reformed tradition, the *Kairos Document*,[31] published in September 1985, exerted influence within a broader ecumenical circle. It was signed by black and white Christians from a broad spectrum of South African churches. Instead of *status confessionis*, a term little used among Anglicans and Catholics, it fell back on the biblical term *kairos* (Luke 19:14 and elsewhere) to announce that "the hour of truth" had come for the church and for "all who bear the name 'Christian.'"

The document was issued by the Institute for Contextual Theology (ICT) in Johannesburg, an ecumenical institute which, instructed in part by the experiences of base communities in Latin America, had worked for some years to bring groups of Christians together for theological reflection in terms of their life contexts in South Africa.

30. Press statements issued by the NGK and NGKA in March and April, 1988 respectively.

31. A second edition of the *Kairos Document* with a longer version of chapter 4 and a number of explanatory notes was issued in September 1986.

The *Kairos Document* presents itself as a "Christian, biblical and theological comment on the political crisis in South Africa today"; it not only discusses the situation but itself originated from within the experience of a "situation of death," and seeks to develop a biblical and theological alternative aimed at real change. The document, which was conceived in Soweto following the proclamation of a state of emergency, can be viewed as "people's theology" mediating the cry of fury, powerlessness, and hope arising in the black townships.

It is characterized by the search for a "prophetic theology." This search takes the form of "reading the signs of the times" in the light of what the Bible says about oppression and tyranny. Following the prophets of the Old Testament, the authors neither indulge in abstract reflection nor shun speaking the hard truth, a truth diametrically opposed to what the court prophets are saying. The conclusion they draw from the Bible is that the oppressors are the enemies of the people who are sinning against God's plans for the people. On the basis of their social analysis they conclude that the apartheid regime, which in fact only champions the interests of the white minority, is a *hostis boni communis*, an enemy of the common good, and therefore tyrannical.

By way of a circulatory process of a prophetic reading of Scripture alternating with a critical analysis of the concrete situation in South Africa the *Kairos Document* arrives at the conclusion that the apartheid regime is illegitimate, as such not reformable, and hence to be replaced by another government chosen by the majority. The document offers no blueprint for a new political future of the country, but seeks to be "a challenge to the church" to take the side of the oppressed, following God's own example. It calls for a very different church and a different kind of spirituality. A new form has to be given to all church activities, services, baptismal celebrations, etc., in order to shape them for the prophetic faith that the *kairos* calls for.

The *Kairos Document* unmasks two other prevalent theological models: "state theology" and "church theology." State theology sanctions injustice; it is the theological justification of racism, capitalism, and totalitarianism; it misuses the Bible (i.e., Romans 13) and demands obedience to a god that is an idol. One finds this theology in the white NG Church but also in other groups. What is at issue is not just the now passé theology of apartheid but also the theological legitimation of "all the activities of the State in its attempts to hold on to power."[32] Church theology is found especially in English-speaking churches. This theology restricts itself to speaking superficially about reconciliation, righteousness, and nonvi-

---

32. *The Kairos Covenant* (New York, 1988) 41, n. 7.

olence, without a searching analysis of social reality. Its adherents expect reform from above and do not opt for an alliance with the people of the underclasses to encourage them in their struggle.

Thanks to the *Kairos Document* the Christian faith acquired new relevance for many in the black community who had rejected the church as an institution supporting or legitimating the cruel system of apartheid. The preface to the second edition of the document (September 1986) speaks in this connection of its "missionary dimension." As a cartoon in the ICT paper pictured it, the church of heaven was being dragged down from the clouds and into the black townships.

The church and the liberation movement do not belong to two separate worlds. But that does not mean they coincide. At the same time the church must not be allowed to become a "third force" that takes its place between the oppressor and the oppressed: It must unreservedly be on the side of the latter. But the authors of the document indicate that this means "that the church must participate in the struggle as a *church* and not as a political organization. . . . The church has its own motivation, its own inspiration for participating in the struggle for justice and peace."[33]

The challenge to the church presented by the *Kairos Document* was taken up very seriously by a group of South African "involved evangelical Christians" belonging to evangelical, charismatic, and pentecostal churches. In their booklet *Evangelical Witness in South Africa* (1986), their critique is directed against the practice and theology of their own evangelical churches. They censure as being inconsistent with both Judeo-Christian and African tradition the dualistic attitude of evangelicals who lead pietistic "spiritual" lives while they oppress and exploit their fellow human beings. They observe that their churches have conformed themselves to the existing order and have accepted racial separation as a creation ordinance though it is the task of "born-again Christians" to challenge the status quo and call people to "new life and a new creation."[34]

In numerous places Christians now come together around the Belhar Confession, the *Kairos Document*, and *Evangelical Witness* to give shape in their own communions and with other Christians to a confessing and prophetic church in the dramatic context of South Africa.[35]

But this prophetic theology has also been fiercely attacked. To the Synod of the NG Church this theology has been nothing but a revolution-

33. *Ibid.*, 43, n. 17.
34. *Evangelical Witness in South Africa: A Critique of Evangelical Theology and Practice by Evangelicals Themselves* (Johannesburg, 1986) 9f., 15, 28.
35. *Statement on the Confessing Church Movement* (Johannesburg, 1987) mentions these three documents plus the SACC Message of 1968 as a basis.

ary ideology of liberation: "Liberation in Jesus Christ has degenerated into political liberation." In its eyes "the historical situation" has become the hermeneutical key to understanding the Bible, "while the central theme of Holy Scripture is salvation in Christ and the coming of the kingdom of God to his glory."[36]

Over against such spiritualization of the gospel stands the concrete experience of the black church, in which salvation in Christ is a message of hope in the face of the concrete wretchedness in which people find themselves. "At the center of the church struggle throughout South African history is the struggle of the black church to prove to its fellow blacks that Christianity is not the 'opiate of the people' but the hope for the future and therefore the word of salvation for today."[37]

Black Theology

Black theology as a consciously articulated faith perspective is of recent date. But it gives expression to a long-standing reality in the black church. It is rooted in the suffering and struggle of black people that was expressed earlier in the Ethiopian movement (see above).

Black Consciousness as the Matrix of Black Theology

The Black Consciousness movement arose from a series of events in the sixties that began with the Sharpeville massacre in 1960. This movement, though it linked up with earlier African nationalism, was broader because it included the mixed-race "colored" population and the Indian population. Black consciousness was a collective black repudiation of white domination. There were also external sources of inspiration: the civil rights struggle in the United States, the ideologies of *négritude*, African humanism, and African socialism in newly independent African nations, and the ideas of Frantz Fanon and Paolo Freire. Although African American influence was undeniable, there were also clear differences. Whereas American blacks generally accepted existing political and socioeconomic systems and only demanded that they be fully integrated into them, South Africa Black Consciousness was directed toward radically revolutionizing the structures. Its aim was not integration in a multiracial society but a *non*racial society.

36. Critique of the *Kairos Document* adopted by NGK Synod of October 1986, sections 1.1 and 4.2.

37. De Gruchy, *The Church Struggle in South Africa*, 51.

A number of organizations were started or merged to give shape to the Black Consciousness movement, such as Black Community Programmes (BCP), the Black People's Convention (BPC), the Interdenominational African Ministers Association (IDAMASA), the Black Allied Workers Union, and the Black Women's Federation. Intellectual stimulation and impetus were also given to the movement by the South African Students Organization (SASO), which was created in 1968 and supported by young black intellectuals, among whom was Biko, who died in detention September 12, 1977. For a short time the Black Consciousness movement was viewed by the white regime as a black expression of the official policy of separate development, but this lasted only until the movement's political character became clear. In 1977 the movement and its principal organs of expression were declared illegal. This action prompted a new and intensified phase in the movement.

The Origins of Black Theology

Black Consciousness was fundamentally a movement for political and socioeconomic liberation, though it did acknowledge the religious nature of traditional and modern African culture. Black theology became in many respects the expression of Black Consciousness philosophy, furnishing it with a religious foundation and motivation.

In 1971, prompted by Basil Moore, the University Christian Movement (UCM) started a Black Theology project. The UCM, which began in 1967 as an interracial movement of university students and instructors, conducted an initial seminar at Wilgespruit in 1972. This resulted in the publication of *Essays on Black Theology,* a volume that was immediately banned in South Africa but published elsewhere under different titles.[38] Black theology had made its debut in South Africa. Important authors in this volume included Biko, who served as a link between Black Consciousness and black theology, and Manas Buthelezi, who played a large role in the early phase of black theology. The African American theologian James H. Cone was not present at the seminar, though a taped message of his was heard there. Subsequently he continued to exert influence on South African black theology without, however, being followed in all respects.[39]

In the preface of *Essays on Black Theology,* black theology is described

---

38. M. Motlhabi, ed., *Essays on Black Theology* (Johannesburg, 1972), partially reproduced in B. Moore, ed., *The Challenge of Black Theology in South Africa* (Atlanta, 1974).

39. See Moore, ed., *The Challenge of Black Theology.*

as "a theology of the oppressed, by the oppressed, for the liberation of the oppressed." In Cone's essay it is said of black theology that its significance lies in "the conviction that the content of the Christian gospel is liberation, so that any talk about God that fails to take seriously the righteousness of God as revealed in the liberation of the weak and downtrodden is not Christian language."[40] In the foreword to the Dutch edition Boesak is quoted as saying: "It is our fervent hope that whites will also be liberated," a theme he was to develop in his dissertation, in which he sees black theology as an aid to understanding the history and present condition of both black and white people.[41]

As an organized movement black theology went into virtual hiding following a conference in 1975 organized by Fr. Smangaliso Mkhatshwa and convened at Mazenod, Lesotho. But in the early eighties it again surfaced as a corporate movement.

Some Basic Aspects

Essays on Black Theology dealt with a series of theological concepts from a black Christian perspective: God, the church, corporate personality in ancient Israel and in Africa, black and white worship, and an ethics of hope. Not all aspects of black theology can be discussed here. We shall only comment on the meaning of the word "black" and on liberation, power, and reconciliation.

The Meaning of "Black"

When blacks in South Africa use the word "black" they have in mind both their own will to self-affirmation and the state of being oppressed. For a long time they were called "non-whites," that is, those who fail to meet the norm of humanness, which is whiteness. The moment blacks fully realize that they are created in God's image, blackness can no longer be viewed as a curse. According to Buthelezi blackness remains a symbol of oppression as long as someone else uses the term. But when a person says "*I* am black," it becomes a symbol of liberation and selfaffirmation.[42] Therefore, black theology speaks of the need for blacks to love themselves.

40. *Ibid.*, ix, 52.

41. A. A. Boesak, *A Farewell to Innocence: A Social-Ethical Study of Black Theology and Black Power* (Maryknoll, 1976). Cf. *idem, Black Theology, Black Power* (London, 1978): "in memory of Steve Biko with respect."

42. M. Buthelezi, "The Christian Presence in Today's South Africa," *JThSA* 16 (1976) 7.

Blackness becomes "an awareness, an attitude, a state of mind. It is a bold and serious determination to be a person in one's own right."[43]

Black theology is called "black" in order to create a new black human being and to demythologize white superiority. It is a summons to whites to relinquish their blasphemous sense of superiority and to blacks to relinquish their blasphemous nonbeing so that both may become more human, bearers of God's image. Therefore, the emphasis on being "black" is not reverse racism. It represents a process of conversion for both blacks and whites.[44] Boesak and other black theologians in South Africa therefore reject every notion of "black nationalism" in the sense given to it by the African American theologian Albert Cleage in *The Black Messiah* (1969). Black theology must refuse to make a choice between "black" and "white," between black nationalism and Afrikaner nationalism. It does mean a choice between "blackness" and "nihilism," the nonbeing of both black and white.[45]

Liberation, Power, and Reconciliation

The understanding of blackness in Black Consciousness and black theology is directed toward liberation, both internal and external liberation. Buthelezi speaks of a liberation of the spirit in which the black person decides to become the creator of his or her own history.[46] Black theology is focused, says Boesak, on the present dependence and coming liberation of the oppressed in all their dimensions — psychological, cultural, political, economic, and theological. It is an expression of the belief that because Christ has accomplished liberation people cannot be denied total liberation.

Liberation requires power, and black liberation requires "Black Power." To Boesak "Black Power" is a "watchword" for the continuing efforts in history of black people to force white people in power to change existing structures. Black Power is not the same as the gospel, but it is consistent with the gospel if it "serves the new humanity through liberation and the wholeness of life out of which flow justice, peace, reconciliation, and community."[47]

Reconciliation with God and one's neighbor is a central theme in Christian doctrine and the Christian life. It is not, however, available in isolation, nor does it happen on a purely spiritual plane. To black theology

43. Boesak, *Farewell to Innocence*, 27.
44. *Ibid.*, 29.
45. See A. Small, in Moore, ed., *The Challenge of Black Theology*, 11-17.
46. M. Buthelezi, "The Christian Presence," 7.
47. Boesak, *Farewell to Innocence*, 79.

this is clear: "There is a close relationship between reconciliation and liberation. Unless the hungry are fed, the sick are healed, and justice is given to the poor, there can be no reconciliation."[48]

Black Theology and Ideology

Theologians and church leaders tend to underestimate the power and influence exerted by social structures and processes on human thought and action. They easily lapse into an ideology of "false consciousness," which manages to justify its own interests and privileges, including apartheid, in theological terms. The question is whether a criterion exists to distinguish between a liberating and an alienating use of God's Word. To black theology a thing is true and good if it is beneficial for the poor and oppressed.[49]

Bishop Alphaeus Zulu has pointed out that "black theologians need to guard against equating 'God being on the side of the oppressed' with 'the oppressed being on the side of God.'" The "true consciousness" of the poor is often the result of a long process of struggle, learning, and even conversion. They must be liberated from false, alienating values and discover the real potential present in themselves and their situation.[50]

By keeping open the eschatological perspective, one safeguards every human effort, including theology, from becoming ideologically fixed. Bishop Tutu, as a black church leader and theologian, does not believe change in the political and economic system will necessarily usher in the golden age.

> Liberation theologians have too much evidence that the removal of one oppressor often means replacement by another; yesterday's victim quite rapidly becomes today's dictator. Liberation theologians know only too well the recalcitrance of human nature and so accept the traditional doctrines of the fall and original sin, but they also know that God has provided the remedy in Jesus Christ.[51]

---

48. *Ibid.,* 101.

49. J. Leatt, T. Kneifel, and K. Nürnberger, ed., *Contending Ideologies in South Africa* (Grand Rapids, 1986), chapter 18: "Theology and Ideology," 285-302, especially 296.

50. A. Zulu, "Whither Black Theology?" *Pro Veritate* 11/11 (March 1973) 13; cf. Boesak's reaction in *Farewell to Innocence,* 111f.; on the "true consciousness" of the poor, see Leatt, et al., *op. cit.,* 297.

51. D. Tutu, "The Theology of Liberation in Africa," in K. Appiah-Kubi and S. Torres, *African Theology en Route* (Maryknoll, 1979) 167.

Black theologians, by doing theology as ideological critique, seek to make clear that one cannot retreat to a storm-free zone by postulating a sort of spiritual reconciliation between white and black somewhere far above the brutal realities of society. They are aware that the statements by Zulu and Tutu can be used by whites as an excuse for escaping the "kairos." For black theologians, including Zulu and Tutu, committed struggle for personal and structural change in view of the plight of the poor and oppressed remains imperative. "Liberation" is the hermeneutical key to black theology, not merely as an idea but as a praxis on which to reflect — on the basis of a criticism of ideology and in eschatological perspective.[52]

The Reorientation of Black Theology

Fourteen years after *Essays on Black Theology*, a new volume of essays appeared under the title *The Unquestionable Right to be Free*.[53] It contained the papers presented at two conferences on "Black Theology Revisited" (1983) and "Black Theology and the Black Struggle" (1984). The initiative for these conferences came from ICT. At these conferences the original goals of black theology were confirmed, but, in view of the many new methodological and material viewpoints that were presenting themselves, people began to speak of a new phase of South African black theology.

Shifts in Political Praxis

In the first phase of black theology the philosophy of Black Consciousness was the only internal factor uniting blacks; existing ideological differences were not brought into the open. In the late 1970's however, the ideological conflict present beneath the surface manifested itself in the creation of, on the one hand, organizations that proceeded along the lines of the banned Black Consciousness Movement and excluded whites from the struggle (AZAPO) and, on the other, organizations that sought to involve all

52. On theology and ideology in South Africa, cf. Boesak, *Farewell to Innocence* ch. 4 (80-97); Leatt, et al., *op. cit.*, Part V: "Ideology and Theology" (271-302); for a critique of ideology in the context of North American black theology see T. Witvliet, *The Way of the Black Messiah* (New York, 1987), especially chs. 1 and 6.

53. I. J. Mosala and B. Tlhagale, ed., *The Unquestionable Right to be Free: Essays in Black Theology* (Johannesburg, 1986); the American edition (Maryknoll) has the subtitle *Black Theology from South Africa*. For a concise historical overview, see Robert Vander Gucht, "Black Theology and Black Struggle in South Africa," *International Communications* 42 (1987) 25-32.

democratic and "progressive" people, including whites, in the struggle against the common enemy, the apartheid regime (AZASO, COSAS). Those inspired by Black Consciousness continued to stress the significance of "race" in regard to oppression and the struggle for liberation, but the others used "class" as the key category. In response to the new constitution of 1983, which sought to give apartheid a semblance of democracy, two political groupings emerged: National Forum (NF, June 1983) and the United Democratic Front (UDF, August 1983). Though both had the same goal, the abolition of apartheid, they differed in strategy: NF wanted to reach the goal exclusively with blacks, while UDF sought to unite all opponents of apartheid.

It was in this politically charged context that ICT took the initiative in seeking, with fifty black theologians, the significance and role black theology might have in the black struggle for liberation. The ideological conflict ("race" vs. "class") threatened to divide the black Christian community. At the two conferences on black theology in 1983 and 1984 the ideological differences were not swept under the rug. On the contrary, attempts were made to bring the two sides together by evaluating the intention and goals of each in terms of liberation, justice, and peace.[54]

Historically, the cultural and economic clash between the original inhabitants of what is South Africa — the Khoikhoi and the San, collectively referred to as the Khoisan — and the European settlers had four phases: the Khoisan phase in the seventeenth century, the tribal phase in the eighteenth and early nineteenth centuries, the nationalistic phase in the late nineteenth and early twentieth centuries, and the Black Consciousness phase beginning in the late 1960s. According to Sebidi, in the first two phases the conflict was mainly over economic interests, specifically land. In the second and third phases it was mainly over color or race. After 1977, however, the prevailing view was that class analysis brings out the root of the conflict. In his paper Sebidi demonstrates that every ideological position in and of itself fails to do justice to the South African realities, which after all consist of the double bondage of racial *and* economic oppression. Apartheid is buttressed by differences of both race and class, that is, by racial capitalism. "This is the sin that Black Theology wants to uncover and eradicate in God's name."[55]

---

54. On the background and context of the second phase of black theology, see Editorial Note, Introduction, and Foreword in *The Unquestionable Right*, v-xix.

55. L. Sebidi, "The Dynamics of Black Struggle and its Implications for Black Theology," in *The Unquestionable Right*, 35.

Developments in Method and Content

A sharper analysis of the situation brought black theologians closer to Latin American liberation theology. The relationship between praxis and reflection came into view. Some, like Mosala, Mofokeng, Sebidi, and Thlagale, began to make use of Marxist analysis. This was a new departure, one that was virtually absent until then in both South African and North American black theology. Shunmugam Perumal Govender was the first black theologian in South Africa who — in *In Search of Tomorrow: The Dialogue between Black Theology and Marxism in South Africa* (Kampen, 1987) — analyzed more systematically the significance of a critical Marxist theory (Gramsci) for the method and content of theology.

This insight that concrete reality influences human thought and conduct also had an impact on biblical hermeneutics. The final communication of the 1983 conference states that theologians had too long been dependent in their exegesis on theoretical instruments derived from the world against which the struggle for liberation is directed. The conference underscored "the need to urge rereadings and reappropriations of the Bible in the interest of the oppressed and exploited classes of our society. This is particularly significant in view of the general conviction among the participants in the Conference that salvation is historical."[56]

Black theologians became aware of their own class-based character as a group of ordained male academics. On the basis of a sharper analysis of their situation they discovered that they were operating from too narrow a base and also that they had kept large parts of reality outside their field of attention. Under the influence of ICT they became more alert to the values and potential in the culture and tradition of the black people — more specifically to the values of traditional religion and cultural practices assimilated in the life and experience of the independent churches. Black theologians also came to the conviction that "the true measure of liberation in any society is the extent to which women are liberated."[57] They declared that black theology cannot be a theology of liberation unless feminist theology constitutes an essential part of a broad movement of black liberation theology. *The Unquestionable Right to be Free* includes contributions on the relevance and challenge of traditional African religions to black theology and on the roots of the African independent churches and two contributions by women.[58] At the same time black theology aims

56. Notes on the Black Theology Seminar, Wilgespruit Ecumenical Center, South Africa, August 16-19, 1983, in *Voices from the Third World* 6 (1983) 29 (= Excerpts from *ICT News* 1 [1983]).

57. *Ibid.*, 30.

58. Cf. B. I. Mosala, "Black Theology and the Struggle of the Black Woman in

to do more research and to write more from within such specialized disciplines as ecclesiology and christology.

Black, African, and Contextual Theology

As a result of the ideological conflict, a sharper analysis of the South African situation, and a dose of healthy self-criticism, black theology has undergone a metamorphosis. It has been asked whether the term "black" still adequately represents the nature of this theology. By paying more attention to input from African culture, traditional religion, and the independent churches, black theology has come closer to being *African* theology,[59] without, however, surrendering its focus on liberation. By seeking connections with the experience and world of the common people and by recognizing in principle the importance of women, black theology now faces a broader horizon and more clearly deserves the name "contextual theology."

"Black theology" could also be called African contextual theology of liberation. In a statement issued on the occasion of the founding of the Ecumenical Association of African Theologians of the Southern African Region (EAATSA) at Hammanskraal in May 1983, the term "black theology" did not occur.[60] The ICT views its "black theology" project as a component of contextual theology, which is regarded as an umbrella concept. Many theologians in South Africa, nevertheless, consciously stick to the term *black* theology. Lebamang Sebidi writes: "The term 'black' must perforce remain prefixed to 'theology' because for the past 117 years 'blackness' in this country has been the symbol of economic class exploitation. That prefix emphasizes this crucial point, which no black can forget in a hurry."[61]

Preoccupation with the socioeconomic and political situation of injustice makes black theology a contextual theology par excellence. But

---

Southern Africa," and B. Bennett, "A Critique on the Role of Women in the Church," both in *The Unquestionable Right*.

59. African theology has always had its practitioners in South Africa itself, e.g., H.-J. Becken, ed., *Relevant Theology for Africa* (Mapumulo, 1973). G. Setiloane, with *Der Gott meiner Väter und mein Gott. Afrikanische Theologie im Kontext der Apartheid* (Wuppertal, 1988), is a South African practitioner of African theology who has come closer to black theology.

60. B. Goba in *Voices from the Third World* 6 (1983) 17-20.

61. *The Unquestionable Right*, 35. The "117 years" are the period from 1867 to 1984, i.e., from the discovery of diamonds and the entry of world capitalism to the ICT conference in 1984 where Sebidi presented his lecture.

as theology it views the "context" in the light of the biblical promises and Christian hope, even while it speaks of the church as the suffering and persecuted people of God. In order for the confessing and prophetic church to persevere, a spirituality of liberation is needed. In his book on black christology Takatso A. Mofokeng regards the cross as the high point and starting point on the road to liberation. He links Jesus' cry of dereliction on the cross to the swelling crescendo of the cries of the poor and oppressed, who often experience God's absence more than his power to liberate. And still — with that cry from the cross Jesus gained new followers:

> He calls them to take that ultimate action, like him, to endure torturing and crucifixion for justice and fraternity and triumph because He has triumphed as His resurrection reveals. . . . Their faith shall be a faith against the destruction of faith, their love shall be love against hatred and bitterness and their hope in the coming of the new society shall be a "hope against hope."[62]

---

62. T. A. Mofokeng, *The Crucified among the Crossbearers: Towards a Black Christology* (Kampen, 1983) 259-63. Cf. *Kairos Document* (1986²), §§ 4-6.

CHAPTER 21

Asia: The Search for Identity as a Source of Renewal

A. G. Honig

Identity and Renewal

In the course of their development in the twentieth century Asian churches have received impulses for renewal from a variety of sources. Especially in this century the invasion of the West (in the form of imperialism and colonialism) has begun to show its aftereffects, namely, the violation of old life patterns and understandings. Social structures have been disrupted and a new disposition toward one's fellow humans and the world developed out of socioeconomic changes, themselves the results of secularism and the technological revolution. Many people began to feel that they had been deeply affected in their identity, personhood, and understanding of life.

The initial reaction to all this was seen already in the nineteenth-century rise of the nationalist movement, which was coupled with renewed reflection on the collective religious and cultural heritage. During the rise of the struggle for national liberation this reflection was pursued with increasing momentum. The liberation of most Asian countries from foreign domination, which occurred nearly everywhere immediately after World War II, made the search for a collective identity all the more intense. It was on the basis of this search, after all, that the road toward the formation of the new free person in a new society and under a new constitution would have to be traveled. It was in this context that opportunity was found for the resurgence of ancient religions. Intensive study was made of ancient views of life and the world, and philosophical writings from times immemorial were given fresh attention.

Although the materialism of Western colonialism had left indelible marks on Asian society, there was no desire to abandon the old spirituality.

And though Marxism had also played a large role in Asia and had opened the eyes of many to what had happened in the socioeconomic sphere in modern times, it was itself drawn firmly into the old atmosphere and the old spirituality.[1]

Remarkably, though Christian churches constituted minute minorities, the gospel was also given an important place in national reflection.[2] Familiar and very striking examples are the high esteem in which Mahatma Gandhi held the teachings of Jesus[3] and the impressive address of President Sukarno to the assembly of the Indonesian Council of Churches in 1960 on "Jesus, the Good Shepherd."[4] Many other examples could be mentioned. The gospel has not only set people in motion as individuals; its impact has also strongly influenced national development in many countries.

M. M. Thomas has pointed this out repeatedly, for example, in his address in Bangkok to the 1972 World Conference on Mission and Evangelism sponsored by the Commission on World Mission and Evangelism of the WCC.[5] He stated that the striving of the people of India for a new society is due in part to the transformation of traditional spirituality under the influence of the gospel. In his judgment this influence came not only through Christian mission but also by way of Western culture and later by the cultural renaissance in India. Although the false gods of the West have also had their influence (even through Christian mission!), no historian can deny that the gospel played a decisive role, says Thomas.

It must be noted that the historical development in India has been very special. Ram Mohan Roy's book *Precepts of Jesus*, which came out in 1820, was present at the cradle of India's national renaissance, and since then all the important national leaders have been intensely occupied with Jesus. But that this gospel influence is demonstrable can in fact be said of every country in Asia.

From these historic processes the churches in Asia have also received a variety of fresh impulses. Their aim has not been just to under-

1. A noteworthy example occurred when President Sukarno of Indonesia stated his political philosophy in his proclamation of NASAKOM (an acronym for nationalism, religion [agama], and communism). Its intention was to reinforce the unity of the state. Cf. J. S. Mintz, *Mohammed, Marx and Marhaen* (New York, 1965) 163, 185, 203.

2. A good example can be found in India in S. J. Samartha, *The Hindu Response to the Unbound Christ: Towards a Christology in India* (Madras, 1974).

3. Cf. S. Radhakrishnan's quotation of Gandhi in *Eastern Religions and Western Thought* (London, 1940): "I believe in the Bible as I believe in the Gita."

4. I did not succeed in finding the text of this address anywhere.

5. M. M. Thomas, "The Meaning of Salvation Today — A Personal Statement," *International Review of Mission* 62 (1973) 158-69.

stand their own role and significance but also — and even more — to find a way of making their own contribution. The goal of the churches has been to participate positively and critically in the revolutionary struggle for a society freeing itself from foreign domination and from bondage to a fatalism arising from a particular understanding of cosmic laws mediated by the tradition. The churches have been thrust back on themselves in the struggle for liberty, and this became a source of renewed reflection and creativity for them. Consequently Christians everywhere, with all the energies at their disposal, have thrust themselves into the revolution.

It is no wonder then that during the 1972 conference in Bangkok people sought to reflect on the meaning of well-being, salvation, and liberation in the modern age. In the liberation that had come they glimpsed something of the work of Jesus. But precisely what was it? And in what regard did a false interpretation and a pseudo-religiosity occasion a new fall into sin in the historical process? M. M. Thomas pointed out these matters also. It was the aim of the Asian churches to sound a note of their own and to let the gospel have a voice in what was happening. In this they saw the missionary task of the churches vis-à-vis the well-being and wholeness of the people, the land, and the world. And in a great variety of ways the churches went to work to give shape and content to the Christian message, all the while participating in the ongoing development of their nations.[6]

The Fundamental Shift in Theology

People had by no means been unaware of the liberating power of the preaching of the gospel when they heard it from Western missionaries. Though the missionaries strongly emphasized individual salvation, they also brought out the social significance of the gospel — though they stopped at the boundary of politics! But this emphasis on personal salvation had a strongly isolating effect. To become a Christian meant in many respects to withdraw from one's own society. This understanding was due in part to the form in which the gospel was communicated by Western missionaries. It could hardly be otherwise. Christian faith in the Western world had become largely a matter of "the spiritual life," something private. In mission-based churches the necessity to break out of this isolation was felt to be urgent.[7]

6. Cf. U. M. Dehn, *Indische Christen in der gesellschaftlichen Verantwortung* (Frankfurt, 1985).
7. From this mindset one can understand why objections were lodged in every

A fundamental shift in theology was called for: an attempt to re-assess the Asian spiritual heritage. People have no longer been willing to view themselves as belonging to a pagan world that is hostile to God. They have come to understand themselves rather as those who are incorporated in the history of God's salvific action in the world. In the process there arose reflection on the particularity and universality of salvation. What is the connection between the "two histories," salvation history and secular history? People no longer want to be subject solely to the Judeo-Christian tradition. They want to find traces of God's work also in their own history and tradition.[8]

But they also have no desire to lose an understanding of the special line of God's salvific action in Israel and the church. For all their concentration on their own heritage, the yearning to become rooted in the church of the ages has not disappeared.[9] To design new christologies from within their own philosophy did not imply detachment from the treasures of the church laid down in the ancient ecumenical creeds, if for no other reason than that for the Asian churches, which as a rule form but extremely small minorities in their national communities, the sense of being part of a worldwide fellowship is immensely encouraging. But more than this, in this fellowship there grows a strong awareness of the cosmic significance of Christ and his identity as Lord of history. It is not surprising that a WCC assembly held in Asia (New Delhi, 1961) posed precisely these themes and yielded very specific elaborations of them by Asian theologians.[10]

The issue is by no means just that of finding new dogmatic formulations from within new options. On the contrary: What is at stake is a new and liberating reflection on Christian action in the context of the

---

possible way against the "church growth movement" of Donald McGavran and similarly in 1985-86 against his "A Giant Step in Christian Mission." For the text and reactions to it see *A Monthly Letter on Evangelism* (WCC CWME), August 1985 to April 1986. See also "Strategy for World Mission" by Raymond Fung, the editor of the *Monthly Letter,* June and July 1986, based on Isa. 65:17-23. And see *International Review of Mission* 75/299 (July 1986).

8. Cf. my article in *Exchange: Bulletin of Third World Christian Literature* 11 (1982) 5-9.

9. The "Confession of Alexandria," issued by the the All Africa Conference of Churches and reprinted in *Mission Trends No. 3: Third World Theologies,* ed. G. H. Anderson and T. F. Stransky (New York and Grand Rapids, 1976) 132-34, also sought to be rooted in the ancient church of North Africa to which Mark had preached the gospel (*Mission Trends 3,* 133). The idea, after all, is to contextualize the message of the gospel, says Shoki Coe. The context is of real importance in terms of the content.

10. Cf. my *De kosmische betekenis van Christus in de oecumenische discussies van het laatste decennium, speciaal met betrekking tot de zending* (Kampen, 1968) and *De kosmische betekenis van Christus in de hedendaagse Aziatische theologie* (Kampen, 1984).

all-embracing national struggle to mold character and to build up the nation. From the beginning the churches were challenged — and still are — to show where they stand. Accordingly, they work toward a theology of witness in the actual context of contemporary life.[11] For that reason this theology is called a work of "double struggle": a struggle to make the gospel relevant to the reality of the present situation and a struggle to find traces of God's work in this reality.[12] Accordingly, this theology must be a theology in dialogue with tradition, with the contemporary thought world and its ideologies, and with the reviving ancient religions.

Examples of What Has Been Achieved

I shall make no attempt to arrive at a total overview of the practice of theology in Asia. Asian theologians have over the years created a library full of books. Elsewhere I have tried to point out the complex of connected themes.[13] Here I seek to provide an interpretive sketch of the missionary character of certain Asian theologies in relation to ecclesiastical missionary initiatives and to missionary forms in the spheres of the local congregation and of spirituality. I have had to choose among many interesting examples, and such a choice is inevitably arbitrary.

An added problem is that there are no good criteria for what is really representative in a given country. That must be determined partly by one's personal values. In Korea, is Jung Young Le's proposal regarding the Yin-Yang way of thinking as a possible method for an ecumenical theology[14] more representative of what is going on in Korean theology than *Minjung* theology?[15] Is the Immanuel theology of Takizawa Katsumi,[16] who

---

11. In his account of the "Asiatic critical principle" Nacpil sums up its four most important components and also mentions the fundamental aim of mission theology, which is to equip people with a "missio," a message that not only illumines Asian reality with the light of the gospel but also enables people to gain control over changes and to lead them in directions consistent with the gospel and its view of human life. Cf. also my article cited in n. 8 above, 11. On Nacpil, see D. J. Elwood, ed., *What Asian Christians Are Thinking* (Quezon City, 1976) 3.

12. S. Coe, *Working Political Statement for the Implementation of the Third Mandate of the Theological Education Fund* (Geneva, 1972).

13. In *Exchange* 32 and 33, 5-9.

14. J. Y. Lee, "The Yin Yang Way of Thinking: A Possible Method for Ecumenical Theology," *Mission Trends 3*, 29-38.

15. Commission on Theological Concerns of the Christian Conference of Asia, *Minjung Theology: People as the Subjects of History* (Maryknoll, 1983).

16. Takizawa Katsumi, "Zen-Buddhismus und Christentum im gegenwärtigen Japan," in *Gott in Japan*, ed. Yagi Seichi and U. Luz (Munich, 1973) 139-59.

speaks of Immanuel as the primordial datum underlying humanness, less characteristic of Japanese contextual theology than Masao Takenaka's *God Is Rice*?[17] Is Samartha's christology based on Vedanta philosophy[18] a more or less mature Indian theology than, for example, Sam Amirtham's *Theology of the People*?[19]

Emerito Nacpil has written about the "Asian critical principle"[20] but also acknowledges that this concept will only acquire the correct content in a more complete development of Asian theology in the light of the *missio Dei*. But he goes on to say that this must not be stressed at the expense of catholicity. Catholicity is given by the Word made flesh. True catholicity is a gift we receive only if we derive our basic energies from the gospel of the incarnate Word. By contextualization the multi-hued character of the gospel comes to expression.

Samartha concludes his book on the "Unbound Christ" by saying that the contextualization of christology must not lead to the binding of Christ to a specific culture so that christology again becomes provincial in significance. This temptation must be resisted by those who in their confession of Christ are caught between the inheritance of the worldwide church and their loyalty to the culture of their own land and are pulled back and forth by these two forces.

Nacpil points out that in Asia there exists such great diversity of cultures that it is very difficult to describe precisely what Asian theology really is. He restricts himself geographically to Southeast Asia. But even there the differences are great. What precisely does it mean to be Asian? Furthermore, old patterns have been affected by the invasion of Western culture and technology, coupled with all-pervasive secularization. Thus from every angle one finds it extremely difficult to determine just how representative a given theology is.

Korea: Minjung *Theology*

Minjung theology attracted considerable interest in the early 1980s, most of all, probably, because it was seen as an Asian counterpart to Latin American liberation theology. The search for some form of liberation theology has been conducted in many ways in many Asian countries, always

17. Masao Takenaka, *God Is Rice: Asian Culture and Christian Faith* (Geneva, 1986).
18. Samartha, *op. cit.* (n. 2 above).
19. S. Amirtham, *Theology of the People* (Geneva, 1986).
20. E. Nacpil, "Das asiatische kritische Prinzip," in D. J. Elwood, *Wie Christen in Asien denken* (Frankfurt, 1979).

with some reference to the unacceptability of what had been created earlier in Latin America. Secular social analysis and critique à la Marx does not fit with a view of society rooted in a religious consciousness that despite all the consequences of secularization is still all-pervasively present in Asia.

Minjung theology is rooted in a primordial Korean understanding of life. On that basis an attempt is made to understand the social and political role of the church in today's Korea as it seeks to fulfill its missionary task. *Minjung* is a Korean word but it is composed of two Chinese characters: *min*, which can be translated as "people," and *jung*, which means "mass" (Greek *ochlos*). As has been said repeatedly, it is not a simple matter to describe precisely what is meant by *minjung* in Korea. Kim Yong Bock has said that it "expresses a living reality which is dynamic, changing, and complex." This living reality "defines its own existence," he writes, and makes a place for itself in history. "It refuses in principle to be defined conceptually."[21] There is a consensus, however, that "it designates a people politically oppressed, economically poor, socially and culturally alienated, yet seeking to be the artisan of its own destiny in an active way."[22] One comes to know the identity and reality of the *minjung* best from their life stories — stories that they themselves create and that therefore can best be told by them.[23] They tell their stories in the face of the power structure that controls them. In the stories, power is the antagonist and the *minjung* is the protagonist.

Kim Yong Bock illumines his account by elaborating two points. First, he cautions that one must not equate *minjung* with the "proletariat" in Marxism. The proletariat is materialistically "confined" by socioeconomic determination and therefore bound to "the internal logic of history." The *minjung* are people who suffer these restrictions, but as historical subject "the *minjung* transcends the socio-economic determination of history and unfolds its stories beyond mere historical possibilities to historical novelty — a new drama beyond the present history to a new and transformed history." "This difference between the minjung and the proletariat," therefore, "entails a different view of history." "Minjung history has a strong transcendental or transcending dimension . . . which is often expressed in religious

21. Kim Yong Bock, "Messiah and Minjung, Discerning Messianic Politics over against Political Messianism," in *Minjung Theology*, 184.

22. *Towards a Relevant Theology in Asia* (Asian Report Group, Fifth International Conference of the Ecumenical Association of Third World Theologians [EATWOT], New Delhi, 1981). Cf. V. Fabella and S. Torres, ed., *Irruption of the Third World: Challenge to Theology* (Maryknoll, 1983) 70.

23. The idea comes vividly to expression in the chapter by Suh Nam Dong, "Towards a Theology of 'Han,' " in *Minjung Theology*, 55.

form. . . . Even if minjung history does not involve religious elements in an explicit manner, its folklore or cultural elements play a transcending function similar to religion in the perception of history."

Another difference between *minjung* and the proletariat is who belong to each. *Minjung* is "a dynamic, changing concept." A woman belongs to *minjung* when she is politically dominated by a male or by men. "An ethnic group is a minjung group when it is politically dominated by another group." *Minjung* might be, therefore, some dominated race. "But also when intellectuals are suppressed by the military power elite they belong to the minjung." The same applies to workers and farmers. "However, the proletariat is rigidly defined in socio-economic terms in all political circumstances. It is even a name through which a totalitarian political dictatorship is justified." "Historically, the minjung is always in the condition of being ruled, a situation which they seek to overcome." Its existence never justifies a dictatorship. Kim believes that "in many ways this view of history has an affinity with the cultural values of Western democracy; but the constituency of the minjung is the poor and the suppressed who are alienated in their political and socio-economic condition."

Secondly, Kim asks what the subjection of the *minjung* actually is in historical terms. It is not an idea that slipped in from North Korean communism. For there "subjection" refers to the autonomy of the national dictatorship, which misuses the name of the proletariat. The subjection of the *minjung* is their position between what exists and what is to be. It is "realized in the struggle against oppressive powers and repressive social structures." This struggle fills the life history of the *minjung.* But there is no reason to glorify the *minjung* or to absolutize them as in communism because they suffer under their political plight. History is not the history of rules as, for example, in Confucian historiography, but must be read from below. "History is the process in which the minjung realize their own destiny to be the free subjects of history and to participate in the Messianic Kingdom." Kim thus uses the idea of the messianic kingdom to develop a *minjung* perspective on history. "The messianic aspirations of the people arise out of the historical confrontation between the people and the powers." The messianic kingdom is not a dream. It is, rather, the core of history "for which the suffering people, the poor and oppressed, struggle." Accordingly, the reference is to a messiah *of the people,* one who is viewed by the people as belonging to them. "The messiah emerges from the suffering people and identifies with the suffering people."[24]

24. The quotations from Kim Yong Bock in the preceding paragraphs are from *Minjung Theology,* 184-86.

The concept of *"han"* therefore plays an important role. *Han* refers to the pain of someone who has experienced repression in his own life and that of others. Such a feeling of helpless suffering and of being oppressed constitutes the core of the life story of the individual Korean. And this feeling of *han*, the suffering and helplessness of the oppressed, is a collective feeling in the social life-history of the oppressed.[25]

But *han* has not only this negative meaning of resignation to fate or to political oppression. There is in it also a transforming, dynamic element that provides the energy for revolution. Suh reproduces a social biography of the *minjung* of Korea as this comes out in their literature, their pathos, and their plays and then offers a moving account of their history. He depicts the Korean mask dance as a *minjung* drama that depicts *han* as the tenacity of purpose for life. Young Shak Hyun, referring to this mask dance, writes that in it and by it the *minjung* express critical transcendence over this world and laugh at its absurdity.[26] They view themselves as standing above the entire world — which includes not only rulers but also themselves and their religion. Hyun notes something here of the experience of what Paul Tillich called "God above God." And he states that his "understanding of God's incarnation was deepened in more concrete and existential terms. God is working and revealing his will in and through the minjung of Korea, especially the minjung's history and culture."[27]

Kim also arrives at the idea that the messiah and the people actualize the victory of God's justice over evil. This historical process is a process of "radical transformation." "Messianism is an eschatological phenomenon closely linked to an apocalyptic perception of history." "The content of the Messianic Kingdom is *justice, koinonia,* and *shalom.*" A distinction has to be made between "power-messianism and Jesus-messianism, ruler-messianism and minjung-messianism":[28]

> Jesus-messianism or messianic servanthood is a radical challenge to all forms of political, royal, and power messianism. It is concerned with saving and transforming the minjung so that its subjecthood may be realized. Hence, all powers must be under the rule of Jesus the Messiah who came to be the servant of the minjung, who died for them and who rose from the dead so that the minjung may rise from the power of death historically and not just at the end of time.

25. Suh Dwang-sun David, "Minjung: A Biographical Sketch of an Asian Consultation," in *Minjung Theology,* 27-29.
26. Young Shak Hyun in *Minjung Theology,* 47-54.
27. *Ibid.,* 54.
28. Kim Yong Bock in *Minjung Theology,* 186f.

Kim once stated in a debate that he was not so much interested in the mission of the church as it derives its impetus from within the church; his real concern was "with the mission of the people to the church — their cries and their sufferings . . . which should elicit from the churches not a 'churchy' response but a 'people' response."[29] In view of all this it does not surprise us that when Kim sets out to describe the *minjung* movements in Korea he also includes those of Buddhist origin. The *missio Dei* is much broader than the mission history of the church.

It is clear that this theology is a theology of liberation. But it is equally clear that in its profoundly cosmic sense of life its character is typically Asian. The authentically Korean nature of this theology is manifest in the attempt to show how it is rooted in Korean messianic movements that have from time immemorial been a part of the history of the people. Over and over, say the authors of *Minjung Theology*, the messianic kingdom broke through in these historic processes.

It is also apparent that this theology is totally missionary in character. We shall again let Kim explain to us in what sense this is the case:[30] The first task of the Christian church is "to expose the long history of political messianism which has enslaved us and to struggle against it." It may be the *special* task of Third World theology "to purge elements of political messianism from our Christian confessions, proclamations, and theologies." After all, messianic traditions, even those of Christians, "are not immune to influences from political messianism," especially not when the Christian community has bound itself to the ruling power. "We know of this process in the history of Christianity which has justified absolute power like that of the Divine Right of the King."

Kim attempts to offer the Christian community a Christian political perspective. It is based on "the general resurrection of the people (bodily as well as spiritual) understood in terms of the messianic subjectivity of the people," *shalom* in the relationship between North and South Korea, and "*koinonia* (participation) and justice in relation to the social and political development of the Korean people." "Jesus the Messiah was resurrected as a foretaste and affirmation of the raising of all the dead minjung to inaugurate the messianic rule of justice, *koinonia* and *shalom*."

The language of the Korean Christian *koinonia*, as it developed in 1970s, "is a new language for the Korean people," says Kim.[31]

29. D. Preman Niles, in *Minjung Theology*, 9.
30. Kim Yong Bock, *Minjung Theology*, 192f.
31. *Ibid.*, 117f.

The complete . . . system of the messianic language in Korean society, in the midst of intensifying historical contradictions, brought about a revolutionary change in the culture and language of the people. This messianic language as the language of the oppressed people was a counter-language, subversive of the established and ruling ideology. . . . The language was utopian and at the same time transformative. But most important, the messianic language in Korea was concerned with historical transformation. The application of the messianic language to the historical experiences of the Korean people was bound to historicalize and secularize the Christian language.

Thus it moved beyond the boundaries of the Christian church. In this manner the language found expression in active participation in current historical processes.

Sri Lanka, India, and Taiwan: The Cosmic Meaning of Christ

Kim's *minjung* theology reminds Niles of the theology of the cosmic significance of Christ. He refers to M. M. Thomas, who wrote about revolution in Asia from the perspective of such a theology.[32] Thomas himself explains in "Christ-centered Syncretism"[33] how his thinking moved in this direction: As a non-theologian he entered theology through his involvement in the struggle for political and social justice. He gained an appreciation for Kraemer's view that the gospel comes from God and must always keep the Christ of God at the center. But he did not want to overlook what A. T. van Leeuwen had stressed, namely, that the gospel is for people. Consequently the gospel — divine truth — must not be separated from human values and social ideology. A christocentric humanism is part of the gospel and has a witnessing dimension of its own. Christocentric theology may not be set over against anthropology.[34] From the perspective of the revolutionary process in Asia, the aim of which is to build up societies that actualize the highest possible quality of human life, Thomas viewed other religions not primarily in terms of their religiosity but in terms of their potential for the transformation and building up of

32. It is especially because of Thomas's writings, says Niles, that Asian theologians began to perceive the presence of the cosmic Christ in the Asian revolutionary process. He begins by citing a pronouncement from the East Asia Christian Conference held in Rangoon in 1959. In Asia this view represents a breakthrough from the post-Kraemer era.

33. M. M. Thomas, "Christ-centered Syncretism," in *Varieties of Witness*, ed. Niles and Thomas (Singapore, 1980).

34. *Ibid.*, 13.

such societies. He regarded these religions as "religions in renaissance," in which one can discern "a partial knowledge and recognition of Christ."

Thomas regarded secular ideologies in the same way. Consequently he regarded the struggle for human dignity as a preparation for the gospel, since Christ is present in that struggle despite the distortions that slip into every revolutionary movement. Thomas, like D. P. Niles, depicts the ethos or ideology of the Asian struggle as "an integral humanism, spiritually informed by the insights of the prophetic Christian faith and of the humanism of Asia's indigenous religions and cultures."[35] Niles cites his father in this connection:[36] In nations that had just freed themselves from the colonial era, the goal was now national construction: "character and nation building." Under the influence of Christianity and secular ideologies ancient Asian religions were enjoying a renaissance. These religions, too, wanted to make a contribution to a truly human society. The challenge to the churches was therefore to say what it meant to them to be a missionary church. It was a time of rising expectations and great aspirations in which the Christian hope could be articulated.

In the 1970s the mood shifted and became much more pessimistic. Independence had not delivered what had been expected of it. It had not brought relief to the suffering masses. The unity experienced in the struggle for liberation made way for increasingly sharper ideological and religious polarizations. Military dictators used these developments to stay in power. Because Christians had identified with the people, they also intensely experienced these conflicts together with the *minjung*, who had to carry heavy burdens. This new missionary attitude also raised questions concerning the theological and ideological reflection of Christians. Had it not been the aim of theology to work for the people? And had it not listened too little to the historic expectations and feelings of the people themselves?

Niles gives sharp expression to this theological shift when he points out that the wealth of Asia is its people: Asian peoples have a long history and have initiated great religious movements in historical processes spanning thousands of years. He states that it is no longer possible to view the history of the people from a Christian perspective. One should rather view Christian history from the perspective of the people.

These ideas have been elaborated most fundamentally by Choan-Seng Song of Taiwan in, for example, his book on the reconstruction of Christian mission.[37] But this point of view comes out over and over as

35. D. P. Niles, "Christian Action in the Asian Struggle," in *What Asian Christians are Thinking* (n. 11 above) 451.

36. D. T. Niles, *Ideas and Services* (Singapore, 1968) 7f.

37. Choan-Seng Song, *Christian Mission in Reconstruction: An Asian Analysis*

basic to his later books. As late as 1983 he wrote in a letter to me that he regards his own theology as an attempt to place God's acts of creation and redemption, as well as the events of the incarnation, in history, regardless of where these events occurred. He therefore struggles against much of Western salvation-historical theology,[38] which focuses on the incarnation and has paid too little attention to the place assumed in creation by the Logos. Linking creation and redemption leads Song directly into history, into what people experience in their own history and culture, the history and culture from which they themselves have emerged. Only thus does he see the way clear to get to the root, the meaning of the incarnation. And there he finds the focus of his theology.

The problem for this theology of the cosmic Christ is what to do with Israel. The effort is made to maintain Israel's special place in the history of salvation, but then Israel turns into little more than a mirror by which people can see more clearly how God's redemptive action has also taken place in the history of their own people.[39]

What Kim, Niles, Song, and Ting have in common in their very different theologies is the attempt to identify in historical processes something of God's redemptive action through the cosmic Christ — or something of the cosmic significance of Christ (the phrase that Song prefers). And they are certainly representative of virtually all Asian theologies. Sometimes these theologies, for example that of Samartha, have a strong ontological cast. Samartha stresses that in Western theology such a heavy emphasis has been put on the historical significance of Christ that Christ's ontological significance has been eclipsed. Earlier we mentioned that he begins his christological work in the ontology of the Vedanta. Sometimes, as with Niles, Christ's lordship over history is pivotal.[40]

Whereas in the 1960s this conveyed a touch of triumphalism, which was in keeping with the mood of those times, in the 1970s, when pessimism was rising (and the Christian church was able to counter with a testimony of Christian hope), the Lord of history was confessed as the suffering Servant who identified with the suffering *minjung*, the poor and oppressed. In the situation of Asia today theology can only be relevant if

---

(Madras, 1975). Cf. also Bishop K. H. Ting (president of the Council of Churches in China), "Theological Mass Movements in China," *International Bulletin of Missionary Research* 9 (1985) 98-102.

38. In a personal letter dated June 19, 1983.

39. D. P. Niles, "A Suffering People Called to be Suffering Servant: The Political Vision of Second Isaiah," in *Toward the Sovereignty of the People*, 43-88.

40. In that case it is more correct to speak of the cosmic significance of Christ. Christ as Lord of history was a central theme at the 1961 WCC assembly at New Delhi. See my *De kosmische betekenis van Christus* (n. 10 above).

it offers an answer to the cries of a suffering people. Critical analysis is not enough. Response to the suffering of the people requires participation in their groaning. From this arises another kind of critique alongside criticism of ideology. What emerges are the longings and symbols, the elements of a political vision, which point to and are the bearers of the significance of a new future. A Christian theology ought, with its own inherited themes and symbols, to respond to these elements.[41]

From such a theology renewing power will come forth and have its impact on the church. To regain its lost authority the church in Asia must give up its alliances with power. The church will have to "be humble enough to be baptized in the Jordan of Asian religiosity" and bold enough to be nailed to the cross of Asian poverty. Its fear of losing its identity makes the church a servant of mammon. Its refusal to die keeps the church from living. What it needs is a theology and praxis of participation. Aloysius Pieris of Sri Lanka asserts that the church's desperate search "for the Asian face of Christ can find fulfillment only if we participate in Asia's own search for it in the unfathomable abyss where religion and poverty seem to have the same common source: God, who has declared Mammon his enemy (Matthew 6:24)."[42]

> What then is the locus of this praxis? Certainly not the Christian life lived within the church in the presence of non-Christians; rather, it is the God-experience (which is at once the human-concern) of God's own people living beyond the church and among whom the church is called to lose itself in total participation. That is to say, *theology in Asia is the Christian apocalypse of the non-Christian experiences of liberation.*[43]

The Philippines: The Threatened Position of Theology

Theology has been challenged by the death of the poor and by the claim of life represented by the resistance of the oppressed,[44] as we noted above. But as a result of the stress on the *minjung* as the subject of history (Korea) and on participation (Sri Lanka), a very different challenge to theology has come into being. It is the question, raised in Asia, to what degree and

41. D. P. Niles, *op. cit.*, 45.

42. A. Pieris, "Towards an Asian Theology of Liberation: Some Religio-cultural Guidelines," in *Asia's Struggle for Full Humanity*, ed. V. Fabella (Maryknoll, 1980) 93f.

43. *Ibid.*, 24.

44. S. Rayan, "Irruption of the Poor: Challenges to Theology," *Option for the Poor: Challenge to the Rich Countries*, ed. L. Boff and V. P. Elizondo (Concilium; Edinburgh, 1986) 106.

in what sense "professional theology" still has any right to exist. This challenge is posed throughout the report on the Asian Theological Conference held in 1979 at Wennapuwa, Sri Lanka, which is titled *Asia's Struggle for Full Humanity: Towards a Relevant Theology.* We have already cited this volume.

The crisis in theology comes out sharply in the paper submitted by Carlos H. Abesamis of the Philippines, who describes the broad-based reflection that took place in the churches in preparation for the conference:

> For one who begins to do theological work in Asia today, the realization of the radically threatened position of theology is an indispensable psychological prerequisite. Moreover, at the very outset, the theologian will have to realize (1) that theology is response rather than dogma; (2) that what theology can eventually say is an inadequate second word in response to the question first spoken by the history of Third World peoples in our lands; (3) that one must go beyond Vatican II and even the recent theological developments elsewhere and proceed to make our peoples' contemporary history and God within that history the main preceptors of faith; and (4) that commitment to that Asian history and struggle is a prerequisite for one who engages in Asian theology today.[45]

In the traditional Christianity of the Philippines Vatican II prompted a movement toward a freer spirituality and "the indigenization of prayers, liturgy and church architecture."

> But there has also emerged . . . a new enfleshment of Christianity which goes beyond the concern for the salvation of souls or for the integral human development of the individual person. It is a form of Christianity that is concerned with the history of our people. It looks into the concrete historical forces working in the lives of men and women. . . . It is committed to the struggle of the poor, deprived, and oppressed for full humanity. . . . Its apostolates of lay leadership, family life, health, media, prayer sessions, and Bible reflections have a thrust towards total human development, salvation, and liberation; and it concretizes this thrust by undertaking a conscientizing education and by catalyzing the organization of the oppressed for self-affirmation, self-determination, and self-reliance.[46]

45. C. H. Abesamis in *Asia's Struggle for Full Humanity,* 123-39 (quotation is from p. 124); cf. *Voices from the Third World* 7/2 (December, 1984) 16-22; *ibid.* 1/1 (December, 1978) 19f.

46. Abesamis, in *Asia's Struggle,* 125.

To put together a preparatory paper for the conference in Wennappuwa the leaders went to work with people of the grassroots who had reflected on a social analysis of the situation in their own country and for whom the faith was oriented to the Bible and to the history in which God is actively present in his "concern for total life and salvation." At the very outset the question arose: Who is the theologian? And the collective answer that emerged was: "Assuming that it is worthwhile developing a theology, the theologians should be the grassroots poor themselves." They are not the *objects* of relevant theology but its *subjects*. And what can those who belong to the middle class contribute as catalyzers and facilitators?

When this group began to ask themselves what the components of theological reflection are, they arrived at the conclusion that theological reflection is an activity of interpreting present life in the light of the faith; and accordingly that theological reflection is based on the contemporary life-situation and history, which are to be seriously analyzed and viewed in the light of a biblical-historical faith with the help of native wisdom and local religion. Such theological reflection must lead to transforming action. And those who do theological reflection, "the creators of a real Filipino theology," are "the grassroots poor themselves."[47]

In the consultation in which the group arrived at formulations, Abesemis relates, the transition from a theology created within the old contexts — a domesticating theology — to a liberated and liberating theology came about especially through the biblical-historical framework in which the group saw theology operating.

> The biblical faith primarily confesses God's salvific involvement in historical events: in the exodus from the slavery of Egypt, in the possession of the land, and especially in the health-giving deeds of Jesus, in his life-giving death and resurrection, in his anticipated "second coming" which will usher in the "new heaven and the new earth" where people, nations, and the whole of creation will no longer know mourning nor tears nor suffering nor pain, because God will be all in all, and all things will be made new.[48]

Theology, accordingly, interprets the life of people with the help of analysis, Scripture, and indigenous wisdom or religion. These three elements relate to each other dialectically and complement and correct each other. Analysis can complement Scripture by a scientific understanding of human beings and society.

47. *Ibid.*, 128.
48. *Ibid.*, 131.

Scripture can say that God and religion are concerned for justice, but it is social analysis that will uncover the structural injustices of our times. On the other hand, Scripture can complement social analysis by underlining the importance of the individual person, the reality of sin, the place of the psycho-spiritual aspects of life.

The religion that is native to a region can help create a more vivid picture of the purpose of the struggle for justice by stressing the values of inner liberation and personal conversion. Similarly, native wisdom can complement the results of social analysis by showing "that any genuine reading of reality and any liberational action must take into account the culture of the people, the ethos, and way of behaving and thinking of the masses." The question remains: Which of these elements corrects which? In other words, what are the criteria for judging among them? Abesamis looks for such criteria by asking what is "life-giving, liberating, humanizing, bringing about people's total salvation?" Even more important: What do the grassroots poor judge to be life-giving and humanizing?[49]

It is clear by now that in all this we are dealing with more than what was earlier called the adaptation, accommodation, or indigenization of the gospel. There the idea was to find a way of *approaching* the people. Abesamis speaks of a crisis in theology because theology is literally turned upside-down: Real theology has to be done from below, from the grassroots. In what Abesamis says about Philippine goals there is on this point much resemblance with what we saw in the *minjung* theology of Korea, which places so much emphasis on the *minjung* as the *subject* of history.

Abesamis does not mention any results achieved on the basis of what was strongly emphasized in the consultation, which was that the real theologians are the grassroots poor. He does ask what would have to happen if the poor were not interested in the creation of a grassroots theology or refused to cooperate in creating it. In that case, says Abesamis,

> I think it would be better to have a respectful and fruitful silence rather than fill the vacuum with alienating theologies proceeding from alienated consciousnesses. The fact, however, is that there already exist grassroots communities of farmers, fisherfolk, workers, poor urban dwellers where one finds the ingredients for the making of a relevant theology.[50]

He therefore expects the emergence of theological results. I suspect that there is now already more theological work being done in the base com-

49. *Ibid.*, 133.
50. *Ibid.*, 138.

munities than Abesamis saw. My suspicion is based on experiences in Indonesia in 1980.

Indonesia: The Emergence of Grassroots Theology

Whoever is listening closely to the churches of Indonesia will hear the beginning — in a variety of forms — of a "church" theology that is closely bound up with the search for Christian identity in the context of national liberation from colonial domination and of ecclesiastical liberation from the dominance of Western missions. Here I will describe some of this, largely on the basis of incidental experiences and also on the basis of research done by Hans-Ruedi Weber in 1972-74, in which members of Reformed and Presbyterian churches in various parts of the world were asked: What is the significance of Christ's crucifixion in personal life?[51]

In the course of a journey through various parts of Indonesia (Sumatra, Java, and Sulawesi) I was struck by the extent to which people were reflecting on their relationship to the dead. This occurred not only in the countryside but also among academics who had had training abroad. One of the best-known leaders even assured me that the answer to questions in this regard would decide the direction of the churches' development. We are not now talking about reflection apart from contemporary history, apart from historical development, apart from the socioeconomic and political problems with which the country is struggling. On the contrary, theological reflection and the experience of faith in the churches are concentrated on this point as the crystallization of the search for a group identity as Christians in the midst of national construction. What is our relationship to our ancestors? How far do the effects of Christ's atoning work extend? What is there for us as Christians to do in the construction of our state in its development on the basis of our cultural and religious heritage into the modern era?

I traveled by car from Medan into the interior of North Sumatra to visit several churches, and that journey brought out these questions. At several places images of ancestors were in view,[52] each time accompanied by a cross and a Bible text. I asked an Indonesian colleague what such a monument meant in the contemporary Christian life of faith. The answer

---

51. H.-R. Weber, *The Cross: Tradition and Interpretation* (Grand Rapids, 1979). Cf. B. F. Drewes, "Het verstaan van het kruis op Midden — Java," *Vox Theologica* 46 (1976); *idem* in *Vandaar* (1975, 3)

52. For Batak-Tapanuli, cf. L. Schreiner, *Adat und Evangelium. Zur Bedeutung der altvölkischen Lebensordnungen für Kirche und Mission unter den Batak in Nordsumatra* (Gütersloh, 1972).

was that people related to the dead in the same way as the author of Hebrews, who speaks of a "cloud of witnesses" around us (12:1). One may regard past generations as incorporated into redemption in Christ. Now that people have come to Christ and have been baptized, they have also been baptized for the dead, as Paul says (1 Cor. 15:29). After all, after his death on the cross the Lord himself descended into the realm of the dead to involve even the dead of Noah's day in his redemption (1 Pet. 3:20). Communion with one's ancestors is experienced in a special way at the Lord's Supper. Those who have died dwell with the Lord (2 Cor. 5:8), while in the Lord's Supper we are granted the most intimate communion with Christ. That we are baptized into one body is thus experienced in a total way (1 Cor. 12:13).

This answer to my question about the images of ancestors shows that the break with previous generations, with the ancient religious and cultural inheritance, that was experienced as a result of conversion to the Christian faith has been overcome. Identity — rootedness in one's own ethnic group and culture — has reemerged whole. Consequently, the inspiration to work at the construction of a more humane society has returned.

Soundings that I took at various levels, even among people who obtained university degrees abroad and in ethnically and culturally disparate churches, indicated not only that people everywhere were preoccupied with these problems but also that the insights and consciousness that they have acquired has a large measure of similarity. Where and how and with whom I encountered all this cannot be told here. My sources are highly personal conversations. Though I have sought to keep my account here as neutral as possible, enough has been said, I think, to indicate the line of thought and the experience of faith of people in this huge land with its fast-growing churches, which are the basis of the rootedness of the churches in society and their solidarity with it.

It is harder to get close to the new "mind" that grows out of being rooted in Christ, the experience of God and everything that is associated with it. The "sense of life" (Lebensgefühl) that is born of the encounter with Christ depends largely on whether one's background is that of tribal religion, Hinduism, Buddhism, Islam, or Confucianism. This is the reason (according to people in a position to know) that in the ecumenical movement, which sought from the beginning in Indonesia to create one single church for the whole country, unification proved so difficult, even though confessional differences were minimal.

Weber's research was focused in part on Middle Java, and it is most instructive to see, with the aid of B. F. Drewes, how grassroots theology has developed there.[53] These churches were born out of Dutch Reformed

53. See Drewes, "Het verstaan."

mission work and therefore grew up theologically on the Heidelberg Cate-chism. So the theology unearthed by Drewes's study is soundly Reformed, though the "forensic significance" of Christ's death (the acquittal of sin-ners on the basis of Christ's sacrifice) does not seem to loom large. The blood of Christ interpreted as a "fountain of life" finds a much deeper response.

With reference to the significance of Christ's death on the cross for the believer's daily life, Drewes reports that an essential value of Javanese culture comes out, namely, a sense of stability, balance, serenity, and patience. This leads to a model focused on harmony and to an emphatic rejection of any kind of model focused on conflict. In the struggle and chaos of life in society Christ furnishes balance and victory over the experience of being hurled back and forth between the powers that surround us. The fruit of Christ's work affords the believer rest, peace, and a feeling of being in harmony with the surrounding world. Therefore, the unifying NASAKOM ideology (see n. 1) found a ready and fruitful reception on Java.

Besides, Jesus teaches us patience and gives us power to endure suffering. His patience in suffering is exemplary. In this connection Drewes cites the systematic theology of Harun Hadiwijono (1985), professor at the Theological School in Yogyakarta: "Christ's dying on the cross is a dying for us and together with us. It is not only the case that Christ died for us believers but also that we believers participate in his dying (Rom. 6:5). The resurrec-tion of Christ brings us to life together with him (Eph. 2:15)."[54] Such a view corresponds completely to the ancient Javanese saying, sometimes spoken at Christian funerals, that "we must accomplish death in the midst of life and life in the midst of death." Drewes cites Budiman's dissertation and then says: "In this book there is a strong emphasis on communion with Christ's suffering . . . and with the suffering of all Christians. . . . In the Javanese view of life there is a recognition that for people to arrive at honor and glory they must first suffer. This view is still perceptible in the church."[55]

Patience in suffering always stands in the framework of harmony and balance in human lives and in the world. Drewes touches the core of the matter when he writes:

> This applies in both the life of society and one's personal life. To utter a blunt "no" to somebody is impolite; it disturbs the harmony. Every-thing that disturbs the harmony is judged negatively. On the occasion of significant events a "slametan," a *shalom* meal, is held as a way to

54. H. Hadiwijono, *Iman Kristen* (Jakarta, 1973) 249.
55. Drewes, "Het verstaan"; R. Budiman (at the time also in Yogyakarta), *De realisering der verzoening in het menselijk bestaan. Een onderzoek naar Paulus' opvatting van de gemeenschap van Christus' lijden als een integrerend deel der verzoening* (Delft, 1971).

restore the threatened balance, both socially and personally. . . . It is striking that many regard the cross as a balance-restoring point of rest. . . . Alongside the break with one's environment one experiences stability in life as a gift of the crucified Christ.[56]

Here the message of reconciliation between God and human beings is set within a new context apart from any conscious goal-directed activity to confess it situationally. In this connection Weber speaks of hearing the message of the cross situationally.[57]

In this line of thought does union with the Supreme Being, as it is known in Javanese mysticism, also play a role? In the opinion of Drewes this is not the case in reflection on the meaning of the cross. Still, in my opinion, his own account of a work of art by a Javanese guru in Yogyakarta points in another direction. About this depiction of the crucified Christ Drewes writes:

> The superscription on the cross is not INRI but "my own self." The reference is to Christ, indeed, but also to us. The bowed head literally looks at the dilated chest. He submits totally and honestly to God. The opened chest suggests introspection: People turn to what is within them to discover the secret of the self and the world.[58]

Is not this secret God? In the theology of the people this is undoubtedly a factor. In the story of Bimo Sutji did not Bimo ultimately find the divine secret within? I do not know the extent of this in the theology of the people, but one catches it in the way in which people sing during church services, even when they are singing Western melodies. For that reason alone participation in a Javanese church service is a moving experience: New Testament riches bloom here that we in the West have largely lost.

The results of this research undertaken in Middle Java are not simply applicable in other regions of Indonesia. They are certainly not to be found in the same clear forms. But in relating joint reflection in the Indonesian Council of Churches to current social and political problems one is struck by the degree to which there is a search under way for a model focused on harmony.

That fact is not always well received outside Indonesia. For years it has been stressed in Third World theology that theological contextualization will have to take place in the context of contemporary interdependence, which links the patterns of past and present with the possibilities

56. Drewes, "Het verstaan."
57. Weber, *op. cit.*
58. Drewes in *Vandaar* (1975, 3).

of the future. Contextualization, it has been said, must take place in response to the urgent issues in one's own context, in one's own place and time.[59] It has been assumed that it would sometimes be necessary to make a clear choice against dominant tendencies, government policies, and the like. As examples one can point to events in Korea, the Philippines, and Japan. Old Takizawa once told me how his conversion to Christian faith automatically brought with it for him a commitment to the revolutionary student movement in Japan. Not only in the Netherlands but also at Asian theological conferences, Indonesian Christians receive the criticism that at critical moments they do not sufficiently show their colors.

But in my view a model focused on harmony, entwined as it is with the deepest, cosmically-rooted life convictions of people, is primordially Asian. Much of the social and political activism in some Asian countries can be explained exclusively in terms of the effects of secularization, which in varying degrees in different locations contributes to detachment from ancient religions, ancient cultural attitudes, and the ancient inherited understanding of life.

The development of theology in China, as it is conveyed, for example, through Bishop Ting, clearly points to a harmony model. This is apparent from the way in which the churches have positioned themselves amid the historical processes. It would be interesting to explore the degree to which ancient Chinese yin-yang philosophy is present in the churches' positions and the degree to which the theology of Jung Young Lee presents a fruitful elaboration of it.[60]

One may also wonder what the background of Korea's *minjung* theology is. Ostensibly a conflict model is manifest in it. But this is not the whole story, which is implicit in the view of historical processes in this theology, in which the people (the *ochlos*) are the subject. On this view history is largely a cosmic occurrence. Accordingly, the conclusion is inevitable that here too the yin-yang scheme, along with the entire cosmic classification system, is present in the background. The rejection of the Confucian concept of history need not be inconsistent with this conclusion: Presumably that only means that Confucius had a mistaken view of the relationship between yin and yang in history.

Hendrik Kraemer is reported to have said that the church has only become established in a given "ethnic unit" when "heresies" are born there. In his time that was perhaps the way to put it, and presumably that statement referred to what we now call contextualization. But what is really happening could be defined as "the expression of one's own expe-

---

59. Cf. S. Coe, *Working Political Statement*.
60. Cf. n. 14 above.

rience as a believer." In the theology of the people the "foreign husk" of the gospel, which came with the missions, has dropped off.

It would be worth the effort to examine what people are thinking in other areas of Indonesia. A new "native" confession like that of the Toraja-Rantepao church on Celebes certainly does not bring out what people think and feel in the churches. The inquiry — initiated a long time ago — into the relationship of Toraja culture to the Christian faith and vice versa in the present situation will undoubtedly yield important information.

Japan: "Ha-hah" versus "Ya-yah"

Japanese theologian Masao Takenaka has achieved world renown with his book *Christian Art in Asia*.[61] His later book *God Is Rice*[62] is concerned with questions surrounding the relationship between culture and the Christian faith. In all theological reflection in Japan the purpose is to let the Christian faith strike root in Japanese culture. *God Is Rice* seeks to understand how the gospel summons us to live in harmony with nature and our fellow human beings, to establish a just society, and to be open to renewal.

The national renaissance of Japan will be derailed if a nostalgic return to old patterns is allowed. A positive use of traditional culture originates in a contemporary expression of that culture. One of the most important factors in the cultural renaissance is the rediscovery of the individual and the freedom to release the energies of self-expression. The self has become conscious of being a part of the continuous flow of cultural history. It exists and struggles in the contemporary social context and looks forward to the future. In traditional culture, too, there have been oppressive elements. Consequently, if one wants to attach oneself to tradition — which includes negative factors like feudalism and conservatism — one must be critically conscious of oneself. The link to tradition will have to be sought in its positive aspects. In many respects the same applies to the contextualization of the gospel.

Takenaka favors the "ha-hah" approach: "Whenever I participate in theological discussions I often sense an atmosphere of debate. This is particularly true in the West where the approach through rational argument is to destroy other people's concept of God."[63] To him this resembles

---

61. M. Takenaka, *Christian Art in Asia: Artistic Expressions of Christian Faith in Asian Context Today* (Kyoto, 1975).

62. *Idem, God Is Rice: Asian Culture and Christian Faith* (Geneva, 1986).

63. *Idem,* "A Christian Reflection on Beauty in the Japanese Cultural Context," *Reformed World* 38/7 (1985) 357-65.

a Japanese sword fight. This is a "ya-yah" approach, "ya-yah" being the cry a fighter shouts after announcing his name and before he begins to fight. In Western theology one discerns "an approach of deductive metaphysics rather than of inductive learning, an approach of confrontation rather than mutual sharing." When Takenaka instead proposes a "ha-hah" approach, his intention is to look for a way of "personal appreciation and mutual acknowledgement of what's going on in the living reality of life." In the story of Jacob's robbery of Esau's birthright and blessing and of Esau's fury over this, one has an account of a terrible confrontation. After his first night as a fugitive, when he wakes up at Bethel, Jacob says, "Surely the LORD is in this place — and I did not know it!" (Gen. 28:10-17). To Takenaka this is a vivid example of what he means by the ha-hah approach: discerning God's presence in the world.

In *God Is Rice* Takenaka uses examples from Japanese writings, Christian art, and Japanese customs such as the tea ceremony and floral arrangements to arrive at a unique Asian understanding of the person, work, and teachings of Jesus.

Another appealing example can be found in *Mount Fuji and Mount Sinai*, written by an equally well-known Japanese theologian, Kosuke Koyama.[64] This book is his report on a personal pilgrimage: He attempts to bring together his historical experience arising within the Japanese tradition as it moves into modern times and his personal confession of faith — or rather how by God's grace he was brought to a dialogue between his own historical experience and the theology of the cross. "I came to realize that it is the theology of the cross that can really level a sharp and, at the same time, helpful critique against idolatry." The mountains referred to in the title are the two great poles of Koyama's critique of idols. Fuji stands for the traditional Japanese religious cultural inheritance, which is centered in nature, or to use a term employed earlier, in the experience of cosmic unity. Sinai represents the traditional Semitic religious cultural inheritance, which is oriented to history and eschatology.

Koyama's theological pilgrimage began in 1945, the year of Hiroshima. With his own eyes he saw Tokyo reduced to a wilderness by the constant bombings. "This seeing the wilderness of Tokyo has become, over the years, a 'theological' experience." In those years four biblical themes became central for him:

1. "And all its cities were laid in ruins before the LORD, before his fierce anger" (Jer. 4:26).

64. K. Koyama, *Mount Fuji and Mount Sinai: A Pilgrimage in Theology* (London, 1984).

2. Reflection on the Japanese cities lying in ruins leads Koyama in Part II of his book to a critical evaluation of the culture oriented toward nature and centered on emperor worship and the cult of the sun. "Out of this critique arose the intriguing challenge of the Bible that 'my help comes from the maker of heaven and earth [Ps. 121:2],' not just from 'heaven and earth.'"

3. Exod. 20:7: "You shall not make wrongful use of the name of the LORD your God." In Part III Koyama attempts to "provide a historical background to the discussion of idolatry in Japanese culture. Have the Japanese people taken the name of the Lord God in vain? In what way can it be said they did?"

4. Hos. 11:8: "My mind is turning over inside me. My emotions are agitated all together" (Koyama's translation). "Part IV focuses on the meaning of our faith in the God who is passionately involved in history. Behind our history is the agitated mind of God because of God's love for us."

"All these four biblical themes are deeply 'disturbing' to the spiritual orientation of the East." On their basis Koyama moved toward a theology of the cross that gave him "the fundamental orientation in which to engage in theology while living in a world dangerously fragmented by violent militarism, racism, and nuclearism." He wrote "with a keen awareness of the global peril of nuclear war." Wars are waged, he says, "in the name of God," that is, with "theological" justification. This justification is idolatry. All nations busily quote "the names of their gods to justify what they are doing." Koyama himself experienced this during the time of the emperor cult in Japan. "In the name of our own Solar Goddess we appointed ourselves to be the Righteous Nation that possessed the fulness of morality! One of the fundamental functions of theology is to expose idolatry."[65]

Idols — ideologies, totalitarianism, nuclear weapons, the striving for power and glory, national security, economic efficiency and productivity, and the rest — all fall under the judgment of the cross. The God who speaks the last word over the world and over history exposes all our idolatries at the cross. Jesus Christ, who comes to us through the word of the cross, is opposed to all idolatry. This God, who in Jesus Christ comes to the edge of human life — to the publicans and sinners, to the place where no honor, prestige, or power can be gained, where the orphans, widows, and refugees are, where people die of hunger — this God reveals the truth of Immanuel, God with us. God with us on the cross speaks to us about *ēthos*, ethical involvement, and *pathos*, the passion of God, whose

65. All the quotations are from the Preface of *Mount Fuji and Mount Sinai*.

attention is focused on our history, the God of brokenness, compassion, and sharing, not of greed, power, and domination.

Therefore, in accord with Amos 4:9f. (cf. vv. 6-8), people are summoned to return from their idolatry. They have ended up on the periphery, but God, who accuses them of not having returned to him despite all the judgment he has sent upon them, is still the one who brings his people back to himself on eagles' wings (Exod. 19:4). Jesus Christ deepens the prophetic call to turn back to the Lord.

Koyama asks in what direction we would move if the refrain in Amos read: "I have sent the Buddha, who taught you to battle against your own greed, yet you did not return to me." The question is unavoidable to all Christians who seek after theological illumination upon their own relationship with the people of other faiths. Theology must engage itself in a task of relating the Buddha's teaching on battle against human greed and the agitated mind of the God of Israel who says, "yet you did not return to me." I am suggesting *theological* bridging between the two.

A quick answer to this problem would be found in the view that Buddhists are "anonymous Christians." They have anonymously returned to God. This may sound acceptable to Christians but arrogant and imperialistic to the ease of the Buddhists. They would object to this "extension" programme of Christianity.[66]

"The theology of the cross which is inspired and maintained by the words: 'the foolishness of God is wiser than men and the weakness of God is stronger than men,' is a theology which is able to meet the claim that other faiths make." The Christ who confirms his centrality by going "to the periphery is the Christ who can establish a healing tie with the other faiths. . . . The theology of the cross suggests to us that interreligious discussion must be seen from the perspective of the 'refuse of the world' which defines an apostolic quality of life and message."[67]

Thus it is not opposition but connection that is the starting point, not that which destroys boundaries but that which speaks of healing and return. In the same way Koyama also works out the difference between cosmologically-oriented traditional Japanese religion and the biblical view of the cosmos: Mount Fuji is the *axis mundi*, the central axis of the world, "the womb of the primal pair-gods, the brain of the world, the sacred place of the harmony of the sexes and the symbol of the new Miroku-era" in which people will help each other. Mount Sinai, on the other hand, does not speak

---

66. *Ibid.*, 255.

67. *Ibid.*, 255f. It is fascinating to place these statements alongside those of Sjohi Tsutomu, "Not the Chrysanthemum, but the Crown of Thorns: A New Vision of Mission in Japan," *International Review of Mission* 75 (1986) 383-90.

of a stationary God, one who is cosmologically experienced as enthroned upon the axis of the world. "The God who meets the people at Mount Sinai will meet them again" at other critical moments of their history. He journeys with them. Despite the difference Koyama still wants to search for interaction between cosmological and theological concepts of "center symbolism." God symbolizes the center of salvation. This center symbolism expressed in the pillar of cloud and the pillar of fire (Exod. 13:12) travels with the people. Wherever this God is in the world, that is the center of salvation. "Not to be at the center but to be with God is salvational." Understanding of the difference can be attained, but not by confrontation, only by interaction.[68]

Thus here also the fundamental pattern of much Asian theology — or of all of it — comes out.

Concluding Remarks

In this chapter I have attempted to furnish some insight into Asian theology. This theology is developing in churches that are becoming rooted in their native soil and are attempting to find a way toward a witness of faith in their own situations. The reader may have noticed that I have mentioned no confessional distinctions. Pieris as a Catholic, Niles as a Methodist, and Song as a Presbyterian — just to mention some — barely differ in the fundamental patterns of their theology. The reason for this might be that theology is done not from an Augustinian but from an Irenaean perspective on salvation history.[69] All three of these theologians view Christ as the One who brings the completion of creation. But Catholic theology has always been more invested in this perspective than Protestant theology.

I have not discussed Asian theology done by evangelicals, which strongly rejects the movement toward links with the national religious and cultural inheritance.[70] In this framework contextualization becomes something very different and means what used to be called "the approach of adaptation." Discussion of this evangelical theology would demand a separate chapter. I have also left undiscussed the undoubtedly still influential theologies imported by the missions. Some theological training centers use very old handbooks and commentaries. The theology of the base groups always avoids this older framework.

---

68. Koyama, *Mount Fuji and Mount Sinai*, 87f.
69. See my *De kosmische betekenis van Christus* (n. 10 above) 17ff.
70. E.g., "The Seoul Declaration: Towards an Evangelical Theology for The Third World," *International Bulletin of Missionary Research* 7 (1983) 64f.

CHAPTER 22

Latin America: Evangelization on a Christian Continent

R. G. VAN ROSSUM

Historical Background

Today's missionary movement in Latin American churches cannot be evaluated in depth without insight into the manner in which Christianity was introduced and planted in Latin America and into the involvement, beginning in the nineteenth century, of European and North American Catholic and Protestant churches in the development of Latin American Christianity. It is only on the basis of an understanding of this history that we can understand the genuine missionary élan that now animates — and divides — many Latin American churches.[1]

No one standing within, or seeking information about, the present-day missionary movement in Latin America can forget that the mission history of Latin America bears the marks of ethnocide.[2] Generally speaking, Catholic missionaries did not come to the region they were to name

---

1. For more thorough treatments see E. Dussel, *A History of the Church in Latin America: Colonialism to Liberation (1492-1979)* (Grand Rapids, 1981); P. Richard, *Death of Christendom, Birth of the Church: Historical Analysis and Theological Interpretation of the Church in Latin America* (Maryknoll, 1987); and H. J. Prien, *Die Geschichte des Christentums in Lateinamerika* (Göttingen, 1978). These studies serve as a good introduction to the ambitious series *Historia General de la Iglesia en America Latina*, published by the Comision De Estudios De Historia De La Iglesia en America Latina (1985; see R. M. K. van der Grijp, "Kerkgeschiedenis schrijven in Latijns Amerika: een strijd tegen complexen, waanideeën, chantage," *Wereld en Zending* 12 [1983] 48-54). All these studies represent what is most relevant in regard to mission and consistently attempt to move beyond the kind of church history in which everything that happens outside Europe is viewed as and limited to an extension of European church history.

2. O. Maduro, "Notes for a South-North dialogue in Mission from a Latin American Perspective," *Missiology* 15/2 (April, 1987) 61-75.

America because they were called from within the "New World." They
came because they belonged to a culture that was materially, militarily,
and spiritually equipped to destroy the riches of the thousands of cultures
that flourished there. This overwhelming culture, with its extreme destructive potential, was that of the European elite, whose members were urban,
male, and wealthy. When it could find no better way, this elite imposed
its religious system by fire and sword. It built up a military, administrative,
commercial, and educational infrastructure in Latin America that was
totally foreign to the experiences and needs embodied in existing structures.

Catholic missions in Latin America were part and parcel of the
European machine of pillage. Slavery, the displacement and dismantling
of local communities, mass murder, torture, and extermination were all
made possible by the cooperation of military, civil, and ecclesiastical
leaders. There were exceptions, such as Montesino, Bartholomé de Las
Casas, Bishop Valdivieso, and the system of *reducciones*, which were self-
sufficient settlements directed by the religious orders and found mainly
in and around Paraguay. With these men and in these communities there
were departures from the dominant pattern, exceptions to the rule of
usurpation and oppression, eloquent in their protest and therefore often
subject to torture, imprisonment, or murder — with the consent and
cooperation of church authorities.[3] Generally the missionaries were the
sacral right hand of the European colonial enterprise in Indian America.

Fortunately, in sharp contrast to this mission history, a new way of
evangelization is coming to the fore. It is "new" even though it owes much
to the development of European aid, which began in the nineteenth century. It is strongly influenced by the ideas of Pope John XXIII, Vatican II,
and the World Council of Churches, and it is new because it owes much
to the documents of the Latin American bishops' conferences of Medellín
and Puebla,[4] to the base communities, and to contacts that Latin American
liberation theologians have had with theologians in the rest of the Third
World.[5] It is new most of all because of the power of the witness of its
martyrs. This newness in evangelization is best expressed in the phrase
"good news for the oppressed."

To grasp the full scope and depth of this new understanding of

3. M. Mörner, *The Expulsion of the Jesuits from Latin America* (New York, 1965).
4. *Medellin 1968: La Iglesia en la actual transformación de América Latina a la luz
del Concilio* (Bogotá 1968); *A Evangelizaçao no presente e no futuro da America Latina,
conclusoes. Puebla. Texto official da CNBB* (São Paulo, 1979).
5. J. van Nieuwenhove, "De vele contexten in de derde wereld: discussie over
bevrijdingtheologie onder derde wereld-theologen," *Tijdschrift voor Theologie* 27 (1987)
21-36.

evangelization would require a broader account than we are able to give of the earlier evangelization imposed on Latin America and of the manner in which the common people responded to this "official mission" with their own mission. This mission of the "little" people, which actually did spread the gospel, appears to be uninterruptedly continued in today's base communities and explains to some degree why evangelical Protestant movements have found such fertile soil in Latin America. Evangelization in Latin America today can best be studied in the framework of the still all-determining relationships between church and state and between "Christianity" and "new Christianity."[6]

Our purpose here is to show how out of the crisis of "new Christianity" a new way of doing and understanding mission is being worked out. Its agents and carriers are no longer the movements that in the 1960s went down to defeat along with Catholic Action. Its creative forces are located especially in the base pastorate, which to a degree is turning the Catholic Church into a church of the people, which speaks most eloquently in the base communities, and which challenges both Catholic and Protestant churches. In their missionary impulse the base communities receive indispensable support from many theologians who advance their work in and through liberation theology. This theology is a specifically missionary theology and is also the first real Latin American and ecumenical theology. But we cannot conclude this introduction without referring briefly to that other Catholic missionary movement which bills itself as "the theology of reconciliation" and which, with strong support from the Vatican, is manifesting itself in numerous new movements.

The key concept in Pablo Richard's historical analysis is "Christendom," defined as a "particular kind of relationship between the *church* and *civil society*," a relationship in which the state is the primary agent of mediation.[7] In the course of history "Christendom" has had various faces. On the basis of this concept Richard divides history into three periods, which we will follow in the next three subsections.

---

6. E. Hoornaert, *Historia da Igreja no Brasil. Ensaio de interpretaçao a partir do Povo* (Petropolis, 1979); J. Rietveld, *O senhor gosta d'aqui* (Heerlen, 1984); R. van der Ploeg, *Bevrijding en Bekering: over de optie van de Latijnsamerikaanse kerk voor de armen* (Utrecht, 1982).

7. In this section we draw primarily on the work of Hoornaert and on P. Richard's outstanding interdisciplinary work (see n. 1 above), which is fundamental to our view of evangelization in Latin America.

Colonial Christianity: 1492-1808

Latin American history of this early period can be viewed from the stand-point of "Catholic feudalism." But from the conquest on, because of the riches of its resources, Latin America was caught up in the development of mercantile capitalism, that is, in the domination of foreign capital. Increasingly dependent Latin America saw the development of its class structure within the context of that capitalism. Richard lists four social classes:

- those bound together by vague and contradictory capitalistic pro-duction relationships,
- those bound together by vague and contradictory feudal and pre-capitalistic production relationships,
- the dominant classes, those linked to the development of an auton-omous or national capitalism, and
- those who were marginalized and exploited.

The fundamental contrast was not between the first and second of these classes but between the first three and the fourth.

Colonial Christianity had to define its Christian and social specificity within the context of the alternatives of oppression and liberation, but it did not do this with any finality. Consequently it bears the marks of both integra-tion with and resistance to the state. "Christendom" was marked by capital-ism, dependence, and class contrasts mediated by the state. Integration was marked by royal patronage. The manner in which the Jesuits championed the cause of the Indians by isolating and protecting them as much as possible in their own societies, the *reducciones*, constitutes the best example of resistance. In the end, in 1759, the Jesuits, too, had to yield to the state.

"New Christianity": 1808-1960

When in the first decades of the nineteenth century Latin American coun-tries achieved independence, colonial Christendom entered a crisis be-cause it had always been bound to Spain and Portugal. The church was not rejected, but its linkage with the colonial powers was.

The independent states had four broad groups of people:

- conservatives, who wanted to preserve the links with the mother country, i.e., the landed aristocracy and those who monopolized agrarian trade,

- liberals who exchanged dependence on Spain and Portugal for dependence on British capitalism and who therefore favored free trade, consisting especially of the mining interests and the petty bourgeoisie,
- liberals who advocated complete independence and fought for autonomous national development, including the rising artisans, and
- the dominated, exploited, and marginalized Amerindians, blacks, poor whites, and those of mixed race.

The new states began to use the church to legitimate themselves and to foster national unity. Catholicism became the state religion and royal patronage was converted, without Vatican involvement, into national patronage. In the second half of the nineteenth century the struggle among the four groups just named was won by the second, the bourgeoisie, those who wanted to become integrated further into the free market capitalistic system, which was oriented to the export of raw materials.

"Christendom" disintegrated and went in search of a new identity. Almost every state had its "religious issue" brought by a church seeking greater independence but accustomed to being under state domination.[8] Since most of the new states pursued development on the model of European positivism, the ecclesiastical world was labeled "anti-scientific" and "Christendom" became something of the past. Few church people welcomed the separation of church and state, and they did not join with the array of popular movements that were resisting the modernization process. Church leadership was fixated on safeguarding the privileges of the church and on the political coalitions that could guarantee those privileges.[9] With the aid of numerous European orders and congregations Rome was Romanizing the churches, and this process was strongly favored by Latin American church leaders, who understood that where the church could no longer lean on the state, it needed the people in order to have a voice in the affairs of the state.

Generally speaking, Latin American churches were on the defensive — against rising Protestantism and against the liberalism and positivism of the oligarchy, which was dependent on international capitalism to buy its agricultural exports. In the 1930s capitalism entered a crisis and the United States replaced Britain as the major market. Industrialization began

8. Some sort of "religious issue" appeared in practically all Latin American countries the moment Latin American bishops trained in Europe began to experience as negative the subordination of the church to a variety of secular societies. A similar "religious issue" marks the Romanization of the Latin American churches.

9. Dussel, *History,* 117-23.

in various places in Latin America, which resulted in the rise of a new middle class. The church allied itself with this new class and so reinforced its position in society.

The period from 1930 to 1955 was marked by populism. In opposition to the large landowners, political leaders sought popular support for their industrialization policies. The church's alliance with these leaders won it a number of rights, including education subsidies, religious education in all schools, and recognition of church marriages. This alliance strengthened both church and populist state in their struggles against Marxism, atheism, and Protestantism.

But in the church itself there was much disunity. An "integralist" school of thought disagreed with the subordinate place of the church and of Christian culture, and "social Christianity" (Maritain) sought to make believers into apostles in their own setting. "Social Christianity" was promoted by a variety of Catholic Action groups.[10] Through these channels the church leadership gained contact with the views of the middle class on social and political problems and "new Christianity" reached its high point. The "problems of development" became a fixed point on the church's agenda.

The socialist alternative that took shape in Cuba pushed the Christian social alternative to such lengths that it faded away. Radicalizing groups within Catholic Action sought radical social reforms and rejected "Catholic social doctrine" as inadequate. Their focus shifted from the social to the political, with the faith remaining as the ultimate meaning of history.

The Latin American Catholic churches led even their European sister churches in the formation of a new kind of organization, that of the national bishops' conferences. Thereby they created a new instrument for operating nationally and especially for addressing national problems. The national bishops' conferences were brought together in the Latin American bishops' conferences, the first such meeting occurring in 1955 in Rio de Janeiro.

In the feverish Latin America of the 1960s, "new Christianity" proved to have opened itself up to social issues. But it continued to cling to a Christian-influenced development orientation, which viewed itself as supplementary to what the state was doing or should be doing. As a result "new Christianity" entered a deep crisis.[11]

---

10. J. O. Beozzo, "A Igreja entre a revoluçao de '30 e a redemocratiçao (1930-1945)," in *Historia Geral de Civilizaçao Brasileira* II (1984) 304-17; E. de Kadt, *Catholic Radicals in Brazil* (New York, 1970); cf. above, pp. 112-15.
11. Richards, *op. cit.*, 128ff.; Dussel, *op. cit.*, 137ff.

The Crisis of New Christianity: 1964-78

As a result of that crisis, imposed by reality and by the polarized Christian response to that reality, "new Christianity" began to vanish and in its place came a church with a face of its own, free from the state. Typical of this process was the second general assembly of the Latin American Bishops' Conference in 1968 in the Colombian city of Medellín. The existence of military dictatorships accelerated this process, confronting the church with the choice between submission and resistance.

Elsewhere in this volume we have described at some length the crisis of "new Christianity" and the deepening conflict between the military state and the oppressed, specifically in Brazil (chapter 7 above). There we noted that out of the church's internal conflicts experienced in its confrontation with social and political reality a church originated that was close to the problems of the people.[12]

Similar developments occurred in other Latin American countries, however different the patterns of church-state relations may have been. One important difference among Latin American churches arose from the way in which assistance from the European church led to a sort of "Roman restoration," by which churches such as those of Chile and Peru were much more heavily influenced than those of Colombia, Argentina, or Central America. This assistance, accompanied by an increasingly strong emphasis on the social relevance of the church and consequently resulting in new relations with emerging groups, now determined the measure of openness to the movements generated in the 1970s by liberation theology.

Protestant Christianity

In the period of "Christendom" Protestant churches were kept from developing in Latin America outside Western European settlements in the Caribbean. In the nineteenth century, the century of mission for Protestant churches, Latin America was not considered an appropriate sphere of activity for Protestant mission. Immigrants, especially in Chile, Argentina, Uruguay, and southern Brazil, founded the first Protestant churches in Latin America, but limited their churches to their own people. Most Latin American governments eagerly enlisted the aid of English-speaking — and therefore Protestant — educational institutions, which they deemed more useful for the modernization of Latin America than Catholic insti-

---

12. Cf. R. van Rossum and J. van Engelen, *Kerk op zoek naar haar volk: Braziliaanse reisnotities* (Baarn, 1976) 49-75.

tutions, which generally followed French models and had students from among the traditional elite. Individual Latin Americans who found their own way into Protestantism were as Latin Americans spiritually far removed from the immigrant churches and from the Presbyterian, Methodist, and Anglican middle-class churches in the larger cities.[13]

But already early in the twentieth century, Pentecostalism took shape in the Assembleias de Deus in Chile and Brazil.[14] (This strongly missionary form of popular Protestantism should not be simply lumped together with the North American Pentecostal sects that began to be active in Latin America especially after World War II.) As the Pentecostal churches developed, North American churches had fewer scruples about doing mission work in Latin America than European churches, to which Latin America still remained a Catholic "backyard." North Americans saw the Latin American world as an extension of their own continent. John Mackay's *The Other Spanish Christ: A Study in the Spiritual History of Spain and South America*, which appeared in English in 1932 and in Spanish in 1933, quieted many Protestant misgivings. It furnished a legitimation that went much deeper and is much more authentic than the shallow post–World War II fear of Communism. When the curtain dropped on China as a huge mission field, Latin America for the first time really came to the attention of many mission movements. The parallel with the interest shown by the Vatican in Latin America is more than striking.

It was of great importance for the reception of Protestant mission initiatives after World War II that the old immigrant Protestant churches were now integrated into the Latin American world enough to furnish at least some form of guidance — even theological guidance — to these Protestant initiatives and to find their way to the international platforms of the World Council of Churches and of Reformed world organizations. The first Latin American appearance in such a forum occurred at the Church and Society meeting at Geneva in 1966. Since then the voices of Latin American Protestant Christians have been a self-evident contribution.[15]

13. E. Léonard, *O protestantismo brasileiro. Estudo de eclesiologia en historia social* (São Paulo, 1963); E. Conde, *Historia das Assembleias de Deus no Brasil* (Rio de Janeiro, 1960).

14. C. Lalive d'Epinay, *O refugio das masas. Estudo sociologico do protestantismo chileno* (Rio de Janeiro, 1970).

15. H. Borrat, "Der Einfluß des Protestantismus auf den Katholizismus aus katholischer Sicht," in *Explosives Lateinamerika* (Berlin, 1969); J. Míguez Bonino, *Doing Theology in a Revolutionary Situation* (Philadelphia, 1975); J. de Santa Ana, *Protestantismo, Cultura y Sociedad* (Buenos Aires, 1970).

Evangelization in Latin America Today

The missionary dimension in recent Latin American Catholic developments arises from the refusal of broad sectors in the Catholic Church to profit from or lean on the power of the state or on the socioeconomic and military groups that control the state. Instead, these Catholics seek out and lean on "the faith of the people," thus distancing themselves from "Christendom."

The missionary dimension in the historic Protestant churches has a different point of departure and a different perspective. They have been minority churches and have, each at its own time, sought genuine integration into the local culture. Their missionary perspective is focused on the development of a fully ecumenical church and on openness to those forms of folk Protestantism that, together with the Catholic base communities, are often the only Christian presence in the world of the poor that has grown up on the fringes of the large cities.

Latin American liberation theology, both Catholic and Protestant, renders invaluable service to the missionary development of what has been rightly called the "church from below." But Catholic Latin America still has many missionary groups that fundamentally cling to the old idea of "Christendom."

Medellín, 1968

The Medellín Conference was organized by CELAM[16] in order to apply the results of the Second Vatican Council to the churches of Latin America. Its members read the council decrees in the context of their own situation and in accordance with the pattern of Catholic Action: look — judge — act. The pastoral constitution *Gaudium et Spes* played a large role, as did the vow made by a number of bishops in the catacombs at Rome, by which they dedicated themselves to the cause of the poor.[17] Two things especially stand out in this vow:

16. The Conferencia Episcopal Latinoamericana (CELAM) was founded in Rio de Janeiro in 1955 under the impetus of Msgr. Montini (later Pope Paul VI) and Dom Helder Camara. Use was made of the organization of the thirty-sixth International Eucharistic Congress, a typically Catholic device for bringing masses of people together. The original purpose of CELAM was to save Latin America for Catholicism against the threats of Communism and Protestantism.

17. H. J. Prien, *Die Geschichte des Christentums in Lateinamerika* (Göttingen, 1978) 895-906, presents a fine overview of the reception of Vatican II in Latin America and how it prepared the way for Medellín.

- In the light of the gospel the bishops no longer read the Latin American situation from a European frame of reference, according to which one said, "For some reason we are underdeveloped; how, then, can we link up with development so that we ourselves can become developed?" Now the situation was read from this perspective: "We are kept in a state of economic, social, and political dependence, and that dependence does not give us space to build a just society."
- And in regard to the question of the Church's action, the answer had come to be: The ideal pastor is not the agent of development, not one who follows a European or American model, but one who releases the energies of the people, one who liberates, one who turns the people themselves into agents of faith.

It was especially these two changes in perspective that began to operate at Medellín. The pathos of Medellín was as important as its papers, and what was of the greatest weight pastorally was that the voice that came through was that of Latin America itself, a voice in accord with the ancient mystical tradition of the New World in which the Church presents itself as the protector of the Indians — the protector *and spokesperson* for the "little ones."[18]

Thus Medellín, more implicitly than explicitly, bade farewell to the old harmonization of opposites, to the basic adherence to European notions of progress. That farewell came just when the reform governments of the early 1960s, which felt threatened by Cuba, were succeeded by a variety of military governments, which no longer read their mandate as one of development, but as one of security in the face of mostly internal enemies. The armies saw themselves as the voices of true national interest and to that end gave free rein to the technocrats, to the exclusion of the people.

After Medellín two realities met: the spiritual reality of the church in search of the people and the sociopolitical reality of the regimes of national security, which repelled the people. Thus, to a degree much greater than Medellín ever foresaw, the Church became a place of freedom, an open space where people could make their own voices heard. And so, again to a degree much greater than Medellín ever thought, the Church found itself positioned against the national security state and against groups that supported the state.[19]

---

18. J. Comblin, "Notas sobre el documento básico para la II Conferencia General del Celam," *CM* 17 (1968) 47-59.

19. J. Comblin, *Le pouvoir militaire en Amérique Latine: l'idéologie de la sécurité nationale* (Paris, 1977).

These developments were represented in a letter from the bishops and religious superiors of northeastern Brazil titled "I have Heard the Cry of My People."[20] The major decision represented by the letter was this: *Before we listen to any other, we will listen to the poor. Of what use is that security or development to them? That is what we will tell the pharaohs of this day. And like Moses those pharaohs will tell us: "Were you not on our side? You have even betrayed your brothers." And like him we must acknowledge that history and, nevertheless, join the people in their exodus.*

The Consequences of Medellín for Pastoral Work

In the parishes Medellín — together with the sociopolitical realities — decreased confidence in the kind of pastorate that did things *for* people but little *with* people other than those whom the pastors identified with, that is, the middle classes. It also decreased anxiety over getting around to administration of the sacraments, which had locked the small number of clergy into a narrow round of activity. There was now courage to set standards of formation and understanding for administration of the sacraments, recognition of the success that sects had had with the Bible among the common people, and less fear of the religiosity of the people.

The social pastorate, the sacrament joined to evangelization, and folk religion, all together, bring the pastorate into a new world of experience and understanding. And all this is beginning to work. The pastorate is now seeking to view itself as an offer of aid to the faith of the common people. A certain way of believing, a way — one that belongs to the people — of understanding and expressing the faith not only in verbal explanations but also in gestures and symbols, is permitted to thrust itself on the pastors.

Folk life in Latin America has a strongly collective character and its own historic consciousness. It understands itself as the heir of a long process of suffering and exploitation and of a barely successful struggle for existence. Faith experienced and expressed in this context has its own way of articulating the experience of God, in which God is not *my* God, the God of my internal spiritual life, but the God of the people, the God of the poor, the one who leads and accompanies God's people through history, who loves them and gives them life in a concrete sense. This articulation of religious experience does not refer to a supernatural life that is simply added on to normal human life. On the contrary, it views and experiences all of life as the place of encounter with God.

20. *Catholic Mind* 72 (1974) 39-64.

How can such a manner of life, such a language of faith, and such a way of believing become the possession of the pastor as well? That came to be the call and challenge of the pastorate, and the Bible played an enormous role in this learning process. Through this kind of pastorate the poor make the gospel their own.[21] That is to say, during the celebration of the eucharist and the observance of the other sacraments they do not merely listen to a few short passages of the gospel along with the priests' explanations. The people themselves, groups of young people and groups of adults, actively take hold of the gospel and read the story of Jesus as the story of someone who lived at a certain time and in a certain historical, social, religious, and cultural setting, who lived among the people, who took risks, and who made concrete choices in relation to those who held religious or military power.

The common people are in the process of discovering all this. They do not oppose the Jesus of history to the Christ of faith, as is done in European exegetical and theological schools. The background of their discovery is rather their traditional faith in the mysterious depth of the person of Jesus. Against that background they are discovering a new and liberating insight, one that gives them much joy: They are so close to that Jesus, who lived in situations very much like their own. He was born poor. He was one of the poor, simple, ignorant, and despised people. He preached a message of universal liberation — and did so with both feet on the ground. He did not need to go to the poor from the outside like the pastors, because he was born poor. He was one of the truly poor of this world. The people have been discovering this, and such a discovery is liberating. They feel they have good ground beneath their feet through their faith in Jesus Christ, who was poor like them, who is close to them, and who risked his life for them.

This confrontation of poor people with the gospel of Jesus, with the witness of his life, and with his way of being the Messiah and spokesman for his people is an important and new basis for pastoral care. It topples a good deal of theology and forces people to adopt a very different starting point. That is a problem not only for the Vatican but also for theologians and pastors in general.[22] The Brazilian episcopate is clearly aware of this, and these words from the introduction to the pastoral guidelines of 1982-85 of the Chilean Bishops' Conference speak volumes as well:

21. E. Cardinal, *The Gospel in Solentiname* (4 vols.; Maryknoll, 1976-82); C. Mesters, *God, Where Are You? Meditations on the Old Testament* (Maryknoll, 1972); *idem, Eden: Golden Age or Goad to Action* (Maryknoll, 1974).

22. See the Vatican documents *Libertatis Nuntius* (1984) and *Libertatis Conscientia* (1986). Cf. M. Greinachter, *Konflikt um die Theologie der Befreiung. Diskussion und Dokumentation* (Zurich, 1985).

The theological line of action for these pastoral directives is based on the historical Jesus, on his way of evangelizing, on his preference of the poor, and on his manner in relation to conflicts in the society of his time. This constant reference to the person, manner, and history of Jesus is the basis for unity in the actions of the church in its entirety.

In this official document of the Chilean church, the authors repeated what many pastors had long known: that this choice makes heavy demands on the church. In this way the pastors attested to their endorsement of the cause of the poor, that is, of what comes out of that complex of values and aspirations present in the heart of the people as they look toward the creation of a new society, of a new way of structuring life in society.

For the pastors themselves all this points to a challenge to be genuine carriers of the Good News of Jesus to the poor, not only in sermons better adapted to the audience but also, and much more, by a manner of life that has again become credible to the poor in their situations of life-or-death struggle. It calls for a pastorate of the concrete gesture, that is, of the decision to live among the people. This gesture makes it possible for the people to say: "The pastors are really in earnest." There are groups of pastors doing just this and also asking their congregations, their dioceses, and the Church to follow them.

The issue for pastors is not just to work *for* the poor. They actually go to the poor, try to understand them from the inside, their world with all the cultural injustices it embraces, and the human, cultural, and religious values peculiar to that world. The farther one goes on this road, the better one grasps the pastoral task and does it differently. One thus understands that it is not just that the pastors instruct the people: The people themselves are where God is present. The goal is not to establish a base church, a people's church as opposed to an official and hierarchical church. The goal is to view the whole church from the ecclesiological standpoint of the poor.[23] Or in the words of Puebla: "As bishops we must more deliberately put ourselves in the service of that entire movement of faith, of the concrete love of neighbor that the Spirit prompts in us, prompts in our people and gives them depth. Jesus Christ is present in his church, especially among the poorest."[24]

---

23. C. Mesters, *Zending van een volk dat lijdt* (Nijmegen); R. Muñoz, *Evangelho e Libertação na América Latina. A teologia pastoral de Puebla* (São Paulo, 1981).

24. *Puebla and Beyond: Documentation and Commentary*, ed. J. Eagleson and P. Scharper (Maryknoll, 1979) 69.

Puebla

The effects of Medellín called forth such contradictory responses in both Church and society that the third meeting of the bishops' conference, planned for 1978 but actually assembled in 1979 in Puebla, Mexico, was eagerly anticipated. Already at the intervening meeting in San José, Costa Rica, in 1973 the bylaws had — partly at the instigation of the papal commission for Latin America — been so altered that in 1972 the conservative Colombian bishop Lopez Trujillo was elected secretary general. Gradually most parts of the Church in Latin America were brought under the conservative spell of Bogota. There was clearly an attempt to restructure the orientation of Medellín.[25]

The opening address of Pope Paul John II at Puebla also left little room for misunderstanding. He opposed any genuine representation from the Conference of Latin American Religious (CLAR) or of any liberation theology. But representatives of both were present, and their ties with the bishops were strong enough to prevent the conference from explicitly restructuring Medellín and from condemning liberation theology or the base communities. The texts of the conference were better than expected, though significant alterations were made in the offices of the Vatican.

Since Puebla the leadership of CELAM has been waging a struggle against liberation theology and against the church from below. Within Latin American Catholicism CELAM has become an tool of restoration. The distance that the Brazilian episcopate maintains toward CELAM is significant.[26]

Santo Domingo

On the island where Columbus landed in 1492, CELAM held its fourth general assembly in 1992 on the theme of "The New Evangelism." A heated debate took place regarding the initial evangelism of 500 years earlier. Some wanted to leave the past for what it was and concentrate on the so-called Latin American Catholic substratum, which, it was felt, is threatened by new cultural developments. Others were concerned to em-

25. Fr. Houtart, "A Historia do CELAM ou a Esquecimento das origens," *Revista Eclesiastica Brasileira* 47 (1987) 655-65 (in French in *Archives de Sciences Sociales des Religions* 62 [1986] 93-105).

26. This is the background of the Vatican's banning of L. Boff's *Church: Charism and Power. Liberation Theology and the Institutional Church* (New York, 1985).

phasize the abiding importance of discussing that past, the shortchanging of Indians and African Americans, and the concept of evangelism in a multicultural America. The closing document of the assembly offers an unworkable mixture of these two points of view, but also recognizes in the paragraph on inculturation the Indian and African contributions to Latin American life and society.

The Base Communities

The missionary development that is coursing through Latin American churches is most dramatic in the base communities. Often stimulated from within missionary parishes, the base communities themselves have conveyed important missionary impulses back to the parishes.[27]

The six national conferences of ecclesial base communities held from 1975 to 1986 brought into view the interplay between sociopolitical changes and developments in the base communities as they read and assimilated "the signs of the times."[28] Leonardo Boff's work has been fundamental in Brazil, as has Gutiérrez's in Peru, Sobrino's in Central America, and Muñoz's in Chile. Rover van der Ploeg has spoken of the base communities, in the course of a theological assessment of the ecclesial praxis of the poor, as "a true feast of tabernacles":

> One could say that the embryonic phase is past. The ecclesial base communities have been born. Thank God they were born healthy: They belong totally to Jesus Christ. Now we also know whether it is a baby boy or a baby girl that was born. It turned out to be a baby girl! The ecclesial communities are female on account of their composition — certainly 75% of their active members are women — and on account of their manner of existence: religious and testifying to an unshakable faith and a tenacious struggle for the protection of life.
>
> At the same time these ecclesial base communities are to a high

27. The best Protestant book on the ecclesial base communities, G. Cook's *The Expectation of the Poor: Latin American Base Ecclesial Communities in Protestant Perspective* (Maryknoll, 1985), is written from an emphatically missionary perspective. See also CNBB, *Communidades eclesiais de base no Brasil* (Estudos da CNBB 23; São Paulo, 1984); G. Deelen, *Kirche auf dem Weg zum Volke. Soziologische Betrachtungen über kirchliche Basisgemeinde in Brasiliën* (Mettingen, 1981); J. van Nieuwenhove, "Kerkelijke basisgemeenschap in Brazilië," in J. van Lin, ed., *Parochie en gemeenschap* (Hilversum, 1987) 74-97; Rogier van Rossum, "Basispastoraat in Brazilië. Parochie en kerkelijke basisgemeenschap," *Wereld en Zending* 16 (1987) 134-43.

28. B. K. Goldewijk, "De zes landelijke bijeenkomsten van de kerkelijke basisgemeenschap in Brazilië, 1975-1986," *Wereld en Zending* 16 (1987) 154-63.

degree — and it is well to take a sober look at this reality — newborn children. They are still to a significant degree dependent on the presence and investment of pastoral workers, theologians, and bishops who nurture them and attempt to shape their future direction. The joy with which they are incorporated into pastoral planning on all levels — from the parish to the episcopal conferences — could well be the euphoric joy of new parents, a joy that will pass as the child grows up and tries to find its own way as an ecclesial base community with an autonomous leadership exercised by the people themselves. We still know a few adolescent ecclesial base communities that give their parents trouble because they have an outside friend whom dad does not like and because they want a more fraternal relationship at home, in which there would no longer be "parents" or "fathers," but all would be brothers and sisters, laypersons, members of the same "laos," the people of God. The word "Father" would be used only of the Heavenly Father (Matt. 23:9).[29]

By means of this comparison Van der Ploeg seeks to clarify the believing political activism of the communities themselves and the problems of priestly leadership — subjects left virtually undiscussed in Latin America itself.

It would take us too far afield to mention all those institutions and movements with which the Latin American church equipped itself from the late 1960s and beyond in order to guarantee the depth and continuity of its own missionary impulses. It exchanged complete dependence on European churches for a creativity of its own which then crossed the boundaries of the continent. An indigenous pastorate to the Indian population in the Andes was created, as was the CIMI (mission councils for the Indians), Operation Anchieta, the committees for human rights, rural pastorates, and the vicariates of solidarity. What had been brought from Europe was also restuctured. All this represents the unique vitality of the Latin American Catholic Church. In just a few years European and North American churches became followers instead of leaders.

The Protestant Churches

The short history of the Protestant churches explains much of the ambivalence that the Catholic evangelization movement (which is not a separate activity but the church's lifeline) feels in regard to Protestants: Cath-

29. Rover van der Ploeg, "De basisgemeenschappen in Trinidade. Een waarachtig loofhuttenfeest," *Wereld en Zending* 16 (1987) 105-14.

olic missionaries are delighted because they recognize so much of what they see, but they also feel uneasy.[30]

The success of the historic Protestant churches has been connected with the rise of their converts on the social ladder, which has been visible to all. The same thing happened more collectively with the second and third generations of transplanted ethnic churches. Protestant churches typically became middle-class. Fortunately, they were pulled along in the 1960s by their connection with the World Council of Churches and the great Protestant world federations with their theological and other programs. These associations were the context of fruitful debate with Catholics on the global agenda of Christianity, while at the same time the church in Latin America was taken by surprise from below — by ordinary believing people and their disbelief in the modernizing, development, and secularization schemes of the wider world.

It was not just the middle-class character of the Protestant churches that made it difficult for them to share in each other's lives and programs. It also seemed that the legitimacy of being a Protestant church in Latin America was itself at stake. Protestant leaders were staring, so to speak, into the same dark hole into which many European Catholic Church workers were looking. With their superior knowledge of the faith and their superior methods of service they felt taken by surprise by a "political church," a "church from below," not to say "a pre-Enlightenment church."

Stagnation is as much a threat for these Protestant churches as it is for the middle-class segment in the Catholic Church, the segment that knows itself to be out of the limelight. In a continent kept underdeveloped like Latin America, the middle groups generally remain at a great distance from their "natural" position. Because they are constantly threatened socioeconomically, middle-class Christians naturally feel more attracted to spiritual revival movements. It is they who keep Protestant churches away from any real contact with the Pentecostal Assembleias de Deus, which, as already stated, are the only groups other than the Catholic base communities with any relevance in the slums, where mediumistic religions and an array of sects seem to attract the religious element.

Granted: Real contact cannot be forced. As a reaction to a Protestantism that is strongly intellectual and organized and has salaried ministers and numerous social and educational institutions, Pentecostal churches remain genuine base groups. Since they have no "pastoral mediation," they have direct access to the means of grace. Their future lies in folk Catholicism, though the Pentecostal movement will never acknowledge it because it lives from pronounced differences: their use of the Bible and a

---

30. Prien, *Geschichte*, 1128-53.

strong ethical opposition to a worldly existence. But however vigorously Pentecostal movements distance themselves from Catholicism, it often seems easier to understand their religious culture with all its ethical rigorism on the personal plane from within folk Catholicism than from the perspective of the Protestant churches that developed in the nineteenth century. The bridge between Pentecostals and folk Catholicism is a biblicism with affinities with a fundamentalist way of handling the Bible. Both Catholic and Protestant observers regard a more contextual handling of the Word of God as the proper missionary perspective for Latin American churches; though still a future perspective for the churches themselves, this is for numerous individual Protestants a part of their own understanding.

Haan, summarizing Cook's conclusions, writes:

> Mission theology, in true Protestant fashion, must start from God's action in history, and from Scripture, the church, and the world. Fundamentalist Protestantism operates with too narrow a concept of Scripture. The Reformation never intended by "sola scriptura" to make the Bible into "a sealed and impregnable box containing all the changeless truths that we ought to know about the life and mission of the church." Traditional Catholicism and Protestant church institutionalism, added to prevailing church growth thinking, absolutize the church as a starting point. A secular theology that takes its point of departure exclusively in the world also fails to meet the demands of the "holistic mission theology" we need.[31]

For Protestants the emphasis in this connection will lie on the Spirit.

> Not until we are willing to let the Spirit work freely — not only in our personal lives, but also in far-reaching ecclesial change — and not until we can make ourselves recognize that the Spirit is working within movements of social change (even those that do not bear a specifically Christian name), shall we begin to understand the vastness and complexity of the Spirit's work and attempt to be a part of it. This too is a lesson we are learning through the Catholic grassroots communities.[32]

In the ecumenical circle that publishes the Brazilian periodical *Estudios Biblicos* this lesson has been clearly practiced, just as Míguez Bonino has carried it on for years in his theological work. This work of patient labor, maintained both by genuine contact with "the faith of the people" and by the support it receives from the worldwide ecumenical movement, demonstrates the importance of these relationships for an

31. R. Haan, *Wereld en Zending* 16 (1987) 179f.
32. Cook, *Expectation*, 233f.

undeniably necessary Protestant presence. Alves is missing this openness to relationships in his own keen inquiry.[33]

"New Christianity"

An initial introduction to "Evangelization in Latin America" cannot be complete without some reference to a very different missionary movement within the Catholic Church in Latin America, one that in principle seeks to adhere to the ideal of the "new Christianity." It receives strong support from the Vatican and is carried forward in the main by the so-called "new movements."

The beginning and goal of this movement is the church with its historic position in Latin America viewed as an Iberian society. It is the old "Spanish" position that, by contrast with an "indigenistic" position, continues to view Latin America as an extension of European Catholic culture. Its advocates believe that, notwithstanding this, they will never — unless it be incidentally — regard the Indian cultures negatively. After all, they say, the Church always championed the cause of the Indians. They repudiate the violent character of Iberian colonization just as they reject the whole of liberation theology. Their emphasis lies wholly on the historically integrative role of the Catholic Church. Even more strongly: They locate the Church outside this history and thus see it as functioning best as the bearer of *hispanidad* in its several national variations. Accordingly, the Church at bottom has a confirming and harmonizing role — even with regard to the popular values enshrined in traditional Catholicism.

The architect of this approach is the extremely competent Colombian cardinal Lopez Trujillo, who, after its initially progressive period, managed to swing the top leadership of CELAM his way. With the support of the Vatican Trujillo was able not only to bring his opposition to the level of the whole Church but also, through congresses, to equip it with a counter-theology, the "theology of reconciliation," which embraces many elements from Catholic social doctrine. Nicaragua was made a showcase of this ecclesiastical counter-policy.

Because the Latin American religious, united in CLAR *(Conferencia Latina Americana dos Religiosos)*, have been written off for such a missionary offensive, they lean heavily on lay movements such as Opus Dei, the work of Schönstadt, Comunhão e Libertação, and others. More spiritual movements, like those of the Cursilhos, the Neocatechumenate, and the Focolare move-

---

33. R. A. Alves, *Protestantism and Repression: A Brazilian Case Study* (New York, 1985).

ment, easily link up with the religious. In the Italian paper *Trenta Giorni* (with editions in Spanish and Portuguese) they have created a network of international relationships. In that way they were able, in February 1987, to set the tone and direction of the Roman congress convened to prepare the synod on "the layperson in the church."[34] During the 1992 CELAM gathering in Santo Domingo, Opus Dei managed to have a hispanic point of view incorporated into the historical section of the final document and to prevent the inclusion in it of any reference to the missionary method so dear to the heart of the contemporary Latin American church: observe — judge — act.

Liberation Theology

In the preceding section on missionary developments I have attempted to bring out — entirely within the modus operandi and self-understanding of liberation theology — how theology as thought about liberation originates, what its locus and laboratory is, and in what learning process it is caught up. It is not the theology of the seminary or the university.[35]

Liberation theology views itself as believing reflection on the reality and historic action of the people of God, which carries the work of Jesus forward in the proclamation and realization of the kingdom of God. In its self-understanding liberation theology is an act of the people of God, who as disciples of Jesus seek to follow him and together with him attempt to bring the world of God into living contact with the world of humanity. The reflective character of liberation theology does not deprive it of being an *act* of the people of God. Liberation theology is rooted in historical events and seeks to lead to historical events. It lives from the conviction of faith that God is present among the people, especially among the people of God.

In that way it recalls the primacy of the future, the primacy of expectation. The gospel is meaningful only to one who lives in the future and in terms of the future, one who lives from expectation, the expectation of a new world. First comes hope, then faith, since the gospel gives evi-

34. J. Comblin, "Os 'movimentos' e a pastoral latino-americana," *REB* 43 (1983) 227-62.

35. L. Boff and C. Boff, *Introducing Liberation Theology* (Maryknoll, 1987), offers, in the words of its authors, "an overall, non-technical, and objective account of this new way of 'doing theology' " (xi). T. Witvliet, *A Place in the Sun: Liberation Theology in the Third World* (Maryknoll, 1985), is written out of a sense of Western vulnerability and in the context of the continuation of world mission. A good introduction to this theology is *The People of God Amidst the Poor,* edited by L. Boff and V. Elizondo, with contributions by Boff, P. Richard, E. Dussel, G. Gutiérrez, and E. Schillebeeckx (Concilium; Edinburgh, 1984). A special issue of *Tijdschrift voor Theologie* (27/1 [1987]) considers among other things the possible significance of liberation theology for the practice of theology in Europe.

dence of itself on the basis of hope. Faith exists as affirmation of the true significance of the signs of the kingdom of God.

Accordingly, liberation theology distances itself from the "Greek tradition" in theology, a tradition that leads one away from the historic course of the Word of God, as though God had disclosed a number of abstract "truths" — information about hidden realities with which faith establishes a connection. We note this distancing from that tradition not only in the work of Gutiérrez, the father of liberation theology, but also in the church history of Dussel, Hoornaert, and Richard. But what comes into view first for us in the North Atlantic countries is liberation theology's critique of ideology, the assistance of Marxism in that critique, and the distance that liberation theology goes beyond European political theology.

To European eyes Latin American liberation theology offers an almost impossible synthesis of premodern and modern thought. In this chapter's sketch of developments in the missionary pastorate, I have deliberately taken pains to show how God's action in the world — to us a premodern element — and group solidarity are of decisive significance and how such a faith is the motor of social liberation. In "the wisdom of the people" God is not insensitive to the suffering of the people. We are dealing here with the capacity — which seems "pre-Enlightenment to our minds — the religious capacity to see real suffering in the light of the God who really exists and acts." "God provokes resistance." The God of human life provokes the preferential option for the poor.

This inclusive manner of thinking has been adopted by liberation theology and developed into a transformative consciousness. The religion of the poor is shown a way toward a religion that liberates. Bonds of oppression and dependence are being cast off. The poor must view themselves as a class and must bring forth from within themselves the emotional, ethical, and religious forces that will enable them to be strong and to resist. People for whom suffering is a way of life must become agents of change.

In this context Marxism has been of service by teaching that human thinking is always situated in a socioeconomic setting and is a reflection of tensions in society, and this is also true for religious thinking. A religiously estranged consciousness can only become a liberated consciousness when it engages in the praxis that seeks the economic basis for misery. In this respect the ideologically conditioned folk religion promoted by the rich has not been spared. The mystification that God is a God of the rich is being punctured theologically.

In the nature of the case such theological work is not done in an ivory tower. We have seen how, in order to serve the cause of God and the poor, pastors have to enter the world of the poor and from within that world read and interpret the gospel — and so risk a break with what has been.

CHAPTER 23

Latin American Liberation Theology

F. VAN DER HOFF

Talking and writing about Latin American liberation theology is a precarious undertaking, one that easily degenerates into vague generalities. Just what are we talking about —

- the theological reflections of academically trained theologians, of which there are fortunately many in liberation theology,
- the many informal and formal reflections of Christian base communities, based on and animated by their experiences, or
- reflections, photocopied over and over, by church staffs involved in base pastorates in the slums or in the mountains with Indian peasants?

Of course there are connections between these, and a good academic theologian will not be able to construct a decent reflection without being in touch with the many forms of base level work. Furthermore, even the academic theologian is limited and must work within self-imposed restrictions. Such a theologian will be the first to state that his or her theology is only the tip of the iceberg and has a different color from the great mass of ice below the surface.

But it is worthwhile to mention some of the characteristic features of this systematic liberation theology.[1] Liberation theology developed from within a new view of reality as it is seen through the eyes of oppressed people in the light of the gospel of Jesus. It is a view "from below," one that leads to a new way of understanding the Bible and to a reinterpretation of the Christian tradition in the service of liberating people to full

---

1. See further L. Boff and C. Boff, *Introducing Liberation Theology* (Maryknoll, 1987), select bibliography on pp. 97-99; R. M. Brown, *Theology in a New Key: Responding to Liberation Themes* (Philadelphia, 1978), annotated bibliography on pp. 199-208.

humanity. Accordingly, liberation theology differs in many respects from classical Western theology.

Liberation theology is marked by a pretheological step of gaining direct knowledge of oppression by entering into solidarity with the poor and by a threefold method of mediation:

- the mediation of social analysis, aimed at gaining more insight into the situation of the poor,
- the mediation of biblical hermeneutics, aimed at gaining a clearer view of God's plan for humanity, especially the oppressed, and
- practical mediation to discover possible lines of action and involvement to move past situations of poverty and oppression in keeping with God's plan.

All this amounts to saying that there is no pure theology. The first action of theology is dedication and involvement. The second action, that of theological reflection, is focused on the first action. Then this praxis, once it has been reflected on, must lead to *renewed* commitment and involvement. A professional theologian can pursue liberation theology only on the basis of other levels of involvement and reflection — the sort of involvement that is carried out by pastoral workers (in pastoral theology) and by the oppressed and poor themselves, those who are the initial bearers of the liberation movement (in popular or folk theology).

Much that presents itself as biblical and Christian is viewed by liberation theologians with "hermeneutical suspicion." By setting the radical biblical demand for justice in the center, liberation theology finds many current theological interpretations wanting and sees them as so much ideological underpinning for the group or class interests of the powerful and rich. Still, to liberation theologians faith cannot be reduced to liberating action: Faith also includes "movements of contemplation and of profound thanksgiving." "Liberation theology also leads one up to the Temple. And from the Temple it leads back once more to the practice of history, now equipped with all the divine and divinizing powers of the Mystery of the world." And so, in the main, liberation theology is geared to action, "action for justice, the work of love, conversion, renewal of the church, transformation of society."[2] Beyond the very necessary "hermeneutic of suspicion" the theology of liberation develops a "hermeneutic of hope," leading to a hope for liberation, a hope that leads to fulfillment.[3]

It has often been said that the story of Latin American liberation

---

2. Boff and Boff, *op. cit.*, 39.
3. B. Melano Couch (an Argentine theologian) in Brown, *op. cit.*, 88f.

theology is like the story of coffee: Coffee-drinkers sometimes sniff revolutionary aromatic fragrances, often with no sense of where coffee comes from or of how it is produced by the labor and sweat of small coffee growers or picked on large plantations by poor and landless seasonal laborers. These laborers never see the profits made off their work. But even worse, they are the unknowns in the coffee-producing process, the anonymous mass of those who in harvest time trek through the mountains like an army of ants.

The real producers of liberation theologies, the good soil from which those theologies come, remain vague or obscured behind structural analyses of injustice, exploitation, and oppression, all of which are objectively true even while they remain subjects of those very structures and keep running on the treadmills of those structures. The producers and the original soil of liberation theology always have been and still are the believing and exploited people with all their baroque religious expressions. It is these believing and oppressed people (oppressed in all the various forms of being uprooted, impoverished, bullied, etc.) who come together in little groups (called lease communities) and organizations and dare to think and experience and sometimes blurt out: "God cares about us, and that not because we are so pathetic, but because, out of sheer grace, he is with us. He simply has his preference." That is what they hear and (sometimes) read in the tradition of their ancestors but also in the Bible and from each other. Pastors — bishops, priests, religious, and laypersons — and theologians who hear and see this run to their typewriters, not to fill up sheets of paper with this material (more mental and environmental pollution!) but to let the Spirit that they have jointly called forth shine through, to testify, often in academic terms, to what they have "seen and heard." When anyone writes this theology outside its actual lived context, that is absolutely dangerous to the believing people who are the ground out of which it grew: They are thus robbed of their product, just like the coffee workers, and others rake in the profit of their faith. That outcome has to be prevented.

Another, more internal, problem is that a kind of "clerical treason" is occurring in the treatment of Latin American liberation theology: Base communities and organizations are made dependent or kept dependent, but this time by progressive church politicians putting on revolutionary and demagogic airs. Theology as critical reflection on the faith as it is actually lived can easily lead to upside-down conclusions, the wish being the father of the thought. Writings on and surveys of liberation theology sometimes elicit the thought: "It would be nice if this were true on the grassroots level of believing, exploited people." In these writings *about* liberation theology one all too often misses the pathos of the faith of the people — and of the believing Latin American liberation theologian who at times has to correct and modify his or her own position and tune in again to the wavelength of ordinary believing people. To think for the people is and remains a sin against the second commandment. To love my neighbor and to make him dependent on my good intentions is a nice way of patronizing and controlling him, but certainly not the way to leave him free. Again, it is like the story of coffee: Among the middlemen there are nice people, even socially sensitive people. But keeping the growers in a state of dependence is something such middlemen view as necessary to the proper functioning of their profitable enterprise.

Sometimes, in speaking of Latin American liberation theology, people present it as a new way of doing theology, as something new under the ecclesiastical sun, as a new discovery or invention or a totally new approach. That is historically inaccurate. In Latin America there has been a long tradition of theologizing, even though, sometimes for centuries, it worked underground. Naturally there was also much imitation theology. But we can clearly distinguish three periods in which a Latin American theology containing elements of liberation came to the surface. These periods of theological production coincide with times of popular militancy. Accordingly, they are theologies that are clearly in contrast with theologies of domination and with rulers who preferred to ape Western theologies in their own manner and in their own interest.

The first creative moment was the movement of prophetic theology that began when the conquest of the continent began. The cry of oppressed and mistreated people, heard by Dominican monks, was made the subject of theological reflection. They remembered the ancient word: "And God heard the cry of his people." This theological labor was personified in Bartholomé de las Casas, but he was not its only representative. These monks were prophets and theologians who saw the suffering of the indigenous population and who gave a believing response to it. The cry — a theological category of the first order — was spelled out in words and accordingly became flesh.

The second era of theological creativity occurred in the period of national emancipation from European political domination. This tended to be a theology of political liberation.

The third period began with the crisis of the developmentalist model in the 1950s and 1960s. It is a theology in which the central focus is more explicitly that of liberation and in tone and thrust is even set forth as such.

Of essential importance in the several worthwhile historical investigations of this Latin American legacy is the "discovery" by church and theology of popular religiosity as a serious source of inspiration for Christian institutions and community. This has required a totally different way of evaluating and thinking on the part of theologians, one that gave liberation theologians difficulty at first, but which they have now clearly integrated into their own way of doing theology. The result is that the dangerously elitist character of liberation theology has been overcome.

Naturally this discovery is not devoid of danger for the believing and oppressed people. The dialogue with culture, with suppressed and accumulated religious thought, feeling, and action, with a popular Christian legacy, is not always conducted within the context of solidarity among the dialogue partners — academically trained theologians, pastors, *and* the impoverished people of the shanty towns and of the countryside — with all setting out with complete equality on a common journey, celebrating the faith. There have been, and still are, numerous interruptions of the journey. The best of intentions, in the guise of romanticism, moralism, or revolutionary exhibitionism, have sometimes led to the destruction of the religion of the people. Or their piety was subjected to ideals of ecclesiastical or pastoral domination, usually under the guise of progress and liberation slogans. There have been casualties, unnecessarily.

Serious dialogue and a common journey with the believing and oppressed people is possible only in concrete situations and for those who accept risks. What is needed is a unity of heart, soul, and common sense, a free and liberating view of folk religiosity. The church of the people carries with it not only its own situation but also its own struggle, its own ways of engaging in struggle, and hope that takes certain concrete forms. In economics a distinction is made between macroeconomic and microeconomic realities — and the two are sometimes set in direct opposition to each other — and just so in speaking about Latin American liberation theology one must distinguish macrotheology and microtheology. The latter perhaps deserves preference since it is where "God's benefits" are concretely experienced.

Talk about Latin American liberation theology is often prompted by very good intentions, that is, as a challenge to one's own Western theology and as a proof of humility. But this kind of talk too easily restricts itself to certain circles of people who attempt, by borrowing, to make up for their own poverty and their own lack of concrete engagement with those who lack opportunity, with those who have been beaten into silence, or with those who are newly poor in the society of the talkers themselves. This is not what anybody wishes for, of course, but sometimes spiritual impotence and lack of faith assume this form despite our intentions.

CHAPTER 24

After the Glasnost Revolution: Soviet Evangelicals and Western Missions

WALTER SAWATSKY

By 1975 Soviet Christians[1] had realized that the state effort to eradicate religion would not succeed. Encouraged by the revised legislation on religion of that year, evangelical and Orthodox leaders shed their survival mentality and began to squeeze concessions from the state. They experienced growing pressure from the grass roots for more Bibles, then other religious literature, then extended Bible correspondence courses and the addition of music courses, and then increased circulation of denominational journals. Soon delegates to the All Union Council of Evangelical Christian-Baptists (AUCECB) national congress were even clamoring for special attention to youth. These initiatives began before *glasnost* became official policy, and well in advance of 1988, the year Soviet Christianity first experienced the impact of *perestroika*.

Exceptions to this trend of concessions from the state occurred among dissident groups, including the Council of (unregistered) Churches of Evangelical Christian-Baptists (CCECB), independent Pentecostals, and Adventists, which felt intensified pressure by the Soviet security forces. In fact, the CCECB's list of imprisoned leaders began to grow again after 1979.[2]

Once the authorities agreed to permit the 1988 millennial celebra-

---

1. Terminology since the dissolution of the USSR is problematic. CIS (Commonwealth of Independent States) and FSU (former Soviet Union) seem temporary, but at least FSU is precise in referring to what was. I will concentrate largely on the Russian Republic and will also refer to Ukraine and Belarus when referring to "Slavic Christians."

2. For a detailed treatment see my *Soviet Evangelicals Since World War II* (Scottdale: Herald, 1981), updated in my "Protestantism in the USSR," in *Christianity Under Stress III: Protestantism and Politics in Eastern Europe and Russia: The Communist and Postcommunist Eras*, ed. S. P. Ramet (Durham: Duke University Press, 1992) 237-75.

tion of Russian-Ukrainian Christianity, the limits to religious expansion so long imposed by the state seemed to disappear. The restrictive law of cults, in effect till September 30, 1990, virtually ceased to function as a point of reference by the end of 1988. Enterprising evangelicals, both locally and centrally, kept asking officials for ever more concessions, and no one ordered it to stop. Sometime in late 1989 it became possible to import large shipments of religious literature without bothering with permits. Indeed, so much relief aid was entering the country, initially for Armenian earthquake victims but also for hospitals generally, that if something was declared to be for charity (*miloserdie* became the magic word) it was waved through customs.[3]

Christian aid and missionary efforts rose to avalanche proportions in 1990. Soon Western mission agencies were seeking to obtain office space and working out joint ventures with Soviet evangelicals, often mixing evangelism with such enterprises as furniture factories, printing plants, and agricultural projects. In the space of about a year, church offices in Moscow and other cities that had functioned with a few typewriters and telephones, and perhaps a lone photocopy machine if they were in the capital city, suddenly were equipped with computers and fax machines (though not yet with filing cabinets).

The inundation of Western mission representatives[4] was such that local pastors sometimes failed to preach to their own congregations for months on end, due to the custom of deferring to visiting preachers. In fact, church leaders met so many guests offering new partnership projects that they rarely found time to follow through on anything agreed upon with previous visitors.

New relationships were developed, often with individuals and groups in the West who had spent the previous decades supporting the Cold War by looking for mission opportunities in other places. Younger leaders, many without much knowledge of their churches' recent histories, took financial retainers from Western agencies in order to pursue projects that they — or successful-looking Westerners — deemed important. The resultant disarray extended to disturbed relationships with Western parachurch agencies and denominational bodies that had long maintained ties

3. Here was a rediscovery of language, for the word *miloserdie* (compassion or charity) had been a taboo under Soviet Communism until the writer Granin called for its return in 1988.

4. The proliferation can be traced in M. Elliott, *East European Missions Directory* (Wheaton: Institute for the Study of Christianity and Marxism, 1989, second edition 1992), and its successor, S. Linzey, M. H. Ruffin, and M. R. Elliott, ed., *East-West Christian Organizations* (Evanston: Berry, 1993), which lists nearly seven hundred organizations.

to Soviet churches. There also developed a new sense of denominational competition, including the formation of new Protestant denominations.[5]

Under these circumstances, it should not be surprising if complaints were heard that the older generation was passive. As younger leaders took the churches in unknown new directions, the older generation could not help wondering if time had passed it by.

Ministry Priorities before *Perestroika*

By beginning with 1975 rather than 1985, the year Gorbachev announced *perestroika*, I am emphasizing that there was a period when church leaders were learning to consult, to set priorities, and to take new initiatives more than a decade before Western mission entrepreneurs began to flood in. The political transformations of 1989-91 did not suddenly give a captive church its freedom. Those freedoms were being claimed gradually, at an uneven pace, all across eastern Europe.

Furthermore, the priorities and progress of evangelicals in that period serve as a guide for assessing the current proliferation of activity. We must ask which Western-initiated projects represent a response to definite needs and broadly supported visions, and which are merely standard tools of the trade for Western missions. For example, even though Soviet evangelicals have a long tradition of reliance on the traveling evangelist as a key means of reaching the lost, by now there is a keen awareness that the one thing clearly not needed is more generalist evangelists from the West who neither speak the language nor understand the culture.

The list of priorities for Soviet evangelicals between 1975 and 1985 was simple. The first order of business was to get more Bibles. Since by 1975 most evangelical preachers had at least a New Testament, the main interest was to supply each believing household, then each believer (often at the time of baptism), with a personal copy of Holy Scripture. With the explosion of Bible importation after 1988, the new need then was to make the Scriptures available to the general public. In 1989-90 it was thought that twenty million Bibles would be needed before the excessive black market prices would start to drop.[6] By at least 1990 it became increasingly evident that not only was there a major need for a Bible especially for

5. M. Elliott, "Protestant Theological Education in the Former Soviet Union," *IBMR* 18 (1994) claimed that twenty-five Protestant bodies were now active.

6. M. Elliott, "New Openness to USSR Prompts Massive Bible Shipments to Soviet Christians in 1987-1988: A Statistical Overview," *News Network International*, March 20, 1989, 24-31.

children, but that the vast majority of the seeking Soviet public was so severely illiterate in terms of religious culture that only a Bible for children would be understood.

Next to the Bible, Soviet evangelicals wanted Christian literature to help believers grow in their faith and to assist preachers in interpreting the Bible. That also meant a serious emphasis on theological education. Since 1979 Soviet Baptists had been announcing plans to open a seminary, and they received official approval in 1987. As an interim measure they had managed to expand the intake for their correspondence course, and some of the courses had been upgraded. In 1990 they also organized regional Bible school level courses (mainly by correspondence and weekends of intensive lectures on a quarterly basis).

In September 1991 the first Pentecostal Bible school was started in the Ukrainian city of Rovno, with thirty-two students. By this time also, several parachurch agencies, Soviet and Western, had begun such Bible schools (often misleadingly labeled seminaries).

Theological education was widely perceived as the major task for establishing an orderly church life. The Russian Orthodox Church expanded its seminaries to eight from three, began offering a two-year training course for Christian education of children, and was associated with a variety of ventures in theological higher education through universities and institutes. Slavic evangelicals in the former Soviet Union had established over fifty theological schools (nineteen claiming at least a full year of study) involving 1,667 students plus an additional 3,184 correspondence or TEE registrants by 1994. Several obtained excellent campus facilities and showed promise for the future. In addition, at least several dozen outstanding students were studying in Western seminaries with the intention of returning to teach in Soviet seminaries. A new Protestant university was announced to begin classes in September 1994 with an initial class of sixty students.[7]

Related to the teaching and ministry task was the problem of information flow — how to improve church communication within geographic regions and maintain regular contact with local churches. The first step was to increase the distribution of the AUCECB bimonthly journal from 5,000 to 8,000 and finally to 20,000. After the millennial year of 1988, regional church papers of varying quality emerged. Now there are so many church papers that an overview of them has become impossible.

---

7. For details see my "Visions in Conflict: Starting Anew through the Prism of Leadership Training Efforts," in N. Nielsen, *Religion After Communism in Eastern Europe* (Boulder: Westview, 1994); and regular updating through Jack Graves of the Overseas Council for Theological Education and Missions, Greenwood, Indiana.

One can find public voices as early as 1974 asking for help in special ministries to youth and even to children, even though religious work with children was illegal. By 1985, both legal (AUCECB, "registered") churches and illegal (CCECB, "unregistered") churches had de facto activity but minimal program materials, and no specially trained staff. So by 1990 the major priority became the organization of training seminars for Sunday schools, then the introduction of graded lessons and organized projects for youth. New publishing houses in St. Petersburg and Odessa began printing Sunday school curricula.

Information Scarcity Compounds
the Problems of Ministry

Much of the initial post–World War II mission activity in the Soviet Union and eastern Europe was like a stab in the dark. Lack of information made one prey to political manipulation and produced a climate of charge and countercharge, as, for example, between the Bible smugglers and the United Bible Societies.

In the early 1970s three research centers emerged as attempts to collect and analyze information systematically and to publish it openly: the missiological and ecumenical center in Utrecht, headed by Dr. Hans Hebly; Glaube in der zweiten Welt (G2W) in Zurich, represented by Pfarrer Eugen Voss; and Keston College in England, founded by Canon Michael Bourdeaux. Hebly's center had less influence because its primary language was Dutch, but several of his monographs have been translated. G2W was long the major source of information for the German-speaking world. In 1986, however, its news service was terminated, and only a monthly journal and a book-publishing program continued. For the English-speaking world Keston News Service and Keston's quarterly journal *Religion in Communist Lands* have been widely recognized for their comprehensive and accurate treatment. But Keston lost much of its funding base as a casualty of the end of the Cold War. In September 1991 the news service was terminated. Only three of the staff continued at the new research center in Oxford, and the future of Keston's rare library and archive was uncertain. Staff member Jane Ellis hoped to resume a new service in Moscow.

A spinoff of the Open Doors Mission of Brother Andrew, the now independent *News Network International* (now available only by paid subscription) is a regular source for developments in eastern Europe. Unfortunately its coverage is much more episodic and of uneven quality. During the past decade *Religion in Eastern Europe (REE*, formerly *Occasional Papers on Eastern Europe)*, edited by Paul Mojzes and sponsored by Christians Associated for Relationships with Eastern Europe (CAREE) has developed a solid reputation. *REE* consists of articles written for the general reader and increasingly includes contributions by eastern European writers.

Sources of information within the Soviet Union have undergone several changes. In October 1991 the Baptist Union closed down its English-language information bulletin (as well as its international department), and the Orthodox patriarchate was also financially unable to circulate as much in foreign languages as in the early years of *perestroika*. Because of these developments there is in the former Soviet Union no central place for keeping track of religious developments. Soviet evangelical leaders indicated that they would be unable to make information exchange a meaningful priority for the next several years because of lack of resources.

But the explosion of newspapers, alongside the decline of Soviet newspapers such as *Pravda* and *Izvestia*, included new religious leaflets and magazines. Among the major efforts at providing an overview of religious events across the country, an independent publishing house named "Protestant" became widely known for its informational and inspirational weekly paper of the same name, which was among the first and most venturesome in providing general religious news coverage. Headed by Alexander Semchenko, a gifted entrepreneur, the company purchased a large press and became a major producer and distributor of books.

Gradually certain individuals parted ways with Semchenko's dominant leadership. Several pursued a vision to establish a new religious information service for Russians called *Khristianskoe Chtenie* (Christian Readings), which in early 1994 became independent of its English-language sponsor, the Christian Resource Center, headed by Sharon Linzey. Both the Russian and English-language versions attempted, in spite of tremendous difficulties, to offer coverage of all Christian confessions, even if the result was partial.

Perestroika Brings Unexpected Issues

As a result of *perestroika*, Soviet evangelicals found themselves confronted with three major issues that they had not thought much about. In the first place, with the cessation of state hostility toward Christianity, they needed to clarify how they should relate to the state in the future. Gorbachev's invitation to the churches to contribute to the moral rebuilding of society legitimized the role of the Christian community (recalling the equally dramatic shift in Roman society following the conversion of Constantine in 312). Will Soviet evangelicals continue to think in terms of separation of church and state? And will that be understood as the separation doctrine of sixteenth-century Anabaptism, namely, the state not interfering in the life of the church, or more in terms of the separation doctrine of the First Amendment to the American Constitution, the main intent of which is to keep religion from controlling the state? Thus far, as I write this, Soviet evangelicals have not been elected to political office, as have Orthodox clergy, but they have participated in discussions of alternative democratic party formations.

The second unexpected and troubling issue was the way in which Christians were invited to think of their role in society. No longer ignored as second-class citizens, in 1989 they were encouraged to participate in the newly permitted charitable societies. That led to an ever-increasing variety of social services, from "meals on wheels," to drug treatment centers, senior citizens homes, and counseling ministries to prisoners. Christians had to decide whether to join secular service agencies or confine themselves to their own Christian agencies, and they needed to decide how much effort they would devote to social ministries over against the task of evangelism. In other words, Soviet evangelicals were in the process of forming their alignment on the evangelism–social action, or word-deed spectrum.

Perhaps even more surprising was the new expectation that Christians, specifically Protestants, would contribute to economic reconstruction. Initially they were expected to draw on their established network with affluent Western churches, nonprofit relief agencies, and individual businessmen in order to obtain hard currency investment for joint ventures. In 1990 Soviet evangelical businessmen — a diversity of individual entrepreneurs — met for a conference in Kiev. Within a year they then organized an Association of Christian Businessmen, opened an office in Moscow, and formed an informal partnership with the Soviet Union Network (SUN), an ad hoc consortium of Canadian and American evangelical businessmen. These Soviet Christians also began giving thought to their roles in a market economy and particularly to business ethics.

The role of Christians in the economic well-being of society has been highlighted by Dr. Alexander Zaichenko and others who, as economic advisers to former Soviet President Gorbachev, emphasized the critical role that faith and values play in the success of a national economy. Zaichenko, himself an evangelical Christian, and other economists looked favorably on the Weberian "Protestant work ethic" thesis. They argued that if the success of capitalism is related to the Protestant work ethic, then perhaps what Russia and the new Commonwealth of Independent States needed was a critical mass of Protestants before it could develop a free-market economy. Hence, such economists favored a strong Protestant missionary thrust, through which a better business climate might emerge. At the same time, of course, warnings were heard about misreading Weber and about the inherent ethical dangers of a free-market economy.

Missiological Approaches of Western Missions

As a result of the sudden popularity of religion, especially Christianity, Soviet evangelical leaders now feel that their greatest challenge is evangelism and mission. This includes responding adequately both to the demands of the public to know more about the Christian faith and to the pressure from Western missions eager to launch major evangelism and mission projects. In order to understand the nature of this challenge, we must sketch out the origins of the evangelical community in Russia and the approaches to the Russian people that Western missions have taken. As we shall see, many missions are already very influential in shaping the evangelistic task, in creating alternative religious cultures (including the potential Americanization of Soviet evangelicals), and in fostering greater denominational diversity and competition.

A fact not recognized by many new missions to Russia, Ukraine, and other members of the CIS is that evangelical mission to the Soviet peoples has a history. The first part of that history consisted of a late blooming of the general Pietist missionary impulse, which contributed to the formation of "Neo-Protestant" churches in eastern and central Europe.[8] Bible colporteurs traveled about, Bible schools were organized (even during the first few years of the Soviet era), and the YMCA mobilized the university youth. The second part of evangelical mission history occurred after World War II, with its major focus on finding ways to help Soviet Christians survive state-sponsored suppression and persecution. It was mission in an emergency situation.

A brief schematic of mission approaches during this latter period can be developed by contrasting the programs of Underground Evangelism (UE) and the Slavic Gospel Association (SGA). Organized in 1960 by Joe Bass, a young Pentecostal entrepreneur, UE (under a variety of names) became by 1970 one of the largest and flashiest fund-raising international missions. It smuggled Bibles to the underground church — that was its most publicized program. Radio broadcasting into the Soviet Union was

---

8. Best summarized in Wilhelm Kahle, *Evangelische Christen in Rusland und der Sowjetunion* (Wuppertal: Oncken, 1978).

a major expense. UE used generic persecution stories and a computerized mass market mailing system. Its board was self-perpetuating. A number of board members were financially dependent on UE, and therefore the board could not exercise the necessary control. Not surprisingly, financial scandal became a persistent problem.

SGA, on the other hand, had its base in an earlier period of ethnic immigration. Peter Deyneka, Sr., who founded the association in 1934, was a White Russian emigrant, who became part of the North Atlantic network of the Evangelical Christian Union, an evangelical church union first started under the leadership of Ivan Prochanov in Russia. A major wing of the AUCECB consists of second- and third-generation evangelical Christians. During the decades of silence and isolation, Deyneka's mission concentrated on evangelism and training among Slavic immigrants in North and South America, as well as cooperation with evangelicals in Poland. When contact with the Soviet Union resumed after 1956, the SGA mission pursued a cautious line of relationship building.

Under the leadership of Peter Deyneka, Jr., who served as executive director beginning in the 1970s, the mission has operated as a supporting arm for Soviet churches. SGA provided literature, particularly teaching materials requested by Soviet evangelicals, and its radio broadcasts were heard through much of the Soviet Union. Whereas UE tended to finance independent gospel preachers without setting a program direction, SGA became a leader after the mid-seventies in identifying a differentiated listening market — teaching programs for believers, and new programs of dialogue with culture in order to attract literate unbelievers less likely to be reached by local churches.

SGA came to typify a core of medium-sized missions (with budgets under $250,000 per year) that relied on an ethnically or denominationally related constituency for support and guidance and that sought to work in partnership with Soviet evangelical leaders. UE came to typify high-budget missions with a simplistic approach that idealized the suffering church and provided largesse to isolated individuals across the Soviet Union and Eastern Europe. Under the greater openness and opportunities of *perestroika*, a new generation of UE types — flashy and culturally insensitive — has arrived, while the SGA types have been struggling with their own transformation.[9]

Not all the mission societies now active in the former Soviet Union

9. *East West Christian Organizations* (see n. 4 above) includes five essays by Anita Deyneka, Kent Hill, Serge Duss, Peter Kuzmic, and Mark Elliott offering advice and suggestions on missiological and financial considerations based on a survey of recent experience (pp. 22-47).

can be classified as one of these two types. Nevertheless, thinking Soviet evangelicals identify some or all of the characteristics of these two types in almost all of the new missions. The new missions might have been established for ministry elsewhere, as, for example, Campus Crusade, Luis Palau Evangelism, or the Gideons, or they may have been organized by an individual or congregation after a visit to the Soviet Union or after hosting a Soviet visitor. Although some are more subtle and sophisticated, the common assumption is that there is an evangelism program, package, or doctrinal framework that is right and that the Soviet partner must now follow. When moving in with a program, some missions have been reported as saying that they will deliver their part (literature, videotapes, sound tapes, seminars, and the like) only if the partner works exclusively with these materials. Hence they are contributing to a culture of conflict and separatism. Bypassing the formerly established Soviet church leadership in order to work with independent and younger persons, they have also claimed that the official leaders have compromised themselves by functioning under communism and that the Western partners of these leaders are also suspect as coming from the world of ecumenism or from churches that lack the spiritual vibrancy of their own, more fundamentalist churches.

Meanwhile, the established missions, including denominational missions such as those of the Baptists, Pentecostals, and Mennonites, have continued to stress the partnership model, but the specifics have become more difficult. Established partnership understandings have come undone as the newer missions have breezed in and offered more money and quicker action. The established missions have also needed to ask themselves how they should relate to leaders who were appropriate to the difficulties of the 1970s, but who lack the readiness for the creativity and risk taking needed for the new opportunities. Should Western partners support the central leadership, or should the balance be tipped in favor of regionalization? Furthermore, since parachurch organizations — special mission and service agencies — have now become possible inside the Soviet Union (there are now over 2500 of them[10]), should these be the new partners? Can a Western entity work to support both parachurch agencies and the established denominational bodies? The supporting constituencies of these established Western agencies are chafing under an apparent slowness of response, in contrast to the new self-confident fundraising missions with their ethos of hurry.

10. As of March 1994 according to the Russian data base of indigenous organizations maintained by Sharon Linzey of the Moscow Christian Resource Center, excerpted in *East-West Church and Ministry Report* (Wheaton) 2 (1994) 6.

Still another critical feature of the partnership question is the matter of relating to the Russian Orthodox community. By far the largest confessional body, the Russian Orthodox Church is receiving the great majority of persons turning to Christianity. Open Doors International, a prominent European-American mission with a Pentecostal orientation, found itself in 1989-90 organizing a shipment of over one million New Testaments to the Russian Orthodox Patriarchate. (The Russian Orthodox Church has found it necessary to work with Protestant agencies and in cooperation with the World Council of Churches, of which it is a member, because Orthodox church bodies abroad are generally poor and not particularly organized to provide assistance.) Working with the Orthodox has also raised the question whether one should provide the specialized theological and philosophical literature the Russian intelligentsia are asking for.

On these partnership issues the SGA experience might be instructive. Deyneka's commitment to partnership led him to transfer as much of the work as possible to a Soviet base with ownership by Soviet believers. Specifically that meant more radio program production within the former Soviet Union, while maintaining heavy financial support from America. But SGA Board members and some staff in North America, looking at the necessity of publicity to sustain the skyrocketing budget, felt that North American control of program was essential. As a result of this tension, Peter and his wife Anita terminated their relationship with SGA, as did several other staff members, and formed a new ministry based in Moscow. By invitation of Soviet evangelical leaders, the Deynekas moved to Moscow in January 1992 in order to facilitate a better network of relationships between Soviet and Western agencies and to function as consultants on ministry.[11] The SGA mission then began a series of reorganizations and may be unrecognizable in the future.

Incarnational or "Presence" Ministry

In mission circles a ministry of "presence" has long been considered less effective than open proclamation or persuasion. In authoritarian countries however, it was acknowledged that a ministry of presence might be the only option available. The experience of Soviet Christians in the past several decades, which has led to the current dramatic expansion of mission opportunities, invites careful reflection on presence ministry.

11. Initially called Deyneka Ministries, USSR. See A. Deyneka, "Good Things Come to Those Who Network," *Evangelical Missions Quarterly* 28 (1992) 42-45.

Those who thought of presence ministry in the former Soviet Union as an unfortunate necessity quickly shifted to a more aggressive proclamation ministry after *perestroika*.

Those who are committed to a presence ministry even in environments of relative freedom, who view a presence ministry as more in keeping with Christ's own approach, have needed to keep some differentiations in mind. When missionary presence is seen as a natural combination of living and speaking the Christian gospel, the need for solidarity with local Christians, and even for making common cause with all others claiming to follow Christ, becomes paramount. Yet there is an obvious difference between the demands on local Christians and the demands on foreign missionaries. For the former there are greater risks and there is no opportunity to go away and rest awhile. Yet the primary witness across eastern Europe and the former Soviet Union that accounts for the dramatic positive change in societal attitudes to Christianity is the result of the silent suffering and serious Christian living, especially in its ethical and fellowship qualities, of local believers.

At the same time, the presence witness of the foreigner may draw attention to some desirable differences. For instance, the foreigner may be better equipped to show how faith and scholarship can be integrated or how reconciliation can be achieved through love and understanding. Local believers may thereby be encouraged to take responsible leadership and to work for cooperation among rivals. At a recent conference reviewing mission in eastern Europe, the most striking phrase from an eastern European was the reminder that people watch "your walk as much as your talk."

Representatives of this kind of ministry emphasize the importance of facilitating the "authentic self-determination of Christians in eastern Europe in the matter of their own spiritual development."[12] This requires that the missionary be the learner, able to provide links for finding specialized resources but never making the mistake of thinking of Soviet and eastern European believers as junior Christians. Sad to say, the spiritual and cultural or racial arrogance of some missionaries to the former Soviet Union has been unmistakable. More attractive is the confession of one person after living in eastern Europe for some years:

> I learned humility in the presence of many east European Christians who are of tremendous spiritual depth. . . . These are folks who have successfully integrated the gospel with local life and are instrumental

12. So Rom Maczka at the Mennonite Council of International Ministries consultation on Eastern Europe, December 1990.

in helping others to do so. Most of them are quiet. They are unobtrusive. . . . They are generally not very flashy. . . . [They are] people with spiritual depth and experiences who have been in ministry and understand how to contextualize the Gospel.[13]

What Will Last?

The Soviets have learned to use the word "lasting" to indicate a major value in assessing something. So much of past workmanship and scholarship lacked integrity and quality. To say something *budet stoit*, that it will last, is the ultimate compliment.

Much of the missionary energy now being expended in the former Soviet Union is based on the theory that in the great cosmic war between God and Satan, there is a temporary respite. Soon the door of opportunity may be closed again. Therefore, we must get the minimal proclamation to as many as possible. Missionaries who think this way are too busy to wonder whether their style of work might be a precipitating factor in closing doors.

Most Western missionaries are preoccupied with evangelism, with denominational competition, and possibly with alternative cultural expressions of faith (in contrast to those of the rather ingrown Soviet evangelical congregations). These missions show minimal interest in church and state questions, the social role of Soviet Christians, or their potential contributions to economics and national education. Yet the capacity of Soviet evangelicals to respond to such issues will determine whether they will be a serious factor in Soviet society, or become increasingly irrelevant. Many concerned evangelical leaders recognize this and are seeking discussion partners who might help them think through their roles on the basis of lessons from other cultures and periods of Christian history.

Since at least the time of Peter the Great, Russians have wrestled with the question of borrowing from the West over against the opposite extreme of stressing their Eastern uniqueness. One obvious conclusion, applied to Marxism as an import from the West, is that what is imported will not last unless it can be adapted to fit the context. Western missionary imports will also not last, unless appropriately contextualized.

In mid-October 1991, Grigorii Komendant, President in Moscow of the AUCECB, commented on the current situation and on the role of Western missions:

13. *Ibid.*

We find ourselves involved in a very large process of ministry where we are experiencing great blessing and also great difficulty. All possible doors to ministry are open; that is not the difficulty. Currently there are 314 missions working here — 14 of them are actually working; the other 300 are just collecting money. They are collecting money for very large projects costing millions of dollars, but only about ten percent of this will get approved by local authorities and get completed. With some missions we have close cooperation, whereas others are quite exclusive. What is vital is that such persons truly work for the kingdom of God, which also means that new converts must be taught to relate to a local church. Mission without ecclesiology is not sound.[14]

I pondered those observations as I returned that evening to the Izmailov hotel complex, where 1200 people aged sixteen to their mid-twenties had gathered for three days of charismatic preaching (by American evangelists speaking through an interpreter) and Bible study before returning to their homes across the vast reaches of the then Soviet Union. Such meetings were happening monthly. It seemed wonderful and astonishing — so many young people in jeans, with or without cigarettes, carrying their Bibles without embarrassment. Would they find their way to churches? Would it last?

A Short Bibliographic Guide

Much of the earlier analytical and descriptive material now seems dated. Nevertheless some of the basic monographs on Soviet evangelicals and Orthodox believers recommended in M. R. Elliott, ed., *Christianity and Marxism Worldwide: An Annotated Bibliography* (Wheaton: Institute for the Study of Christianity and Marxism, 1988), or P. Mojzes, ed., *Church and State in Postwar Eastern Europe* (New York: Greenwood, 1987), remain the most important sources.

The current standard treatments on Orthodoxy are J. Ellis, *The Russian Orthodox Church: A Contemporary History* (Bloomington: University of Indiana Press, 1986), and D. P. Pospielovsky, *The Russian Church under the Soviet Regime 1917-1982* (2 vols.; Crestwood: St. Vladimir's Seminary Press, 1985).

Perhaps the most comprehensive reference work now available is a three-volume series, *Christianity under Stress*, ed. P. (Sabrina) Ramet (Durham, NC: Duke University Press, 1988-92). Volume I is titled *Eastern Chris-*

14. My paraphrase from notes, October 10, 1991.

tianity and Politics in the Twentieth Century, volume II is *Roman Catholicism and Politics in the Soviet Union and Eastern Europe,* and volume III is *Protestantism and Politics in the Soviet Union and Eastern Europe.*

Two handy book-length descriptions using the 1988 millennial celebrations to highlight religious developments are M. Bourdeaux, *The Gospel's Triumph over Communism* (Minneapolis: Bethany House, 1991; the British title is *Glasnost, Gorbachev and the Gospel*), and J. Forest, *Religion in the New Russia* (New York: Crossroad, 1990). Also helpful for an overall presentation of changes under *perestroika* is the second edition of K. Hill, *The Soviet Union on the Brink: An Inside Look at Christianity and Glasnost* (Portland: Multnomah, 1991; the title of the first edition was *The Puzzle of the Soviet Church*).

Several new publications speak to the role of religion in the revolutions of 1989-91 and the task of the churches: N. Nielsen, *Revolutions in Eastern Europe: The Religious Roots* (Maryknoll: Orbis, 1991); J. M. Bailey, *The Spring of Nations: Churches in the Rebirth of Central and Eastern Europe* (New York: Friendship, 1991); R. Davies, *After Gorbachev: How Can Western Christians Help?* (Eastbourne: MARC [Monarch Publications], 1991); P. Mojzes, *Religious Liberty in Eastern Europe and the USSR: Before and After the Great Transformation* (Boulder: East European Monographs, 1992).

See also Walter Sawatsky, "Truth Telling in Eastern Europe: The Liberation and the Burden," *The Journal of Church and State* 33 (1991) 701-29; M. Elliott, "New Opportunities, New Demands in the Old Red Empire," *Evangelical Missions Quarterly* 28 (1992) 32-39; W. Triggs, "The Soviet Union: A Different Kind of Mission Field," *Evangelical Missions Quarterly* 26 (1990) 432-41.

Illustrative of recent symposia assessing the nature and direction of Christian renewal are S. Batalden, ed., *Seeking God: The Recovery of Religious Identity in Orthodox Russia, Ukraine, and Georgia* (DeKalb: University of Northern Illinois Press, 1993), and N. Nielson, ed., *Religion after Communism in Eastern Europe* (Boulder: Westview, 1994).

CHAPTER 25

American Protestants in Pursuit of Mission: 1886-1986

GERALD H. ANDERSON

In 1886 Dwight L. Moody convened the first Mount Hermon summer conference for college students at Northfield, Massachusetts, which led to the formation of the Student Volunteer Movement for Foreign Missions (SVM) in 1888, with John R. Mott as chairman. Also in 1886 Arthur Tappan Pierson, who addressed the Mount Hermon conference, published the major missionary promotional book of the era, *The Crisis of Missions;* Josiah Strong published *Our Country: Its Possible Future and Its Present Crises;* and Strong became general secretary of the Evangelical Alliance for the United States, for which Philip Schaff served as honorary corresponding secretary. The missionary enterprise in the United States was entering a period of enormous vitality with a crusading spirit fueled by duty, compassion, confidence, optimism, evangelical revivalism, and premillennialist urgency.[1]

Manifest Destiny in Missions

The overarching motive for missions at this time was love of Christ and obedience to the Great Commission for the salvation of souls.[2] Underneath, however, was the compelling idea, developing since the 1840s, of America's Manifest Destiny — of a national mission assigned by Providence for extending the blessings of America to other peoples. Herman

---

1. Cf. C. J. Phillips, "The Student Volunteer Movement and Its Role in China Missions, 1886-1920," in *The Missionary Enterprise in China and America,* ed. J. K. Fairbank (Cambridge, MA, 1974) 93-98.

2. Cf. R. P. Beaver, "Missionary Motivation through Three Centuries," in *Reinterpretation in American Church History,* ed. J. C. Brauer (Chicago, 1968) 141ff.

374

Melville had written in 1850, "We Americans are peculiar, chosen people, the Israel of our times; we bear the ark of the liberties of the world."[3] Until the 1890s Manifest Destiny was thought of primarily in terms of continental expansion, of "winning the West," with the absorption of settlers into citizenship and statehood. In the 1890s, however, when the United States had reached the limits of prospective continental expansion, there developed agitation for expansion beyond North America. There was a conviction that the United States was a nation divinely chosen or predestined to be "the primary agent of God's meaningful activity in history."[4] The doctrine of Manifest Destiny had its roots in the concepts of Anglo-Saxon racial superiority, America as the center of civilization in the westward course of empires, the primacy of American political institutions, the purity of American Protestant Christianity, and the desirability of English becoming the language of humanity.[5]

Until late in the nineteenth century American churches concentrated their missionary efforts in "home missions," evangelizing the pioneers on the frontier, Indians, Hispanic Americans, African Americans, and new immigrants in the cities. "In 1874, for example, the Missionary Society of the Methodist Episcopal Church (Northern) supported in whole or in part more than 3,000 missionaries in the United States. In the same year . . . that same church had 145 missionaries overseas."[6]

Of special significance in shaping the mind and mood of American Protestant churches regarding the new frontiers of Manifest Destiny were the published writings of the Reverend Josiah Strong (1847-1916), who came out of a background of work with the Congregational Home Missionary Society. His books, especially *Our Country* (1886) and *The New Era; or, The Coming Kingdom* (1893), "did much to develop the idea of the part America should play in fulfilling Anglo-Saxon destiny as a civilizing and Christianizing power."[7] Austin Phelps, professor emeritus at Andover Seminary, wrote the introduction to *Our Country*, in which he said that Americans should "look on these United States as first and foremost the

3. Quoted by E. M. Burns, *The American Idea of Mission: Concepts of National Purpose and Destiny* (New Brunswick, NJ, 1957) 1, from Melville's *White-Jacket*.

4. J. E. Smylie, "National Ethos and the Church," *Theology Today* 20 (1963) 314.

5. See G. H. Anderson, "Providence and Politics behind Protestant Missionary Beginnings in the Philippines," *Studies in Philippine Church History* (Ithaca, 1969) 280.

6. W. R. Hogg, "The Role of American Protestantism in World Mission," in *American Missions in Bicentennial Perspective*, ed. R. P. Beaver (South Pasadena, 1977) 364.

7. A. P. Stokes, *Church and State in the United States* (New York, 1950) II, 311. See also J. E. Reed, "American Foreign Policy, the Politics of Missions and Josiah Strong, 1890-1900," *Church History* 41 (1972) 230-45.

chosen seat of enterprise for the world's conversion. Forecasting the future of Christianity, as statesmen forecast the destiny of nations, we must believe that it will be what the future of this country is to be. As goes America, so goes the world, in all that is vital to its moral welfare."[8]

This small volume — which sold 175,000 copies over a period of thirty years — emphasized the superiority of the Anglo-Saxon race in general and of Americans in particular as God's chosen people. The Anglo-Saxon, Strong asserted, was "divinely commissioned to be, in a peculiar sense, his brother's keeper."[9] In the closing pages of *The New Era,* Strong summarized his "enthusiasm for humanity" in these words: "Surely, to be a Christian and an Anglo-Saxon and an American in this generation is to stand on the very mountain-top of privilege."

Leaders in the Forward Movement of Missions

While Strong probably did more than anyone else at that time to get Americans interested in the application of Christianity to the problems of the nation, A. T. Pierson, a Presbyterian, is judged to have been "the foremost spokesperson for foreign missions in the late nineteenth century."[10] Of particular importance was Pierson's leadership at the 1886 Mount Hermon summer conference, which was attended by 251 students from nearly ninety colleges, including John R. Mott, Luther D. Wishard, Robert P. Wilder, and Charles K. Ober. Speaking on "God's Providence in Modern Missions," Pierson urged that "All should go, and go to all." By the last day of the conference, 100 young men — "The Mount Hermon Hundred" — dedicated themselves to foreign missionary service.[11] Two students — Robert Wilder and John N. Forman — were delegated to visit American colleges during 1886-87 to enlist further student support for foreign missions. By the time 450 students assembled at Northfield in June 1887 for the second student conference, the number of volunteers had increased to more than 2,100 — 1,600 men and 500 women. During the second year (1887-88), even with no organized deputation to campuses, the number of volunteers who had signed a declaration, "I am willing and desirous, God permitting, to become a foreign missionary," swelled to

8. P. 11. References to *Our Country* are from the revised edition of 1891, as reprinted and edited by J. Herbst (Cambridge, MA, 1963).

9. *Ibid.*, 200-202.

10. D. L. Robert, "Arthur Tappan Pierson and Forward Movements of Late-Nineteenth-Century Evangelism" (Ph.D. diss., Yale University, 1984) 165.

11. J. R. Mott, *History of the Student Volunteer Movement for Foreign Missions* (Chicago, 1892) 6-11.

nearly 3,000. The story of the student missionary uprising generated a revival of missionary interest in the churches. President James McCosh of the College of New Jersey at Princeton, commenting on the new student offering of life for missionary service, asked, "Has any such offering of living young men and women been presented in our age, in our country, in any age, or in any country, since the day of Pentecost?"[12]

In 1887 Pierson became editor of *Missionary Review of the World*, and he is credited with formulating the watchword, "The Evangelization of the World in This Generation," adopted by the SVM in 1889.[13] Pierson initiated a call in 1885 for a world missions conference and council that was realized initially with the London Centenary Missions Conference in 1888, attended by 1,579 delegates from 139 missionary societies, including Philip Schaff of the Evangelical Alliance, who addressed the conference. Pierson also helped to begin the Kansas-Sudan movement in 1889 and the Africa Inland Mission in 1895 as faith missions.

Pierson and Adoniram Judson Gordon — prominent pastor of Clarendon Street Baptist Church in Boston and author of *The Holy Spirit in Missions* (1893) — were "the fathers of faith missions" in America.[14] Gordon founded the Boston Missionary Training Institute in 1889 (which later evolved into Gordon College and Gordon-Conwell Theological Seminary). In this institute the emphasis was on training in Bible and mission methods for laypersons, especially women, to provide laborers for the mission fields, which were viewed as "ripe unto harvest." While Pierson and Gordon were premillennialists, the main motives for founding faith missions in the late nineteenth century were not theological or sectarian but practical — to decentralize missionary responsibility for greater efficiency, to overcome denominational separatism, and to supplement the work of denominational agencies. It was not until the fundamentalist-modernist controversy intensified after World War I that theological issues became more pronounced and the American Protestant missionary consensus disintegrated.

12. Quoted by Mott, *History of the Student Volunteer Movement* 29. Cf. C. P. Shedd, *Two Centuries of Student Christian Movements* (New York, 1934) 267.

13. D. L. Robert, "The Legacy of Arthur Tappan Pierson," *International Bulletin of Missionary Research* 8 (1984) 120; *idem*, "The Origin of the Student Volunteer Watchword: 'The Evangelization of the World in This Generation,'" *International Bulletin of Missionary Research* 10 (1986) 146ff.

14. D. L. Robert, " 'The Crisis of Missions': Premillennial Mission Theory and the Origins of Independent Evangelical Missions," in *Earthen Vessels: American Evangelicals and Foreign Missions, 1880-1980*, ed. J. A. Carpenter and W. R. Shenk (Grand Rapids, 1990) 33; also Robert, "Arthur Tappan Pierson and Forward Movements," 303-12, and "The Legacy of Adoniram Judson Gordon," *International Bulletin of Missionary Research* 11 (1987).

Two other late nineteenth-century premillennialists are important for their contributions to American missions: Albert Benjamin Simpson and Cyrus Ingerson Scofield.[15] Simpson was a Presbyterian minister who in 1887 founded two affiliated organizations: The Christian Alliance as a nondenominational fellowship, and the Evangelical (later International) Missionary Alliance for foreign mission work. They merged in 1897 as the Christian and Missionary Alliance, and their workers were trained at the Missionary Training Institute and later at the Jaffray School of Missions (now Nyack College and Alliance Theological Seminary in Nyack, New York). What Simpson established was a missionary agency that became a missionary denomination. Missions in the alliance are the reason for which congregations exist; thus today the CMA has far more members overseas than in the United States.[16]

Scofield was a Congregationalist who founded the Central American Mission as a faith agency in 1890. He is best remembered, says Dana L. Robert, "as the editor of the *Scofield Reference Bible*, an annotated King James Bible that encapsulated the hermeneutical system known as premillennial dispensationalism. What is almost never mentioned about the *Scofield Reference Bible* is that its purpose was not to codify a theological system but to be a one-volume reference work for missionaries who had no access to theological libraries."[17]

Mott — who graduated from Cornell University in 1888 and became intercollegiate secretary for the North American Student YMCA — was invited to speak at commencement exercises at the University (later College) of Wooster in Wooster, Ohio, in 1890 by a graduating senior, John Campbell White. "Cam" White became Mott's assistant, later served a term in India, and was subsequently general secretary of the Laymen's Missionary Movement and president of Wooster. His brother, W. W. White, was the founder and long the president of Biblical Seminary in New York. Mott married their sister, Leila, in 1891.[18]

In 1892 Mott could report that already "several thousands of students" had been inspired by the Volunteer Movement to declare their purpose to become foreign missionaries; that "over five hundred volunteers have already gone to the foreign field under the various missionary agencies, and fully one hundred more are under appointment. . . . Moreover, a large majority of the volunteers are still in various stages of

15. Robert, " 'The Crisis of Missions,' " 44.

16. R. L. Niklaus, J. S. Sawin, and S. J. Stoesz, *All for Jesus: God at Work in the Christian and Missionary Alliance over One Hundred Years* (Camp Hill, 1986) 68ff.

17. Robert, " 'The Crisis of Missions,' " 44.

18. C. H. Hopkins, *John R. Mott, 1865-1955: A Biography* (Grand Rapids, 1979) 83-86.

preparation." He reported also that "missionary intelligence" had been taken into three hundred colleges and there were now nearly six times as many students in these colleges who expect to become missionaries as there were before the movement. Furthermore, he said, missionary studies and interest had been intensified in forty-five seminaries, and "carefully selected missionary libraries have been introduced into fully seventy-five institutions. . . . It would be difficult now to find an institution where there are not now two or more missionary periodicals on file."[19]

Documentation for reference and research was enhanced with the publication in 1891 of the two-volume *Encyclopedia of Missions*, edited by Edwin M. Bliss, who had worked in the Middle East for the American Bible Society. This was followed by the publication in 1897-99 of the two-volume work *Christian Missions and Social Progress: A Sociological Study of Foreign Missions* by James S. Dennis, a former missionary in Syria. Dennis sought to show "the larger scope of missions" with "the dawn of a sociological era in missions." He examined the ability of Christianity "to uplift society and introduce the higher forces of permanent social regeneration and progress." His thesis was that non-Christian society, "left to its own tendencies, uniformly and persistently goes the way of moral deterioration and sinks into decadence, with no hope of self-reformation," whereas Christianity "has been invariably the motive force in all noble and worthy moral development" in any "attempt to civilize barbarous races" (II, 3).

In a statistical supplement, published in 1902 as *Centennial Survey of Foreign Missions*, Dennis provided massive documentation on the turn-of-the-century status of Protestant foreign missions, which he defined as "any more or less organized effort to lead the natives of unevangelized lands to the acceptance of a pure and saving form of Christian truth, and to lift their daily living into conformity with it."[20] His work has been judged "a landmark in the history of American foreign missions as a dividing point between the old stress on snatching the heathen from the jaws of Hell and the new view of missions as a humanitarian agency" — where "conversion of the heathen was gradually becoming a means to an end, namely an improved society."[21]

---

19. Mott, *History of the Student Volunteer Movement*, 28-33.

20. J. S. Dennis, *Centennial Survey of Foreign Missions* (New York, 1902) 1. See also H. P. Beach, *A Geography and Atlas of Protestant Missions* (2 vols.; New York, 1902-06); J. S. Dennis, H. P. Beach, and C. H. Fahs, ed., *World Atlas of Christian Missions* (New York, 1911); H. P. Beach and B. St. John, ed., *World Statistics of Christian Missions* (New York, 1916); H. P. Beach and C. H. Fahs, ed., *World Missionary Atlas* (New York, 1925).

21. P. A. Varg, "Motives in Protestant Missions, 1890-1917," *Church History* 23 (1954) 75, 77.

In May 1893 Mott declined an invitation from Moody to head up his recently established Bible Institute in Chicago. Later that summer at the World's Parliament of Religions (where many evangelicals refused to participate), held in conjunction with the Chicago World's Fair ("Columbian Exposition"), Moody conducted an evangelistic campaign, and Mott delivered there his first speech to an international audience; then they were on the Northfield platform together for another summer student conference.[22]

Providence, Politics, and the Philippines

The potent blend of Providence, piety, politics, and patriotism surged in support of foreign missions in 1898-99 with the Spanish-American War, especially with regard to the Philippines.[23] Anti-Roman Catholic sentiment was also a factor. In an article on "The Philippine Islands" in the *Christian Advocate* for September 1898, the Reverend R. G. Hobbs appealed to fellow Methodists: "Break the clutch which Rome has put upon those people, and give them a chance for a civilization which is something more than Christianized paganism."

The faith that America's course of action had approval of divine Providence seemed to be confirmed by the swift and complete triumph of American arms in Manila.[24] Rudyard Kipling urged Americans to "Take up the white man's burden." Religious leaders saw parallels between the American victories and those of Israel in biblical times. The editor of *Christian and Missionary Alliance* said that the story of Admiral Dewey's victory "reads almost like the stories of the ancient battles of the Lord in the times of Joshua, David, and Jehoshaphat." Alexander Blackburn, writing in *The Standard*, a Baptist publication, said, "The magnificent fleets of Spain have gone down as marvelously, I had almost said, as miraculously, as the walls of Jericho went down," and he maintained that the nation now had a duty "to throw its strong protecting arms around . . . the Philippine Islands" and to practice an "imperialism of righteousness."

Within a few weeks after Dewey's victory a Presbyterian writer could say that the religious press was practically unanimous "as to the

---

22. Hopkins, *John R. Mott*, 104, 107.

23. The definitive study is K. J. Clymer, *Protestant Missionaries in the Philippines, 1898-1916: An Inquiry into the American Colonial Mentality* (Champaign, 1986).

24. For discussion and documentation on clergy sentiments about taking possession of the Philippines, see Anderson, "Providence and Politics," 284ff.; also W. S. Hudson, "Protestant Clergy Debate the Nation's Vocation," *Church History* 42 (1973) 110-18.

desirability of America's retaining the Philippines as a duty in the interest of human freedom and Christian progress." Methodist Bishop John Fletcher Hurst concurred: "The missionary aspirations of the American Church will add this new people to its map for conquest. . . . Never before has there fallen, at one stroke of the bell of destiny, such a burden upon the American people." The *Baptist Union* agreed that "The conquest by force of arms must be followed by conquest for Christ." Anticipating the acquisition of the Philippines by the United States, the Methodist editors of *World-Wide Missions* rejoiced that "we are no longer compelled to go to a foreign country to seek raw heathen. When patriotism and evangelism can go hand in hand, the one strengthens the other. . . . How glorious it would be to think that we have one Mission in the heathen world with the starry flag afloat above it."

On the side of the government, President William McKinley (who once said, "I am a Methodist and nothing but a Methodist") was not indifferent to this sentiment. To a delegation from the general missionary committee of the Methodist Church that called on him in his office in November 1899, the President described how he had arrived at his decision — despite opposition and controversy — to retain the Philippines as a mission of "benevolent assimilation":

> I walked the floor of the White House night after night until midnight; and I am not ashamed to tell you, gentlemen, that I went down on my knees and prayed Almighty God for light and guidance more than one night. And one night late it came to me this way — I don't know how it was, but it came: . . . that there was nothing left for us to do but to take them all, and to educate the Filipinos, and uplift and civilize and Christianize them, and by God's grace do the very best we could by them, as our fellow-men for whom Christ died.

Senator Albert J. Beveridge delivered a Senate speech in January 1900 on his return from a tour of the Philippines and the Far East in which he concluded that "God marked the American people as His chosen nation to finally lead in the regeneration of the world." Not only was the Christian mission linked with national purpose, but the mission *to* America became subservient to the mission *of* America, and the nation replaced the church as the new Israel.[25] Clearly the mood at the turn of the century in both church and state was forward-looking in terms of progress and expansion, with a triumphant expectation that this would be "the Christian century."

25. Cf. C. L. Chaney, *The Birth of Missions in America* (South Pasadena, 1976) 298.

Other Voices and Views

A rather unusual self-critical note was sounded by William Newton Clarke, a prominent liberal theologian at Colgate Theological Seminary in Hamilton, New York, in his *Study of Christian Missions*, published in 1900. Clarke affirmed that "Christianity deserves possession of the world. It has the right to offer itself boldly to all men, and to displace all other religions, for no other religion offers what it brings. It is the best that the world contains" (p. 19). But, he cautioned, "Mankind has entered one of its periods of passion and unrest. . . . The present atmosphere of the world is not inspiring to missionary zeal: it is too full of something opposite" (pp. 193-94). Further, it was Clarke's judgment that there was a "crisis in missions . . . a sense of pause . . . signs of weakening . . . and of uncertainty. . . . Something has happened, to chill the ardor" (pp. 170-71). Criticism was rife, financial support was wanting, retrenchment was diminishing the work. The problems were created, he said, by romantic, unrealistic expectations of a swift and complete triumph of the gospel (pp. 172-73), by material interests, a warlike spirit, racial antagonisms, and national ambitions in a period of passion and unrest. "What we occidentals call civilization," Clarke observed, "too often carries to heathen people the wrong gift" (p. 243). Renewal of commitment in this "period of great transition" required a recognition that the task of missions — especially to overcome the ancient non-Christian religions — was "a far greater undertaking than our fathers thought" (p. 185). To recover momentum in missions, American Christians needed to requicken their faith, to simplify the Christian message, and to adopt "the long and exacting work of making Christianity the religion of the world." While he appreciated those who were motivated by the SVM watchword, Clarke had questions about its meaning and goal. "It might be as difficult to tell when the world has been evangelized," he said, "as to know when the present generation is past. . . . It is quite impossible that within the lifetime of a generation Christ should become intelligently known by all men" (pp. 73-74).

In contrast, John R. Mott in 1900 wrote his classic text, *The Evangelization of the World in This Generation*, in which he defined and defended the SVM watchword, then surveyed the possibilities and resources for accomplishing the task. The watchword, he said, "means the giving to all men an adequate opportunity of knowing Jesus Christ as their Saviour and of becoming His real disciples" (p. 4). This is what Christ implied in the Great Commission. It means preaching the gospel to those who are now living; it does not mean the conversion of the world, according to Mott. There were approximately 15,000 Protestant missionaries throughout the world in 1900. Mott proposed there was a need for one missionary to every 20,000 heathen; therefore he called for an increase in the missionary task force from 15,000 to 50,000 — though he agreed with Professor Gustav Warneck that there was no need for more than the 537 Protestant mission agencies already in existence.

Robert E. Speer began his remarkable forty-six-year tenure as secretary of the Board of Foreign Missions of the Presbyterian Church in the U.S.A. in 1891. Profoundly influenced during student days at Princeton College by Pierson and Moody, Speer was an SVM traveling secretary for one year following graduation from Princeton in 1889, then attended Princeton Seminary for a year, but never graduated. Like Mott, he was never ordained and never served as a foreign missionary; they were "detained volunteers." Yet his influence in American missions — and beyond — in the first third of the century would be enormous. A prolific author (sixty-seven books and countless articles) and eloquent speaker, Speer was a preeminent interpreter of foreign missions. While Mott was the missionary statesman, Speer was the prophet.[26] His leadership of the Presbyterian board "contributed to an increase in Presbyterian foreign missionaries from 598 when he joined the board in 1891 to a peak of 1,606 in 1927," and at 1,356 shortly before he retired in 1937 it was the largest of any American agency at that time.[27] John A. Mackay, later president of Princeton Seminary and himself an influential figure in American missions, testified that Speer was "one of the greatest figures in American Christianity. Judged by any standard intellectual or spiritual, Dr. Speer was incomparably the greatest man I have ever known."[28] The Robert E. Speer Library building at Princeton Seminary is a tribute to his legacy.

Speaking in 1900, Speer said that "the aim of foreign missions [is] to make Jesus Christ known to the world with a view to the full salvation of men, and their gathering into true and living churches." There should be no confusion of the aim with the methods and results of missions. It is a "mischievous doctrine," he said, to suggest that missions "must aim at the total reorganization of the whole social fabric"; this may be a result of missions, but it is not the aim of missions.[29]

---

26. S. Eddy, *Pathfinders of the World Missionary Crusade* (Nashville, 1945) 260.

27. J. A. Patterson, "Robert E. Speer and the Crisis of the American Protestant Missionary Movement, 1920-1937" (Ph.D. diss., Princeton Theological Seminary, 1980) 185.

28. Quoted by H. M. Goodpasture, "Robert E. Speer's Legacy," *Occasional Bulletin of Missionary Research* 2 (1978) 38. See also R. P. Beaver, "North American Thought on the Fundamental Principles of Missions during the Twentieth Century," *Church History* 21 (1952) 348, and Patterson, "Robert Speer," 185ff.

29. R. E. Speer, "The Supreme and Determining Aim," *Ecumenical Missionary Conference, New York, 1900: Report* (New York, 1900) I, 74-78.

Along with Mott and Speer as a major figure in this period and later was George Sherwood Eddy. Eddy graduated from Yale in 1891 with Henry W. Luce (father of the founder of *Time*) and Horace T. Pitkin. The three of them were student volunteers, they were roommates at Union Theological Seminary, and they planned to spend their lives in China. Pitkin went and was beheaded during the Boxer Rebellion in 1900. After finishing his seminary studies at Princeton with Eddy, Luce went to China and eventually became vice president of Yenching University. But Mott prevailed on Eddy to go to India with the YMCA. After fifteen years in India, Eddy served another fifteen years as YMCA secretary for Asia doing student evangelistic work, then went on to become an influential world citizen as lay evangelist and advocate of the social gospel, socialism, and pacifism in his lectures, travel seminars, and thirty-six books. In his autobiography, Eddy testified that his conversion under Moody at Northfield and his association with Mott and Speer were dominant in shaping his life. It was difficult for students in later generations, he said, "to realize how impelling was the appeal of the Volunteer Movement for us in those days."[30]

Ecumenical Missionary Conference, 1900

In planning for the Ecumenical Missionary Conference to be held in New York City in 1900, William E. Dodge expressed a common conviction, "We are going into a century more full of hope, and promise, and opportunity than any period in the world's history. We want to seize upon these opportunities."[31] The ten-day conference in April 1900 "was the largest missionary conference that has ever been held,"[32] with 200 mission societies from Europe, Britain, and the United States represented and nearly 200,000 people attending the various sessions. Those who could not get into sessions at Carnegie Hall went to overflow meetings at nearby Calvary Baptist Church, Central Presbyterian Church, and other churches. President William McKinley, at the opening, spoke of "the missionary effort which has wrought such wonderful triumphs for civilization."[33] He was followed on the program by the governor of the state of New York,

30. S. Eddy, *Eighty Adventurous Years: An Autobiography* (New York, 1955) 29.
31. *Ecumenical Missionary Conference: Report* I, 11.
32. W. R. Hogg, *Ecumenical Foundations: A History of the International Missionary Council and Its Nineteenth-Century Background* (New York, 1952) 45; also C. W. Forman, "Evangelization and Civilization: Protestant Missionary Motivation in the Imperialist Era: The Americans," *International Bulletin of Missionary Research* 6 (1982) 54.
33. *Ecumenical Missionary Conference: Report* I, 39.

Theodore Roosevelt, and former President Benjamin Harrison, who was honorary president of the conference.

The 1900 conference was indicative of the momentum in support of interdenominational cooperation in missions, at home and abroad, that had been developing especially since the 1880s — to avoid competition, to realize better stewardship of resources, and to provide more effective witness to non-Christians. For instance, the Intercollegiate YMCA Movement, founded in 1877 with Luther D. Wishard as the first secretary, was a pioneering effort, and the Interseminary Missionary Alliance (later the Interseminary Movement), founded in 1880, "prepared the ground for the Mount Hermon awakening in 1886" and was the forerunner of the SVM.[34]

Of special significance for comity and cooperation was the formation in 1893 of the Interdenominational Conference of Foreign Mission Boards and Societies in the United States and Canada (which became the Foreign Missions Conference of North America in 1911, the Division of Foreign Missions of the National Council of Churches in 1950, and the Division of Overseas Ministries, NCC, in 1965).[35] This was followed by a number of ecumenical organizations that were founded for coordination and cooperation in support of missions. Some of the more important were the Central Committee on the United Study of Foreign Missions, 1900; the Young People's Missionary Movement, 1902 (which became the Missionary Education Movement in 1911); and the Laymen's Missionary Movement, 1907 (which some church officials at the time declared was "the most epoch-making [movement] that has occurred in the Christian world since the Protestant Reformation"), which was absorbed in 1919 by the Interchurch World Movement and collapsed a year later in a financial fiasco.[36]

The number of American Protestant overseas missionary personnel increased dramatically from a relatively small number prior to 1880, to 2,716 in 1890, to 4,159 in 1900, to 7,219 in 1910, and over 9,000 in 1915.[37] Participation in foreign missions had become "an identifying mark of mainstream Protestantism."[38] Mott announced in 1910 that it was "the

---

34. Hogg, *Ecumenical Foundations*, 84.

35. S. M. Cavert, *Church Cooperation and Unity in America: A Historical Review, 1900-1970* (New York, 1970) 52, 202. In 1990, it became the Church World Service and Witness Unit of the NCC.

36. V. H. Rabe, *The Home Base of American China Missions, 1880-1920* (Cambridge, Massachusetts, 1978) 26, 30.

37. E. M. Bliss, ed., *Encyclopaedia of Missions* (New York, 1891) II, 626; Dennis, *Centennial Survey*, 257; Hogg, "The Role of American Protestantism in World Mission," 369.

38. R. P. Beaver, *American Protestant Women in World Mission: History of the First*

decisive hour of Christian missions," that there was a "rising spiritual tide" in the non-Christian world, and that "on the world-wide battlefield of Christianity . . . victory is assured if the present campaign be adequately supported and pressed."[39]

Women in Mission

In addition to the significant contribution of the SVM was the remarkable role of women in the American missionary enterprise. Women undergirded the missionary movement with prayer, study, financial support, personnel, and diffusion of information. Their periodicals included the Congregationalist *Light and Life for Heathen Women* (shortened to *Life and Light for Women* in 1876), the Methodist *Heathen Woman's Friend* (which became *Woman's Missionary Friend* in 1896), both founded in 1869, the Free Baptist *Missionary Helper* (1878), the Presbyterian *Woman's Work for Woman* (1871, merged with *Our Mission Field* in 1886 and the name was changed to *Woman's Work* in 1905), the Southern Methodist *Woman's Missionary Advocate* (1880), the United Brethren *Woman's Evangel* (1881), the Methodist Protestant *Woman's Missionary Record* (1885), and the United Presbyterian *Woman's Missionary Magazine* (1887). However, the women faced opposition, discrimination, and lack of recognition by men. When Rufus Anderson, foreign secretary of the American Board and one of the outstanding American mission strategists of the nineteenth century, retired in 1866, he told his successor, "I cannot recommend bringing women into this work; but you are a young man, go and do it if you can."[40] In response to this situation, women formed their own mission boards, such as the Woman's Union Missionary Society of America for Heathen Lands (1860). At the Centenary Conference of 1888 in London, American women — led by Abbie Child — initiated the formation of the World's Missionary Committee of Christian Women, which has been described as "the first international ecumenical missionary agency."[41] In connection with the Columbian Exposition at Chicago in 1893, there was a Congress of Missions for Women and a Conference of Women's Missionary Societies. The first meeting of the Interdenominational Conference of Woman's Boards of Foreign Missions of the United States and Canada (which became the

Feminist Movement in North America (rev. ed., Grand Rapids, 1980) 87. First published in 1968 under the title *All Loves Excelling: American Protestant Women in World Mission*.

39. Mott, *The Decisive Hour of Christian Missions* (London, 1910) 78-79, 112.
40. Quoted by Beaver, *American Protestant Women*, 87.
41. *Ibid.*, 145.

Federation of Woman's Boards of Foreign Missions in 1916 and merged with the Foreign Missions Conference in 1934) was held in 1896. It was a parallel organization to the Interdenominational Conference of Foreign Mission Boards, from which the women's boards were excluded.[42]

By 1890 there were 34 American women's societies supporting 926 missionaries in various fields, and together with the married women of the general missionary boards, they composed 60% of the total American missionary force.[43] By 1900 there were 41 women's agencies supporting over 1,200 single women missionaries. In 1910 the women's foreign missionary movement claimed a total supporting membership of two million.[44] While their general concern was for all people, their particular focus was on work with women and children. As the number of women missionaries outnumbered the men on many fields, the women's movement came to be viewed as a threat to the general boards, and women were reminded to keep their proper place. The prevailing sentiment was expressed in 1888 by the secretary of the American Baptist Missionary Union: "Woman's work in the foreign field must be careful to recognize the headship of man in ordering the affairs of the Kingdom of God."[45] After 1910 most of the women's agencies were gradually merged into the general denominational boards, where they came under more ecclesiastical control and were dominated by men.[46] This led eventually to "the destruction of the women's foreign missionary movement," because — as R. Pierce Beaver has observed — "the voluntary principle is essential to world mission," whereas denominational and ecumenical structures "frown upon spontaneous action and establishment of direct relationships which they do not initiate or administer."[47]

African Americans in Mission

An aspect of American missions that is not widely recognized is the pioneering role and contribution of African Americans. "Although the golden age of Black foreign missions did not come until the late 1870s,"

---

42. *Ibid.*, 149-54.

43. J. Hunter, *The Gospel of Gentility: American Women Missionaries in Turn-of-the-Century China* (New Haven, 1984) xiii.

44. P. R. Hill, *The World Their Household: The American Woman's Foreign Mission Movement and Cultural Transformation, 1870-1920* (Ann Arbor, 1985) 195.

45. Quoted by Beaver, *American Protestant Women*, 114, and Hunter, *Gospel of Gentility*, 14.

46. Beaver, *American Protestant Women*, 184ff.

47. *Ibid.*, 205.

according to Gayraud S. Wilmore, "as early as 1782 former slaves such as David George, George Liele, Amos Williams, and Joseph Paul sought to transplant their churches from South Carolina and Georgia to Nova Scotia, Sierra Leone, Jamaica, and the Bahamas. . . . These men became the first unofficial Afro-American missionaries before the American foreign missionary movement had been solidly launched."[48] Lott Carey and Colin Teague were sent to Liberia in 1820 by the black Baptists of Richmond, and numerous other initiatives were taken by African Americans in missions during the nineteenth century, especially to Africa.[49] After the "Great Century," however, "with the struggle against virtual genocide in an era of racial hatred and violence at home, together with the distractions of World War I and the Great Depression, black church support of missions gradually declined and much was left in disarray."[50] A notable continuing black mission agency is the Lott Carey Baptist Foreign Mission Convention, founded in 1897, with headquarters in Washington, D.C., which is an ecumenical mission serving denominations of Baptist tradition.

Textbooks

Books by Speer and William Owen Carver in the first decade of the century became standard texts for the study of missions. Staunchly evangelical, ecumenical, and sensitive to new insights, Speer published in this decade *Missionary Principles and Practice* (1902), *Missions and Modern History* (2 vols., 1904), and *Christianity and the Nations* (1910).

Carver, professor of missions at Southern Baptist Theological Seminary in Louisville from 1899, published *Missions in the Plan of Ages* (1909) and *Missions and Modern Thought* (1910). Of his twenty-one published books, *Missions in the Plan of Ages* — described by R. Pierce Beaver as "representative of American thought on the eve of the Edinburgh Conference" — was Carver's most important and influential book.[51]

48. G. S. Wilmore, "Black Americans in Mission: Setting the Record Straight," *International Bulletin of Missionary Research* 10 (1986) 98.

49. *Ibid.*, 98ff. See also S. M. Jacobs, ed., *Black Americans and the Missionary Movement in Africa* (Westport, 1982), W. L. Williams, *Black Americans and the Evangelization of Africa, 1877-1900* (Madison, 1982), and S. D. Martin, *Black Baptists and African Missions: The Origins of a Movement, 1880-1915* (Macon, 1989).

50. Wilmore, "Black Americans," 100.

51. Beaver, "North American Thought," 347. See also H. H. Culpepper, "The Legacy of William Owen Carver," *International Bulletin of Missionary Research* 5 (1981) 119-22.

Edinburgh 1910

The milestone event at this early point in the century was the World Missionary Conference at Edinburgh in 1910, where American leaders such as Mott, Speer, James L. Barton, Harlan Beach, Bishop Charles H. Brent, Arthur Judson Brown, Henry Sloane Coffin, Sherwood Eddy, Douglas Mackenzie, Frank Mason North, Bishop James Thoburn, J. Campbell White, and Samuel Zwemer were prominent. It came at a time of high enthusiasm in the missionary endeavor, and the missionary obligation was considered a self-evident axiom to be obeyed, not to be questioned. Edinburgh was primarily concerned with strategy, consultation, and cooperation to complete the task of evangelizing the world; the Great Commission of Christ was the only basis needed for missions. Speer challenged the assembly at the opening service to prepare for "the immediate conquest of the world." Ten days later in his closing address Mott said, "The end of the conference is the beginning of the conquest." A Continuation Committee was appointed, with Mott as chairman, and in 1921 at Lake Mohonk, New York, it formed the International Missionary Council (IMC, merged with the World Council of Churches in 1961). This became the major international forum and vehicle for ecumenical cooperation in Protestant missions.

Two important journals were launched following Edinburgh 1910: the *Moslem World* began publication in 1911 with Zwemer as editor, and the *International Review of Missions* was started in 1912. Another remarkable fruit of Edinburgh was the founding in 1914 of the Missionary Research Library in New York City under the leadership of Dr. Mott. Initial funding came from John D. Rockefeller, Jr., and in 1914 Mott wrote to Charles H. Fahs, who was to be the secretary (later changed to curator) of the new library, "We are now ready to go ahead full steam on the plan to secure the most complete and serviceable missionary library and archives in the world. I desire it to be thoroughly interdenominational, ecumenical, and international. It should be preeminently rich in source material." In 1929, when larger quarters were needed, Union Theological Seminary agreed to house the library in partnership with the Foreign Missions Conference of North America, and for years the library ranked as the best collection of its kind in the world.[52]

---

52. R. P. Beaver, "The Missionary Research Library and the Occasional Bulletin," *Occasional Bulletin of Missionary Research* 1 (1977) 2; also Hopkins, *John R. Mott*, 425.

The Teaching of Missions

At the Ecumenical Missionary Conference in 1900, Charles Cuthbert Hall, president of Union Theological Seminary, reported that "the study of missions is slowly rising to the rank of a theological discipline."[53] By the time of the Edinburgh Conference there were four professorships for the teaching of missions in American seminaries: Episcopal Theological Seminary (Cambridge, Massachusetts), Omaha (Presbyterian) Theological Seminary (Nebraska), Southern Baptist Theological Seminary (Louisville, Kentucky), and Yale Divinity School.[54] In the decade following Edinburgh, six new professorships were established at Bethany Biblical Seminary in Chicago, Boston University School of Theology, Candler School of Theology at Emory University, Drew University Theological School, Princeton Theological Seminary, and Union Theological Seminary in New York. In the 1920s eleven more seminaries established professorships of missions.[55] In 1911 the Hartford School of Missions was founded, later known as the Kennedy School of Missions of the Hartford Seminary Foundation (1913), where "for decades the greatest concentration of missions scholars were found."[56]

About 1917 informal meetings of those teaching missions and related subjects began along the eastern seaboard, and this became the Fellowship of Professors of Missions of the Middle Atlantic Region.[57] But

---

53. *Ecumenical Missionary Conference: Report* I, 151.

54. World Missionary Conference, 1910, *Report of Commission VI: The Home Base of Missions* (New York, 1910) 175. It was reported at the Edinburgh Conference that "at Yale University the 'Courses of Study of the Missionary Department' number one hundred-and-three items under thirteen heads!" (W. H. T. Gairdner, *"Edinburgh 1910": An Account and Interpretation of the World Missionary Conference* [Edinburgh, 1910] 227). O. G. Myklebust lists only three professorships at the time of Edinburgh in vol. II (p. 71) of his study, but lists four (and explains the discrepancy) in vol. I (p. 373) of his work, *The Study of Missions in Theological Education* (2 vols.; Oslo, 1955, 1957).

55. Myklebust, *Study of Missions* II, 71-72.

56. R. P. Beaver, "The Meaning and Place of Missiology Today in the American Scene" (a paper given at the European Consultation on Mission Studies, Selly Oak Colleges, Birmingham, England, April 1968) 3. Beaver adds this critical judgment about Hartford: "That school, however, consistently rejected responsibility for theoretical and theological concern in missions."

57. Myklebust, *Study of Missions* II, 71, 185. As the source of his information Myklebust cites a typescript by D. J. Fleming, "History of the Fellowship of Professors of Missions," and a letter from R. P. Beaver, dated Nov. 29, 1955. In response to my inquiry in November 1986, the library at Union Theological Seminary, New York, reported that there is no copy of the Fleming typescript in the Fleming file or papers. In response to a similar inquiry, Professor Myklebust wrote in a letter dated Dec. 10, 1986, "I am afraid I have to disappoint you. The documents to which you refer are not

missiology would not be recognized in North America as a proper theological discipline for another fifty years. At this early stage, says James A. Scherer, missions instruction was

> plagued by a certain immaturity and obscurity with regard to definition, methodological basis, and objectives. In retrospect, it appears that the credibility of the claims of world missions to a rightful place in theological education was weakened by a failure to think through the nature and requirements of the infant discipline and the manner in which these were to be represented in the curriculum. Was world missions merely an appendage to ecclesiology or practical theology? . . . Or did world missions have a solid theoretical and methodological basis which allowed it to challenge and to interact with other disciplines? What were the aims of the new subject? Were they related primarily to motivation and training, or did they have basic theological understanding as their object?[58]

As yet there was no consensus.

The End of the "Great Century"

The outbreak of World War I marked the beginning of a new era in the missionary enterprise. Kenneth Scott Latourette maintained that the twentieth century, in the sense of a distinct change from the nineteenth century, really began in 1914 with the outbreak of the World War of 1914-18, and it marked the end of the "Great Century" of Christian expansion.[59] The break, of course, did not happen overnight, and some of the earlier trends continued to fruition in the new era. But the general spirit of confidence in the capacities of humanity, in inevitable progress in history, and in the scientific method as the key to the solution of evil in the world was increasingly replaced by skepticism, cynicism, and pessimism.

---

in the archives of the Egede Institute. The secretary and the librarian have searched the files, but in vain. . . . Neither Fleming's 'History' or Beaver's letter of Nov. 29, 1955 are there. However, I can assure you that the quotations from Fleming's 'History' are through and through correct." Cf. R. P. Beaver, "The American Protestant Theological Seminary and Missions: An Historical Survey," *Missiology* 4 (1976) 84.

58. J. A. Scherer, "Missions in Theological Education," in *The Future of the Christian World Mission: Studies in Honor of R. Pierce Beaver*, ed. W. J. Danker and Wi Jo Kang (Grand Rapids, 1971) 145.

59. See K. S. Latourette, *A History of the Expansion of Christianity* IV: *The Great Century in Europe and the United States of America, A.D. 1800–A.D. 1914* (New York, 1941) 7.

Following the war's disruption, the sending and support of overseas missionary personnel came to a point of culmination. "Most of the major sending agencies reached a peak in the number of missionaries in the field during the early 1920s which was not approached again until after World War II."[60] Similarly the predepression high point in North American foreign mission contributions was reached in 1921.[61] The growth was impressive. In 1911 only one-third of the 21,000 Protestant foreign missionaries scattered around the world came from North America (including Canada).[62] By 1925 there were over 29,000 Protestant missionaries, and approximately half of them came from North America (there were more than 3,300 American missionaries in China alone). Income for foreign missions from living donors of fifteen major denominations in the United States soared from $5,300,100 in 1901 to $21,288,749 in 1919.[63]

Some prewar negative trends also continued to confront the missionary enterprise. Criticism of missions from secular sources escalated with charges of cultural and political imperialism. Issues that came out in the debate over the annexation of the Philippines, and the controversy surrounding the Boxer Rebellion of 1900, were carried forward by critics who cast aspersions on the motives and methods of foreign missions.

Debate over the theology of missions — fueled by the fundamentalist-modernist controversy — also became more serious and led to fragmentation. Two articles that appeared in the *Harvard Theological Review* in 1915 by James L. Barton and J. P. Jones, both of the American Board of Commissioners for Foreign Missions, were indicative of the changes in missionary thinking occurring in those churches and agencies that came under the sway of liberal theology and the social gospel movement. Barton and Jones came to these general conclusions: (1) There was a change in the attitude of missionaries to the non-Christian religions, which were no longer thought to be entirely false but instead to have elements of truth in them; (2) there was a change of emphasis in missions from the individual to society, with less stress upon the number of admissions to the church than on the leavening influence of Christian truth in the community as a whole; (3) there was a broader range of activities for the missionary, which meant less direct preaching of the gospel and more attention to the transformation of one's life as well as one's heart; and (4) there was

60. V. H. Rabe, "Evangelical Logistics: Mission Support and Resources to 1920," in Fairbank, ed., *The Missionary Enterprise in China and America*, 71.

61. *Ibid.*, 388, no. 80.

62. F. W. Price and K. E. Moyer, "A Study of American Protestant Foreign Missions in 1956," *Occasional Bulletin from the Missionary Research Library* 7 (1956) 1.

63. Rabe, "Evangelical Logistics," 88.

a change of emphasis in the missionary message, which formerly stressed salvation in the world to come but now laid more stress on salvation for life in the present world.[64]

Faith Missions

In contrast to the mainline denominational mission agencies that reflected these theological developments were the conservative faith missions that formed the Interdenominational Foreign Mission Association (IFMA) in 1917 as a "fellowship of missions without denominational affiliation" and with a statement of faith adhering to "the fundamental doctrines of the historic Christian faith." Among the founding agencies of the IFMA were Africa Inland Mission, Central American Mission, China Inland Mission, South Africa General Mission, and Sudan Interior Mission. Theologically conservative faith missions flourished and numerous new agencies were established, such as Orinoco River Mission (1920), Latin America Mission (1921), Iran Interior Mission, Oriental Boat Mission, and Gospel Mission of South America (all in 1923), West Indies Mission (1928), and the India Mission (1930). Bible institutes — especially Moody in Chicago and others in Toronto, Massachusetts (Gordon), Nyack, Philadelphia, Providence, and Los Angeles — provided large numbers of personnel for the conservative missions.

Theological controversy led to schism in the work of the United Christian Missionary Society (Disciples of Christ) in the Philippines in 1926. In 1927 the Association of Baptists for Evangelism in the Orient (later Association of Baptists for World Evangelization) was formed by personnel formerly related to the American Baptist Foreign Mission Society. The Independent Board for Presbyterian Foreign Missions was organized in 1933 by J. Gresham Machen and his followers in their dispute with the Presbyterian Board of Foreign Missions. The resignation of Pearl S. Buck in 1933 as a Presbyterian missionary in China because of critical attacks on her theological views from fundamentalist sources was widely publicized.[65]

---

64. J. L. Barton, "The Modern Missionary," *Harvard Theological Review* 8 (1915) 1-17; J. P. Jones, "The Protestant Missionary Propaganda in India," *ibid.*, 18-44. The articles are summarized in *International Review of Missions* 4 (1915) 308-9.

65. *Christian Century*, Nov. 23, 1932, 1434. On the rise of evangelical-fundamentalist missions, see *Earthen Vessels* (n. 14 above); also the editor's introduction to *Modernism and Foreign Missions: Two Fundamentalist Protests*, ed. J. A. Carpenter (New York, 1988).

Decline of the SVM

The Student Volunteer Movement was in decline and the watchword was in the twilight of its influence. Mott had resigned as chairman in 1920; it was the end of an era. Nearly 13,000 volunteers actually sailed for overseas service, it was claimed, between 1886 and 1936. But questions about missions and a desire for a broader approach to Christian internationalism affected the SVM. At a student conference under the auspices of the SVM at Northfield in 1917, the participants asked, "Does Christ offer an adequate solution for the burning social and international questions of the day?" There was a growing sense that foreign missions were not the only channel through which Christians should work to bring about the healing of the nations. "A radical reorientation in the thinking and methods of the SVM" occurred at conventions in 1919 and 1923 where students called for "a radical change in the assumptions and methods underlying future SVM activity and conventions," to accommodate "the students' new-found interest in issues of race, war, and the social order."[66]

The *Christian Century* reported that at the SVM Convention in Detroit at the end of 1927 Sherwood Eddy "finally and publically repudiated that famous war-cry: 'The evangelization of the world in this generation.' No one challenged him; no one attempted to maintain that what is still needed is — to use the Eddyian phrase — 'a Paul Revere's ride across the world.'"[67] Other factors in the decline of the SVM, says Clifton J. Phillips, included the growing fundamentalist-modernist split, the Great Depression of the 1930s, which undercut the financial support of foreign missions, the rising secularism in American higher education, the spread of the social gospel, "and perhaps most important of all, a developing crisis in missionary thinking, which in the 1920s and later shifted even farther away from evangelization of the non-Christian world by Americans and Europeans in the direction of partnership and cooperation among the older and younger churches in the building of a Christian world order."[68]

As the SVM declined and changed its orientation in the 1930s, evangelicals formed the Student Foreign Missions Fellowship in 1936 (exactly fifty years after Mount Hermon in 1886), and in 1939 the first Inter-Varsity Christian Fellowship chapters in the United States were estab-

---

66. Shedd, *Two Centuries*, 405. Cf. N. D. Showalter, "The End of a Crusade: The Student Volunteer Movement for Foreign Missions and the Great War" (Th.D. diss., Harvard University, 1990).

67. "Youth and Missions," editorial in *Christian Century*, Jan. 12, 1928, 40.

68. Phillips, "Student Volunteer Movement," 109.

lished. In 1945 the two movements merged and the SFMF became the missionary arm of the IVCF.[69] They sponsored a student missionary convention at Toronto in 1946, where Samuel Zwemer reminded participants of the watchword and the earlier student movement. Two years later a second missionary convention was held on the campus of the University of Illinois at Urbana. The Inter-Varsity Urbana conventions became triennial events that would attract as many as 19,000 students, who claimed the tradition of the SVM and the watchword as their own.

The crucial issues in missions that had emerged since Edinburgh 1910 were debated at the Jerusalem meeting of the International Missionary Council in 1928, where the focus of discussion was on "The Christian Life and Message in Relation to Non-Christian Systems of Thought and Life." Secularism and syncretism were seen as the two major challenges to missions. In addition to Mott and Speer, Americans who were prominent at Jerusalem included Ralph Diffendorfer, E. Stanley Jones, Rufus Jones, William Ernest Hocking, Bishop Francis J. McConnell, John A. Mackay, Luther A. Weigle, and Samuel Zwemer. The European participants were generally critical of the Americans on two points: their emphasis on social concerns, i.e., the "social gospel," and their allowance for the possibility of revelation in non-Christian religions. One of the lessons learned at the Jerusalem meeting, according to John A. Mackay, was that "the missionary movement must become more theological, not primarily for those to whom missionaries go, but for the Church herself and the missionaries who represent her."[70]

Daniel Johnson Fleming, former missionary in India and professor of missions at Union Theological Seminary in New York City from 1918, dealt with the missionary attitude and approach to people of other faiths in his books *Attitudes toward Other Faiths* (1928) and *Ways of Sharing with Other Faiths* (1929). Fleming — an influential liberal theoretician of missions — urged a sympathetic approach to people of other faiths, with a desire to share the knowledge of Jesus and his spirit, but he placed little emphasis on the need for conversion. By contrast, Samuel M. Zwemer, professor of missions at Princeton Seminary and regarded as the "Apostle to Islam," held to a staunchly evangelical position of "salvation in no other name" in his numerous publications.

69. D. M. Howard, *Student Power in World Missions* (2nd ed., Downers Grove, 1979) 110. See also H. W. Norton, *To Stir the Church: A Brief History of the Student Foreign Missions Fellowships, 1936-1986* (Madison, 1986).

70. J. A. Mackay, "The Evangelistic Duty of Christianity," *The Christian Life and Message in Relation to Non-Christian Systems of Thought and Life*, vol. I of *The Jerusalem Meeting of the International Missionary Council, March 24–April 8, 1928* (New York, 1928) 390.

The Hocking Report

The most significant event of the period in terms of creating controversy in American missions was the publication in 1932 of *Re-Thinking Missions*, the Report of the Commission of Appraisal of the Laymen's Foreign Missions Inquiry, edited by the chairman of the commission, William Ernest Hocking, professor of philosophy at Harvard University. The report was the culmination of a massive survey and research project funded by John D. Rockefeller, Jr. While the report did not deny that missions should continue, it suggested that important changes had taken place that required the missionary enterprise to reconsider its motives, methods, message, and aims. These changes were: an altered theological outlook, the emergence of a basic world culture, and the rise of nationalism. The report proposed that the aim of missions should be "to seek with people of other lands a true knowledge and love of God, expressing in life and word what we have learned through Jesus Christ"; that "the Christian will regard himself as a co-worker with the forces which are making for righteousness within every religious system"; that "the relation between religions must take increasingly hereafter the form of a common search for truth"; and that the missionary "will look forward, not to the destruction of these [non-Christian] religions, but to their continued co-existence with Christianity, each stimulating the other in growth toward the ultimate goal, unity in the completest religious truth."

This was a radical departure from the traditional concept of missions, the role of the missionary, and the relation of Christianity to other religions. As such, the report provoked basic rethinking of the issues, but was itself widely criticized for its tone of optimism and relativism and was not representative of American thinking on missions. Robert E. Speer and John A. Mackay published critiques that rejected the theological views of the report. Mackay said it presented a theological viewpoint that was already outdated — "the sunset glow of nineteenth-century romanticism."[71] The only mission board in America to respond favorably to the theological tone of the report was the American Board of Commissioners for Foreign Missions. Hocking later elaborated on his thought about the way toward a single world faith — not by means of "radical displacement" but by "synthesis" leading to "reconception" — in his book *Living Religions and a World Faith* (1940).

Among the few mission scholars who were sympathetic with the viewpoint of the Hocking Report were Archibald G. Baker at the Univer-

---

71. "The Theology of the Laymen's Foreign Missions Inquiry," *International Review of Missions* 22 (1933) 178.

sity of Chicago and Hugh Vernon White, secretary of the American Board of Commissioners for Foreign Missions. Baker, in his book *Christian Missions and a New World Culture* (1934), presented a position of nearly complete religious relativism. His justification for missions was that the experiments of Christianity with the problems of life had been more fruitful than the experiments of other religions. Therefore Christianity had a mission to share the results of this cultural experiment with other cultures by means of "the interpenetration or cross-fertilization of cultures" (p. 293). White, in *A Theology for Christian Missions* (1937) and *A Working Faith for the World* (1938), affirmed the position of the Laymen's Inquiry and said that "the Christian mission should be a man-centered enterprise," with "the service of man as the regulative aim of Christian missions."

The malaise in mission theology — reflected in Hocking, Baker, and White — was matched by a decline in financial support for foreign missions. By the mid-1930s the economic depression "threw the whole Protestant missionary enterprise in reverse."[72] It was symptomatic of the "American religious depression," described by Robert Handy as "a nationally observable spiritual lethargy evident in the 1920s and 1930s."[73] More specifically, as Charles W. Forman has observed, "the story . . . of the '20s and '30s suggests that missiology failed to meet the test. Instead of holding together and going deeper in response to many new challenges, it seemed to become shallower and to wander off into vague uncertainties or else to react defensively."[74]

Reaction to Hocking

In 1938, on the eve of World War II, the International Missionary Council met at Madras. In preparation for the conference, the Dutch missiologist Hendrik Kraemer published *The Christian Message in a Non-Christian World*, which was said to have been "provoked by, and written in direct refutation of, the thought of Professor W. E. Hocking of Harvard."[75] Kraemer took

72. Beaver, "The American Protestant Theological Seminary and Missions," 84. This was more true of mainline denominational mission agencies than of faith missions. Between 1929 and 1931 China Inland Mission sent out over 200 new missionaries; World Radio Missionary Fellowship was founded in 1931; and Wycliffe Bible Translators was founded in 1934.

73. R. T. Handy, "The American Religious Depression, 1925-1935," *Church History* 29 (1960) 13.

74. C. W. Forman, "A History of Foreign Mission Theory in America," in *American Missions in Bicentennial Perspective*, ed. R. P. Beaver, 103.

75. H. P. Van Dusen, "The Missionary Message since Madras," *Christendom* 9 (1944) 27.

the position that Christianity was *"the* religion of revelation" (p. 23), and he stressed a radical discontinuity between the realm of what he called "biblical realism" (which critics said was neither biblical nor realistic) and the whole range of non-Christian religious experience. All non-Christian religions, philosophies, and worldviews, he said, are merely "the various efforts of man to apprehend the totality of existence," and are doomed to failure (pp. 111-12). The only point of contact between non-Christian religions and Christian revelation is "the disposition and the attitude of the missionary" (p. 140).

Kraemer's views regarding the relationship between Christianity and other faiths and the role of the church were vigorously debated at the conference and for a generation following. After the conference there was a spirited exchange between E. Stanley Jones and Henry P. Van Dusen in the pages of the *Christian Century* that indicated both a vitality of thought and strategy among missionaries overseas and a sharp difference of perspective between Jones, the veteran missionary, and Van Dusen, the North American seminary professor who had no overseas experience. Jones — a Methodist missionary in India who was well known for his books *The Christ of the Indian Road* (1925, sold over 600,000 copies in twelve languages) and *Christ at the Roundtable* (1928) — said that "Madras missed the way" because it had used the church as its starting point instead of the kingdom of God.[76] Van Dusen, who had been chairman of Section I at Madras, wrote a stinging rebuke, "What Stanley Jones Missed at Madras." He maintained that Jones had missed the proper church emphasis and that the conference had given appropriate attention to the kingdom, but not as an instrumentality for a new social order, as Jones advocated. Many "sincere students of the New Testament," according to Van Dusen, would "deny that [the kingdom] has any direct and indisputable implication for economic and international life," whereas "almost every Christian movement for radical social reform has come out of the heart of the church."[77] Jones, in his reply, acknowledged that he missed the church at Madras:

> I missed a church which started from where Jesus started, the Kingdom of God, and found instead a church which started with itself, and therefore largely ended with itself and with the saving of its fellowship. . . . I missed a church which, while conscious of its mission as the chief instrument of the Kingdom of God, also was humble enough

76. E. S. Jones, "Where Madras Missed Its Way," *Christian Century*, March 15, 1939, 351.

77. *Christian Century*, March 29, 1939, 411.

to rejoice that God was using other instruments to bring in the King-dom.[78]

A kingdom perspective in mission, such as Jones was urging, would come more than forty years later at the World Mission Conference sponsored by the World Council of Churches at Melbourne in 1980 under the theme "Your Kingdom Come."

The most important contribution to mission theory to appear during the war years was *The Philosophy of the Christian World Mission* by Edmund Davison Soper, a former Methodist missionary, who was profes-sor of missions at Garrett Biblical Institute in Evanston, Illinois, when the book was published in 1943. Soper, representing the prevailing view in North America, took a middle position between Hocking and Kraemer. He affirmed the absolute uniqueness of the revelation in Christ over against the relativism of Hocking, yet recognized the spiritual values in other religions over against the radical discontinuity of Kraemer. He aptly described Kraemer's position as "uniqueness without continuity" and Hocking's as "continuity with doubtful uniqueness," then set forth his own position of "uniqueness together with continuity" (pp. 223, 225ff.).

Also published in this period was Kenneth Scott Latourette's monu-mental seven-volume study, *A History of the Expansion of Christianity* (1937-45). After graduation from Yale, Latourette — a Baptist — served as travel-ing secretary for the SVM, then briefly as a missionary in China until poor health forced his return to the States in 1912. His teaching career at Yale (1912-53) as professor of missions and Oriental history was marked by a steady stream of publications that established his international reputation as a leading historian and apologist of Christian missions. The thesis of his study of the expansion of Christianity was that

> throughout its history it has gone forward by major pulsations. Each advance has carried it further than the one before it. Of the alternating recessions, each has been briefer and less marked than the one which preceded it. This has been the case by whichever of the criteria the advance and recession have been measured — geographic extent, the new movements issuing from Christianity, or the influence upon the human race.[79]

It was Latourette's judgment that "in A.D. 1944 Christianity was affecting more deeply more different nations and cultures than ever before." Yet

---

78. *Christian Century*, May 31, 1939, 707.
79. Latourette, *A History of the Expansion of Christianity* VII: *Advance through Storm: A.D. 1914 and After, with Concluding Generalizations* (New York, 1945) 494.

"when he died in the late 1960s," says one of his students, "he was not prepared to say whether the period of history from 1914 to 1960 was a period of missionary 'advance' or 'retreat.' "[80]

Postwar Renewal

After World War II a new wave of missionary vitality surged through the American churches. The immediate task was that of getting missionaries back to the field. In 1946 the American President Ship Lines allotted over 1,000 spaces on two former troop ships to be prorated among the various boards belonging to the Foreign Missions Conference of North America for transporting missionaries back to Asia. Mainline boards began to rebuild after a twenty-year period of decline and disruption, but they would never fully recover. For instance, the peak year of the Presbyterian Board before the depression was 1926 with 1,606 missionaries. That number had gradually decreased until 1942, when there were only 1,134 on the roll. During 1946-47, 100 new missionaries were commissioned and the total rose to 1,209.[81]

It was also a period of rapid growth for conservative evangelical missions, both in existing agencies and in a proliferation of new agencies: Missionary Aviation Fellowship (founded 1944), Far East Broadcasting Company (1945), United World Mission (1946), Far Eastern Gospel Crusade (1947), Greater European Mission (1949), and Overseas Crusades (1950). Another conservative evangelical association of mission agencies, the Evangelical Foreign Missions Association (EFMA), was formed in 1945 by the National Association of Evangelicals (established in 1942), to serve and foster the work of conservative denominational missions as well as some of the independent groups.[82]

Three influential scholars of conservative evangelical missions at the time were Robert Hall Glover, director for North America of the China

---

80. T. K. Jones, Jr., "History's Lessons for Tomorrow's Mission," *International Bulletin of Missionary Research* 10 (1986) 51. See also E. T. Bachmann, "Kenneth Scott Latourette: Historian and Friend," in *Frontiers of the Christian World Mission since 1938: Essays in Honor of Kenneth Scott Latourette,* ed. W. C. Harr (New York, 1962) 231-80; K. S. Latourette, "My Guided Life," *ibid.,* 281-93 (with select bibliography of his published writings); and Latourette, *Beyond the Ranges: An Autobiography* (Grand Rapids, 1967).

81. W. R. Wheeler, ed., *The Crisis Decade: A History of the Foreign Missionary Work of the Presbyterian Church in the U.S.A., 1937-1947* (New York, 1950) 285-96.

82. H. Lindsell, "Faith Missions since 1938," in Harr, ed., *Frontiers of the Christian World Mission since 1938,* 219ff. In 1991 the name of the Evangelical Foreign Missions Association (EFMA) was changed to Evangelical Fellowship of Mission Agencies.

Inland Mission; Harold Cook, director of the missions department at Moody Bible Institute; and Harold Lindsell, dean of Fuller Theological Seminary. Glover's book *The Progress of World-Wide Missions* (1924) was still widely used as a text in Bible institutes and colleges; *The Bible Basis of Missions* (1946) was published the year before he died. Both books were viewed as classics by evangelicals. Cook's *Introduction to the Study of Christian Missions* (1954) was a standard textbook, and his *Missionary Life and Work* (1959) went through twenty-four printings. Lindsell's *A Christian Philosophy of Missions* (1949) and *Missionary Principles and Practice* (1955) were pioneering, systematic expositions of conservative evangelical mission theory and strategy. From an uncritical biblical perspective, Lindsell maintained that all those who have either rejected Jesus Christ or never heard of him are doomed to eternal hell. The only way to salvation, he said, is through faith in Jesus Christ; there is no real value in the non-Christian religions.

In 1952 there were 18,599 North American Protestant missionaries working overseas, which was more than half of the total Protestant missionary task force worldwide. By 1956 the number of North American personnel increased 25% to 23,432. The Methodist Board was the largest with 1,513 foreign missionaries.[83] In less than fifty years the North American percentage of the total Protestant missionary task force was reversed. "Whereas in 1911 about two-thirds of the foreign missionaries came from outside North America, in 1956 it was the other way around."[84] But a shift in the configuration of the North American missionary force was taking place. Whereas in 1952 the mainline boards related to the National Council of Churches supplied 50% of North American Protestant missionaries, by 1958 it was only 41%, while the percentage of personnel sent by other associations and independent groups, unrelated to the NCC, increased nearly 9%.[85] The trend in both directions would continue precipitously.

In 1952 the Associated Missions of the International Council of Christian Churches (TAM-ICCC) was formed, representing extreme right-wing fundamentalism, inspired by Carl McIntire. Several agencies withdrew from TAM in 1969 and formed a new association known as the Fellowship of Missions (FOM). Both are small separatist associations that are militantly anti-ecumenical and do not cooperate with any other groups.

---

83. Price and Moyer, "Study of American Protestant Foreign Missions in 1956," 2.

84. H. Lindsell, "An Appraisal of Agencies Not Co-operating with the International Missionary Council Grouping," *International Review of Missions* 47 (1958) 202.

85. F. W. Price, "World Christian and Missionary Statistics," *Occasional Bulletin from the Missionary Research Library* 9 (May 6, 1958); F. W. Price and C. E. Orr, "North American Protestant Foreign Missions in 1958," *Occasional Bulletin from the Missionary Research Library* 9 (Dec. 8, 1958).

A New Context

There was a radically new context for world mission in the post-1945 period, with the resurgence of non-Christian religions, the shift of cultural and political power, and the emergence of indigenous national churches in nearly every country of the world. The first postwar meeting of the IMC at Whitby, Canada, in 1947, called for "partnership in obedience" — a new relationship between Western mission agencies and the indigenous "younger churches." The Whitby meeting, followed by the inaugural assembly of the World Council of Churches at Amsterdam in 1948, marked the end of the "Vasco de Gama Epoch," the era of Western penetration and domination. The Communist revolution in China in 1949 and the expulsion of all missionaries from that country were dramatic evidence of the new reality. The change was clear, but the way forward was less clear. At the next meeting of the IMC in Willingen, Germany, in 1952, Max Warren of the Church Missionary Society acknowledged the difficulty: "We know with complete certainty that the most testing days of the Christian mission in our generation lie just ahead. . . . We have to be ready to see the day of missions, as we have known them, as having already come to an end."[86]

In preparation for the Willingen meeting on the theme "The Missionary Obligation of the Church," a series of studies was commissioned by the Division of Foreign Missions of the NCC under the direction of the Committee on Research in Foreign Mission. More than fifty papers were prepared by mission executives and seminary professors from the United States and Canada on five subjects: (1) the biblical and theological basis of mission, (2) the missionary vocation, (3) North American mission boards and their task, (4) the missionary task in the present day, and (5) policy for today. Each subject was assigned to a commission to prepare papers and a report. Charles W. Forman, a member of the commission on policy, says, "Nothing so ambitious was ever attempted before — or since — in the way of mission studies, and the product of that effort may well stand as a landmark, an Ebenezer, for American missiology of 150 years."[87] Of special interest and importance is the report of Commission I, chaired by Paul Lehmann, entitled "Why Missions?" It defined the aim of mission as "the obligation to make God as He is revealed in Jesus Christ so known

86. M. A. C. Warren, "The Christian Mission and the Cross," in *Missions under the Cross: Addresses Delivered at the Enlarged Meeting of the International Missionary Council at Willingen, Germany, 1952,* ed. N. Goodall (New York, 1953) 40. R. P. Beaver said, "World War II marked the end of the old order of overseas missions" ("The American Protestant Theological Seminary and Missions," 84).

87. C. W. Forman, "A History of Foreign Mission Theory in America," 109.

as to be faithfully served by all men" (1.2). A study of the messages and statements of the great church/missionary conferences from Edinburgh to Amsterdam, they said, showed that "the missionary movement in the twentieth century has . . . been following its apostolic prototype in the trinitarian direction of its thought and life. . . . From vigorous Christo-centricity to thoroughgoing trinitarianism — this is the direction of mis-sionary theology, missionary strategy, and missionary obligation" (1.6). The report sounded a cautionary note, however, on the task of mission:

> Missionary obligation, grounded in the reconciling action of the triune God, is not the duty to save souls (after all only God does that, *ubi et quando visum est Deo*) but the sensitive and total response of the church to what the triune God has done and is doing in the world. It is the business of the Christian missionary to "make straight in the desert a highway for our God" (Is. 40:3), not blow Gabriel's horn. Obviously, this does not mean that theological formulae, secretarial administra-tion, and saving of souls are expendable. It only means that they are peripheral and must remain so, if the missionary movement is not to become something else. (1.6)

The inability of the Willingen conference to adopt an agreed state-ment on "The Missionary Obligation of the Church" was not surprising; it was an indication of the depth of disagreement over the direction of mission. To one participant it was another symptom of "a disastrous failure of nerve in the western missionary movement. . . . The sickness, however diagnosed, was essentially spiritual."[88]

Ecumenical Challenge and Change

If "the day of missions" was at an end, it was the beginning of a new day for the one mission of the church. With the home base for mission wherever the church existed around the world, mission was no longer a one-way enterprise from the Western churches to Asia, Africa, and Latin America (a three-continent view); rather mission was the whole church, with the whole gospel, to the whole world (a six-continent view).[89] The integration of the IMC with the World Council of Churches at New Delhi

---

88. M. Warren, *Crowded Canvas: Some Experiences of a Life-Time* (London, 1974) 154.

89. W. R. Hogg, "New Thrusts in the Theology and Life of the Christian Mis-sion," in *Christian Mission in Theological Perspective*, ed. G. H. Anderson (Nashville, 1967) 207.

in 1961 was endorsed by mainline mission boards in the United States as symbolizing in structure a theological view of mission as integral to the nature of the church. A similar structural change had already occurred in the United States in 1950 when the Foreign Missions Conference of North America joined the newly created National Council of Churches as the Division of Foreign Missions.

The Theology of the Christian Mission, an ecumenical symposium edited by Gerald H. Anderson, which appeared on the eve of the 1961 New Delhi Assembly of the WCC, presented a broad range of international scholarship on crucial issues — in biblical and historical perspective — that anticipated future developments. In addition to Barth, Cullmann, Kraemer, Warren, and others from Europe and Britain, the twenty-five contributors included an imposing array of Americans across the theological spectrum from Tillich to Lindsell, together with Orthodox, Roman Catholic, and Third World voices. Bishop Lesslie Newbigin, general secretary of the IMC, wrote the Foreword. In his Introduction, Anderson traced the progressively deepening thrust of mission theology among Protestants in the twentieth century, from the point of asking simply "How missions?" at the time of Edinburgh 1910, to the point of asking "What is the Christian mission?" at the time of the Ghana meeting of the IMC in 1957.[90]

Christianity Today magazine (April 24, 1961) viewed the volume with such alarm that it devoted an eleven-page article by the editors — "A New Crisis in Foreign Missions?" — to a critique of the book because, they said, it "discloses far-reaching influences now divergently shaping the philosophy of the Christian mission around the world" and "inevitably raises searching questions for the Protestant ecumenical movement" at a time when "discussion of contemporary mission strategy promises to dominate the theological horizon" (pp. 2-3). Comparing it to the earlier works by Hocking and Kraemer, the editors said the new volume "may rock the Christian world missionary venture afresh." Especially the essays on the relation of Christianity to other faiths, they said, would make the volume "a center of debate for some time," and it would be "required reading . . . even for fundamentalist critics" (pp. 3-4). Despite the fact that "it contains some first-rate biblical theology," the editors worried that "the book could significantly influence reformulation of missions: 1. by its tenuous connection of the missionary task to a nebulous trinitarian theology; 2. by relating the ideal completion of mission to the WCC-IMC-identified Church; and 3. by viewing Christianity as the fulfillment (rather than antithesis) of pagan religions" (p. 4). By way of final appraisal, *Christianity Today* assailed the volume

90. G. H. Anderson, "The Theology of Mission among Protestants in the Twentieth Century," in *The Theology of the Christian Mission* (New York, 1961) 4-7.

because, in the judgment of this conservative evangelical journal, "confidence in the Hebrew-Christian religion as the one true and saving religion is being shattered; Christianity and other world religions are viewed . . . as different in degree rather than in kind" (p. 13).

Other indications of foment in ecumenical perceptions of mission occurred at the 1960 conference of the World Student Christian Federation (WSCF), in Strasbourg. Students at the conference felt there was "too much speaking about the life of the church; what students wanted was action in the world. And there seemed to be too much mission; what students wanted was a welcome to this world."[91] Hans Hoekendijk — later professor of missions at Union Theological Seminary in New York — urged the participants at Strasbourg "to begin radically to desacralize the church" and to recognize that Christianity is "a secular movement," not "some sort of religion."[92] It was the decade of the secular, and the world set the agenda of the church. The struggles for justice, liberation, and human development not only were part of the ecumenical definition of mission, but seemed to take precedence over the need for people to be converted, baptized, and brought into the church.[93]

The radical challenge was voiced on the American scene by M. Richard Shaull, former Presbyterian missionary in Latin America, in his installation address as professor of ecumenics at Princeton Seminary in 1963:

> Theologically speaking, the church may be a missionary community. In actual fact, however, it has become a major hindrance to the work of mission. . . . Our ecclesiastical organizations are not the most striking examples of dynamic and flexible armies which direct their energies primarily toward witness and service to those outside. Missionary boards and organizations, in their justified desire to turn over increasing responsibility to their daughter churches, have become so bound to relatively static ecclesiastical organizations that, with rare exceptions, they have shown little possibility of thinking imaginatively about the vast new frontiers of mission or becoming engaged in new ventures on them.[94]

91. D. L. Edwards, "Signs of Radicalism in the Ecumenical Movement," in *The Ecumenical Advance: A History of the Ecumenical Movement, 1948-1968*, ed. H. E. Fey (Philadelphia, 1970) 400.

92. H. Hoekendijk, "Christ and the World in the Modern Age," *Student World* 54 (1961) 75, 81-82.

93. This was the judgment of Lesslie Newbigin, a prominent participant in the ecumenical missionary events of that decade, in his *Unfinished Agenda: An Autobiography* (Grand Rapids, 1985) 198.

94. M. R. Shaull, "The Form of the Church in the Modern Diaspora," *Princeton*

Another American voice calling for radical change was Keith R. Bridston, former Lutheran missionary in Indonesia and staff member of the World Council of Churches. In his book *Mission Myth and Reality* (1965), Bridston predicted that "the latter half of the twentieth century . . . may prove to be as radical in its implications for the missionary outlook of the Christian church as the Copernican revolution was for the scientific cosmology of its day" (p. 13). Traditional forms of mission, he said, "embody a response to a world that no longer exists and express a theological under-standing of the relation of the world to God that is now felt to be fallacious" (p. 17). The vocational category of "foreign missionary" was, he suggested, "irrelevant and theologically unjustified," and mission boards were "socio-logically anachronistic and ecclesiologically questionable" (p. 18). The church was "still at the first stage of discovering the right questions — in considering the nature and form of the Christian mission today" (p. 18).

Norman A. Horner was right when he observed in 1968 that "the Protestant missionary enterprise has undergone more radical change in the last fifteen years than in the previous century."[95]

Conservative Evangelical Resurgence

Conservative evangelicals were distressed by developments in the ecu-menical movement that they felt were compromising — if not replacing — the task of evangelism in mission and calling into question the continu-ing mandate of the Great Commission. In a series of major conferences, evangelicals rallied around a revival of the SVM watchword.[96] In 1960, at the IFMA Congress on World Missions at the Moody Church in Chicago, evangelicals saw themselves in continuity with Edinburgh 1910, affirmed that "the total evangelization of the world may be achieved in this genera-tion," and issued a call for 18,000 additional missionaries.[97] Similarly, in 1966 at Wheaton, Illinois, a joint EFMA/IFMA Congress on the Church's Worldwide Mission declared, "We . . . covenant together . . . for the evan-

---

Seminary Bulletin (March 1964), reprinted in *New Theology No. 2*, ed. M. E. Marty and D. G. Peerman (New York, 1965) 266-67.

95. N. A. Horner, ed., *Protestant Crosscurrents in Mission: The Ecumenical-Conservative Encounter* (Nashville, 1968) 10.

96. See D. Lotz, *"The Evangelization of the World in This Generation": The Resur-gence of a Missionary Idea among the Conservative Evangelicals* (Th.D. diss., University of Hamburg, 1970) 231ff.

97. A. F. Glasser has described the "IFMA parochialism" at the Chicago Con-gress as "the last attempt of dispensationalist-separatists to dominate the American

gelization of the world in this generation, so help us God!" Also in 1966, the World Congress on Evangelism in Berlin, sponsored by *Christianity Today* magazine, with Billy Graham as honorary chairman, concluded, "Our goal is nothing short of the evangelization of the human race in this generation." For conservative evangelicals the spirit of Edinburgh 1910 was alive and well in 1966 — a crucial year of new dynamism.

In 1968 the Association of Evangelical Professors of Missions was organized. Of the evangelical missiologists, the most productive author was J. Herbert Kane at Trinity Evangelical Divinity School, who had served with China Inland Mission. After revising and enlarging Glover's *Progress of Worldwide Missions* in 1960, Kane published *A Global View of Christian Missions* (1971), *Understanding Christian Missions* (1974), *Christian Missions in Biblical Perspective* (1976), *A Concise History of the Christian World Mission* (1978), *Life and Work on the Mission Field* (1980), and other books, which were all used extensively as texts in evangelical schools.

After publishing *The Bridges of God* (1955) and *How Churches Grow* (1959), on strategies that lead to quantitative church growth in missionary situations, Donald A. McGavran — a graduate of Yale Divinity School and longtime missionary in India — established the Institute of Church Growth at Northwest Christian College in Eugene, Oregon, in 1961. His Institute moved in 1965 to Fuller Theological Seminary, where it became the School of World Mission. By the 1980s this evangelical school had developed into the largest graduate faculty of missiology in North America. Following McGavran's emphasis on evangelism for church growth among people groups (homogeneous units) — formed along lines of ethnic, caste, racial, and other existing social relationships — the school is noted for its study of strategies to foster success in discipling converts and multiplying churches among those who are receptive to the gospel. Spin-offs from McGavran's movement include the *Global Church Growth Bulletin* (which he edited), Ralph Winter's U.S. Center for World Mission, which focuses on "reaching un-reached people groups," Win Arn's Institute for American Church Growth, and several church growth research centers in Third World countries. Critics of the emphasis on establishing homogeneous churches as a strategy for church growth, such as René Padilla in Argentina, maintain that it has no biblical foundation, that it is contrary

---

missionary movement. And it fell far short of being a success. . . . a curious mixture of triumphalism and pessimism . . . the platform was dominated by the old guard. It was a depressing scene" (A. F. Glasser and D. A. McGavran, *Contemporary Theologies of Mission* [Grand Rapids, 1983], 117-18). See also Glasser, "The Evolution of Evangelical Mission Theology since World War II," *International Bulletin of Missionary Research* 9 (1985) 9-13.

to the New Testament emphasis on breaking down barriers and building up unity in the body of Christ, and that it reinforces the status quo.[98] Others worry that concern for social justice is secondary and warn that the pragmatic emphasis of the church growth movement is in danger of turning it into mere "spiritual technology."[99]

A growing appreciation for the insights of linguistics and anthropology among missionaries — especially evangelicals — was influenced by the pioneering work of Eugene A. Nida, secretary for translations in the American Bible Society, through his books *God's Word in Man's Language* (1952), *Customs and Cultures* (1954), *Message and Mission: The Communication of the Christian Faith* (1960), and *Religion across Cultures* (1968). In the 1950s Nida gave encouragement and contributed to the development of the journal *Practical Anthropology*, edited by William Smalley, for missionaries with special interests in anthropology.[100]

The pentecostal and charismatic movements are another vital stream in American evangelical missions. The Assemblies of God, founded in 1914 with lineage to the Azusa Street, Los Angeles, revival of 1906-09, is the largest Pentecostal denomination in the United States. With a strong emphasis on missions (1,500 missionaries in 1986), the Assemblies had nearly ten times as many members in Latin America as in North America by the mid-1980s. Melvin L. Hodges — field director for Latin America and later professor of missions at the Assemblies of God Theological Seminary in Springfield, Missouri — expounded their emphasis on indigenous-church principles and a pentecostal perspective on missions in his books *The Indigenous Church* (1953) and *A Theology of the Church and Its Mission* (1977).[101]

98. C. R. Padilla, "The Unity of the Church and the Homogeneous Unit Principle," *International Bulletin of Missionary Research* 6 (1982) 29-30.

99. See T. Stafford, "The Father of Church Growth," cover story on McGavran in *Christianity Today*, Feb. 21, 1986, 19-23; reprinted with comments and response by McGavran and R. D. Winter in *Mission Frontiers* 8 (1986) 5-10; also McGavran, "My Pilgrimage in Mission," *International Bulletin of Missionary Research* 10 (1986) 53-58.

100. See M. Black and W. A. Smalley, ed., *On Language, Culture, and Religion: In Honor of Eugene A. Nida* (The Hague, 1974); also Nida, "My Pilgrimage in Mission," *International Bulletin of Missionary Research* 12 (1988)

101. See G. B. McGee, "Assemblies of God Mission Theology: A Historical Perspective," *International Bulletin of Missionary Research* 10 (1986) 166-70; idem, *This Gospel Shall Be Preached: A History and Theology of Assemblies of God Foreign Missions* (2 vols.; Springfield, 1986, 1989); L. G. McClung, Jr., ed., *Azusa Street and Beyond: Pentecostal Missions and Church Growth in the Twentieth Century* (South Plainfield, 1986); S. M. Burgess and G. B. McGee, ed., *Dictionary of Pentecostal and Charismatic Movements* (Grand Rapids, 1988).

Confusion and Transition

By 1973 evangelical agencies were providing 66.5% of the funds and 85% of the personnel for American Protestant overseas missions. Meanwhile, mainline boards were in a period of painful transition. It was "a theological transition with notable operational consequences," says W. Richey Hogg.

> The shift marks a move away from a Western Christian evangelistic crusade to the world and toward an engagement with the world in what is regarded as a total evangelistic response to the world's needs and the religious beliefs of its people. . . . It views the North American role in world mission not in terms of large numbers of professional missionaries, but rather through fewer skilled specialists and particularly through the work and witness of the world-wide lay Christian diaspora in secular posts.[102]

There was confusion, however, about what exactly it meant to speak of mission in terms of "engagement with the world" in "a total evangelistic response to the world's needs." People in the pews were getting mixed messages about the future of the missionary enterprise. Bishop Stephen Neill warned that "if everything is mission, nothing is mission." Adding to the confusion in the early 1970s was a call for a moratorium on Western missionaries by some ecumenical church leaders in the Third World,[103] and a new anti-Americanism in many parts of the world fueled by the war in Vietnam. A neo-isolationism in American society led to a wave of defeatism and a loss of momentum in mission boards of denominations in the National Council of Churches.

This affected the teaching of mission in mainline, ecumenical seminaries as well. In addition to the earlier Fellowship of Professors of Missions of the Middle Atlantic Region (now the Eastern Fellowship), a national Association of Professors of Missions (APM) was founded in 1952[104] and a Midwest Fellowship of Professors of Missions began to meet

---

102. W. R. Hogg, "The Role of American Protestantism in World Mission," 388.

103. See G. H. Anderson, "A Moratorium on Missionaries?" *Christian Century,* Jan. 16, 1974, 43-45.

104. Beaver is mistaken when he says that the APM "came into existence in 1950" ("The American Protestant Theological Seminary and Missions," 85); also J. A. Scherer (when he cites Beaver), "The Future of Missiology as an Academic Discipline in Seminary Education: An Attempt at Reinterpretation and Clarification," *Missiology* 13 (1985) 448. See N. A. Horner, who was present at the founding meeting in Louisville in 1952 and was elected the first secretary-treasurer of the APM ("The Association of Professors of Missions in North America: The First Thirty-five Years, 1952-1987," *International Bulletin of Missionary Research* 11 [1987] 120-24).

informally sometime during the 1950s and was formally organized in 1957.
By 1968, however, R. Pierce Beaver — professor of missions at the University of Chicago Divinity School — could report that "students are now
cold, even hostile, to overseas missions" and that the place of missiology
as a discipline in the seminary curriculum "is most precarious, and I expect
its rapid decline and even its elimination from most denominational seminaries."[105] Only sixteen professors attended the meeting of the national
APM in 1970. The decade 1963-73 saw the demise of mission studies and
training at the Kennedy School of Missions at Hartford Seminary, at
Scarritt College for Christian Workers in Nashville, at the Missionary
Orientation Center in Stony Point, New York, and at the Lutheran School
of Missions near Chicago.

Revitalization of Missiology

In response to this situation, an ad hoc gathering of mission leaders and
academicians in 1972 founded the American Society of Missiology (ASM)
as a broadly inclusive professional society for the study of world mission.
In 1973 the ASM began publishing a new quarterly, *Missiology*, that incorporated the journal *Practical Anthropology*. The ASM — bringing together
conservative evangelicals, conciliar Protestants, and Roman Catholics in
remarkable fashion — fostered a renewal of missiology and facilitated the
recognition of the discipline by the academic community in North America.[106] By 1986 the ASM had over 500 members, the various associations
of professors of mission had taken on new life, and *Missiology* had a
circulation in excess of 2,200. Also contributing to the revitalization of
missiology were the *Evangelical Missions Quarterly*, published by IFMA and
EFMA since 1964; the *International Bulletin of Missionary Research* (successor
to the *Occasional Bulletin* from the Missionary Research Library, 1950),
published by the Overseas Ministries Study Center; Orbis Books, the publishing imprint established in 1970 by Maryknoll; the Missions Advanced
Research and Communication Center (MARC) of World Vision, founded

---

105. Beaver, "The Meaning and Place of Missiology Today in the American
Scene," 4-5.

106. When the Council on the Study of Religion voted to accept the American
Society of Missiology as one of its constituent member societies, effective Jan. 1, 1976,
L. J. Luzbetak, S.V.D., then president of the ASM, declared, "This is a historic landmark;
on this day 'missiology' becomes a fully recognized academic discipline in North
America" ("Missiology Comes of Age," *Missiology* 4 [1976] 11). See also the discussion
of this event and developments in the years that followed, by J. A. Scherer, "The Future
of Missiology," 455ff.

in 1967; William Carey Library, an evangelical missions publishing firm in Pasadena, California, founded in 1969; the Billy Graham Center, established at Wheaton College in 1974; new graduate schools of mission and evangelism at Trinity Evangelical Divinity School, Columbia (South Carolina) Biblical Seminary, Nazarene Theological Seminary, and Asbury Theological Seminary; and approval by the Association of Theological Schools in 1986 of standards for offering the Doctor of Missiology (D.Miss.) as a professional academic degree. A survey of doctoral dissertations on mission topics for the Ph.D., Th.D., S.T.D., and Ed.D. degrees revealed nearly 1,000 such dissertations accepted at theological schools and universities in the United States and Canada in the period 1945-81, with Boston University, the University of Chicago, and Columbia University leading the list. An increase from 211 dissertations accepted in 1960-69 to 462 dissertations in 1970-79 was further evidence of revitalization.[107]

In a 1985 survey of missiology as an academic discipline in American seminaries, James A. Scherer reported "a qualitative improvement in the climate for the teaching of missions, and a quantitative increase in programs and activities, especially in the decade from 1975 to 1985." He concluded that the discipline of missiology "is at last respectable, possesses a birth certificate, has gained some peer recognition, and shows signs of a promising future."[108] Those teaching in the discipline in the mid-1980s, as reported by Scherer, saw the contribution of missiology as being "an integrating and permeating role" — a catalyst — within the theological curriculum, "to keep theological education open to the whole world, and to keep the world's needs at the heart of seminary life"; to increase "awareness of the role and contributions of churches in the two-thirds world"; and to give leadership "in the dialogue with people of other faiths."[109]

It was a remarkable turnaround in less than two decades from Beaver's alarming forecast, and Beaver himself — the doyen of American missiologists in the period — contributed much to help bring about the change. After missionary service in China with the Evangelical and Reformed Church, and internment by the Japanese during World War II, he taught missions at Lancaster Theological Seminary, then was director of the Missionary Research Library for seven years and professor of missions at the University of Chicago Divinity School from 1955 until his retirement in

---

107. "Doctoral Dissertations on Mission," *International Bulletin of Missionary Research* 7 (1983) 97ff.

108. J. A. Scherer, "The Future of Missiology," 455.

109. *Ibid.*, 457-58; see also Scherer, "Missiology as a Discipline and What It Includes," *Missiology* 15 (1987) 507-22.

1971, after which he served as director of the Overseas Ministries Study Center for three years. A prolific author, Beaver wrote several pioneering studies that became standard references: *Ecumenical Beginnings in Protestant World Mission: A History of Comity* (1962), *Pioneers in Mission: The Early Missionary Ordination Sermons, Charges, and Instructions* (1966), *Church, State, and the American Indians* (1966), and especially *All Loves Excelling: American Protestant Women in World Mission* (1968; rev. 1980, title *American Protestant Women in World Mission*). A large symposium he edited for the ASM in 1976, *American Missions in Bicentennial Perspective,* was judged by Robert T. Handy to be "one of the most important books in the field of religion to arise out of the bicentennial celebration . . . a landmark in the development of missiology in America."[110] Like Latourette — warmly evangelical, yet firmly ecumenical, a historian with impeccable academic credentials — Beaver was trusted across the theological spectrum and served as a "bridge person" in bringing scholars together to advance the cause of missiology. *The Future of the Christian World Mission* (1971), a festschrift in his honor, was testimony to his effectiveness. Beaver maintained that "every seminary needs a professor of missions, whatever his personal discipline may be, to be a living symbol of the church's worldwide mission and to be the agent who summons students and faculty to engagement in it."[111] It was the case that most of those who taught missiology in university theological faculties in the postwar period were historians.

Ecumenical and Evangelical Crosscurrents

The impact of the postwar transition and the contrast between ecumenical and evangelical missions is described by Wilbert R. Shenk:

> That part of the missionary movement most closely identified with the Christendom thrust of the Great Century rapidly lost momentum after 1945, while independent and Free Church groups surged forward. The latter often acted as if they were still living in the nineteenth century. They treated sociopolitical issues simplistically and interpreted the missionary call as the simple and unambiguous action of saving souls.[112]

The situation for evangelicals began to change, however, following the International Congress on World Evangelization at Lausanne in 1974

110. *Occasional Bulletin of Missionary Research* 2 (1978) 28.
111. R. P. Beaver, "The Meaning and Place of Missiology Today," 5.
112. W. R. Shenk, "The 'Great Century' Reconsidered," *Missiology* 12 (1984) 142.

(a sequel to the 1966 Berlin Congress on Evangelism), the Consultation on World Evangelization, sponsored by the Lausanne Committee at Pattaya, Thailand, in 1980, and the Consultation on Evangelism and Social Responsibility in 1982 at Grand Rapids, Michigan — jointly sponsored by the Lausanne Committee and the World Evangelical Fellowship. In response to a challenge largely from Third World and young evangelicals, it was acknowledged within the Lausanne movement and the World Evangelical Fellowship that evangelism and social action are integrally related in mission, though a debate continues as to whether evangelism has *priority*. Arthur P. Johnston of Trinity Evangelical Divinity School, in his book *The Battle for World Evangelism* (1978), disagreed with these developments and warned that it was a drift toward the "evangelistic sterility in the WCC." He argued that "historically the mission of the church is evangelism alone" (p. 18), and he criticized members of the Lausanne Committee and other evangelicals who redefine mission in terms of holistic evangelism that includes social action.

In contrast to this debate among evangelicals, ecumenical mission theology maintains that it is artificial and unbiblical to dichotomize or prioritize the witness of word and deed to the single reality of the reign of God.[113] Especially as Christians encounter oppression under authoritarian regimes, they are aware — once again — that evangelism is inseparable from concerns for justice and peace, and that faithfulness in mission is measured as much by the *quality* of discipleship as it is by the *quantity* of disciples.

The scandal of divided witness among Protestants (not to mention other Christian traditions) continues to plague the missionary endeavor. This was highlighted on a global scale in 1980 when two world mission conferences were held within thirty days of each other; one by the WCC at Melbourne, Australia, and the other by the Lausanne Committee at Pattaya, Thailand. The modern ecumenical movement had its genesis in the missionary movement of the nineteenth century — as recounted by William Richey Hogg in his definitive study *Ecumenical Foundations* (1952) — but convergent forces are more than matched by divergent forces, so that unity in mission remains elusive.

---

113. See L. Newbigin, "Cross-currents in Ecumenical and Evangelical Understandings of Mission," *International Bulletin of Missionary Research* 6 (1982) 146ff., with responses by P. G. Schrotenboer and C. P. Wagner and a reply by Newbigin.

Historical Research in American Missions

John King Fairbank in 1968 lamented "the neglect of missionaries in American historiography," and described the missionary as "the invisible man of American history."[114] Historical research in American missions is a goldmine for exploring scholars, yet — as Pierce Beaver once observed — "most writing in the history of missions is not being done by church historians, but by general historians and area experts in the universities and colleges."[115] A selection of studies published in the 1980s indicates that this situation largely continues: Suzanne Wilson Barnett and John King Fairbank, eds., *Christianity in China: Early Protestant Missionary Writings* (1985); Adrian A. Bennett, *Missionary Journalist in China: Young J. Allen and His Magazines, 1860-1883* (1983); Nancy Boyd, *Emissaries: The Overseas Work of the American YWCA, 1895-1970* (1986); Kenton J. Clymer, *Protestant Missionaries in the Philippines: 1898-1916* (1986); Patricia R. Hill, *The World Their Household: The American Woman's Foreign Mission Movement and Cultural Transformation, 1870-1920* (1985); Jane Hunter, *The Gospel of Gentility: American Women Missionaries in Turn-of-the-Century China* (1984); William R. Hutchison, *Errand to the World: American Protestant Thought and Foreign Missions* (1987); Sylvia M. Jacobs, ed., *Black Americans and the Missionary Movement in Africa* (1982); and Walter L. Williams, *Black Americans and the Evangelization of Africa: 1877-1900* (1982). James Eldin Reed chides church historians for their "scholarly neglect" of the history of missions, and says, "No doubt the religious core of the missionary movement will remain invisible until (and unless) the church historian comes to the rescue. Until then, . . . we will be forced to view the inner meaning of the missionary enterprise as through a glass darkly."[116]

Another problem in the history of missions as an academic discipline is that up to this point most of it has been written by Western scholars. It has been written, said Stephen Neill, "far too much from the side of the operators and far too little from that of the victims. . . . We know fairly well what it feels like to be a missionary; we know much less of what it feels like to be the object of the missionary's attentions."[117] In a similar vein, African theologian John Mbiti says to Western church

114. J. K. Fairbank, "Assignment for the '70's," *American Historical Review* 74 (1969) 876-79.

115. Editorial Foreword, *Mo Bradley and Thailand* by D. C. Lord (Grand Rapids, 1969) 7.

116. J. E. Reed, "American Foreign Policy," 245.

117. S. C. Neill, "The History of Missions: An Academic Discipline," in *The Mission of the Church and the Propagation of the Faith,* ed. G. J. Cuming (London, 1970) 160.

historians, "We feel deeply affronted [that you have] more meaningful . . . academic fellowship with heretics long dead than with living colleagues of the church today in the so-called Third World."[118]

Missionary Personnel

There were more North American Protestant missionaries serving overseas in 1985 than ever before — over 39,000 career persons and nearly 28,000 short-termers — from 764 agencies with income in excess of $1 billion. The growth in missionary personnel was uneven, however, as shown in the following table prepared by Robert T. Coote, based on data in the thirteenth edition of the *Mission Handbook: North American Protestant Ministries Overseas* (1986), compared with data from earlier editions of the *Mission Handbook*.[119]

North American Overseas Protestant
Career Missionary Personnel Totals

Affiliation	1953	1968	1985
NCC/DOM	9,844	10,042	4,349
Canadian Council of Churches/CWC	572	1,873	234
EFMA	2,650	7,369	9,101
IFMA	3,081	6,206	6,380
Independent/Unaffiliated	3,565	11,601	19,905
(less doubly affiliated)	-1,113	-2,941	-660
Total	18,599	34,150	39,309

The continuing decline of personnel in mainline — or old-line — boards related to the NNN/DOM (11.5% of the total in 1985) was more than offset by the continuing increase of personnel in evangelical agencies, though that is also a mixed picture. In his analysis of the data, Coote shows that for EFMA/IFMA taken as a whole, 1968 marked the beginning of a plateau, and this plateau has prevailed for almost two decades.[120] The

118. J. S. Mbiti, "Theological Impotence and the Universality of the Church," in *Mission Trends No. 3: Third World Theologies*, ed. G. H. Anderson and T. F. Stransky (New York and Grand Rapids, 1976) 17.

119. R. T. Coote, "Taking Aim on 2000 A.D.," in *Mission Handbook: North American Protestant Ministries Overseas*, ed. S. Wilson and J. Siewert (13th ed., Monrovia, 1986) 39.

120. *Ibid.* See also R. T. Coote, "The Uneven Growth of Conservative Evangelical Missions," *International Bulletin of Missionary Research* 6 (1982) 118-23.

really dramatic growth in evangelical personnel occurred in unaffiliated evangelical or fundamentalist agencies, especially the three largest — Southern Baptist Foreign Mission Board (1984: 3,346 career missionaries), Wycliffe Bible Translators (3,022, Canadian personnel included), and New Tribes Mission (1,438). In 1985 the annual Lottie Moon Christmas offering in Southern Baptist churches for support of foreign missions amounted to nearly $67 million (toward a total foreign missions budget of $162 million in 1986), and 429 new Southern Baptist missionaries were named.

Agenda of Issues

The place of persons in mission is an issue that faces mission agencies with increasing urgency as many areas of the Third World become closed to North American missionaries. While sending men and women to proclaim the gospel in cross-cultural situations may be an abiding reality at the heart of mission, it does not necessarily follow that "more missionaries mean more mission"; faithfulness in mission is measured in larger terms than the number of missionaries sent. The need to reconceptualize the role of the missionary is high on the agenda for the future, taking into account the increasingly significant role of Third World mission agencies with more than 20,000 non-Western Protestant missionaries in 1986.[121]

Also on the agenda for further investigation is the theology of mission — the basic presuppositions and underlying principles that determine, from the standpoint of Christian faith, the motives, message, methods, strategy, and goals of mission.[122] Of particular importance for this task is the contribution of Third World scholars, such as the late Orlando E. Costas at Andover Newton, Kosuke Koyama at New York's Union Theological Seminary, Samuel Escobar at Eastern Baptist, Lamin Sanneh at Yale, Wi Jo Kang at Wartburg Seminary, Tite Tienou at Alliance Seminary, Thomas Thangaraj at Candler, and C.-S. Song at Pacific School of Religion, as well as those who are overseas.

121. L. D. Pate and L. E. Keyes report that "there are over 20,000 non-Western missionaries today," and they anticipate "there will be more than 100,000 . . . by the year 2000" ("Emerging Missions in a Global Church," *International Bulletin of Missionary Research* 10 [1986] 156). See also Keyes, *The Last Age of Missions* (Pasadena, 1983); Pate, *From Every People: A Handbook of Two-Thirds World Missions, With Directory, Histories, Analysis* (Monrovia, 1989); and Pate, "The Changing Balance in Global Mission," *International Bulletin of Missionary Research* 15 (1991) 56-61.

122. See R. C. Bassham, *Mission Theology: 1948-1975* (Pasadena, 1979), and J. A. Scherer, *Gospel, Church and Kingdom: Comparative Studies in World Mission Theology* (Minneapolis, 1987).

The most critical aspect of this task deals with the Christian attitude toward religious pluralism and the approach to people of other faiths. In ecumenical scholarship it is generally recognized that Christ is present and active among non-Christians, but the crucial question is whether Christ is present in non-Christian religions as such, and whether they may thereby be considered ways of salvation. It is one thing to recognize that Christ is present in other faiths; it is quite another to say that this provides salvific efficacy to other faiths, and that people of other faiths may be saved *in* their religions or even *through* their religions, without explicit affirmation of faith in Christ. Since Vatican Council II, Protestants have been pressed in this direction by Catholic scholars, such as Paul F. Knitter in his book *No Other Name? A Critical Survey of Christian Attitudes toward the World Religions* (1985), and the radical relativism represented in *The Myth of Christian Uniqueness*, edited by John Hick and Paul F. Knitter (1987). Related to this discussion is the role of dialogue versus evangelism in mission to people of other faiths — an increasingly controversial topic. Conservative evangelical scholars are only beginning to address these issues with fresh thinking.

Evangelicals have given leadership, however, in attention to issues of gospel and culture, and contextualization in mission, especially in the work of missionary anthropologists such as Alan Tippett and Charles Kraft at Fuller Seminary, Paul Hiebert at Trinity Evangelical Divinity School, Linwood Barney at Alliance Seminary, Donald Larson and William Smalley at Bethel College, Charles Taber at Emmanuel School of Religion, and Darrell Whiteman at Asbury Seminary.[123]

Another issue of continuing concern are the echoes of chauvinism and jingoism from the Spanish-American war era that are still heard in some American churches and missions. It was especially obvious during the Vietnam war, the Sandinista-Contra conflict, and the struggle in South Africa. The uncritical pro-American attitude that some missionaries carry abroad, in terms of United States foreign policy and economic interests, compromises their witness to the gospel.[124]

It is also important for American missionaries and mission agencies to understand the theological upheaval in the Third World, especially as represented by liberation theology. The challenge of this theological approach was expressed by the Ecumenical Association of Third World Theologians (EATWOT) at its organizing meeting in 1976 at Dar es Salaam,

---

123. See also the papers and report from the Willowbank Consultation on Gospel and Culture, sponsored by the Lausanne Committee in 1978, *Down to Earth: Studies in Christianity and Culture*, ed. J. Stott and R. T. Coote (Grand Rapids, 1980).
124. I am grateful to J. E. Goff for his counsel in expressing these concerns.

Tanzania: "We reject as irrelevant an academic type of theology that is divorced from action. We are prepared for a radical break in epistemology which makes commitment the first act of theology and engages in critical reflection on the praxis of the reality of the Third World."[125] At its New Delhi conference in 1981, EATWOT stated that "for the Third World, [Western] theology has been alienated and alienating. It has not provided the motivation for opposing the evils of racism, sexism, capitalism, colonialism, and neocolonialism. It has failed to understand our religions, indigenous cultures, and traditions, and to relate to them in a respectful way."[126]

A Shifting Center of Ecclesiastical Gravity

Of special significance for the study and understanding of mission in the remaining years of the twentieth century is the fact that the center of ecclesiastical gravity in the world is shifting from the northern to the southern hemisphere. The Swiss Catholic missiologist Walbert Bühlmann, in his book *The Coming of the Third Church* (1977), observed that whereas at the beginning of this century 85% of all Christians lived in the West, there has been a shift in the church's center of gravity so that by the year 2000 about 58% of all Christians — and about 70% of all Catholics — will be living in the Third World. Bühlmann considers the coming of this church of the Third World and the third millennium — the so-called Third Church — to be *"the* epoch-making event of current church history."[127]

Once again the old centers of strength and influence in the church are becoming the new peripheries, as the areas of greatest church growth and theological creativity are found in the Third World. This suggests that we are in one of the most important periods of church history — a period of ferment and transition. In certain respects, as Tracey K. Jones, Jr., has observed, "The Christian mission around the world today is in colossal confusion." Rather than despair, however, this should be seen as a sign of vitality and hope, says Jones, because "untidiness and confusion have characterized the great periods of missionary expansion."[128] To paraphrase

125. S. Torres and V. Fabella, ed., *The Emergent Gospel: Theology from the Underside of History. Papers from the Ecumenical Dialogue of Third World Theologians, Dar es Salaam, August 5-12, 1976* (Maryknoll, 1978) 269.

126. V. Fabella and S. Torres, ed., *Irruption of the Third World: Challenge to Theology. Papers from the Fifth International Conference of the Ecumenical Association of Third World Theologians, August 17-29, 1981, New Delhi, India* (Maryknoll, 1983) 197.

127. W. Bühlmann, *Courage, Church!* (Maryknoll, 1978) 131. See also *idem, The Church of the Future: A Model for the Year 2001* (Maryknoll, 1986).

128. T. K. Jones, Jr., "History's Lessons for Tomorrow's Mission," 50.

something that Wilfred Cantwell Smith once said about Islam, we could say that the most exciting chapter in church history is the one that is currently in the process of being written.

The Unfinished Task

Reliable data about the whole church in the whole world up to 1982 are available in the *World Christian Encyclopedia*, a fact-filled, 1,010-page volume, edited by David B. Barrett, former Anglican missionary in Africa, now serving as a research consultant for the Southern Baptist Foreign Mission Board. While Barrett's work documents the dramatic expansion of Christianity around the world, especially during the last one hundred years, it gives no basis for complacency. There were approximately 1.6 billion Christians in a world of 5 billion people in 1986, but the percentage of Christians in the world's population had decreased by 2% since the beginning of the twentieth century — from 34.4% to 32.8% in 1980 — and half of that decrease occurred between 1970 and 1980.[129] With far more non-Christians in the world in 1988 than on the day when Jesus was crucified, the unfinished task of world evangelization is immense. The stated goal of some American evangelical agencies has been to establish work among the 17,000 so-called unreached people groups in the world by the year 1995, and to achieve "A Church for Every People by the Year 2000."

Can the West Be Converted?

There is a serious "missionary problem" in the United States, however, as in Britain and Western Europe. It is the spread of nominalism in the church and secularism in society. An American Lutheran theologian has observed that "the single most striking fact in the life of main-line U.S. churches over the last twenty years is the rapid erosion of concern about whether people believe in Jesus. . . . The point is not that people no longer believe in Jesus. It is rather that those who do believe seem to care much less than they did twenty years ago about whether those who do not believe come to the place where they do. And this lack of care," he says, "is no simple thoughtlessness; it is an energetic rejection of such care."[130]

129. D. B. Barrett, "Annual Statistical Table on Global Mission: 1986," *International Bulletin of Missionary Research* 10 (1986) 23.

130. J. H. Burtness, "Time for Change," *Lutheran Standard*, Oct. 7, 1983, 4. An

In his Warfield Lectures at Princeton Theological Seminary in 1984 — titled "Can the West Be Converted?" — Lesslie Newbigin said, "Surely there can be no more crucial question for the world mission of the church than the one I have posed. Can there be an effective missionary encounter with *this* culture — this so powerful, persuasive, and confident culture which (at least until very recently) simply regarded itself as 'the coming world civilization.'"[131] Similarly, recognizing the spiritual crisis in churches of the West, Australian Methodist evangelist Alan Walker says, "The Western world is now the toughest mission field on earth. The whole church must come to the aid of stricken, declining Western churches. . . . Now the missionary age is moving into reverse, and the rest of the world must reach out to the West."[132] With nearly one hundred million unchurched people, the United States is not only one of the toughest but one of the largest mission fields in the world.

The Christian mission is simultaneously directed to "Jerusalem . . . and to the ends of the earth."[133] That mission to all the nations includes — for all the nations — the United States. This is a fruit, in part, of what American Protestants in pursuit of mission have helped to bring about — a world church for world mission.

---

expanded version appeared in *Dialog* (Summer, 1982) under the title "Does Anyone Out There Care Anymore Whether People Believe in Jesus?"

131. L. Newbigin, "Can the West Be Converted?" *International Bulletin of Missionary Research* 11 (1987) 2. See also *idem, The Other Side of 1984* (Geneva, 1983), and *Foolishness to the Greeks: The Gospel and Western Culture* (Grand Rapids, 1986).

132. A. Walker, *World Parish* (November, 1985). Quoted by Coote, "Taking Aim on 2000 A.D.," 57.

133. Acts 1:8. See R. P. Beaver, *The Missionary between the Times* (Garden City, 1968) 12.

PART V

Mission, Ecumenicity, and Missiology

The world as it is today demands greater commonality in missiological reflection. That need is the theme of this section. Although from the past and from our own traditions we carry with us a large legacy of separateness, interpretation of the "signs of the times" forces us toward a greater degree of joint participation in missionary witness and missiology. The tension between what is peculiar to each of our own confessions and denominations and the call — both biblical and historical — to commonality is clearly discernible in the following chapters. In a postscript on "Prospects for the Future," an attempt is made to get past traditions that stand in the way and then, on the basis of existing challenges and trends, to gain a clear and radical view of the future of both mission and missiology.

CHAPTER 26

The Genesis of a Common Missiology:
A Case Study of Protestant and Catholic
Mission Studies in the Netherlands,
1877-1988

F. J. VERSTRAELEN

The first introduction to missiology produced in the Netherlands defined missiology as "the science of a praxis."[1] This definition has a touch of the modern in it when one considers that Latin American theologies of liberation have made praxis the starting point for theological deliberations.

In this chapter I will first discuss the conditions under which Protestant and Catholic missiologies emerged in the Netherlands. Then I will examine the ecumenical rapprochement of these disciplines, en route, perhaps, to a common missiology.

The Four Sources of Missiology

The term "mission" in Protestantism and Catholicism has meant specifically foreign missions. This has assumed the existence of a home base, trained missionaries, and missionary work done in a mission field. Therefore, missiology has had to work at different levels and with different purposes, seeking to explain the "why," "what," and "how" of missions in relation to all three of these areas: the home base, the training of missionaries, and their work. But the reflection undertaken on these three points has produced a more systematic study of all aspects of mission.

After a time, this consideration acquired university status as mis-

1. F. E. Daubanton, *Prolegomena van Protestantsche Zendingswetenschap* (Utrecht, 1911) 139.

siology became a subject in the field of theological studies. Faculties of theology have become, then, the fourth element of missionary studies.

The Home Base

Missionary work has needed the support of the home base in terms of both personnel and money. To obtain this support, it has had to inform others about the work of missionaries, to say that it is important, difficult, heroic, and successful. In the beginning, this information was pure propaganda and was provided by innumerable missionary periodicals — more than 500 Protestant periodicals and at least 277 Catholic periodicals having been published in the Netherlands in the nineteenth and twentieth centuries.[2] Their titles give an idea of the missionary spirit of the age. Along with information, missionary societies also gave a sort of missionary training to the faithful to persuade them that missions were a duty given to us by Christ. At the beginning of the twentieth century, W. J. Gunning, director of the school of Protestant missions, tried to introduce a slightly more critical mindset into the Protestant concept of missions. Between 1910 and 1912, a series of very thoughtful brochures was published under the title "De protestantsche zending." The magazine *Mededelingen*, founded in 1857 by the Dutch Society of Missions, became in 1912 a "journal of missiology." It was so well received that it was said that Lévy-Bruhl learned Dutch so that he could read it.

On the Catholic side, each order or missionary congregation had its own newspaper. There were many missionary orders: At the end of the period from 1915 to 1940, which has been called "the great hour of missions,"[3] there were ninety-one missionary orders — thirty societies of priests, ten of brothers, and fifty-one of nuns — with a total of 8,806 missionaries in 1963. Each missionary organization tried to preserve its share of the market by trumpeting its exploits.

2. See J. A. B. Jongeneel, "Protestantse Zendingsperiodieken uit de negentiende eeuw en twintigste eeuw," *Documentatieblad van de Nederlandse Kerkgeschiedenis van de negentiende eeuw* 16 (1983) 26-42; 21 (1985) 5-22; (1988) 28-49. This listing of periodicals was resumed and completed in Jongeneel's *Protestantse zendingsperiodieken uit de negentiende en twintigste eeuw* (IIMO Research Publications 30; Leiden and Utrecht, 1990). Titles of Catholic missions periodicals have been computerized by the Katholiek Documentatie Centrum, Katholieke Universiteit, Erasmusplein 36, 6525 GG Nijmegen.

3. Cf. Jan Roes, *Het Groote Missieuur, 1915-1940* (Bilthoven, 1974). Roes presented his research at the colloquium of the CREDIC of Nijmegen; see his abstract in J.-F. Zorn, ed., *L'appel à la mission. Formes et évolution, XIXe-XXe siècles. Actes de la IXe session du CREDIC, Nimègue, 14-17 juin 1988* (Lyons, 1989) 141.

Side by side with this very limited and self-centered information were a few magazines that were more open-minded, for example, *De Katholieke Missiën*, founded in 1874, then *Het Missiewerk*, published by the Missionary Union of Clergy after 1919. In 1946, *Het Missiewerk* was divided into two distinct publications, *Missieactie*, to inform and educate the faithful, and a new *Het Missiewerk*, a journal of scholarly missiology.

The challenges of the new situation created by the Second World War brought about the creation of new journals reflecting a "Copernican revolution"[4] in mission thought and action. On the Protestant side, the review *De Heerbaan* began to appear in 1948; it adopted the subtitle "review of missiology" in 1966. On the Catholic side, several reviews of missions merged; one was *Missie Integraal*, starting in 1964 and emphasizing the close relationship between missions and development. Another was *Rerum Ecclesiae*, which began in 1968. In the same year a dozen missionary newsletters, including *De Katholieke Missien*, which dated back to 1874, were consolidated to form the monthly *Bijeen*.

So on all fronts simple propaganda gave way little by little to broader and more scholarly reflection.

Along with this, students created very influential missionary groups. For example, in 1846 state university students created the group Eltheto, which had its own newsletter. In 1928, a student missionary commission was created to carry out mission activities among students. Catholics had had an association for Catholic students since 1919, the MIA (Missie Interacademiale). Another association was created in 1947 for laypersons leaving the university; it laid the groundwork for the recruitment of doctors, technicians, and agronomists.

A final note concerning vocabulary: Among Protestants, "missionary studies" are distinguished from missiology or the "science of missions," a term that has been used since 1876. Catholics have distinguished missionary action ("missieactie") done at the home base from mission work ("missiewerk") done overseas. It was only in the 1920s that they came to give more systematic consideration to actual mission work.

The Training of Missionaries

There is a great difference between Protestants and Catholics with regard to training of missionaries. Protestant missionary activity has been organized by missionary societies. The first such society was founded in 1797,

---

4. E. J. Schoonhoven, "Terugblik op 23 jaar Zendingshogeschool," *De Heerbaan* 23 (1970) 2-19.

and nine others were founded subsequently. These ten societies joined together in 1897. In 1892, the free Reformed Churches of the Netherlands[5] created a missions department directly responsible to their synod. The other societies remained independent of the synod of the state church, the Dutch Reformed Church, until 1951.

For a long time Protestant missionary candidates did not have a very high level of education. After 1905 they were trained at a joint missionary school founded in Rotterdam in that year. In 1917 the school moved to Oegstgeest, where the proximity of the University of Leiden allowed a better education. University professors came to the school to give courses in theology, oriental languages, ethnology, and Islam (for example, Professor Snouck Hurgronje). After 1946, a bachelor's degree in theology was required for entrance into the mission school. Missiology had an important place in the curriculum.[6]

In contrast to Protestant missionaries, who were trained for their future tasks in Indonesia, Catholic priests who were to become missionaries received no specific missionary or missiology training. All priests, whether missionaries or not, followed the same curriculum: After six years of secondary education (or the equivalent), including Greek and Latin, they had six or seven years of philosophy and theology. Until the 1960s, this theology was of a scholastic type and assumed that a single ecclesiological model was valid in all places. It was, therefore, of little use for the mission field. In short, missionary priests received a classical training, augmented by a little information about possible adaptations of canon law in mission situations. Religious brothers and sisters were given traditional professional training in their particular fields — for example, teaching, health care, or agriculture.

But Catholic missionaries were not entirely without resources. They received a kind of on-the-job training. Seminaries, both small and large, had missions clubs and, most important, welcomed missionaries on furlough. Since all the orders and congregations had their particular fields, each training house was most interested in the particular mission field that had become a kind of "family property." Missionaries who were sent there felt at home.

In sum, the training of missionary priests for their mission work was not at all academic, a fact that did not keep it from producing some

---

5. The Gereformeerde Kerken (plural "churches") in Nederland. The adjective *gereformeerd* is sometimes translated as "re-reformed" in order to distinguish it from *hervormd*, which is used in the name of the former national church, the Nederlandse Hervormde Kerk (singular "church"), i.e., the Dutch Reformed Church.

6. C. Van Randwijck, *Handelen en denken in dienst der Zending. Oegstgeest 1897-1942* (The Hague, 1981) 675-715.

notable personalities.[7] Until the 1960s there was no coordination among the thirty training houses. Each missionary family trained its members in philosophy and theology with its own resources, which were naturally limited. This contrasts with the ten Protestant missionary societies, which, as we have seen, had a joint training center after 1905. The Catholic centers remained separate from each other, undoubtedly because they each had a large number of missionary candidates to train and because Catholics were very generous toward missions. But in the early 1960s, missionary vocations became rare. A vast reorganization of theological training was undertaken: Large seminaries and missionary houses were replaced by four Catholic faculties of theology, of which only one, in Heerlen, gave a significant place to missiology.

Missiology in the Field

The mission field has been decisive for both Protestants and Catholics. It is there where the rubber meets the road, so to speak. There missionaries from the Christian West encounter non-Christians and there the gospel reaches non-Christian cultures and religions. But what has been at stake has been very different for Catholics and Protestants.

Protestant mission fields — or one should say *the* field, since there was essentially only Indonesia — were staffed by first-class people, several of whom possessed doctorates. In principle, the mission was not seen as a means of exporting the various trends of the Dutch Reformed Church. The desire was, rather, to serve Indonesian interests. Dr. A. C. Kruyt (1869-1949) played a pioneering role in improved interpretations of Indonesian religions and civilization. Dr. N. Adriani (1865-1926) and Dr. Hendrik Kraemer (1888-1965) were experts in oriental languages and Indonesian ethnology; they were sponsored by the Dutch Bible Society. Adriani emphasized dialogue and service.

Kraemer was interested in the modern nationalism of the Indonesian elite and exercised great influence on the movement toward autonomy of local churches in Java from 1922 to 1935.[8] On returning to the Netherlands, he became a professor at the University of Leiden (1937-46),

7. Cf. Rogier Van Rossum, "Opleiden tot missionaris vroeger en nu," *Wereld en Zending* 14 (1985) 209-14.

8. See H. Kraemer, *From Mission Field to Independent Church: Report on a Decisive Decade in the Growth of Indigenous Churches in Indonesia, with an Introductory Note by Dr. W. A. Visser 't Hooft* (London, 1958). This work is a translation of the principal reports on the mission situation in Indonesia edited by Kraemer during his stay in the islands from 1922 to 1935.

but retained his interest in missions and in the missionary renewal of the Dutch Reformed Church. He foresaw the saying "missions from everywhere to everywhere" by noting that the mission field was not only Indonesia but also his own country.[9]

We must also mention Dr. J. H. Bavinck (1895-1964), a missionary of the Reformed Churches to Java. Well versed in traditional Javanese mysticism, he tried to open it to the gospel, notably in his book *Soeksma Soepana*.[10] A professor at the Theological College of Yogyakarta from 1931 to 1939, Bavinck put into the curriculum of future Javanese and Chinese pastors the study of Javanese religions and cultures. On his return to the Netherlands, he taught missiology at the Reformed faculties of theology in Kampen and Amsterdam. In 1953 he published his introduction to the Protestant science of missions, a work that continues to serve as a reference tool.[11]

It is important to note that Protestant missionaries were still in the prime of their lives when they came back to their homeland for family reasons, particularly the education of their children; thus they were able to participate in a powerful way in the development of missiology in the Netherlands. Kraemer and Bavinck were considered veritable gurus by many Dutch Protestants. Since Protestant missions gave independence to indigenous churches much sooner than did Catholic missions, the traditional concept of missions was challenged much sooner among Protestants. Moreover, Protestant participation in the International Council of Missions and later in the World Council of Churches, where the voices of the Third World were becoming more and more dominant, provided occasions for exchanges of viewpoints and experiences in a more lively manner than in the Catholic Church, where everything was rather centralized.

In Catholic mission fields, missionary thought was much more diverse. Besides Indonesia, Brazil and central Africa attracted large numbers of missionaries. Therefore, the perspective was from the outset more international and not purely colonial. One trait of the Catholic missionary reflection was the enormous weight of regulations formulated by Rome rather than out of the situation on the field. The need to call into question the traditional idea of missions was not felt with the same urgency as on the Protestant side. Lastly, the fact that the Bible played only a marginal

9. H. Kraemer, "Ervaringen en gedachten. III," *Rondom ons zendingsveld* 4 (1937) 82ff., cited by Van Randwijck, *op. cit.,* 775. See also Kraemer, *The Christian Message in a Non-Christian World* (London, 1938) 6-17.

10. J. H. Bavinck, *Soeksma Soepana* ("Ecstasy of the Soul"; n.p., 1933; 3rd edition, 1956). See also his *Christus en de mystiek van het Oosten* (Kampen, 1934).

11. J. H. Bavinck, *Inleiding in de Zendingswetenschap* (Kampen, 1954; reprinted 1990); English translation *An Introduction to the Science of Missions* (Philadelphia, 1960).

role in Catholic missionary work meant that there were no scholars comparable to Adriani and Kraemer.

Since Catholic missionaries did not return to the Netherlands except at the ends of their careers, they no longer had the strength to participate in intellectual exchange for the sake of progress in a Catholic missiology in the Netherlands. But some of them did make important contributions, which were spread through missionary newsletters, of which the most serious-minded was *Het Missiewerk*, published after 1919. The situation changed after the Second World War: Missionaries trained at the institute of missiology erected at the Catholic University of Nijmegen in 1948, as well as the institute's professors, began to publish. Reflection deepened and was concentrated on the problem of accommodation. On the whole, Dutch Catholic missionaries had been more active than reflective. The Jesuit F. van Lith in Java was without doubt the most explicit in his experience with accommodation,[12] but there were among the Catholics no charismatic persons like Kraemer and Bavinck.

The Study of Missions at the University Level

In Dutch, Protestants and Catholics have different names for missiology: *Zendingswetenschap* and *Missiewetenschap*. It was not until the mid-1960's that the term *Missiologie* became dominant, thanks to the ecumenical climate of the era. Missiology includes three essential elements: the fundamentals of missions, their history, and their methods, all in their social, economic, religious, and cultural context.

On the Protestant side, from the time of the origins of the universities of the United Provinces (Leiden, 1575), a few professors of theology took an interest in missions: Adrianus Saravia (1531-1613) and Antonius Walaeus (1573-1639) in Leiden, Gisbertus Voetius (1589-1676) in Utrecht, and Johannes Hoornbeek (1617-1666) in Utrecht and Leiden. Much later, in 1876, a reform of the faculties of theology in the state universities created a dual system of teaching, the "duplex ordo," offered by two categories of professors. Professors appointed by the state taught Christianity from a purely scientific perspective, while professors named by the churches taught Christianity from a theological and confessional viewpoint. It was within this latter approach that the study of missions was introduced into the curriculum of the faculties of theology. In 1877, the synod of the Netherlands Reformed Church created a course of study on the *"historia*

---

12. See L. Van Rijckevorsel, S.J., *Pastoor F. van Lith. De Stichter van de missie in Midden-Java (1863-1926)* (Nijmegen, 1952).

propagationis religionis christianae" in the universities of Leiden, Gronigen, and Utrecht. This arrangement remained in place until 1951. The history of missions was also taught in mission schools, which were not considered to have university status.[13] The first chair of missiology in a state university was created in 1961 with Professor Evert Jansen Schoonhoven in Leiden. We must note that already in 1939, J. H. Bavinck was teaching missiology at the Free University of Amsterdam and at the Faculty of Reformed Theology *(gereformeerde)* of Kampen.

The effects of the Second World War forced on missions new methods and a greater openness to the world and to the Kingdom of God. Missions began to be thought of more as "the work of God in this world"[14] than as an ecclesiastical activity. The Reformed Church introduced the term "apostolate" in its new constitution of 1951 in Article VIII, which dealt with missions, evangelization, and dialogue with Israel.[15] The new name of the course work being taught was "the nature and history of the apostolate." The term "apostolate" freed "mission" from its colonial connotations, though "mission" remained in use among Protestant missiologists.[16] J. C. Hoekendijk, J. Blauw, A. T. Van Leeuwen,[17] E. J. Schoonhoven, J. M. Van der Linde, and J. Verkuyl[18] all wrote prolifically in the new missiology review *De Heerbaan.* The meetings of the World Council of Churches, as well as world missionary conferences, put into circulation the idea of mission from everywhere to everywhere (the "six continents approach") and of common apostolic action.

The first chair of missiology in the Netherlands was created in the Catholic Faculty of Theology at Nijmegen in 1930, and Alphons Mulders was named to it. It would, in fact, be the only Catholic chair of missiology, a rather small effort when compared to the eventual five Protestant chairs. In fact, Catholic missiology developed more in the large seminaries, for example, in the diocesan seminary of Hoeven, where Father Anton Freitag, S.V.D., taught. Father Freitag had been a student of Josef Schmidlin (1876-1944) at Münster

13. The problems involved in training of Protestant missionaries by the missions themselves and by university faculties are studied by Van Randwijck, *op. cit.,* 694-700.

14. An allusion to the title of J. Blauw, *Gottes Werk in dieser Welt. Grundzüge einer biblischen Theologie der Mission* (Munich, 1961).

15. Cf. E. Jansen Schoonhoven, *Het apostolaat en de uitwendige zending* (Oegstgeest, 1951); *idem,* "Der Artikel 'Vom Apostolat der Kirche' in der Kirchenordnung der niederlandischen Reformierten Kirche," in *Basileia. Walter Freytag zum 60. Geburtstag* (Stuttgart, 1959) 278-84.

16. The "theology of apostolate" in the Netherlands is discussed by M. Spindler in his thesis *La mission, combat pour le salut du monde* (Neuchâtel and Paris, 1967) 82-92.

17. A. T. Van Leeuwen, *Christianity in World History: The Meeting of the Faiths of East and West* (London, 1964).

18. Author of *Contemporary Missiology: An Introduction* (Grand Rapids, 1978).

in Westphalia.[19] A third missiologist, Hubert Ahaus, had a great influence through the mission association Missie Interacademial. With Freitag, he published a work strongly linking missions and the kingdom of God.[20]

After his nomination to Nijmegen, Mulders gave new life to the journal *Het Missiewerk,* which was valued for its annual bibliography. The missiology institute, founded in 1948, enlarged the base of missiology by putting into the curriculum related sciences such as the comparative history of religions, islamology, ethnology, and the study of oriental languages, notably Indonesian and Javanese.[21] Mulders did not provide a practical missiology manual.

Mulders's successor, Father Arnulf Camps, O.F.M., taught from 1963 until 1990. He tried to bring missiology into closer touch with missionary practice. While Mulders's method was deductive, Camps tried to work inductively and "empirically."[22] He succeeded in gathering a team of teaching researchers, each one a specialist in Africa, Latin America, Asia, or missions planning. This decentralized approach replaced the relative monotony that had until then characterized Catholic missiology in the Netherlands. The missiology branch of the Nijmegen faculty produced many missiologists, in particular 18 doctors of missiology between 1930 and 1984. The competition with Protestant missiology began to bear its fullest fruits; during the same period, the Protestant faculties of missiology had produced 54 doctorates on subjects directly missiological in nature.[23]

19. See *De Katholieke Missie in wezen en ontwikkeling* (Hoeven, 1924); *Emigranten voor God. Wereldbetekenis van het Nederlandse Missiewerk* (Ruremonde, 1949); *Moderne missiebibliografische handleiding* (Alverna, 1954); *Bijdrage tot een Missiedogmatiek* (Teteringen, 1955).

20. A. Freitag, S.V.D., and H. Ahaus, MMH, *Het Godsrijk* (Steyl, 1940).

21. Mulders's teachings are found in his two classic manuals: *Missiegeschiedenis* (Bussum, 1957, revised and augmented in German as *Missionsgeschichte. Die Ausbreitung des katholischen Glaubens*); *idem, Missiologisch Bestek. Inleiding tot de katholieke missiewetenschap* (Hilverstum/Antwerp, 1962).

22. Cf. A. Camps, "Vier sleutelbegrippen voor een meer empirische missiologie," and J. M. Van Engelen, "Godsdienst, sociale verandering en conflict. Een missiologische case study over Noordoost Brazilië," *Vox Theologica* 42 (1972) 218-31 and 232-53.

23. J. A. B. Jongeneel and E. Klootwijk, *Faculteiten der Godgeleerdheid, Theologische Hogescholen en de Derde Wereld* (Leiden, 1986) 49-88 contains a list of all theses since 1876 that deal with the Third World or were written by persons from the Third World. Many white South Africans are cited. Not all of these theses are strictly missiological.

Relations between Protestant and Catholic Missiology: From Rivalry to Cooperation

The history of relations between Protestant and Catholic missiologies can be divided into three periods: 1797 to 1940, 1940 to 1967, and 1967 to the present.

1797-1940: Noncooperation and Rivalry

The first modern Protestant missionary society in the Netherlands was founded in 1797. Until the Second World War, Catholic and Protestant missions and missionary studies were almost entirely separate and were in competition with each other. The Reformed Church was at that time the only official church. Catholics were considered second-class citizens, and their church was not able to reconstitute itself with its normal hierarchy until 1853. In fact, however, Catholics had always been very numerous in the Netherlands, but the myth of Protestant Holland did not allow Catholics there or in the Dutch colony of Indonesia to attain the political and missionary responsibilities that they were capable of assuming. At the beginning of the nineteenth century, there were only a handful of secular priests in the Dutch colonies — in Indonesia, Curaçao, and Suriname. The revival of the religious orders after 1853 gave greater and greater force to Catholic missions. In 1896, there were 50,000 Catholics in Indonesia, compared to 260,000 Protestants. But in 1925, the Protestant missionary periodical *Mededelingen* was alarmed by Catholic progress, noting that there was one Dutch Catholic missionary (male or female) for every 675 Dutch Catholics; Protestants were far behind this number. In 1934, the director of the Protestant missionary school in Oegstgeest spoke of a veritable Catholic menace for Protestant missions.[24]

A spirit of rivalry, if not of "battle against Rome," developed, all the stronger because the Catholic side held that Protestantism was a heresy and had no right either to exist or (all the more) to evangelize. On the field, Catholics had never accepted the principle of spheres of influence (comity agreements) and demanded the right to do mission work even in areas assigned to Protestant missions. In Indonesia there had been two official representatives of missions accredited to the colonial government: the Protestant Mission Consulate, created in 1906, and the Central Catholic Mission Bureau, established in 1931. These two organizations never met,

---

24. J. Rauws, "De nieuwe zending," in H. D. Boissevain, ed., *De zending in Oost en West. Verleden en heden* I (The Hague, 1934) 89.

even after the invasion of the Netherlands by Germany in May 1940.[25] But some dreamed that it would be otherwise.[26]

1940-67: Redirection

The Second World War caused a massive upheaval. Interned together in Japanese concentration camps in Java and Indonesia, Catholic and Protestant missionaries learned to know and respect each other. Elsewhere in the world, an ecumenical reconciliation was in progress. In addition, new Protestant missionary scholars were creating a new ecumenical and missionary climate.[27] On the Catholic side, there was no such opening yet; missions were being rebuilt on the pre-war model, without any thought to possible relations with Protestants. In addition, the Nijmegen missiologist of the era, A. Mulders, considered Protestant mission thought unusable,[28] even though he conscientiously cited Protestant missiologists in his bibliographies! One of his Protestant counterparts, J. H. Bavinck, held similar opinions about Catholic missiology because of the total difference of opinion between Protestants and Catholics about paganism.[29]

On the other hand, J. C. Hoekendijk, a professor at the University of Utrecht, was much more open to Catholic missionary thought. His mission theology was in fact radically different: His central categories were the kingdom of God and the world, and he believed that church and mission had only secondary roles in God's plan of salvation. The church could not be the goal of mission, but rather a function of mission.[30]

During Vatican II (1962-65), Catholic missiologists came to be more and more interested in ecumenism in missions.[31] In 1962 *De Katholieke Missiën* devoted a special issue to the churches of the Reformation, with seven articles by Protestant authors. In a review of G. H. Anderson's *The Theology of Christian Mission*, Father E. Loffeld, CSSP, wrote longingly,

---

25. Maria C. Jongeling, *Het zendingsconsulaat in Nederlands-Indië 1906-1942* (Arnhem, 1966) 180.

26. The Protestant journal *Nederlands Zendingsblad* 20 (1937) 181 was thrilled by the presence of Father P. H. Geurtjens, a famous Catholic missionary in New Guinea, at the Protestant mission jubilee in Oegstgeest in 1937.

27. See, e.g., L. Zielhuis, "Rooms-Katholieke Inleidingen tot de Zendingswetenschap. Van Schmidlin naar Seumois," *De Heerbaan* 9 (1956) 107-15.

28. A. Mulders, *Missiologisch Bestek* (1962) viii.

29. J. H. Bavinck, *Inleiding in de Zendingswetenschap*, 175.

30. See P. Van Gurp, *Kerk en zending in de theologie van J. C. Hoekendijk (1912-1975). Een plaatsbepaling* (thesis, Haarlem, 1989).

31. A. Camps, "Oecumenische contacten tussen missie en zending," *Oecumene* 1 (1962) 34.

"This book shows us how much missionary problems are parallel. We could do well to search together for solutions."[32]

1967 to the Present: The Ecumenical Breakthrough

The Second Vatican Council brought a decisive opening of Catholicism toward other Christian churches and permitted an ecumenical break-through in the realm of missions. Two meetings took place in 1967 after which it became impossible to do Catholic and Protestant missions studies separately. The first of these was held January 3-5 at Driebergen at the Protestant study and meeting center Kerk en Wereld ("Church and World") under the auspices of the St. Willibrord Catholic Association. Its theme was "Ecumenical Evangelization." The second meeting was organized by the Protestant Missionary Council of the Netherlands and was held at the missions school at Oegstgeest on May 24 on the theme "Catholic and Protestant Missions after Vatican II." The link between these two meetings was made obvious by the participation of the same missiologists at both. The reports of the Oegstgeest meeting appeared in the Protestant missiology review De Heerbaan, and the Catholic journal Missie Integraal called the event "historic." Professor J. M. van der Linde of the University of Utrecht wrote: "Catholic and Protestant missions can no longer continue in isolation. The documents of Vatican II invite separated Churches to consider in a spirit of real communion what the mission of God means for the entire world, what the will of God and Christ demands of them, and how their structures have responded."[33]

The Catholic-Protestant reconciliation had its beginnings in the war years, and it was Vatican II that gave it an official character. For that reason the Council became a common reference point for both Catholics and Protestants, as Professor E. Jansen Schoonhoven noted in 1969: "The Second Vatican Council makes it impossible to do missiology any longer in separate camps."[34]

The way was open to missionary and missiology cooperation. I will limit myself to pointing out some initiatives in the realm of missiology.

---

32. E. Loffeld in Het Missiewerk 41 (1962) 192ff.; cf. idem, "Convergerende tendenzen in de hedendaagse missietheologie," Het Missiewerk 41 (1962) 129-54.

33. J. M. van der Linde, "Van vervreemding tot beraad," De Heerbaan 20 (1967) 255.

34. E. J. Schoonhoven, "Terugblik op 22 jaar Zendingshogeschool," De Heerbaan 23 (1970) 15; see also J. Verkuyl, "Over de mogelijkheden van practische samenwerking tussen 'Zending en Missie,'" De Heerbaan 20 (1967) 219.

The Founding of the Interuniversity Institute of Missiological and Ecumenical Research (IIMO), June 23, 1969.

The idea of the Interuniversity Institute was born in the Protestant Missionary Council, which had a study and documentation bureau where medical missions, the biblical basis of missions, and social aspects of missions (C. L. van Doorn, Mady A. Thung) were addressed. In a memo addressed to the Protestant Missionary Council in 1962, Hoekendijk proposed to enlarge the field of study in an ecumenical direction, including the Catholic world. He drew up the plan of an institute of basic research on missions and ecumenism. The idea was accepted in principle by the Protestant Missionary Council on the condition that appropriate financing be found. The university reforms in the Netherlands foresaw the creation of Interuniversity Institute as a way of linking the world of research and the world of work. Missions and universities seized the opportunity and created the IIMO.

The Institute was interconfessional but not under the authority of the churches, and was meant to supply university-level research financed essentially by the state. Its administrative council, even today, comes from six universities, four faculties of theology, and five Catholic and Protestant missions and church organizations. The IIMO has two departments: missiology in Leiden, ecumenism in Utrecht. The University of Utrecht manages the Institute. The department of missiology has created a documentation section and a specialized library; since 1972 it has published a journal, *Exchange: Bulletin of Third World Christian Literature*,[35] and since 1979 a series of scientific monographs, IIMO Research Pamphlets.[36] Two missions study societies function under the auspices of the IIMO: a missiology society founded in 1954 by Protestants and later enlarged to include Catholics, and a working group of missiology professors, founded in 1965.

A New Journal of Missiology

In 1972 the Catholic missiology journal *Het Missiewerk* and the Protestant missiology journal *De Heerbaan* joined together to give birth to a new

35. Since 1990, the journal's field has enlarged and its name has become *Exchange: Journal of Missiological and Ecumenical Research*.

36. The name of the series became IIMO Research Publications in 1987. Forty titles had appeared by 1994. On the history of IIMO see A. J. van den Berg, "Het Interuniversitair Instituut voor Missiologie en Oecumenica 1969-1994," *Terugblik en Perspectief Unteruniversitair Instituut voor Missiologie en Oecumenica 1969-1994* (Utrecht and Leiden, 1994) I-38.

quarterly journal, *Wereld en Zending*. Its editorial committee is named on an equal basis by the Catholic and Protestant Missionary Councils. The subjects undertaken are always treated from an ecumenical perspective. The journal allows exchange of reflection and missionary experiences from both sides of the confessional border. The initiatives of Third World Christians receive much attention in the belief that they are also pertinent for Western situations. Each year the journal publishes a missiology bibliography for the Netherlands and Flemish Belgium, prepared by the document researcher of the IIMO.

The Ecumenical Introduction to Missiology

1988 saw the publication of *Oecumenische Inleiding in de Missiologie*, on which the present volume is based. This event crowned years of collaboration between Protestant and Catholic missiologists in the framework provided by the IIMO.

This *Oecumenische Inleiding* was the eighth in a series of introductions to missiology produced in the Netherlands since 1879.[37] During the first era, there was Neurdenburg and Daubanton; in the second, Bavinck and Mulders; in the third, Verkuyl, Versteeg, and Jongeneel.

This new textbook had a number of characteristics not found elsewhere: It was written by an interconfessional team, and with no preconceived idea of setting out once and for all the content and the form of missions. It tries to discover the meaning of missions in the interaction of texts and contexts, as the subtitle indicates: "Texts and Contexts of World Christianity." It recognizes the pluralism of interpretations of the Christian message found in different cultures. It proposes a global approach to missions, with Europe and North America considered as mission fields on a par with the other continents. It understands unity of mission not as uniformity but as dynamic development based on mutual assistance and reciprocal correction and enrichment, increasingly involving the Third World Church.[38]

In brief, mission takes shape in a resonating dialogue that affects all parties. Mission in a pluralistic world can only be pluralistic. It must

37. Cf. J. M. Van der Linde, "Honderd jaar zendingswetenschap in Nederland 1875/6-1975," *Nederlands Theologisch Tijdschrift* 31 (1977) 227-57, reprinted in *idem, Gods Wereldhuis. Voordachten en opstellen over de geschiedenis van zending en oecumene* (Amsterdam, 1980) 167-85.

38. Cf. F. J. Verstraelen, "Heil als heelheid van leven. Impulsen uit Afrika voor heling van Europees Christendom," in *Heil voor deze wereld* (Kampen, 1984) 143-59; Jan Van Lin, ed., *Parochie en gemeenschap. Kerkopbouw in Nederland: een grensverleggende verkenning in Indonesië, Zaïre en Brazilië* (Hilversum, 1987).

take root in local contexts in order to respond to the needs and aspirations of the people. So it is a task to be undertaken above all by local Christians. Yet unity is an essential dimension of the Christian faith, so local missions must be involved in global mission through a process of sharing. Christian mission for today's world can be relevant only if it is fundamentally ecumenical without losing its mooring in the person of Jesus Christ and his message of healing, salvation, and liberation.[39]

The ecumenical breakthrough that I have discussed here has limits of which I am painfully aware. We have not succeeded in formulating an ecumenical missiology. Certain missionary milieux remain apart from our undertaking. I am thinking in this case of fundamentalist Protestants, who would certainly have something to contribute and to learn, and of conservative elements in the older churches who are aiming at restoring confessional identities rather than developing a common witness. Christians feel embarrassed in our secularized world. Perhaps this discomfort will be the occasion of a new ecumenical breakthrough by a shared conversion to the essentials, leaving aside the ballast of historical constructs falsely held as sacred. Such a common conversion would in the final analysis be a solid base for a joint mission, and consequently for a shared missiology, truly evangelical and truly ecumenical. The struggle continues!

---

39. Cf. *Common Witness: A Study Document of the Joint Working Group of the Roman Catholic Church and the World Council of Churches* (Geneva, 1981).

CHAPTER 27

Contemporary Currents in Missiology

J. A. B. Jongeneel and J. M. van Engelen

By "contemporary currents in missiology" one could mean all those movements that manifested themselves in the field of missiology in this century
after the groundwork was laid for missiology as an academic discipline
by Gustav Warneck (1834-1910), the author of the three volumes of *Evangelische Missionslehre* (1892-1903), on the Protestant side, and Joseph
Schmidlin (1876-1944), the author of *Einführung in die Missionswissenschaft*
(1917², 1925), on the Roman Catholic side. But here we have in mind only
those movements that have, either for the first time or yet again, made
themselves felt since the turbulent 1960s.

That decade saw a sea change in Western culture and hence also in
Christian theology. Thinking of the work of Bishop John A. T. Robinson,
Paul Van Buren, Dorothee Sölle, and others, J. Sperna Weiland remarked:

> I believe we have to say that what is really occurring here, even though
> it is not without continuity with the tradition, is a new theological
> experiment in which the issue is "the secular meaning of the gospel."
> It appeared that we were no longer in agreement about system and
> method and that the consensus was no longer intact.[1]

In those years great changes occurred also in the field of missiology.
The "secular meaning" of mission, that is, of cooperation in development,
became a fixed feature on the agenda of the church and its mission agencies. The negative valuation of secularization by the mission conferences
of Edinburgh (1910), Jerusalem (1928), and Tambaram (1938) consciously
yielded to a "yes to the secular" in Mexico City (1963).[2] This "yes to the

---

1. *Oriëntatie; nieuwe wegen in de theologie* (Baarn 1971) 12. Van Buren is the author
of *The Secular Meaning of the Gospel* (London, 1963).
2. J. Verkuyl, *De taak der missiologie en der missionaire methodiek in het tijdperk van
saecularisatie en saecularisme* (Kampen, 1965) 21.

world" produced joy in the hearts of many but at the same time disturbed not only evangelical theologians but also people like W. A. Visser 't Hooft, past Secretary General of the World Council of Churches. On the Roman Catholic side, the positive valuation of secularization came about somewhat differently — as a result of (and after) the Second Vatican Council.[3] But major shifts in the field of missiology were not limited to the complex of issues associated with secularization but extended to the issue of the "theology of religions": More than ever the term "the absoluteness of Christianity" (from Ernst Troeltsch and others) and the idea it represented were, with other things, called into question.

These shifts in theology and missiology naturally have consequences for missionary organization and for what the church says about mission. They also put a stamp on two mileposts of the 1960s: First, in 1961 the third assembly of the World Council of Churches (WCC) was held at New Delhi. Eastern Orthodox churches joined the Council and the International Missionary Council, which had come into being in 1921, was integrated into the Council.[4] There it continued to exist in an ecumenical context as the Commission for World Mission and Evangelism. Second, in 1962 to 1965 the Second Vatican Council (Vatican II) was held in Rome. In a spirit of renewal *(aggiornamento)* it produced not only *Nostra aetate* and *Lumen gentium* but also the decree on the church's missionary activity *(Ad gentes)* and the pastoral constitution on the church in the modern world *(Gaudium et spes)*.

On the basis of this history we will divide this chapter into three parts:

- the first half of the twentieth century, beginning with Warneck and Schmidlin,
- the 1960s, beginning with the third assembly of the WCC at New Delhi in 1961, and
- the present situation since Vatican II and the fourth assembly of the WCC at Uppsala in 1968.[5]

---

3. Cf. G. Evers, *Mission — nichtchristliche Religionen — Weltliche Welt* (Münster, 1974) 164.

4. Arthur F. Glasser saw the "absorption" of the International Missionary Council by the WCC as the "starting point" for evangelical mission theology (A. F. Glasser and D. A. McGavran, *Contemporary Theologies of Mission* [Grand Rapids, 1983] 8).

5. Cf. J. M. van Engelen's division in "Missiology at a Turningpoint," *Mill-Hilliana* 30 (1978) 5-24: (1) the preconciliar concept of mission, (2) the conciliar theology of mission, and (3) the postconciliar concept of mission. Cf. also David Bosch, *Transforming Mission: Paradigm Shifts in Theology of Mission* (Maryknoll, 1991).

The emphasis naturally falls on the third and last period — where we are today.

The First Half of the Twentieth Century

Just as F. D. E. Schleiermacher (1768-1834) stood at the cradle of nine-teenth-century Protestant theology, so Karl Barth (1886-1968) stood at the beginning of Protestant theology in our century. Warneck and Schmidlin, however, belong to the pre-Barthian era of theology. Their lasting impor-tance is that they made it possible for missiology to be practiced on an academic level and accepted as an academic discipline.

Barth's dialectical theology had important implications for missi-ology, which were drawn out especially by Hendrik Kraemer (1888-1965). This practitioner of the science of religion and theologian of mission made a distinction between naturalist religions of self-realization and prophetic religions of revelation. Belonging to the latter category were Judaism, Christianity, and to some extent Islam. Christianity as an empirical religion was not absolute for Kraemer, but the unique revelation of God in Christ was. Mission in the non-Christian world is imperative "because only in the light of the revelation in Christ are the greatness and misery of man adequately unveiled."[6]

Kraemer consistently stressed the discontinuity between the Chris-tian faith — which is the human response to the revelation of God in Christ — and non-Christian religions. At the world mission conference at Tam-baram in 1938 he clashed on this issue with the American philosopher-theologian William Ernest Hocking (1873-1966), who had been chairman of the commission that in 1932 had produced the report entitled *Rethinking Missions*. In this controversial report all religions were understood as roads to God and Christianity was summoned to join with other religions in the struggle against secularism. According to the report, the task of missions was to express the desire of Christians to share with non-Christians the highest spiritual norms and values and to cooperate with them in building a world culture. The American Edmund D. Soper, whose own position was somewhere between those of Hocking and Kraemer, summed up their viewpoints by calling that of Kraemer "uniqueness without continuity" and Hocking's "continuity with doubtful uniqueness."[7]

6. H. Kraemer, *The Christian Message in a Non-Christian World* (London, 1938) 146.

7. Edmund D. Soper, *The Philosophy of the Christian World Mission* (New York, 1943) 223. Soper's own viewpoint can be summed up in the words "uniqueness with continuity" (228).

Rudolf Bultmann (1884-1976) also influenced the theology of mission in this period, though on a much smaller scale than Barth.[8] Here we have in mind specifically the work of Walter Holsten (1908-82), professor at Mainz, who viewed missiology, along with the science of religion, in the light of the *kerygma*, "the message of the action of God in Christ, which is decisive and which calls to decision."[9] Holsten does not position himself against Hocking but against Ernst Troeltsch (1865-1923), the systematician of the history-of-religions school, because in Holsten's opinion Troeltsch replaces the *kerygma* as eschatological occurrence with the Enlightenment concept of "the essence of Christianity." The foundation of mission is not "the essence of Christianity within us" *(in nobis)* but the *kerygma* outside us *(extra nos)*, a *kerygma* that is dynamic and that calls on every person to make existential decisions.

On the Roman Catholic side discussion of mission has been carried on between representatives of the school of Münster (Schmidlin) and that of Leuven (Pierre Charles, S. J.). The former, following Warneck at some distance, stresses the great importance of conversion and evangelism; the latter emphasizes church planting *(plantatio ecclesiae)*.[10] But both occupied themselves with and based themselves on various papal encyclicals and apostolic documents of the time, specifically *Maximum illud* (1919) from Benedict VI, *Rerum ecclesiae* (1926) from Pius XI, *Evangelii praecones* (1951) and *Fidei donum* (1957) from Pius II, and *Princeps pastorum* (1959) from John XXIII. A central focus in the discussions preceding Vatican II was the complex of issues associated with the theme of the "adaptation" or "accommodation" of church and theology to the non-Christian world. A more marginal issue was the question, raised by Yves M. J. Congar, O.P., whether the church is necessary to salvation (is there really "no salvation outside the church"?).[11]

The missiology of Münster as well as Leuven was more ecclesiocentric than those of the Protestant missiologists that we have mentioned. Protestant concepts of mission in this period were more theocentric or — under the influence of Barth — more christocentric. Until the late 1950s

8. Paul Tillich (1887-1965), the third important Protestant systematic theologian of the first half of this century, had even less influence on missiology than Bultmann. Not a single prominent book on missiology is based on his theology.

9. W. Holsten, *Das Kerygma und der Mensch. Einführung in die Religions- und Missionswissenschaft* (Munich, 1953) 43.

10. Cf. Evers, *op. cit.*, 4-9, 11-16; J. Mitterhöfer, *Thema Mission* (Vienna, 1974) 68; R. G. van Rossum, "Missiologie-gedachten in de Katholieke Kerk," *De Heerbaan* 20 (1967) 272.

11. Van Rossum, *op. cit.*, 264, calls the appearance of Congar's book, *Chrétiens désunis*, in 1937 a "breakthrough" in theology (but not yet in missiology!).

Roman Catholic missiology, despite the contrast between Münster and Leuven, was much more unified than Protestant missiology, which was divided into "camps." But in Catholic reflection before Vatican II on what constitutes mission there was certainly a discernible radicalization of thought. One of the most provocative and controversial writings of this period was that of Henri Godin and Y. Daniel: *La France, pays de mission?* (Paris, 1943), which applied missiological categories to the French situation and thus for the first time raised with urgency, *pars pro toto*, the question of "mission in Europe."

As the 1960s approached there was still no Roman Catholic or Protestant Third World theology as a distinct current. The Western church and mission had done no more than listen to "theological voices"[12] that were raised especially in Asia beginning in the 1930s. It was in Asia after all that in 1938 the important Third World mission conference took place at Tambaram. There delegates from North and South came into contact not only with the theology of Western missionaries active in India but also with the "Indian theology" of Vengal Chakkarai Chetty (1880-1958), Pandipeddi Chenchiah (1886-1959), Aiyadurai Jesudasen Appasamy (1891-1975), and others,[13] which can be considered one of the earliest forms of well thought-out Third World theology. There they could also observe that "Indian theology," with its tendencies towards mysticism and syncretism, did not simply accept Kraemer's tome *The Christian Message in a Non-Christian World* (1938).

The 1960s

Johannes Christiaan Hoekendijk (1912-1975), for one, picked up the theme of Godin and Daniel. His missiological work can be viewed not only as characteristic of the transition from the 1950s to the 1960s, but also as directive of the process of transition from one decade to the other. According to Hoekendijk, the kingdom, not the church, is central in missiology. The church cannot and may not be more than a function of the apostolate. Moreover, the apostolate must be more than merely a cog in the wheels of systematic and practical theology. Already in 1950 (in an article on "the call to evangelism") he indicated his belief that in some schools of Prot-

---

12. The term is from H.-W. Gensichen, G. Rosenkranz, and G. Vicedom, ed., *Theologische Stimmen aus Asien, Afrika und Lateinamerika* (3 vols., Munich, 1965-68), one of the first collections of Third World theology published in the West.

13. See H. Wagner, *Erstgestalten einer einheimischen Theologie in Südindien. Ein Kapitel indischer Theologiegeschichte als kritischer Beitrag zur Definition von "einheimischer Theologie"* (Munich, 1963).

estant and Catholic theology the "apostolate" was becoming the pervasive center of thought, which he considered a theological revolution.[14]

The course that missiology must take in the postcolonial period, says Hoekendijk, is one that moves from theology of mission, as a division of systematic and practical theology (along with dogmatics, ethics, liturgics, pastoral theology, and the like), to a missionary theology, that is, the whole of systematic and practical theology permeated by the spirit of apostolate.[15] Kraemer, on the other hand, writes of a transition "from mission field to independent church," which, translated into the idiom of missiology, is a transition from "a western theology of mission" to "third-world theology."[16] The theological and missiological shift that occurred in the 1960s has also been characterized as a move from a theology of mission to a theology of development, which the commission for "Society, Development, and Peace" (Sodepax), formed by Rome and Geneva, has suggested,[17] and as a move from a theology of mission to a theology of dialogue, which came to the fore especially after the fourth assembly of the WCC at Uppsala (1968).[18] There a council division set up by Stanley J. Samartha for "Dialogue with people of living faiths (and ideologies)" began its work, in which the focus is not "mission among non-Christians" but "dialogue with people of other faiths." Here "faith" no longer has the meaning it had for Barth, Kraemer, and others since it is no longer contrasted with religion, but is rather more or less identified with religion.[19]

This metamorphosis of missiology in the 1960s uncovered certain tendencies that existed here and there, but not everywhere, in Protestant-

14. J. C. Hoekendijk, *The Church Inside Out* (Philadelphia, 1964) 14.

15. *Idem, Kirche und Volk in der Deutschen Missionswissenschaft* (Munich, 1967), 339. Cf. G. Coffele, *Johannes Christiaan Hoekendijk. Da una teologia delle missione ad una teologia missionaira* (Rome, 1976).

16. H. Kraemer, *From Mission Field to Independent Church: Report on a Decisive Decade in the Growth of Indigenous Churches in Indonesia* (London, 1958).

17. Cf. G. Bauer, *Towards a Theology of Development: An Annotated Bibliography Prepared for Sodepax* (Geneva, 1970). F. J. Verstraelen, "Theologie in actie voor ontwikkeling," in H. H. Berger, W. Goddijn, et al., ed., *Tussentijds. Theologische Faculteit te Tilburg, bundel opstellen bij gelegenheid van haar erkenning* (Tilburg, 1974) 251, adds to this: "Now interest in an all-embracing 'theology of development' is diminishing."

18. Cf. A. Camps, *Partners in Dialogue: Christianity and Other World Religions* (Maryknoll, 1981) 29f.; he poses a "theology of adaptation" over against the theology of development.

19. The terminological development was from "heathens" to "non-Christians" and then from "non-Christians" to "fellow believers." Cf. the historical notes of J. C. Hoekendijk in *Kerk en volk in de Duitse zendings-wetenschap* (Amsterdam, 1948) 77, on C. H. C. Plath (1829-1901): "Mission is no longer depicted as the final means of salvation . . . but as a means of education. [Plath] typically prefers to replace 'heathen' with 'non-Christian.' In essence 'non-Christians' have already become the 'uneducated.' "

ism and sparsely in the Catholic Church. That decade was not purely an era of the avant garde, one in which colonialist and imperialist forms of mission were radically left behind and a resolute breakthrough was made to "mission in six continents" (Mexico City, 1963) and to an apostolate focused in the Western world on "the new man." This "new man" is categorized by Hoekendijk as "post-Christian, post-ecclesiastical, post-bourgeois, post-personal (with, as an open question, post-religious?)."[20] There was non-avant garde development among both Protestant evangelicals and theologians in the Catholic Church.

The decade of the 1960s was a time when the evangelical movement made itself known forcefully. One evangelical declaration followed another in rapid tempo: Wheaton 1966, Berlin 1966, Frankfurt 1970, and others. The Frankfurt Declaration, composed mainly by Peter Beyerhaus, attracted particular attention because of its fierceness:

> We therefore oppose the false teaching (which is circulated in the ecumenical movement since the Third General Assembly of the World Council of Churches in New Delhi) that Christ himself is anonymously so evident in world religions, historical changes, and revolutions that man can encounter him and find salvation in him without the direct news of the Gospel.[21]

The idea of "anonymous Christianity" also appeared in Roman Catholic theology. It was propagated especially by Karl Rahner[22] and neither adopted by Vatican II nor repudiated as it was in the Frankfurt Declaration. It can be seen as a manifestation of the view that the relation of Christianity to non-Christian religions can no longer be thought of as that of truth to error but as the dynamic relation of a part of truth to all of truth.[23] To be sure, in *Ad Gentes* one can find formulations that are consistent with a "theology of anonymous Christianity," as for example the remark that Christians have an obligation to so reveal the power of the Holy Spirit that others might "more perfectly perceive the true meaning of human life and the universal solidarity of mankind" (Art. 11), but that is as far as it goes.[24]

20. Hoekendijk, *The Church Inside Out*, 50.

21. As translated in Won Yong Ji, "Evangelization and Humanization," *Concordia Theological Monthly* 42 (1971) 165.

22. Evers, *op. cit.*, 107-17.

23. So van Rossum, *op. cit.*, 268. Van Rossum calls the doctrine of createdness in Christ and the idea of "anonymous Christianity" "the two primary theological foci of the reversal that occurred in the 1950s in Roman Catholic missiology" (267).

24. Van Rossum, *op. cit.*, 275, remarks that the *Declaration on the Relation of the Church to Non-Christian Religions* deliberately did not describe non-Christian reli-

What Vatican II did resolve was the opposition between the schools of Münster and Leuven. In Art. 6 of *Ad Gentes* we read concerning mission activity: "The special end of this missionary activity is the evangelization and the implanting of the church among peoples or groups . . . ," which amounted to an equal endorsement of both schools.

We can make four summary statements about missiological developments in the 1960s as they were experienced differently in the Catholic Church and among Protestants: First, developments in the Roman Catholic Church, in contrast with the WCC, were evolutionary rather than revolutionary. True, a variety of new emphases arose at Vatican II, which would not have been found in the documents of the *Congregatio de Propaganda Fide* published before that time. But there was no palace revolution. By contrast, the evangelical movement regarded the events at and after the third assembly of the WCC at New Delhi (1961) as a dethronement of "a proclamation of the Gospel which aims at conversion" (Frankfurt Declaration 6).

Second, conflict between "evangelicals" and "ecumenicals" dominated Protestant missiology after 1961 and certainly after 1968. In the Catholic Church conflict became more evident after 1972, that is, after the publication of Gustavo Gutiérrez's *A Theology of Liberation* (Maryknoll, 1973).

Third, the spirit of *aggiornamento* (renewal) at Vatican II led to positive contacts between Catholics and Protestants. Among the results were, in the Netherlands for example, the first consultation between Catholic and Protestant missionary councils at Oegstgeest in 1967, the founding of the Interuniversitair Instituut voor Missiologie en Oecumenica (IIMO) in 1969, and the merging of Catholic and Protestant mission journals into *Wereld en Zending* in 1972. From that time forward the two missions, despite differences in missionary outlook,[25] no longer operated polemically in opposition to each other but stood irenically side by side in the performance of the one indivisible missionary task.

Fourth, with regard to the emancipation of Third World theology, after 1961 Third World theologians were given an increasing number of responsibilities in the WCC. M. M. Thomas of India was appointed president of the Central Committee as well as of the Executive Committee, where he remained until the fifth assembly of the WCC at Nairobi in 1975. In the Catholic Church this emancipation process was completed some-

---

gions as "ways of salvation" (this formulation was deleted in the final edition of the text).

25. E. Jansen Schoonhoven, *De Heerbaan* 20 (1967) 253-315, noted seven points of resemblance and three points of difference in missiological thought between Catholics and Protestants.

what later, though the first Chinese and African bishops had been consecrated at Rome or elsewhere already before World War II. But it was only as a result of Vatican II that the bishops of the Third World were assigned many responsibilities of their own.

The Situation Today

The situation after New Delhi, Uppsala, and Vatican II can be described, following Rodger C. Bassham, as a land of three streams: ecumenical, evangelical, and Roman Catholic.[26] But one can also describe it, as do Glasser and McGavran, as a land of four streams: ecumenical (or conciliar), evangelical, Roman Catholic, and liberationist.[27]

But since we are writing less about missionary streams than about missiological streams, we must go beyond these divisions. There are a number of missiologists who cannot be easily classified within them. Stephen Neill, Lesslie Newbigin, Johannes Verkuyl, Gerhard Rosenkranz, Hans-Werner Gensichen, Gerald Anderson, Bengt Sundkler, Eric Sharpe, Mortimer Arias, John Mbiti, and Olav Myklebust cannot be simply classified as "ecumenical" as opposed to "evangelical."[28] There are a number of subdivisions: Peter Beyerhaus, professor at Tübingen, distinguishes no fewer than six groups of evangelicals.[29] Within liberation theology we must distinguish those who are in dialogue with Western theology and remain in the Catholic Church, such as Gustavo Gutiérrez, from those who more consciously seek a path of their own in alliance with Marxism, such as Juan Luis Segundo and Pablo Richard.

We cannot possibly enter on a discussion of all these groups and divisions. We have to limit ourselves here to the main lines. Moreover, we are looking for distinctions that relate primarily to missiology. In this regard we are aided by Joseph Amstutz, who, in his survey of mission theologies, distinguishes three groups, the first seeing mission as God's initiative, the second seeing it as an activity of the church, and the third seeing it as redemptive history.[30] We would characterize the first of these

---

26. R. C. Bassham, *Mission Theology, 1948-1975: Years of Worldwide Creative Tension, Ecumenical, Evangelical and Roman Catholic* (Pasadena, 1979).

27. Glasser and McGavran, *op. cit.*

28. So D. J. Bosch, *Witness to the World: The Christian Mission in Theological Perspective* (London, 1980) 29.

29. Cited in Bosch, *op. cit.*, 30.

30. J. Amstutz, *Kirche der Völker. Skizze einer Theorie der Mission* (Freiburg, 1972) 12-44. Mitterhöfer, *op. cit.*, 65ff., builds further on Amstutz, as does T. Kramm, *Analyse und Bewährung theologischer Modelle zur Begründung der Mission* . . . (Aachen, 1979) 39ff.

three groups as the continuation of the "classic" or "traditional" theory of mission, which looks for support in the text of the Bible and perhaps also in church tradition. Over against such missiologies "from above" one can position "modern" views, which derive the agenda of missiology primarily from the world context and so speak of mission as "presence" or "humanization," as "dialogue," and as "liberation."

We will discuss first missiologies "from above" and then missiologies "from below." In distinction from Amstutz, we will look at what he calls "redemption-historical mission" immediately after "mission of the *missio Dei*" (and not after "ecclesiocentric mission") because "redemption history" is directly bound up with the *missio Dei* and because it is broader in conception than church or mission history. Finally, referring back to Glasser and McGavran's sketch of the land of four streams, we can state in general that the official Roman Catholic theory of mission and that of the evangelical movement are in essence missiologies "from above" while those of the ecumenical movement and of liberation theology are contextual missiologies — missiologies "from below."[31]

Missio Dei *Theology*

There has been a considerable amount of missiological literature on *missio Dei*. The term gained general currency as a result of the Willingen mission conference in 1952, but it had been forged earlier by the "Barthian" Karl Hartenstein. He viewed mission not as a responsibility of the missionary, the mission society, or the sending church, but as a cause of the triune God. Accordingly, he replaced the "liberal" anthropocentric view of mission with a radically theocentric view, which was worked out in great detail a few years later by Georg F. Vicedom: Mission is God's own work.[32] Helmut H. Rosin, having examined the function of the term *missio Dei* in contemporary missiology, concluded:

> For this after all indicates an action, which does not point indiscriminately to all kinds of happenings in the world, but only to one incomprehensible event, namely that God, the creator of all things, sub-

31. Without speaking of missiologies "from above" and "from below" Glasser and McGavran in fact take the same direction. "Here the answers depend exclusively on whether the Bible is regarded as God's one authoritative revelation. . . . Conciliar and liberationist theologies of mission are on one side of the watershed. Evangelical and Roman Catholic theologies of mission are on the other side" (*op. cit.*, 9f.).

32. G. F. Vicedom, *Missio Dei. Einführung in eine Theologie der Mission* I (Munich, 1960; English tr. St. Louis, 1965).

merged himself in his own world as a stranger, as a displaced person, an outcast, in solidarity with other outcasts and strangers, who in this world pursues a very special, hidden road in order to liberate it.[33]

After Willingen the concept of *missio Dei* conquered the ecumenical world. Not only did it receive support in the Third World from people like the Sri Lankan Daniel T. Niles (1908-70),[34] but it was also welcomed with approval by several Roman Catholic authors, for example, Frans J. Verstraelen of Leiden.[35]

Although *missio Dei* is not a theological construct of liberal origin (Vicedom signed the Frankfurt Declaration), the evangelical Arthur F. Glasser nevertheless subjected this "neologism" to severe criticism. Among other things, he stated that in the WCC the secularized version of *missio Dei* had gained the upper hand and that consequently this concept had become (that is, had degenerated into) a green light for revolutionary thought and action. Glasser speaks in this connection of "structural revolt," "proclamation revolt," and "hermeneutical revolt" in the WCC.[36]

Glasser's criticism of the concept of *missio Dei*, whether or not it was warranted, makes it clear that *missio Dei* became no longer the exclusive possession of missiologies "from above" as opposed to those "from below." Contextual theologians have used it frequently. Shoki Coe of Taiwan, who introduced the concept of contextuality, defines contextuality as "that critical assessment of what makes the context really significant in the light of the *Missio Dei*."[37]

Salvation-Historical Missiologies

In neither Barth nor Bultmann and consequently in neither Kraemer nor Holsten is salvation history pivotal. But Oscar Cullmann made it the heart

33. H. H. Rosin, *'Missio Dei': An Examination of the Origin, Contents and Function of the Term in Protestant Missiological Discussion* (Leiden, 1972) 34.

34. D. T. Niles, *Upon the Earth: The Mission of God and the Missionary Enterprise of the Churches* (London, 1962, ²1963).

35. F. J. Verstraelen, "World and Mission: Towards a Common Missiology," *Mission Studies* 1 (1984) 34-47. Nonetheless, G. A. C. van Winsen, *Missio 1900-1970, fasen van Roomskatholieke bezinning op een kerngedachte* (Leiden, 1971) 58, concludes that "the concept as such is not used in Catholic literature."

36. Glasser and McGavran, *op. cit.*, 94-98: "The Feeble Offspring of MISSIO DEI."

37. Shoki Coe, "Contextualizing Theology," in G. H. Anderson and T. F. Stransky, ed., *Mission Trends No. 3: Third World Theologies* (New York and Grand Rapids, 1976) 21.

of theology: In his view salvation history was not concluded by the incarnation of the Word but continues until the second coming. Until then, mission is not merely a preparation for the end but also a sign of the end.[38] Cullmann influenced, among others, Johannes Blauw, Karl Hartenstein, Walter Freytag, David J. Bosch, Manfred Linz, and José Miguez-Bonino. (Under Cullmann's influence Hartenstein even detached himself from Barth's eschatology.)

As one of the most prominent missiologists oriented toward salvation history, Bosch wants to present neither a "narrow salvation-historical interpretation," nor a "desacralization" of salvation history, which in any case only leads to a "sacralization of world history" (P. Beyerhaus).[39] Accordingly, he seeks to steer a middle course between evangelical views of salvation history, which are "too narrow," and the views of ecumenical and liberation theologians, which are "too broad."

"Salvation history" is not pivotal in the thinking of all evangelicals. In the Lausanne Covenant (1974) and the Thailand Declaration (1984) the concept is not even mentioned. There is reference only to "the plan of salvation" and to "witnessing to Christ and his salvation." Still, the concept of salvation history is of cardinal importance for the evangelical movement. This is evident, for example, from the following passage in the Lausanne Covenant: "Those who reject Christ repudiate the joy of salvation and condemn themselves to eternal separation from God" (Art. 3).[40] Accordingly, "salvation history" and "eternal life" belong essentially together, just as "standing outside the history of salvation," that is, "standing only in the secular history of the world," belongs together with "eternal lostness."

Amstutz distinguishes between "implicit" and "explicit" salvation history.[41] In the latter, salvation history is "restricted" to the history of God with Israel and the works of God in and through the church (cf. the classic Catholic statement: There is no salvation outside the church). But "explicit" salvation history is extended to include the whole of world history. This point of view has been adopted not only by ecumenical missiologists like Hoekendijk, but also by Roman Catholic authors such as Karl Rahner, Heinz Robert Schlette, and Ludwig Rütti. The ideas of "anonymous Christianity," of non-Christian religions as "ways of salvation," and similar

38. O. Cullmann, *Christ and Time* (Philadelphia, 1950). Cf. C. E. Braaten, *The Flaming Center: A Theology of Christian Mission* (Philadelphia, 1977), who at some length calls for attention to Cullmann (pp. 34-36).

39. Bosch, *op. cit.*, 230f.

40. J. Stott, *The Lausanne Covenant: Exposition and Commentary* (Minneapolis, 1975) 14.

41. Amstutz, *op. cit.*, 25ff. Cf. Mitterhöfer, *op. cit.*, 67f.

notions advanced by these theologians are intended as corrections of an all too explicit view of salvation history present in classical Catholic teaching.[42]

In sum, we can say that today not only missiologies "from above" but also missiologies "from below" speak of "salvation history." Roman Catholic missiology and evangelical missiology oppose the equation of world history with salvation history, while ecumenical missiology and liberation theology resist the separation of salvation history and secular history.

Ecclesiocentric Missiologies

Roman Catholic missiology has always been ecclesiocentric, at least since the founding of the *Sacra Congregatio de Propaganda Fide* in 1622. The Second Vatican Council did not change this. It did, however, develop a dynamic concept of "churchness" and consequently made the relationship between church and mission more flexible. Roman Hoffman views the church of Rome today as a "worldwide missionary fellowship."[43]

Ecclesiocentric conceptions also underlie the idea of "the mutual assistance of churches" or "interchurch assistance," terms that were used frequently for a decade, not only in the Catholic Church after Vatican II but also in the WCC. In the 1970s, however, this idea fell out of favor for a number of reasons. The IIMO study of the concept demonstrated, for example, that it had become problematic because of the predominance of European Christianity in the world church and the historically rooted structures of (both Catholic and Protestant) mission.

In Protestantism the rise of dialectical theology in opposition to "liberal" culture-Protestantism produced a move in the direction of an ecclesiocentric missiology. But Hoekendijk, with his stress on the kingdom of God, belongs among those who started a countermovement. In the WCC we encounter ecclesiocentric tendencies, due partly to Orthodox influence,[45] side-by-side with anti-ecclesiocentric tendencies, as in the WCC document *Mission and Evangelism: An Ecumenical Affirmation*.[46]

Developments among evangelicals are noteworthy. Here especially

42. Cf. Evers, *op. cit.*, 107ff., 117ff., 208ff.

43. Cited in van Engelen, *op. cit.*, 300.

44. E. Jansen Schoonhoven, *Wederkerige assistentie van kerken in missionair perspectief.* IIMO-Leiden 1977, 183.

45. I. Bria, ed., *Go Forth in Peace: Orthodox Perspectives on Mission* (Geneva, 1986).

46. *Mission and Evangelism: An Ecumenical Affirmation. A Study Guide for Congregations* (Geneva, 1983).

Donald A. McGavran is responsible for the "church growth movement," which was initiated in 1961 with the founding of the Institute of Church Growth, which later became the School of World Mission of Fuller Theological Seminary in Pasadena, California. For McGavran and his colleagues not "winning souls for the Lamb" (Count von Zinzendorf) but "multiplying churches" is primary, because in their view "the church is a central component in God's redemptive plan."[47] The church growth movement must be regarded as the most important contemporary missiological current of evangelical origin. It is to be categorized without qualification as "ecclesiocentric."

Missiologies "from above" are as a rule more "ecclesiocentric" than missiologies "from below." The latter are generally more in favor of the scheme "God-world-church" than the scheme "God-church-world,"[48] in part because they are fearful of institutionalism and the kind of hierarchical theologizing exemplified by Pope John Paul II, who describes himself as "a frontline missionary," "the primary evangelist," and "the traveling catechist."[49] Many missiologies "from below" prefer the concept of the kingdom of God over that of the church. One may not conclude from this, however, that the notion of the kingdom of God is unimportant to missiologies "from above." The opposite is true. In his account of the biblical theology of mission Glasser regards the notion of the kingdom of God as "the unifying theme."[50] Furthermore, John Paul II still finds mission activities in that sense necessary and irreplaceable: "Without them the realization of God's plan and the extension of the kingdom to the ends of the earth would not even be conceivable."[51] We can say in conclusion that missiologies "from above" as a rule think about the kingdom of God from within the church, while missiologies "from below" as a rule think of the church from within the kingdom.

47. Glasser and McGavran, *op. cit.*, 104.
48. Cf. Mitterhöfer, *op. cit.*, 78 and the literature cited there.
49. J. M. van Engelen, *De zending van de kerk in onze tijd. Een onderzoek naar de missievisie van paus Johannes Paulus II* ('s Hertogenbosch, 1985) 36.
50. Glasser and McGavran, *op. cit.*, 31. Cf. van Engelen, "Missiologie op een keerpunt," *Tijdschrift voor Theologie* 15 (1975) 300ff., where the emerging advocacy of mission as "interchurch assistance" is expressly repudiated as an ecclesiocentric version of mission. Van Engelen opts for a "missiology of the kingdom of God."
51. Van Engelen, *De zending van de kerk*, 32.

Missiologies in the Context of Secularization: Presence, Humanization, and Other Concepts

In 1964 the World Student Christian Federation held an important conference at which the word "presence" was used as the key concept for correctly understanding the missionary mandate in the university world.[52] This conference was not the first to use the notion of "presence." Before that it was used by Jacques Ellul, author of *The Presence of the Kingdom* (Philadelphia, 1981), and by Canon Max A. C. Warren, publisher of the Christian Presence series beginning in 1959.[53] In the same period it gained currency as a result of the realization of the idea of presence in the Benedictine settlement Toumliline in Morocco,[54] in the Christian kibbutz Nesh Ammim in Israel, and in other such communities.[55]

"Mission by presence" was later treated systematically, for example, by Calvin E. Shenk in his brochure *A Relevant Theology of Presence*, the result of a panel discussion in 1982.[56] He noted, to be sure, that a "theology of presence" is involved in answering the question how God is present in non-Christian religions, but then indicates that after facing that question he and the others involved in the discussion worked out the idea of presence for the definition of the church's place in the First, Second, and Third Worlds, with particular attention to the context of secularization.

Criticism of the notion of presence was expressed before and after the appearance of the Frankfurt Declaration by the evangelicals Glasser and McGavran, who viewed "presence" only as a means, not as an end.[57] The attitude of a number of Roman Catholic authors is different: Rather than enter upon a critical discussion of a "theology of presence," they pass it by in silence.[58]

Roughly in the same period or somewhat later other key concepts

---

52. See J. A. C. Rullmann, " 'Présence chrétienne' als legitieme zendingsmethode," *De Heerbaan* 24 (1971) 297; H.-W. Gensichen, *Glaube für die Welt. Theologische Aspekte der Mission* (Gütersloh, 1971) 208-10: "Präsenz der Gemeinde."

53. Rullmann, *op. cit.*, 296, 306. Warren, like McGavran and H. J. Margull, spoke about "presence" at the first European consultation of missiologists at Selly Oak, Birmingham, England (1968). On that consultation see A. Camps, "Presence en proclamation," *De Heerbaan* 21 (1968) 223-32; Gensichen, *op. cit.*, 209.

54. Rullmann, *op. cit.*, 295. This was preceded by the "presence" work of Charles de Foucauld, who died in 1916.

55. *Ibid.*, 295. Cf. S. Schoon, *Christelijke presentie in de joodse staat* (Kampen, 1982), especially ch. 5.

56. Elkhart, 1982.

57. Glasser and McGavran, *op. cit.*, 96: "the 'presence' fever burnt itself out quickly with the rapid decline of the WSCF."

58. "Presence" does not appear in Evers's index *(op. cit.).*

for understanding the task of the church and theology in the context of secularization were proposed: "humanization," "pro-existence," "conscientization," and the like, with "humanization" perhaps the most important. The fourth assembly of the WCC at Uppsala in 1968 especially gave the concept of humanization currency. Still it gained universal recognition no more than "presence" did. In one of his books on the missionary encounter of the gospel with modern Western culture, Lesslie Newbigin ascribed to neither "presence" nor "humanization" a central place, nor did he launch a new key concept (ignoring for the moment "dialogue").[59]

So we must conclude that though there exists a great volume of missiological literature on the issues associated with secularization — from Godin and Daniel to Newbigin — it is not possible to categorize it all under one heading. Perhaps, then, there is in missiology still no consensus on an adequate reaction to the situation of "desacralization" and "deconfessionalization" that has come into being in the West and elsewhere. "Presence," "humanization," "pro-existence," and the like all represent attempts to do theology with relevance in the context of secularization. The evangelical movement, though it has criticized the functioning of these key concepts, has neglected to offer an alternative of its own.

Missiologies in the Context of Non-Christian Religions: Dialogue

The word "dialogue" has more recently come into vogue for the relationship of Christianity to non-Christian religions and subsequently also to nonreligious worldviews and ideologies. It is now possible to speak of "dialogue theology." This theology has become one of the most significant missiological currents, one that has found a firm place of acceptance not only in the WCC (which established, along with a Division for World Mission and Evangelism, a Division for Dialogue), but also in the Roman Catholic Church.[60]

In recent decades much has been written on "dialogue" by missiologists and non-missiologists alike.[61] In 1971 Stanley J. Samartha noted that it was no longer a matter of talk about dialogue among Christians but of involvement by Christians in dialogue with others.[62] In recent years

59. L. Newbigin, *Foolishness to the Greeks: The Gospel and Western Culture* (Grand Rapids, 1986).

60. Cf. Camps, *Partners in Dialogue.*

61. See A. W. Musschenga, ed., *De dialoog kritisch bezien. Studies over de plaats van de waarheidsvraag in de dialoog met gelovigen uit andere kulturen* (Baarn, 1983).

62. J. A. B. Jongneel, ed., *Ganges en Galilea. Een keuze uit het werk van Stanley J. Samartha* (Kampen, 1986) 89.

the WCC and the Roman Catholic Secretariat for non-Christians have initiated a number of contacts with Jews, Muslims, Hindus, and others and have convened bilateral and multilateral conferences. At these conferences there has been either implicit or explicit references to the meaning of "dialogue" and its relation to "witness," "mission," and other terms.

In the evangelical movement protests have been registered against the theology of "dialogue" just as against the theology of "presence." There is no objection to these words as such. The problem is, rather, that they often serve as replacements for key words of Scripture. In the Frankfurt Declaration, for instance, it is stated: "We refute the idea that 'Christian presence' among the adherents of the world religions and a give-and-take dialogue with them are substitutes for a proclamation of the Gospel which aims at conversion. Such dialogues simply establish good points of contact for missionary communication."[63]

Vatican II, with its broad and integral conception of mission, did not, like the Frankfurt Declaration, express itself negatively on the subject of "dialogue." In section 11 of *Ad Gentes*, under the heading "Christian Witness," it is said that Christians should converse with non-Christians "that through sincere and patient dialogue these men might learn of the riches which a generous God has distributed among the nations. They must at the same time endeavor to illuminate these riches with the light of the Gospel, set them free, and bring them once more under the dominion of God the Saviour."

In sum: missiologies "from above" and the theology of dialogue are not always and everywhere mutually exclusive.

Missiologies in the Context of Oppression and Violence: From Development to Liberation

More radical than the ideas of "presence" and "dialogue" is that of "liberation," which replaced the Western concept of "development." "Presence" barely aims at transformation at all; "dialogue" aims at the transformation of relations among peoples; "liberation" seeks nothing less than a transformation of the social order, beginning with the church.

Gustavo Gutiérrez is the best-known exponent of the theology of liberation. His book *A Theology of Liberation* harks back to a lecture he gave at a national conference of the ONIS movement of priests meeting at Chimbote, Peru, in 1968. In this lecture he replaced the word "development," which stems from the First World, with "liberation," saying that

63. See Won Yong Li, "Evangelization and Humanization," 166.

the latter expresses what the former does not, namely, the inescapable break with the past.[64] He distinguishes three levels of meaning for the word. Liberation is:

- an expression of the desires of oppressed peoples, classes, and social sectors
- a historical process in which humanity deliberately takes its destiny into its own hands, and
- a biblical concept: Christ liberates people and makes them truly free.

By contrast with the currents that we have been describing, this movement (cf. the theology of the poor) originated in the Third World. Its influence, not only in Latin America but also in Africa (black theology) and Asia (*minjung* theology), has not remained within the Catholic Church but has achieved ecumenical character. In his monograph on the theology of liberation Theo Witvliet has made this sufficiently plain.[65]

Not only Rome (Cardinal Ratzinger vs. Leonardo Boff and others) has criticized the theology of liberation but also various evangelical missiologists. Glasser and McGavran distance themselves from what they call "the liberationist theology of mission," because it breaks with traditional Christianity and transforms the *missio Dei* into politics.[66] However, one must definitely not infer from this that in official Roman Catholic documents and those of the evangelical movement the word "liberation" is taboo. The opposite is true. In *Ad Gentes,* section 8, Christ is called "liberator," and in the fourth article of the Lausanne Covenant there is mention of "the liberating gift of the Holy Spirit."

Accordingly, also in the case of this last current, we have to be careful with our conclusions. Liberation theology is contextual theology, missiology "from below." The interaction between missiologies "from above" and those "from below" is such, however, that even in official Roman Catholic missiology and in evangelical theology there is room for elements of liberation theology.

---

64. Gustavo Gutiérrez, *A Theology of Liberation* (second ed., Maryknoll, 1988).
65. T. Witvliet, *A Place in the Sun: Liberation Theology in the Third World* (Maryknoll, 1985).
66. Glasser and McGavran, *op. cit.,* 165.

A Summary and Perspective

In brief, we can say the following about contemporary missiological currents:

- The church growth movement, the theology of dialogue, and liberation theology are the main missiological currents of recent years.
- Liberation theology has made it clear that the "third church" (Walter Bühlmann) manifestly and penetratingly helps shape the face of contemporary missiology.

Dialectical theology of mission and the theology of mission that is oriented to salvation history, though they originated in an earlier period, remain as important parallel currents in contemporary missiology. Mission theology oriented to salvation history is based either on a special history of salvation (Israel and the church) alongside secular history (missiology "from above") or on an all-embracing history of salvation (missiology "from below").[67] Unfortunately, there is no missiological current that — in the manner of the theology of dialogue and the theology of liberation — clearly shows the way to church and theology in defining their posture toward secularization. Despite attempts made in this direction by the theology of presence, the theology of humanization, and the like, individual schemes continue to dominate the scene.

Two comments remain to be made: First, combinations of the missiologies "from above" and "from below" are conceivable and do in fact exist: A dialectical theology of dialogue that takes its starting point from the fact that God in Christ has begun his dialogue with the world is equally possible and as much a reality as an evangelical theology of liberation. Especially in the Third World we encounter all sorts of combinations since there people are relatively adverse to making distinctions and classifications. (Exceptions to this rule exist: Bong Rin Ro of Korea sharply distinguishes a biblically oriented theology from any syncretistic theology, accommodationist theology, or situation-oriented theology.[68])

Second, many are looking for a way to transcend the distinctions among all these positions in missiology, especially the opposition between missiology "from above" and missiology "from below." Contributions to

---

67. Apart from the writings of Amstutz and Mitterhöfer that have been mentioned, see also T. Kramm, *Analyse und Bewährung theologischer Modelle zur Begründung der Mission* (Aachen, 1979), on which van Engelen, *De Zending van de kerk*, 38ff., builds.

68. "Contextualisation: Asian Theology," in D. J. Elwood, ed., *What Asian Christians Are Thinking: A Theological Source Book* (Quezon City, 1976) 52.

that end are seen in publications such as *Common Witness: A Study Document of the Joint Working Group of the Roman Catholic Church and the World Council of Churches* (Vatican City and Geneva, 1980), the publications of the Interuniversitair Instituut voor Missiologie en Oecumenica at Leiden and Utrecht, publications of consultative bodies such as the Gunster-steinberaad at Breukelen mediating so-called "church missions" (ecumenical) and "faith missions" (evangelical),[69] and the like. If there is ever to be something like a common missiology,[70] it is almost certain that it will be produced by such joint deliberative and cooperative bodies.

69. See J. J. van Capelleveen, I. H. Enklaar, and others, *Overleg onderweg. Kerkelijke zending en geloofszending* (Kampen, 1979).

70. Cf. Verstraelen, *op. cit.*, 34-47; J. A. B. Jongeneel, *The Philosophy, Science, and Theology of Mission in the Nineteenth and Twentieth Centuries: A Missiological Encyclopedia* (Frankfurt, 1995).

CHAPTER 28

The Missionary Movement and Missionary Organizations

M. R. SPINDLER

One may well ask whether a separate chapter needs to be devoted to the organization of the missionary movement. On the one hand, one is everywhere told that the whole church, beginning with the local congregation, is missionary in its entirety. This implies that *all* ecclesiastical structures must have a missionary dimension and that the link binding specialized organizations for certain forms of mission to the church must always be clearly explained. If we followed this out, then it would be the purpose of this chapter to examine the entire life of the church and to measure the missionary content of its various parts. But that would be going beyond our intention here.

Stress is also laid on the mobility of Christianity in its missionary impact and influence. To qualify as "missionary" requires mobility in the tension between the world (the *oikoumene*) and the kingdom of God. Organizations tend by nature toward immobility. They develop an inertia that increasingly slows down and sometimes even paralyzes the missionary movement that they hope to represent. In Dutch discussions a distinction has been made between mission as movement and *a* mission, that is, a particular organization.[1] Some have expressed the suspicion that the latter serves as an alibi for the lack of genuine missionary movement among Dutch Protestants.

Among Dutch Catholics as well there is discernible tension between missionary organizations, which embody the mobility of a high missionary ideal, and church leadership, which cannot permit mission to occur without a lawful mandate from the successors of the apostles and which seek as much as possible to streamline all missionary activities.

---

1. See *Visie en werkelijkheid. Nota van de Raad voor de Zending aangeboden aan de Generale Synode van de Nederlandse Hervormde Kerk* (Oegstgeest, 1983) 123-37 (appendix: "De zending en 'De Zending' ").

In this chapter we will look at all these tensions and sketch a picture of the organizations that do the work of "mission," in the broad sense of that word. The missionary movement takes concrete shape in a spectrum of institutions. Institutionalization is unavoidable and legitimate. We will not deal with the problem of the "eschatology" of institutions, namely how an organization moves toward its end and is finally ended. Since the days of Henry Venn essays have been devoted to the "euthanasia of mission," that is, of mission as institution.[2] But no satisfactory model for killing off the organization has been constructed. In all likelihood mission will always, even to the end of the world, remain somewhat organizational.

Globally speaking, missionary organizations can be divided into three large groups: Roman Catholic missions and missionary organizations, Protestant organizations that acknowledge the moral authority of the World Council of Churches (WCC), and evangelical organizations, which hold to more conservative viewpoints. There is no overarching ecumenical mission organization, though there have been attempts at rapprochement among representatives of these three orientations. The Catholic Church, or, to be precise, the Secretariat for the Promotion of Christian Unity, has since 1985 had a permanent observer at the Commission for World Mission and Evangelism at the WCC headquarters in Geneva. From 1977 to 1984 a series of discussions took place between Catholic and evangelical mission representatives, which resulted in 1986 in an important document seeking mutual clarification of missionary ideas and practice.[3]

Consultation and division of tasks do, of course, take place in specific cases, especially where a missionary initiative takes shape in the context of government planning or requires communication or transportation facilities. At times specialized missionary organizations provide facilities for an entire local community. In parts of Zaire missions have offered the most reliable radio connections with the capital and with other countries. In Irian Jaya mail service and transportation to the interior have been provided in the small planes of the Missionary Aviation Fellowship, an international evangelical mission organization. In Madagascar the geographic department of the government has had its maps printed by a Lutheran mission. Numerous examples exist of services rendered by missionary organizations of various orientations.

2. M. R. Spindler, "La pensée d'Henry Venn," in *Naître et grandir en Église. Le rôle des autochtones dans la première inculturation du christianisme* (Lyons, 1987) 103-14.
3. *The Evangelical-Roman Catholic Dialogue on Mission 1977-1984*, ed. B. Meeking and J. Stott (Grand Rapids, 1986).

The Roman Catholic Mission

The Second Vatican Council, in line with the papal bull *Cum inter multiplices* (1622), entrusted general oversight of mission to a single authority, the pope, who of course delegates his powers to a large number of agencies. "There should be only one competent congregation for all missions and missionary activity, namely that of the 'Propagation of the Faith,' which would direct and coordinate missionary work and missionary cooperation throughout the world. The rights of the Eastern Churches must, however, be safeguarded." This congregation that governs mission should be "subject to the authority of the Pope [and should] exercise supreme control over all missionary work" (*Ad Gentes*, section 29). The name of this department of the curia, which since 1622 had been *Congregatio de propaganda fide*, was changed in 1967 to the Congregation for the Evangelization of the Peoples.

In reality Catholic mission work proceeds organizationally along two tracks. Primarily it is done by the religious orders and congregations, especially those that have a specific purpose or "charisma." There are renowned missionary organizations such as the Franciscans, the Jesuits, the missionaries of the Society of the Divine Word, the White Fathers, the Benedictines of St. Ottilian, the members of the Congregation of the Immaculate Heart of Mary, the missionaries of the Sacred Heart of Jesus, and others. Missionary orders and congregations include more female than male members. Their number of both men and women runs in the hundreds and is growing, thanks to the founding of independent new orders and congregations in countries that were earlier called mission fields and now have national church structures. In the course of the history of the Church the religious have supported and performed the essential work of mission. New and risky missionary initiatives are still being successfully developed throughout the world by the religious and their orders and congregations. Deserving of mention besides the increasing internationalization of existing orders and congregations is the growing number of new societies in the churches of the Third World: The "Third Church" is becoming missionary.[4]

The second track along which Catholic missionary work proceeds is the missionary endeavor and involvement of the secular clergy, beginning with the local hierarchy as soon as it is established in each new place. The bishop in his diocese has proper authority over missionary activities: "All missionaries, even exempt religious,[5] are subject to this authority in

---

4. Cf. O. Degrijse, *Going Forth: Missionary Consciousness in Third World Catholic Churches* (Maryknoll, 1984).

5. "Exempt" refers to those who are not under the jurisdiction of the local bishop. See "Exemption, History of," in *New Catholic Encyclopedia* V, 716f.; O. Stoffel,

all the various activities which have to do with the exercise of the sacred apostolate" (*Ad Gentes*, section 30). In practice this stipulation means that every religious order and congregation enters into a contract with the local bishop to secure certain institutional liberties. The practice varies considerably and depends on who is involved: Sometimes the bishop gives the missions carte blanche, sometimes he operates very patronizingly, and sometimes he creates new missionary possibilities on his own initiative.

At first sight the organization of Roman Catholic missions appears quite tight, but in reality it is so complicated that there is a good measure of room for new initiatives. A missionary reformer or prophetess can come into his or her own with the support of diverse, sometimes even opposing, forces. Father Vincent Lebbe in China was able to do his work thanks to the support of the pope and his local representative and against the wishes of the local missionary leadership. Father Jean-Marc Ela in Cameroon was able to do his theological work and to draw inspiration from the grassroots level thanks to the support of international networks, despite the polite indifference of the local bishop. Mother Theresa in Calcutta fell completely outside the established patterns of the missionary organization of her order and so founded a new religious congregation.

In broad terms one can distinguish the following organizational systems. They actually function along parallel lines, though in principle this takes place under the coordinating guidance of the curia.

- There is, of course, the system of bishops appointed by and in communion with the pope. But all the bishops are responsible for the entire apostolate in their respective dioceses.
- There are also the pope's direct representatives, specifically the nuncios, and diplomats with other titles, who are stationed in most countries and who have considerable authority to act both in the sphere of politics and in that of the church.
- Then there are the male and female religious orders, congregations, and institutions, whose central leadership or general superiors are usually in Rome.
- And there is the system of papal mission works, which have the responsibility of raising and distributing funds on behalf of the numerous missions and "younger" churches. This centralization of funding began in 1822 in Lyons and was brought to Rome in 1922. Most Western countries have one or two networks of this system. Naturally, the financial side of this work is supplemented by infor-

---

"Der ekklesiale Standort der Missionsgesellschaften im CIC von 1983," *NZM* 43 (1987) 81-97, especially 89.

mation seminars and efforts to raise consciousness and encourage study.

Beside these Church systems there are numerous organizations and coordinating agencies in which Roman Catholics cooperate with other social or religious partners for an implicit or explicit missionary purpose in the broad sense of the word. When it concerns the welfare of the world, specifically that of the Two-Thirds World, an objective that has been unqualifiedly recognized as a missionary goal, mention must be made of organizations occupied with development projects and programs. The episcopal "Fast" program, the Catholic organization for joint financing of development programs (or CEBEMO), the interchurch program for Latin America or Solidaridad, are all sensitive to the missionary implications of their work and consequently also have permanent contacts with the organizations mentioned earlier.

Deserving of mention, finally, are various special international Catholic organizations: trade unions, political movements such as the Christian democratic association, and associations of laypersons, doctors, academics, journalists, and others. All of them make a worthwhile contribution to the content and work of the "mission" of the Catholic Church.

Protestant Organizations with an Ecumenical Orientation

Protestant Christianity has no global center of missionary administration. The administration of mission work is divided along national and confessional lines. The most commonly used organizational model is the "missionary society," a structure which assumed its classic form at the end of the eighteenth century.[6] The multiplicity and diversity of missionary societies generally present a picture of fragmentation and competition that impresses the outsider as typically Protestant. National governments sometimes experience difficulty with the elusiveness of Protestant missionary activities. Successful attempts at making mission more ecumenical have been described in ch. 17 above.

In the twentieth century Protestant mission acquired a common organ in the International Missionary Council (IMC, 1921). It was a struc-

---

6. On the origin and missiological significance of missionary societies, see H.-W. Gensichen, *Glaube für die Welt. Theologische Aspekte der Mission* (Gütersloh, 1971) 173-86; J. R. Reid, "The Voluntary Missionary Association," *International Review of Mission* 70 (1981) 276-79; J. Boneschansker, *Het Nederlandsch Zendeling Genootschap in zijn eerste periode. Een studie over opwekking in de Bataafse en Franse tijd* (Leeuwarden, 1987).

ture for consultation and joint study rather than an operational body. Nevertheless, during World War II the IMC functioned as the official representative of all Protestant missionary corporations, thanks to a commission for international affairs formed in 1938 under the joint auspices of the IMC and the WCC, which was in the process of being founded. In 1961 the IMC became part of the WCC, which had been officially organized in 1948. The activities of the IMC were continued by the Commission on World Mission and Evangelism (CWME) of the WCC.

A new dimension from that point was the participation of the Eastern Orthodox churches in this worldwide missionary consultation. The new commission is, therefore, not strictly "Protestant," though the missionary tradition of the IMC still plays a strong role. Orthodox participation has contributed to the CWME the missionary radiance of their liturgy, and the Orthodox understanding of mission has assimilated new elements from this cooperation.

The CWME has played a decisive role in policy decisions of the participating churches and of missionary organizations, specifically in regard to coordination of their work with that of other churches and agencies. It must be kept in mind that the CWME membership includes churches and other bodies that do not belong to the WCC.

When the WCC was restructured in 1991, CWME was replaced by new commissions. The evangelistic and missionary concern was transferred from Program Unit I (Faith and Witness) to Program Unit II, the name of which was changed from *Mission, Education, and Witness* (1991) to *Life, Education, and Mission* in 1992 and then to *Life, Education, and Witness* in 1994. Many missionary programs in the field fall under one of the other three program units of the WCC: Gospel and Culture belongs to Unit I, International Affairs is part of Unit III, and Sharing and Service is the name of Unit IV. The world mission of the church clearly entails more than just the program of a single commission or WCC unit. And it should be noted that the WCC and its commissions do not make binding decisions for member churches. Only in certain programs does the WCC act on behalf of the member churches.

The WCC operates not only in the framework of the established churches but also in contact with parachurch and secular organizations and action groups. Here, too, an attempt is made to do justice to the broad missionary dimension of being a Christian. The WCC has committed itself to carry on the work of the IMC (WCC Constitution, art. III) and is now preparing for a new Conference on World Mission and Evangelism to be held in Salvador Bahia, Brazil, in November 1996, the eleventh in the series of world missionary conferences that began at Edinburgh in 1910.

The ecclesiastical networks of consultation mentioned above do not, of course, cover the entire missionary dimension of the Protestant churches. As mentioned above in relation to Roman Catholic mission work, there are various organizations and overarching bodies that can rightly be considered missionary in nature without being so designated. Protestant churches have a counterpart to CEBEMO: the Interchurch Coordinating Commission for development projects (ICCO). They also have a Foundation for Ecumenical Help. In addition there are many other committees and ad hoc groups, as well as international Protestant and confessional associations that play an important role in the "mission" of the churches of the Reformation.[7]

Especially deserving of mention is the cooperation between churches of North and South, that is, between old and new churches, on administrative levels through new corporations. The Communauté Evangélique d'Action Apostolique (CEVAA) replaced the Paris Evangelical Missionary Society in 1971 and now embraces forty-seven churches as it carries on a common missionary engagement on a basis of equality for a mission "from and to everywhere."[8] The Council for World Mission (CWM) replaced the London Missionary Society in 1977 and now unites thirty churches from the South Pacific to the North Sea, from the English Channel to the Indian Ocean.[9] In these new associations all continents are viewed as "mission regions" and treated as such, and all churches participate in accordance with their means in missionary programs at home and abroad.

Evangelical Organizations

Evangelicals and ecumenicals worked together within the framework of the IMC until a "separation of minds" occurred with the integration of the IMC with the WCC in 1961. A large number of mission bodies objected to this "churchifying" of mission and to the lack of doctrinal commitment that they believed existed in the Council. At the time new umbrella or-

7. Cf. G. de Gans, "Kerkelijke organisaties en het wereldvoedselvraagstuk. Inventarisatie en verbindingslijnen," *Wereld en Zending* 17 (1988) 18-28.

8. S. Ada, "CEVAA: From a Mission Society to a Community of Churches in Mission," *International Review of Mission* 76 (1987) 505-20. Since December 1989 CEVAA has published a quarterly news bulletin in English and French, *Info CEVAA News.*

9. See B. Thorogood, "Towards Mutuality in Mission: The Council for World Mission," *International Review of Mission* 66 (1977) 163-68; M. Evans, "Council for World Mission's Partnership in Mission Model," *International Review of Mission* 76 (1987) 458-74 (other articles on this model of mission work can be found in the same issue of *International Review of Mission*). Since 1977 CWM has published a bimonthly, *News Share.*

ganizations were formed and older ones were strengthened, such as the Evangelical Foreign Missions Association (EFMA) and the Interdenominational Foreign Mission Association (IFMA).

It is often characteristic of evangelical bodies that mission personnel themselves must secure financial support from their own backers: This is what is meant by "faith missions." The missionary is not a functionary of an organization but depends on the "faith" and enthusiasm of the sending church. To counter the financial difficulties that sometimes result from this system, evangelical mission bodies have created special accountability networks, such as the Evangelical Council for Financial Accountability (ECFA).

Not only large organizations that send out or support thousands of missionaries but also very small groups that independently send out one or two people or support them with prayer and material gifts to carry out projects at home and abroad operate under the evangelical wing. It appears that these nonaffiliated missionaries and mission societies outnumber all other Protestant and larger evangelical organizations. 52% of American mission personnel belongs to independent missions. It seems that this pattern of independent mission also predominates in the Third World. The boundary between "organization" and "movement" cannot be clearly marked here. Normal lay activity and Christian creativity are given every opportunity. Besides evangelism and church planting, "development cooperation" and "world diaconate" are undertaken by evangelical mission organizations, for example, on the international level, World Vision, with its development projects and programs, and The Evangelical Alliance Relief Fund (the TEAR Fund).

Mission historian Ralph Winter has attempted to interpret the enormous growth in the number of missionary bodies since 1950. His model is based on a survey of the historical development of modern organized mission since the eighteenth century. A first wave of creativity began around 1792; at that time missionary bodies as a rule operated in the coastal regions of the so-called non-Christian continents. A second wave of creativity began around 1865; at that time the aim of mission was to evangelize the interior of non-Christian lands. The third wave of creativity took off around 1934 when Cameron Townsend founded the International Association of Wycliffe Bible Translators. Target groups now were forgotten or hidden population groups, but the intent has been especially to accomplish specialized tasks more efficiently. Contemporary administrative principles of efficiency, division of labor, and concentration are also applied to the missionary movement! It is remarkable that specialization of missionary activities is found, broadly speaking, in all branches of the faith. The evangelical world has no monopoly in this regard. Ecumenicals also create specific organizations or action groups for, say, coordinating the struggle for peace and education for peace or exposing the use of torture. Winter's interpretive key is certainly not the last word. But his model does have the merit of placing the tension among organizations or types of organizations in a broader framework and thus helping to reduce it.

In numerous places in the world we see examples of a new direction in the missionary movement: the abandonment of an exclusively national basis, which was characteristic of the majority of Protestant mission organizations until 1945. Now we are seeing the emergence of a growing number of transnational mission societies, with all their advantages and disadvantages.[10]

It has not been our intent here to equate the Christian missionary movement with how it is organized. In large part "mission" is an unorganized and spontaneous movement of Christians and Christian groups and churches. Still, one must not and cannot overlook the enormous capacity for organization displayed by "mission" in its three major manifestations. The danger exists that too much weight will be attached to the organization. Accordingly, every organization should fundamentally remain a *"precarious* organization."[11]

---

10. A sharp critique of this development can be found in V. Samuel and C. Sugden, "Mission Agencies as Multinationals," *International Bulletin of Missionary Research* 7 (1983) 152-55.

11. An allusion to M. A. Thung, *The Precarious Organisation: Sociological Explorations of the Church's Mission and Structure* (The Hague, 1976).

The Ecumenical
Development of Missiology:
Texts and Contexts of Global Christianity
in the Twenty-First Century

AN AFTERWORD BY THE EDITORS

Global Christianity has detached itself from the formerly predominant framework of Western missionary expansion. That is the twentieth century's most important lesson for the mission movement and for missiology. The globalization and contextualization involved in this detachment will undoubtedly be extended and deepened in the twenty-first century, and this trend will have far-reaching consequences for the understanding of the faith and of the formation of community. In this connection some speak of a new Reformation. Because cultural and religious interaction is no longer controlled from a single center, a great variety of insights and experiences has surfaced, and they may, in principle, enrich all contexts. But this enrichment is not automatic. It calls for initiatives in communication, translation, encounter, dialogue, and shared study.

In this development, one in which the meaning of *oikumene* will at last come into its own, missiology will have to play a role for which it has not been completely prepared by its past. It will have to act as the initiator and mediator in dealing with the new challenge that theology will face on every side. New discussions will be launched on soteriology, christology, and ecclesiology, on creation and eschaton, and on ethical issues. Missiology cannot include all these discussions in its own agenda, but it can do much preparatory and supportive work — precisely because in the twentieth century it has learned to study a mobile and pluriform Christianity from the vantage point of the unity of its own starting point and expectations. Therefore, study of that plurality is one of the tasks on which it will have to concentrate in the near future.

Even more deepening of the concept of *oikoumenē* is possible and will be relevant for the future development of missiology. The globalization of Christianity means that the problems of global society enter into the understanding of the faith and of the formation of community, that wherever

Christian faith is there arises a solidarity with people and communities that particularly bear the burden of those social problems. The tensions between small communities seeking to maintain and defend their homogeneous cultures and traditions and the leveling tendencies of global society will increase in the twenty-first century and will give rise to a variety of problems among Christians as well. Furthermore, the struggle for justice and peace, which is carried on with such intensity in some places, and the sufferings which are the fruit of injustice and conflict will challenge believers to levels of solidarity far exceeding the sharing of "insights and experiences" mentioned earlier. Here contextuality and globality are particularly joined.

If missiology wants to hold to the formula that its task is to study the movement of Christianity from the point of view of unity, then it will have to do its work of renewal at precisely these points. Concepts like "contextuality" and "contextualization" are in a sense twentieth-century inventions, and they have prompted a range of complex discussions. In the twenty-first century the relation between particularism and universalism will have to receive greater theological depth, and theological reflection on the problems of global society will have to be further developed. Issues of social ethics will demand more attention from missiologists than they have in the past. And it is true here also that in these areas missiology will have to do groundwork for theology as a whole and be supportive of theology as a whole.

In the globalization or "ecumenizing" mentioned above, Christianity in the twenty-first century will be confronted more than ever with questions about the foundation and future of human life. In this diverse world, which is intended to be one, what are the common roots of our humanity? The problems of global society, the development of interreligious dialogue, and the increasing circulation of religious and ideological convictions are challenging Christianity to devote its attention to fundamental anthropological questions. In this connection, problems of servitude and liberation will undoubtedly be central. When are cultural, social, political-economic, and religious systems enslaving and oppressive? When, on the other hand, do they give people the space in which to develop forms of community that point to the unity of humankind?

To the degree that in posing this question we are dealing with religious systems, the theology of religions will be increasingly determined by it. There is still a great deal of confusion and uncertainty about the basis and possibility of interreligious dialogue: This is one of the most important unexplored fields awaiting the work of the twenty-first century. Therefore, the theology of religions will rank high on the future agenda of missiology.

But within the discipline of the theology of religions itself a point of special consideration will have to be that in the final analysis the aim of mission and dialogue is not to establish the validity of theological concepts associated with the interests of a specific group, but to develop perceptions of truth that together can establish a foundation for human life and strengthen that foundation. The question of the enslaving and liberating aspects of religion will prove to be unavoidable in this context.

The breakup of ecclesiastical forms and activities belonging to an age that is past will continue and the demand for contemporary forms of witness and presence will grow stronger. Churches will not only have to be a haven for people of very diverse cultural and social origins but will also need to project their distinctive features adequately in society. Therefore, churches that differ in, for example, theological education, education in the faith, and the making of political choices will have to work together. Everywhere in the world the distance between the church and the civil government is increasing, and the need for a common strategic concept of politically relevant witness grows accordingly.

For missiology that means a new accent on ecclesiological questions, on, that is, questions concerning the missionary character of denominations and churches. The relationship between church and state will have to be restudied because the concepts of the past are no longer adequate. Churches have to deal not only with national governments but also with the spread of the power of multinational corporations, with their political and economic systems, which practically embrace and dominate the whole world. The challenges produced by all this for the church's confession and for new ways of being the church will have to be attended to more in the future than it is now.

If in the midst of all these concerns missiology is not to saw off the branch on which it is sitting, then eschatology will have to remain central. It is expectation of God's kingdom that has marked the mission movement throughout its history, and in its best moments a spirituality of expectation has overshadowed and stamped any other interests that were present within it. From the beginning of the mission movement the expectation of God's kingdom has carried the church through time and from place to place. In an era of globalization and "ecumenizing," with the radical changes these processes entail for every part of the church, all this remains true. This expectation of the kingdom is the golden thread that binds together all the different forms of gospel proclamation that keep Christianity mobile. And in the proclamation of the gospel the mission movement sees its most important reason for being.

This means that missiology must give attention to the ways in which the spirituality of expectation is alive in all the different parts of Christianity, to, that is, the different eschatological paradigms employed among Christians. These paradigms are at the root of the polarization that has afflicted Christianity in the second half of the twentieth century. A thorough joint study precisely of the content and manner of these forms of expectation may enable missiology to test critically the variety of intermediate goals pursued by the mission movement and to work in such a way as to promote the unity of the mission movement.

Selected Bibliography

Most of the works listed here are of general significance. For works of specific interest, see the footnotes in the chapters above.

Bibliographies

Abstracts: European Muslims and Christian-Muslim Relations. Birmingham, 1979-85.

Bibliografia Missionaria. Roma, annually since 1933.

Bibliographical Introduction to Church History. Leuven, 1982.

"Bibliography on World Mission and Evangelism," quarterly in *International Review of Mission(s)* since 1912.

Bibliotheca Missionum. Freiburg, 1913-74 (I-XXX).

"Fifteen Outstanding Books for Mission Studies," annually in the January issue of *International Bulletin of Missionary Research.*

A History of the Church in Southern Africa I: *Select Bibliography of Published Material to 1980.* Pretoria, 1986.

"Literaturschau zur Fragen der Weltmission," annually in *Beiheft der Zeitschrift für Mission* since 1968.

Missionalia (Pretoria), triennially since 1973; with short articles and reviews.

Missions and Evangelism: A Bibliography Selected from the ATLA Religion Database, ed. P. D. Pedersen. Chicago, 1985.

Répertoire Bibliographique des Institutions Chrétiennes (Strasbourg), annually since 1968.

"Selected Annotated Bibliography of Missiology," in *Missiology* since vol. 14 (1986).

Spindler, M. R., and P. Middelkoop, *Bible and Mission: A Partially Annotated Bibliography 1960-1980.* Leiden, 1981.

Theologie im Kontext (Aachen), since 1979 = *Theology in Context*, since 1984.

Dictionaries, Encyclopedias, and Collections of Documents

Concise Dictionary of the Christian World Mission, ed. S. Neill, G. H. Anderson, and J. Goodwin. London and Nashville, 1970.

Dictionary of the Ecumenical Movement, ed. N. Lossky, et al. Geneva and Grand Rapids, 1990.

A Dictionary of the Jewish-Christian Dialogue, ed. L. Klenicki and G. Wigoder. New York, 1984.

Dizionario di missiologia. Bologna, 1993.

The Encyclopedia of Religion, ed. M. Eliade, et al. New York, 1987, 16 vols.

Jongeneel, J. A. B., *The Philosophy, Science, and Theology of Mission in the Nineteenth Century: A Missiological Encyclopedia*. Frankfurt, forthcoming.

Lexikon Missions-Theologischer Grundbegriffe, ed. K. Müller and T. Sundermeier. Berlin, 1987.

Ökumene Lexikon. Kirchen, Religionen, Bewegungen, ed. H. Krüger, W. Löser, and W. Müller-Römheld. Frankfurt am Main, 1983.

Rzepkowski, H., *Lexikon der Mission. Geschichte, Theologie, Ethnologie*. Graz, 1992.

Scherer, J. A., and S. B. Bevans, ed., *New Directions in Mission and Evangelization* I: *Basic Statements 1974-1991*. Maryknoll, 1992. II: *Theological Foundations*. Maryknoll, 1994.

Spindler, M., "Mission Reaffirmed: Recent Authoritative Statements of Churches Around the World (1982-1991)," *Exchange* 20 (1991) 161-258.

Wietzke, J., ed., *Mission erklärt. Ökumenische Dokumente von 1972 bis 1992*. Leipzig, 1993.

World Christian Encyclopedia: A Comparative Survey of Churches and Religions in the Modern World AD 1900-2000, ed. D. B. Barrett. New York, 1982.

Periodicals

Africa

AFER — The African Ecclesial Review (Kenya, 1959-)
Africa Theological Journal (Tanzania, 1968-)
African Christian Studies (Kenya, 1987-)

Aspects du Christianisme à Madagascar (Madagascar, 1946-)
Au Coeur de l'Afrique (Burundi, 1969-)
Bulletin de Théologie Africaine (Zaire, 1979-)
Bulletin on Islam and Christian-Muslim Relations in Africa (U.K., 1983-)
Cahiers Bibliques Africains (Kenya, 1987-)
Cahiers des Religions Africaines (Zaire, 1968-)
East Africa Journal of Evangelical Theology (Kenya, 1981-)
Journal of Black Theology in South Africa (South Africa, 1987-)
Journal of Religion in Africa (The Netherlands, 1967-)
Journal of Theology for Southern Africa (South Africa, 1972-)
Missionalia (South Africa, 1973-)
Pro Mundi Vita Dossiers. Africa Dossier (Belgium, 1976-)
Revue Africaine de Théologie (Zaire, 1977-)
Revue Zairoise de Théologie Protestante (Zaire, 1986-)
Spearhead (Kenya, 1977-)

Asia

Asia Journal of Theology (Singapore, 1987-)
Bangalore Theological Forum (India, 1968-)
Chinese Theological Review (U.S., 1984-)
Ching Feng (Hong Kong, 1957-)
Dialogue (new series, Sri Lanka, 1974-)
East Asia Pastoral Review (Philippines, 1963-)
Evangelical Review of Theology (India, 1976-)
Indian Church History Review (India, 1967-)
The Indian Journal of Theology (India, 1955-68)
Indian Missiological Review (India, 1979-)
Inter-Religio (Japan, 1983-)
The Japan Christian Quarterly (Japan, 1926-)
The Japan Missionary Bulletin (Japan, 1946-)
Jeevadhara (India, 1971-)
Logos (Sri Lanka, 1979-)
Pro Mundi Vita Dossiers. Asia-Australasia Dossier (Belgium, 1976-)
Religion and Society (India, 1953-)
Theological Review (Lebanon, 1978-)
Vidyajyoti (India, 1975-)
Voices from the Third World (Sri Lanka, 1977-)

Oceania

Catalyst (Melanesia, 1971-)
Melanesian Journal of Theology (Papua-New Guinea, 1987-)

Latin America

Caribbean Journal of Religious Studies (Jamaica, 1979-)
Christianismo y Sociedad (El Salvador, 1962-)
Estudios Teologicos (Brazil, 1960-)
Informes de Pro Mundi Vita. Latinoamericana (Belgium, 1976-)
Latin American Pastoral Issues (Costa Rica, 1973-)
Medellín (Columbia, 1975-)
Misión (Costa Rica, 1981-)
Revista Eclesiastica Brasileira (Brazil, 1940-)
Revista Latinoamericana de Teología (El Salvador, 1984-)
Theological Fraternity Bulletin (Argentina, 1982-)

North America

Evangelical Missions Quarterly (U.S., 1964-)
International Bulletin of Missionary Research (U.S., 1977-)
Missiology (U.S., 1972-)
Urban Mission (U.S., 1983-)

Europe

Ateísmo y diálogo — Atheism and Dialogue (Vatican City, 1966-)
Bulletin Secretariatus Pro Non Christianis (Vatican City, 1966-)
The Ecumenical Review (Switzerland, 1948-)
Evangelikale missiologie (Germany, 1985-)
Exchange: Bulletin of Third World Christian Literature and Ecumenical Research
    (The Netherlands, 1972-)
International Review of Mission(s) (Switzerland, 1912-)
Kosmos en Oekumene (The Netherlands, 1971-)
Liaisons Internationales (Belgium, 1974-)
*Media Development: Journal of the World Association for Christian Communica-
    tion* (U.K., 1982-)
Misiones Extranjeras (Spain, 1947-)

Mission Studies, Journal of the IAMS (Germany, 1984-)
Neue Zeitschrift für Missionswissenshaft (Switzerland, 1945-)
Perspectives Missionnaires (Switzerland, 1981-)
Pro Mundi Vita Dossiers. Europa/North American Dossier (Belgium, 1976-)
Soteria. Evangelische Theologische Bezinning (The Netherlands, 1984-)
Spiritus (France, 1959-)
Studia Missionalia (Italy, 1952-)
Wereld en Zending. Tijdschrift voor Missiologie en Missionaire Praktijk (The Netherlands, 1972-)
Zeitschrift für Mission (Germany and Switzerland, 1975-)
Zeitschrift für Missionswissenshaft und Religionswissenshaft (Germany, 1911-)

Atlases

Beach, H.P., and C. H. Flahs, *World Atlas of Christian Missions*. New York, 1911.

Chadwick, H., and G. Evans, *Atlas of the Christian Church*. London, 1988.

Emmerich, H., Svd, *Atlas Hierarchicus. Descriptio geographica et statistica Ecclesiae Catholicae tum occidentis tum orientis*. Mödling-Austria, 1968.

Faruqi, I. R. al, and D. E. Sopher, *Historical Atlas of the Religions of the World*. New York, 1974.

Freitag, A., *Die Wegen des Heils. Bildatlas zur Geschichte der Weltmission*. Salzburg, 1960. Dutch adaptation by F. J. Verstraelen: *Historische Wereldatlas van het Christendom*. Hasselt, 1960.

Jedin, H., K. S. Latourette, and J. Martin, *Atlas zur Kirchengeschichte. Die Christlichen Kirchen in Geschichte und Gegenwart*. Freiburg, 1970; revised edition, 1987.

Johnstone, P., *Operation World*. Fifth ed., Grand Rapids, 1993.

Littell, F. H., *The Macmillan Atlas of the History of Christianity*. New York, 1976.

Other Works

Abraham, W. J., *The Logic of Evangelism*. Grand Rapids, 1989.

L'Accueil et le refus du christianisme. Historiographie de la conversion. Colloque du CREDIC — Stuttgart Septembre 1985. Lyon, 1986.

Amirtham, S., and S. W. Ariarajah, ed., *Ministerial Formation in a Multifaith Milieu: Implications of Interfaith Dialogue for Theological Education*. Geneva, 1986.

Anderson, G. H., ed., *Asian Voices in Christian Theology*. Maryknoll, 1976.

Anderson, G. H., J. M. Philips, and R. T. Coote, ed., *Mission in the 1990s.* Grand Rapids/New Haven, 1991.

Anderson, G. H., R. T. Coote, N. A. Horner, and J. M. Philips, ed., *Mission Legacies: Biographical Studies of Leaders of the Modern Missionary Movement.* Maryknoll, 1995.

Anderson, G. H., and T. F. Stransky, ed., *Christ's Lordship and Religious Pluralism.* Maryknoll, 1981.

Anderson, G. H., and T. F. Stransky, ed., *Evangelization.* Mission Trends 2; New York/Grand Rapids, 1975.

An-Na'im, A., and J. D. Gort, et al., ed., *Human Rights and Religious Values: An Uneasy Relationship?* Currents of Encounter 8; Grand Rapids, 1995.

Ariarajah, S. W., *The Bible and People of Other Faiths.* Geneva, 1985.

————, *Gospel and Culture: An Ongoing Discussion within the Ecumenical Movement.* Geneva, 1994.

Arias, M., *Announcing the Reign of God: Evangelization and the Subversive Memory of Jesus.* Philadelphia, 1984.

————, and A. Johnson, *The Great Commission: Biblical Models for Evangelism.* Nashville, 1992.

Armstrong, J., *From the Underside: Evangelism from a Third World Vantage Point.* Maryknoll, 1981.

Bakke, R., and J. Hart, *The Urban Christian: Ministry in Today's Urban World.* Downers Grove, 1987.

Bassham, R. C., *Mission Theology, 1948-1975: Years of Worldwide Creative Tension, Ecumenical, Evangelical and Roman Catholic.* Pasadena, 1979.

Bavinck, J. H., *An Introduction to the Science of Missions.* Philadelphia, 1960.

Bellagamba, A., *Mission and Ministry in the Global Church.* Second ed. Maryknoll, 1994.

Bertsch, L., and F. Schlösser, *Evangelisation in der Dritten Welt. Anstösse für Europa.* Freiburg, 1981, 1982[2].

Bevans, S. B., *Models of Contextual Theology.* Maryknoll, 1992.

Beyerhaus, P., *Krise und Neuaufbruch der Weltmission. Vorträge, Aufsätze und Dokumente.* Bad Liebenzell, 1987.

Blauw, J., *The Missionary Nature of the Church: A Survey of the Biblical Theology of Mission.* New York, 1962.

Boer, H. R., *Pentecost and Missions.* Grand Rapids, 1964 = *Pentecost and the Missionary Witness of the Church.* Franeker, 1955.

Boesak, A., *Farewell to Innocence: A Social-Ethical Study of Black Theology and Black Power.* Maryknoll, 1976.

Boff, L., *Ecclesiogenesis: The Base Communities Reinvent the Church.* Maryknoll, 1986.

————, *Passion of Christ, Passion of the World: The Facts, Their Interpretation, and Their Meaning, Yesterday and Today.* Maryknoll, 1987.

Bonk, J. J., *Missions and Money: Affluence as a Western Missionary Problem.* Maryknoll, 1991.

Borrmans, M., *Guidelines for Dialogue between Christians and Muslims.* Rome, 1990.

Bosch, D. J., *Transforming Mission: Paradigm Shifts in Theology of Mission.* Maryknoll, 1991.

————, *Witness to the World: The Christian Mission in Theological Perspective.* London, 1980.

Boulaga, F. E., *Christianity without Fetishes: An African Critique and Recapture of Christianity.* Maryknoll, 1984.

Braaten, C. E., *No Other Gospel! Christianity among the World's Religions.* Minneapolis, 1992.

Brandon, S. G. F., ed., *The Saviour God: Comparative Studies in the Concept of Salvation.* Manchester, 1963.

Braun, H. J., *Indische Religionen und das Christentum in Dialog.* Zurich, 1986.

Brennan, J. P., *Christian Mission in a Pluralistic World.* Middlegreen, 1990.

Bria, I., *Go Forth in Peace: Orthodox Perspectives on Mission.* Geneva, 1986.

Brown, D., *To Set at Liberty: Christian Faith and Human Freedom.* Maryknoll, 1981.

Burridge, K., *In the Way: A Study of Christian Missionary Endeavors.* Vancouver, 1991.

Burrows, W. R., ed., *Redemption and Dialogue: Reading "Redemptoris Missio" and "Dialogue and Proclamation."* Maryknoll, 1993.

Camps, A., *Partners in Dialogue: Christianity and Other World Religions.* Maryknoll, 1983.

Carpenter, J., and W. R. Shenk, ed., *Earthen Vessels: American Evangelicals and Foreign Missions 1880-1980.* Grand Rapids, 1990.

Carrier, H. *Evangelizing the Culture of Modernity.* Maryknoll, 1993.

Castro, E., *Freedom in Mission: The Perspective of the Kingdom of God. An Ecumenical Inquiry.* Geneva, 1985.

————, *A Passion for Unity: Essays on Ecumenical Hopes and Challenges.* Geneva, 1992.

Christensen, T., and W. R. Hutchison, ed., *Missionary Ideologies in the Imperialist Era: 1880-1920.* Arhus, 1982.

The Church for Others: Two Reports on the Missionary Structure of the Congregation. Geneva, 1967.

Clarke, A. D., and B. W. Winter, ed., *One God, One Lord in a World of Religious Pluralism.* Cambridge, 1991.

Cone, J., *A Black Theology of Liberation*. Maryknoll, 1986.

Conn, H. M., *A Clarified Vision for Urban Mission: Dispelling the Urban Stereotypes*. Grand Rapids, 1987.

Cook, G., *The Expectation of the Poor: Latin American Basic Ecclesial Communities in Protestant Perspective*. Maryknoll, 1985.

Coote, R. T., "Taking Aim on 2000 AD," *13th Mission Handbook: North American Protestant Ministries Overseas*, ed. S. Wilson and J. Siewert (Monrovia, 1986), 35-80.

Costa, R. O., ed., *One Faith, Many Cultures: Inculturation, Indigenization, and Contextualization*. Maryknoll and Cambridge, 1988.

Costas, O. E., *Christ Outside the Gate: Mission Beyond Christendom*. Maryknoll, 1982.

————, *The Integrity of Mission: The Inner Life and Outreach of the Church*. New York, 1979.

————, *Liberating News: A Theology of Contextual Evangelization*. Grand Rapids, 1989.

Cox, H., *Religion in the Secular City: Toward a Postmodern Theology*. New York, 1984.

Cracknell, K., *Towards a New Relationship: Christians and People of Other Faiths*. London, 1986.

————, and C. Lamb, *Theology on Full Alert*. Second ed. London, 1986.

Dayton, E. R., and D. A. Fraser, *Planning Strategies for World Evangelization*. Grand Rapids, 1990.

D'Costa, G., ed. *Christian Uniqueness Reconsidered: The Myth of a Pluralistic Theology of Religions*. Maryknoll, 1990.

Degrijse, O., *De Derde Kerk wordt missionair*. Brugge, 1983.

Delumeau, J., *Le Christianisme va-t-il mourir?* Paris, 1977.

Dickson, K. A., *Uncompleted Mission: Christianity and Exclusivism*. Maryknoll, 1991.

————, and P. Ellingworth, ed., *Biblical Revelation and African Beliefs*. London, 1969.

Donavan, V. J., *Christianity Rediscovered: An Epistle from the Masai*. London, 1978.

Douglas, J. D., ed., *Proclaim Christ Until He Comes: Calling the Whole Church to Take the Whole Gospel to the Whole World. Lausanne II in Manila: International Congress on World Evangelization*. Minneapolis, 1990.

Drummond, L. A., *The Word of the Cross: A Contemporary Theology of Evangelism*. Nashville, 1992.

Drummond, R. H., *Toward a New Age in Christian Theology*. New York, 1985.

DuBose, F. M., ed., *Classics of Christian Mission*. Nashville, 1979.

————, *God Who Sends: A Fresh Quest for Biblical Mission*. Nashville, 1983.

Duchrow, U., *Global Economy — A Confessional Issue for the Churches?* Geneva, 1987.

Dunn, J. G. D., *Unity and Diversity in the New Testament*. Philadelphia, 1977.

Dupuis, J., *Jesus Christ at the Encounter of World Religions*. Maryknoll, 1991.

Dussel, E. D., *A History of the Church in Latin America: Colonialism to Liberation*. Grand Rapids, 1982.

Edgar, W., *Taking Note of Music*. London, 1988.

Ela, J.-M., *Ma foi d'Africain*. Paris, 1985.

Ellison, C., ed., *The Urban Mission: Essays on the Building of a Comprehensive Model for Evangelical Urban Ministry*. Grand Rapids, 1974.

Elwood, D. J., ed., *Asian Christian Theology: Emerging Themes*. Philadelphia, 1980.

Emerging Models of Christian Mission: A Special Consultation, Ventnor, New Jersey, May 11-14, 1976. Ventnor, 1976.

England, J. C., *Living Theology in Asia*. London, 1981.

Evans, A. F., et al., *The Globalization of Theological Education*. Maryknoll, 1993.

Evers, G., *Mission — nichtchristliche Religionen — weltliche Welt*. Münster, 1974.

Fabella, V., ed., *Asia's Struggle for Full Humanity: Toward a Relevant Theology. Papers from the Asia Theological Conference*. Maryknoll, 1985.

Fabella, V., and S. Torres, ed., *Irruption of the Third World: Challenge to Theology. Fifth International Conference of EATWOT (New Delhi, 1981)*. Maryknoll, 1983.

————, *Doing Theology in a Divided World. Sixth International Conference of EATWOT, Geneva, 1983*. Maryknoll, 1985.

Fackre, G., *Ecumenical Faith in Evangelical Perspective*. Grand Rapids, 1993.

————, *Word and Deed: Theological Themes in Evangelism*. Grand Rapids, 1975.

Fey, H. E., ed., *The Ecumenical Advance: A History of the Ecumenical Movement*, vol. II: *1948-1968*. Geneva, 1986[2].

Freytag, W., ed., *Mission zwischen Gestern und Morgen*. Stuttgart, 1952.

Frohnes, H., and U. W. Knorr, ed., *Kirchengeschichte als Missionsgeschichte*, vol. I: *Die Alte Kirche*. Munich, 1974.

Fung, R., *The Isaiah Vision: An Ecumenical Strategy for Congregational Evangelism*. Geneva, 1992.

Gensichen, H. W., *Missionsgeschichte der neueren Zeit*. Göttingen, 1976[3].

Gittins, A. J., *Bread for the Journey: The Mission of Transformation and the Transformation of Mission*. Maryknoll, 1993.

Glasser, A. F., and D. A. McGavran, *Contemporary Theologies of Mission*. Grand Rapids, 1983.

Goodall, N., ed., *Missions under the Cross: Addresses and Statements of Willingen 1952*. London, 1953.

Gort, J. D., *Your Kingdom Come: Melbourne, Australia 12-25 May 1980.* Amsterdam, 1980.

————, ed., *Zending op weg naar de toekomst. Essays aangeboden aan J. Verkuyl.* Kampen, 1978.

Gort, J. D., H. M. Vroom, et al., ed., *Dialogue and Syncretism: An Interdisciplinary Approach.* Currents of Encounter 1; Grand Rapids/Amsterdam, 1989.

Gort, J. D., H. M. Vroom, et al., ed., *On Sharing Religious Experience: Possibilities of Interfaith Mutuality.* Currents of Encounter 4; Grand Rapids/Amsterdam, 1992.

Gospel and Culture: The Willowbank Report. Lausanne Occasional Papers 2; Wheaton, 1978.

Green, M., *Evangelism in the Early Church.* London, 1970.

Greenway, R. S., and T. M. Monsma, *Cities: Mission's New Frontier.* Grand Rapids, 1989.

Groot, A. de, *De Bijbel over het heil der volken.* Roermond, 1964.

Gutiérrez, G., *A Theology of Liberation: History, Politics and Salvation.* Maryknoll, 1973.

Hahn, F., *Mission in the New Testament.* London, 1965.

Hammond, P. E., ed., *The Sacred in a Secular Age: Toward Revision in the Scientific Study of Religion.* Berkeley, 1985.

Hanks, T. D., *God So Loved the Third World: The Bible, the Reformation and Liberation Theologies.* Maryknoll, 1983.

Hastings, A., *African Catholicism: Essays in Discovery.* London, 1989.

Hebly, H., *Eastbound Ecumenism: A Collection of Essays on the World Council of Churches and Eastern Europe.* New York, 1986.

Hesselgrave, D. J., *Today's Choices for Tomorrow's Mission: An Evangelical Perspective on Trends and Issues in Missions.* Grand Rapids, 1988.

Hick, J., *Problems of Religious Pluralism.* London, 1985.

————, and P. F. Knitter, ed., *The Myth of Christian Uniqueness: Toward a Pluralistic Theology of Religions.* Maryknoll, 1987.

Hoedemaker, L. A., *Met Christus bij anderen. Opmerkingen over dialoog en apostolaat.* Baarn, 1978.

Hoefer, H. E., ed., *Debate on Mission: Issues from the Indian Context.* Madras, 1979.

Hoekendijk, J. C., *Kerk en volk in de Duitse zendingswetenschap.* Groningen, 1948. Abridged German edition: *Kirche und Volk in der deutschen Missionswissenschaft,* with appendix, "Zur Frage einer missionarischen Existenz." Munich, 1967.

Honig, A. G., Jr., *What is Mission? The Meaning of the Rootedness of the Church in Israel for a Correct Concept of Mission.* Kampen, 1982.

Jansen Schoonhoven, E., *Wederkerige assistentie van Kerken in missionair perspectief. Samenvatting en evaluatie van een studieproject (1970-1976).* Leiden, 1977. Abridged English edition: *Mutual Assistance of Churches in a Missionary Perspective.* IIMO Research Pamphlet 1; Leiden, 1979.

————, et al., *Heil voor deze wereld. Studies aangeboden aan prof. dr. A. G. Honig Jr.* Kampen, 1984.

Jedin, H., and J. Dolan, ed., *History of the Church.* Vols. V-X. New York, 1965-81.

Jenkinson, W., and H. O'Sullivan, ed., *Trends in Mission: Toward the Third Millennium.* Maryknoll, 1991.

Jeremias, J., *Jesus' Promise to the Nations.* Studies in Biblical Theology 24; Naperville, 1958.

Jongeneel, J. A. B., *Missiologie, I: Zendingswetenschap.* The Hague, 1986. II: *Missionaire Theologie.* The Hague, 1991.

The Kairos Document. Grand Rapids, 1986.

Kane, J. H., *The Christian World Mission Today and Tomorrow.* Grand Rapids, 1981.

Kateregga, D. D., and D. W. Shenk, *Islam and Christianity: A Muslim and a Christian in Dialogue.* Grand Rapids, 1980.

Kertelge, K., et al., *Mission im Neuen Testament.* Freiburg, 1982.

Keyes, L. E., *The Last Age of Missions: A Study of Third World Missionary Societies.* Pasadena, 1983.

Klein Goldewijk, B., and J. van Nieuwenhove, ed., *Theologie in de context van de derde wereld: Een vergelijkende studie.* Kampen, 1993.

Knitter, P. F., *No Other Name? A Critical Survey of Christian Attitudes toward the World Religions.* Maryknoll, 1985.

Koyama, K., *Mount Fuji and Mount Sinai: A Pilgrimage in Theology.* London, 1984 = *Mount Fuji and Mount Sinai: A Critique of Idols.* Maryknoll, 1985.

Kraemer, H., *The Christian Message in a Non-Christian World.* London, 1938.

————, *From Mission Field to Independent Church: Report on a Decisive Decade in the Growth of Indigenous Churches in Indonesia.* The Hague, 1958.

Kraft, C. H., *Communication Theory for Christian Witness.* Maryknoll, 1991.

Kramm, T., *Analyse und Bewährung theologischer Modelle zur Begründung der Mission. Entscheidungskriterien in der aktuellen Auseinandersetzung zwischen einem heilsgeschichtlich-ekklesiologischen und einem geschichtlich-eschatologischen Missionsverständnis.* Aachen, 1979.

Krass, A. C., *Evangelizing Neopagan North America: The Word that Frees.* Scottdale, 1982.

Kritzinger, J. J., P. G. J. Meiring, and W. A. Saayman, *On Being Witnesses.* Johannesburg, 1994.

Kroeger, J. H., *Living Mission: Challenges in Evangelization Today.* Maryknoll/Quezon City, 1994.

Lagerwerf, L., et al., _Changing Partnership of Missionary and Ecumenical Relationships._ Zoetermeer, 1995.

Lanooy, R., ed., _For Us and Our Salvation: Seven Perspectives on Christian Soteriology._ IIMO Research Publications 40; Utrecht/Leiden, 1994.

Latourette, K. S., _A History of the Expansion of Christianity._ New York, 1937-45, seven vols.

Laubach, F., _Aufbruch der Evangelikalen._ Wuppertal, 1972.

Legrand, L., _Unity and Plurality: Mission in the Bible._ Maryknoll, 1990.

————, J. Pathrapankal, and M. Vallanickal, _Good News and Witness: The New Testament Understanding of Evangelization._ Bangalore, 1974.

Linthicum, R. C., _City of God, City of Satan: A Biblical Theology of the Urban Church._ Grand Rapids, 1991.

Löffler, P., et al., _Secular Man and Christian Mission._ Geneva, 1968.

Luzbetak, L. J., _The Church and Cultures: New Perspectives in Missiological Anthropology._ Maryknoll, 1988.

Martin-Achard, R., _Israël et les nations. La perspective missionnaire de l'Ancien Testament._ Neuchâtel, 1959.

Marty, M. E., _Varieties of Unbelief. From Nihilism to Atheism, from Agnosticism to Apathy._ New York, 1964.

Meeking, B., and J. Stott, ed., _The Evangelical-Roman Catholic Dialogue on Mission 1977-1984._ Grand Rapids, 1986.

Mensen, B., ed., _Schuld und Versöhnung in verschiedenen Religionen._ Sankt Augustin, 1986.

Messer, D. E., _A Conspiracy of Goodness: Contemporary Images of Christian Mission._ Nashville, 1992.

Mission and Evangelism: An Ecumenical Affirmation. Geneva, 1982.

Mitton, C. L., _Your Kingdom Come._ Grand Rapids, 1978.

Mott, S., _Jesus and Social Ethics._ Nottingham, 1984.

Mouw, R. J., _Called to Holy Worldliness._ Philadelphia, 1980.

————, _Political Evangelism._ Grand Rapids, 1973.

————, _Politics and the Biblical Drama._ Grand Rapids, 1976.

Mulders, A., _Missiegeschiedenis._ Bussum, 1957 = _Missionsgeschichte. Die Ausbreitung des katholischen Glaubens._ Regensburg 1960.

————, _Missiologisch Bestek. Inleiding tot de katholieke missiewetenschap._ Hilversum, 1962.

Müller, K., _Mission Theology: An Introduction_ (with contributions by H.-W. Gensichen and H. Rzepkowski). Nettetal, 1987.

Muzorewa, G. H., _The Origins and Development of African Theology._ Maryknoll, 1985.

Nacpil, E. P., and D. J. Elwood, ed., _The Human and the Holy: Asian Perspectives in Christian Theology._ Quezon City, 1978.

Namwera, L., et al., _Towards African Christian Liberation._ Nairobi, 1990.

Neill, S. C., *A History of Christian Missions*. The Pelican History of the Church, vol 6; Harmondsworth, 1986², revised by O. Chadwick.

Netland, H. A., *Dissonant Voices: Religious Pluralism and the Question of Truth*. Grand Rapids, 1991.

Newbigin, L., *Foolishness to the Greeks: The Gospel and Western Culture*. Grand Rapids, 1986.

————, *The Gospel in a Pluralist Society*. Grand Rapids/Geneva, 1989.

————, *The Other Side of 1984: Questions to the Churches*. Geneva, 1983.

————, *Truth to Tell: The Gospel as Public Truth*. Grand Rapids/Geneva, 1991.

————, *Unfinished Agenda*. Grand Rapids, 1985.

————, *A Word in Season: Perspectives on Christian World Missions*. Grand Rapids, 1994.

Nissen, Johannes, *Poverty and Mission: New Testament Perspectives on a Contemporary Theme*. IIMO Research Pamphlet 10; Leiden, 1984.

Noll, M. A., and D. Wells, ed., *Christian Faith and Practice in the Modern World: Theology from an Evangelical Point of View*. Grand Rapids, 1988.

Oduyoye, M. A., *Hearing and Knowing: Theological Reflections on Christianity in Africa*. Maryknoll, 1986.

Ohm, T., *Machet zu Jüngern alle Völker: Theorie der Mission*. Freiburg im Breisgau, 1962.

Orchard, R. K., *Out of Every Nation: A Discussion of the Internationalizing of Missions*. London, 1959.

Padilla, C. R., *Mission between the Times*. Grand Rapids, 1985.

————, ed., *The New Face of Evangelicalism*. London, 1976.

Parratt, J. K., *Reader in African Theology*. London, 1993.

Pathrapankal, J., ed., *Service and Salvation: Nagpur Theological Conference on Evangelization*. Bangalore, 1973.

Peters, G. W., *A Biblical Theology of Missions*. Chicago, 1972.

————, *Missionarisches Handeln und biblischer Auftrag: Eine Theologie der Mission*. Bad Liebenzell, 1977.

Phillips, J. M., and R. T. Coote, ed., *Toward the Twenty-First Century in Christian Mission*. Grand Rapids, 1993.

Pieris, A., *An Asian Theology of Liberation*. Maryknoll, 1988.

Pixley, George V., *On Exodus: A Liberation Perspective*. Maryknoll, 1987.

Pobee, J. S., ed., *Religion in a Pluralistic Society* (Leiden, 1976).

————, *Toward an African Theology*. Nashville, 1979.

Pope-Levison, P., *Evangelization from a Liberation Perspective*. New York, 1991.

Pranger, J., *Dialogue in Discussion: The World Council of Churches and the Challenge of Religious Plurality between 1967 and 1979*. IIMO Research Publications 38; Utrecht/Leiden, 1994.

Prokop, D., ed., *Massenkommunikationsforschung*. I: *Produktion*. Frankfurt, 1973.

Poupard, P., et al., *L'indifférence religieuse*. Paris, 1983.

Rabas, J., *Kirche in Fesseln*. Munich, 1984.

Rainer, T. S., *The Book of Church Growth: History, Theology, and Principles*. Nashville, 1993.

Raiser, K., *Ecumenism in Transition: A Paradigm Shift in the Ecumenical Movement?* Geneva, 1991.

Rendtorff, T., ed., *Europäische Theologie. Versuche einer Ortsbestimmung*. Gütersloh, 1980.

Rétif, A., *Initiation à la mission* (Paris, 1960)

Richard, P., *Mort des Chrétientés et Naissance de l'Église*. Paris 1978.

Rommen, E., *Namenschristentum. Theologisch-Soziologische Erwägungen*. Bad Liebenzell, 1985.

Rosin, H. H., and G. van Winsen, *Missio Dei, term en functie in de zendings-theologische discussie*. Leiden, 1971.

Rouse, R., and S. C. Neill, ed., *A History of the Ecumenical Movement 1517-1948*. London, 1986[3].

Saayman, W., *Christian Mission in South Africa: Political and Ecumenical*. Pretoria, 1991.

Samartha, S. J., *Courage for Dialogue. Ecumenical Issues in Inter-Religious Relationship*. Geneva, 1981.

————, *One Christ — Many Religions: Toward a Revised Christology*. Maryknoll, 1991.

Samuel, V., and C. Sugden, ed., *Sharing Jesus in the Two Thirds World*. Grand Rapids, 1984.

Samuel, V., and A. Hauser, ed., *Proclaiming Christ in Christ's Way*. Oxford, 1989.

Sanneh, L., *Translating the Message: The Missionary Impact on Culture*. Maryknoll, 1990.

Scharpff, P., *History of Evangelism: Three Hundred Years of Evangelism in Germany, Great Britain, and the United States of America*. Grand Rapids, 1966.

Scherer, J. A., *Gospel, Church, and Kingdom: Comparative Studies in World Mission Theology*. Minneapolis, 1987.

Schoen, U., *Das Ereignis und die Antworten. Auf der Suche nach einer Theologie der Religionen heute*. Göttingen, 1984.

Schottroff, L., and W. Schottroff, ed., *Wer ist unser Gott? Beiträge zur einer Befreiungs-theologie im Kontext der "ersten" Welt*. Munich, 1986.

Schreiter, R. J., *Constructing Local Theologies*. Maryknoll, 1985.

————, *Reconciliation: Mission and Ministry in a Changing Social Order*. Maryknoll, 1992.

Scott, W., *Bring Forth Justice: A Contemporary Perspective on Mission*. Grand Rapids, 1980.

Segundo, J. L., *The Liberation of Theology*. New York, 1976.

Senior, D., and C. Stuhlmueller, *The Biblical Foundations for Mission*. Maryknoll, 1983.

Severino-Croatto, J., *Exodus: A Hermeneutics of Freedom*. Maryknoll, 1981.

Sharing in One World Mission: Proposals for the Council for World Mission. London, 1975.

Shenk, W. R., ed., *The Transfiguration of Mission: Biblical, Theological, and Historical Foundations*. Scottdale, 1993.

Sider, R. J., *Evangelism and Social Action in a Lost and Broken World*. London, 1993.

————, ed., *Evangelicals and Development: Toward a Theology of Social Change*. Philadelphia, 1981.

Sidjabat, W. B., *Religious Tolerance and the Christian Faith*. Jakarta, 1965.

Smalley, W., *Translation as Mission: Bible Translation in the Modern Missionary Movement*. Macon, 1991.

Song, C.-S., *Christian Mission in Reconstruction: An Asian Analysis*. Maryknoll, 1979.

————, *Tell Us Our Names: Story Theology from an Asian Perspective*. Maryknoll, 1984.

Soukop, P., *Communication and Theology: Introduction and Review of the Literature*. London, 1983.

Spindler, M. R., *La mission combat pour le salut du monde*. Neuchâtel, 1967.

Stackhouse, M. L., et al., *Apologia: Contextualization, Globalization, and Mission in Theological Education*. Grand Rapids, 1988.

Stamoolis, J. J., *Eastern Orthodox Mission Theology Today*. Maryknoll, 1986.

Starkey, P. M., *Salvation as a Problem in Christian Theology of Religions*. New York, 1978.

Steenbrink, K. A., *Dutch Colonialism and Indonesian Islam: Contacts and Conflicts 1596-1950*. Currents of Encounter 7; Amsterdam, 1994.

Stein, G., ed., *The Encyclopedia of Unbelief*. New York, 1985.

Stoffel, O., *Die katholischen Missionsgesellschaften. Historische Entwicklung und konziliare Erneuerung in kanonischer Sicht*. Immensee, 1984.

Sugirtharajah, R. S., ed., *Voices from the Margin: Interpreting the Bible in the Third World*. London, 1991.

Swidler, L., ed., *Towards a Universal Theology of Religion*. Maryknoll, 1987.

Taber, C. R., *The World Is Too Much with Us: "Culture" in Modern Protestant Missions*. Macon, 1991.

Takizawa, K., *Das Heil im Heute. Texte einer Japanischen Theologie*. Theologie der Ökumene, 21; Göttingen, 1987.

Taylor, J. V., *The Go-Between God: The Holy Spirit and the Christian Mission*. Sixth ed. London, 1975.

Terry, J. M., *Evangelism: A Concise History*. Nashville, 1994.

Thomas, M. M., *The Acknowledged Christ of the Indian Renaissance*. London, 1969.

Thung, M. A., et al., ed., *Exploring the New Religious Consciousness: An Investigation of Religious Change by a Dutch Working Group*. Amsterdam, 1985.

Trompf, G. W., *The Gospel Is Not Western: Black Theologies from the Southwest Pacific*. Maryknoll, 1987.

Turner, S., *Hungry for Heaven: Rock 'n Roll and the Search for Redemption*. Eastbourne, 1988.

Vajta, V., *Die diakonische Theologie im Gesellschaftssystem Ungarns*. Frankfurt am Main, 1987.

van Buren, P. M., *A Christian Theology of the People of Israel*. New York, 1983.
————, *Discerning the Way*. New York, 1980.

van der Linde, J. M., *Gods wereldhuis. Voordrachten en opstellen over de geschiedenis van zending en oecumene*. Amsterdam, 1980.

Van Engen, C., *God's Missionary People: Rethinking the Purpose of the Local Church*. Grand Rapids, 1991.
————, D. S. Gilliland, and P. Pierson, ed., *The Good News of the Kingdom: Mission Theology for the Third Millennium*. Maryknoll, 1993.

van Leeuwen, A. T., *Christianty in World History: The Meeting of the Faiths of East and West*. London, 1964.

van Ruler, A. A., *Theologie van het Apostolaat*. Nijkerk, 1954.

Verkuyl, J. *Contemporary Missiology: An Introduction*. Grand Rapids, 1978.
————, *Met moslims in gesprek over het evangelie*. Kampen, 1985.

Verstraelen, F. J., *An African Church in Transition: From Missionary Dependence to Mutuality in Mission. (A Case-study on the Roman-Catholic Church in Zambia)*. Leiden, 1975.
————, et al., ed., *"Rewriting" the Bible: The Real Issues: Perspectives from within Biblical and Religious Studies in Zimbabwe*. Gweru, 1993.

Verstraelen-Gilhuis, G., *From Dutch Mission Church to Reformed Church in Zambia: The Scope for African Leadership and Initiative in the History of a Zambian Mission Church*. Franeker, 1982.
————, *A New Look at Christianity in Africa: Essays on Apartheid, African Education, and a New History*, ed. and introduced by F. J. Verstraelen. Gweru, 1992.

Vicedom, G. F., *Missio Dei, Einführung in eine Theologie der Mission*. Munich, 1958.

Vischer, L., ed., *Toward a History of the Church in the Third World: Papers and Report of Consultation Working Commission on Church History, EATWOT, Geneva 17-21 July 1983*. Bern, 1985.

Vroom, H. M., *Religions and the Truth: Philosophical Reflections and Perspectives*. Currents of Encounter 2; Grand Rapids/Amsterdam, 1989.

Wallis, J., *Call to Conversion: Rediscovering the Gospel for These Times*. San Francisco, 1982.

Warren, M., *Social History and Christian Mission*. London, 1967.

Watson, D., *I Believe in Evangelism*. London/Grand Rapids, 1976.

Wessels, A., *"Een soort bijbel." Vincent van Gogh als evangelist*. Baarn, 1990.

———, *Europe: Has It Ever Been Really Christian?* London, 1994.

———, *Images of Jesus: How Jesus Is Perceived and Portrayed in Non-European Cultures*. Grand Rapids, 1990.

Wilmore, G., and J. H. Cone, ed., *Black Theology: A Documentary History, 1966-1979*. Maryknoll, 1979.

Wind, A., *Zending en Oecumene in de twintigste eeuw. Handboek over de geschiedenis van zending en oecumene aan de hand van de grote conferenties en assemblees*, vol. 1: *Van Edinburgh 1910 tot en met Evanston 1954*. Kampen, 1984. Vol. 2a: *Van Ghana 1957/58 tot en met Uppsala 1968*. Kampen, 1991.

Winter, G., *The New Creation as Metropolis: A Design for the Church's Task in an Urban World*. Second ed. New York, 1964.

Wirt, S. E., *The Social Conscience of the Evangelical*. London, 1968.

Witvliet, T., *A Place in the Sun: An Introduction to Liberation Theology in the Third World*. Maryknoll, 1985.

———, *The Way of the Black Messiah*. New York, 1987.

Yates, T., *Christian Mission in the Twentieth Century*. Cambridge, 1994.

Yewangoe, A. A., *Theologia Crucis in Asia: Asian Christian Views on Suffering in the Face of Overwhelming Poverty and Multifaceted Religiosity in Asia*. Amsterdam, 1987.

Zverina, Josef, *Ich habe mich entschieden. Mut zum Glauben*. Freiburg, 1980.

Contributors

Gerald H. Anderson taught theology in Manila, the Philippines, and is now director of the Overseas Ministries Study Center in New Haven, Connecticut, and editor of the *International Bulletin of Missionary Research*.

Arnulf Camps taught theology at the Regional Seminary of Pakistan in Karachi and is emeritus professor of missiology at the Catholic University of Nijmegen, the Netherlands.

Adrianus de Groot, now retired, taught theology and missiology in Teteringen, the Netherlands, and served as provincial prior of the Dutch-Belgian province of the Missionaries of the Divine Word (SVD).

Jerald D. Gort is associate professor of missiology in the Faculty of Theology of the Free University in Amsterdam and an editor of the interdisciplinary series *Currents of Encounter*.

Jan Heijke, now retired, was study secretary of the Dutch Roman Catholic Church Province and associate professor of African theology and church history in the Faculty of Theology of the Catholic University of Nijmegen, the Netherlands.

Libertus A. Hoedemaker is professor of ethics, missiology, and ecumenics in the Faculty of Theology of the University of Groningen, the Netherlands, and is a member of the Commission on Faith and Order of the World Council of Churches.

Anton G. Honig, now retired, taught theology in Yogyakarta and Ujung Pandang, Indonesia, and served as professor of missiology at the Theological University of Kampen, the Netherlands.

Jan A. B. Jongeneel taught systematic theology in Ujung Pandang and Tomohon, Indonesia, and is currently professor of missiology in the Faculty of Theology of the University of Utrecht, the Netherlands.

Rob H. Matzken is a lecturer in missiology at various institutions of theological education in the Netherlands and serves as consultant to the Dutch evangelical organization Bible and Education.

Walter Sawatsky is associate professor of church history at Associated Mennonite Biblical Seminary, Elkhart, Indiana.

Marc R. Spindler, now retired, was professor of missiology and ecumenics at the University of Leiden, the Netherlands, and director of the missiology division of the Dutch Interuniversity Institute for Missiological and Ecumenical Research (IIMO).

Karel A. Steenbrink taught Christian theology at the Islamic State University in Jakarta and Yogyakarta, Indonesia, and is now adjunct director of the missiology division of the IIMO in Utrecht, the Netherlands.

Frans van der Hoff worked as a missionary in Chili and Mexico, taught missiology at the University of Ottawa, and now serves as representative of Mexican Indian farmers' organizations in the Diocese of Breda, the Netherlands.

Jan M. van Engelen worked as a missionary in Brazil and served as associate professor of missiology in the Faculty of Theology of the Catholic University of Nijmegen, the Netherlands. He is now theological adviser for the (Catholic) Mission Council of the Netherlands.

Jan van Lin serves as chairman of the Section for Interreligious Encounter of the Dutch Council of Churches and is director of the Missiological Institute of Nijmegen-Heerlen, the Netherlands.

Before his death in 1995 **Jan van Raalte** taught theology in Suriname and until his retirement served as Secretary for Study and Policy of the Working Group for a Pluriform Society of the Dutch Council of Churches.

Rogier G. van Rossum was rector of the University for Theology and Pastorate (UTP) in Heerlen, the Netherlands, and is currently professor of missiology at the UTP and in the Faculty of Theology of the Catholic University of Nijmegen.

Frans J. Verstraelen worked as a missionary in Ghana, was adjunct director of the missiology division of the IIMO, served as general secretary of the IAMS, and is currently professor of religious studies at the University of Zimbabwe.

Guerdina M. Verstraelen-Gilhuis was on the staff of the IIMO and taught at the Near East School of Theology in Beirut, Lebanon. At the time of her death in 1989, she was serving as senior lecturer in the history of African Christianity at the University of Zimbabwe.

Anton Wessels taught at the Near East School of Theology in Beirut, Lebanon, and is currently professor of missiology and religious studies in the Faculty of Theology of the Free University of Amsterdam.

Anne Wind, now retired, worked as a missionary in Indonesia, taught at the Near East School of Theology in Beirut, Lebanon, and was associate professor of missiology at the Theological University of Kampen, the Netherlands.

Index